MODERN
BRITISH AND AMERICAN
PRIVATE PRESSES (1850-1965)

HOLDINGS OF THE BRITISH LIBRARY

PUBLISHED FOR

THE BRITISH LIBRARY

BY

BRITISH MUSEUM PUBLICATIONS LIMITED

© 1976 The British Library Board

ISBN 0 7141 0367 5

Published by
BRITISH MUSEUM PUBLICATIONS LTD.,
6 BEDFORD SQUARE, LONDON WC1B 3RA

Printed by offset in Great Britain by
William Clowes & Sons, Limited, London, Beccles and Colchester

Preface

There is a need for a comprehensive bibliography of modern private presses. Between the appearance of Will Ransom's *Private presses and their books*, published in 1929, partly supplemented by his *Selective check lists of press books*, issued in parts between 1945 and 1950, and that of the first annual issue of *Private press books* in 1959, no attempt was made to cover this field, though of course a number of bibliographies of individual presses appeared.

Whether the British Library will be able to undertake the production of a "Gesamtkatalog" is open to doubt, but it is hoped that this list of the Library's own holdings of books printed between *ca.* 1850 and 1965 will be a useful source book for bibliographers, librarians and others interested in the modern private press movement.

Although the holdings of the British Library are by no means complete even in the field of private press books printed in Great Britain, they are probably as full as those of any other library in this country. Naturally, the holdings of works printed at private presses in America are less full, but here too they compare favourably with those of other British libraries.

For some years a card catalogue of private press holdings in the English language has been maintained, originally based on lists in Ransom and on bibliographies of individual presses, as well as on the items found in the yearly issues of *Private press books*, supplemented by others selected from booksellers' catalogues and elsewhere. The present list is based on entries in the General Catalogue of the British Library, arranged (i) alphabetically, by presses; (ii) chronologically within each press; (iii) alphabetically by author or other heading within each year under each press. The entries have been made over a long period, and consequently changes in catalogue practice are reflected by differences in style.

Books printed at one press but published by another are recorded under each press. The list includes works in English published by private presses in non-English speaking countries.

In the case of some presses, the list contains only a selection of the Library's holdings. This is because bibliographers have not agreed on the exact definition of the term "private press". Some presses which began as "private" later became wholly or partially commercial. Other firms, like the Chiswick and Curwen presses, which produced work of typographical excellence, could not be omitted from a list of this nature, although they were never strictly "private". It is necessarily a matter of opinion whether their work, or part of it, should be included.

The work of compilation has been done by Mr. P. A. H. Brown.

October, 1975

D. T. RICHNELL
Director-General,
Reference Division,
The British Library

ABBEY PRESS, Edinburgh

BIBLE.—*Job.* [*English.*]
—— The Book of Job. (Drawings by R. T. Rose.) pp. 99. *G. Bell & Sons: London ; Abbey Press: Edinburgh,* 1902. 4⁰. **3052. c. 17.**
Printed on hand-made paper.

SHAKESPEARE (WILLIAM) [*Merry Wives of Windsor.*] Comedy of the Merry Wives of Wiudsor. (The Abbey Shakespeare.) pp. 134. *George Bell & Sons: London,* 1902. 4⁰. **11765. r. 7.**

ADAGIO PRESS, Grosse Pointe Park, Harper Woods, Michigan

PRINTING.
—— Printing in Privacy. (A review of recent activity among American private presses. The editorial contents prepared by Leonard F. Bahr [and others].) *Private Press of Leonard F. Bahr: Grosse Pointe Park,* 1960. 8⁰. **Cup. 510. pg. 1.**

RUSKIN (JOHN) [*Letters.*]
—— The Contemptible Horse. The text of John Ruskin's letter to 'My Dear Tinie' written from the Bridge of Allan on 31 August 1857. With an introductory essay by Norman H. Strouse and five pen-and-ink illustrations by Adele Bichan. pp. 46. *Adagio Press: [Detroit,]* 1962. 8⁰. **Cup. 510. pg. 2.**

ADAGIO PRESS.
—— Adagio. (An introduction to the Adagio Press.) A statement of purpose, a description of equipment and bibliographic notes on the early work of one private press. [By Leonard F. Bahr.] pp. 12. *Leonard F. Bahr: Harper Woods,* 1963. 8⁰. **Cup. 510. pg. 3.**

BOHM (ANTON)
—— A Tribute to Anton Bohm and his work at the Sans Souci Press. [By Leonard F. Bahr.] pp. 7. *Printed by Leonard F. Bahr at his private press, Adagio: Harper Woods,* 1964. 16⁰. **Cup. 510. pg. 5.**

HAND (LEARNED)
—— The spirit of liberty. [*Harper Woods, Mich.:*] *printed by Leonard F. Bahr at his private press, Adagio,* 1964. **Cup. 510. pg. 7.**

Pages not numbered. 21 cm. △
An address. Reprinted from "The spirit of liberty", a collection of Judge Hand's papers and addresses.

ZAUN (ALLAN A.)
—— But the greatest of these is love. The text of the sermonette delivered by the Reverend Allan A. Zaun at the wedding of Ann and Leonard Bahr, Jefferson Avenue Presbyterian Church, Detroit, Michigan, October 1, 1960. [*Harper Woods, Mich.:*] *printed for presentation to their friends by Ann and Leonard Bahr,* 1964. **Cup. 510. pg. 6.**

Pages not numbered. 25 cm. △

JOHNSON (SAMUEL) LL.D. [*The Rambler.*]
—— The Spring of the year. (An essay from The Rambler of April 3, 1750.) *Printed by Ann & Leonard Bahr at their private press, Adagio: [Harper Woods,]* 1965. 8⁰. **Cup. 510. pg. 4.**

ADAMS (John), Hawkesbury

ABBS (PETER)
—— A Fisherman of this Sea. First poems. pp. 15. *John Adams: Hawkesbury,* 1965. 8⁰. **Cup. 510. d. 1.**

ALBION HAND PRESS, Chelsea, London

BUDAY (GYÖRGY)
—— George Buday's Little book, *etc.* [*Privately printed;*] *London,* 1955. 12⁰. **Cup. 510. cek. 1.**

ALCESTIS PRESS, New York

BISHOP (JOHN PEALE)
—— Minute Particulars. [Poems.] pp. 70. *Alcestis Press: New York,* 1935. 8⁰. **Cup. 510. nac. 3.**

TATE (JOHN ORLEY ALLEN)
—— The Mediterranean and other poems. pp. 56. *Alcestis Press: New York,* 1936. 8⁰. **Cup. 510. nac. 2.**

WILLIAMS (WILLIAM CARLOS)
—— An Early Martyr and other poems. pp. 68. *Alcestis Press: New York,* 1935. 8⁰. **Cup. 510. nac. 1.**

ALCUIN PRESS, Chipping Campden, Glos.

WHITFIELD (CHRISTOPHER) The Village, and other poems. pp. v. 49. *Alcuin Press: Chipping Campden,* 1928. 8⁰. **11643. m. 56.**
No. 78 of an edition of 100 copies.

FINBERG (ALEXANDER JOSEPH) An Introduction to Turner's Southern Coast. With a catalogue of the engravings ... and a full transcript ... of Turner's marginal notes and instructions to the engravers. pp. xxii. 80. *Cotswold Gallery: London*, 1929. fol.
L.R. **41**. c. **11**.

HOUSMAN (ALFRED EDWARD)
—— Last Poems. pp. 67. *H. P. R. Finberg: Chipping Campden*, 1929. 8°. **11643**. n. **24**.

HOUSMAN (ALFRED EDWARD) A Shropshire Lad. pp. 91. *Richards Press: London*, 1929. 8°.
11643. n. **25**.

CAVENDISH (GEORGE)
—— The Life and Death of Thomas Wolsey, *etc.* pp. 192. *Alcuin Press: Chipping Campden*, 1930. 4°. **4863**. f. **24**.

DAVID (JACOB VILLIERS PEVERIL)
—— The guardsman and Cupid's daughter, and other poems ... The decorations by John Austen. *London: Humphrey Toulmin [at] the Cayme Press*, 1930. Cup. **510**. caf. **1**.
pp. 54. 23 cm. △
Printed at the Alcuin Press, Campden, Glos.

HOBBY HORSE.
—— The Hobby Horse. no. 1–7. March 1930–March 1932. *Southampton*, 1930–32. 23 cm. Cup. **510**. caf. **4**.
No. 1–4 were issued by the Hampshire Branch of the English Folk Dance Society; no. 5–7 were issued by the Wiltshire Branch and published at Steeple Langford.

LA TOUR LANDRY (GEOFFROY DE) The Book of the Knight of La Tour Landry. Edited by G. S. Taylor, *etc.* pp. xii. 172. *Verona Society: London*, 1930. 8°. Cup.**510**.caf.**9**.

LERMONTOV (MIKHAIL YUR'EVICH) The Demon. Translated . . . by Gerard Shelley. With an introduction by Prince Mirsky. pp. 56. *Richards Press: London*, 1930. 8°. **011586**. l. **76**.

NASH (THOMAS) *Satirist.*
—— The Unfortunate Traveller . . . Edited by Philip Henderson. Illustrated by Haydn Mackey. pp. xxvi. 161. *Verona Society: London*, 1930. 8°. C. **99**. h. **27**.

PARTRIDGE (ERIC HONEYWOOD) The First Three Years. An account and a bibliography of the Scholartis Press. pp. ix. 54. *Scholartis Press: London*, 1930. 8°. **011900**. b. **22**.

ALEXANDER, *Aphrodisæus.* Ἀλεξάνδρου Ἀφροδισιεως προς τους αὐτοκρατορας περι εἱμαρμενης. Alexander of Aphrodisias on Destiny, addressed to the Emperors. Translated ... by Augustine FitzGerald. *Gr. & Eng.* pp. 163. *Scholartis Press: London*, 1931. 8°.
08458. b. **11**.

BENINGTON (WILSON)
—— Love in London, and the Tidal Town. [Poems.] pp. v. 100. *Scholartis Press: London*, 1931. 8°.
11644. k. **57**.

BLAKESTON (OSWELL) and **BRUGUIÈRE** (FRANCIS) Few are Chosen. Studies in the theatrical lighting of life's theatre. [With plates.] pp. 116. *Eric Partridge: London*, 1931. 8°. **12625**. pp. **6**.

CAMPBELL (IGNATIUS ROY DUNNACHIE)
—— The Georgiad. A satirical fantasy in verse. pp. 64. *Boriswood: London*, 1931. 8°. Cup. **510**. caf. **2**.

DIGBY (Sir KENELM)
—— Tamarisk and Sanicle. Being the essence distilled from Sir Kenelme Digby's excellent directions for cookery. [Extracted from "The Closet of ... Sir Kenelme Digby Kt. opened."] pp. 11. *Alcuin Press: Chipping Campden*, 1931. 8°.
7945. cc. **35**.

FITZGERALD (AUGUSTINE) Peace and War in Antiquity. A selection of passages from ancient Greek and Latin authors, presented in English, with the originals appended, by A. Fitzgerald. [Edited by Alexander Souter.] pp. 123. *Scholartis Press: London*, 1931. 8°. **08425**. f. **37**.

GIRVAN (I. WAVENEY)
—— A Bibliography and a Critical Survey of the Works of Henry Williamson, *etc.* pp. 56. *Alcuin Press: Chipping Campden*, 1931. 8°. **011900**. bb. **95**.

GROSE (FRANCIS) *F.A.S.* A Classical Dictionary of the Vulgar Tongue...Edited with a biographical and critical sketch and an extensive commentary by Eric Partridge. pp. ix. 396. *Scholartis Press: London*, 1931. 8°. **12980**. dd. **25**.
Issued for private subscribers.

PHELPS (WILLIAM HENRY) Tones High & Low. [Verse.] pp. 61. *Alcuin Press: Campden*, 1931. 8°.
11644. l. **17**.

BINDER (FRANK) Dialectic ; or, the Tactics of thinking. pp. 299. *Eric Partridge: London*, 1932. 8°.
08458. bb. **49**.

CAMPBELL (IGNATIUS ROY DUNNACHIE)
—— Pomegranates. A poem, *etc.* *Boriswood: London*, 1932. 8°. Cup.**510**.caf.**6**.

HENDERSON (PHILIP)
—— A Wind in the Sand. Poems by P. Henderson and drawings by Jean Shepheard. pp. 24. *Boriswood: London*, 1932. 8°. **11640**. h. **7**.
One of an edition of 65 copies.

HERRICK (ROBERT) *the Poet.* [*Smaller Collections.*]
—— Verses from the Hesperides of Robert Herrick. *Campden, Glos.: printed by Basil Fairclough at the Alcuin Press,* 1932.
Cup. **510**. caf. **3**.

Pages not numbered. 24 cm. △

MILTON (JOHN) [*Paradise Regained.*]
—— Paradise Regained . . . Newly edited with an introduction and commentary by E. H. Blakeney. pp. ix. 187. *Eric Partridge: London,* 1932. 8°. **11633**. h. **20**.

B., W. M.
—— Love-Letters of a Sentimentalist. By W. M. B. [i.e. W. M. Bocquet. In verse.] pp. 22. *Scholartis Press: London,* 1933. 8°. **011641**. cc. **118**.

CAMPBELL (IGNATIUS ROY DUNNACHIE)
—— Flowering Reeds. Poems. pp. 47. **F.P.** *Boriswood: London,* 1933. 8°. **11640**. i. **47**.

GROOM (G. LAURENCE)
—— Grecian Nocturne. Poems. pp. 64. *Scholartis Press: London,* 1933. 8°. **011641**. e. **10**.

MONTGOMERIE (WILLIAM)
—— Via. Poems. pp. 62. *Boriswood: London,* 1933. 8°.
Cup.**510**.caf.**7**.
One of 20 copies printed on hand-made paper.

THEOCRITUS. [*Greek and English.*]
—— The Festival of Adonis. Being the xvth Idyll . . . Edited with a revised Greek text, translation and . . . notes by E. H. Blakeney . . . to which is added a rendering in English verse of the Lament for Adonis attributed to Bion. pp. 37. *Eric Partridge: London,* 1933. 8°. **11340**. ee. **13**.

ASHBEE (CHARLES ROBERT)
—— Kingfisher out of Egypt. A dialogue in an English garden. [In verse. Preceded by brief biographies of the speakers in the dialogue. With illustrations.] pp. 51. *Oxford University Press: London,* 1934. 8°.
011653. o. **22**.

CAMPBELL (IGNATIUS ROY DUNNACHIE)
—— Broken Record. Reminiscences. pp. 208. *Boriswood: London,* 1934. 8°. Cup.**510**.caf.**10**.
One of an edition of fifty copies printed on hand-made paper and signed by the author.

GOETHE (JOHANN WOLFGANG VON) [*Faust.—Thl. 1.—English.*]
—— The First Part of Goethe's Faust. Translated . . . by John Shawcross, *etc.* pp. vi. 189. *Eric Partridge: London,* 1934. 8°. **20018**. d. **9**.

JEFFERY (SYDNEY)
—— Desires and Adorations. [Verses.] pp. 46. *Alcuin Press: Campden,* 1935. 8°. **11655**. aa. **74**.

EARLE (JOHN) *successively Bishop of Worcester and of Salisbury.*
[*Micro-cosmographie.*]
—— Character of a cooke, 1628. *Campden, Glos.: A. B. R. Fairclough,* 1938. Cup. **510**. caf. **5**.

Pages not numbered. 15 cm. △

Reprinted from "Micro-cosmographie".

ALDERBRINK PRESS, Chicago

IRIS (SCHARMEL)
—— A Singing reed. [Poems. With a portrait.] pp. xi. 64. *Ralph Fletcher Seymour: [Chicago,* 1963.] 8°.
X. **900/3735**.
Author's presentation copy.

ALLENHOLME PRESS, Wylam, Northumberland

PERIODICAL PUBLICATIONS.—*Wylam.*
—— Bulmer Papers. *Wylam,* 1960– . 8°. P.P. **1621**. ae.

ALLISON (Steve L.), Birmingham

ALLISON (STEVE L.)
—— Whynotitle? (Literary editor, Steve Allison.) [With illustrations.] pp. 26. *S. L. Allison: Birmingham,* 1965. 16°. Cup. **510**. cup. **1**.

ANGEL ALLEY PRESS, Winter Park, Florida

GROVER (EDWIN OSGOOD) The Angel Alley Press. A foot note to the history of printing. pp. 13. *Angel Alley Press: Winter Park, Fla.,* [1929.] 16°.
11900. a. **38**.

ANVIL PRESS, Lexington, Kentucky

SHAKESPEARE (WILLIAM) [*Sonnets.*]
—— Shake-speares Sonnets. (Printed after the Praetorius facsimile from the copy of the first Quarto—1609—in the British Museum.) *Anvil Press: Lexington, Ky.,* 1956. 4°.
Cup. **510**. nev. **1**.

HESIOD. [*Opera et Dies.—Greek and English.*]
—— Fable of the Hawk and the Nightingale, translated from Hesiod's Works and Days—lines 202-212—by Robert Graves. *Stamperia del Santuccio: Lexington, Ky.,* 1959. 4°.
Cup. **510**. nev. **3**.
Broadside. no. 1. No. 93 of an edition of 100 copies.

MENCIUS.
—— The Ox mountain parable. [From the translation by I. A. Richards. With an introduction by Thomas Merton.] *Stamperia del Santuccio: Lexington, Ky.,* 1960. 4°.
Cup. **510**. nev. **4**.
Broadside. no. 2.

CHAPTERS.

—— Chapters on writing and printing. Calligraphy for the printer, [by] Paul Standard. Digressions on the Roman letter, [by] Victor Hammer. Printing from the blocks of Thomas Bewick, [by] R. Hunter Middleton. Notes on the Stamperia del Santuccio, [by] Carolyn R. Hammer. [With plates.] pp. 70.   *Anvil Press: Lexington, Ky.,* 1963. 8°.   Cup. **510**. nev. **2.**
Anvil Press Publications. no. 7.

APPLEDORE PRIVATE PRESS,
New Haven, Connecticut; Hamden, Conn.

FAMINE. Famine : a masque. [By William James Linton.] pp. 20.   [*Appledore Press : New-Haven, Conn.,*] 1875. 8°.   **011652**. m. **13**. (**1.**)

REID (ABEL) *pseud.* [i.e. WILLIAM JAMES LINTON.]
—— Broadway ballads. Collected for the centennial commemoration of the Republic, 1876 . . . Author's edition. [*New Haven, Conn. : Appledore Private Press,* 1876].
                                11687. f. **44.**
   pp. 2, 126 ; illus. 22 cm.   △
   One of an edition of fifty copies.

REID (ABEL) *pseud.* [i.e. WILLIAM JAMES LINTON.]
—— [Another copy.] Broadway ballads, *etc.* [1876].
                          011652. m. **13**. (**2.**)

LINTON (WILLIAM JAMES)
—— James Watson. A memoir of the days of the fight for a free press in England and of the agitation for the people's charter. [*New Haven, Conn. :*] *Appledore Private Press,* 1879.   **10826**. ee. **10.**
   pp. 76. 21 cm.   △
   Author's presentation copy to the British Museum. In this copy a mounted photograph of James Watson precedes the titlepage.

LINTON (WILLIAM JAMES)
—— [Another issue.] James Watson : a memoir, *etc.* 1879.
                              10827. e. **7.**
   pp. 76 ; port. 21 cm.   △
   In this copy the portrait precedes the first page of the text.

LINTON (WILLIAM JAMES) Slanderers [a letter to the Editor of " The Nineteenth Century," in answer to an article by G. Howell in that periodical, entitled : " History of the International Association "].
[1879?] 8°.   **1414**. h. **21**. (**5.**)

VOICES.

—— Voices of the dead. Charlotte Corday and Marat. Mazzini and the Countess Ossoli. Delescluze on the barricade. [By W. J. Linton.]   [*New Haven, Conn. : Appledore Private Press,* 1879].   **11652**. cc. **11**. (**21.**)
   pp. 14. 21 cm.   △

HUGO (VICTOR MARIE) *Viscount.* [*Selections and Extracts.*] Translations : Hugo—Béranger—Mickiewicz. [By William James Linton.]
                   A[*ppledore*]. P[*rivate*]. P[*ress :*
New-Haven, Conn.,] 1881. 8°.   **011652**. m. **13**. (**3.**)

LINTON (WILLIAM JAMES)
—— Golden apples of Hesperus. Poems not in the collections. [The editor's dedicatory statement signed : W. J. Linton.] [*New Haven, Conn. :*] *Appledore Private Press,* 1882.   C. **30**. h. **11.**
   pp. xvi, 187 ; illus. 24 cm.   △

LINTON (WILLIAM JAMES)
—— Rare poems of the sixteenth and seventeenth centuries : a supplement to the anthologies. Collected and edited with notes by W. J. Linton. *New Haven, Conn. : Appledore Private Press,* 1882.   C. **30**. h. **12.**
   pp. xvii, 264 ; illus. 24 cm.   △
   One of an edition of five copies.

WINDFALLS.

—— Windfalls. Two hundred and odd. [Edited by W. J. Linton.] [*Hamden, Conn. : Appledore Private Press,* 1882].   **11781**. aa. **12.**
   Pages not numbered. 16 cm.   △
   Quotations, in verse, " from characters in various dramas ". Presentation copy from the editor to the British Museum.

CATULLUS (CAIUS VALERIUS) [*Nulli se dicit.—Latin and English.*]
—— In dispraise of a woman. Catullus, with variations. [*Hamden, Conn.*] : *Appledore Private Press,* 1886.
                                11649. f. **21.**
   Pages not numbered. 23 cm.   △
   Verses in imitation of Catullus's Carmen LXX, with the Latin text. One of an edition of twenty-five copies.

FAMINE. Famine, a Masque. [By William James Linton.] pp. 20. [1887.] 8°.   **11779**. bb. **21**. (**1.**)

LINTON (WILLIAM JAMES)
—— Love-Lore. [*Hamden, Conn. :*] *Appledore Private Press,* 1887.   **11651**. aa. **62.**
   pp. 125. 15 cm.   △
   Poems. One of an edition of fifty copies.

BROWN (HATTIE) *pseud.* [i.e. WILLIAM JAMES LINTON.]
—— Catoninetales, *etc.* [*Hamden, Conn.*] : *Appledore U.S. Press,* [1892].   **011652**. m. **13**. (**4.**)
   pp. 100 ; illus. 21 cm.   △

HELICONUNDRUMS.

—— Heliconundrums. [By W. J. Linton.]   [*Hamden, Conn. :*] *Appledore U.S. Press,* [1892].   **11652**. cc. **7.**
   pp. 91 ; illus. 23 cm.   △
   Poems. One of an edition of twenty-five copies.

HELICONUNDRUMS.

—— [Another issue.] Heliconundrums. [1892]. 21 cm.
                          011652. m. **13**. (**5.**)
                                        △

LINTON (WILLIAM JAMES) The Religion of Organization, *etc.* pp. 39.   *Appledore Private Press : New Haven, Conn.,* 1892. 8°.   **4379**. g. **10.**

LINTON (WILLIAM JAMES) [Another copy.] The Religion of Organization.   *Appledore Private Press : New-Haven, Conn.,* 1892. 8°.   **4379**. g. **11.**

LINTON (WILLIAM JAMES) Love-Lore and other early and late poems. pp. vi. 255. *Appledore Press: Hamden, Conn., 1895.* 8°.   **11652. k. 50.**

MOLLUSC.

—— Of a mollusc. [*Hamden, Conn.:*] *Appledore Private Press*, 5095 [1895].   **11601. a. 59. (7.)**

 Pages not numbered. 12 cm. △

 Verses.

VERBA. Ultima Verba. [In verse. By W. J. Linton?] *Appledore Private Press*, 1895. 16°.   **011652. h. 23.**

DARWIN (CHARLES ROBERT) [*Appendix.*]

—— Darwin's Probabilities. A review of his "Descent of Man". [By William J. Linton.] pp. 15. *Appledore Press: Hamden, Conn., 1896.* 8°.   **7006. c. 15.**

—— [Another copy.]   **7004. de. 25. (1.)**

AQUILA PRESS, London

HOWARD (HENRY) *Earl of Surrey.* The Original Poems of Henry Howard, Earl of Surrey. pp. 96. *Aquila Press: London*, 1929. 8°.   **Cup. 510. caz. 1.**

LERMONTOV (MIKHAIL YUR'EVICH)

—— A song about Tsar Ivan Vasilyevitch, his young body-guard, and the valiant merchant Kalashnikov . . . Translated by John Cournos. With decorations by Paul Nash. pp. 23. iiii. *Aquila Press: London*, 1929. 8°.   **C. 98. h. 30.**

MARLOWE (CHRISTOPHER) *the Dramatist.*

—— Edward the Second. [Reprinted from the edition of 1594.] *Aquila Press: London*, 1929. fol.   **Cup. 510. caz. 2.**

 No. 24 of 50 copies printed on hand-made paper and with the shields blazoned by hand.

RODKER (JOHN)

—— Adolphe 1920. pp. 131.   *Aquila Press: London*, 1929. 8°.   **012604. bb. 55.**

CUNARD (NANCY)

—— Poems—Two—1925, *etc.*   *Aquila Press: London*, 1930. fol.   **Cup. 510. caz. 3.**

LASSO DE LA VEGA (GARCÍA) *the Poet.* The Odes and Sonnets of Garcilaso de la Vega. An English verse rendering by James Cleugh. pp. 94. *Aquila Press: London*, 1930. fol.   **L.R. 38. a. 9.**

ARCADIAN PRESS, Egremont, Cumberland

FRONTIERS.

—— New Frontiers, *etc.* [An anthology of poems by various authors.] *Arcadian Press: Egremont, Cumberland*, [1963.] 4°.   **Cup. 510. cag. 1.**

 Printed on one side of the leaf only.

GUNSTONE (KATHLEEN)

—— A Garland for you. [Poems.] pp. 16. *Arcadian Agency: Egremont*, [1963.] 8°.   **Cup. 510. cag. 2.**

READE (NAN)

—— For Friendly Folk. [Poems.] pp. 16. *Arcadian Agency: Egremont, Cumberland*, [1964.] 8°.   **Cup. 510. cag. 3.**

ARGONAUT PRESS, London

DRAKE (Sir FRANCIS)

—— The World encompassed and analogous contemporary documents concerning Sir Francis Drake's circumnavigation of the world. (Editor: N. M. Penzer.) With an appreciation of the achievement by Sir Richard Carnac Temple. *London: Argonaut Press*, 1926.   **10496. dd. 17.**

 pp. lxv, 235 ; illus., maps. △

 Printed on Japon vellum.

CHARDIN (Sir JOHN)

[Journal du voyage.]

—— Sir John Chardin's Travels in Persia. With an introduction by . . . Sir Percy Sykes. (Editor: N. M. Penzer.) *London: Argonaut Press*, 1927.   **10077. p. 5.**

 pp. xxx, 287 : plates ; port. 27 cm. △

 Printed on Japon vellum.

DAMPIER (WILLIAM) [*New Voyage Round the World.*]

—— A new voyage round the world . . . With an introduction by Sir Albert Gray. [The editor's preface, containing a bibliographical note, signed: N. M. Penzer.] *London: Argonaut Press*, 1927.   **010028. k. 7.**

 pp. xxxvii, 376 : plates ; illus., maps, port. 27 cm. △

 A reprint of the edition of 1729. Printed on Japon vellum.

BARTHEMA (LODOVICO)

—— The Itinerary of Ludovico di Varthema of Bologna from 1502 to 1508, as translated . . . by John Winter Jones . . . With a Discourse on Varthema and his travels in Southern Asia, by Sir Richard Carnac Temple. (Editor: N. M. Penzer.) [With maps.] pp. lxxxv. 121. *Argonaut Press: London*, 1928. 4°.   **010028. k. 8.**

RALEIGH (Sir WALTER) The Discoverie of the large and bewtiful Empire of Guiana . . . Edited . . . with introduction, notes and appendixes . . . by V. T. Harlow. (Editor: N. M. Penzer.) [With a portrait and maps.] pp. cvi. 182. *Argonaut Press: London*, 1928. 4°.   **9551. l. 18.**

POLO (MARCO) [*English.*] The Most Noble and Famous Travels of Marco Polo, together with the Travels of Nicolò de' Conti. Edited from the . . . translation of John Frampton, with introduction, notes and appendixes [including passages from Ramusio] by N. M. Penzer. [With maps.] pp. lx. 381. *Argonaut Press: London*, 1929. 4°.   **10058. s. 9.**

WILLIAMSON (JAMES ALEXANDER) The Voyages of the Cabots and the English Discovery of North America under Henry VII and Henry VIII . . . Illustrated with thirteen maps. (Editor: N. M. Penzer.) pp. xiii. 290. *Argonaut Press: London*, 1929. 8°.   **9551. l. 20.**

COLOMBO (CRISTOFORO) [*Collected Writings.*]

—— The Voyages of Christopher Columbus: being the journals of his first and third, and the letters concerning his first and last voyages, to which is added the account of his second voyage written by Andres Bernaldez . . . Newly translated and edited, with an introduction and notes, by Cecil Jane. Illustrated with five maps. pp. 347. *Argonaut Press: London,* 1930. 4°. 9551. l. 23.

HAMILTON (ALEXANDER) *Captain.* A New Account of the East Indies . . . Edited with introduction and notes by Sir William Foster. (General editor: N. M. Penzer.) [With maps.] 2 vol. *Argonaut Press: London,* 1930. 4°. L.R. 39. a. 1.

SUTIL, *Ship.* A Spanish Voyage to Vancouver and the North-West Coast of America, being the narrative of the voyage made in the year 1792 by the schooners Sutil and Mexicana to explore the Strait of Fuca. Translated . . . with an introduction by Cecil Jane . . . With a folding map and six illustrations. (General editor: N. M. Penzer.) pp. xiv. 142. *Argonaut Press: London,* 1930. 4°. 9551. l. 24.

DAMPIER (WILLIAM) [*Voyages and Descriptions.*]

—— Voyages and discoveries . . . With an introduction and notes by Clennell Wilkinson. (Editor: N. M. Penzer.) *London: Argonaut Press,* 1931. 10028. g. 28.

pp. xxxv, 311 ; maps. 26 cm. △

A reprint of the edition of 1729. *Printed on Japon vellum.*

HARLOW (VINCENT TODD)

—— Ralegh's Last Voyage. Being an account drawn out of contemporary letters and relations, both Spanish and English . . . concerning the voyage of Sir Walter Ralegh . . . to Guiana in the year 1617 and the fatal consequences of the same . . . Illustrated with a portrait and two maps. pp. 379. *Argonaut Press: London,* 1932. 4°. 9551. m. 7.

DARTON (FREDERICK JOSEPH HARVEY)

—— Dickens. Positively the first appearance. A centenary review. With a bibliography of "Sketches by Boz." [An account of the publication in "The Monthly Magazine" of "A Dinner at Poplar Walk," of which a revised version was afterwards included in "Sketches by Boz" under the title "Mr. Minns and his Cousin." With the text of the original contribution and of the revisions. With a portrait and facsimiles.] pp. x. 145. *Argonaut Press: London,* 1933. 8°. 10861. de. 43.

HAWKINS (*Sir* RICHARD)

—— The Observations of Sir Richard Hawkins. Edited from the text of 1622, with introduction, notes and appendices. By James A. Williamson . . . Illustrated with four maps. pp. xci. 190. *Argonaut Press: London,* 1933. 8°. 010028. k. 24.

CARON (FRANS)

[Beschrijvinghe van het machtigh Coninckrijcke Japan.]

—— A True Description of the Mighty Kingdoms of Japan & Siam. By François Caron & Joost Schouten. (Rendred into English by Roger Manley.) Reprinted from the English edition of 1663. With introduction, notes and appendixes by C. R. Boxer. *London: Argonaut Press,* 1935. 10058. s. 20.

pp. cxxix, 197 : plates ; maps. 26 cm. bibl. pp. 167–185. △

Printed on Japon vellum.

BEST (GEORGE) *Captain.*

—— The Three Voyages of Martin Frobisher in Search of a Passage to Cathay and India by the North-West, A.D. 1576–8. From the original 1578 text of George Best. Together with numerous other versions, additions, etc. Now edited, with preface, introduction, notes, appendixes and bibliography, by Vilhjalmur Stefansson . . . with the collaboration of Eloise McCaskill . . . together with numerous maps and illustrations [including a portrait]. (General editor: N. M. Penzer.) 2 vol. *Argonaut Press: London,* 1938. 4°. 10026. tt. 7.

GUARMANI (CARLO CLAUDIO)

—— [Il Neged settentrionale.] Northern Najd. A journey from Jerusalem to Anaiza in Qasim . . . Translated from the Italian by Lady Capel-Cure. With introduction and notes by Douglas Carruthers. [With plates and maps.] pp. xliv. 134. *Argonaut Press: London,* 1938. 4°. 010076. i. 19.

DAMPIER (WILLIAM) [*Collections.*]

—— A Voyage to New Holland. [With " A Continuation of a Voyage to New Holland." Both reprinted from the 1729 collection of Dampier's " Voyages round the World."] Edited, with introduction, notes and illustrative documents, by James A. Williamson . . . 32 illustrations [including a portrait]. pp. lxxv. 266. *Argonaut Press: [London,]* 1939. 8°. 10025. s. 5.

ARIES PRESS, Eden, N.Y.

MIDDLETON (RICHARD BARHAM)

[The ghost ship and other stories.]

—— The ghost ship . . . From The ghost ship and other stories. With original preface by Arthur Machen and a biographical note by Laurence J. Gomme. *Eden, N. Y.: Aries Press,* 1926. Cup. 510. nil. 1.

pp. xix, 20. 22 cm. △

ARK PRESS, St. Ives (later Marazion), Cornwall

LAWRENCE (DAVID HERBERT)

—— Life . . . With engravings by Ru Van Rossem. [An essay.] *Ark Press: Saint Ives,* 1954. 8°. Cup. 510. bbd. 1.

BECKETT (L. C.)

—— Neti, neti. Not this, not that. [On mystical theories and experiences.] pp. 112.　*Ark Press: Marazion.* 1955. 8°.　　　　　　　　　Cup.510.bbd.2.
　　A slip bearing the imprint " John M. Watkins: London" has been pasted over the original imprint.

MORLAND (HAROLD)

—— The Singing Air. Poems . . . Drawn by Cyril Satorsky. pp. 40.　*Ark Press: Marazion,* 1956. 8°.
　　　　　　　　　　　　　Cup.510.bbd.3.

LAWRENCE (DAVID HERBERT)

—— Look ! We have come through . . . With an introduction by Frieda Lawrence & with illustrations by Michael Adam. pp. 108.　*Ark Press: Marazion,* 1958. 8°. Cup.510.bbd.4.

ADAM (MICHAEL)

—— A Matter of Death & Life. An essay in autobiography . . . With drawings by Ben Shahn. pp. 48.　*Ark Press: Marazion,* 1959. 8°. [*Ark Series.* no. 1.]
　　　　　　　　　　　　11437. p. 1/1.

BECKETT (L. C.)

—— Unbounded Worlds, *etc.*　　*Ark Press: Marazion,* 1960. 8°.　　　　　　　　　8478. r. 7.

PEATTIE (DONALD CULROSS)

[An Almanac for Moderns.]

—— Glory on the Earth. Wood-engravings by Otto Rohse, *etc.* (Extracts from the author's "An Almanac for Moderns.") pp. 46.　*Ark Press: Marazion, Cornwall,* 1960. 8°. [*Ark Series.* no. 2.]　11437. p. 1/2.

PEATTIE (DONALD CULROSS)

—— [Another copy.] Glory on the Earth.　*Marazion,* 1960. 8°.　　　　　　Cup. 510. bbd. 6.

MORLAND (HAROLD)

—— David dancing. [Poems.] Illustrations by Mort Baranoff. pp. 46.　*Ark Press: Marazion,* 1961. 8°.
　　　　　　　　　　　　Cup. 510. bbd. 5.

ADAM (MICHAEL)

—— The Labour of Love. One aspect of the autobiography of Michael Adam. With woodcuts by Robert Wyss. pp. 86. *Ark Press: Marazion,* 1962. 8°. [*Ark Series.* no. 3.]
　　　　　　　　　　　　11437. p. 1/3.

ZUKOFSKY (LOUIS)

—— Bottom: on Shakespeare. (vol. 1. By L. Zukofsky.— vol. 2. Music to Shakespeare's Pericles by Celia Zukofsky. [With the text.]) 2 vol.　*Published by the Ark Press for the Humanities Research Centre, University of Texas: Austin,* 1963. 8°.　　　　　　　Cup. 503. g. 19.

JAN ARNOLFINI PRESS, Bridgwater, Somerset

HERMAN (JOSEF)

—— A Welsh Mining Village. Written and illustrated with works by J. Herman. pp. 12.　*Jan Arnolfini Press: Bridgwater,* 1956. 8°.　　Cup.510.acc.2.
　　One of an edition of twenty copies.

ZULAWSKI (MAREK)

—— Dawn, Noon and Night. [An essay on London. With lithographs.] pp. 14.　*Jan Arnolfini Press: [Bridgwater,]* 1958. 8°.　　Cup.510.acc.1.
　　Printed for private circulation. One of an edition of eighty copies.

ART SOCIETY PRESS, Wimbledon

PRIDDLE (ROBERT)

—— Victoriana. The second edition. The original text by R. Priddle. Additional text by R. D. Robinson. [With illustrations.] pp. 67.　*Art Society Press: Wimbledon,* 1963. *obl.* fol.　　　　Cup. 510. cav. 1.

ASHENDENE PRESS, Ashendene, Herts; Chelsea, London

DANTE ALIGHIERI. [*Vita Nuova.—Italian.*]

—— La Vita nuova di Dante Alighieri fiorentino. pp. xiii. 91. **L.P.**　*C. H. St. J. H. & E. M. S. H.: Ashendene,* 1895. 4°.　　　　C. 99. i. 5.
　　The printers' names are disclosed in the colophon as C. H. St. J. Hornby & E. M. S. Hornby. Privately printed. No. 47 of an edition of fifty copies.

MILTON (JOHN) [*Minor Poems.*] Three Poems of John Milton (L' Allegro.—Il Penseroso.—Hymn on the Morning of Christ's Nativity). pp. 42.
Privately printed: Ashendene, Hertford, 1896. 4°.
No. 35 of 50 copies printed.　　C.99.d.3.

TODHUNTER (JOHN)

—— Ye minutes of ye CLXXVIIth meeting of ye Sette of Odde Volumes, extracted from ye Diary of Samuel Pepys . . . translated by Bro. John Todhunter, *etc.* [*London,*] 1896.
　　　　　　　　　　　　Ac. 9128.

　　pp. 30. 16 cm. (Privately printed opuscula issued to the Sette of Odd Volumes. no. 42.)　　△
　　Privately printed by C. St. J. Hornly at the Ashendene Press.

BACON (FRANCIS) *Viscount St. Albans.* [*Essays.*]

—— Two Essays of Francis, Lord Bacon: Of Building & Gardens. pp. 32.　*Ashendene Press: [Ashendene,]* 1897. 4°.　　　　　　C. 103. f. 9.
　　No. 14 of an edition of sixteen copies.

CHAUCER (GEOFFREY) [*Canterbury Tales.—Single Tales.— Prologue.*]

—— The Prologue to the Tales of Caunterbury. [With reproductions of the woodcuts in Caxton's second edition.] pp. 38. *Ashendene Press: Herts.,* 1897. 4°. C. 99. d. 23.
　　No. 38 of an edition of fifty copies printed for private circulation.

HORNBY (CHARLES HARRY SAINT JOHN) [*Appendix.*]

—— Hymns and Prayers to be sung and said at the Marriage of St John Hornby and Cicely Barclay in the Parish Church Bayford on January XIX, MDCCCXCVIII. pp. 10. *Printed at the Ashendene Press by the above-named St John Hornby and Cicely Barclay, etc.:* [*Ashendene,*] 1898. 8°.
C. 99. c. 52.

DANTE ALIGHIERI. [*Divina Commedia. —Inferno. —Italian.*] Lo Inferno di Dante Alighieri Fiorentino. [The text as revised by Dr. Edward Moore, with woodcuts designed by R. Catterson Smith after the originals of the edition of 1491.] *Nella stampera di Ashendene: Chelsea,* 1902. 4°.
C.99.e.11.

BERNES (JULYANS) *Dame.*

—— A Treatyse of Fysshynge wyth an Angle. pp. 48. *Ashendene Press: London,* 1903. 4°. C. 99. e. 12.
A reprint of the edition of 1496.

HORATIUS FLACCUS (QUINTUS) [*Carmina.— Selections.—Latin.*] Quinti Horati Flacci Carmina Alcaica. pp. 69. *In Aedibus St. J. Hornby: Chelsea,* 1903. 4°.
C.99.b.10.

HORATIUS FLACCUS (QUINTUS) [*Carmina.— Selections.—Latin.*] Q. Horati Flacci Carmina Sapphica. pp. 46. *Ashendene Press: Chelsea,* 1903. 4°.
C.99.b.9.

BIBLE.—*Old Testament.—Selections.* [*English.*]

—— A Book of Songs and Poems from the Old Testament and the Apocrypha. pp. 62. *Ashendene Press: Chelsea,* 1904. 8°. C. 99. c. 2.

DANTE ALIGHIERI .[*Divina Commedia.—Purgatorio.— Italian.*]

—— Lo Purgatorio di Dante Alighieri fiorentino. [In the text prepared for the "Oxford Edition" of Dante by Edward Moore. With woodcuts after those contained in the 1491 Venice edition of the Divina Commedia.] pp. 242. *Nella stamperia di Ashendene: Chelsea,* 1904. 4°.
C. 99. e. 9.

Privately printed.

FRANCIS [BERNARDONI], *of Assisi, Saint.* [*Appendix.— I Fioretti di San Francesco.*]

—— Un Mazzetto selto di certi Fioretti del glorioso Poverello di Cristo San Francesco di Assisi insieme col Cantico al sole del medesimo. [With illustrations.] pp. 40. *Stamperia di Ashendene: Chelsea,* 1904. 4°. C. 99. k. 20.

DANTE ALIGHIERI. [*Divina Commedia.–Paradiso. —Italian.*] Lo l'aradiso di Dante Alighieri. (Lettere rubricate da mano sono l'opera di Graily Hewitt, e le incisioni in legno di W. Hooper e C. Keates secondo i disegni dell' edizione stampata in Venezia nell' anno 1491.—Il testo di questa edizione è quello rivisto ed emendato dal reverendo Dottore E. Moore.) pp. 243.
St. John and Cicely Hornby, Ashendene Press: Chelsea, 1905. 4°. C.99.e.10.

THOMAS [MORE], *Saint, Lord High Chancellor of England.* [*Utopia.—English.*]
A Fruteful and Pleasaunt Worke of the Beste State of a Publique Weale, and of the newe yle called Utopia... Translated into Englyshe by Raphe Robinson ... Imprinted at London by Abraham Wele ... anno MDLI. pp. 161. *Printed by St. John Hornby, at the Ashendene Press: Chelsea,* 1906. fol. C.99.k.14.
Only 120 copies printed.

DANTE ALIGHIERI. [*Works.*]

—— Tutte le opere di Dante Alighieri fiorentino, nuovamente rivedute nel testo e diligentemente emendate dal reverendo dottore Edoardo Moore. [With woodcuts by Charles Gere.] pp. xiv. 392. *Nella Stamperia Ashendeniana: Chelsea,* 1909. fol. C. 99. l. 1.

STORY.

—— The Story without an End. Translated from the German [i.e. from "Das Märchen ohne Ende" by F. W. Carpové] by Sarah Austin. pp. vi. 60. *Ashendene Press: Chelsea,* 1909. 8°. C. 102. a. 18.
One of an edition of thirty copies printed for Diana Hornby on her ninth birthday by her father, St. John Hornby. A presentation copy to Sir Sydney Cockerell.

VIRGILIUS MARO (PUBLIUS) [*Works.*] Publii Vergilii Maronis Opera. pp. 468. *In aedibus C. H. St. John Hornby: Chelsea,* 1910. fol.
C.99.i.10.

ARTHUR, *King of Britain.* [*Sir Thomas Malory's Morte darthur.*]

—— The Noble and Joyous Book entytled Le Morte Darthur ... Whiche book was reduced in to Englysshe by Syr Thomas Malory, Knyght. (The text is that of Southey's reprint of Caxton's edition, with a few minor variations.) [With illustrations by Charles M. Gere and Margaret Gere.] pp. xxii. 500. *Ashendene Press: Chelsea,* 1913. fol. C. 43. i. 3.

H., B.

—— The Children's Garden. A memory of the Old Porch House. By B. H. pp. 7. *Printed by St John & Cicely Hornby at the Ashendene Press:* [*London,*] 1913. 8°.
C. 99. b. 42.

LUCRETIUS CARUS (TITUS) [*Latin.*]

—— T. Lucreti Cari de rerum natura libri sex. *Chelsea: in aedibus St. J. Hornby,* 1913. C. 43. g. 12.
pp. 256. 29 cm. △

BRIDGES (ROBERT SEYMOUR)

—— Poems written in the year MCMXIII. pp. 20. *Printed by St. John Hornby at the Ashendene Press: Chelsea,* 1914. 4°. K.T.C. 30. a. 22.
One of an edition of ninety-one copies.

BOCCACCIO (GIOVANNI) [*Decamerone.— Italian.*]

—— Il Libro ... chiamato il Decameron, *etc.* pp. xi. 360. *Stamperia Ashendeniana: London,* 1920. fol.
C. 99. l. 7.

JAMES (HENRY) *Novelist.* Refugees in Chelsea. (Reprinted from 'The Times Literary Supplement.') pp. 11. *Printed...by C. H. St. J. Hornby at the Ashendene Press: Chelsea,* 1920. 4°. L.R. **37. b. 7.**
One of 50 copies printed for private circulation.

VERINO (UGOLINO) Vita di Santa Chiara Vergine ...Reprinted from the original manuscript with an introduction and notes by Walter W. Seton. pp. xvi. 95. *Ashendene Press: Chelsea,* 1921. 8°. K.T.C. **20. a. 10.**

FRANCIS [BERNARDONI], *of Assisi, Saint.* [*Appendix.—I Fioretti di San Francesco.*]
—— I fioretti del glorioso poverello di Cristo S. Francesco di Assisi. *Chelsea: St. John Hornby nella sua officina privata di Ashendene,* 1922. C. **99. e. 33.**
  pp. viii. 239. 23 cm. △

SPENSER (EDMUND) [*Faerie Queene.*] The Faerie Queene, *etc.* pp. 406. *Ashendene Press: London,* 1923. fol. C. **99. l. 8.**

APULEIUS (LUCIUS) *Madaurensis.* [*Asinus Aureus.—English.*] The XI. Bookes of the Golden Asse...Translated...by William Adlington. pp. vii. 230. *Ashendene Press: London,* 1924. 4°. C. **99. k. 18.**

TOLSTOI (LEV NIKOLAEVICH) *Count.* [Где любовь, там и Бог.]
—— Where God is, Love is. [Translated by Louise & Aylmer Maude.] pp. 26. *Ashendene Press: Chelsea,* 1924. 8°. C. **98. a. 6.**
  Printed as a Christmas greeting for friends by St. John and Cicely Hornby, 1924. *Presentation copy to A. D. Power.*

WILDE (OSCAR FINGALL O'FLAHERTIE WILLS) The Young King, and other tales. pp. 110. *Ashendene Press: Chelsea,* 1924. 8°. C. **99. e. 36.**
  One of 65 copies printed on paper.

ASHENDENE PRESS. A Hand-list of the Books printed at the Ashendene Press MDCCCXCV–MCMXXV. *Chelsea,* 1925. 8°. C. **99. d. 56.**

SPENSER (EDMUND) [*Smaller Collections of Poems.*] Spenser's Minor Poems. Containing the Shepheardes Calender, Complaints, Daphnaida, Colin Clouts come Home again, Amoretti, Hymnes, Epithalamion, Prothalamion, Sonnets, and sundrie other verses. pp. 216. *Ashendene Press: London,* 1925. fol. C. **99. l. 9.**

CERVANTES SAAVEDRA (MIGUEL DE) [*Don Quixote.—English.—Shelton's Translation.*]
—— The first (second) part of the history of the valorous and wittie knight-errant Don-Quixote of the Mancha. Translated ... by Thomas Shelton, MDCXII. *London: Ashendene Press,* 1927, 28. Cerv. **724.**
  2 vol. 44 cm. △
  One of twenty copies printed on vellum.

—— [Another copy.] C. **99. l. (17.)**

HORNBY (MICHAEL CHARLES SAINT JOHN)
—— Hymns and Prayers for use at the Marriage of Michael Hornby and Nicolette Ward at St. Margaret's Church, Westminster, November xv, MCMXXVIII. *Printed by the Father of the Bridegroom at his Private Press: Chelsea,* 1928. 8°. C. **102. i. 7.**

MILTON (JOHN) [*Ode on the Morning of Christ's Nativity.*]
—— Hymn on the Morning of Christ's Nativity. *Printed by St. John & Cicely Hornby for their friends: Chelsea,* 1928. fol. C. **98. h. 32.**
  Printed as a Christmas greeting. Presentation copy to A. D. Power.

THUCYDIDES. [*English.*] Thucydides. Translated...by Benjamin Jowett. pp. 363. *Ashendene Press: London,* 1930. fol. C. **102. l. 1.**

BIBLE.—*Ecclesiasticus.* [*English.*]
—— The Wisdom of Jesus, the son of Sirach, commonly called Ecclesiasticus. [Collated by Arnold D. Power and based upon the Authorised and Revised Versions.] pp. 182. *Ashendene Press: Chelsea,* 1932. fol. C. **102. h. 7.**

LONGUS.
—— Les Amours pastorales de Daphnis et Chloe. Traduction de Messire J. Amyot, éditée et corrigée par Paul-Louis Courier. [With woodcut illustrations by Gwendolen Raverat.] pp. iv. 163. *Ashendene Press: London,* 1933. 4°. C. **102. e. 5.**

ASHENDENE PRESS.
—— A Chronological List, with prices, of the forty books printed at the Ashendene Press. MDCCCXCV–MCMXXXV. *London,* 1935. fol. C. **102. l. 17.**

ASHENDENE PRESS.
—— A Descriptive Bibliography of the Books Printed at the Ashendene Press MDCCCXCV–MCMXXXV. [Compiled by C. H. St. J. Hornby.] pp. 172. *Ashendene Press: London,* 1935. fol. C. **102. l. 16.**

ASPHODEL PRESS, London

CIPPICO (ANTONIO) *Count.*
—— Carme umanistico. [With woodcuts by Phyllis Gardner.] pp. 7. *Asphodel Press: London,* 1923. 4°. Cup. **510. ald. 3.**

FRY (EDITH M.) Short Poems. pp. 19. *The Author*[: London], 1923. 4°. Cup. **510. ald. 1.**

GARDNER (DELPHIS)
—— The tale of Troy. Retold in seven books by Delphis Gardner . . . Illustrated with woodcuts by Phyllis & Delphis Gardner. (Preface by R. W. Chambers.) *London: Asphodel Press,* 1924, 25. Cup. **510. ald. 4.**
  9 pt. 26 cm. △
  With an index.

GARDNER (MARY) *Writer of Verse.*
—— Songs of the Broads . . . Woodcuts by Phyllis Gardner. ff. 16. *Asphodel Press: London,* 1924. 8º.
Cup. **510**. ald. 2.
No. 15 of 25 copies printed.

APOSTLES' CREED. [*English.*]
—— The Apostles' Creed. With illustrations cut on wood by Phyllis and Delphis Gardner. *Maidenhead: Asphodel Press,* 1929. Cup. **510**. ald. 5.
Pages not numbered. 15 cm. △

ASTOLAT PRESS, Guildford

GREEN (ARTHUR ROMNEY)
—— Poems. pp. vii. 96. *A. C. Curtis: Guildford; Brimley Johnson: London,* 1901. 8º. **11658**. aaa. **201**.

BUNYAN (JOHN) [*Pilgrim's Progress, Pt. 1, 2.—English.*]
—— The Pilgrim's Progress . . . Eight illustrations by Victor W. Burnand. pp. 259. *A. C. Curtis: Guildford,* 1902. 8º. Cup. **510**. ced. **1**.
One of an edition of thirty copies printed on Japanese vellum.

'UMAR KHAIYĀM. [*English.—FitzGerald's Version.*]
—— Rubaiyat of Omar Khayyam . . . Translated into English verse by Edward Fitzgerald. pp. 58. *Astolat Press: Guildford,* 1902. 32º. **11659**. a. **2**.
Printed on Japanese vellum.

ARTHUR, *King of Britain.* [*Sir Thomas Malory's Morte darthur.—Abridgments and Selections.*]
—— The Story of Elayne, the Fair Maid of Astolat. By Sir Thomas Malory. pp. 41. *Astolat Press: London,* 1903. 8º. [*Oakleaf Series.*] **11648**. eee. **65/2**.

BACON (FRANCIS) *Viscount St. Albans.* [*Essays.—Single Essays.*]
—— On Gardens. Two essays by Francis Bacon and Abraham Cowley. (The Garden. To J. Evelyn Esquire. By A. Cowley.) pp. 23. *A. C. Curtis: Guildford,* 1903. 8º. 11648.eee.65/10.

BROWNING (ROBERT) *the Poet.* [*Smaller Collections.*]
—— Songs selected from the Works of Robert Browning. pp. 32. *Astolat Press: London,* 1903. ·8º. [*Oakleaf Series.*] **11648**. eee. **65/3**.

EMERSON (RALPH WALDO) Friendship. pp. 25. *Astolat Press: London,* 1903. 8º. 11648.eee.65/9.

HERRICK (ROBERT) *The Poet.* [*Smaller Collections.*]
—— Songs from the Hesperides. *Guildford: A. C. Curtis,* 1903. **944**. bb. **2**.
pp. 78. 11 cm. △
On vellum.

KEATS (JOHN) [*Single Poems.*]
—— The eve of Saint Agnes. *Guildford: A. C. Curtis,* 1903. **11648**. eee. **65/4**.
pp. 23. 19 cm. (Astolat oakleaf series.) △

TENNYSON (ALFRED) *Baron Tennyson.* [*Selections and Extracts.*]
—— Songs. Selected from the works of Lord Tennyson. *London: Astolat Press,* 1903. **11648**. eee. **65/8**.
pp. 27. 19 cm. (Oakleaf series.) △

ARTHUR, *King of Britain.* [*Sir Thomas Malory's Morte darthur.—Abridgments and Selections.*]
—— The Book of Sir Galahad and the achievement of the adventure of the Sancgreal. By Sir Thomas Malory. pp. 42. *Astolat Press: London,* 1904. 8º. [*Oakleaf Series.*] **11648**. eee. **65/1**.

HERRICK (ROBERT) *the Poet.* [*Smaller Collections.*]
—— Songs from the Hesperidies [*sic.*]. [*London:*] *Astolat Press,* 1904. K.T.C. **12**. a. **11**.
pp. 78. 10 cm. △
On vellum.

LOWELL (JAMES RUSSELL)
—— The Vision of Sir Launfal. *London: Astolat Press,* 1904. **11648**. eee. **65/6**.
pp. 18. 19 cm. (Oakleaf series.) △

MILTON (JOHN) [*Poetical Works.*] The Poetical Works of John Milton. Etchings, mezzotints and copper engravings by William Hyde. pp. 194. *Astolat Press: London,* 1904. 4º. **11609**. l. **5**.

SHAKESPEARE (WILLIAM) [*Selections and Extracts.*] Songs from the Plays of William Shakespeare. pp. 63. *Astolat Press: London,* 1904. 32º. K.T.C. **12**. a. **13**.
Printed on Japanese vellum.

SYLVA (CARMEN) *pseud.* [i.e. PAULINA ELIZABETH OTTILIA LOUISA, *Queen Consort of Charles I., King of Roumania.*]
—— How I spent my sixtieth birthday. By "Carmen Sylva". Translated into English by H. E. Delf. Second edition. *Mirfield: John H. Fearnley,* 1904. Cup. **510**. ced. **2**.
pp. 14: plate. 18 cm. △
Printed by the Astolat Press, Guildford.

EMERSON (RALPH WALDO) Character. pp. 25. *Astolat Press: London,* 1905. 8º. 11648.eee.65/12.

EMERSON (RALPH WALDO) An Emerson Treasury. Edited by J. Pennells. pp. 95. *Astolat Press: London,* 1905. 16º. **12295**. aa. **14**.

SOUTHEY (ROBERT) [*Life of Nelson.*] The Battle of Trafalgar. [Extracted from "The Life of Nelson."] . . . Introductory note by A. C. Curtis. pp. 47. *Astolat Press: London,* 1905. 8º. 11648.eee.65/11.

KEATS (JOHN) [*Selections.*]
—— The Odes of John Keats. *London: Siegle, Hill & Co.,* [1908]. **11648**. eee. **65/5**.
pp. 19. 18 cm. (Oakleaf series.) △

ROSSETTI (DANTE GABRIEL)
—— Hand & soul. *London: Siegle, Hill & Co.,* [1908]. **11648**. eee. **65/7**.
pp. 22. 18 cm. (Oakleaf series.) △

ASHBEE (Charles Robert)

—— Peckover. The Abbotscourt Papers, 1904–1931. Edited by C. R. Ashbee. Illustrated by Reginald Savage. pp. xi. 268. *Astolat Press: London*, 1932. 4º.
12349. w. 3.

AUERHAHN PRESS, San Francisco

MAC CLURE (Michael)

—— Hymns to St. Geryon and other poems. pp. 54. *Auerhahn Press: San Francisco*, 1959. 8º.
Cup. 510. ne. 2.

WHALEN (Philip)

—— Self-portrait, from another direction. [In verse.] *Auerhahn Press: San Francisco*, 1959. *s. sh.* fol.
Cup. 510. ne. 4.

WHALEN (Philip)

—— Memoirs of an interglacial age. [Poems.] pp. 49. *Auerhahn Press: San Francisco*, 1960. 4º.
Cup. 510. ne. 5.

MAC CLURE (Michael)

—— Dark brown. [Poems.] *Auerhahn Press: San Francisco*, 1961. 8º.
Cup. 1000. c. 8.

OLSON (Charles)

—— Maximus, from Dogtown—I, *etc.* [A poem.] *Auerhahn: San Francisco*, 1961. 4º.
Cup. 510. ne. 3.

ANTONINUS, *Dominican Lay Brother* [William Everson].

—— The Poet is Dead. (A memorial for Robinson Jeffers.) *Auerhahn Press: San Francisco*, 1964. 4º.
Cup. 510. ne. 1.
With the author's signature.

AZANIA PRESS, Medstead

WAINWRIGHT (Elizabeth) *Mrs.* The Receipt Book of a Lady of the Reign of Queen Anne. With a foreword by John Shirley-Fox. pp. x. 100. *Azania Press: Medstead*, 1931. 8º.
07943. h. 98.

MIĶDĀD IBN AL-ASWAD, *al-Kindī.*

—— The story of Miqdad & Mayasa. From the Swahili-Arabic text. By Alice Werner. *Medstead: Azania Press*, 1932.
11657. cc. 101/1.
pp. 90: plates. 20 cm. (The Azanian classics.) △
Swahili & English.

KUPONA BINT MSHAM.

—— The Advice of Mwana Kupona upon the Wifely Duty. From the Swahili texts by Alice Werner . . . and William Hichens. pp. 95. *Azania Press: Medstead*, 1934. 8º. [*Azanian Classics.* no. 2.]
11657.cc.101/2.

BANYAN PRESS, Pawlet, Vermont

STEIN (Gertrude)

—— Two Poems, hitherto unpublished. *Gotham Book Mart: New York*, [1948.] 8º.
Cup. 510. nay. 1.

STEVENS (Wallace)

—— A primitive like an orb. A poem . . . with drawings by Kurt Seligmann. [*New York:*] *printed for the Gotham Book Mart at the Banyan Press*, 1948.
Cup. 510. nay. 5.
Pages not numbered; plates. 26 cm. (A Prospero pamphlet.) △

EBERHART (Richard)

—— Brotherhood of Men. pp. 11. *Banyan Press: Pawlet*, 1949. 8º.
Cup. 510. nay. 2.

GIDE (André Paul Guillaume)

—— Persephone. Translated by Samuel Putnam. *New York: Gotham Book Mart*, 1949.
Cup. 510. nay. 4.
pp. 20. 21 cm. △
Printed at the Banyan Press, Panlet, Vt.

STEIN (Gertrude)

—— Things as they are. A novel in three parts, *etc.* pp. 87. *Banyan Press: Pawlet, Vt.*, [1950.] 8º.
Cup. 510. nay. 3.

BARKER (Leslie), Chesham, Bucks

GRAY (Thomas) *the Poet.* [*Elegy written in a Country Churchyard.*]

—— The Elegy written in a Country Churchyard. pp. 11. *Leslie Barker: Chesham*, 1961. *obl.* 16º. Cup. 510. cas. 1.

TENNYSON (Alfred) *Baron Tennyson.* [*Selections and Extracts.*]

—— Three Songs. *Leslie Barker: Chesham*, 1962. 16º.
Cup. 510. cas. 2.
Classic reprint. no. 2.

BARLEYN PRESS, Bristol

BYRON (George Gordon Noel) *Baron Byron.* [*Don Juan.—Cantos I–XVI.*]

—— Don Juan. (The Campion edition.) [*London:*] *A. M. Philpot*, 1924.
C. 98. g. 9.
pp. 426. 26 cm. △
Printed at the Barleyn Press, Bristol. No. 5 of twenty-five copies in Niger leather.

BATTLE PRESS, Nevilles Cross, Durham

PERIODICAL PUBLICATIONS.—Newcastle-upon-Tyne.—*Newcastle Magazine.*

—— Personal choice. Being extracts from the Newcastle Magazine, 1747–1760. *Printed by Ian Leake at his Battle Press: Nevilles Cross, Durham, 1964.* 8°.
Cup. **510**. dag. **1**.
One of an edition of seventy-five copies. Printed on blue paper.

BAYBERRY HILL PRESS, Meriden, Conn.

MUSSON (M. E.)

—— Muss's little tours ; or, London on a quid ... Illustrated by W. Haynes Fitzgerald. pp. 69. *Bayberry Hill Press: Meriden, 1965.* 8°. Cup. **510**. nec. **1**.

BEAUMONT PRESS, London

DE LA MARE (Walter John)

—— The Sunken Garden, and other poems. pp. 39. *C. W. Beaumont: London, 1917.* 8°. C. **57**. i. **15**.
No. 8 of twenty copies printed on Japanese vellum.

DRINKWATER (John) *Poetical Writer.* Tides: a book of poems. pp. 36. *The Beaumont Press: London, 1917.* 8°. K.T.C. **101**. a. **26**.
One of 20 copies printed on Japanese vellum.

DAVIES (William Henry)

—— Raptures. A book of poems. pp. 38. *Cyril William Beaumont: [London,] 1918.* 8°. C. **57**. i. **16**.
No. 17 of twenty-two copies printed on Japanese vellum.

DRINKWATER (John) *Poet.*

—— Loyalties. A book of poems. pp. 41. *Beaumont Press: Westminster, 1918.* 8°. Cup. **510**. bee. **1**.

IGOR SVYALOSLAVICH, *Prince.* The Tale of Igor. Adapted from the old Russian legend by Helen de Vere Beauclerk. With six illustrations designed and hand-coloured by Michel Sevier. pp. 23. *C. W. Beaumont: London, 1918.* 8°. C. **57**. f. **9**.
One of 25 copies printed on Japanese vellum.

NICHOLS (Robert Malise Bowyer)

—— The Budded Branch. (Poems and a play.) pp. 40. *Beaumont Press: Westminster, 1918.* 8°.
Cup. **501**. aa. **19**.
Handprinted. The binding executed by Sangorski and Sutcliffe.

NICHOLS (Robert Malise Bowyer)

—— [Another copy.] The Budded Branch. *Westminster, 1918.* 8°. Cup. **510**. bee. **2**.
No. 1 of thirty copies printed on Japanese vellum, signed by the author and artist.

PUSHKIN (Aleksandr Sergyeevich) [Сказка о золотомъ пѣтушкѣ.] The Golden Cockerel...Rendered into English verse by Nicholas Katkoff. With eight illustrations by Michel Sevier. pp. 19. *C. W. Beaumont: London, 1918.* 8°. C. **57**. i. **17**.
No. 61 of 65 copies printed on Japanese vellum, with the illustrations coloured by hand.

ALDINGTON (Richard)

—— Images of War . . . Poems. (Decorations designed by Paul Nash.) pp. 46. *C. W. Beaumont : London, 1919.* 8°.
C. **100**. g. **4**.
No. 30 of 30 copies printed on Japanese vellum.

CONRAD (Joseph) *pseud.* [i.e. Teodor Józef Konrad Korzeniowski.] [*Single Works.*]

—— One Day more. A play in one act. pp. 48. *Cyril William Beaumont: Westminster, 1919.* 8°.
Cup. **510**. bee. **3**.

LAWRENCE (David Herbert)

—— Bay. A book of poems. pp. 43. *Beaumont Press: Westminster, 1919.* 8°. Cup. **510**. bee. **7**.

READ (Sir Herbert Edward)

—— Eclogues. A book of poems. (Decorations designed by Ethelbert White.) *Westminster: Cyril W. Beaumont, 1919.* C. **100**. g. **3**.
pp. 35. 20 cm. △
No. 23 of thirty copies printed on Japanese vellum, signed by the author and the illustrator.

GIBSON (Wilfrid Wilson)

—— Home. A book of poems. pp. 41. *Beaumont Press: Westminster, 1920.* 8°. Cup. **510**. bee. **6**.

NICHOLS (Robert Malise Bowyer) The Smile of the Sphinx. (Decorations...by Ethelbert White.) pp. 58. *C. W. Beaumont: London, 1920.* 8°.
C. **100**. g. **2**.
No. 11 of thirty-five copies printed on Japanese vellum.

DE LA MARE (Walter John) Crossings. A fairy play, *etc.* [With musical notes.] (Decorations by Randolph Schwabe.) pp. 131. *Beaumont Press: London, 1921.* 8°. C. **100**. g. **7**.
Printed on Japanese vellum.

WILDE (Oscar Fingall O'Flahertie Wills) After Reading. Letters...to Robert Ross. [With woodcuts.] pp. 59. **F. P.** *C. W. Beaumont: London, 1921.* 8°. C. **100**. g. **6**.

GOLDONI (Carlo) [Le Donne di buon umore.] The Good-Humoured Ladies . . . Translated . . . by Richard Aldington. To which is prefix'd an essay on Carlo Goldoni, by Arthur Symons. The whole embellish'd with cuts by Ethelbert White. pp. xxiii. 76. **F. P.** *C. W. Beaumont: London, 1922.* 8°. C. **100**. g. **12**.
One of six extra copies specially printed for presentation.

WILDE (Oscar Fingall O'Flahertie Wills) After Berneval. Letters ... to Robert Ross. [Edited by More Adey.] pp. 65. *C. W. Beaumont: London, 1922.* 8°. C. **100**. g. **8**.
Printed on Japanese vellum.

BLUNDEN (EDMUND CHARLES)
—— To Nature. New poems. pp. 50. **F.P.**
Beaumont Press: London. 1923. 8°.   C. **100. g. 11.**

SYMONS (ARTHUR) The Café Royal, and other essays. (Decorations designed by Randolph Schwabe.) pp. 62. **F. P.** *C. W. Beaumont: London.* 1923. 8°.
          Cup.510.bee.4.

BEAUMONT (CYRIL WILLIAM)
—— The Mysterious Toyshop. A fairy tale . . . With decorations by Wyndham Payne. (Edition de luxe.) pp. 32. *C. W. Beaumont: London,* 1924. 8°.
          012809. ccc. 64.

CLARE (JOHN) *Poet.*
—— Madrigals & Chronicles. Being newly found poems . . . Edited with a preface and commentary by Edmund Blunden. (Illustrations . . . by Randolph Schwabe.) [With portraits.] pp. xiii. 102. **F.P.** *Beaumont Press: London,* 1924. 8°.   C. **100. g. 10.**

CONSTANTINI (ANGELO)
—— The Birth, Life and Death of Scaramouch . . . Translated . . . by Cyril W. Beaumont. Together with Mezzetin's [i.e. Constantini's] dedicatory poems and Loret's rhymed news-letters concerning Scaramouch, now first rendered into English verse by Edmund Blunden, *etc.* pp. xlii. 83. pl. IV. **F.P.** *C. W. Beaumont: London,* 1924. 8°.   C. **100. g. 14.**
Eighty copies of this edition were printed on hand-made parchment paper and in addition three extra copies were printed for presentation, of which this is one.

ARBEAU (THOINOT) *pseud.* [i.e. JEHAN TABOUROT.]
—— Orchesography. A treatise in the form of a dialogue . . . Now first translated from the original edition published at Langres, 1588, by Cyril W. Beaumont. With a preface by Peter Warlock. pp. 174. *C. W. Beaumont: London,* 1925. 8°.   C. **100. g. 13.**

BLUNDEN (EDMUND CHARLES)
—— Masks of Time. A new collection of poems, principally meditative. pp. 58. **F.P.** *Baeumont Press: London,* 1925. 8°.   C. **100. g. 9.**
One of eighty copies printed on Japanese vellum.

BLUNDEN (EDMUND CHARLES)
—— Shelley and Keats as they struck their contemporaries. Notes partly from manuscript sources. Edited by E. Blunden. pp. 94. **F.P.** *C. W. Beaumont: London,* 1925. 8°.   Cup.510.bee.5.

BEAUMONT (CYRIL WILLIAM)
—— The History of Harlequin . . . With a preface by Sacheverell Sitwell . . . and illustrations from contemporary sources. pp. 155. *C. W. Beaumont: London,* 1926. 4°.
          L.R. 40. b. 2.

BEAUMONT (CYRIL WILLIAM)
—— The Strange Adventures of a Toy Soldier. A fairy tale . . . With decorations by Wyndham Payne. pp. 32. **F.P.** *C. W. Beaumont: London,* 1926. 8°.
          C. **100. g. 16.**

FLECKER (JAMES ELROY) [*Letters.*]
—— The letters of J. E. Flecker to Frank Savery. [The editor's foreword signed: Hellé Flecker.] *London: Beaumont Press,* 1926.   C. **100. g. 17.**
   pp. 125 ; illus. 23 cm.   △
No. 30 of eighty copies printed on parchment vellum, and signed by the editor, artists, and publisher.

LLOYD (ROBERT) *Poet.* The Actor...To which is prefix'd an essay by Edmund Blunden. The whole embellish'd with theatrical figures by Randolph Schwabe. pp. 42. *C. W Beaumont: London,* 1926. 8°.   C.**100.g.15.**
No. 58 of 60 copies printed on Japanese vellum.

PAYNE (WYNDHAM) Town & Country. A collection of designs and decorations, *etc.* **F. P.** *C. W. Beaumont: London,* [1926.] 4°.   **7860. dd. 16.**
One of 60 copies printed on hand-made paper.

SYMONS (ARTHUR) Parisian Nights. A book of essays. **F. P.** pp. 49. *Beaumont Press: London,* 1926. 8°.   012352. cc. 25.
No. 69 of 80 copies printed.

BEAUMONT (CYRIL WILLIAM)
—— The First Score . . . An account of the foundation and development of the Beaumont Press and its first twenty publications. pp. 96. pl. IV. *Beaumont Press: London,* 1927. 8°.   C. **100. g. 18.**
No. 18 of 80 copies printed on hand-made parchment vellum.

BEAUMONT (CYRIL WILLIAM)
—— The Wonderful Journey. A fairy tale . . . With illustrations by Wyndham Payne. pp. 87. *C. W. Beaumont: London,* 1927. 8°.   C. **100. g. 19.**

POLUNIN (VLADIMIR) The Continental Method of Scene Painting... Edited by Cyril W. Beaumont. pp. xiii. 84. pl. 16. *C. W. Beaumont: London,* 1927. 4°.   C. **100. g. 20.**

BLUNDEN (EDMUND CHARLES)
—— Japanese Garland. (The cover and decorations designed by Eileen Mayo.) pp. 39. , *Beaumont Press:* [*London,*] 1928. 8°.   C. **99. d. 33.**
No. 78 of eighty copies signed by the author, artist and publisher.

LAMBRANZI (GREGORIO) New and Curious School of Theatrical Dancing . . . With all the original plates by Johann Georg Puschner. Translated . . . by Derra de Moroda. Edited with a preface by Cyril W. Beaumont. *C. W. Beaumont: London,* 1928. 8°.   C. **100. k. 15.**

WILLIAMSON (HENRY) *Novelist.* The Wet Flanders Plain. (Cover and title-page designed by Randolph Schwabe.) [Thoughts on the European War, 1914–18.] pp. 95. *Beaumont Press: London,* [1929.] 8°.   C. **100. g. 21.**
No. 79 of 80 copies printed on handmade parchment vellum, and signed by the author, artist and publisher.

BEAUMONT (Cyril William)

—— Toys. Rhymes by C. W. Beaumont. Decorations by Eileen Mayo. pp. 48.   *C. W. Beaumont: London,* 1930. 8°.   **C. 100. g. 25.**
    No. 39 of 100 copies signed by the author and artist, with the decorations hand-coloured by the latter.

BLUNDEN (Edmund Charles)
—— A Summer's Fancy. [A poem.] (Illustrations and decorations designed by Randolph Schwabe.) pp. 53. *Beaumont Press: London,* 1930. 8°.   **C. 100. g. 24.**
    No. 71 of eighty copies printed on fine paper and signed by the author and illustrator.

NOVERRE (Jean Georges) Letters on Dancing and Ballets...Translated by Cyril W. Beaumont, *etc.* [With plates, including a portrait.] pp. xiii. 169. *C. W. Beaumont: London,* 1930. 8°. **C. 100. g. 22.**

BLUNDEN (Edmund Charles)
—— To Themis. Poems on famous trials. With other pieces. pp. 58. *Beaumont Press: London,* 1931. 8°.
        C. 100. g. 27.
    No. 26 of eighty copies printed on hand-made paper.

RAMEAU (P.) The Dancing Master...Translated by Cyril W. Beaumont, *etc.* [With illustrations.] pp. xx. 150.   *C. W. Beaumont: London,* 1931. 8°.
        C. 100. g. 26.

AJELLO (Elvira) The Solo Irish Jig. Described by E. Ajello, *etc.* pp. 30.   *C. W. Beaumont : London,* 1932. 4°.   **C. 99. h. 33.**

BEAUMONT (Cyril William)
—— Anna Pavlova. [With portraits.] pp. 24. *C. W. Beaumont: London,* 1932. 8°.   **C. 100. g. 36.**

BEAUMONT (Cyril William)
—— Vaslav Nijinsky. [With portraits.] pp. 28. *C. W. Beaumont: London,* 1932. 8°. **C. 100. g. 34.**

GAUTIER (Théophile) *the Elder.*
—— The Romantic Ballet as seen by Théophile Gautier. Being his notices of all the principal performances of ballet given at Paris during the years 1837–1848 [extracted from " Histoire de l'art dramatique en France depuis vingt-cinq ans "]. Now first translated . . . by Cyril W. Beaumont. [With plates.] pp. 93. *C. W. Beaumont: London,* 1932. 8°.   **C. 100. g. 35.**

BEAUMONT (Cyril William)
—— A Short History of Ballet. [With plates.] pp. 40. *C. W. Beaumont: London,* 1933. 8°.   **C. 100. g. 37.**

BEAUMONT (Cyril William)
—— A Miscellany for Dancers. Compiled and translated by C. W. Beaumont, *etc.* pp. 196. *C. W. Beaumont: London,* 1934. 12°.   **C. 99. b. 33.**

BEAUMONT (Cyril William)
—— Three French Dancers of the 18th Century. Camargo—Sallé—Guimard. [With portraits.] pp. 31. *C. W. Beaumont: London,* 1934. 8°.   **C. 100. e. 13.**

BEAVER PRESS, Laleham, Middlesex

ANDERSEN (Hans Christian) *the Novelist.* [*Eventyr.—Single Tales.*]
—— [Det gamle Hus.] The Old House. [With illustrations by Hugh Wallis.] pp. 18. *Beaver Press: Laleham,* 1904. 8°.   **12813. v. 20.**

MAG.
—— Mag. [A tale.] pp. 12.   *Beaver Press: Laleham,* 1905. 8°.   **012629. de. 59.**

BEE & BLACKTHORN PRESS, Beckenham, Kent

BONE (David Harbord)
—— The bees of Swanland. A poem . . . With drawings by Arthur Coombes and the author. *Beckenham: Bee & Blackthorn Press,* 1957.   **Cup. 510. baf. 1.**
    pp. 158. 26 cm.   △

BONE (David Harbord)
—— A Lenten Pie. [Poems.] pp. xv. 134.   *Bee & Blackthorn Press: Beckenham,* 1960. 8°.
        Cup. 510. baf. 2.

ANDERSON (John Redwood)
—— While the Fates allow . . . 1952–61. [Poems. With a portrait.] pp. xi. 81. *Bee & Blackthorn Press: Beckenham,* 1962. 8°.   **Cup. 510. baf. 3.**

BELL & BAKER PRESS, London

KOPS (Bernard)
—— Poems. (Lino cuts by Dellar.) *Privately printed by the Bell & Baker Press: [London ?],* 1955. 8°.
        Cup. 510. bbb. 1.
    " *A Grove Edition." Printed on one side of the leaf only. No. 34 of a limited edition of 100 copies Author's presentation copy to Wrey Gardiner.*

BETWEEN HOURS PRESS, New York

GRAUER (Ben)
—— How Bernal Díaz's " True History " was reborn. (Reprinted from Bouillabaise [*sic*] for Bibliophiles.) [With fascimiles.] *New York,* 1955 [1960]. 8°.
        Cup. 500. c. 53.

BIRMINGHAM GUILD OF HANDICRAFT, Birmingham

HUTTON (EDWARD)
—— My Lady's Sonnets. pp. 26. *Privately printed for her Ladyship: London*, 1896. 16º. Cup. **510**. cea. **1**.

HUTTON (EDWARD)
—— Dalliance : a book of essays. *Birmingham : privately printed at the Press of the Birmingham Guild of Handicraft,* [1897]. Cup. **510**. cea. **2**.
pp. 122. 19 cm. △

BLACK ARCHER PRESS, Chicago

SAROYAN (WILLIAM)
—— Those who write them and those who collect them. *Black Archer Press: Chicago*, 1936. 16º.
Cup. **510**. pad. **1**.
One of an edition of fifty copies.

BLACK CAT PRESS, Chicago

HAAS (IRVIN)
—— Bibliography of Modern American Presses. Compiled and edited by I. Haas, *etc.* pp. 95. *Black Cat Press: Chicago*, 1935. 8º. **011904**. aa. **84**.

MAUGHAM (WILLIAM SOMERSET)
—— My South Sea Island. pp. 12. *Ben Abramson: Chicago*, 1936. 8º. Cup.510.nib.1.
Printed on one side of the leaf only. One of an edition of fifty copies.

HAAS (IRVIN)
—— A Bibliography of Material relating to Private Presses, *etc.* pp. xvi. 57. *Black Cat Press: Chicago*, 1937. 8º. **011899**. b. **91**.

ORTON (VREST)
—— Goudy, Master of Letters . . . With an introduction by Frederic W. Goudy. [With portraits and facsimiles.] pp. 101. *Black Cat Press: Chicago*, 1939. 8º. **10888**. c. **12**.

BLACK KNIGHT PRESS, Bath

ROEBUCK (JIM)
—— The Poppy's Song . . . Illustrated by Deirdre Carr. *Black Knight Press: Bath*, 1965. 8º. Cup. **510**. cum. **1**.

BLACK MANIKIN PRESS, Paris

BAUDELAIRE (CHARLES PIERRE) [*Single Works.*]
[Petits poèmes en prose.]
—— Little Poems in Prose. Translated by Aleister Crowley. With several added versions of the Epilogue by various hands with twelve copper plate engravings from the original drawings by Jean de Bosschère. pp. xi. 147. *Edward W. Titus: Paris*, 1928. 8º. Cup. **403**. m. **5**.

BLACK SUN PRESS, Paris

CROSBY (CARESSE) *pseud.* [i.e. MARY PHELPS CROSBY.]
—— **Crosses of Gold. A book of verse. [With illustrations.] pp. 93. *Léon Pichon: Paris*, 1925. 8º. Cup. 403. b. 3.**
No. 83 of an edition of 100 copies.

CROSBY (HARRY)
—— Sonnets for Caresse. (Second impression.) *Herbert Clarke: Paris*, 1926. 8º. **11643**. h. **67**.
One of an edition of twenty-seven copies.

CROSBY (CARESSE) *pseud.* [i.e. MARY PHELPS CROSBY.]
—— Painted Shores . . . [Poems.] Illustrated with three water-colors by François Quelvée. *Éditions Narcisse: Paris*, 1927. 4º. Cup.510.fa.18.

CROSBY (HARRY)
—— Red Skeletons . . . Illustrated by Alastair. [Poems.] *Editions Narcisse: Paris*, 1927. 4º. Cup.510.fa.1.

CROSBY (HARRY)
—— Shadows of the Sun. [A diary.] 2 pt. *Black Sun Press: Paris*, 1928, 29. 8º. Cup.510.fa.2.

JAMES (HENRY) *Novelist.* [*Letters.*]
—— Letters of Henry James to Walter Berry. *Black Sun Press: Paris*, 1928. 4º. Cup.510.fa.5.
No. 20 of an edition of 100 copies, to be sold at the bookshop of Harry Marks, New York.

POE (EDGAR ALLAN) *Poet.* [*Tales.*]
—— The Fall of the House of Usher . . . Illustrations by Alastair. Introduction by Arthur Symons. pp. xix. 50. *Éditions Narcisse: Paris*, 1928. 4º. Cup.510.fa.4.

WALLOP (GERARD VERNON) *Earl of Portsmouth.*
—— Gît le cœur. Poems by Lord Lymington. *Editions Narcisse: Paris*, 1928. 8º. **11392**. a. **38**.

BOYLE (KAY)
—— Short Stories. pp. 55. *Black Sun Press: Paris*, 1929. 8º. Cup.510.fa.7.

CHODERLOS DE LACLOS (Perre Ambroise François)
—— Les liaisons dangereuses . . . With illustrations by Alaskir. (Translated by Ernest Dowson.) *Paris: Black Sun Press*, 1929. Cup. **510. fa. 9.**
2 vol. 30 cm. △
English. The date on the spine of vol. 2 is 1930.

CROSBY (Harry)
—— Tirades. (With a drawing by Caresse Crosby.) pp. 73. *Black Sun Press: Paris*, 1929. 8°. Cup.510.fa.8.
The title on the cover reads: " Mad Queen. Tirades. No. 62 of an edition of one hundred copies.

CROSBY (Harry)
—— Transit of Venus. Poems. (Second edition.) pp. 62. *Black Sun Press: Paris*, 1929. 8°. Cup.510.fa.6.

JOLAS (Eugene)
—— Secession in Astropolis. pp. 84. *Black Sun Press: Paris*, 1929. 8°. Cup.510.fa.11.

JOYCE (James Augustine Aloysius)
[Finnegan's wake.]
—— Tales told of Shem and Shaun. Three fragments from Work in progress. [The preface signed: Charles K. Ogden.] *Paris: Black Sun Press*, 1929. C. 99. e. 46.
pp. xv. 55. 21 cm. △
Contents: The Mookse and the Gripes.—The muddest thick that ever was heard dump.—The Ondt and the grace-hoper.

LAWRENCE (David Herbert)
—— [The Man who died.] The Escaped Cock . . . With decorations in color by the author. pp. 95. *Black Sun Press: Paris*, 1929. 4°. Cup.510.fa.12.
Privately printed.

MAC LEISH (Archibald)
—— Einstein. (With a drawing of the author by Paul Emile Becat.) [A poem.] *Black Sun Press: Paris*, 1929. 4°. Cup.510.fa.13.
No. 19 of an edition of 100 copies. With the author's autograph signature.

STERNE (Lawrence) [*Sentimental Journey.*]
—— A Sentimental Journal through France and Italy . . . With illustrations by Polia Chentoff. pp. 191. *Black Sun Press: Paris*, 1929. 8°. Cup.510.fa.10.

WALLOP (Gerard Vernon) *Earl of Portsmouth.*
—— Spring Song of Iscariot. Poem. pp. 27. *Black Sun Press: Paris*, 1929. 8°. Cup.510.fa.14.

CRANE (Harold Hart)
—— The Bridge. A poem . . . With three photographs by Walker Evans. *Black Sun Press: Paris*, 1930. 4°. Cup.510.fa.15.

MAC LEISH (Archibald)
—— New Found Land. Fourteen poems. *Black Sun Press: Paris*, 1930. 8°. Cup. 400. c. 22.
No. 61 of an edition of one hundred copies.

POUND (Ezra Loomis)
—— Imaginary Letters. pp. 56. *Black Sun Press: Paris*, 1930. 8°. Cup.510.fa.16.

PROUST (Marcel) 47 Lettres inédites de Marcel Proust à Walter Berry. (Traduites en anglais par Harry et Caresse Crosby.) [With a portrait.] *Fr. & Eng. Paris*, 1930. 4°. Cup.510.fa.17.

CREVEL (René)
—— [Babylone.] Mr. Knife, Miss Fork (being a fragment of the novel Babylone) . . . Translated by Kay Boyle. Illustrated by Max Ernst. pp. 38. *Black Sun Press: Paris*, 1931. 8°. 11411. gg. 60.

CROSBY (Harry)
—— The Collected Poems of Harry Crosby. 4 vol.
vol. 1. Chariot of the Sun . . . Introduction by D. H. Lawrence pp. xviii. 68.
vol. 2. Transit of Venus . . . With a preface by T. S. Eliot. pp. ix. 62.
vol. 3. Sleeping together. A book of dreams . . . With a memory of the poet by Stuart Gilbert. [With a portrait.] pp. 65. ix.
vol. 4. Torchbearer . . . With notes by Ezra Pound. [With a portrait.] pp. 44. viii.
Black Sun Press: Paris, 1931. 4°. Cup.510.fa.3.

HEMINGWAY (Ernest)
—— In our time. Stories. pp. 220. *Crosby Continental Editions: Paris*, 1932. 8°. X. 907/5679.
Modern masterpieces in English. no. 6.

HEMINGWAY (Ernest)
—— The Torrents of spring. A romantic novel in honor of the passing of a great race. pp. 176. *Crosby Continental Editions: Paris*, 1932. 8°. X. 907/5680.
World-wide masterpieces in English. no. 1.

PHILIPPE (Charles Louis)
—— Bubu of Montparnasse . . . Translated by Laurence Vail, *etc.* pp. 218. *Paris*, 1932. 8°. 12516. r. 31.

RADIGUET (Raymond)
—— [Le Diable au corps.] Devil in the Flesh . . . Translated by Kay Boyle, *etc.* pp. 253. *Crosby Continental Editions: Paris*, 1932. 8°. 12516. r. 33.

SAINT EXUPÉRY (Antoine de)
—— Night-Flight . . . Translated by Stuart Gilbert. pp. 189. *Crosby Continental Editions: Paris*, 1932. 8°. 12516. r. 32.

JOYCE (James Augustine Aloysius)
—— Collected Poems of James Joyce. [With a portrait.] pp. lxv. *Black Sun Press: New York*, 1936. 8°. Cup.510.pk.3.

BLACK VINE PRESS, San Francisco

MORISON (STANLEY)
—— Typographic Design in Relation to Photographic Composition, etc. pp. 32. *Book Club of California: San Francisco*, 1959. 8º. Cup. **510**. nat. **1**.

BLACKAMORE PRESS, London

PUSHKIN (ALEKSANDR SERGYEEVICH) The Queen of Spades. (Translated by J. E. Pouterman and C. Bruerton.) Engravings in colour by A. Alexeieff, *etc.* pp. 109. *Blackamore Press: London; Argenteuil* printed, 1928. 4º. C. 98. f. 18.
No. III of XXXV copies not for sale. With a duplicate set of plates.

GIDE (ANDRÉ PAUL GUILLAUME)
—— Montaigne. An essay in two parts. (Translated by Stephen H. Guest & Trevor E. Blewitt.) *London: Blackamore Press; New York: Horace Liveright*, 1929. **11823**. p. **10**.

pp. 128. 20 cm. △
Printed in France.

GREEN (JULIEN) The Pilgrim on the Earth. (Translated by C. Bruerton.) 12 wood engravings in colour by René Ben Sussan. pp. 120. *Blackamore Press: London; Harper & Bros.: New York; Argenteuil* printed, 1929. 4º. C. 98. f. 19.
No. III of XXXV copies not for sale. With a duplicate set of plates.

MILTON (JOHN) [*Prose Works.—Brief History of Moscovia.*] A Brief History of Moscovia . . . To which are added other curious documents, with an introduction by Prince D. S. Mirsky. Illustrations by A. Brodovitch. pp. 120. *Blackamore Press: London*, 1929. 8º. 9454. d. 35.

BAUDELAIRE (CHARLES PIERRE) [*Journals.*]

—— Intimate Journals. Translated by Ch. Isherwood. Introduction by T. S. Eliot. [With plates from drawings by Baudelaire.] pp. 125. *Blackamore Press: London; Random House: New York*, 1930. 8º. 012352. ee. 60.

HUDSON (STEPHEN) *pseud.* [i.e. SYDNEY SCHIFF.]
—— Céleste, and other sketches . . . Wood engravings by John Nash. pp. 101. *Blackamore Press: London*, 1930. 8º. 12643. w. 43.

BLAKENEY (E. H.), Ely; Winchester

BLAKENEY (EDWARD HENRY)
—— Poems by Two Friends: E. H. Blakeney and D. Morrieson Panton. pp. vi. 44. *J. Palmer: Cambridge; G. J. Palmer: London*, 1892. 8º. Cup. 510. aba. 2 (15)

BLAKENEY (EDWARD HENRY)
—— A Death on the Prairie. [*Ely*,] 1909. 8º. *Printed by the Author:* Cup. 510. aba. 14.
Printed on one side of the leaf only.

HALL (FRITZ-EDWARD)
—— A Note on Fitzgerald. [The editor's preface signed: W. F. P., i.e. William Francis Prideaux.] ff. 5. *Printed by E. H. Blakeney at his Private Press: Ely*, 1909. 8º. Cup. 510. aba. 2. (10.)
One of an edition of twenty-five copies. Printed on one side of the leaf only.

PRIDEAUX (WILLIAM FRANCIS)
—— Omar and his Translator. ff. 5. *Printed by E. H. Blakeney at his Private Press: Ely*, 1909. 8º. Cup. 510. aba. 1 (3.)
Printed on one side of the leaf only.

BLAKENEY (EDWARD HENRY)
—— Footsteps of Autumn, and other poems. ff. 56. *Printed by the Author: Ely*, 1912. 8º. Cup. 510. aba 15
Printed on one side of the leaf only.

PRIDEAUX (WILLIAM FRANCIS)
—— A Cameo of Provence. *Printed at his private press by Edward Henry Blakeney: Ely*, 1912. 8º. Cup. 510. aba. 2. (9.)
Printed on one side of the leaf only. One of an edition of thirty-five copies.

BLAKENEY (EDWARD HENRY)
—— Romance: an address to girls. ff. 7. *Printed by the Author: Ely*, 1914. 8º. Cup. 510. aba. 16.
Printed on one side of the leaf only.

BLAKENEY (EDWARD HENRY)
—— To the Day: a poem. [*Ely*], 1914. 8º. *Printed by the Author:* 011649. ee. 41.

KIPLING (RUDYARD) [*Single Tales and Poems.*]
—— Ulster. A poem. *Ely: printed by E. H. Blakeney at his private press*, 1914. C. 71. c. 24.
Pages not numbered. 20 cm. △
Printed for private circulation, on one side of the leaf only.

—— [Another copy.] Ashley 1001.

BLAKENEY (EDWARD HENRY)
—— Collected War Poems. pp. 12. *Printed by the Author: Ely*, 1915. 8º. Cup. 510. aba. 13.

BLAKENEY (EDWARD HENRY)
—— Memorabilia Latina. Compiled by E. H. Blakeney. *E. H. Blakeney: Ely*, [c. 1915.] 32º. Cup. 510. aba. 2. (1.)

BLAKENEY (Edward Henry)

—— Poems in Peace and War: 1912–1918. ff. 29. *Printed by the Author at his Private Press: Ely*, 1918. 8°.
Cup.510.aba.17.

Printed on one side of the leaf only. One of an edition of sixty-five copies.

BLAKENEY (Edward Henry)

—— In the Vale of Years. Verses on various occasions. *Printed by the Author: Winchester*, 1926. 8°.
Cup.510.aba.18.

Printed on one side of the leaf only.

BIBLE.—*Judges.*—*Selections.* [*English.*]

—— The Song of Deborah and Barak. (A partial revision of the A.V. rendering.) *Privately printed by E. H. Blakeney: Winchester*, 1927. 8°. Cup.510.aba.26.

One of an edition of thirty copies.

BLAKENEY (Edward Henry)

—— Mountain Memories. [Verses.] *Printed by the Author: Winchester*, 1927. 8°. Cup.510.aba.21.

One of an edition of thirty copies. Printed on one side of the leaf only.

PLATO. [*Doubtful and Supposititious Works.—Epigrammata.—English.*]

—— The Light of the Dead: a newly discovered poem by Percy Bysshe Shelley. (From the Greek of Plato [Ἀστέρας εἰσαθρεῖς ἀστηρ ἐμος].) *Printed by Edward Henry Blakeney at his Private Press: Winchester*, 1927. 16°.
Cup. 510. aba. 2. (2.)

Printed on one side of the leaf only. One of an edition of thirty copies.

SHELLEY (Percy Bysshe) [*Miscellaneous.*] The Celandine. A newly discovered poem. *Printed by E. H. Blakeney at his private press: Winchester*, 1927. 8°. Cup.510.aba.29.

One of an edition of 30 copies.

PATER (Walter Horatio) The Chant of the Celestial Sailors. An unpublished poem. *Printed at the private press of E. H. Blakeney: [Winchester,]* 1928. 8°. Cup.510.aba.30.

Printed on one side of the leaf only. One of an edition of 30 copies.

PATER (Walter Horatio)

—— Inscription for the Life of Walter Pater. To the reader. (Inserted by Pater in front of a book of MS. poems begun March 1859.) *Printed by E. H. Blakeney at his private press: Winchester*, 1928. 4°. Cup.510.aba.33.

BLAKENEY (Edward Henry)

—— Alpine Poems. pp. 37. *Printed at the Author's private press: Winchester*, 1929. 8°. Cup.510.aba.19.

One of an edition of sixty copies.

GOSSE (Sir Edmund William)

—— Two Unpublished Poems. (Hesperus.—Saint Peter.) *E. H. Blakeney: Winchester*, 1929. 8° Cup.510.aba.25.

One of an edition of fourteen copies. Printed on one side of the leaf only.

LANDOR (Walter Savage) [*Letters.*]

—— A letter, believed to be hitherto unpublished, by W. S. Landor. *Winchester: printed by E. H. Blakeney at his private press*, 1929. Cup. 510. aba. 2. (6.)

Pages not numbered. 21 cm.

Addressed to Mrs. Southey. Dated 2 Jan. 1843. Part of an edition of twenty-one copies. Printed on one side of the leaf only.

B., E. H.

—— The Dial. A sonnet. [Signed: E. H. B., i.e. E. H. Blakeney.] [*Printed by the Author: Winchester*, 1930.] 4°.
Cup.510.aba.2.(5.

DOBSON (Henry Austin) Three Unpublished Poems. *Mr. Blakeney's private press: Winchester*, 1930. 8°. 011644. i. 81.

One of an edition of 25 copies; printed on one side of the leaf only.

GISSING (George Robert)

—— Hope in Vain. [A poem.] *Printed by E. H. Blakeney at his private press: [Winchester,]* 1930. 8°.
Cup. 510. aba. 24.

Printed on one side of the leaf only. One of 16 copies printed.

SASSOON (Siegfried Loraine)

—— On Chatterton: a sonnet. *Printed at Mr. Blakeney's Private Press: Winchester*, 1930. 4°.
Cup.510.aba.1.(2.)

One of an edition of fourteen copies.

SERJEANT (Farel Viret Calvin)

—— 'There is a City Bright.' *Lat.* [*E. H. Blakeney: Winchester, c.* 1930.] *s. sh.* 8°. Cup.510.aba.2(4.

KIPLING (Rudyard) [*Single Tales and Poems*]

—— Memories. [A poem.] *Printed by E. H. Blakeney for private circulation: Winchester*, 1932. 8°.
Ashley 3501.

One of fifteen copies printed.

BLAKENEY (Edward Henry)

—— Falling Leaves: or, Wayside musings in verse. ff. 24. *Printed by the Author: Winchester*, 1933. 8°.
Cup.510.aba.32.

Printed on one side of the leaf only.

B., E. H.

—— Monday, May 6, 1935. [A poem. Signed: E. H. B., i.e. Edward Henry Blakeney.] [*Winchester,* 1935.] 8°.
11655. bb. 10.

One of an edition of twenty-five copies privately printed by the author. The wrapper bears a MS. title reading: " Lines to commemorate the King's Jubilee, 1935."

BLAKENEY (Edward Henry)

—— In a Winchester Garden. A sonnet. *Printed at the Author's private press: Winchester*, 1935. 8°.
Cup.510.aba.4.

BLAKENEY (Edward Henry)
—— In Memoriam Rudyard Kipling. [A sonnet.]
The Author: [Winchester,] 1936. 8°. Cup.510.aba.5.
One of an edition of fifteen copies.

HOOD (Thomas) *the Elder.*
—— Sonnet . . . to . . . Marianne Reynolds, the friend of John
Keats. *Printed by E. H. Blakeney at his Private Press:*
Winchester, 1936. 8°. Cup.510.aba.2.(3.)
One of an edition of fifteen copies.

MEREDITH (George)
—— George Meredith on John Morley. Glasgow University
Rectorial Election, 1902. [A letter addressed to John
Bain.] *Printed at Mr. Blakeney's Private Press:*
Winchester, 1936. 8°. Cup.510.aba.22.

NOYES (Alfred)
—— The Cormorant. A poem. *E. H. Blakeney: Winchester,*
1936. 4°. Cup.510.aba.34.
Printed on one side of the leaf only.

SHELLEY (Percy Bysshe) [*Letters.*]
—— A Shelley Letter, unfinished, unsigned, undated. [In
verse.] *Printed by E. H. Blakeney at his Private Press:*
Winchester, 1936. 8°. Cup. 510. aba. 27.
One of an edition of fourteen copies.

BLAKENEY (Edward Henry)
—— Occasional Verses. *Printed at his Private Press:*
Winchester, 1937. 16°. Cup.510.aba.3.
Printed on one side of the leaf only.

NOYES (Alfred)
—— Youth and Memory. A poem . . . Read to the Youth
of the Empire at the Albert Hall Rally, on 18 May, 1937.
E. H. Blakeney: Winchester, 1937. 8°. Cup.510.aba.35.
One of an edition of thirty copies privately printed.

NOYES (Alfred)
—— Wizards. A poem. *Printed by E. H. Blakeney at his*
Private Press: Winchester, 1938. 4°.
Cup.510.aba.1(4.)
For private circulation.

BLAKENEY (Edward Henry)
—— At the Day's End. Verses on various occasions. ff. 29.
At the Author's Private Press: Winchester, 1939. 8°.
Cup.510.aba.6.
Printed on one side of the leaf only.

GALE (Norman Rowland)
—— His Testament, and Settled. [Two poems.] *At the*
Private Press of Edward Henry Blakeney: Winchester,
1939. 8°. Cup.510.aba.2.(11.)
One of an edition of thirty copies.

BLAKENEY (Edward Henry)
—— Seven Epigrams, *etc.* *Printed by the Author:*
Winchester, 1940. 8°. Cup.510.aba.12.

NOYES (Alfred) [*Letters.*]
—— Unpublished Letters from the collection of Alfred Noyes.
[By Joseph Mazzini and others.] *Printed by E. H.*
Blakeney at his Private Press: Winchester, 1940. 8°.
Cup. 510. aba. 1. (7.)

ROOSEVELT (Theodore) *President of the United States of*
America. [*Letters.*]
—— A Hitherto Unpublished Letter from Theodore Roose-
velt [to Alfred Noyes]. (Nov. 28, 1914.) *Printed by*
E. H. Blakeney at his Private Press: Winchester, 1940. 8°.
Cup. 510. aba. 28.

BLAKENEY (Edward Henry)
—— My Cats. A collection of verses. *Printed by the Author:*
Winchester, [1941.] 16°. Cup.510.aba.7.

HOUSMAN (Alfred Edward) [*Letters.*]
—— Letters from A. E. Housman to E. H. Blakeney.
[Edited by E. H. Blakeney.] *Printed at Mr. Blakeney's*
Private Press: Winchester, 1941. 4°.
Cup. 510. aba. 23.
No. 4 of an edition of eighteen copies.

BLAKENEY (Edward Henry)
—— Malta to-day. [Signed: E. H. B., i.e. E. H. Blakeney.]
[1942]. 18 cm. Cup. 510. aba. 1. (9.)
△
A single-sheet poem.

BLAKENEY (Edward Henry)
—— Now and Then. A sheaf of epigrams. *The Author:*
Winchester, 1942. 16°. Cup.510.aba.20.

BLAKENEY (Edward Henry)
—— Collected Hymns. *Printed by the Author at his private*
Press: Winchester, 1943. 8°. 03433. aa. 2.

BLAKENEY (Edward Henry)
—— The Last Load Home. Verses written in war-time.
Printed by the Author at his private press: Winchester,
1943. 8°. Cup.510.aba.9.

BLAKENEY (Edward Henry)
—— Between Times. Gleanings by the wayside. [Mainly
verse translations from the Greek.] *Printed by the author*
at his private press: Winchester, 1944. 8°.
Cup.510.aba.10.

BLAKENEY (Edward Henry)
—— Hitler, in 1944. [By E. H. Blakeney.] [1944].
93 mm.×15 cm. Cup. 510. aba. 1. (8.)
△
A single-sheet verse.

BLAKENEY (EDWARD HENRY)
—— Hours in a Study. [A poem.] [*The Author:*] *Winchester,* 1944. 16°.   Cup.510.aba.8.
Printed on one side of the leaf only.

BLAKENEY (EDWARD HENRY)
—— My Cats, *etc.* (Second edition, enlarged.) FEW MS. CORRECTIONS. *Printed by the author at his private press : Winchester,* 1944. 8°.   C. **109**. m. **40**. (6.)
One of an edition of twenty-seven copies.

BROWNING (ROBERT) *the Poet.* [*Smaller Collections.*]
—— The Sonnets of Robert Browning. [The postscript signed: E. H. B., i.e. Edward Henry Blakeney.] *Printed by E. H. Blakeney at his Private Press : Winchester,* 1944. 8°.   Cup. **510**. aba. **2**. (8.)
Printed on one side of the leaf only. One of an edition of fifteen copies.

BLAKENEY (EDWARD HENRY)
—— Collected Hymns . . . Second, enlarged, edition. *Printed by the Author at his Private Press : Winchester,* 1945. 8°.   Cup.510.aba.2. (12.
Printed on one side of the leaf only.

BLAKENEY (EDWARD HENRY)
—— In a Railway Carriage. [A poem.]   *Printed by the Author : Winchester,* 1945. 8°.   Cup.510.aba.11.

ESDAILE (ARUNDELL JAMES KENNEDY)
—— Four Poems of the Second World War.   *Printed at Mr Blakeney's Private Press : Winchester,* 1945. 8°.   11657. c. 81.

ESDAILE (ARUNDELL JAMES KENNEDY)
—— Shadow of Power. A sonnet.   [*E. H. Blakeney : Winchester,* 1945 ?] *obl.* 8°.   Cup.510.aba.1. (1.)

BLAKENEY (EDWARD HENRY)
—— Four New Hymns.   *The Author at his Private Press : Winchester,* 1947. 8°.   3437. i. 25.
One of an edition of twenty-one copies.

BLAKENEY (EDWARD HENRY)
—— Collected Hymns.   *Printed by the Author at his private press : Winchester,* 1949. 8°. Cup.510.aba.2. (13.)
Printed on one side of the leaf only. One of an edition of thirty-five copies.

BLAKENEY (EDWARD HENRY)
—— My Cats, *etc.* (Third issue.) pp. 12.   *Winchester,* 1949. 8°.   C. **109**. m. **40**. (5.)
One of an edition of thirty copies, printed on one side of the leaf only. With additional material inserted.

B., E. H.
—— In the Garden at Lisle Combe, *etc.* [A poem. Signed: E. H. B., i.e. E. H. Blakeney.] *Printed by the Author at his Private Press : Winchester,* 1950. 8°.   Cup.510.aba.2(7.)
One of an edition of fifteen copies.

NOYES (ALFRED)
—— The Assumption. An answer. [A poem.]   *Printed by E. H. Blakeney at his Private Press : Winchester,* 1950. 8°.   Cup.510.aba.1. (5.)
One of an edition of thirty copies.

NOYES (ALFRED)
—— A Roehampton School Song.   *Printed by E. H. Blakeney at his Private Press : Winchester,* 1950. 8°.   Cup.510.aba.1. (6.)

TOPLADY (AUGUSTUS MONTAGUE)
—— Two Hymns. Translated into Latin verse by William Ewart Gladstone, *etc.* (' Rock of Ages,' by Toplady. ' Art thou weary,' from the Greek, by J. M. Neale.) *E. H. Blakeney : Winchester,* 1951. 8°.   3425. i. 1.
Privately printed.

BLUE MOON PRESS, Friern Barnet; London

SCRANNEL (ORPHEUS) *pseud.* [i.e. TERENCE IAN FYTTON ARMSTRONG.]
—— An Unterrestrial Pity. Being contributions towards a biography of the late Pinchbeck Lyre.   *Blue Moon Press : Friern Barnet,* 1931. 8°.   11654. c. 21.

GAWSWORTH (JOHN) *pseud.* [i.e. TERENCE IAN FYTTON ARMSTRONG.]
—— Epithalamium. For 'H. E. Bates, Esq., of Ashforde and his lady wife, *etc.* *Press of the Blue Moon : Friern Barnet,* 1931. 8°.   11644. l. 23.

MOORE (OLIVE)
—— Further Reflections on the Death of a Porcupine. [An essay on D. H. Lawrence.] pp. 34.   *Blue Moon Press : London,* 1932. 4°.   C. 98. i. 13.
One of an edition of 99 copies.

COPPARD (ALFRED EDGAR)
—— These hopes of heaven.   *London : Blue Moon Press,* 1934.   Cup. **502**. n. **59**.
    Pages not numbered ; illus.   21 cm.   △
Privately printed for Albert Parsons Sachs.

BOAR'S HEAD PRESS, Manaton, Devon

SANDFORD (CHRISTOPHER) The Cegs. [A tale.] pp. 13. *Christopher Sandford : London,* 1930. 16°.
No. 5 of an edition of 25 copies. Cup.510.av.9.

SANDFORD (CHRISTOPHER) *and* **SANDFORD** (LETTICE)
—— The magic forest. A story told printed and illustrated by Christopher and Lettice Sandford. *London : Christopher & Lettice Sandford at the Chiswick Press,* 1931.   Cup. **510**. av. **24**.
    pp. 32.   27 cm.   △
No. 35 of an edition of one hundred copies, signed by the authors. A four-page folder, containing advertisements for " Books published at the Sign of the Boar's Head in Heathercombe " has been inserted in this copy.

BERSAN (H.) Maya. Fifty-five sonnets. pp. 31.
Boar's Head Press: Manaton, 1932. 8°.
Cup.510.aga.5.

BOOTH (Digby Haworth) Kleinias. Poems. pp. 30.
At the Sign of the Boar's Head: Manaton, 1932. 8°.
Cup.510.aga.2.

LYLE (Marius)
—— The Virgin. A tale of woe. pp. 45.
Boar's Head Press: Manaton, 1932. 8°.
Cup.510.aga.3.

SANDFORD (Christopher) and (Lettice)
—— Clervis & Belamie. A story told, illustrated & published
by C. and L. Sandford. pp. 26. *C. & L. Sandford:
Heathercombe, 1932.* 4°. Cup.510.aga.1.
One of an edition of 100 copies.

SAPPHO.
—— Sappho. The text arranged with translations, an intro-
duction & notes, by E. M. Cox. (Illustrations by Lettice
Sandford.) pp. 81. *Boar's Head Press: Manaton,
1932.* 8°. C. 99. d. 41.
No. 8 of 25 copies printed on Japanese vellum.

SPENSER (Edmund) [*Prothalamion.*]
—— Thalamos; or, The Brydall Boure, being the Epitha-
lamion & Prothalamion of Edmund Spenser. *Manaton:
Christopher & Lettice Sandford, to be sold at the sign of the
Boar's Head, 1932.* C. 98. i. 11.
pp. 34; illus. 27 cm. △

UBSDELL (A. R.)
—— East & West. Poems. pp. 58. *Boar's Head Press:
Manaton, 1932.* 8°. Cup.510.aga.4.

BARWELL (Peggy) and MORLAND (Nigel)
—— Salome before the Head of Saint John . . . Illustrated
by Lettice Sandford. (Reprinted from ' Cachexia.')
Boar's Head Press: Manaton, 1933. 8°.
Cup.510.aga.10.

BINGLEY (Barbara)
—— Tales of the Turquoise . . . Wood-engravings by
Lettice Sandford. pp. 94. *Boar's Head Press: London,
1933.* 8°. C. 100. b. 4.

SANDFORD (Christopher)
—— Few were Chosen. A sequence of poems. *Boar's
Head Press: London, 1933.* 8°. Cup.510.aga.8.
One of an edition of 100 copies.

LONDON.—III. *First Edition Club.*
—— Dreams & Life. Le rêve et la vie. By Gérard de Nerval.
Translation by Vyvyan Holland. pp. 86. *First Edition
Club: London; Boar's Head Press: Manaton, 1933.* 8°.
Ac. 9670. c/13.

SANDFORD (Christopher)
—— Immortality, and other poems. *Boar's Head Press:
London, 1933.* 8°. Cup.510.aga.7.
One of an edition of 100 copies.

SANDFORD (Christopher)
—— Primeval Gods. [Verses.] (With illustrations by Blair
Hughes-Stanton.) pp. 30. *Boar's Head Press: [London,
1934.]* 8°. Cup.510.aga.6.

BINGLEY (Barbara) The Painted Cup . . . [Poems.]
Wood-engravings by Lettice Sandford. pp. 63.
Boar's Head Press: London, 1935. 8°. C. 100. b. 5.

YOUNGER (William Anthony)
—— Madonna and other poems. pp. 39 *Boar's Head Press:
London, 1935.* 8°. Cup.510.aga.9.
*No. 28 of an edition of 100 copies. Author's presentation
copy to Mr. & Mrs. C. R. Ashbee. With an autograph letter
from the author to C. R. Ashbee inserted.*

BOOTHAM PRESS, York

CHINESE PHILOSOPHY.
—— Some Fragments of Chinese Philosophy. (Illustrations
by Rigby Graham.) *Bootham Press: York, 1961.* 8°.
Cup. 510. bet. 1.
One of an edition of seventy copies.

BOURBON PRESS, London

BALZAC (Honoré de)
—— Selections from the Droll Stories of Honoré de Balzac.
Arranged and translated by: André de Lignolles, with 20
illustrations by Cees Woltman. pp. 115. *Bourbon Press:
London, 1948.* 8°. C. 103. b. 12.

BOWLING GREEN PRESS, New York

MOORE (George) *Novelist.*
—— The Making of an Immortal. A play in one act. pp. 59.
Bowling Green Press: New York, 1927. 8°.
11791. g. 31.

DE LA MARE (Walter John) [*Single Works.*]
—— The Captive and other Poems. pp. 19. *Bowling Green
Press: New York, 1928.* 8°. 11392. a. 48.
Printed on grey paper.

DRINKWATER (JOHN) *Poet.*

—— The World's Lincoln. pp. 34.   *Bowling Green Press:*
New York, 1928. 8º.   C. **103**. e. **25**.

SCOTT (TEMPLE) *pseud.* [i.e. J. H. ISAACS.] Oliver
Goldsmith, bibliographically and biographically con-
sidered. Based on the collection of material in the
library of W. M. Elkins, Esq., *etc.* [With portraits.]
pp. xix. 368.   *Bowling Green Press:*
New York, 1928. 8º.   **11907**. dd. **27**.

WOLFE (HUMBERT) The Silver Cat, and other
poems.   *Bowling Green Press:*
New York; Ernest Benn: London, 1928. 8º.
  Printed on one side of the leaf only.   **11643**. l. **24**.

COOPER (JAMES FENIMORE) [*Single Works.—The Spy.*]

—— The spy ... With a general introduction by Henry Seidel
Canby, also with illustrations by William Cotton. *New
York: Bowling Green Press,* 1929.   **012601**. ee. **39**.
  3 vol.: plates. 17 cm.   △

BOWNESS PRESS, Horsell

FLOCCINAUCINIHILIPILIFICATION.

—— Floccinaucinihilipilification, or Virile '65. [Poems by
various authors.]   *Bowness Press: Horsell; Beaumont
College: [Old Windsor,]* 1965. 8º.   Cup. **510**. cus. **1**.

BRACEBRIDGE PRESS, Four Oaks, Warwickshire

ENGLAND.—*Justices of the Peace.*

—— The Boke for a Justyce of Peace neuer soo wel and dili-
gently set forthe. [The text of the edition printed by
Thomas Berthelet in 1536.] (Produced by W. T. Wiggins-
Davies.) pp. 39.   *Bracebridge Press: Four Oaks,*
1942. fol.   **6283**. d. **1**.

BREMER PRESSE, Munich

EMERSON (RALPH WALDO)

—— Nature. pp. 86.   *Bremer Presse: München,* 1929. fol.
               C. **98**. e. **21**.

FIELD (WILLIAM B. OSGOOD) John Leech on my
Shelves. [A catalogue of books illustrated by Leech,
of original drawings, etc. by him, and of books relating
to him, in the collection of W.B.O. Field. With a
portrait and facsimiles.] pp. 313.
      Privately printed at the Bremer Presse:
Munich, 1930. fol.   L. R. **40**. c. **5**.

HOFMILLER (JOSEF)

—— Ballads and Songs of Love. (Ausgewählt und herausgegeben von J. Hofmiller.) *Eng.* pp. 136. *Bremer Presse:*
München, 1930. fol.   C. **102**. h. **5**.

HOFMILLER (JOSEF) and **SPINDLER** (ROBERT)

—— Sonnets. [By various English writers.] (Herausgegeben
von J. Hofmiller und R. Spindler.) pp. 238. *Bremer Presse:*
München, 1931. fol.   C. **102**. h. **4**.

FIELD (WILLIAM B. OSGOOD)

—— Edward Lear on my Shelves. [A catalogue of the drawings, paintings and literary works of Lear in the collection
of W. B. O. Field. With a portrait and facsimiles.]
pp. 455.   *Printed by the Bremer Press for William B.
Osgood Field: Munich,* 1933. fol.   C. **103**. h. **5**.
  Privately printed.

MÊNG CHIANG NÜ.

—— The lady of the Long Wall ... A Ku Shih or drum song
of China [entitled: Mêng Chiang Nü]. Translated ... by
Genevieve Wimsatt and Geoffrey Chen—Chen Sun-han.
New York: Columbia University Press, 1934.
              11101. d. **6**.
  pp. 84; illus. 27 cm.   △
  Printed at the Bremmer Presse, Munich.

MÊNG CHIANG NÜ.

—— [Another copy.] The lady of the Long Wall, *etc.* 1934.
             11101. d. **21**.
               △

BREWHOUSE PRESS, Wymondham, Leicestershire

G., P. M.

—— An Autumn Anthology. Illustrations by Rigby Graham.
[The compiler's note signed: P. M. G., i.e. Patricia M.
Graham.]   *Privately printed by the Cistercians of Mount
Saint Bernard Abbey: Coalville,* 1964 [1965]. 8º.
           Cup. **510**. coz. **2**.

TYCHBORNE (CHIDIOCK)

—— Chidiock Tichbourne. His last letter to Agnes his wife
and his Elegy, together with an Answer to Mr Tichbourne
and a biographical note. Illustrated by Rigby Graham.
Brewhouse Press: Wymondham, 1964. 8º.
           Cup. **510**. cov. **1**.

GRAHAM (RIGBY ALFRED)

—— A Note on the Book Illustrations of Paul Nash. [With
reproductions, including self-portraits.]   *Brewhouse
Press: Wymondham,* [1965.] 8º.   Cup. **510**. cov. **2**.

BRONZE SNAIL PRESS, London

BEERNINK (ERNST) The Phœnix. [In verse.] *Capell:*
London, [1930.] 8º.   Cup. **510**. bex. **1**.

DAVIES (Rhys) *Novelist.*

—— A Woman. pp. 39. *Capell: London,* 1931. 8°.
　　　　　　　　　　　　　　　Cup.510.bex.2.
One of thirty-two copies printed on Japanese vellum.

BROOKS PRESS, Wirksworth

COLERIDGE (Samuel Taylor) [*Single Works.—Christabel, Kubla Khan, etc.*]

—— Christabel: a poem. *Wirksworth: Brooks Press,* 1920.
　　　　　　　　　　　　　　11642. bbb. 74.

　　pp. 44. 16 cm. △

BAY (Celia Hansen) A Little Book about Wirksworth. [With plates.] pp. 26. *Brooks Press: Wirksworth,* 1924. 8°. 10360. cc. 69.

BAY (Celia Hansen) Sonnets and Occasional Verses. pp. 36. *Brooks Press: Wirksworth,* 1927. 8°.
　　　　　　　　　　　　　　011644. ee. 45.

BROTHERS OF THE BOOK, Chicago

STONE (Wilbur Macey) Some Children's Book-plates. An essay in little. [With plates.] *Brothers of the Book: New York,* 1901. 8°.
　　　　　　　　　　Cup.510.pf.1.

CRAM (Ralph Adams)

—— The Great Thousand Years. Written in the year 1908, and first printed in Pax, the magazine of the Benedictines of Caldey, in December 1910. To which is added a brief commentary written in January, 1918, and called Ten Years After. pp. 67. *Brothers of the Book: Chicago,* 1918. 8°. Cup. 510. pf. 2.
No. 44 of an edition of fifty-three autographed copies.

BURLEIGH PRESS, Bristol

SQUIRE (*Sir* John Collings)

—— The Clown of Stratford. (A comedy in one act.) pp. 21. *Burleigh Press: Bristol,* 1926. 8°. Cup. 510. cem. 1.
Printed for private circulation only.

ALCOFORADO (Marianna)

—— The Letters of a Portuguese Nun. Translated . . . by E. Allen Ashwin. pp. xi. 36. *Francis Walterson: Dyffryn,* 1929. 8°. 010902. f. 44.

BUSY BEE, Utrecht

GAY (John) *the Poet.*
[*Fables.*]

—— The Fox at the Point of Death. (Reprinted from the edition of his Fables of 1828.) *The Busy Bee:* [*Utrecht,*] 1945. 12°. Cup. 510. gd. 10.
Clandestinely published.

BYWAY PRESS, Cincinnati

THÓRIR, called Hænsa-Thórir. The Saga of Hen Thorir. Done into English out of the Icelandic by William Morris and Eirikr Magnusson. With decorations by A. E. Goetting. pp. 87. *Byway Press: Cincinnati, Ohio,* 1903. 8°. 12411. aa. 21.

CAMELOT PRESS, London

GIBBINGS (Robert John)

—— Iorana! A Tahitian journal . . . With wood-engravings by the author. pp. 142. *Duckworth: London,* 1932. 8°. 10492. ff. 33.

BATES (Herbert Ernest)

—— Down the River . . . With 83 engravings on wood by Agnes Miller Parker. pp. 150. *Victor Gollancz: London,* 1937. 4°. 010352. i. 39.

CANDLE PRESS, Dublin

PIM (Herbert Moore)

—— Selected Poems of Herbert Moore Pim. pp. 23. *Candle Press: Dublin,* 1917. 8°. Cup. 510. bbf. 6.
Poetry Booklets. no. 1.

PLUNKETT (Geraldine)

—— Magnificat . . . Illustrated by Jack Morrow. *Dublin: Candle Press,* 1917. Cup. 510. bbf. 8.
　　pp. 14. 17 cm. △
Poems.

MAC BRIEN (Peter)

—— Poems. *Dublin: Candle Press,* 1918.
　　　　　　　　　　　　Cup. 510. bbf. 4.
　　pp. 23. 22 cm. (Poetry booklets. no. 3.) △

MAC BRIEN (Peter)

—— [Another copy.] Poems. *Dublin,* 1918. 22 cm.
　　　　　　　　　　　　Cup. 510. bbf. 7.
　　　　　　　　　　　　　　　　　△

O'BYRNE (Dermot) *pseud.* [i.e. *Sir* Arnold Edward Trevor Bax, *K.C.V.O.*]

—— A Dublin Ballad, and other poems. pp. 23. *Candle Press: Dublin,* 1918. 8°. Cup. 510. bbf. 5.
Poetry Booklets. no. 2.

WILSON (Florence M.)

—— The coming of the Earls, and other poems. *Dublin: Candle Press,* 1918. Cup. 510. bbf. 3.
　　pp. 22. 22 cm. (Poetry booklets. no. 4.) △

YOUNG (Ella)

—— The Rose of Heaven. Poems . . . decorated by Maud Gonne. pp. 53. *Candle Press: Dublin,* 1920. 4°.
　　　　　　　　　　Cup.510.bbf.1.

YOUNG (ELLA)

—— [Another copy.] The Rose of Heaven, *etc.*   *Dublin,*
1920.   Cup. **510**. bbf. **2.**

△

*Author's presentation copy to Seumas O'Sullivan. With
a MS. poem, inscribed on a blank leaf.*

CANTERBURY COLLEGE OF ART,
Canterbury, Kent

BOORDE (ANDREW)

[Dyetary of Helth.]

—— Thoughts before Building . . . [Selections from Dyetary of
Helth.] With an introduction and notes by H. Edmund
Poole. pp. 14.   *College of Art Press : Canterbury,*
1961. 4º.   Cup. **510**. bep. **1.**
*Privately printed. No. 34 of an edition of one hundred
copies.*

MILES (HERBERT WILLIAM)

—— Corolla Cantiana. A garland of wild flowers. With text
by Herbert W. Miles. pp. 45.   *Privately printed at the
College of Art Press : Canterbury,* 1963. 8º.
                                        Cup. **510**. bep. **2.**

No. 5 of an edition of fifty copies.

CARADOC PRESS, Chiswick; London

EPHEMERIDES. [*Unnamed Ephemerides.*]

—— [Calendar for 1900, with verses.] Written, designed, cut
on wood and printed by H. D. and H. G. Webb, *etc.*
H. D. & H. G. Webb : Chiswick, 1899. obl. 32º.
                                         Cup. **510**. bb. **1.**

BOY.

—— The old ballad of the Boy and the Mantle. (From the
text of Bishop Percy. The ornaments designed . . . by
H. D. and H. G. Webb.) pp. 17.   *H. D. & H. G. Webb :
London,* 1900. 8º.   Cup.510.bb.**3.**

EPHEMERIDES.

—— The Caradoc Kalendar, MDCCCCI (1902). (Written by
H. D. and H. G. Webb.) [Verses. 1902. By H. D.
Webb.] *Caradoc Press : Chiswick,* 1900, 01. obl. 8º.
                                         Cup. **510**. bb. **2.**

AMOR .

—— Quia amore langueo. (This poem of unknown author-
ship is printed . . . from a manuscript in the Library at
Lambeth Palace . . . written early in the xv century.—
The borders initials and ornaments designed and cut on
wood and the whole printed . . . by H. D. & H. G.
Webb.) *H. D. & H. G. Webb : Chiswick,* 1902. 8º.
                                         K.T.C. 30. a. 12.

YEATS (WILLIAM BUTLER) Cathleen Ni Hoolihan.
A play in one act and in prose. pp. 29.
Caradoc Press : London, 1902. 8º. Cup.510.bb.**4.**

BIBLE. *Selections. [English.]*

—— In Praise of Wisdom. (Extracted from the canonical and
uncanonical books of the Bible.) pp. 34. *H. G. Webb :
London,* 1902. 12º.   Cup.510.bb.**5.**

GOLDSMITH (OLIVER) *the Poet.* [*The Vicar of
Wakefield.*] The Vicar of Wakefield, *etc.* (Republished
from the text of the first edition by H. G. Webb and . . .
Hesba D. Webb.) pp. 211.   *Caradoc Press :
Chiswick,* 1903. 8º.   Tab. **537.** a. **4.**

BERNARD, *Saint, Abbot of Clairvaux.* [*Supposititious
Works.—De Regimine Domus.*]

—— The Proverbys of Saynt Bernarde. (The Doctrynall
Principlis and Proverbys Iconomic or Howsolde Keeping,
sent from Saynte Bernard unto Raymonde, Lord of
Ambrose Castelle.—Le Regisme de mesnaige selon saint
Bernard.) *Eng. & Fr.* pp. 31. *Caradoc Press : London,*
1904. 16º.   Cup.510.bb.**6.**

HOBSON (GEORGE ANDREW) The Life of Sir James
Falshaw, Bt., Lord Provost of the City of Edinburgh,
1874–1877, *etc.* pp. viii. 231.   *Caradoc Press :
Chiswick,* 1905. 8º.   Cup.510.bb.**7.**
Printed for private circulation.

WALTON (IZAAK) *the Angler.*

—— The Compleat Angler, *etc.* (Reprinted from the first
edition, printed at London in 1653. The ornaments,
initials and etchings designed and engraved by H. G. Webb.)
pp. 155. *Caradoc Press : London,* 1905. 8º.
                                         Cup. **510**. bb. **8.**

GREVILLE (FULKE) *Baron Brooke.*

—— The Life of the Renowned Sir Philip Sidney, *etc.* [With a
portrait.] pp. iv. 167.   *Gibbins & Co. : London,*
1906. 8º.   Cup. **510**. bb. **10.**

JAMES I., *King of Scotland.*

—— The King's Quair. ON VELLUM. pp. 78. *Caradoc Press :
Chiswick,* 1906. 8º.   Cup. **510**. bb. **9.**

SIDNEY (SIR PHILIP)

—— The Defence of Poësie and certain sonnets. pp. viii. 107.
Caradoc Press : London, 1906. 8º. Cup.510.bb.**11.**

CARAVEL PRESS, London

PAUL (LESLIE ALLEN)

—— Exile, and other poems. [With wood-engravings.]
pp. 39. *Caravel Press : London,* [1951.] 8º.
                                         Cup.510.age.**3.**

WALLIS (Cedric)
—— Charles d'Orléans and other French poets. Rondels. Chosen and translated by Cedric Wallis. Wood-engravings and decorations by Guy Worsdell. *London: Caravel Press*, 1951. Cup. 510. age. 2.

pp. 75. 20 cm. △

French & English.

GOLDSMITH (Oliver) the Poet. [*The Deserted Village.*]
—— The Deserted Village ... Wood-engravings by Stephanie Maberly Smith. pp. 34. *Caravel Press: London*, 1953. 8°. Cup. 510. age. 1.

KEOWN (Anna Gordon)
—— Collected Poems . . . Four wood-engravings and decorations by Guy Worsdell. pp. 71. *Caravel Press: London*, 1953. 8°. Cup.510.age.4.

CARTER (Sebastian), Cambridge

SHIRE (Helena Mennie)
—— Poems from Panmure House. Edited, with an introduction, by H. M. Shire. pp. 23. *Sebastian Carter: Cambridge*, 1960. 8°. Cup.510.ac.19.

LYKIARD (Alexis Constantine)
—— Lobsters. [Poems.] *Sebastian Carter: Cambridge*, 1961. 8°. 011768. w. 8.

LYKIARD (Alexis Constantine)
—— Journey of the Alchemist. *Sebastian Carter: [Brighton,]* 1963. 8°. X. 909/783.

CAXTON PRESS, Christchurch, N.Z.

CAXTON PRESS.
—— Printing Types. A second specimen book of faces commonly in use at the Caxton Press, Christchurch, New Zealand. pp. 75. *[Caxton Press: Christchurch,]* 1948. 8°. Cup.510.ve.3.

BENSEMANN (Leo)
—— A Second Book of Leo Bensemann's Work exemplified in twenty drawings in pen & pencil, together with six engravings on wood, and specimens of calligraphy and typography, etc. pl. XXXI. *Printed by the Artist at the Caxton Press: Christchurch*, 1952. 4°. Cup.510.ve.4.

COLERIDGE (Samuel Taylor) [*Lyrical Ballads.—Rime of the Ancient Mariner.*]
—— The Rime of the Ancient Mariner. (Frontispiece by Leo Bensemann.) pp. 39. *Caxton Press: Christchurch*, 1952. 4°. C. 100. a. 11.

COLERIDGE (Samuel Taylor) [*Lyrical Ballads.—The Rime of the Ancient Mariner.*]
—— [Another copy.] The Rime of the Ancient Mariner. *Christchurch*, 1952. 4°. Cup.510.ve.1.

SWIFT (Jonathan) Dean of St. Patrick's. [*Miscellaneous Single Works.*]
—— A Letter to a very Young Lady on her Marriage. pp. 24. *Caxton Press: Christchurch*, 1954. 8°. Cup.510.ve.2.

BELL (Colin Kane)
—— Why birds don't cry ... (A legend in the Maori manner.) With a Maori translation by Arapeta Awatere, etc. *Christchurch, N.Z.: Caxton Press*, 1960. Cup. 510. ve. 5.

pp. 19; illus. 25 cm.

PALMER (Charles Oscar)
—— Thirty poems. *[Christchurch:] printed at the Caxton Press for private publication*, 1964. Cup. 510. ve. 6.

pp. 42. 23 cm.

CAYME PRESS, London

D., R.
—— A Little more Nonsense. The author, R. D. [i.e. Randall R. H. Davies.] [Limericks, illustrated by woodcuts reproduced from "Specimens of Early Wood Engraving" by William Dodd.] *Cayme Press: London*, 1923. 8°. 012330. k. 63.
Printed on one side of the leaf only.

OGILVIE (Alexina) Profitable Proverbs ... Five and twenty woodcuts illustrating as many proverbs. *Cayme Press: London*, 1923. 4°. Cup.510.acb.7.

CAMPION (Thomas)
—— The maske by Thomas Campion, as produced at Hatfield Palace on May 30th. & 31st. 1924, for the benefit of the Hertfordshire County Nursing Association. (Produced [and edited] by Kathleen Talbot.) *Kensington: privately printed at the Cayme Press for the Chelsea Publishing Co.*, 1924. Cup. 510. acb. 13.

pp. 39: plates. 26 cm. △

GRAHAM (James) 1st Marquis of Montrose.
—— Love Verses, etc. [A reprint of the poem beginning: "My dear and only love."] *Philip Sainsbury: London*, 1924. 8°. Cup. 510. acb. 10.

HAYNES (Edmund Sidney Pollock) Fritto Misto. [Literary essays.] pp. 217. *Cayme Press: London*, 1924. 8°. 11850. ppp. 18.

LOVER. The Lover's Quarrel, or Cupid's Triumph. [A ballad.] Reprinted. *Chelsea Publishing Co.: [London,]* 1924. 8°. 11632. de. 40.

PENNY, *Sir.*

—— Sir Peny. [A ballad.] Reprinted. *Chelsea Publishing Co.: London,* 1924. 8⁰.　　**11632. de. 39**

SAMSON (Hillel) The Island Set Apart; preceded by a record of the Truth-seekers' Club. pp. 47. *Cayme Press: London,* 1924. 8⁰.　　**12630. dd. 12.**

SIEVEKING (Lancelot de Giberne)

—— Stampede! [A tale.] . . . With illustrations by G. K. Chesterton. pp. 305. *Cayme Press: London,* 1924. 8⁰.　　**012603. aaa. 24.**

THUMB (Tom) The Life and Death of Tom Thumbe. [A ballad.] *Chelsea Publishing Co.: London,* 1924. 8⁰.　　**11632. de. 38.**

ADVICE.

—— Advice to the Rich. [By Joseph Hilaire Pierre Belloc ?] *Cayme Press: Kensington,* 1925. 4⁰. Cup. **510. acb. 11.**

ANSTEY (Christopher) The Birth of Fashion. A modern ode. pp. 14.　　*Cayme Press: London,* 1925. 12⁰.　　**011644. de. 35.**

BLUNT (Reginald)

—— The Crown & Anchor. A Chelsea Quarto. Edited by R. Blunt. [With plates.] pp. xii. 108.　　*Chelsea Publishing Co. & Cayme Press: London,* 1925. 4⁰.　　**12352. h. 23.**

CHRISTY (Josephine Z.) Weathercock Stories of London Town . . . Illustrated by Alexina Ogilvie. pp. 45. *Cayme Press: London,* 1925. 8⁰.　　**12805. p. 49.**

D., R.

—— A lyttel booke of nonsense. (New edition.) [The compiler's preface " To the reader " signed: R. D., i.e. Randall Davies.] *Kensington: Cayme Press,* 1925.　　**11645. dd. 29.**

ff. 76; illus.　23 cm.　　　　　　　　　　△

GORGES (Sir Arthur)

—— The Olympian Catastrophe. [A poem.] . . . With an introduction by Randall Davies. pp. 61. *Cayme Press: London,* 1925. 8⁰.　　**11631. g. 50.**

GREEN (Matthew) The Spleen, and other poems. [A type-facsimile of "The Spleen," 1725, and "The Grotto," 1733, edited by R. K. Wood.] pp. 83. *Cayme Press: London,* 1925. 8⁰.　　**11633. c. 63.**

JOHNSON (Charles) *Captain.*

—— A general history of the pirates [vol. 1.] . . . Edited, with a preface, by Philip Gosse. Adorn'd with cuts by Alexina Ogilvie. *Kensington: printed & sold by Philip Sainsbury,* 1925, 27.　　**8804. h. 7.**

2 vol.　30 cm.　　　　　　　　　　　　△

KEOWN (Anna Gordon)

—— The Bright-of-Eye. [Poems.] . . . With a preface & pictures by L. de Giberne Sieveking. pp. 76.　*Cayme Press: London,* 1925. 8⁰.　　**11643. cc. 24.**

LA MOTHE (Marie Catherine) *Countess d'Aulnoy.* The White Cat. . .Illustrated by Alexina Ogilvie. pp. 56. *Philip Sainsbury: London,* 1925. 8⁰.　　**12430. p. 2.**

NISHIWAKI (J.) Spectrum. [Poems.] pp. 77. *Cayme Press: London,* 1925. 8⁰.　　**11643. k. 38.**

SAINSBURY (Hester) Meanderlane. Tales & wood engravings. pp. 27.　　　　*Cayme Press: London,* 1925. 4⁰.　　**012634. n. 50.**

YUSUPOVA (Elena) *Countess Elston.* The Amorous Rabbit. . .Illustrated, *etc.* pp. 22. *Chelsea Publishing Co.: London,* [1925.] 8⁰.　　**12632. e. 34.**

BELLOC (Joseph Hilaire Pierre)

—— Mrs. Markham's New History of England, *etc.* pp. 109. *Cayme Press: London,* 1926. 4⁰.　　**012316. h. 6.**

BELLOC (Joseph Hilaire Pierre)

—— Short Talks with the Dead and Others. pp. 208. *Cayme Press: London,* 1926. 8⁰.　　**012352. ff. 56.**

BRAY (Ruth) Sir Thomas More's House at Chelsea. [A play.] pp. 61. *Cayme Press: London,* 1926. 8⁰.　　**011781. e. 7.**

BROSTER (Dorothy Kathleen)

—— The Happy Warrior [A. C. de Brunet, Count de Neuilly]. pp. 34. *London,* 1926. 8⁰. [*Cayme Press Pamphlets.* no. 1.]　　**12207. dd. 1/1.**

GURNEY (Diana) Verses. pp. 41. *Cayme Press: London,* 1926. 8⁰.　　**011645. h. 102.**

IVES (George Cecil)

—— The Græco-Roman View of Youth. pp. 90. *Philip Sainsbury: [London,]* 1926. 8⁰.　**20020. eee. 5.**

LEAR (P. G.) and **O., L.**

—— The Strange and Striking Adventures of Four Authors in Search of a Character. pp. 20.　　*Cayme Press: London,* 1926. 8⁰. [*Cayme Press Pamphlets.* no. 2.]　　**12207. dd. 1/2.**

POLLOCK (Sir JOHN) *Bart.*

—— Anatole France & Mrs. Grundy . . . With passages hitherto unpublished from Anatole France en pantoufles by J. J. Brousson. *Kensington: Cayme Press,* 1926.

12207. dd. **1/3**.

pp. 32. 22 cm. (Cayme Press pamphlets. no. 3.) △

POLLOCK (Sir JOHN) *Bart.*

—— Twelve One-Actors. pp. 330. *Cayme Press: London,* 1926. 8º. **011779**. f. **88**.

SAINSBURY (HESTER)

—— Noah's Ark. (Reprinted.) [*London:*] *Cayme Press,* 1926. Cup. **510**. acb. **15**.

Pages not numbered ; illus. 23 cm. △

Poems.

WAUGH (ALEXANDER RABAN) On Doing What One Likes. pp. 156. *Cayme Press: London,* 1926. 8º. **12356**. dd. **25**.

ANSTEY (CHRISTOPHER)

—— The new Bath guide. [The preface signed : Philip Sainsbury.] *Kensington: Cayme Press,* 1927.

11633. cc. **22**.

24 pp. xv, 118 ; port. 24 cm. △

With wood-engravings of the edition of 1804, and lithographs of the edition of 1807.

B., P. G.

—— Achilles in Scyros. A classical comedy. [The preface signed : P. G. B., i.e. P. G. Bainbrigge ?] pp. 29. 1927. 8º. Cup. **503**. n. **1**.

CHRISTINA, *Queen of Sweden.*

—— The history of the intrigues & gallantries of Christina, Queen of Sweden, *etc.* [By C. G. Franckenstein. The translator's dedicatory epistle signed: Phil. Hollingworth.] (The illustrations . . . are by Alexina Ogilvie.) *London: Cayme Press,* 1927. **010760**. k. **5**.

pp. 223: plates; ports. 26 cm. △

A reprint of the 1697 edition.

COLMAN (GEORGE) *the Younger.*

—— The Rodiad . . . Now re-printed with a preface by Yvon Nicobas. [Spurious.] pp. 31. *Kensington,* 1927. 8º. [*Cayme Press Pamphlets.* no. 4.]

C.116.bb.25.

DAVIES (RANDALL ROBERT HENRY)

—— Notes upon some of Shakespeare's Sonnets. [With a portrait.] pp. 46. *Cayme Press: London,* 1927. 4º. [*Cayme Press Pamphlets.* no. 6.] **12207**. dd. **1/6**.

DOBRÉE (BONAMY)

—— Sir John Denham. A conversation between Bishop Henry King and Edmund Waller, *etc.* pp. 17. *London,* 1927. 4º. [*Cayme Press Pamphlet.* no. 8.]

12207. dd. **1/8**.

ELLIS (STEWART MARSH) The Solitary Horseman ; or, the Life & Adventures of G. P. R. James. [With portraits and a bibliography.] pp. 303. *Cayme Press: London,* 1927. 8º. **010855**. h. **8**.

HAYNES (EDMUND SIDNEY POLLOCK)

—— Much Ado about Women. pp. 18. *London,* 1927. 8º. [*Cayme Press Pamphlets.* no. 5.] **12207**. dd. **1/5**.

HOLLAND (VYVYAN BERESFORD)

—— The Mediæval Courts of Love, *etc.* pp. 46. [*London,*] 1927. 16º. [*Sette of Odd Volumes. Privately Printed Opuscula.* no. 82.] Ac. **9128**.

NAPIER (ELMA) Nothing So Blue. [Travel sketches.] pp. 186. *Cayme Press: London,* 1927. 8º. **010025**. df. **38**.

POLLOCK (Right Hon. Sir FREDERICK) *3rd Bart.*

—— Outside the Law. Diversions partly serious. [In prose and verse.] pp. 127. *Cayme Press: London,* 1927. 8º. **012273**. d. **7**.

REYNOLDS (Sir JOSHUA)

—— Johnson & Garrick. Two dialogues . . . With an introduction by R. Brimley Johnson. pp. 31. *London,* 1927. 4º. [*Cayme Press Pamphlet.* no. 9.] **12207**. dd. **1/9**.

SAVILE (GEORGE) *Marquis of Halifax.*

—— The Lady's New-Years-Gift; or, Advice to a daughter . . . Reprinted with . . . wood-engravings by Hester Sainsbury. [With a preface by Bonamy Dobrée.] pp. 68. *Cayme Press: London,* 1927. 4º. Cup. **510**. acb. **8**.

No. 16 of 75 copies printed on hand-made paper.

BOOK.

—— A Book with Seven Seals. [By Agnes Maud Mary Douton. A novel.] pp. 343. *Cayme Press: London,* 1928. 8º. Cup.510.acb.14.

LESLIE (Sir JOHN RANDOLPH SHANE) *Bart.*

—— The Poems of Shane Leslie. pp. 95. *Cayme Press: London,* 1928. 8º. Cup.510.acb.9.

NICHOLSON (WILLIAM HEDLEY HOPE) The Mindes Delight ; or, Variety of memorable matters worthy of observation. Collected by H. Hope-Nicholson. pp. xvi. 275. *Cayme Press: London,* 1928. 8º. **12298**. e. **4**.

SUMMERS (ALPHONSUS JOSEPH-MARY AUGUSTUS MONTAGUE)

—— The Discovery of Witches. A study of Master Matthew Hopkins, commonly call'd Witch Finder Generall . . . Together with a reprint of The Discovery of Witches from the rare original of 1647. pp. 61. *London,* 1928. 8º. [*Cayme Press Pamphlet.* no. 7.] **12207**. dd. **1/7**.

WALKER (Thomas) *M.A., Barrister-at-Law.* The Art of Dining . . . With an introduction by Filson Young, *etc.* pp. xv. 80.　　　　*Cayme Press:* *London,* 1928. 8°.　　**Cup.510.acb.12.**

WYNDHAM (Guy Richard Charles)
—— A Book of Towers and other Buildings of Southern Europe. A series of dry-points engraved by R. Wyndham. With an introduction and brief descriptions by Sacheverell Sitwell. pp. xii. 101. *Cayme Press: London,* 1928. 8°. [*Haslewood Books.*]　　　　**C.102.k.1/9.**
With a duplicate set of the plates.

DAVID (Jacob Villiers Peveril)
—— The guardsman and Cupid's daughter, and other **poems** . . . The decorations by John Austen. *London: Humphrey Toulmin* [*at*] *the Cayme Press,* 1930.　**Cup.510.caf.1.**
pp. 54. 23 cm.　　　　　　　　　　△
Printed at the Alcuin Press, Campden, Glos.

HARDY (Thomas) *O.M.* The Three Wayfarers. A play in one act...Dramatized from..."The Three Strangers." Illustrated by William H. Cotton. pp. 34. *Fountain Press: New York; Cayme Press: London,* 1930. 4°.　　　**11781.i.35.**

DUFF (Charles St. Lawrence)
—— Handrail and the Wampus. Three segments of a polyphonic biogriad. pp. 46. *London,* [1931.] 4°. [*Cayme Press Pamphlets.* no. 10.]　　**12207.dd.1/10.**

CEDAR TREE HOUSE PRESS, Cambridge

BIBLE.—*Jonah.* [*English.*]
—— The book of the prophet Jonah . . . Reprinted from the Authorised Version. [With an introduction by R. S. Dawson.]　　*Cambridge: R. S. Dawson at Cedar Tree House,* 1942.　　　**Cup.510.bm.1.**
Pages not numbered. 25 cm.　　　　△
One of an edition of forty-five copies.

CENTAUR PRESS, London

BOLITHO (Henry Hector)
—— The Queen's tact. *London: Centaur Press,* [1933].　　　　　　　　**Cup.510.be.10.**
Pages not numbered; illus. 25 cm.　　△
A poem. No. 43 of an edition of one hundred copies for the author's private circulation only.

GOLDING (Louis) *Novelist.*
—— Poems drunk and drowsy.　*London: Centaur Press,* [1933].　　　　　　**Cup.510.be.9.**
Pages not numbered. 25 cm.　　　　△
One of an edition of one hundred copies. Author's presentation copy.

BELL (Adrian Hanbury)
—— Seasons, *etc.* [Poems.]　*Centaur Press: London,* 1934. 8°. [*Centaur Booklet.* no. 2.] **Cup.510.be.1/2.**

BOLITHO (Henry Hector)
—— The Queen's Tact. [A poem.]　　*Centaur Press:* *London,* 1934. 8°. [*Centaur Booklet.* no. 1.]　　　　　　　　**Cup.510.be.1/1.**

COTGRAVE (Peri)
—— The Little Centaur . . . Illustration by Hugh Easton. *Centaur Press: London,* 1934. 8°.　[*Centaur Booklet.* no. 6.]　　　　**Cup.510.be.1/6.**
One of an edition of which twenty-five copies were for sale.

FIRBANK (Arthur Annesley Ronald)
—— The artificial princess . . . Illustrated by Hugh Easton. *London: Centaur Press,* 1934.　　**Cup.510.be.8.**
pp. 84. 23 cm.　　　　　　　　△
A copy " out of series " to an edition of sixty copies.

GOLDING (Louis)
—— Black Frailty . . . Illustrations by Ulrica Hyde. pp. 49. *Centaur Press: London,* 1934. 8°.
One of a series of 75 copies.　　**Cup.510.be.3.**

GOLDING (Louis)
—— Poems Drunk and Drowsy, *etc. Centaur Press: London,* 1934. 8°. [*Centaur Booklet.* no. 4.]　　　　　　　　**Cup.510.be.1/4.**

HASLIP (Joan)
—— Peonies and Magnolias, *etc.* [A poem.] *Centaur Press: London,* [1934.] 8°. [*Centaur Booklet.* no. 3.]　　　　　　　**Cup.510.be.1/3.**

KENNARD (Sir Coleridge Arthur Fitzroy)
—— Farewell to Eilenroc. [A tale.] pp. 23. *Centaur Press: London,* 1934. 8°.　**Cup.510.be.4.**

MAUGHAM (William Somerset)
—— The Judgement Seat, *etc.* pp. 17.　*Centaur Press:* *London,* 1934. 8°.　　　　　**Cup.510.be.7.**

O'CONOR (Minna Margaret) *Lady.*
—— Silver Wedding. [A tale.] pp. 14.　*Centaur Press:* *London,* [1934.] 8°.　　　　**Cup.510.be.2.**

BELL (Adrian Hanbury)
—— Poems. pp. 23.　　*Cobden-Sanderson: London,* 1935. 8°.　　　　　　**Cup.510.be.6.**
No. 27 of an edition of thirty copies printed on hand-made paper.

COTGRAVE (Peri)
—— The Little Centaur and other verses. pp. 32. *Centaur Press: London,* 1935. 8°.　**Cup.510.be.5.**

CENTAUR PRESS, Philadelphia

LAWRENCE (David Herbert) Reflections on the
Death of a Porcupine, and other essays. pp. 240.
Centaur Press: Philadelphia, 1925. 8°. 012352. ff. 49.

COPPARD (Alfred Edgar)
—— Yokohama Garland, and other poems . . . Vignettes
by Wharton Esherick. ff. 74. *Centaur Press:
Philadelphia*, 1926. 8°. **11645. i. 10.**
Printed on one side of the leaf only.

WELLS (Oliver)
—— An Anthology of the Younger Poets. Edited by O. Wells.
With a preface by Archibald MacLeish. pp. xiv. 184.
Centaur Press: Philadelphia, 1932. 8°. 011388. e. 13.

ANDERSON (Sherwood)
—— No Swank. [Essays.] pp. ix. 130. *Centaur Press:
Philadelphia*, 1934. 8°. **11589.v.89.**

CENTAUR PRESS, San Francisco

RUKEYSER (Muriel)
—— Orpheus. [A poem.] *Centaur Press: San Francisco*,
1959. 8°.
Cup.510.saa.1.

CERNEL PRESS, Cerne Abbas

SMART (Christopher)
—— My Cat Jeoffry. (Wood engravings by Eleanor Meadow-
croft.) [*Cernel Press: Cerne Abbas*,] 1962. 4°.
Cup. 510. cos. 2.
No. 7 of an edition of twenty copies.

WINE.
—— Good Wine. A fifteenth century song. *Cernel Press:
Cerne Abbas*, 1963. 8°. **Cup. 510. cos. 1.**
No. 29 of an edition of thirty-six copies.

CHAMPOEG PRESS, Portland, Oregon

BEAVER (Herbert)
—— Reports and Letters of Herbert Beaver, 1836–1838 . . .
Edited by Thomas E. Jessett. pp. xxiv. 148. *Champoeg
Press: Portland, Ore.*, 1959. 8°. **4769. gg. 5.**

CIPRIANI (Leonetto) *Count.*
—— California and overland diaries of Count Leonetto
Cipriani, from 1853 through 1871 . . . Translated and
edited by Ernest Falbo. [With a portrait.] pp. 148.
Champoeg Press: Portland, Or., 1962. 8°. **X. 802/462.**

CHISWICK PRESS, London

LOCKER, afterwards LOCKER-LAMPSON (Frederick)
—— London Lyrics. pp. viii. 134. *John Wilson: London*,
1868. 8°. **Cup.510.av.18.**
*Not published. Author's presentation copy to Richard
Garnett. Inserted in this copy is a leaflet containing
reviews of works by the author.*

LONGUS.
—— Daphnis et Chloé. Traduction d'Amyot. Précédée d'une
préface par Alexandre Dumas fils. *Londres: Louys Glady*,
1878. **1074. b. 37.**
pp. xxiv, 157. 16 cm. △
*Presentation copy to the British Museum. Printed, in red
and blue ink, at the Chiswick Press. Only 333 copies issued.*

PRÉVOST D'EXILES (Antoine François)
—— Histoire de Manon Lescaut et du Chevalier des Grieux.
Précédée d'une préface par Alexandre Dumas, fils . . .
Texte revu par Anatole de Montaiglon. *Londres: Louys
Glady*, 1878. **1459. a. 56.**
pp. xxxv, 221. 16 cm. △
*Printed at the Chiswick Press. Presentation copy to the
British Museum.*

T., G. W. Verses from Japan. [By G. W. T., i.e.
George William Thomson. Reprinted from the
" Japan Weekly Mail."] pp. 59. *London*, 1878. 8°.
011650. eo. 69. (2.)

LAWLEY, afterwards WIEL (Hon. Alethea Jane)
Two Doges of Venice: being a slight sketch of the
lives and times of T. Moconigo and F. Foscari.
pp. 142. *The Chiswick Press: London*, 1891. 8°.
10629. d. 14.

JACOBI (Charles Thomas) Some Notes on Books
and Printing. A guide for authors and others.
Whittingham & Co.: London, 1892. 8°. 11899. cc. 3.

BLISS (Frank E.)
—— In Praise of Bishop Valentine. [Selections in verse,
with an introduction by R. Le Gallienne.] pp. xiii. 158.
Printed for private circulation: London, 1893. 8°.
K.T.C. 1. a. 3.
One of twenty-five copies printed on Japanese vellum.

HORNER (Burnham W.)
—— Life and Works of Dr. Arne, 1710–1778, *etc.* [With a
portrait.] pp. 43. *Chiswick Press: London*, 1893. 16°.
Hirsch 2077.
*Privately Printed Opuscula. Issued to the Members of
the Sette of Odd Volumes.* no. 31.

TILLIEFOURE.

—— Tilliefoure. [A history. By Francis Gregson. With illustrations.] *Chiswick Press: London*, 1894. 8°.
Cup. 510. av. 23.

Privately printed.

ANWILL (CATHERINE)

—— Catherine Anwill: Her Book. [A collection of poems compiled in MS. by C. Anwill, c. 1650. The editor's preface signed: L., i.e. A. L. Humphreys.] pp. xxvi. 25. *Privately printed for Arthur L. Humphreys: London*, 1895. 16°.
Cup.510.av.8.

WILDE (OSCAR FINGAL O'FLAHERTIE WILLS)

—— The Soul of Man. (Reprinted from the Fortnightly Review.) pp. 97. *Privately printed: London*, 1895. 8°.
Cup.510.av.16.

MORRIS (WILLIAM) *Poet.* The Well at the World's End. A tale. 2 vol. *Longmans & Co.: London*, 1896. 8°. K.T.C. 101. a. 5.

MORRIS (WILLIAM) *Poet.*

—— [Another copy.] The Well at the World's End, *etc.* London, 1896. 8°. Cup. 510. av. 14.
With an extra set of preliminary leaves, including a titlepage bearing the imprint: "Reeves & Turner: London, 1894," inserted in each volume.

POEMS.

—— Poems. [By Goldsworthy Lowes Dickinson.] pp. vi. 67. *Privately printed at the Chiswick Press: London*, 1896. 8°.
Cup. 510. av. 20.

Inscribed by the author.

GRAVES (ALGERNON) and CRONIN (WILLIAM VINE) A History of the Works of Sir Joshua Reynolds. [With plates.] 4 vol. *H. Graves & Co.: London*, 1899–1901. 4°. L.R. 33. a. 1.
The pagination is continuous throughout.

HIND (CHARLES LEWIS)

—— Things Seen. (Reprinted from "The Academy.") pp. vii. 47. *Printed for private circulation: London*, 1899. 12°.
Cup.510.av.12.

BRADLEY (JOHN WILLIAM) B.A.

—— Notes on a Book of Hours for the "use" of the metropolitan diocese of Reims. Probably commissioned by the Abbess of St. Remy. Circa 1450–1460. *London: Chiswick Press*, [ca. 1900].
Cup. 510. av. 26.
pp. 12: plates. 24 cm. △

BRADLEY (JOHN WILLIAM) B.A.

—— Notes on the de Maillard livre de prières. *London: Chiswick Press*, [ca. 1900]. Cup. 510. av. 28.
pp. 23: plates. 24 cm. △
On a book of hours prepared for the special use of the diocese of Geneva.

BRADLEY (JOHN WILLIAM) B.A.

—— Notes on the Lyte family Book of Hours, circa 1390. *London: Chiswick Press*, [ca. 1900]. Cup. 510. av. 27.
pp. 15: plates. 24 cm.

THACKERAY (FRANCIS ST. JOHN)

—— Occasional poems. *London: privately printed at the Chiswick Press*, 1900. Cup. 510. av. 29.
pp. viii, 61. 20 cm. △
Author's presentation copy.

DOBSON (HENRY AUSTIN)

—— Carmina Votiva, and other occasional verses. pp. xi. 99. *Printed for private circulation: London*, 1901. 4°.
Cup.510.av.4.
With an autograph letter of Sir Edmund Gosse inserted.

MORRIS (WILLIAM) *Poet.* The Roots of the Mountains, *etc.* pp. vi. 284. *Longmans & Co.: London*, 1901. 4°. C.43.f.23.
Printed at the Chiswick Press with Kelmscott Press type.

SANDERSON (THOMAS JAMES COBDEN) Ecce Mundus. Industrial Ideals, and The Book Beautiful. *Hammersmith Publishing Society: London*, 1902. 8°.
Cup.510.av.1.

KEATS (JOHN) Isabella, and the Eve of St. Agnes ... With illustrations by R. A. Bell. pp. 69. *George Bell & Sons: London*, 1902. 8°. 011652. i. 36.

MACKAIL (JOHN WILLIAM)

—— William Morris. An address delivered the XIth November MDCCC . . . before the Hammersmith Socialist Society. *Hammersmith: Hammersmith Publishing Society*, 1902.
Cup. 510. av. 2.
Pages not numbered. 22 cm. △
Printed at the Chiswick Press.

BLAKENEY (EDWARD HENRY)

—— 'Twixt the Gold Hour and the Grey. [Poems.] pp. viii. 86. *Chiswick Press: London*, 1903. 4°.
11658. g. 186.

BLAKENEY (EDWARD HENRY)

—— [Another copy.] 'Twixt the Gold Hour and the Grey. F.P. *London*, 1903. 4°. Cup.510.av.5.

HERBERT (GEORGE) *the Poet.*

—— The temple, *etc.* *London: George Bell & Sons*; [printed by the] *Chiswick Press*, 1904. 11607. ee. 16/1.
pp. 243; port. 23 cm. (The Chiswick quartos.) △

KEATS (JOHN) [*Poetical Works.*]

—— The poems of John Keats. (Edited by Mr. George Sampson.) *London: printed at the Chiswick Press for George Bell & Sons*, 1904. 11607. ee. 16/2.
2 vol; port. 23 cm. (Chiswick quartos.) △
The titlepage of each volume is engraved.

YOUNG (ALEXANDER BELL FILSON) Venus and Cupid: an impression in prose after Velasquez in colour. [With a frontispiece.] *Elisina Grant Richards: London*, 1906. fol. L.R.408.c.17.

BLUNT (Wilfrid Scawen)

—— Secret History of the English Occupation of Egypt. Part II. India. Being a personal narrative of events. pp. 599. *Chiswick Press: London*, 1907. 8°.
09061. h. 36.

Privately printed.

IMAGE (Selwyn)

—— An Address delivered by request in the Hall of Clifford's Inn before the Art Workers' Guild on the twenty-fifth anniversary of the Guild's foundation, Friday the fifteenth of January, MCMIX. pp. 19. *Charles T. Jacobi at the Chiswick Press: London*, 1909. 8°. Cup. 510. av. 13.

LAMB (Charles) The Child Angel. A dream. [From the "Last Essays of Elia."] *P. J. Smith: Dulwich*, 1910. 8°. 012352. bbb. 32.
Printed on handmade paper.

AMYNTAS.

—— Amyntas. A mystery. [By Siegfried Sassoon.] pp. 24. MS. ALTERATIONS [by the author]. *Charles Whittingham & Co.: London*, 1912. 8°. C. 131. de. 14.
Not published. With the author's signature on the front wrapper.

MELODIES.

—— Melodies. [By Siegfried Sassoon.] pp. 17. *Charles Whittingham & Co.: London*, 1912. 4°. Cup. 510. av. 11.
Author's presentation copy to Sir Sydney Cockerell with autograph inscription on the titlepage and MS. corrections by the author.

NEW YORK. *Grolier Club.*

—— Levis (Howard Coppuck) Bazilиωlogia. A booke of kings. Notes on a rare series of engraved English royal portraits from William the Conqueror to James I. (Issued by Henry Holland in 1618.) [With plates.] pp. xviii. 188. *New York; London* [printed], 1913. 4°.
K.T.C. 28. b. 21.

TREVELYAN (Robert Calverley)

—— The new Parsifal. An operatic fable. *London : printed for the author at the Chiswick Press*, 1914.
Cup. 510. av. 19.

pp. 74. 23 cm. △

BLUNT (Wilfrid Scawen)

—— History of the Crabbet Estate in Sussex, etc. pt. 1. pp. vi. 124. *Chiswick Press: London*, 1917. 8°.
09915. t. 23.
Printed for private circulation. No more published.

LEVIS (Howard Coppuck) The British King who tried to fly: extracts from old chronicles and histories relating to Bladud, the ninth King of Britain, together with several portraits. pp. viii. 123. pl. XIII. *Chiswick Press: London*, 1919. 4°. Cup. 510. av. 15.
One of 100 copies printed for private distribution.

HARDY (Thomas) O.M.

—— "And there was a Great Calm." 11 November 1918. [A poem.] pp. 5. *Chiswick Press: London*, 1920 [1921]. 4°. Ashley 3352.
"Twenty-five copies printed for Florence Emily Hardy." no. 15.

MASEFIELD (John Edward)

—— Animula. *London: privately printed at the Chiswick Press*, 1920. Cup. 510. av. 30.

pp. 16. 24 cm. △

A copy from John Masefield's library.

DRINKWATER (John) *Poet.*

—— The World and the Artist. pp. 43. *Office of "The Bookman's Journal": London*, 1922. 8°.
Cup.510.av.17.

RECREATIONS.

—— Recreations. [Poems. By Siegfried Sassoon.] pp. 40. *Printed for the Author: London*, 1923. 8°.
Cup.510.av.10.
One of an edition of seventy-five copies. Author's presentation copy to Sir Arnold Bax, with autograph signature on verso of the titlepage.

HARDY (Thomas) O.M. The Dynasts. An epic-drama of the war with Napoleon, etc. [With a portrait.]. 3 vol. L. P. *Macmillan & Co.: London*, 1927. 8°. Cup.510.av.25.

JANNON (Jean) The 1621 Specimen of Jean Jannon, Paris & Sedan, designer & engraver of the caractères de l'Université...Edited in facsimile with an introduction by Paul Beaujon. *Chiswick Press, for Stanley Morison: London*, 1927. 8°. C. 98. f. 13.
One of 10 copies printed on hand-made paper.

DAVIES (Rhys) *Novelist.*

—— The Stars, the World, and the Women. With a fore-word by Liam O'Flaherty and an illustration by Frank C. Papé. pp. 53. *William Jackson: London*, 1930. 8°. [*Furnival Books.* no. 4.] 012604. d. 18/4.

SANDFORD (Christopher) and **SANDFORD** (Lettice)

—— The magic forest. A story told printed and illustrated by Christopher and Lettice Sandford. *London: Christopher & Lettice Sandford at the Chiswick Press*, 1931.
Cup. 510. av. 24.

pp. 32. 27 cm. △

No. 35 of an edition of one hundred copies, signed by the authors. A four-page folder, containing advertisements for "Books published at the Sign of the Boar's Head in Heathercombe" has been inserted in this copy.

SASSOON (Siegfried Loraine)

—— Rhymed Ruminations. pp. 30. *Chiswick Press: London*, 1939. 8°. C. 103. a. 2.
One of an edition of seventy-five copies.

ABBEY (John Roland)

—— English Bindings 1490–1940 in the Library of J. R. Abbey. Edited by G. D. Hobson. [With plates.] pp. xvi. 201. *Chiswick Press: London*, 1940. fol.
N.L.8. c.
Privately printed. This copy contains the extra plate and leaf of text included in the twenty-five special copies.

WHISTLER (LAURENCE)

—— The Burning Glass. pp. 7.   *Printed for Laurence Whistler, Siegfried Sassoon & Geoffrey Keynes at the Chiswick Press:* [London,] 1941. 8⁰.   Cup. **510**. av. **22**.
No. 22 of an edition of fifty copies. With the author's signature.

CROWLEY (EDWARD ALEXANDER) calling himself ALEISTER CROWLEY.

—— The Fun of the Fair—Nijni Novgorod, 1913 e.v. [With a portrait.] pp. 23.   *O.T.O.: Barstow, Cal., London; printed in England,* 1942. fol.   **11656. g. 43**.

CROWLEY (EDWARD ALEXANDER) calling himself ALEISTER CROWLEY.

—— [Another copy.] The Fun of the Fair, *etc.   Barstow, Cal. & London,* 1942. 8⁰.   Cup. **510**. av. **3**.
In this copy is inserted an additional poem entitled "Political Vote. B - - - - y Secret," reproduced from typewriting.

COWPER (WILLIAM) *the Poet.* [*The Diverting History of John Gilpin.*]

—— The Diverting History of John Gilpin . . . With many illustrations by Ronald Searle. pp. 44.   *Printed at the Chiswick Press for Sir Allen Lane and Richard Lane: London,* 1952. 4⁰.   Cup. **510**. av. **21**.

JOYCE (JAMES AUGUSTINE ALOYSIUS)

—— Joyce the Artificer. Two studies of Joyce's method by Aldous Huxley & Stuart Gilbert; with five collotype reproductions from the proofs of "Ulysses" and "Tales of Shem and Shaun," together with a letter and notes thereon by J. Schwartz.   *Chiswick Press:* [London,] 1952. fol.   **11868**. pp. **16**.
One of an edition of ninety copies printed for private circulation.

SWEDISH LEGEND.

—— Legenda Suecana. Twenty-odd poems. [By Geoffrey Edward Harvey Grigson.] *The Author: London,* 1953. 8⁰.
Cup. **510**, av. **6**.

DUNCAN (RONALD FREDERICK HENRY)

—— Judas . . . Illustrated by John Piper.   *London: Anthony Blond,* 1960.   Cup. **510**. av. **7**.
pp. 37. 26 cm.   △
Printed at the Chiswick Press.

CHOCORUA PRESS, New York

MORLEY (CHRISTOPHER DARLINGTON)

—— The Palette Knife . . . Illustrated by René Gockinga. *Chocorua Press: New York,* 1929. 8⁰.   Cup. **510**. pd. **10**.

CHUBB (R. N.), Curridge, *etc.*

CHUBB (RALPH NICHOLAS)

—— Manhood. A poem . . . Designed & engraved by the author. (2nd edition.)   *Published by R. J. Chubb; printed by L. J. Chubb: Curridge,* 1924. 8⁰.
Cup. **510**. ba. **1**.
Printed on one side of the leaf only.

CHUBB (RALPH NICHOLAS)

—— The Sacrifice of Youth. A poem. pp. 15.   *The Author: Curridge,* 1924 [1925]. 8⁰.   Cup. **510**. ba. **7**.
No. 1 of an edition of forty-five copies printed on hand-made paper.

CHUBB (RALPH NICHOLAS)

—— A Fable of Love & War. A romantic poem . . . Designed & decorated with woodcuts by the author. pp. 36.   *R. N. Chubb: Curridge,* 1925. 8⁰.   Cup. **510**. ba. **5**.

CHUBB (RALPH NICHOLAS)

—— The Cloud & the Voice. A fragment [in verse] . . . With a woodcut by the author. pp. 19.   *The Author: Newbury,* 1927. 8⁰.   Cup. **510**. ba. **10**.
No. 5 of an edition of 100 copies.

CHUBB (RALPH NICHOLAS)

—— The Book of God's Madness. An unfinished poem in three parts, whereof part I slightly abridged was published as the Cloud and the Voice . . . With woodcuts by the author. pp. 32.   *Privately printed:* [Cambridge,] 1928. 8⁰.
Cup. **510**. ba. **6**.
One of an edition of ninety-five copies.

CHUBB (RALPH NICHOLAS)

—— Woodcuts.   *Andrew Block: London,* 1928. 4⁰.
Cup. **510**. ba. **8**.
One of ten copies, with the impressions in two states.

CHUBB (RALPH NICHOLAS) An Appendix . . . A random collection of original ideas, *etc.   The Author: Ashford Hill,* 1929. fol.   Cup. **510**. ba. **11**.
No. 2 of an edition of fifty copies. Reproduced from MS.

CHUBB (RALPH NICHOLAS)

—— Songs of Mankind . . . Decorated with wood-engravings by the author. pp. 48.   *Privately printed: Newbury,* 1930. 8⁰.   Cup. **510**. ba. **9**.
No. 6 of an edition of 100 copies.

CHUBB (RALPH NICHOLAS)

—— The Sun Spirit. A visionary phantasy . . . Designed & decorated by the author. pp. 16.   [*The Author: Newbury,* 1931.] fol.   Cup. **803**. f. **9**.
No. 5 of an edition of thirty copies. This copy is one of six coloured by hand.

CHUBB (RALPH NICHOLAS)

—— The Heavenly Cupid; or, the True paradise of loves . . . Designed, illustrated, composed, & printed in script by the author, *etc.   The Author: Kingsclere,* [1934.] fol.
Cup. **803**. f. **10**.
No. 3 of an edition of forty-three copies. This copy is one of seven coloured by hand.

CHUBB (RALPH NICHOLAS)

—— Songs Pastoral and Paradisal. ff. 28.   *Tintern Press: Brockweir,* 1935. fol.   Tab. **535**. b. **14**.
Engraved throughout. One of an edition of 100 copies.

CHUBB (RALPH NICHOLAS)

—— Water-Cherubs. A book of original drawings & poetry. *The Author: Kingsclere Woodlands*, 1936. fol.

Cup. **803**. f. **11**.

No. 5 of an edition of thirty copies. This copy is one of six painted in water colours.

CHUBB (RALPH NICHOLAS)

—— The Secret Country : or, Tales of vision . . . Designed, lettered and illustrated by the author. *The Author: Kingsclere Woodlands*, 1939. fol. Cup.**803**.f.**12**.

No. 1 of an edition of thirty-seven copies. This copy is one of seven in which some of the illustrations are painted in water-colour.

CHUBB (RALPH NICHOLAS)

—— The Child of Dawn ; or, the Book of the Manchild . . . Design'd, letter'd, illustrated, hand-printed . . . by the author. *The Author: Ashford Hill*, [1948.] fol.

L.R.**37**.c.**10**..

No. 19 of an edition of thirty copies and no. 7 of the painted copies.

CHUBB (RALPH NICHOLAS)

—— Flames of Sunrise. A book of the man child concerning the redemption of Albion . . . Design'd ; illustrated ; letter'd ; hand-printed . . . by the author. ff. 197. *The Author: Ashford Hill*, [1954.] 4°. Cup.**510**.ba.**2**.;

No. 1 of an edition of twenty-five copies. This copy is one of six in which the titlepage and certain illustrations are painted in watercolour.

CHUBB (RALPH NICHOLAS)

—— Treasure Trove. Early tales & romances, with poems . . . Design'd, illustrated, letter'd, hand-printed & published by the author. pp. 103. *The Author: Newbury*, [1957.] fol. Cup. **510**. ba. **3**.

No. 16 of an edition of twenty-one copies, and one of seven with certain illustrations painted in watercolour.

CHUBB (RALPH NICHOLAS) [*Collections.*]

—— The Golden City, with Idylls & Allegories . . . Design'd, illustrated, letter'd, hand-printed . . . by the author. *The Author: Newbury*, 1958-60. 4°. Cup.**510**.ba.**4**.

Printed on one side of the leaf only. No. 5 of an edition of eighteen copies.

CLERK'S PRIVATE PRESS, Cleveland, Ohio

JOHNSON (LIONEL PIGOT)

[*Ireland, with other poems.*]

—— Four poems or Christmas songs wherein is set forth the birth of our holy & blessed Redeemer. [Selected by C. C. Bubb.] *Cleveland: printed at The Clerk's Private Press*, 1917. Cup. **510**. nik. **1**.

pp. 19. 15 cm. △

No. 91 of an edition of one hundred copies.

SOLOGUB (FEDOR) *pseud.* [i.e. FEDOR KUZ'MICH TETER-NIKOV.]

—— Little tales . . . An authorised translation from the Russian by John Cournos. *Cleveland [Ohio]: printed at the Clerk's Private Press*, 1917. **12590**. aa. **42**.

pp. 28. 13 cm. (Russian translations. no. 2.) △

No. 40 of an edition of forty copies printed on hand-made paper.

CLEVERDON (Douglas), Bristol

GILL (ARTHUR ERIC ROWTON)

—— Art & Love. [With plates.] pp. 26. *Douglas Cleverdon: Bristol; Golden Cockerel Press: Waltham Saint-Lawrence*, 1927. 8°. C. **99**. c. **35**.

No. 23 of 35 copies issued with an extra set of the engravings.

LÉLY (GILBERT) Allusions, ou poèmes. pp. 57. *Douglas Cleverdon: Bristol; Paris* printed, 1927. 8°. **011483**. bb. **37**.

One of 9 copies printed on fine paper.

ANDERSEN (HANS CHRISTIAN) *the Novelist.* [*Eventyr.—Single Tales.—De rode Skoe.*] The Red Shoes . . . With coloured wood-engravings by Willi Harwerth. pp. 30. F. P. *Douglas Cleverdon: Bristol; Offenbach a. M.* printed, 1928. 8°. **012403**. df. **40**.

One of ten copies printed on hand-made paper, with two duplicate sets of the engravings, one coloured by hand.

COLERIDGE (SAMUEL TAYLOR) [*Lyrical Ballads.—Rime of the Ancient Mariner.*]

—— The rime of the ancient mariner. With ten engravings on copper by David Jones. pp. 37. *Bristol: Douglas Cleverdon*, 1929. C. **100**. k. **20**.

pp. 37. 33 cm. △

One of a limited issue signed by the artist and containing a set of the engravings in first state, a set in final state, and proofs of the discarded engravings.

FARQUHAR (GEORGE)

—— The Beaux Stratagem. A comedy. With seven engravings on copper by J. E. Laboureur, and an introduction by Bonamy Dobrée. pp. xxvii. 127. *Douglas Cleverdon: Bristol*, 1929. 8°. C. **100**. e. **14**.

Containing an extra set of the engravings.

GILL (ARTHUR ERIC ROWTON) Engravings by Eric Gill. A selection . . . representative of his work to the end of . . . 1927, with a . . . chronological list of engravings and a preface by the artist. [With a portrait.] pp. 49. pl. 103. *Douglas Cleverdon: Bristol*, 1929. fol. L.R. **262**. b. **11**.

One of 10 copies printed on Japanese vellum. The extra set of the engravings, and proofs of the self-portrait are in the Dept. of Prints.

POWYS (THEODORE FRANCIS) Uncle Dottery. A Christmas story . . . With two wood-engravings by Eric Gill. pp. 20. F. P. *Douglas Cleverdon: Bristol*, 1930. 8°. **012604**. cc. **64**.

With a duplicate set of the engravings.

SASSOON (Siegfried Loraine)
—— Vigils. **L.P.** [*Douglas Cleverdon : Bristol,*] 1934. 4º.
C. 100. g. 46.
Engraved. No. 22 of an edition of 23 copies.

CLOANTHUS PRESS, Cambridge

HUNT (Vincent Leigh)
—— Letters to Leigh Hunt from his Son Vincent, with some replies. Edited with a memoir of Vincent by A. N. L. Munby. pp. 61. *Cloanthus Press : Cambridge,* 1934. 8º.
010920. b. 16.

CLUETT (F. A.), Gravesend

CLUETT (Frederick A.)
—— A historical hash. Made and printed by F. A. Cluett. *Gravesend,* [1962]. Cup. 510. aza. **2.**
Pages not numbered. 14 cm. △

COG PRESS, Aylestone, Leicester

GRAHAM (Rigby Alfred)
—— Cogs in Transition. Selections from a mechanical sketchbook. *Cog Press : Aylestone,* 1963. 8º.
Cup. 510. cod. **1.**
Privately printed.

COLLEGE OF ST. COLUMBA PRESS, Dublin

FARRINGTON (Brian)
—— Midnight Poems ... with decorations by Michael Biggs. *College of St. Columba Press :* [*Dublin ?*] 1943. 8º.
Cup. 510. con. **1.**

COLT PRESS, San Francisco

WALKER (Franklin)
—— Ambrose Bierce, the Wickedest Man in San Francisco. [With a portrait.] pp. 45. *Colt Press :* [*San Francisco,*] 1941. 4º.
10888. n. 21.

COPTIC PRESS, London

DOWSON (Ernest Christopher)
—— Verses. *London : Coptic Press,* 1965.
Cup. 510. coy. **1.**
pp. xii, 57. 21 cm. △

SCOTS VERSE.
—— Scots Verse. [An anthology.] pp. 13. *Coptic Press : London,* 1965. 8º.
Cup. 510. coy. **2.**

CORVINUS PRESS, London

CHRISTMAS MISCELLANY.
—— An Xmas Miscellany. [A collection of short stories.] *Viscount Carlow : London,* 1936. 8º. C. 106. c. **7.**

GOLDING (Louis)
—— Adventures in Architecture. pp. 27. *Corvinus Press :* [*London,*] 1936. 4º. Cup. 510. bda. **7.**
No. 6 of an edition of forty copies, signed by the author.

HART (Sir Basil Henry Liddell)
—— Lawrence of Arabia. (Speeches made at a luncheon given in memory of Lawrence.) By Capt. Liddell Hart and Sir Ronald Storrs. *Corvinus Press :* [*London,*] 1936. 4º. Cup. 510. bda. **6.**
Lord Carlow's presentation copy to Jonathan Cape. Bound by Sangorski and Sutcliffe.

STRONG (Leonard Alfred George)
—— Two Stories. [*Corvinus Press : London,* 1936.] 8º.
Cup. 510. bda. **19.**
No. 40 of an edition of sixty copies. Author's presentation copy to George Lazarus.

BIBLE.—*Song of Solomon.* [*English.*]
—— The Song of Songs. (Newly interpreted and rendered as a masque by Louis Golding.) *Corvinus Press :* [*London,*] 1937. 4º. Cup. 510. bda. **2.**

DE LA MARE (Walter John) [*Single Works.*]
—— Poems. [*Lord Carlow : London,* 1937 ?] 8º.
C. 103. b. **25.**
Printed on one side of the leaf only. No. 6 of an edition of 40 copies, privately printed.

GOLDING (Louis) *Novelist.*
—— The dance goes on. (The frontispiece is an original lithograph by Miss Pearl Binder.) *London : Corvinus Press,* 1937. Cup. 510. bda. **14.**
pp. 381. 25 cm. △
No. 26 of an edition of thirty-three copies on Simili Japon paper, signed by the author and the artist.

LAWRENCE, afterwards **SHAW** (Thomas Edward)
—— The Diary of T. E. Lawrence, 1911, during a visit to Northern Syria. [With plates.] *Corvinus Press :* [*London,*] 1937. 4º. C. 102. g. **6.**

LAWRENCE, afterwards **SHAW** (Thomas Edward) [*Single Works.*]
—— An Essay on Flecker. *Corvinus Press :* [*London,*] 1937. fol. Cup. 510. bda. **18.**
No. 15 of an edition of thirty copies.

STRONG (Leonard Arthur George)
—— Common sense about drama. *London : Corvinus Press,* 1937. Cup. 510. bda. **10.**
pp. ix, 131. 20 cm. △
No. 10 of an edition of thirty copies, signed by the author.

WOLFE (HUMBERT)
—— Don J. Ewan. *London: Corvinus Press*, 1937.
Cup. 510. bda. 3.

pp. 119. 26 cm. △
A poem. No. 24 of an edition of thirty copies, signed by the author.

BLUNDEN (EDMUND CHARLES)
—— On Several Occasions. By a Fellow of Merton College. (Edmund Blunden.) [Poems.] *Corvinus Press:* [*London,*] 1938. 8º. Cup.510.bda.4.
Printed on one side of the leaf only. No. 17 of an edition of 60 copies, signed by the author.

GOLDING (LOUIS) *Novelist.*
—— In the steps of Moses the lawgiver, a record of travel in Egypt and the Sinai Peninsula. [*London:*] *Corvinus Press*, 1938. Cup. 510. bda. 21.

pp. ix, 355 : plates. 24 cm. △
No. 17 of an edition of thirty copies on hand-made paper, signed by the author.

TILLERY (JOHN)
—— A Diary of the Travels of John Tillery with his fellow sufferers thro' Syria and Egypt while prisoners with Gen. Bonoparte, 1799. pp. 94. *Corvinus Press:* [*London,*] 1938. 8º. Cup.510.bda.13.
One of an edition of 40 copies.

WAGNER (WILHELM RICHARD) [*Der Fliegende Holländer.*]
—— The Flying Dutchman. *Eng. & German. Corvinus Press:* [*London,*] 1938. 4º. Cup.510.bda.5.

CORVINUS PRESS.
—— A List of Books printed at the Corvinus Press. [1939?] 8º. Cup. 510. bda. 1.
PHOTOCOPY *of a copy, with MS. notes, additions, and corrections, in the Bodleian Library.*

JACKSON (HOLBROOK)
—— The Story of Don Vincente. *Corvinus Press:* [*London,*] 1939. 8º. C. 103. b. 26.
One of an edition of sixty copies.

OUIDA, *pseud.* [i.e. MARIE LOUISE DE LA RAMÉE.]
—— A Tale of a Toad. [By] Ouida. (Printed from the original manuscript in the possession of Lord Carlow.) *Corvinus Press:* [*London,*] 1939. 4º. C. 104. k. 3.
No. 18 of an edition of twenty-four copies. Printed on one side of the leaf only.

BATES (HERBERT ERNEST)
—— The Beauty of the Dead, and one other short story. *Corvinus Press:* [*London,*] 1941. 8º. Cup. 510. bda. 17.
No. 10 of an edition of twenty-five copies. With the author's signature.

DOUGLASS (GEORGE NORMAN)
—— Summer Islands. pp. x. 106. *Corvinus Press:* [*London,*] 1942 [1944]. 8º. Cup. 510. bda. 12.
No. 8 of thirty copies printed on an Auvergne handmade paper.

TOMLINSON (HENRY MAJOR)
—— Ports of Call. *Corvinas Press:* [*London,*] 1942. 8º. Cup. 510. bda. 11.
No. 10 of an edition of thirty copies. Presentation copy to Robert Lutyens.

HOGG (NEIL)
—— Zodiac with Interludes. *Corvinus Press:* [*London,*] 1943. 8º. Cup. 510. bda. 16.
No. 10 of an edition of thirty copies.

COLERIDGE (SAMUEL TAYLOR) [*Lyrical Ballads.—Rime of the Ancient Mariner.*]
—— The Rime of the Ancient Mariner. *Corvinus Press:* [*London,*] 1944. 8º. Cup. 510. bda. 15.
No. 12 of an edition of thirty-nine copies.

VERLAINE (PAUL)
—— Fêtes galantes. *Corvinus Presse:* [*London,*] 1944. 8º. Cup.510,bda.8.
No. 6 of an edition of 37 copies.

ALAND ISLANDS.
—— The Diary of a Journey to the Åland Islands during the winter of 1940-1941. [By Viscount Carlow.] [*Corvinus Press: London,* c. 1945.] 8º. Cup. 510. bda. 20.

DAMER (GEORGE LIONEL SEYMOUR DAWSON) *Viscount Carlow.*
—— Lapland Diary. [With an introductory note signed: P.C., i.e. Peggy Carlow ?] [*Corvinus Press: London,* c. 1945.] 8º. C. 103. c. 18.
The title appears only on the spine of the binding.

MONDAY.
—— Monday, September 8th. [By Viscount Carlow.] [ca. 1945]. Cup. 510. bda. 22.
Pages not numbered. 23 cm.
On the author's journeys in Scandinavia in 1941. One of a few copies of an incomplete work, privately printed at the Corvinus Press, but not published. The title is taken from the dropped-head title on the recto of the first printed leaf.

CORYDON PRESS, Cambridge

BIRCH (JACK ERNEST LIONEL) Between Sunset and Dawn, etc. [Poems.] pp. 40. *Corydon Press: Cambridge,* [1929.] 8º. 011644. g. 97.

CRAFT PRESS, Penzance

CATNACH (JAMES) [*Appendix.*]
—— The Life of Old Jemmy Catnach, Printer. (Taken from a book published sometime in the early 1860's [entitled " The Full, True, & Particular Account of the Life . . . of Old Jemmy Catnach "].) pp. 12. *Craft Press: Penzance,* 1965. 8º. Cup. 510. cuf. 1.
Privately printed.

CRANACH PRESS, Weimar

VIRGILIUS MARO (PUBLIUS) [*Bucolica.—Polyglott.*]
—— The Eclogues of Vergil ... With an English prose translation by J. H. Mason: & with illustrations drawn and cut on the wood by Aristide Maillol. pp. 110. **F.P.** *Emery Walker: London: Weimar* printed, 1927. 4º.
C. **98. gg. 14.**
No. XVII of 33 copies printed on Imperial Japanese paper.

SHAKESPEARE (WILLIAM) [*Hamlet.*] The Tragedie of Hamlet...Edited by J. Dover Wilson... from the text of the Second Quarto...With which are also printed the Hamlet stories from Saxo Grammaticus and Belleforest and English translations therefrom. Illustrated by Edward Gordon Craig. pp. 186.
Cranach Press: Weimar, 1930. fol. C. **100. l. 16.**

RILKE (RAINER MARIA) Duineser Elegien. Elegies from the Castle of Duino. Translated ... by V. Sackville-West and Edward Sackville West. *Eng. & Germ.* pp. 132. *Hogarth Press: London*, 1931. 8º.
11526. g. 24.

CRANFORD PRIVATE PRESS, Aldershot, Hants

SIMPSON (JAMES) *M.A., Ph.D.*
—— Problems of Swarming Behaviour. A lecture given to the Central Association of Bee-Keepers on 18 November 1959. pp. 7. *Central Association of Bee-Keepers: Ilford*, 1960. 8º. **7211. ttt. 27.**

CRESSET PRESS, London

LAWSON (WILLIAM) *Horticulturist.*
—— A New Orchard and Garden ... With the Country House-wifes Garden ... Reprinted from the third edition with a preface by Eleanour Sinclair Rohde. Whereunto is newly added the Art of Propagating Plants (by Simon Harward), *etc.* pp. xxvi. 116. *Cresset Press: London*, 1927. 4º. C. **99. h. 18.**
One of 50 copies printed on Arnold hand-made paper.

MARKHAM (GERVASE)
—— The Pleasures of Princes; or, Good Mens Recreations. By G. Markham. Together with The Experienced Angler, by Colonel Robert Venables. With a preface by Horace Hutchinson. pp. xxiii. 111. *Cresset Press: London*, 1927. 4º. C. **99. h. 19.**
No. 32 of 50 copies printed on Arnold hand-made paper.

BACON (FRANCIS) *Viscount St. Albans.* [*Essays.*]
—— The Essayes, *etc. London: Cresset Press*, 1928.
C. **99. l. 14.**

pp. 198. 40 cm. △

Containing the 58 essays, the "Meditations", "Of the colours of good and evil" and the fragment of an essay "Of fame".

BUNYAN (JOHN) [*Pilgrim's Progress.—Pt. I., II.*]
—— The Pilgrim's Progress. (The wood-engravings have been cut by Blair, Hughes-Stanton & Gertrude Hermes.) *London: Cresset Press*, 1928. C. **100. l. 7.**

2 vol. 37 cm. △

COX (NICHOLAS) *Bookseller.*
—— The Gentlemans Recreation. With a preface by E. D. Cuming. pp. xxiv. 136. **F.P.** *Cresset Press: London*, 1928. 8º. **7904. e. 26.**

HERRICK (ROBERT) *the Poet.* [*Collections.*]
—— The Poetical Works of Robert Herrick. With a preface by Humbert Wolfe and decorations by Albert Rutherston. 4 vol. *Cresset Press: London*, 1928. 8º. C. **99. c. 43.**

HOMER. [*Iliad.—English.*] The Iliad...The first twelve staves translated...by Maurice Hewlett. [With a preface by Lascelles Abercrombie.] pp. xiii. 227. *Cresset Press: London*, 1928. fol. C. **98. h. 17.**

OVIDIUS NASO (PUBLIUS) [*Epistolæ Heroidum. —English.*] The Heroycall Epistles ... Translated ... by George Turbervile. With ... illustrations by Hester Sainsbury. Edited, with an introduction and glossary, by Frederick Boas. **F. P.** pp. xxiv. 349. *Cresset Press: London*, 1928. 4º. C. **98. h. 22.**

BIBLE.—*Apocrypha.* [*English.*]
—— The Apocrypha according to the Authorized Version. With wood-engravings by Blair Hughes-Stanton [and others], *etc.* pp. 406. *Cresset Press: London*, 1929. fol.
C. **100. l. 11.**
One of an edition of thirty copies printed on hand-made paper, with an extra set of the engravings on special paper in a portfolio.

BLOME (RICHARD)
—— Hawking; or, Faulconry. [From pt. 2 of "The Gentleman's Recreation". With a preface by E. W. D. Cuming.] pp. xxxii. 123. *Cresset Press: London*, 1929. 8º.
7904. e. 28.
No. 20 of fifty copies printed on handmade paper.

BRETON (NICHOLAS)
—— A Mad World My Masters, and other prose works ... Edited by Ursula Kentish-Wright. 2 vol. *Cresset Press: London*, 1929. 8º. **12274. d. 8.**

GOGOL' (NIKOLAI VASIL'EVICH) [Записки сумашедшаго.]
—— The Diary of a Madman. Translated by Prince Mirsky. Illustrated with aquatints by A. Alexeieff. [With a portfolio of plates.] pp. 81. *Cresset Press: London*, 1929. 4º. C. **100. c. 7.**

PAINTER (WILLIAM)
—— The Palace of Pleasure. With an introduction by Hamish Miles, and illustrations by Douglas Percy Bliss. 4 vol. *Cresset Press: London*, 1929. fol.
C. **100. k. 22.**
One of 30 copies printed on hand-made paper.

HEINE (HEINRICH) [*Poetical Works.—Selections.*] Portrait of Heine. Translations by Humbert Wolfe. *Germ. & Eng.* pp. xiv. 201. *Cresset Press: London*, 1930. 8º. **11527. ccc. 77.**

LAWRENCE (DAVID HERBERT)
—— Birds, Beasts and Flowers ... With wood-engravings by Blair Hughes-Stanton. pp. 144. *Cresset Press: London*, 1930. fol. C. **100. l. 20.**
One of 30 copies on hand-made paper, containing an extra set of the engravings.

SPENSER (EDMUND) [*Shepheardes Calender.*]
—— The Shepheardes Calender, *etc.* (Illustrations by **Mr.**
John Nash.) *London: Cresset Press*, 1930.   C. **98**. c. **6**.
   pp. xxiii, 133. 33 cm.   △
   With an additional titlepage decorated by the illustrator.

SWIFT (JONATHAN) *Dean of St. Patrick's.* [*Gulliver's*
Travels.]   Gulliver's Travels ... Illustrated by Rex
Whistler. 2 vol. *Cresset Press: London*, 1930. fol.
                                          C. **100**. l. **14**.

WARNER (SYLVIA TOWNSEND)
—— Elinor Barley. With illustrations in dry point by I. R.
   Hodgkins. pp. vii. 107. **F. P.**   *Cresset Press:*
   [*London*,] 1930. 8°.   C. **100**. c. **11**.
   With an additional set of plates.

JOHNSON (ALFRED FORBES)
—— Decorative Initial Letters. Collected and arranged with
   an introduction by A. F. Johnson. pp. xxiii. 247. *Cresset*
   Press: London, 1931. 4°.   L.R. **40**. c. **4**.

MILTON (JOHN) [*Paradise Lost.*]
—— Paradise Lost, *etc.* [With engravings by D. E. Galanis.]
   pp. xii. 441. *Cresset Press: London*, 1931. fol.
                                          C. **102**. l. **6/1**.

MILTON (JOHN) [*Paradise Regained.*]
—— Paradise Regain'd, *etc.* [With engravings by D. E.
   Galanis.] pp. 87. *Cresset Press: London*, 1931. fol.
                                          C. **102**. l. **6/2**.

CRYPT HOUSE PRESS, Gloucester & London

PERIODICAL PUBLICATIONS.—*Dymock.*
—— New Numbers, *etc.* (A quarterly publication of the
   poems of Rupert Brooke, John Drinkwater, Wilfrid
   Wilson Gibson, Lascelles Abercrombie.) vol. 1. no. 1–4.
   Feb.–Dec. 1914. *Dymock*, 1914. 4°.   Cup. **401**. h. **8**.

OVIDIUS NASO (PUBLIUS) [*Ars Amatoria.—English.*]
—— The Lover's Manual of Ovid. Translated into English
   verse by E. Phillips Barker. With drawings by A. R.
   Thomson. pp. vii. 158.   *Basil Blackwell: Oxford*,
   1931. 8°.   Cup. **510**. bj. **2**.

WHITFIELD (CHRISTOPHER) The Wood Gatherer,
and other poems. pp. 70.   *Crypt House Press:*
Gloucester & London, 1931. 8°.   Cup.**510.bj.1.**
No. 35 of an edition of 100 copies.

CUALA PRESS, Dundrum, afterwards Dublin [To 1907 as Dun Emer Press]

E., A.
—— The nuts of knowledge. Lyrical poems old and new.
   By A. E. [i.e. George Russell.]   *Dundrum: Dun Emer*
   Press, 1903.   Cup. **510**. ad. **3**.
   pp. 32. 22 cm.   △

YEATS (WILLIAM BUTLER) In the Seven Woods:
being poems chiefly of the Irish heroic age. pp. 63.
Dun Emer Press: Dundrum, 1903. 8°. Cup. **510**. ad. **2**.

HYDE (DOUGLAS) called AN CRAOIBHÍN AOIBHINN,
President of Eire.   The Love Songs of Connacht:
being the fourth chapter of the Songs of Connacht,
collected and translated by Douglas Hyde. pp. 128.
Elizabeth Corbet Yeats: Dundrum, 1904. 8°.
                              Cup. **510**. ad. **4**.

JOHNSON (LIONEL PIGOT) [*Selections.*]
—— Twenty one Poems ... selected by William Butler Yeats.
   pp. 31. *Dun Emer Press: Dundrum*, 1904. 8°.
                              Cup. **510**. ad. **5**.

YEATS (WILLIAM BUTLER)
—— Stories of Red Hanrahan. pp. 57.   *Dun Emer Press:*
   Dundrum, 1904. 8°.   Cup. **510**. ad. **6**.

ALLINGHAM (WILLIAM) *Poet.*
—— Sixteen Poems by William Allingham : selected by
   William Butler Yeats. pp. 35.   *Dun Emer Press :*
   Dundrum, 1905. 8°.   Cup.**510**.**ad.8.**

E., A.
—— By still waters. Lyrical poems, old and new. By A. E.
   [i.e. George Russell.] *Dundrum: Dun Emer Press*, 1906.
                              Cup. **510**. ad. **10**.
   pp. 32. 22 cm.   △

EGLINGTON (JOHN) *pseud.* [i.e. WILLIAM KIRKPATRICK
   MAGEE.]
——   Some Essays and Passages by
John Eglinton; selected by W. B. Yeats. pp. 56.
Dun Emer Press: Dundrum, 1905. 8°.Cup.**510.ad.7.**

GREGORY (ISABELLA AUGUSTA) *Lady.* A Book of
Saints and Wonders put down here by Lady Gregory
according to the old writings and the memory of the
people of Ireland. pp. 100.
Dun Emer Press: Dundrum, 1906. 8°.
                              Cup.**510**.ad.9

TYNAN, afterwards HINKSON (KATHARINE)
—— Twenty one Poems . . . Selected by W. B. Yeats.
   pp. 33. *Dun Emer Press: Dundrum*, 1907. 8°.
                              Cup. **510**. ad. **11**.

YEATS (WILLIAM BUTLER)
—— Discoveries: a volume of essays. pp. 43.   *Dun Emer*
   Press: Dundrum, 1907. 8°.   Cup. **510**. ad. **12**.

YEATS (WILLIAM BUTLER)
—— Poetry and Ireland: essays by W. B. Yeats and Lionel
   Johnson. pp. 53. *Cuala Press: Dundrum*, 1908. 8°.
                              Cup. **510**. ad. **13**.

SYNGE (JOHN MILLINGTON) Poems and Translations. [With a preface by W. B. Yeats.] pp. xiv. 45. *Cuala Press: Churtown, Dundrum, 1909.* 8°.

Cup.510.ad.14.

SYNGE (JOHN MILLINGTON) Deirdre of the Sorrows: a play. pp. 78. *Cuala Press: Churchtown, 1910.* 4°.

Cup.510.ad.15.

YEATS (WILLIAM. BUTLER) The Green Helmet, and other poems. pp. 32. *Cuala Press: Dundrum, 1910.* 8°.

Cup.510.ad.16.

YEATS (WILLIAM BUTLER)
—— Synge and the Ireland of his time ... With a note concerning a walk through Connemara with him by Jack Butler Yeats. pp. 42. *Cuala Press: Churchtown, 1911.* 8°.

Cup. 510. ad. 17.

DIX (ERNEST REGINALD McCLINTOCK)
—— List of Books, Newspapers and Pamphlets printed in Ennis, Co. Clare, in the eighteenth century. Compiled by E. R. McC. Dix. pp. 31. *Cuala Press: Churchtown, 1912.* 8°.

11927. a. 42.

Irish Bibliographical Pamphlets. no. 8.

MITCHELL (SUSAN L.)
—— **Frankincense and Myrrh. [Poems. With a frontispiece by J. B. Yeats.]** *Cuala Press: [Dundrum, 1912.]* 8°.

Cup. 510. ad. 76.

PLUNKETT (EDWARD JOHN MORETON DRAX) 18*th Baron Dunsany.*
—— Selections from the Writings of Lord Dunsany. [With an introduction by W. B. Yeats.] pp. 98. *Cuala Press: Dundrum, 1912.* 8°.

Cup. 510. ad. 18.

DOWDEN (EDWARD)
—— A Woman's Reliquary. [Poems.] pp. 58. *Cuala Press: Dundrum, 1913.* 8°.

Cup. 510. ad. 65.

YEATS (WILLIAM BUTLER)
—— Poems written in Discouragement ... 1912–1913. *Cuala Press: Dundrum, 1913.* 16°.

Ashley **2289.**

Author's presentation copy to Mrs. Gosse. With a MS. correction in the author's hand.

YEATS (WILLIAM BUTLER) [*Selections.*]
—— A selection from the Love Poetry of William Butler Yeats. pp. 29. *Cuala Press: Churchtown, Dundrum, 1913.* 8°.

Cup. 510. ad. 19.

RAVĪNDRANĀTHA ṬHĀKURA, *Sir.*
—— The post office: a play ... Translated by Devabrata Mukerjea. *Dundrum: Cuala Press, 1914.* **14131. c. 25.**

pp. 37. 22 cm. △

YEATS (WILLIAM BUTLER)
—— The Hour Glass. pp. 34. *Cuala Press: [Dundrum, 1914.]* 8°. Ashley **4679*.**

Privately printed. One of an edition of 50 copies. Author's presentation copy to Edmund Gosse.

YEATS (WILLIAM BUTLER) Responsibilities: poems and a play. pp. 74. *Cuala Press: Dundrum, 1914.* 8°.

Cup.510.ad.20.

MASEFIELD (JOHN EDWARD)
—— John M. Synge: a few personal recollections, with biographical notes. pp. 34. *Cuala Press: Churchtown, Dundrum, 1915.* 8°.

Cup. 510. ad. 21.

YEATS (WILLIAM BUTLER) Reveries over Childhood and Youth. (Plates.) 2 pt. *Cuala Press: Dundrum, 1915.* 8°.

Cup.510.ad.22.

FENOLLOSA (ERNEST FRANCISCO)
—— Certain noble plays of Japan: from the manuscripts of Ernest Fenollosa, chosen and finished by Ezra Pound, with an introduction by William Butler Yeats. *Dundrum: Cuala Press, 1916.* **11094. d. 20.**

pp. xviii, 48. 22 cm. △

YEATS (JOHN BUTLER) [*Letters.*]
—— Passages from the Letters of John Butler Yeats: selected by Ezra Pound. pp. 60. *Cuala Press: Churchtown, Dundrum, 1917.* 8°.

Cup. 510. ad. 24.

YEATS (WILLIAM BUTLER)
—— The Wild Swans at Coole, other verses and a play in verse (At the Hawk's Well). pp. 46. *Cuala Press: Churchtown, 1917.* 8°.

Cup. 510. ad. 23.

GREGORY (ISABELLA AUGUSTA) *Lady.*
—— The Kiltartan Poetry Book. Prose translations from the Irish by Lady Gregory. pp. x. 51. *Cuala Press: Dundrum, 1918.* 8°.

Cup. 510. ad. 73.

YEATS (WILLIAM BUTLER)
—— Two Plays for Dancers. (The Dreaming of the Bones. The Only Jealousy of Emer.) pp. 38. *Cuala Press: Churchtown, 1919.* 4°.

Cup. 510. ad. 26.

YEATS (JOHN BUTLER) Further Letters ... Selected by Lennox Robinson. pp. 81. *Cuala Press: Dundrum, 1920.* 8°.

Cup.510.ad.27.

YEATS (WILLIAM BUTLER) Michael Robartes and the Dancer. [Poems.] pp. 34. *Cuala Press: Churchtown, Dundrum, 1920.* 8°. Cup.510.ad.28.

YEATS (WILLIAM BUTLER)
—— Four Years. (1887–91.) [Reminiscences.] pp. 91. *Cuala Press: Dundrum,* 1921. 8°. Cup. **510**. ad. **29**.

HARMSWORTH (CECIL BISSHOPP) *Baron Harmsworth.*
—— Holiday verses and others : by Cecil & Desmond Harmsworth. *Dublin: Cuala Press,* 1922. Cup. **510**. ad. **78**. pp. 33. 22 cm. △
Authors' presentation copy.

YEATS (WILLIAM BUTLER)
—— Seven Poems and a Fragment. pp. 24. *Cuala Press: Churchtown,* 1922. 8°. Cup. **510**. ad. **30**.

GOGARTY (OLIVER SAINT JOHN)
—— An Offering of Swans. [Poems.] pp. 25. *Cuala Press: Dublin,* 1923. 8°. Cup. **510**. ad. **32**.

YEATS (JOHN BUTLER)
—— Early Memories; some chapters of autobiography. pp. 98. *Cuala Press: Dundrum,* 1923. 8°. Cup. **510**. ad. **31**.

YEATS (WILLIAM BUTLER)
—— The Cat and the Moon, and certain poems. pp. 41. *Cuala Press: Dublin,* 1924. 8°. Cup. **510**. ad. **33**.

FLOWER (ROBIN ERNEST WILLIAM)
—— Love's Bitter-Sweet: translations from the Irish poets of the sixteenth and seventeenth centuries. pp. 34. *Cuala Press: Dublin,* 1925. 8°. Cup. **510**. ad. **25**.

YEATS (WILLIAM BUTLER) The Bounty of Sweden. A meditation, and a lecture delivered before the Royal Swedish Academy and certain notes. pp. 53. *Cuala Press: Dublin,* 1925. 8°. Cup.510.ad.34.

YEATS (WILLIAM BUTLER)
—— Estrangement: being some fifty thoughts from a diary kept . . . in the year nineteen hundred and nine. pp. 39. *Cuala Press: Dublin,* 1926. 8°. Cup. **510**. ad. **35**.

IONIDES (ALEXANDER CONSTANTINE) Iōn. A grand-father's tale. [Reminiscences.] 2 pt. *Cuala Press: Dublin,* 1927. 8°. Cup.510.ad.75.
Privately printed. Pt. 2 printed in England.

PARNELL (THOMAS) *Archdeacon of Clogher.*
—— Poems . . . Selected by L. Robinson. pp. 31. *Cuala Press: Dublin,* 1927. 8°. Cup. **510**. ad. **36**.

YEATS (WILLIAM BUTLER)
—— October Blast. [Poems.] pp. 24. *Cuala Press: Dublin,* 1927. 8°. Cup. **510**. ad. **37**.

GOGARTY (OLIVER SAINT JOHN)
—— Wild Apples. [Poems.] pp. 33. *Cuala Press: Dublin,* 1928. 8°. Cup. **510**. ad. **39**.
One of an edition of 50 copies.

ROBINSON (ESME STUART LENNOX)
——————— Little Anthology of Modern Irish Verse: selected by L. Robinson. pp. 34. *Cuala Press: Dublin,* 1928. 8°. Cup.510.ad.66.

TOLHURST (ROGERS)
—— In the Emperor's Garden and other poems. pp. 29. MS. NOTES [by the author]. *Printed for the Author at the Cuala Press: Dublin,* 1928. 8°. Cup. **510**. ad. **67**.
One of an edition of fifty copies, privately printed. Author's presentation copy.

YEATS (WILLIAM BUTLER) The Death of Synge, and other passages from an old diary. pp. 34. *Cuala Press: Dublin,* 1928. 8°. Cup.510.ad.38.

YEATS (WILLIAM BUTLER) A Packet for Ezra Pound. pp. 37. *Cuala Press: Dublin,* 1929. 8°. Cup.510.ad.60.

GOGARTY (OLIVER SAINT JOHN)
——————— Wild Apples, etc. pp. 30. *Cuala Press: Dublin,* 1930. 8°. Cup.510.ad.72.

HARMSWORTH (DESMOND)
—— Desmond's Poems. pp. 61. *Privately printed for the author at the Cuala Press: Dublin,* 1930. 8°. Cup.510.ad.68.
One of an edition of seventy-five copies.

SHEIL (TERESA)
—— Poems. *Dublin: Cuala Press,* 1930. Cup. **510**. ad. **77**. pp. 45; illus. 22 cm. △
One of an edition of fifty copies, privately printed. A leaf bearing a MS. translation into English by Lord Dunsany of one of the German poems is inserted.

GREGORY (ISABELLA AUGUSTA) *Lady.*
—— Coole. pp. 49. *Cuala Press: Dublin,* 1931. 8°. Cup. **510**. ad. **41**.

YEATS (WILLIAM BUTLER)
—— Stories of Michael Robartes and his friends: an extract from a record made by his pupils: and a play in prose (The Resurrection). pp. 45. *Cuala Press: Dublin,* 1931. 8°. Cup.510.ad.40.

MAXWELL (WILLIAM) *P.R.S.E.*
—— The Dun Emer Press . . . The Cuala Press . . . A complete list of the books, pamphlets, leaflets and broadsides printed by Miss Yeats, with some notes by the compiler. pp. 65. *Privately printed: Edinburgh,* 1932. 8°. Cup. **510**. ad. **1**.

YEATS (WILLIAM BUTLER)
—— Words for Music. Perhaps, and other poems. pp. 41. *Cuala Press: Dublin*, 1932. 8°. Cup.510.ad.42.

ROSSI (MARIO MANLIO)
—— [Viaggio in Irlanda.] Pilgrimage in the West . . . Translated [in an abridged form] by J. M. Hone. pp. 51. *Cuala Press: Dublin*, 1933. 8°. Cup.510.ad.43.

DONAGHY (JOHN LYLE)
—— Into the Light, and other poems. pp. 85. *Privately printed for the author at the Cuala Press: Dublin*, 1934. 8°. Cup.510.ad.69.

YEATS (WILLIAM BUTLER)
—— The King of the Great Clock Tower, Commentaries and Poems. pp. 44. *Cuala Press: Dublin*, 1934. 8°. Cup.510.ad.48.

YEATS (WILLIAM BUTLER)
—— The Words upon the Window Pane. A play in one act, with notes upon the play and its subject. pp. 58. *Cuala Press: Dublin*, 1934. 8°. Cup 510.ad.44.

YEATS (WILLIAM BUTLER)
—— Dramatis Personæ. pp. 88. *Cuala Press: Dublin*, 1935. 8°. Cup. 510. ad. 46.

E., A.
—— Some Passages from the Letters of Æ [George William Russell] to W. B. Yeats. pp. 62. *Cuala Press: Dublin*, 1936. 8°. Cup.510.ad.45.

YEATS (WILLIAM BUTLER)
—— Essays . . . 1931 to 1936. pp. 131. *Cuala Press: Dublin*, 1937. 8°. Cup.510.ad.47.

O'CONNOR (FRANK)
—— Lords and Commons. Translations from the Irish. [Poems.] pp. 40. *Cuala Press: Dublin*, 1938. 8°. Cup.510.ad.49.

YEATS (WILLIAM BUTLER)
—— New Poems. [With musical notes.] pp. 38. *Cuala Press: Dublin*, 1938. 8°. Cup.510.ad.50.

GOGARTY (OLIVER SAINT JOHN)
—— Elbow Room. pp. 32. *Cuala Press: Dublin*, 1939. 8°. Cup.510.ad.51.

YEATS (WILLIAM BUTLER)
—— Last Poems and Two Plays. pp. 58. *Cuala Press: Dublin*, 1939. 8°. Cup. 510. ad. 52.

YEATS (WILLIAM BUTLER)
—— On the Boiler. [Essays and poems.] pp. 46. *Cuala Press: Dublin*, [1939.] 4°. 012274. e. 5.

MASEFIELD (JOHN EDWARD)
—— Some Memories of W. B. Yeats. pp. 29. *Cuala Press: Dublin*, 1940. 8°. Cup.510.ad.53.

O'CONNELL (EILEEN)
—— A Lament for Art O'Leary. Translated from the Irish by Frank O'Connor, with six illustrations by Jack B. Yeats. *Cuala Press: Dublin*, 1940. fol. Cup. 510. ad. 54.

YEATS (LILY)
—— Elizabeth Corbet Yeats. Born March 11th. 1868. Died January 16th. 1940. [*Cuala Press: Dublin*, 1940.] 8°. Cup.510.ad.70.

YEATS (WILLIAM BUTLER)
—— If I Were Four-and-Twenty. (Swedenborg, Mediums, and the Desolate Places.) [Two essays.] pp. 67. *Cuala Press: Dublin*, 1940. 8°. Cup.510.ad.55.

MACDONAGH (DONAGH)
—— Veterans and other poems. pp. 33. *Cuala Press: Dublin*, 1941. 8°. Cup. 510. ad. 56.

O'CONNOR (FRANK)
—— Three Tales. pp. 41. *Cuala Press: Dublin*, 1941. 8°. Cup.510.ad.57.

SHAW (GEORGE BERNARD) [*Letters.*]
—— Florence Farr, Bernard Shaw and W. B. Yeats. [Letters from Shaw and Yeats to F. Farr.] Edited by Clifford Bax. pp. 84. *Cuala Press: Dublin*, 1941. 8°. Cup.510.ad.58.

BOWEN (ELIZABETH DOROTHEA COLE)
—— Seven Winters. [Reminiscences of the author's childhood.] pp. 57. *Cuala Press: Dublin*, 1942. 8°. Cup.510.ad.61.

KAVANAGH (Patrick)

—— The Great Hunger. [A poem.] pp. 33. *Cuala Press: Dublin*, 1942. 8°. Cup. **510**. ad. **74**.

O'CONNOR (Frank)

—— A Picture Book . . . Illustrated by Elizabeth Rivers. pp. 72. *Cuala Press: Dublin*, 1943. 8° Cup. **510**. ad. **62**.

YEATS (Jack Butler)

—— La La Noo. (A play.) pp. 52. *Cuala Press: Dublin*, 1943. 8°. Cup. **510**. ad. **63**.

DAFYDD, *ap Gwilym*.

—— Selected Poems: translated by Nigel Heseltine, *etc.* pp. 44. *Cuala Press: Dublin*, 1944. 8°. Cup. **510**. ad. **64**.

YEATS (William Butler)

—— Pages from a Diary written in Nineteen Hundred and Thirty. pp. 57. *Cuala Press: Dublin*, 1944. 8°. Cup. **510**. ad. **59**.

HUTTON (Annie) *Translator of Archbishop Rinuccini's " Embassy in Ireland".*

—— The Love Story of Thomas Davis, told in the letters of Annie Hutton. Edited with an introduction by Joseph Hone. pp. xiv. 17. *Cuala Press: Dublin*, 1945. 8°. Cup. **510**. ad. **71**.

RIVERS (Elizabeth Joyce)

—— Stranger in Aran. Written and illustrated by Elizabeth Rivers. *Dublin: Cuala Press*, 1946. Cup. **510**. ad. **81**. pp. 77. 22 cm. △

CUCKOO HILL PRESS, Pinner

JEWRY, afterwards **VALENTINE** (Laura)

[The language and sentiment of flowers.]

—— Here's rosemary. A vocabulary, floral and sentimental. (Wood engravings by David Chambers.) [Compiled by Laura Valentine.] *Pinner: Cuckoo Hill Press*, 1959. Cup. **510**. bem. **4**. pp. 14. 16 cm. △

Selections from "The language and sentiment of flowers". No. 36 of an edition of forty-one copies.

JAPANESE PAPERS.

—— Some Decorative Japanese Papers. [Samples, with a description and introduction by David Chambers.] (Second edition.) *Cuckoo Hill Press: Pinner*, 1960. 8°. Cup. **510**. bem. **1**.

One of an edition of 59 copies, privately printed.

CHAMBERS (David) *Printer, at the Cuckoo Hill Press.*

—— The Office Press. [With specimens.] *Printed by David Chambers at Cuckoo Hill Press: Pinner*, 1961. 8°. Cup. **510**. bem. **2**.

One of twelve special copies printed for private circulation.

ELIZABETH II. NUMISMATA.

—— Elizabeth II numismata. *Pinner: Cuckoo Hill Press*, 1964. 93 mm. Cup. **550**. ee. **39**. △

Illustrations of coins, followed by a short descriptive note. One of an edition of one hundred copies.

CUMMINGTON PRESS, Cummington, Mass.

BLACKMUR (Richard Palmer)

—— The Second world. [Poems.] pp. 29. *Cummington Press: Cummington*, 1942. 8°. Cup. **510**. ps. **5**.

BOGGS (Tom)

—— American Decade. 68 poems for the first time in an anthology . . . Edited by Tom Boggs. pp. 93. *Cummington Press: Cummington*, [1943.] 8°. X. **900/1871**.

VENUS.

[Pervigilium Veneris.]

—— The vigil of Venus . . . The Latin text with an introduction and English translation by Allen Tate. *Cummington, Mass.: Cummington Press*, 1943. Cup. **510**. ps. **13**.

Pages not numbered. 25 cm. △

TATE (John Orley Allen)

—— The Winter Sea. A book of poems. *Cummington Press: [Cummington, Mass.,]* 1944. 8°. Cup. **510**. ps. **3**.

STEVENS (Wallace)

—— Esthétique du mal. A poem . . . with pen & ink drawings by Wightman Williams. *Cummington Press: Cummington*, 1945. 8°. Cup. **510**. ps. **9**.

WARREN (Robert Penn)

—— Blackberry winter. A story illustrated by Wightman Williams. *Cummington: Cummington Press*, 1946. Cup. **510**. ps. **11**.

pp. 49. 20 cm. △

BLACKMUR (Richard Palmer)

—— The Good European and other poems. pp. 39. *Cummington Press: Cummington, Mass.*, 1947. 8°. Cup. **510**. ps. **2**.

WILLIAMS (William Carlos)

—— The Clouds, Aigeltinger, Russia, &c. pp. 64. *Published jointly by the Wells College Press and the Cummington Press: [New York,]* 1948. 8°. Cup. **510**. ps. **10**.

CUNNINGHAM (James Vincent)

—— Doctor drink. Poems. *[Cummington, Mass.:] Cummington Press*, 1950. Cup. **510**. ps. **12**.

Pages not numbered; illus. 18 cm. △

EBERHART (Richard)

—— An Herb Basket. *Cummington Press: Cummington*, 1950. 8°. **11689**. g. **13**.

TATE (JOHN ORLEY ALLEN)
—— Two Conceits for the Eye to sing, if possible. *Cummington Press:* [*Cummington, Mass.*,] 1950. 8º. Cup. **510**. ps. **4**.

WINTERS (YVOR)
—— Three Poems. *Cummington Press:* [*Cummington, Mass.*,] 1950. 8º. Cup. **510**. ps. **1**.

DICKENS (CHARLES) [*Letters.*]
—— Dickens in Italy. A letter to Thomas Mitton written in 1844, *etc.* [With a facsimile.] pp. 16. *Pierpont Morgan Library: New York*, 1956. 8º. Cup. **510**. ps. **7**.

AGEE (JAMES RUFUS)
—— Four early stories . . . Collected by Elena Harap and illustrated with intaglio etchings by Keith Achepohl. pp. 43. *Cummington Press: West Branch*, 1964. 4º. Cup. **510**. ps. **8**.

AGEE (JAMES RUFUS)
—— [Another copy.] Four early stories, *etc. West Branch*, 1964. 4º. Cup. **510**. ps. **6**.

CUPID PRESS, Ipswich

HADFIELD (JOHN CHARLES HEYWOOD)
—— Georgian Love Songs. Edited by John Hadfield with decorations by Rex Whistler. pp. xix. 147. *Cupid Press: Preston, Herts.*, 1949. 8º. Cup.510.aca.1.

HADFIELD (JOHN CHARLES HEYWOOD)
—— Restoration Love Songs. Edited by J. Hadfield. With decorations by Rex Whistler. pp. xx. 153. *Cupid Press: Preston near Hitchin*, 1950. 8º. Cup.510.aca.2.

WHISTLER (LAURENCE)
—— The Engraved Glass of Laurence Whistler. (With an introduction by the artist.) pp. 47. pl. 82. *Cupid Press: Hitchin*, 1952. 8º. **7949**. g. **23**.

HADFIELD (JOHN CHARLES HEYWOOD)
—— Elizabethan Love Songs. Edited by J. Hadfield. With lithographs by John Piper. pp. vii. 134. *Cupid Press: Barham, Suff.*, [1955.] 8º. Cup.510.aca.3.

GAINSBOROUGH (THOMAS) [*Letters.*]
—— The Letters of Thomas Gainsborough. Edited by Mary Woodall. (Revised edition.) [With a self-portrait.] pp. 184. pl. 26. *Cupid Press:* [*Ipswich*, 1963.] 4º. Cup. **501**. f. **18**.

CURWEN PRESS, London

NODIER (JEAN EMMANUEL CHARLES)
—— [Trésor-des-Fèves et Fleur-des-Pois.] The Luck of the Bean-Rows. A fairy tale . . . Illustrated by Claud Lovat Fraser. pp. 60. *Daniel O'Connor: London*, [1921.] 8º. C. **108**. c. **9**.
In an inlaid binding by F. C. Austin.

MEIER-GRAEFE (ALFRED JULIUS) Degas. Rendered into English by J. Holroyd-Reece, *etc.* pp. 87. pl. CIII. F. P. *Ernest Benn: London*, 1923. 8º. L.R. **37**. b. **4**.

CURWEN PRESS.
—— Catalogue Raisonné of Books printed at the Curwen Press, 1920–1923. With an introduction by Holbrook Jackson. [With facsimiles.] pp. 27. *Medici Society: London*, 1924. 8º. **011904**. aa. **38**.

YASHIRO (YUKIO) Sandro Botticelli. [With plates.] 3 vol. *Medici Society: London & Boston*, 1925. fol. K.T.C. **121**. b. **8**.

HORATIUS FLACCUS (QUINTUS) [*Carmina.—Latin.*] Horati Carminum Libri IV. (Decorations by Vera Willoughby.) pp. 141. *Impensis Petr. Davies: Londini*, 1926. 8º. C. **99**. h. **12**.

ARMSTRONG (MARTIN DONISTHORPE)
—— Saint Hercules, and other stories . . . With drawings by Paul Nash. pp. 65. *The Fleuron: London*, [1927.] 4º. C. **98**. h. **15**.

HERRICK (ROBERT) *the Poet.* [*Smaller Collections.*]
—— Delighted earth. A selection by Peter Meadows from Herrick's 'Hesperides'. With illustrations by Lionel Ellis. *London: Fanfrolico Press*, 1927. **11633**. f. **54**.
pp. 170. 24 cm. △
Printed at the Curwen Press.

HERRICK (ROBERT) *the Poet.* [*Smaller Collections.*]
—— [Another copy.] Delighted earth, *etc.* 1927. C. **99**. g. **39**.
△
One of twenty-five copies printed on Japanese vellum.

LINDSAY (JACK)
—— Marino Faliero. (A tragedy [in verse].) pp. 104. *Fanfrolico Press: London*, 1927. 4º. C. **98**. f. **8**.

CURWEN PRESS.
—— A Specimen Book of Pattern Papers designed for and in use at the Curwen Press. With an introduction by Paul Nash. *Published for the Curwen Press by The Fleuron: London*, 1928. 4º. **7804**. t. **7**.

OVIDIUS NASO (Publius) [*Epistolæ Heroidum.*
—English.] The Heroycall Epistles . . . Translated
. . . by George Turbervile. With . . . illustrations by
Hester Sainsbury. Edited, with an introduction and
glossary, by Frederick Boas. **F. P.** pp. xxiv. 349.
Cresset Press: London, 1928. 4°.　　C. **98**. h. 22.

BENNETT (Enoch Arnold)
—— Elsie and the child. Drawings by E. McKnight Kauffer.
pp. 85. *London: Cassell & Co.*, 1929.　　C. **100**. e. 5.

　　pp. 85. 26 cm.　　　　　　　　　　△

　　Printed at the Curwen Press. No. 98 of one hundred
copies specially bound, and signed by the author and the
artist.

BLOME (Richard)
—— Hawking; or, Faulconry. [From pt. 2 of " The Gentleman's Recreation". With a preface by E. W. D. Cuming.]
pp. xxxii. 123. *Cresset Press: London*, 1929. 8°.
　　　　　　　　　　　　　　　　　　7904. e. 28.

　　No. 20 of fifty copies printed on handmade paper.

GOGOL' (Nikolai Vasil'evich) [Записки сумашедшаго.]
—— The Diary of a Madman. Translated by Prince Mirsky.
Illustrated with aquatints by A. Alexeieff. [With a portfolio of plates.] pp. 81.　　*Cresset Press: London*,
1929. 4°.　　　　　　　　　　　　C. **100**. c. 7.

CURWEN PRESS.
—— The Curwen Press Miscellany. Edited by Oliver Simon.
[With a " Catalogue Raisonné of Books printed at the
Curwen Press, 1928–1930."] pp. x. 136.　　*Published for*
the Curwen Press, by the Soncino Press: London, 1931. 8°.
　　　　　　　　　　　　　　　　11906. l. 20.

ASHBEE (Charles Robert)
—— Peckover. The Abbotscourt Papers, 1904–1931. Edited
by C. R. Ashbee. Illustrated by Reginald Savage.
pp. xi. 268. *Astolat Press: London*, 1932. 4°.
　　　　　　　　　　　　　　　　12349. w. 3.

BROWNE (Sir Thomas)
—— Urne Buriall and The Garden of Cyrus . . . With
thirty drawings by Paul Nash. Edited with an introduction by John Carter. pp. xx. 146. *Cassell & Co.: London*,
1932. fol.　　　　　　　　　　　C. **98**. gg. 24.

HARDY (Thomas) *O.M.*
—— An Indiscretion in the Life of an Heiress. pp. 89.
Privately printed: London, 1934. 8°.　C. **100**. c. 11
　　No. 13 of an edition of 100 copies.

SHELLEY (Percy Bysshe) [*Miscellaneous.*]
—— Verse and Prose from the Manuscripts of Percy Bysshe
Shelley. Edited by Sir John C. E. Shelley-Rolls, Bart.,
and Roger Ingpen. [With facsimiles.] pp. xiii. 159.
Privately printed: London, 1934. 8°.　　**012272**. bb. 7.

BORROW (George Henry) [*Single Works.*]
—— Lavengro . . . With an introduction by Hugh Walpole.
Illustrated with sixteen lithographs in colour and pen
drawings by Barnett Freedman. 2 vol.　　*Printed for the*
members of the Limited Editions Club at the Curwen Press:
London, 1936. 8°.　　　　　　　　C. **105**. c. 12.
　　One of 15 presentation copies.

GREGORY (Sir Theodore Emanuel Gugenheim)
—— The Westminster Bank through a Century. By T. E.
Gregory, assisted by Annette Henderson, *etc.* [With
plates.] 2 vol.　　*Oxford University Press: London*,
1936. 8°.　　　　　　　　　　　　**8234**. d. 9.

DUMAS (Alexandre) *the Younger.*
—— Camille . . . Translated from the French with an introduction by Edmund Gosse, and twelve drawings by
Marie Laurencin. pp. xi. 213.　　*Printed for the members*
of the Limited Editions Club at the Curwen Press: London,
1937. fol.　　　　　　　　　　　C. **105**. d. 5.

BOSWELL (James) *the Elder.* [*Life of Johnson.*]
—— The Life of Samuel Johnson . . . With marginal comments and markings from two copies annotated by Hester
Lynch Thrale Piozzi. Prepared for publication with an
introduction by Edward G. Fletcher. [With portraits.]
3 vol.　*Printed for the members of the Limited Editions Club*
at the Curwen Press: London, 1938. 8°.　　C. **105**. d. 8.

SIMON (André Louis)
—— Notes on the late J. Pierpont Morgan's Cellar Book, 1906.
pp. 37.　　　*Privately printed for the Author: London*,
1944. 8°.　　　　　　　　　　　　**7082**. r. 12.

ABBEY (John Roland)
—— Scenery of Great Britain and Ireland in aquatint and
lithography, 1770–1860. From the library of J. R. Abbey.
A bibliographical catalogue. pp. xx. 399. pl. xxxiv.
Curwen Press: London, 1952. fol.　　　**2061**.c.
　　Privately printed.

ABBEY (John Roland)
—— [Another copy.] Scenery of Great Britain and Ireland
in aquatint and lithography, 1770–1860. *etc.*　　*London*,
1952. fol.　　　　　　　　　　　**7867**. bb. 24.

HOW (George Evelyn Paget)
—— English and Scottish silver spoons, mediaeval to late
Stuart, and Pre-Elizabethan hall-marks on English plate.
(By Commander George Evelyn Paget How . . . in col-
laboration with Jane Penrice How.　　*London: privately*
printed, 1952–57.　　　　　　　C. **130**. k. 4.

　　3 vol.; illus. 43 cm.　　　　　　　　△

　　No. 4 of fifty copies printed on mould-made paper and
specially bound.

ABBEY (JOHN ROLAND)

—— Life in England in Aquatint and Lithography, 1770-1860. Architecture, drawing books, art collections, magazines, navy and army, panoramas, etc. from the library of J. R. Abbey. A bibliographical catalogue. pp. xxi. 427. pl. XXXII. *Curwen Press: London*, 1953. 4º.

2020.f.

Privately printed.

ABBEY (JOHN ROLAND)

—— [Another copy.] Life in England in Aquatint and Lithography, 1770–1860, *etc. London*, 1953. 4º.
L.R. 298. a. 22.

SHERIDAN (*Right Hon.* RICHARD BRINSLEY BUTLER) [*The Rivals.*]

—— The rivals . . . With an introduction by John Mason Brown and illustrations by René Ben Sussan. *London: printed for the members of the Limited Editions Club at the Curwen Press*, 1953. C. 105. d. 13.

pp. xxi, 149: plates. 28 cm. △

ABBEY (JOHN ROLAND)

—— Travel in aquatint and lithography, 1770–1860. From the library of J. R. Abbey . . . A bibliographical catalogue. *London: privately printed at the Curwen Press*, 1956, 57.
L.R. 402. f. 3.

2 vol.: pp. xiii, xiv, 675: pl. XXXVI. 32 cm. △

LEAR (EDWARD)
[Nonsense Songs.]

—— Le Hibou et la poussiquette. Edward Lear's The Owl and the Pussy-Cat freely translated into French by Francis Steegmuller. With illustrations by Monique-Alika Watteau. *Rupert Hart-Davis: London*, 1961. 8º.
Cup. 502. d. 13.

CYGNET PRESS, Cambridge, Mass.

MAC CORD (DAVID THOMPSON WATSON)

—— Oxford nearly visited. A fantasy. [In verse.] pp. 12. *Privately printed for the Cygnet Press: Cambridge, Mass., by the University Press: Oxford*, 1929. 8º.
Cup. 510. s. 1.
With a prospectus giving a list of publications of the Cygnet Press inserted.

DANIEL PRESS, Frome; Oxford

RICHARD, *Sir.* Sir Richard's Daughter: a Christmas tale, *etc.* [In verse. By Wilson Clement Cruttwell.] pp. 27. *H. Daniel: Frome*, 1852. 16º. C. 99. a. 22.

C., **C. J.** Sonnets: by C. J. C. [i.e. Charles J. Cruttwell.] *Private Press of H. & E. Daniel: Frome*, 1856. 16º.
C. 99. a. 13.

DANIEL (CHARLES HENRY OLIVE)

—— Nomina candidatorum qui termino S. Vacationis A.D. 1874 ab examinatoribus in locis amœnioribus honore digni sunt habiti in unaquaque classe secundum seriem literarum disposita. [Signed: H. Daniel, J. R. Thursfield, H. G. Woods, Examinatores.] [*The Daniel Press: Oxford*, 1874.] 8º. Cup. 510. bc. 1. (1.)

OXFORD.—*University of Oxford.*—*Worcester College.*

—— Notes from a catalogue of pamphlets in Worcester College Library. [Edited by C. H. O. Daniel.] *Oxonii: typis Henrici Daniel*, 1874. C. 99. a. 12.

pp. 79. 15 cm. △

No. 10 of an edition of twenty-five copies.

ERASMUS (DESIDERIUS) [*Colloquia. — Selections.*] Desiderii Erasmi Colloquia duo (Diversoria. Colloquium Abbatis et Eruditæ). Accedit vita. [Edited by C. H. O. Daniel.] pp. xli. *Typis Henrici Daniel: Oxonii*, [1880.] 16º. C.99.a.1.

RACHEL.

—— The Garland of Rachel. By Edmund W. Gosse and divers kindly hands. [Poems addressed to Rachel Anne Olive Daniel on her first birthday, by her father, Charles H. O. Daniel, and others.] pp. 67. *Printed at the private press of H. Daniel: Oxford*, 1881. 8º. Ashley 3277.
"*The number of copies is 36; the title-page of each copy bears the name of a several author.*" With a separately printed note to the contributors, signed: H. D., and beginning "*I have the pleasure of sending you at last a copy of 'The Garland of Rachel.'*"

DANIEL (CHARLES HENRY OLIVE)

—— Hymni ecclesiae cura Henrici Daniel. pp. vii. 71. *Typis Henrici Daniel: Oxonii*, 1882. 8º. C. 99. d. 58.

BRIDGES (ROBERT SEYMOUR)

—— Prometheus the Firegiver. pp. 72. *Printed at the private press of H. Daniel: Oxford*, 1883. 4º. C. 99. d. 13.
One of an edition of 100 copies.

THEOCRITUS. [*English.*] Sixe Idillia (chosen out of . . . Theocritus, and translated into English verse). pp. 39. *H. Daniel: Oxford*, 1883. 4º. C.99.d.12.
One hundred copies printed.

TUSSER (THOMAS) The Months Remembrances... 1580. Excerpsit [from "Five hundred pointes of good Husbandrie"]...H. Daniel. B. L. pp. 62. *H. Daniel: Oxford*, 1883. 16º. C. 99. a. 23.

BRIDGES (ROBERT SEYMOUR)

—— Poems. [24 poems, of which the first 17 are selected from the two preceding works and "Poems by the author of The Growth of Love. Third Series."] pp. 52. *Printed at the private press of H. Daniel: Oxford*, 1884. 4º. C. 99. d. 11.

DIXON (RICHARD WATSON) Odes and Eclogues. pp. 37. *Privately printed by H. Daniel: Oxford*, 1884. 4º. C.99.d.18.
Only 100 copies printed.

PATMORE (Henry John) Poems. [With a bio-graphical note by Gertrude Patmore.] pp. vi. 40. **L. P.** *Henry Daniel: Oxford*, 1884. 4°. C.99.d.16.
125 copies privately printed.

BLAKE (William) *Artist.* [*Selections.*]
—— Songs by William Blake. pp. 31. *H. Daniel: Oxford*, 1885. 24°. C. 99. a. 32.
Wanting the erratum leaf.

WEBSTER (John) *Dramatist.* Love's Graduate. A comedy. [Being the portion by J. Webster, of "A Cure for a Cuckold," written conjointly with W. Rowley, extracted by E. W. Gosse, with a prefatory essay by him. Edited by S. E. S. R. i.e. Stephen Edward Spring Rice.] pp. ix. 69. *At the private press of H. Daniel: Oxford*, 1885. 4°. C.99.d.15.

STAR.
—— *Begin.* Star of the Mystic East. [A poem by C. H. O. Daniel.] [*Daniel Press: Oxford*], 1886. *s.sh.* 8°. Cup. 510. bc. 1. (2.)

DIXON (Richard Watson) Lyrical Poems. **F. P.** pp. 62. [*Privately*] *Printed by H. Daniel: Oxford*, 1887. 4°. C.99.d.24.

DIXON (Richard Watson) The Story of Eudocia and her brothers. **F. P.** pp. vi. 35. *Printed by H. Daniel: Oxford*, 1888. 4°. C.99.d.4.
50 copies only printed.

WOODS (Margaret Louise)
—— Lyrics. pp. 59. *Printed by H. Daniel: Oxford*, 1888. 4°. C. 99. d. 10.

BRIDGES (Robert Seymour) [Single Works.]
—— The Feast of Bacchus. pp. 94. *Privately printed by H. Daniel: Oxford*, 1889. 4°. C. 99. d. 9.

BOURDILLON (Francis William)
—— Ailes d'Alouette. [Poems.] pp. 57. *H. Daniel: Oxford*, 1890. 8°. C. 99. b. 2.
No. 1 of an edition of 100 copies.

BRIDGES (Robert Seymour) [Single Works.]
—— The growth of love. [By R. S. Bridges.] *Oxford: H. Daniel*, 1890. C. 99. f. 6.
pp. lxxix. 23 cm. △
No. 67 of an edition of one hundred copies.

FOUNDERS DAY.
—— Founders Day. A secular ode on the ninth jubilee of Eton College. [By Robert Bridges.] **B. L.** pp. vii. [*Daniel Press: Oxford*, 1891.] 4°. Cup.510.bc.3.
Not published.

HERRICK (Robert) *the Poet.* [*Smaller Collections.*]
—— Christmas from the Noble Numbers of Robert Herrick. pp. 16. *Printed by H. Daniel: Oxford*, 1891. 12°. C. 108. cc. 13.
No. 25 of an edition of sixty copies.
The half-title reads: "Herrick, his Christmas".

HERRICK (Robert) *the Poet.* Herrick, his Flowers. pp. 30. *H. Daniel: Oxford*, 1891. 8°. C. 99. b. 25.
No. 17 of an edition of 100 copies.

BLAKE (William) *Artist*
—— Blake. His Songs of Innocence. pp. 38. *H. Daniel: Oxford*, 1893. 8°. C. 99. b. 30.
No. 1 of an edition of 100 copies. With the addition of a facsimile of the plate entitled "The Lamb."

DANIEL (Charles Henry Olive) Our Memories. Shadows of Old Oxford. Edited ... by H. Daniel. 2 series. *Printed at the Private Press of H. Daniel: Oxford*, 1893-95. 4°. C.99.d.5.
Imperfect; wanting pp. 1-12, 17-24, 49-68, 81-84, 97-100 *of series one.*

WARREN (Sir Thomas Herbert) *K.C.V.O.*
—— A New Years Greeting. [A poem. Signed: Herbert Warren.] *Henry Daniel: Oxford*, 1893. 4°. C. 100. g. 51. (1.)

BRIDGES (Robert Seymour)
[Two or more Works.]
—— Shorter Poems of Robert Bridges. 5 bk. *Printed by Hy. Daniel: Oxford*, 1894 [1893, 94]. 4°. C. 99. d. 6.
Published in parts.

MILTON (John) [*Ode on the morning of Christ's Nativity.*] Milton. Ode on the morning of Christ's Nativity. pp. 21. *H. Daniel: Oxford*, 1894 16°. C.99.b.11.

PATER (Walter Horatio)
—— An Imaginary Portrait. pp. 61. *Printed by H. Daniel: Oxford*, 1894. 8°. C. 99. b. 12.
The running title is: The Child in the House.

BINYON (Robert Laurence) *Keeper of Prints and Drawings, British Museum.*
—— Poems. pp. 52. *Daniel: Oxford*, 1895. 8°. C. 99. d. 8.

KEATS (John) [*Selections.*]
—— Odes Sonnets & Lyrics of John Keats. [With a portrait.] pp. 63. *Daniel: Oxford*, 1895. 4°. C. 68. i. 19.

W., T.H.
—— All amidst the Gardens Fair
Of Hesperus and his Daughters three
That sing about the Golden Tree.
[The text of the poem "Hesperides" by Sir Thomas H. Warren. Signed: T. H. W.] [*Daniel Press: Oxford*, 1895.] 4°. C. 100. g. 51. (2.)

ANODOS, *pseud.* [i.e. MARY ELIZABETH COLERIDGE.]

—— Fancy's Following. [Poems.] By 'Ανοδος. pp. 58. *Daniel: Oxford*, 1896. 8°.   C. **99**. d. **7**.

WOOD (ANTHONY À)

—— The Life of Richard Lovelace. [From vol. 3 of the "Athenæ Oxonienses."] pp. xviii.   *Daniel: Oxford*, 1896. 16°.   C. **99**. a. **27**.
One of an edition of 50 copies.

WOODS (MARGARET LOUISE)

—— Songs. pp. 28. *Daniel: Oxford*, 1896. 8°.
     C. **99**. a. **4**.

CHRISTMAS.

—— Christmas. 1897. (Christmas Carols.) pp. 16. *Daniel: Oxford*, 1897. 8°.   C. **99**. a. **2**.
Printed at the private press of C. H. O. Daniel.

FILIPPI, afterwards **DOWSON** (ROSINA)

—— Three Japanese plays for children . . . Illustrated by Alfred Parsons. *Oxford: H. Daniel*, 1897.
     C. **100**. e. **7**.

pp. 57 : plates. 22 cm.   △

W., H.

—— *Begin.* To the most High, Mightie and Magnificent Empresse . . . Victoria . . . Her most humble servant H. W. [i.e. *Sir* T. H. Warren] doth in all humilitie dedicate, present and consecrate these his verses. [*Daniel Press: Oxford*, 1897.] 8°.   C. **100**. g. **51**. (3.)

WARREN (*Sir* THOMAS HERBERT) *K.C.V.O.* ——————
             By Severn Sea & other poems. pp. 67. *H. Daniel: Oxford*, 1897. 8°.
Only 130 copies printed.   C.**99**.d.**1**.

BRIDGES (ROBERT SEYMOUR)

—— Hymns. (Hymns from the Yattendon Hymnal [written, translated or adapted] by Robert Bridges, with notice of the tunes for which they were written.) pp. 62. *Printed at the private press of Henry Daniel: Oxford*, 1899. 4°.   C. **99**. d. **14**.

FIELD (MICHAEL) *pseud.* [i.e. KATHERINE HARRIS BRADLEY and EDITH EMMA COOPER.]

—— Noontide Branches. A small sylvan drama interspersed with songs and invocations. pp. 44. *Printed at the Private Press of Henry Daniel: Oxford*, 1899. 4°.
     C. **99**. h. **2**.

S., W. Outlines, by W. S. [i.e. William Stebbing.] pp. 61. [*Printed at the Private Press of Henry Daniel*]: *Oxford*, 1899. 8°.   C.**99**.b.**1**.

ROYAL GUEST.

—— A royal guest. Christmas 1900.   [*Oxford: Daniel Press*, 1900].   C. **100**. e. **8**.
Pages not numbered. 21 cm.   △
Poems.

BUCKTON (ALICE MARY)

—— Through Human Eyes. Poems. (With an introductory poem by Robert Bridges.) pp. 53.   *Daniel: Oxford*, 1901. 4°.   C. **99**. h. **1**.

MUSES.

—— The Muses Gardin for Delights, or the fift booke of ayres, onely for the lute, the base-vyoll and the voice. Composed by R. Jones. Edited with an introduction by W. Barclay Squire. [Words only.] pp. vi. 44. *Daniel: Oxford*, 1901. 4°.   C. **99**. h. **13**.

B., R. Peace Ode written on the Conclusion of the Three Years' War. By R. B. [i.e. Robert Bridges], *etc. Daniel Press:* [*Oxford*,] 1902. 4°.   C. **98**. i. **4**.

BOURDILLON (FRANCIS WILLIAM)

—— Ailes d'Alouette. Second series. pp. 68. *Printed at the private press of H. Daniel: Oxford*, 1902. 8°.
     C. **99**. b. **21**.

WIND.

—— Wind along the Waste. [By the Hon. Ethel K. B. Wedgwood. Poems.] pp. 35.   *Daniel: Oxford*, 1902. 4°.   C. **104**. f. **6**.

BACON (*Sir* NICHOLAS)

—— The Recreations of his Age. (Thirty-six unpublished poems.) pp. 39.   *Daniel: Oxford*, 1903, *issued* 1919. 4°.
     C. **99**. e. **31**.
The text printed at the private press of the Rev. C. H. O. Daniel in 1903, with a titlepage and prefatory note printed at the Clarendon Press, Oxford, in 1919.

BRIDGES (ROBERT SEYMOUR)

—— Now in Wintry Delights. [A poem, with a note on prosody, and a facsimile of a page of the author's reformed script.] pp. 23. *Daniel Press: Oxford*, 1903. 4°.
     C. **99**. i. **9**.

ELIZABETH I., *Queen of England.* [*Appendix.*]

—— The Queen's Majesty's Entertainment at Woodstock, 1575. From the unique fragment of the edition of 1585, including the Tale of Hemetes the Hermit, and a comedy in verse, probably by George Gascoigne. With an introduction by A. W. Pollard. pp. xxviii. 32.   *Thomas Cadman: London*, 1585, printed; *H. Daniel & H. Hart: Oxford* reprinted, 1903, 10. 8°.   C. **99**. d. **17**.

OXFORD.—*University of Oxford.—Worcester College.*

—— In laudationem benefactorum. Preces vespertinæ Coll. Vigorn.   *Excudebat C. Henricus Daniel:* [*Oxford*,] 1906. 4°.   C. **100**. g. **52**.
A presentation copy from C. H. Daniel to C. H. Wilkinson.

DANIEL (CHARLES HENRY OLIVE)

—— The Daniel Press. Memorials of C. H. O. Daniel. With a bibliography of the press, 1845–1919 (by Falconer Madan). [With a portrait.] pp. iv. 198. pl. xv. *Daniel Press: Oxford*, 1921. 4°.   C. **99**. f. **31. (1.)**

DANIEL (CHARLES HENRY OLIVE)

—— [Another copy.] The Daniel Press. Memorials of C. H. O. Daniel, *etc.* **L.P.** *Oxford*, 1921. 4°.
Ashley **3613**.

DANIEL (CHARLES HENRY OLIVE)

The Daniel Press.

—— [Another copy, with additional plates.] **L.P.**
C. **99**. i. **16. (1.)**
With specimen leaves, printed by the Daniel Press, inserted.

DANIEL (CHARLES HENRY OLIVE)

—— The Daniel Press. Pulls from formes in the Clarendon Press, 1923. [Edited by Falconer Madan.] pp. 35. [*Oxford*, 1923.] 4°.   Cup.**510.bc.2.**

DARANTIERE (Maurice), Paris

KEATS (JOHN) [*Selections.*]

—— Odes. [Edited by B. Ifor Evans.] *Paris*, 1935. fol.
Cup. **510**. ef. **5.**

HARWOOD (ANTHONY)

—— 8 Poems. *Maurice Darantiere: Paris*, 1952. 8°.
Cup. **510**. fan. **1.**
No. 16 of an edition of 100 copies.

DAWBARN PRESS, Liverpool

CRADDOCK (THOMAS) *of Liverpool.* Charles Lamb. pp. vii. 216.   *Simpkin, Marshall & Co.: London; James Woollard: Liverpool*, 1867. 8°. **10855. aaa. 20.**

DE LA MORE PRESS, London

ROPER (WILLIAM) *Son-in-law of Sir Thomas More.*

—— The mirrour of vertue in worldly greatnes, or the life of Sir Thomas More, Knight. *London: De La More Press*, 1902.   Tab. **535**. b. **9/4.**
pp. 56; port. 31 cm. (The King's Library. De La More Press folios. no. 1.)   △

CHARLES I., *King of Great Britain and Ireland.* [*Doubtful or Suppositious Works.—Eikon Basilike.*]

—— Eikon Basilike or The king's book. Edited by Edward Almack. *London: De La More Press*, 1903.
Tab. **535**. b. **9/5.**
pp. iv, 176; port. 31 cm. (King's Library. De La More Press folios. no. 2.)   △

COUPLAND (*Sir* REGINALD) *K.C.M.G.*

—— Horae iuventutis: essays in prose and verse at Winchester College. *London: De la More Press*, 1903.
Cup. **501**. l. **22.**
pp. x, 155; map. 16 cm.   △
For private circulation.

JONSON (BEN)

—— The alchemist . . . Newly edited by H. C. Hart. *London: De La More Press*, 1903.   Tab. **535**. b. **9/1.**
pp. vii, 232; illus. 23 cm. (The King's Library. De La More Press quartos. no. 1.)   △

LITURGIES.—*Church of England.—Common Prayer.*
—*Communion Office.* [*English.*] The Communion Service . . . Together with the Kalendar. Edited by Vernon Staley. **F. P.** pp. xiii. 272.
De La More Press: London, 1903. 8°. Tab. **538**. b. **8.**

DEKKER (THOMAS) [*The Gull's Horn-book.*]

—— The gull's horn-book. Edited by R. B. McKerrow. *London: De la More Press*, 1904.   Tab. **535**. b. **9/2.**
pp. viii, 107. 23 cm. (King's Library. De la More Press quartos. no. 2.)   △

OVIDIUS NASO (PUBLIUS) [*Metamorphoses.—English.*]

—— Shakespeare's Ovid. Being Arthur Golding's translation of the Metamorphoses, edited by W. H. D. Rouse. *London: De La More Press*, 1904.   Tab. **535**. b. **9/6.**
pp. vi, 321. 31 cm. (The King's Library. De La More Press folios. no. 3.)   △

GAY (JOHN) *the Poet.*

—— The beggar's opera. (Edited by G. Hamilton Macleod.) *London: De La More Press*, 1905.   Tab. **535**. b. **9/3.**
pp. viii, 110; illus. (The King's Library. De La More Press quartos. no. 3.)   △

PERCY (THOMAS) *Bishop of Dromore.*

—— The Percy folio of old English ballads and Romances. (From the text of Dr. F. J. Furnivall and Professor J. W. Hales.) *London: De La More Press*, 1905–10.
Tab. **535**. b. **9/7.**
4 vol.; ports. 31 cm. (The King's Library. De La More Press folios. no. 4.)   △

MORING (THOMAS) One Hundred Book Plates engraved on wood by T. Moring. [With an introduction signed: A. M., i.e. Alexander Moring.] pp. xxv. pl. 100. *Alexander Moring: London*, [1914.] 8°.
09915. c. **26.**

FIRBANK (ARTHUR ANNESLEY RONALD)

—— The artificial princess . . . Illustrated by Hugh Easton. *London: Centaur Press*, 1934.   Cup. **510**. be. **8.**
pp. 84. 23 cm.   △
A copy " out of series " to an edition of sixty copies.

PRESTON (KERRISON)

—— Blake and Rossetti. [With plates, including portraits.] pp. 111. *Alexander Moring: London*, 1944. 4°.
7868. c. **2.**

DE VINNE PRESS, New York

ANDREWS (WILLIAM LORING)

—— Jean Grolier . . . Viscount d'Aguisy : some account of his life and of his famous library. [With plates.] pp. 68. *De Vinne Press: New York,* 1892. 8°.

667. b. 2.

LITURGIES.—*Episcopal Church of America.* [*Common Prayer.—Communion Office.*]

—— The altar book: containing the order for the celebration of the Holy Eucharist according to the use of the American Church: MDCCCXCII. (By Daniel Berkeley Updike and Harold Brown . . . The plain-song is arranged by Sir John Stainer.) *London: A. P. Watt & Son; New York: printed at the De Vinne Press,* 1896. **K.T.C. 41. b. 4.**

Pages not numbered; illus. 39 cm. △

" The type for this volume was set at the Merrymount Press, Boston."

NEW YORK.—*Authors Club.*

—— The Authors Club, etc. [Constitution, list of members, and bibliography.] pp. 103. *New York,* 1896. 8°.

Cup. 510. nas. 3.

STEVENSON (ROBERT LOUIS)

—— Æs triplex. [Reprinted from " Virginibus Puerisque."] With a portrait.] pp. 28. *Printed for the American Subscribers to the Stevenson Memorial: [New York,]* 1898. 8°. **Cup. 510. nas. 1.**

Copy printed for Edmund Gosse. This essay was originally published in " The Cornhill Magazine," April 1878.

NEW YORK.—*Grolier Club.*

—— DE VINNE (Theodore L.) Title-Pages as seen by a Printer. With numerous illustrations in facsimile and some observations on the early and recent printing of books. By T. L. De Vinne. pp. xix. 370. *New York,* 1901. 8°. **011907. h. 1.**

LIVINGSTON (LUTHER SAMUEL)

—— ·A Bibliography of the first editions in book form of the writings of Charles and Mary Lamb, published prior to Charles Lamb's death in 1834. pp. xv. 209. *J. A. Spoor: New York,* 1903. 8°. **011908. i. 6.**

BISHOP (HEBER REGINALD) The Bishop Collection. Investigations and Studies in Jade. [Compiled by H. R. Bishop. With plates.] 2 vol. *Privately printed: New York,* 1906. fol. **C.161.e.1.**

No. 75 of an edition of 100 copies.

MAN.

—— What is Man ? [By S. L. Clemens.] pp. 140. *De Vinne Press: New York,* 1906. 8°. **Cup. 510. nas. 2.**

DE VINNE (THEODORE LOW)

—— Notable Printers of Italy during the Fifteenth Century. Illustrated with facsimiles from early editions and with remarks on early and recent printing. pp. 210. *De Vinne Press: New York,* 1910. 4°. **11906. dd. 9.**

GRANNISS (RUTH SHEPARD) An American Friend of Southey (Maria Gowen Brooks). pp. viii. 58. *Privately printed: New York,* 1913. 8°. **010880. e. 7.**

WIDENER (PETER ARRELL BROWN) *the Elder.*

Pictures in the Collection of P. A. B. Widener at Lynnewood Hall, Elkins Park, Pennsylvania. Early German, Dutch & Flemish Schools. With an introduction by W. R. Valentiner, and biographical and descriptive notes by C. Hofstede de Groot and W. R. Valentiner. *Privately printed : Philadelphia,* 1913. fol. **C.108.m.2.**

Only 200 copies printed ; this is no. 88.

WIDENER (PETER ARRELL BROWN) *the Elder.*

—— Pictures in the Collection of P. A. B. Widener . . . British & Modern French Schools. With introduction, descriptive and other notes by W. Roberts. pl. 52. *Privately printed: Philadelphia,* 1915. fol. **C. 108. m. 4.**

Two hundred copies printed ; this is no. 88.

WIDENER (PETER ARRELL BROWN) *the Elder.*

—— Pictures in the Collection of P. A. B. Widener . . . Early Italian & Spanish Schools. With biographical and descriptive notes on the Italian painters, by B. Berenson, and on the Spanish painters, by W. Roberts. pl. 29. *Privately printed: Philadelphia,* 1916. fol. **C. 108. m. 3.**

Only 200 copies printed ; this is no. 88.

VAN DUZER (HENRY SAYRE) A Thackeray Library . . . A complete Thackeray bibliography. With . . . illustrations. pp. xiii. 198. *Privately printed : New York,* 1919. 8°. **011903. dd. 17.**

GOLDMAN (HENRY) *Collector.*

—— The Henry Goldman Collection [of paintings and sculpture]. By Wilhelm R. Valentiner. [With twenty-two plates.] *Privately printed by the De Vinne Press: New York,* 1922. fol. **K.T.C. 115. a. 9.**

DINGBAT PRESS, New York

KEILEY (JARVIS)

—— Edgar Allan Poe. A probe. pp. 27. *Prometheus Press: New York,* 1927. 8°. **Cup. 502. b. 20.**

DIRTY DUCK PRESS, Ashover; Heswall Hill

SEASALTER.—*Church of Saint Alphege.*

—— Communicants at Seasalter, Kent. 1615–1710 . . . Compiled . . . by C. E. Lugard, etc. *C. E. Lugard: Ashover,* 1929. 8°. **04705. aaa. 69.**

One of an edition of fifteen copies. Printed on one side of the leaf only.

SEASALTER.

—— The Sess of Seasalter. 1653–1678, with index. 1704–1745, with index. And 1821. Compiled . . . by C. E. Lugard. *C. E. Lugard: Ashover*, 1930. 8°.
010360. cc. 51.
No. 4 of an edition of 12 copies. Printed on one side of the leaf only.

ENGLAND.—*Justices of Trailbaston.*

—— Trailbaston. Derbyshire. Compiled by Cecil Edward Lugard. *Ashover: Dirty Duck Press*, 1933, 35.
10358. e. 36.
△
Latin and English. Assize Rolls, containing accounts of cases brought before the Justices of Trailbaston at Derby. No. 10 of an edition of twenty copies.

SOTHERN (Margaret)

—— Sammyander . . . Illustrations by Maud Holden. *Ashover: 'Dirty Duck' Press*, [ca. 1935].
Cup. 510. bga. 1.

Pages not numbered: plates. 16×23 cm. △
A tale. Printed on one side of the leaf only.

ENGLAND.—*Justices in Eyre.*

—— Calendar of the Cases for Derbyshire from Eyre & Assize Rolls preserved in the Public Record Office. Introduction & transcription by Marian K. Dale . . . Henry 3. A.D. 1256–1272. Compiled by Cecil Edward Lugard, pp. xiii. 199. *Cecil Edward Lugard: Heswall Hill*, 1938. 8°.
6120. aaa. 12.
No. 23 of an edition of twenty-six copies.

DIVERS PRESS, Palma de Mallorca

BLACKBURN (Paul)

—— Proensa. From the Provençal, *etc.* [Poems by various authors.] *Divers Press: Palma*, 1953. 8°
Cup. 510. leb. 2.

EIGNER (Larry)

—— From the Sustaining Air. [Poems.] *Divers Press: [Palma de Mallorca?]* 1953. 8°.
Cup. 510. leb. 5.

CREELEY (Robert)

—— The Gold Diggers. [Stories.] pp. 141. *Divers Press: Palma de Mallorca*, 1954. 8°.
Cup.510.leb.6.

BLACKBURN (Paul)

—— The Dissolving Fabric. [Poems.] *Divers Press: Palma*, 1955. 8°.
Cap. 510. leb. 1.

DUNCAN (Robert Edward)

—— Caesar's Gate. Poems, 1949–1950. With collages by Jess Collins. *Divers Press: [Palma de Mallorca]*, 1955. 8°.
Cup. 510. leb. 4.

WOOLF (Douglas)

—— The Hypocritic days. pp. 140. *Divers Press: [Palma de Mallorca,]* 1955. 8°.
Cup. 510. leb. 3.

DIXEY (H. G.), Oxford

DIXEY (Harold Giles)

—— Twenty-three Sonnets. pp. 23. *[The Author:] Oxford*, 1926. 8°.
Cup. 510. cap. 27.
One of an edition of seventy copies, hand-printed by the author.

DIXEY (Harold Giles)

—— Winter Sunshine, and other poems. *[The Author:] Oxford*, 1930. 8°.
Cup. 510. cap. 26.
One of an edition of fifty-three copies, hand-printed by the author.

DIXEY (Harold Giles)

—— Retrospect, and other verses. *H. G. Dixey: Oxford*, 1932. 16°.
Cup.510.cap.1.
One of an edition of 60 copies.

DIXEY (Harold Giles)

—— Versions and Afterthoughts. [Original poems and verse translations.] pp. 52. *Oxford*, 1934. 8°.
One of an edition of 100 copies.
Cup.510.cap.2.

DIXEY (Frederick Augustus)

—— A Posy from the Dust. [Verses. Edited by H. G. Dixey.] pp. 41. *H. G. Dixey: Oxford*, 1937. 8°.
Cup.510.cap.3.
No. 13 of an edition of fifty-five copies.

APOLLONIUS, *Rhodius.* [*English.*]

—— The Way of a Ship according to Apollonius Rhodius: passages from the Argonautica, chosen and paraphrased by Giles Dixey. pp. 9. *H. G. Dixey: Oxford*, 1946. 12°.
Cup.510.cap.4.
No. 56 of an edition of sixty copies.

DIXEY (Harold Giles)

—— Hymns without Faith. pp. 14. *H. G. Dixey: Oxford*, 1946. 8°.
Cup.510.cap.10.
No. 46 of an edition of eighty-three copies.

DIXEY (Harold Giles)

—— Sonnets from Libyan Tripoli. pp. 14. *H. G. Dixey: Oxford*, 1946. 8°.
Cup.510.cap.9.
No. 48 of an edition of eighty-three copies.

DIXEY (Harold Giles)

—— Sonnets from the Levant. pp. 14. *H. G. Dixey: Oxford*, 1946. 8°.
Cup.510.cap.6.
No. 79 of an edition of eighty copies.

DIXEY (Harold Giles)

—— Sonnets from the Western Desert. pp. 14. *H. G. Dixey: Oxford*, 1946. 8°.
Cup.510.cap.7.
No. 76 of an edition of seventy-six copies.

DIXEY (Harold Giles)

—— Sonnets in Sand. pp. 14. *H. G. Dixey: Oxford*, 1946. 8°.
Cup.510.cap.8.
No. 45 of an edition of eighty-three copies.

DIXEY (Harold Giles)

—— The Temple Stair. A fantasia on some aspects of prep-school education between the wars. pp. 32. *H. G. Dixey: Oxford*, 1946. 16°.
Cup.510.cap.11.
No. 49 of an edition of seventy-six copies.

PYTHAGORAS. [*Works ascribed to Pythagoras and the Pythagoreans.*]
—— The Golden Verses of Pythagoras : a paraphrase and imaginary portrait by Giles Dixey after a London text of 1819 and the figure in Milman's Horace. pp. 7. *H. G. Dixey: Oxford*, 1946. 12⁰.　　Cup.510.cap.5.
No. 42 of an edition of fifty-three copies.

DIXEY (HAROLD GILES)
—— Ourselves a Dream. Verses. pp. 23. 　*H. G. Dixey: Oxford*, 1947　8⁰.　　Cup.510.cap.13.
No. 8 of an edition of 83 copies.

DIXEY (HAROLD GILES)
—— Postscripts. [Poems.] pp. 27. 　*H. G. Dixey: Oxford*, 1947. 8⁰.　　Cup.510.cap.12.
No. 5 of an edition of eighty-five copies hand-printed by the author.

DIXEY (HAROLD GILES)
—— Schoolroom Echoes. [Poems.] pp. 23. 　*H. G. Dixey: Oxford*, 1947. 8⁰.　　Cup.510.cap.14.
No. 6 of an edition of ninety-three copies.

DIXEY (HAROLD GILES)
—— Simplicities of an Author-Printer. [With illustrations.] pp. 37. 　*H. G. Dixey: Oxford*, 1947. 8⁰.
　　Cup.510.cap.15.

DIXEY (HAROLD GILES)
—— Clipt Yews. [Poems.] pp. 12. 　*H. G. Dixey: Oxford*, 1948. 8⁰.　　Cup.510.cap.16.
No. 11 of a hand-printed edition of seventy-four copies.

STARK (ROBERT) *Writer of Verse.*
—— Errantes Hederae. A companion to Fashions and Fancies. pp. 26. *H. G. Dixey: Oxford*, 1948. 8⁰.
　　Cup.510.cap.30.
No. 52 of an edition of eighty copies.

DIXEY (HAROLD GILES)
—— Cento Poetae. Sayings from various authors gathered and arranged by G. Dixey. pp. 22. 　*H. G. Dixey: Oxford*, 1949. 8⁰.　　Cup.510.cap.17.

DIXEY (HAROLD GILES)
—— Small Events, and other verses. pp. 36. 　*H. G. Dixey: Oxford*, 1950. 16⁰.　　Cup.510.cap.18.

DIXEY (HAROLD GILES)
—— A View of Poetry. pp. 14. 　*H. G. Dixey: Oxford*, 1950. 8⁰.　　Cup.510.cap.19.

DIXEY (HAROLD GILES)
—— Exigua Musa. pp. 18. *H. G. Dixey: Oxford*, 1956. 8⁰.
　　Cup.510.cap.20.

DIXEY (HAROLD GILES)
—— Rejoinders. Mainly about poetry. pp. 14. 　*H. G. Dixey: Oxford*, 1959. 8⁰.　　Cup.510.cap.21.

DIXEY (HAROLD GILES)
—— Clipt Yews . . . Second edition. pp. 12. 　*H. G. Dixey: Oxford*, 1960. 8⁰.　　Cup.510.cap.22
No. 34 of an edition of fifty-two copies.

DIXEY (HAROLD GILES)
—— Small Events, and other verses . . . Second edition. pp. 26. *H. G. Dixey: Oxford*, 1961. 8⁰. 　Cup. 510. cap. 25.
No. 38 of an edition of fifty-four copies.

DIXEY (HAROLD GILES)
—— Proofs of Endeavour. [Woodcuts and linocuts.] pp. 57. *H. G. Dixey: Oxford*, 1963. 8⁰. 　Cup. 510. cap. 23.

DIXEY (HAROLD GILES)
—— More Haikaics. (Illustrated by the author.) 　*H. G. Dixey: Oxford*, 1964. 8⁰. 　Cup. 510. cap. 24.
No. 25 of an edition of seventy-two copies.

DIXEY (HAROLD GILES)
—— Flashes from the Files of a Section Morse Class in the R N Auxiliary, formerly Minewatching, Service. [With plates.] pp. 27. *H. G. Dixey: Oxford*, 1965. 8⁰.
　　Cup. 510. cap. 28.

DOLMEN PRESS, Dublin

CLIFFORD (SIGERSON)
—— Travelling Tinkers. [Verse.] pp. 22. 　*Dolmen Press: Dublin*, 1951. 8⁰.　Cup.510.ak.1.
No. 84 of an edition of one hundred copies signed by the author.

ROBERTS (H. NEVILLE)
—— Three Carols to Mary. 　*Dolmen Press: Dublin*, 1951. 4⁰.　　Cup.510.ak.2.
No. 4 of twenty-five copies signed by the author.

KENNEDY (MAURICE)
—— Freebooters . . . A story with pictures cut by Michael Morrow. pp. 23. *Dolmen Press: Dublin*, 1952. 4⁰.
　　Cup.510.ak.3.

KINSELLA (THOMAS)
—— The Starlit Eye. Drawings by Liam Miller. [Verses.] pp. 7. *Dolmer Press: Dublin*, 1952. 8⁰.Cup.510.ak.4.

KINSELLA (THOMAS)
—— Three Legendary Sonnets. 　*Dolmen Press: [Dublin,]* 1952. 8⁰.　　Cup. 510. ak. 86.
One of an edition of 100 copies.

MARCUS (David)
—— Six Poems. *Dolmen Press : Dublin,* 1952. 8°.
Cup.510.ak.102

BARRY (Francis James)
—— Who, a Stranger, *etc.* [A poem.] *Dolmen Press.*
Dublin, 1953. 8°. Cup.510.ak.5.

BIBLE.—*Luke.*—*Selections.* [*English.*]
—— The Nativity, from the Holy Gospel according to Saint
Luke. Wood engraving by Michael Biggs. *Dolmen*
Press: Dublin, 1953. 8°. Cup.510.ak.6.

BIBLE.—*John, Gospel of.*—*Selections.* [*Latin.*]
—— Initium S. Evangelii Secundum S. Joannem. (Wood-
engravings by Elizabeth Rivers.) *Dolmen Press :*
[*Dublin,*] 1953. 8°. Cup.510.ak.7.

CLIFFORD (Sigerson)
—— Lascar Rock. A ballad, *etc. Dolmen Press: Dublin,*
1953. 8°. Cup.510.ak.8.
No. 5 of an edition of fifty special copies signed by the
author.

MERRIMAN (Brian)
—— The Midnight Court . . . Newly translated . . . by
David Marcus. *Dolmen Press: Dublin,* [1953.] 8°.
Cup.510.ak.9.
Printed for private circulation.

MILNE (Ewart)
—— Galion . . . A poem . . . Decorated by Mia Cranwill.
L.P. *Dolmen Press: Dublin,* 1953. 8°.
No. 4 of twenty-five signed copies. Cup.510.ak.10.

USSHER (Percy Arland)
—— An Alphabet of Aphorisms. Cuts by Michael Morrow.
Dolmen Press: Dublin, 1953. 8°. Cup. **510**. ak. **11**.
No. 4 of an edition of fifty copies coloured by hand.

CLIFFORD (Sigerson)
—— Travelling Tinkers, *etc.* pp. 30. *Dolmen Press :*
Dublin, 1954. 8°. Cup.510.ak.12.

DOLMEN PRESS.
—— Dolmen Press Ballad Sheets. *Dublin,* 1954- . *s. sh.* 8°.
Cup.510.ak.33.

MAC DONAGH (Donagh)
—— The ballad of Jane Shore. (Design cut by Eric Patton.)
Dublin : Dolmen Press, 1954. Cup. **510**. ak. **115/1**.
Pages not numbered. 25 cm. (Dolmen chapbook. pt 1.)
△

PATRICK, *Saint, Apostle of Ireland.*
—— The Breastplate of Saint Patrick. (Translated by
Thomas Kinsella.) pp. 8. *Dolmen Press : Dublin,*
1954. 8°. Cup.510.ak.13.
No. 8 of an edition of fifteen copies.

STANIHURST (Richard)
—— The Commodities of Aqua Vitæ . . . Here delineated by
Bridget Swinton. (Edited by Lawrence Ryan.) [Ex-
tracted from " A Treatise contayning a playne and perfect
Description of Irelande," the introduction to vol. 1. pt. 3
of Holinshed's "Chronicles of England, Scotland and
Ireland."] *Dolmen Press: Dublin,* 1954. 8°.
Cup.510.ak.14.
No. 4 of thirty hand coloured copies on Milbourn paper.

UISNECH, *Sons of.*
—— Longes mac n-Usnig : being the exile and death of the
sons of Usnech. (Translated by Thomas Kinsella from the
Book of Leinster. The illustrations by Mia Cranwill.)
pp. 32. **L.P.** *The Dolmen Press :* [*Dublin,*] 1954. 4°.
Cup.510.ak.15.
No. 22 of twenty-five large paper copies.

WEXFORD CAROL.
—— A Wexford carol. (Design cut by Leslie MacWeeney.)
Dublin : Dolmen Press, 1954. Cup. **510**. ak. **115/2**.
Pages not numbered ; music. 26 cm. (Dolmen chap-
book. pt. 2.) △

BIBLE.—*Matthew.*—*Selections.* [*English.*]
—— The Genealogy and Nativity of Christ with the offerings
of the wise men. (The text from the Douai version of Saint
Matthew's Gospel. Illustrated by Leslie MacWeeney.)
Dolmen Press: Dublin, 1955. 8°. Cup.510.ak.16.
No. 3 of an edition of fifty hand coloured copies.

GIBBINGS (Robert John)
—— The perfect wife. A fable from France, transmogrified
into the Anglo-Irish idiom & illustrated by Robert Gibbings. *Glenageary : Dolmen Press,* 1955.
Cup. **510**. ak **115/3**.
Pages not numbered. 26 cm. (Dolmen chapbook.
pt. 3.) △

KINSELLA (Thomas)
—— Thirty three triads. Translated by Thomas Kinsella
from the XII century Irish & decorated by Pauline Bewick.
Dublin : Dolmen Press, 1955. Cup. **510**. ak. **115/4**.
Pages not numbered. 26 cm. (Dolmen chapbook.
pt. 4.) △
No. 6 of an edition of seventy-five copies signed by the
translator and the illustrator.

MURPHY (Richard)
—— The Archaeology of Love. [Poems.] pp. 28. *Dolmen*
Press: Glenageary, 1955. 8°. Cup.510.ak .17.

MURPHY (Richard)
—— Sailing to an Island. [A poem.] *Dolmen Press :*
Dublin, 1955. 8°. Cup.510.ak.18.
No. 22 of an edition of thirty-five copies, privately printed.

COGHILL (RHODA)
—— Time is a Squirrel. Poems. pp. 19. *Published for the Author at the Dolmen Press: Dublin*, 1956. 8°.
Cup.510.ak.19.

KINSELLA (THOMAS)
—— The death of a queen . . . With drawings by Bridget Swinton. *Glenageary, Co. Dublin: Dolmen Press*, 1956.
Cup. 510. ak. 115/5.
Pages not numbered. 26 cm. (Dolmen chapbook. pt. 5.)
△

KINSELLA (THOMAS)
—— Poems. pp. 23. *Dolmen Press: Glenageary*, 1956. 8°.
Cup.510.ak.20.

SMART (CHRISTOPHER)
—— [Rejoice in the Lamb.] Out of Bedlam. XXVII wood engravings by Elizabeth Rivers with texts from Christopher Smart. *Dolmen Press: Glenageary*, 1956. 8°.
Cup.510.ak.21.

SPENSER (EDMUND) [*Colin Clout's come home againe.*]
—— The loues of Bregog and Mulla, from Colin Clout's come home againe . . . with monotypes by Leslie MacWeeney. *Dublin: Dolmen Press*, 1956. Cup. **510**. ak. **115/7**.
Pages not numbered. 26 cm. (Dolmen chapbook. pt. 7.)
△

STANIHURST (RICHARD)
—— Aqua Vitæ: its commodities describ'd by R. Stanihurst, *etc.* (Edited by Lawrence Ryan. Reset.) *Dolmen Press: [Dublin,]* 1956. 16°. Cup. 550. b. 6.

USSHER (PERCY ARLAND)
—— The mines of Siberiay. A new ballad of Rooshian Rodie and pawnbroker Liz. By Arland Ussher after Crime and punishment [by Fedor Dostoevsky]. The pictures by Nelson Paine. *Glenageary, Co. Dublin: Dolmen Press*, 1956. Cup. **510**. ak. **115/6**.
Pages not numbered; music. 26 cm. (Dolmen chapbook. pt. 6.)
△

USSHER (PERCY ARLAND)
—— The Thoughts of Wi Wong. *Dolmen Press: Dublin*, 1956. 8°. Cup.510.ak.22
No. 8 of fifty copies signed by the author.

COLUM (PADRAIC)
—— Ten Poems. **F.P.** pp. 23. *Dolmen Press: Dublin*, 1957. 8°. Cup.510.ak.23.
No. 3 of fifty signed and specially bound copies.

KINSELLA (THOMAS)
—— Thirty Three Triads. Translated by T. Kinsella, *etc.* (Reset.) pp. 11. *Dolmen Press: Dublin*, 1957. 8°.
Cup.510.ak.24.

. PATRICK, *Saint, Apostle of Ireland.*
—— Faeth fiadha : the Breastplate of Saint Patrick. Translated by Thomas Kinsella, *etc.* (Revised version.) pp. vii. *Dolmen Press: Dublin*, 1957. 16°. Cup.510.ak.25.
No. 12 of an edition of one hundred copies.

USSHER (PERCY ARLAND)
—— The XXII Keys of the Tarot. . . With the designs drawn by Leslie MacWeeney. pp. viii. 61. *Dolmen Press Dublin*, 1957. 8°. Cup.510.ak.26.
No. 12 of fifty copies, hand-coloured and bound in vellum, signed by the author.

WEBER (RICHARD) *Writer of Verse.*
—— O'Reilly. Poems. *Dublin: Dolmen Press*, 1957.
Cup. **510**. ak. **115/8**.
Pages not numbered; illus. 25 cm. (Dolmen chapbook. pt. 8.)
△

WEBER (RICHARD) *Writer of Verse.*
—— The Time Being. A poem in three parts, *etc.* pp. xviii. *Dolmen Press: Dublin*, 1957. 8°. Cup.510.ak.27.

ADAMS (TATE)
—— The Soul Cages. An Irish legend retold in 20 wood engravings and some words. pp. 20. *Dolmen Press: Dublin*, 1958. 8°. Cup.510.ak.35.

COLUM (PADRAIC)
—— Irish elegies. *Dublin: Dolmen Press*, [1958].
Cup. **510**. ak. **115/9**.
pp. 11; illus. 25 cm. (Dolmen chapbook. pt. 9.) △

COLUM (PADRAIC)
—— [Another copy.] Irish elegies. [1958].
Cup. 510. ak. **115/9a.**
△
No. 7 of fifty large paper copies, signed by the author.

KINSELLA (THOMAS)
—— Another September. [Poems.] pp. 47. *Dolmen Press Dublin*, 1958. 8°. Cup.510.ak.28.
One of an edition of fifty copies signed by the author.

MONTAGUE (JOHN)
—— Forms of Exile. [Verses.] pp. 24. *Dolman Press: Dublin*, 1958. 8°. Cup.510.ak.29.
No. 10 of an edition of fifty signed copies.

RILKE (RAINER MARIA)
—— [Mir zur Feier.] Angel songs. Engellieder. Translated by Rhoda Coghill, *etc.* *Dublin: Dolmen Press*, 1958.
Cup. 510. ak. **115/10.**
pp. 7; illus. 25 cm. (Dolmen Chapbook. pt. 10.) △
English. From " Mir zur Feier ".

TEMPEL (GUDRUN)
—— The Bird that flew away. Ten poems, *etc.* pp. 28. *Dolmen Press: Dublin*, 1958. 8°. Cup.510.ak.101.

TIDINGS.
—— Tidings. [Verses by Jonathan Hanaghan and others.] *Runa Press: Monkstown*, 1958. 8º.   Cup.510.ak.70

MAC ENTEE (MÁIRE)
—— A heart full of thought. Translations by Máire MacEntee from the Irish. *Dublin: Dolmen Press*, 1959.
11392. aa. 94.

pp. 11; illus. 24 cm.   △
Verses.

MAC ENTEE (MÁIRE)
—— [Another copy.] A heart full of thought, *etc.* 1959.
Cup. 510. ak. 40.
△

A copy "out of series" to an edition of one hundred signed copies.

MURPHY (RICHARD)
—— The Woman of the House. An elegy. (In memory of Lady Ormsby, by her grandson.) pp. 01 [10]. *Dolman Press: Dublin*, 1959. 8º.   Cup. 510. ak. 30.
A number out of series of twenty-five copies on handmade paper, signed by the author.

MURPHY (RICHARD)
—— [Another copy.] The Woman of the House, *etc. Dublin*, 1959. 8º.   Cup. 510. ak. 31.
No. 9 of twenty-five copies on handmade paper, signed by the author.

TOMKIN (DIANA)
—— 22 Poems. pp. 34. *Published for the Author at the Dolmen Press: Dublin*, 1959. 8º.   Cup.510.ak.32.

BIGGS (MICHAEL) *Letter-cutter.*
—— A Gaelic Alphabet. Designed & cut by M. Biggs. With a note on Irish lettering by Liam Miller. *Dolmen Press: Dublin*, 1960. 8º.   Cup. 510. ak. 43.
Dolmen Chapbook. pt. 11.

BIGGS (MICHAEL) *Letter-cutter.*
—— [Another copy.] A Gaelic alphabet, *etc.* 1960.
Cup. 510. ak. 115/11a.
△

No 27 of fifty signed and specially bound copies.

HANAGHAN (JONATHAN)
—— Sayings of Jonathan Hanaghan, *etc.* pp. xiv. 122. *Runa Press: Monkstown*, 1960. 8º.   Cup.510.ak.69.

HURKEY (ROOAN)
—— Romances. [Verse.] pp. 30. *Dolmen Press: Dublin*, 1960. 8º.   Cup. 510. ak. 41.
Privately printed.

IRELAND. [PROVISIONAL GOVERNMENT OF THE IRISH REPUBLIC, 1916.]
—— The Easter Proclamation of the Irish Republic, MCMXVI. pp. 7. *Dolmen Press: Dublin*, 1960. 12º.
Cup. 510. ak. 37.

MAC GREEVY (THOMAS)
—— Nicolas Poussin. pp. viii. 47. pl. VI.   *Dolmen Press: Dublin*, 1960. 4º.
Cup. 510. ak. 39.

MONTAGUE (JOHN PATRICK)
—— The Old People. *Dolmen Press: Dublin*, 1960. 8º.
Cup. 510. ak. 34.

TOMKIN (DIANA)
—— 159 Maxims. pp. 24. *Dolmen Press: Dublin*, 1960. 8º.
Cup. 510. ak. 42.
Privately printed.

WILKINS (MAURICE)
—— The Seeker. Poems. pp. 28. *Dolmen Press: Dublin*, 1960. 8º.   Cup. 510. ak. 38.
Privately printed.

CLARKE (AUSTIN)
—— Later Poems. pp. 96. *Dolmen Press: Dublin*, 1961. 8º.   Cup. 510. ak. 36.

COLUM (PADRAIC)
—— Irish Elegies. (Second edition, with additional poems.) pp. 19. *Dolmen Press: Dublin*, 1961. 8º.
Cup. 510. ak. 48.

DUBLIN.—*University of Dublin.—Trinity College.—Library.*
—— Ireland in Maps. An introduction by John Andrews. With a catalogue of an exhibition mounted in the Library of Trinity College, Dublin, 1961, by the Geographical Society of Ireland in conjunction with the Ordnance Survey of Ireland. [With plates.] pp. 36. *Dolmen Press: Dublin*, 1961. 8º.   Maps 34. a. 40.

DURYEE (MARY BALLARD)
—— Words Alone are Certain Good. William Butler Yeats: himself; the poet; his ghost. [Poems.] pp. 43. *Dolmen Press: Dublin*, 1961. 8º.   Cup. 510. ak. 45.

HOLZAPFEL (RUDOLF PATRICH)
—— The rain, the moon. With an introduction by Donald Carroll. ([By] Radi Holzapfel & Brendan Kennelly.) *Dublin: Dolmen Press*, 1961. 8º.   Cup. 510. ak. 75.
pp. 62. 20 cm.   △

KELLS, *Book of*
—— The Book of Kells. A selection of pages reproduced with a description and notes by G. O. Simms. pp. xvi. pl. 20. *Library of Trinity College: Dublin*, 1961. 8º. 2701. s. 4.

KELLS, *Book of.*
—— [The Book of Kells.] Das Buch von Kells. Eine Auswahl von Reproduktionen mit einer Beschreibung und Anmerkungen von G. O. Simms. (Deutsche Uebersetzung: Franz Lösel.) *Dublin: gedruckt von der Dolmen Press für die Bibliothek des Trinity College, Dublin*, 1961. 18 cm.
Cup. 510. ak. 62.

pp. ixx [xix]: pl. xx.   △

MURPHY (RICHARD)
—— The Last Galway Hooker. [A poem.] pp. 12. *Dolmen Press: Dublin*, 1961. 8º.   Cup. 510. ak. 46.

SHAKESPEARE (WILLIAM) [*Sonnets.*]

—— Shakespeare's secret. A new & correct interpretation of Shakespeare's sonnets, which are now for the first time fully explained, with a word-for-word interpretation of each sonnet & a running commentary proving the continuity of the first 126 sonnets, and a re-arrangement of the Dark Lady sonnets. By Rudolf Melander Holzapfel. *Dublin: Dolmen Press for the Melander Shakespeare Society,* 1961. Cup. **510**. ak. **44**.

    pp. xxi, 158: plates; ports. 26 cm. △

    Contending that William Herbert, 3rd Earl of Pembroke, was Shakespeare's son.

    No. 25 of an edition of a hundred signed copies.

SIMMS (GEORGE OTTO) *Archbishop of Dublin.*

[Leaves from the Book of Kells.]

—— Das Buch von Kells. Eine Auswahl von Reproduktionen mit einer Beschreibung und Anmerkungen von G. O. Simms. pp. ixx. pl. 20. *Dublin,* 1961. 8°.
Cup. **510**. ak. **62**.

STRONG (EITHNE)

—— Songs of Living. Preface by Padraic Colum. pp. 69. *Runa Press: Monkstown, County Dublin,* 1961. 8°.
Cup. **510**. ak. **84**.

SYNGE (JOHN MILLINGTON) *Dramatist.*

—— J. M. Synge: Translations. Edited from the original manuscripts by Robin Skelton. pp. vii. 24. *Dolmen Press: Dublin,* 1961. 8°. Cup. **510**. ak. **47**.

ANDERSON (CONSTANCE POWELL)

—— Barren, *etc.* (New edition.) pp. 24. *Dolmen Press: Dublin,* 1962. 8°. Cup. **510**. ak. **67**.

CLARKE (AUSTIN)

—— Forget-me-not. [A poem.] pp. 14. *Dolmen Press: Dublin,* 1962. fol. Cup. **510**. ak. **51**.

FAULKNER (PETER)

—— William Morris and W. B. Yeats. pp. 30. *Dolmen Press: Dublin,* 1962. 8°. Cup. **510**. ak. **50**.

KINSELLA (THOMAS)

—— Another September. (New edition.) [Poems.] *Dolmen Press: Dublin; Oxford University Press: London,* 1962. 8°. Cup. **510**. ak. **72**.

KINSELLA (THOMAS)

—— Downstream. [Poems.] pp. 63. *Dolmen Press: Dublin; Oxford University Press: London,* 1962. 8°. Cup. **510**. ak. **71**.

KIRBY (SHEELAH)

—— The Yeats Country. A guide to places in the west of Ireland associated with the life and writings of William Butler Yeats. Compiled by S. Kirby. Edited by Patrick Gallagher with drawings and maps by Ruth Brandt. pp. 47. *Dolmen Press: Dublin,* 1962. 8°. Cup. **510**. ak. **52**.

LIDDY (JAMES)

—— Esau, my Kingdom for a Drink. Homage to James Joyce on his LXXX birthday. (A memorial address delivered at King's Inns Dublin on 13th February 1962.) pp. 15. *Dolmen Press: Dublin,* [1962.] 8°. Cup. **510**. ak. **73**.

MURPHY (RICHARD)

—— The Last Galway Hooker. (Second edition.) [With a map.] pp. 15. *Dolmen Press: Dublin,* 1962. 8°.
Cup. **510**. ak. **49**.

PYE (PATRICK)

—— Has Art any Meaning? pp. 26. *Dolmen Press: Dublin,* 1962. 8°. Cup. **510**. ak. **87**.

SELIG (RICHARD)

—— Poems. [With an introduction by Peter Levi. With a portrait.] pp. 93. *Dolmen Press: Dublin,* 1962. 8°.
Cup. **510**. ak. **53**.

TOMKIN (DIANA) [*Collections.*]

—— Poetry and Maxims. [With a portrait.] pp. 24. 34. 24. *Dolmen Press: [Dublin,* 1962.] 8°. Cup. **510**. ak. **79**.

COLUM (PADRAIC)

—— Moytura. A play for dancers. pp. 38. *Dolmen Press: Dublin,* 1963. 8°. Cup. **510**. ak. **56**.

DAIKEN (LESLIE HERBERT)

—— Out goes she. Dublin street rhymes. Collected and with a commentary by Leslie Daiken. [With illustrations.] pp. 44. *Dolmen Press: Dublin,* 1963 [1964]. 8°.
Cup. **510**. ak. **64**.

GOGARTY (OLIVER ST. JOHN)

—— William Butler Yeats: a memoir, *etc.* [With a portrait.] pp. 27. *Dolmen Press: Dublin,* 1963. 8°.
Cup. **510**. ak. **60**.

HUTCHINSON (PEARSE)

—— Tongue without Hands. pp. 35. *Dolmen Press: Dublin,* 1963. 8°. Cup. **510**. ak. **61**.

KIRBY (SHEELAH)

—— The Yeats country ... Edited by Patrick Gallagher. (Second edition, revised.) *Dublin: Dolmen Press,* 1963.
Cup. **510**. ak. **117**.

    pp. 48; illus., map. 21 cm. △

MACDIARMID (HUGH) *pseud.* [i.e. CHRISTOPHER MURRAY GRIEVE.]

—— Sydney Goodsir Smith. (A tribute to S. G. Smith at the presentation of the Sir Thomas Urquhart Award by H. MacDiarmid.) pp. 13. *Colin H. Hamilton: Edinburgh; printed at the Dolmen Press: Dublin,* [1963.] 8°.
Cup. **510**. ak. **58**.

MAC LIAIMMHÓIR (MICHEÁL)

—— The Importance of being Oscar ... With an introduction by Hilton Edwards. [With portraits.] pp. xv. 68. *Dolmen Press: Dublin; Oxford University Press: London,* 1963. 8°.
Cup. **510**. ak. **55**.

O'CONNOR (Frank) *pseud.* [i.e. Michael Francis O'Donovan.]
—— The Little Monasteries. Poems [mainly of the VII to XII centuries] translated from the Irish by Frank O'Connor. pp. 43. *Dolmen Press: Dublin; Oxford University Press: London & New York*, 1963. 8°.   Cup. 510. ak. 57.

WATHEN (Ronald James)
—— Bricks. Poems, 1958–60. pp. 24.   *Dolmen Press: Dublin*, 1963. 8°   Cup. 510. ak. 59.

WEBER (Richard) *Writer of Verse.*
—— Lady and Gentleman. pp. 30.   *Dolmen Press: Dublin*, 1963. 8°.   Cup. 510. ak. 54.

DEVLIN (Denis) [*Collections.*]
—— Collected Poems. Edited and with an introduction by Brian Coffey. pp. xxiv. 132.   *Dolmen Press: Dublin*, 1964. 8°.   Cup. 510. ak. 77.

IRVINE (John)
—— A Treasury of Irish Saints. [Poems.] With drawings by Ruth Brandt. pp. 37.   *Dolmen Press: Dublin*, 1964. 8°.   Cup. 510. ak. 76.

KAVANAGH (Patrick)
—— Self Portrait. (Telefís Eireann script.) [With portraits.] pp. 31. *Dolmen Press: Dublin*, 1964. 8°.   Cup. 510. ak. 63.

LIDDY (James)
—— In a Blue Smoke. [Poems.] pp. 40.   *Dolmen Press: Dublin*, 1964. 8°.   Cup. 510. ak. 66.

MURPHY (Michael Joseph)
—— Mountain Year. [Essays.] pp. 63.   *Dolmen Press: Dublin*, 1964. 8°.   Cup. 510. ak. 74.

MYLES, *na gCopaleen, pseud.*
—— An Béal boċt, nó an Milleánach. Droċ-sgéal ar an droċ-ṡaoġal curta i n-eagar le Myles na gCopaleen. (An treas eagar.) pp. 111.   *Cló Dolmen: Áth Cliath*, 1964. 8°.   Cup. 510. ak. 78.

SKELTON (Robin)
—— An Irish Gathering. [Poems.] pp. 22.   *Dolmen Press: Dublin*, 1964. 8°.   Cup. 510. ak. 68.

YEATS (Jack Butler)
—— In Sand. A play, with The Green Wave, a one act conversation piece. Edited and with a preface by Jack Macgowran, and with a drawing by the author. pp. 79. *Dolmen Press: Dublin*, 1964. 8°.   Cup. 510. ak. 65.

ALSPACH (Russell King)
—— Yeats and Innisfree.   *Dolmen Press: Dublin*, 1965. 8°. [*Dolmen Press Yeats Centenary Papers.* no. 3.]   Cup. 510. ak. 83/3.

DOLMEN PRESS.
—— Dolmen Press Yeats Centenary Papers.   *Dolmen Press: Dublin*, 1965– . 8°.   Cup. 510. ak. 83.

FAULKNER (Peter)
—— Yeats & the Irish Eighteenth Century.   *Dolmen Press: Dublin*, 1965. 8°. [*Dolmen Press Yeats Centenary Papers.* no. 5.]   Cup. 510. ak. 83/5.

HANLEY (Mary)
—— Thoor Ballylee—Home of William Butler Yeats. Edited by Liam Miller from a paper given by Mary Hanley to the Kiltartan Society in 1961. With a foreword by T. R. Henn. [With illustrations.] pp. 31.   *Dolmen Press: Dublin*, 1965. 8°.   Cup. 510. ak. 89.

HARRIS (Michael)
—— Poems . . . With an introduction by Sir Compton Mackenzie. pp. 28. *Dolmen Press: Dublin*, 1965. 8°.   Cup. 510. ak. 81.

JACKSON (Robert Wyse) *Bishop of Limerick.*
—— A Memorial Sermon preached at Drumcliffe on the occasion of the centenary of the birth of William Butler Yeats . . . 13 June 1965. pp. iv. *Dolmen Press: Dublin; J. M. Keohane: Sligo*, [1965]. 4°. Cup. 510. ak. 114.

LISTER (Raymond George)
—— Beulah to Byzantium. A study of parallels in the works of W. B. Yeats, William Blake, Samuel Palmer & Edward Calvert. [With plates.] *Dolmen Press: Dublin*, 1965. 8°. [*Dolmen Press Yeats Centenary Papers.* no. 2.]   Cup. 510. ak. 83/2.

MAC AULEY (James John)
—— A New Address. [Poems.] pp. 61.   *Dolmen Press: Dublin*, 1965. 8°.   Cup. 510. ak. 85.

MALINS (Edward)
—— Yeats and the Easter Rising, *etc.* (A lecture delivered to the Yeats International Summer School at Sligo, 17 August, 1962.) [With plates.] pp. 28.   *Dolmen Press: Dublin*, 1965. 8°. [*Dolmen Press Yeats Centenary Papers.* no. 1.]   Cup. 510. ak. 83/1.

MALLARMÉ (Stéphane)
[Un Coup de dés jamais n'abolira le hasard.]
—— Dice thrown never will annul Chance. A translation by Brian Coffey, *etc. Dolmen Press: Dublin*, 1965. 8°.   Cup. 510. ak. 82.

O'DONOVAN (John) *Playwright.*
—— Shaw and the Charlatan Genius. A memoir. [On George Bernard Shaw and George John Lee. With portraits.] pp. 160. pl. xvi. *Dolmen Press: Dublin*, 1965. 8°.   Cup. 510. ak. 88.

SYNGE (JOHN MILLINGTON) *Dramatist.*
—— The Autobiography of J. M. Synge, constructed from the manuscripts by Alan Price. With fourteen photographs by J. M. Synge and an essay on Synge and the photography of his time by P. J. Pocock. pp. 46. *Dolmen Press: Dublin; Oxford University Press: London,* 1965. 8⁰.
Cup. **510**. ak. 80.

TELFER (GILES W. L.)
—— Yeat's Idea of the Gael. *Dolmen Press: Dublin,* 1965. 8⁰. [*Dolmen Press Yeats Centenary Papers.* no. 4.]
Cup. **510**. ak. 83/4.

DOLPHIN PRESS, London

LASSO DE LA VEGA (GARCÍA) *the Poet.* The Odes and Sonnets of Garcilaso de la Vega. An English verse rendering by James Cleugh. pp. 94.
Aquila Press: London, 1930. fol. L.R. **38. a. 9.**

VIRGILIUS MARO (PUBLIUS) [*Georgica.—English.*]
—— The Georgics of Vergil. Translated by R. D. Blackmore . . . With an introduction by R. S. Conway . . . Woodcut illustrations by Edward Carrick. *London: published by G. W. Jones at the Sign of the Dolphin,* 1931.
C. **98. e. 17.**
pp. xxvii, 128. 29 cm. △

JONES (GEORGE WILLIAM) *Printer.*
—— Catalogue of the Library of George W. Jones at the Sign of the Dolphin . . . Gough Square . . . London, E.C.4. [With plates, including a portrait.] pp. ix. 131. *Printed for the Members of the Limited Editions Club by George W. Jones: London,* 1938. fol. C. **105. g. 10.** *Printed for private circulation. Author's presentation copy.*

DOVES PRESS, Hammersmith, London

SANDERSON (THOMAS JAMES COBDEN)
—— The Ideal Book or Book Beautiful, *etc.* pp. 8. *Doves Press: Hammersmith,* 1900. 4⁰. C. **99. g. 1.**

TACITUS (PUBLIUS CORNELIUS) [*Agricola.—Latin.*]
—— Cornelii Taciti de vita et moribus Iulii Agricolae liber. [Edited by J. W. Mackail.] pp. 32. *Doves Press: Hammersmith,* 1900. 4⁰. C. **99. g. 2.**

MACKAIL (JOHN WILLIAM) William Morris. An address delivered the xIth November MDCCCC. . . . before the Hammersmith Socialist Society. pp. 27.
Doves Press: Hammersmith, 1901. 4⁰. C. **99. g. 3.**

MILTON (JOHN) [*Paradise Lost.*]
—— Paradise Lost. A poem, *etc.* *Hammersmith: Doves Press,* 1902. C. **99. g. 5.**
pp. 386. 24 cm. △

TENNYSON (ALFRED) *Baron Tennyson.* [*Selections and Extracts.*]
—— Seven Poems and two Translations. pp. 55. *Doves Press: London,* 1902. 4⁰. C. **99. g. 4.**

BIBLE. [*English.*]
—— The English Bible, containing the Old Testament & the New translated out of the original tongues by special command of His Majesty King James the First and now reprinted with the text revised . . . and edited by the late Rev. F. H. Scrivener. 5 vol. *Doves Press: London,* 1903–05. 4⁰. C. **99. l. 6.** *Version of* 1611. *With Apocrypha.*

MILTON (JOHN) [*Smaller Collections of Works.*] Paradise Regained . . . To which are added Samson Agonistes & Poems both English and Latin compos'd on several occasions. pp. 343. *Doves Press: Hammersmith,* 1905. 8⁰. C. **99. g. 6.**

EMERSON (RALPH WALDO)
—— Essays . . . With preface by Thomas Carlyle. *Hammersmith: Doves Press,* 1906. C. **99. g. 7.**
pp. 311. 24 cm. △

GOETHE (JOHANN WOLFGANG VON) [*Faust.—Thle.* 1, 2.—*German.*]
—— Faust, *etc.* (Tl. 1. Printed . . . from the 1887 Weimar edition. Tl. 2. Printed . . . from the Weimar edition of 1899, specially revised for this edition by Dr. Erich Schmidt.) 2 pt. *Hammersmith: Doves Press,* 1906–10. C. **99. g. 12.**
2 pt. 24 cm. △

SANDERSON (THOMAS JAMES COBDEN) London: a paper read at a meeting of the Art-Workers Guild . . . March 6 1891. pp. 7. *Doves Press:* [*Hammersmith*], 1906. 8⁰. C. **99. g. 11.**

CARLYLE (THOMAS) [*Sartor Resartus.*]
—— Sartor resartus, *etc.* *Hammersmith: Doves Press,* 1907. C. **99. f. 8.**
pp. 341. 24 cm. △

MILTON (JOHN) [*Prose Works. — Areopagitica.*]
—— Areopagitica, *etc.* pp. 73. *Doves Press: Hammersmith,* 1907. 8⁰. C. **99. g. 22.**

RUSKIN (JOHN) Unto this Last, *etc.* pp. xiii. 120. *Doves Press: Hammersmith,* 1907. 4⁰. C. **99. g. 16.**

BROWNING (ROBERT) [*Single Works.*]
—— Men & women. *London: Doves Press,* 1908. C. **99. f. 7.**
2 vol. 24 cm. △
Printed from the first edition, 1855.

SANDERSON (THOMAS JAMES COBDEN)
—— Credo. *Doves Press: Hammersmith,* 1908. 8⁰. C. **99. a. 3.**

SHAKESPEARE (WILLIAM) [*Hamlet.*]
—— The tragicall historie of Hamlet, Prince of Denmarke . . . 1604. 1623. *Hammersmith: printed by T. J. Cobden-Sanderson at the Doves Press,* 1909. C. **99. g. 30.**
pp. 158. 23. 24 cm. △

SHAKESPEARE (WILLIAM) [*Sonnets.*]
—— Shalespeares Sonnets. Tercentenary edition. pp. 84.
Doves Press: Hammersmith, 1909. 8°.   C. **99**. g. **9**.

WINSHIP (GEORGE PARKER) William Caxton. A paper read at a meeting of the Club of Odd Volumes in Boston, Massachusetts, U.S.A., in January M.D.C.C.C.V.I.I.I. pp. 25.   *Doves Press:* *London*, 1909. 4°.   C.99.g.8.

BROWNING (ROBERT)
—— Dramatis personae. *Hammersmith: Doves Press*, 1910.
C. **99**. g. **10**.

pp. 202. 24 cm.   △
Printed from the first edition, 1864.

FRANCIS [BERNARDONI], *of Assisi, Saint.* [*Single Works.*]
—— [Il Cantico del sole.] Laudes creaturarum. (From the ancient Italian text published by Monsieur Sabatier, and from the English translation by the late Matthew Arnold.) *Doves Press: Hammersmith*, 1910. 8°.   C. **108**. n. 5.
Bound in morocco at The Doves Bindery.

FRANCIS [BERNARDONI], *of Assisi, Saint.* [*Single Works.*]
[Il Cantico del sole.]
—— [Another copy.] Laudes creaturarum, *etc. Hammersmith*, 1910. 8°.   Cup. **510**. ada. **3**.
Bound in vellum at the Doves Bindery.

SANDERSON (THOMAS JAMES COBDEN)
—— The City Metropolitan. A letter addressed to The Times, *etc. Doves Press: [London*, 1910.] 8°.
Cup.510.ada.2.

SANDERSON (THOMAS JAMES COBDEN)
—— The City planned. Reprinted from the Westminster Gazette, *etc. Doves Press: [London*, 1910.] 8°.
A presentation copy from the printer with his autograph inscription.   Cup.510.ada.1.

VENUS.
—— Pervigilium Venris. (Edited, rearranged ,and supplemented by J. W. Mackail.) pp. 7. *Doves Press: Hammersmith*, 1910. 8°.   C. **99**. g. **13**.

BIBLE.—*Genesis.* [*Selections.—English.*]
—— In Principio. [Genesis, ch. i.] (Printed from the Authorised Version of the Holy Bible and published on the Tercentenary of its first publication, 1611.) *Doves Press: London*, 1911. 8°.   C. **98**. a. **5**.

DOVES PRESS.
—— Catalogue Raisonné of Books printed & published at the Doves Press, 1900–1911. (Second edition.) pp. 12. *Doves Press: Hammersmith*, 1911. 8°.   C. **99**. g. **24**.

GOETHE (JOHANN WOLFGANG VON) [*Werther.—German.*] Die Leiden des jungen Werther. pp. 187. *Doves Press: Hammersmith*, 1911. 8°. C.99.g.14.

SANDERSON (THOMAS JAMES COBDEN) Shakespearian Punctuation. A letter addressed to the Editor of " The Times," October 26, 1911.   *Doves Press: Hammersmith*, [1911.] 8°.   011765. k. 28. (1.)

WORDSWORTH (WILLIAM) *Poet Laureate.* A Decade of Years. Poems by William Wordsworth, 1798–1807. [Selected by C.-S., i.e. T. J. Cobden-Sanderson.] pp. 230.   *Doves Press:* *Hammersmith*, 1911. 8°.   C.99.g.15.

GOETHE (JOHANN WOLFGANG VON) [*Iphigenie auf Tauris.—German.*] Iphigenie auf Tauris, *etc.* pp. 110. *Doves Press: Hammersmith*, 1912. 8°.
C.99.g.17.

SHAKESPEARE (WILLIAM) [*Antony and Cleopatra.*] The Tragedie of Anthony and Cleopatra. (Printed ... from the text of the First Folio.) **F. P.** pp. 140. *Doves Press: London*, 1912. 4°. C.99.g.18.

SHAKESPEARE (WILLIAM) [*Venus and Adonis.*] Venus and Adonis. (Printed ... from the text of the First Edition imprinted by Richard Field, 1593.) **F. P.** *Doves Press: London*, 1912. 4°.   C.99.g.19.

GOETHE (JOHANN WOLFGANG VON) [*Tasso.—German.*]
—— Torquato Tasso, *etc.*   *Hammersmith: printed by T. J. Cobden-Sanderson at the Doves Press, 1913.*
C. **99**. g. **20**.

pp. 163. 24 cm.   △

SANDERSON (THOMAS JAMES COBDEN) On a Passage in " Julius Caesar." A letter addressed to the Editor of "The Times."   *Doves Press: Hammersmith*, 1913. 8°.
011765. k. 28. (2.)

SHAKESPEARE (WILLIAM) [*Julius Cæsar.*]
—— The Tragedie of Julius Caesar . . . 1623. (From the text of the First Folio.) pp. 111.   *Printed by T. J. Cobden-Sanderson at the Doves Press: Hammersmith*, 1913. 8°.
C. **99**. g. **21**.

KEATS (JOHN) [*Selections.*] Keats. (Selected, arranged and printed by T. J. Cobden Sanderson.) pp. 202. *Doves Press: Hammersmith*, 1914. 8°.
C.99.g.28.

SANDERSON (THOMAS JAMES COBDEN) Amantium Irae: letters to two friends [John, Viscount, and Katharine Louisa, Viscountess Amberley]. pp. 141. *Doves Press: Hammersmith*, 1914. 8°.
C.99.g.27.

SANDERSON (THOMAS JAMES COBDEN) The New Science Museum: a letter, with additions, addressed to the Editor of " The Times." 16 September 1913. *Doves Press: Hammersmith*, 1914. 8°.
C.99.g.32.

SANDERSON (THOMAS JAMES COBDEN) Note on a Passage in Shelley's Ode to Liberty. pp. 6. *Doves Press: [Hammersmith,]* 1914. 8°.

C.99.g.26.

SANDERSON (THOMAS JAMES COBDEN)
—— Wordsworth's Cosmic Poetry. Reprinted from the Westminster Gazette. *Doves Press: [London,* 1914.] 8°.

C.99.g.29.

SHAKESPEARE (WILLIAM) [*Coriolanus.*] The Tragedy of Coriolanus. (From the text of the first folio.) pp. 155. *T. J. Cobden-Sanderson: Hammersmith,* 1914. 8°.

C.99.g.23.

Printed at the Doves Press.

SHELLEY (PERCY BYSSHE) [*Selections.*] Shelley. (Selected...by T. J. Cobden-Sanderson.) pp. 181. *Doves Press: Hammersmith,* 1914. 8°.

C.99.g.25.

SHAKESPEARE (WILLIAM) [*Rape of Lucrece.*] Lucrece, 1594. pp. 76. *Doves Press: Hammersmith,* 1915. 4°.

C.99.g.31.

WORDSWORTH (WILLIAM) *Poet Laureate.* The Prelude: an autobiographical poem ... 1799–1805. pp. 301. *Doves Press: Hammersmith,* 1915. 4°.

C.99.g.33.

DOVES PRESS.
—— Catalogue Raisonné of Books printed & published at the Doves Press, 1900–1916. pp. 96. *Doves Press: Hammersmith,* 1916. 8°.

C.99.g.35.

GOETHE (JOHANN WOLGANG VON) [*Selections.—German.*]
—— Auserlesene Lieder, Gedichte und Balladen. Ein Strauss. (Selected, arranged and printed ... by T. J. Cobden-Sanderson from the Weimar text.) pp. 226. *Doves Press: Hammersmith,* 1916. 8°.

C.99.g.34.

SANDERSON (THOMAS JAMES COBDEN)
—— Towards an Empire of Science. [Signed: T. J. Cobden-Sanderson.] *Doves Press: [London],* 1916. 8°.

C.98.i.16.(1.)

DRAGON PRESS, Ithaca, N.Y.

WINTERS (YVOR)
—— The Journey, and other poems. pp. 29. *Dragon Press: Ithaca, N.Y.,* 1931. 8°.

Cup.402.c.33.

Part of "The Dragon Series."

DROPMORE PRESS, London

BRYANT (Sir ARTHUR WYNNE MORGAN)
—— Historian's Holiday. [A collection of essays.] pp. 84. *Dropmore Press: London,* 1946. 8°. [*Dropmore Essays.* no. 3.]

C.103.g.6/3.

No. 3 of an edition of 25 copies signed by the author and specially bound.

NICOLSON (*Hon. Sir* HAROLD GEORGE) K.C.V.O.
—— The English Sense of Humour. An essay. pp. 70. *Dropmore Press: London,* 1946. 4°. [*Dropmore Essays.* no. 1.]

C.103.g.6/1.

No. 3 of twenty-five copies signed by the author and specially bound.

POPHAM (HUGH HENRY HOME)
—— Three Cantos from To the Unborn—Greetings. *Dropmore Press: London,* 1946. 4°.

11657.eee.23.

No. 5 of an edition of eighty-one copies.

SHANKS (EDWARD BUXTON)
—— The Universal War and the Universal State. pp. 64. *Dropmore Press: London,* 1946. 4°. [*Dropmore Essays.* no. 2.]

C.103.g.6/2.

No. 25 of twenty-five copies signed by the author and specially bound.

SANDEMAN (CHRISTOPHER)
—— Thyme and Bergamot. (The decorations are wood engravings by John O'Connor after various originals chosen by the author.) pp. 58. *Dropmore Press: London,* 1947. 4°. [*Dropmore Essays.* no. 5.] C.103.g.6/5.

SHANKS (EDWARD BUXTON)
—— Images from the Progress of the Seasons ... [Poems.] With decorations by Charles Berry. *Dropmore Press: London,* 1947. 8°.

C.103.f.2.

No. 19 of fifty copies specially bound and signed by the author and the artist.

WEST (*Hon.* VICTORIA MARY SACKVILLE) *afterwards* NICOLSON (*Hon.* VICTORIA MARY) *Lady.*
—— Nursery Rhymes. [An essay.] pp. 66. *Dropmore Press: London,* 1947. 4°. [*Dropmore Essays.* no. 4.]

C.103.g.6/4

No. 25 of twenty-five copies signed by the author.

DE QUINCEY (THOMAS)
—— Revolt of the Tartars ... Illustrated by Stuart Boyle. pp. 96. *Dropmore Press: London,* 1948. 4°.

C.103.g.7.

No. 15 of an edition of fifty copies signed by the artist.

LANDOR (WALTER SAVAGE) [*Selections.*]
—— The sculptured garland. A selection from the lyrical poems of W. S. Landor. (Chosen and arranged by Richard Buxton ... Wood engravings ... by Iain MacNab.) *London: Dropmore Press,* 1948. pp. 54. 27 cm.

Cup.510.bl.1.

NYREN (JOHN) *Author of "The Young Cricketer's Tutor."*
—— The Young Cricketer's Tutor ... Illustrated with wood engravings by John O'Connor. With an introduction by Neville Cardus. pp. xii.89. *Dropmore Press: London,* 1948. 8°.

C.103.e.7.

No. 15 of an edition of fifty specially bound copies.

SHANKS (EDWARD BUXTON)
—— The dogs of war ... With illustrations by S. J. Maiden. *London: Dropmore Press,* 1948.

C.103.g.5.

pp. 67. 27 cm. △

No. 44 of fifty copies specially bound and signed by the author.

THUCYDIDES. [*Selections.—English.*]
—— The Funeral Oration of Pericles. Translated by E. H. Blakeney. pp. 24. *Dropmore Press: London,* 1948. 4°.

C.103.i.13.

COOPER (ALFRED DUFF) *Viscount Norwich.*

—— Translations and Verses. pp. v. 61. *Dropmore Press: London*, 1949. 8°.   C. **103**. b. **16**.
No. 43 of an edition of fifty signed copies.

KNOX (RONALD ARBUTHNOTT) [*Selections.*]

—— A Selection from the Occasional Sermons of the Right Reverend Monsignor R. A. Knox ... Edited by Evelyn Waugh. pp. 102. *Dropmore Press: London*, 1949. 4°.
C. **103**. g. **8**.
No. 19 of fifty copies specially bound and signed by the author.

LOCKHART (*Sir* ROBERT HAMILTON BRUCE) *K.C.M.G.*

—— My Rod my Comfort ... With wood engravings by J. Gaastra. pp. 75. *Dropmore Press: London*, 1949. 8°.
C. **103**. g. **9**.
No. 46 of fifty copies specially bound, with a frontispiece hand-coloured by the artist, and signed by the author and the artist.

SITWELL (*Sir* GEORGE RERESBY) *Bart.*

—— On the Making of Gardens. With an introduction by Sir Osbert Sitwell and decorations by John Piper. pp. xvi. 113. *Dropmore Press: London*, 1949. 8°.
C. **103**. b. **17**.
No. 38 of an edition of 100 copies.

CUBBIN (THOMAS)

—— The Wreck of the Serica. (With wood engravings by John Worsley.) [Introduction by H. M. Tomlinson.] pp. x. 105. *Dropmore Press: London*, 1950. 8°.
C. **103**. b. **18**.
On hand made paper. No. 29 of thirty specially bound copies.

HOWE (ELLIC)

—— The London Bookbinders, 1780–1806. With wood engravings by Gwendolen Raverat. pp. ii. 182. *Dropmore Press: London*, 1950. 8°.   **667**. a. **9**.

SMITH (LOGAN PEARSALL)

—— A Portrait of Logan Pearsall Smith. Drawn from his letters and diaries and introduced by John Russell. pp. 173. *Dropmore Press: London*, 1950. 8°.
C. **103**. e. **12**.

LOCKHART (*Sir* ROBERT HAMILTON BRUCE) *K.C.M.G.*

—— Jan Masaryk. A personal memoir. pp. 80. *Dropmore Press: London*, 1951. 4°.   C. **103**. b. **22**.
No. 34 of one hundred copies specially bound, and signed by the author.

SNAGG (THOMAS)

—— Recollections of Occurrences. The memoirs of Thomas Snagg, or Snagge. With an introduction by Harold Hobson and wood engravings by Kenneth Hunter. pp. xxii. 110. *Dropmore Press: London*, 1951. 8°.
10859. c. **30**.

BAKER (RICHARD ST. BARBE)

—— Famous Trees ... Illustrations by S. R. Badmin. pp. 117. *Dropmore Press: London*, 1952. 8°.
C. **103**. e. **21**.
No. 17 of fifty-three copies specially bound and signed by the author and the artist.

BURY (ADRIAN)

—— Shadow of Eros. A biographical and critical study of the life and works of Sir Alfred Gilbert, *etc.* [With a portrait.] pp. iv. 108. pl. xxiv. *Dropmore Press: London*, 1952 [1953]. 4°.   C. **103**. c. **16**.
No. 14 of fifty-three copies specially bound and signed by the author.

GEORGE VI., *King of Great Britain and Ireland.*

—— The Royal Philatelic Collection. By Sir John Wilson ... Editor: Clarence Winchester. [A catalogue of the collection begun by H.M. King George V and continued by H.M. King George VI. With plates.] pp. viii. 85. 76. 48. 63. 64. 75. *Dropmore Press: London*, 1952. fol.   C. **103**. h. **6**.

SITWELL (HENRY DEGGE WILMOT)

—— The Crown Jewels and other Regalia in the Tower of London ... Edited by Clarence Winchester. [With plates.] pp. xii. 116. *Dropmore Press: London*, [1953.] fol.   C. **99**. l. **20**.
No. 98 of a specially bound edition of 100 copies signed by the author.

BIBLE.—*Appendix.* [*Pictorial Illustrations.*]

—— The Holkham Bible Picture Book. [Facsimiles.] Introduction and commentary by W. O. Hassall. pp. vii. 191. pl. 42. *Dropmore Press: London*, 1954. fol.
C. **103**. h. **8**.
No. 59 of an edition of one hundred copies specially bound and signed by the commentator.

BURY (ADRIAN)

—— Syon House ... With ten original copper-plate engravings by John Buckland Wright and an appreciation of the engraver's work by Henry Rushbury. pp. x. 41. *Dropmore Press: London*, 1955. 4°.   C. **98**. c. **14**.

DRUMALBAN PRESS, Glasgow

GLEN (DUNCAN)

—— The Literary Masks of Hugh MacDiarmid. pp. 10. *Drumalban Press: Glasgow*, 1964. 8°. Cup. **510**. dad. **1**.
Privately printed. No. 54 of an edition of fifty-five copies.

MACDIARMID (HUGH) *pseud.* [i.e. CHRISTOPHER MURRAY GRIEVE.]

—— The Terrible Crystal. A Vision of Scotland. (Two poems.) *Drumalban Press: Skelmorlie*, 1964. 8°.
Cup. **500**. b. **57**.
One of an edition signed by the author, of which fifty-five copies were for sale.

MACDIARMID (HUGH) *pseud.* [i.e. CHRISTOPHER MURRAY GRIEVE.]

—— [Another copy.] The Terrible crystal, *etc.* *Skelmorlie*, 1964. 8°.   Cup. **510**. dad. **2**.
No. 29 of an edition of fifty-five copies.

DUNCAIRN PRESS, Belfast

MORDAUNT (ELIZABETH) *Viscountess Mordaunt.*
—— The priuate diarie of Elizabeth, Viscountess Mordaunt. [The editor's " Memoir of the Viscountess Mordaunt " signed: Roden, i.e. Robert Jocelyn, Earl of Roden. With a note by the printer signed E.M., i.e. Edmund Macrory.] *Duncairn: privately printed.* 1856.   **3456. g. 37.**

    pp. 7, 239: plates; ports. 20 cm.   △

MARY, *the Blessed Virgin.—Churches, etc.—London.—Temple Church.*
—— A few notes on the Temple organ. [By Edmund Macrory.] *Duncairn: privately printed.* 1859.
     7895. a. 26.

    pp. 42.   17 cm.   △

DUNCAN (Harry) and MERKER (Kim), Iowa City

CARRUTH (HAYDEN)
—— Journey to a Known Place. (A poem.) pp. 29.   *New Directions: Norfolk, Conn.,* 1961.   4°.   Cup. **510. sap. 1.**

DUNSTER HOUSE, Cambridge, Mass.

FREEMAN (JOHN) *Poet and Critic.*
—— The Red Path, a Narrative, and the Wounded Bird. (Two poems.) pp. 30.   *Dunster House: Cambridge, [Mass.,]* 1921.   8°.   **11660. f. 51.**
No. 41 of an edition of fifty copies, reserved for sale in Great Britain, and bearing the imprint: " Selwyn & Blount: London " on the half-title.

AIKEN (CONRAD POTTER)
—— Priapus and the Pool.   *Dunster House: Cambridge, Mass.,* 1922.   8°.   **11689. ee. 22.**
Author's presentation copy to John Freeman.

SANTAYANA (GEORGE)
—— Lucifer, or the Heavenly Truce. A theological tragedy. pp. xxi. 128.   *Dunster House: Cambridge, Mass.,* 1924. fol.   Cup.**510.neg.1.**

MAC LEISH (ARCHIBALD)
—— Nobodaddy. A play.   *Cambridge [Mass.]: Dunster House; New York: printed by the Pynson Printers,* 1926.
     11793. b. 2.

    pp. 67.   21 om.   △

BEEBE (LUCIUS MORRIS)
—— Edwin Arlington Robinson and the Arthurian Legend. pp. 30.   *Privately printed for sale at the Dunster House Bookshop: Cambridge, Mass.,* 1927.   8°.
     Cup. **510. nek. 1.**
No. 30 of an edition of 100 copies.

EGOIST PRESS, London

ELIOT (THOMAS STEARNS)
—— Prufrock, and other observations. [In verse.] pp. 40. *The Egoist: London,* 1917.   8°.   Cup. **403. z. 10.**

STORER (EDWARD A.)
—— Terra Italica. Poems written in Italy, *etc.* pp. 52. *Egoist Press: London; Roma* [printed], 1920.   8°.
     011650. g. 53.

COCTEAU (JEAN)
—— [Le Coq et l'Arlequin.] Cock and Harlequin. Notes concerning music ... Translated ... by Rollo H. Myers. With a portrait of the author and two monograms by Pablo Picasso. pp. 57. *Egoist Press: London,* 1921.   8°.
     7894.b.49.

D., H. Hymen. [With other poems.] By H. D. [i.e. Hilda Doolittle, afterwards Aldington.] pp. 46.   *Egoist Press: London,* 1921.   8°.   **011649. i. 101.**

MOORE (MARIANNE)
—— Poems. pp. 23. *Egoist Press: London,* 1921.   8°.
     011649. i. **99.**

JOYCE (JAMES AUGUSTINE ALOYSIUS)
—— Ulysses. pp. 732.   *John Rodker: Paris, for the Egoist Press: London,* 1922.   8°.   C. **116. g. 18.**

ELM TREE PRESS, Woodstock, Vt.

H., R. C.
—— Eczema: a brief account of being over-done. [Signed: R. C. H., i.e. R. C. Hawkins.] pp. 37. *Elm Tree Press: Woodstock, Vermont,* [1909?] 8°.   **07640. ff. 17.**

VIRGILIUS MARO (PUBLIUS) [*Minor Poems.— Copa.*] Copa: the Hostess of the Inn ... [With the text and English translation.] Its reputed authors, Cynthia and Propertius, and the story of Keppler's search [i.e. his attribution of Copa to " Cynthia," identified by him with Hostia]. Edited by Charles L. Dana and John Cotton Dana. pp. 44.
Elm Tree Press: Woodstock, Vermont, 1909.   8°.
     11386. g. 40.

VENUS. Pervigilium Veneris a poeta Latino incognito. In metro eodem Anglice reddidit Elizabetha Hickman du Bois ... Delineamenta a Dela P. Mussey. —The Vigil of Venus. Author unknown. Translated into English in the original metre by Elizabeth Hickman du Bois, *etc.* *Latin & Eng.* pp. 28.
     Typis et sumptibus Preli Ulmei: Woodstock Verdemontani, 1911.   8°.   **11385.k.34.**

FIRMIANUS SYMPOSIUS (CÆLIUS) The Hundred Riddles of Symphosius. Translated into English verse with an introduction and notes by Elizabeth Hickman du Bois. *Lat. & Eng.* pp. 86.
Elm Tree Press: Woodstock, Vermont, 1912.   8°.
     11385. g. 37.

DANA (JOHN COTTON)
—— American Art: how it can be made to flourish. pp. 31.   *J. L. Dana: Woodstock, Vt.,* 1914.   8°.   **07808. h. 55.**

DANA (CHARLES LOOMIS)

—— Poetry and the Doctors. A catalogue of poetical works written by physicians, with biographical notes & an essay on the poetry of certain ancient practitioners of medicine, illustrated with translations from the Latin and by reproductions of the title pages of the rarer works. [With plates.] pp. xxiii. 83. *Elm Tree Press: Woodstock, Vt.,* 1916. 8°.   **011903. cc. 2.**

ELSTON PRESS, New Rochelle, N.Y.

LANGLAND (WILLIAM) The Vision of William concerning "Piers the Plowman." (With illustrations and initial words by H. M. O'Kane.) pp. liv. *Elston Press: New Rochelle,* 1901. fol.   **C. 99. l. 10.**

AUCASSIN.— [*English.*]

—— The Song-Story of Aucassin and Nicolete. Translated from the ancient French by Andrew Lang. pp. 66. *Clarke Conwell: New Rochelle, New York,* 1902. 12°.   **Cup.510.pp.1**

LODGE (THOMAS) *Dramatist.*

—— Rosalynde. Euphues golden legacie, *etc.* (Printed from the edition of 1592, collated with that of 1598.) pp. 123. *Elston Press: New Rochelle, N.Y.,* 1902. 8°.   **Cup. 510. pp. 4.**

MORRIS (WILLIAM) *Poet.*

—— Sir Galahad. A Christmas mystery. (Decorations by H. M. O'Kane.) *Clarke Conwell at the Elston Press: New Rochelle, N.Y.,* 1902. 4°.   **Cup. 510. pp. 3.** *With lists of publications of the Elston Press inserted.*

APOLLONIUS, *Tyrius.*

—— The patterne of painefull adventures . . . gathered into English by Laurence Twine, *etc.* *Rochelle, N.Y.: Clarke Conwell at the Elston Press,* 1903.   **12403. ff. 13.** pp. 76. 25 cm.   △

MILTON (JOHN) [*L'Allegro and Il Penseroso.*]

—— L'Allegro and Il Penseroso. (With decorations cut on wood from designs by H. M. O'Kane.) pp. 28. *Clarke Conwell at the Elston Press: New Rochelle, N.Y.,* 1903. 8°.   **Cup. 510. pp. 2.**

SHELLEY (PERCY BYSSHE) [*The Cenci.*]

—— The Cenci, *etc.* pp. 86. *Elston Press: New Rochelle,* 1903. 8°.   **Cup. 510. pp. 5.**

ERAGNY PRESS, London

RUST (MARGARET)

—— The Queen of the Fishes. An adaptation in English of a fairy tale of Valois . . . With illustrations designed . . . by Lucien Pissarro. *Ch. Ricketts: London,* 1894. 8°.   **Cup. 500. a. 6.**

BIBLE. [*Hagiographa — English.*]

—— The book of Ruth & the book of Esther. With five illustrations designed and cut on the wood by Lucien Pissarro. *Epping: printed by Lucien Pissarro; London: sold by L. Hacon & C. S. Ricketts,* 1896.   **C. 99. b. 6.** pp. lxxxii. 18 cm.   △

LAFORGUE (JULES)

—— Moralités legendaires. *London: en ventre chez Messrs. Hacon & Ricketts; Paris: à la Société du Mercure de France,* 1897, 98.   **C. 99. e. 24.** 2 vol. 22 cm.   △

PERRAULT (CHARLES)

—— La Belle au Bois dormant & Le Petit Chaperon Rouge, *etc.* (Illustrations par L. Pissarro.) pp. 38. *Hacon & Ricketts: London,* 1899. 8°.   **C. 99. c. 1.**

FLAUBERT (GUSTAVE)

[Trois contes.]

—— La légende de Saint Julien l'hospitalier. *London: [printed at the] Eragny Press; en vente chez Hacon & Ricketts,* 1900.   **C. 99. a. 17.** pp. 92; illus. 15 cm.   △ *From "Trois Contes ".*

VILLON (FRANÇOIS) [*Ballades and Miscellaneous Poems.— French.*]

—— Les ballades. (Le frontispice a été dessiné et gravé sur bois . . . la bordure et les lettres ornées ont été dessinées par L. Pissarro.) *London: Hacon & Ricketts,* 1900.   **C. 99. e. 1.** pp. 88. 20 cm.   △ *Printed at the Eragny Press.*

VILLON (FRANÇOIS) [*Ballades and Miscellaneous Poems.— French.*]

—— [Another copy.] Les Ballades. *London,* 1900. 8°.   **C. 108. bbb. 6. (1.)** *In a gold-tooled red morocco binding with green and buff inlays, signed by Sybil Pye, and dated 1928.*

FLAUBERT (GUSTAVE)

[Trois contes.]

—— Hérodias. (Le frontispice a été dessiné & gravé sur bois . . . les bordures et les lettres ornées ont été dessinées par Lucien Pissarro.) *London: en vente chez Hacon & Ricketts,* 1901.   **C. 99. a. 10.** pp. 103. 15 cm.   △ *From "Trois contes ". Printed by E. & L. Pissarro at the Eragny Press.*

FLAUBERT (GUSTAVE)

[Trois contes.]

—— [Another copy.] Hérodias. 1901.   **C. 108. a. 6.**   △

FLAUBERT (GUSTAVE)

[Trois contes.]

—— Un cœur simple. *London: en vente chez Hacon & Ricketts,* 1901.   **C. 99. a. 11.** pp. 113. 15 cm.   △ *Printed at the Eragny Press.*

FLAUBERT (GUSTAVE)
[Trois contes.]
—— [Another copy.] Un cœur simple. 1901. C. **108**. a. **5**.
△

VERHAEREN (EMILE)
—— Les petits vieux. *London: Hacon & Ricketts*, 1901.
C. **99**. a. **19**.
pp. 16. 13×17 cm. △
Poems. Printed at the Eragny Press, on one side of the paper only.

VILLON (FRANÇOIS) [*Ballades and Miscellaneous Poems.— French.*]
—— Autres poésies de Maistre François Villon et de son école. *London: Hacon & Ricketts*, 1901. C. **99**. c. **21**.
pp. 55. 20 cm. △
Printed at the Eragny Press.

VILLON (FRANÇOIS) [*Ballades and Miscellaneous Poems.— French.*]
—— [Another copy.] Autres poesies de Maistre François Villon, *etc. London*, 1901. 8°. C. **108**. bbb. **6**. (2.)

BACON (FRANCIS) *Viscount St. Albans.* [*Essays.—Single Essays.*]
—— Of gardens. An essay. *London: Hacon & Ricketts*, 1902.
C. **99**. b. **3**.
pp. 23. 18 cm. △
Printed at the Eragny Press.

PERRAULT (CHARLES)
[Contes des fées.]
—— Histoire de peau d'âne. (Les trois illustrations ont été dessinées et gravées sur bois par T. Sturge Moore. Le frontispice, les bordures et les lettres ornées ont été dessinés par Lucien Pissarro.) [*London:*] *en vente chez Hacon & Ricketts*, 1902. C. **99**. e. **14**.
pp. 38. 22 cm. △
Printed at the Eragny Press.

RONSARD (PIERRE DE) [*Selections.*]
—— Choix de sonnets de P. de Ronsard. (Le frontispice a été dessiné et gravé sur bois par Lucien Pissarro. La bordure et les lettres ornées ont été dessinées par L. Pissarro et gravées sur bois par Esther Pissarro.) [*London:*] *en vente chez Hacon & Ricketts*, 1902. C. **99**. e. **25**.
pp. 79. 22 cm. △
Printed at the Eragny Press.

AUCASSIN. –[*Old French.*]
—— C'est d'Aucassin et de Nicolete. (Seen through the press and revised by the editor, F. W. Bourdillon. The frontispiece has been designed and engraved by Lucien Pissarro.) [With musical notes.] pp. 55. *Eragny Press: Hammersmith*, 1903. 8°. C. **99**. e. **28**.

ISHTAR. The Descent of Ishtar. [Translated with a frontispiece] by Diana White. pp. 30.
Eragny Press: London; John Lane: New York, 1903. 8°. C.**99**.b.**5**.

MOORE (THOMAS STURGE) A Brief Account of the Origin of the Eragny Press, & a note on the relation of the printed book as a work of art to life. . .A bibliographical list of the Eragny books printed in the Vale type by E. and L. Pissarro, *etc.* [With sixteen woodcuts.] pp. 52. *Eragny Press: Hammersmith, London*, 1903. 8°. C.**99**.e.**13**.

RONSARD (PIERRE DE)
—— Abregé de l'art poetique françois. (Les ornements et les lettres ornées ont été dessinés par Lucien Pissarro et gravés par Esther Pissarro.) *London: Hacon & Ricketts*, 1903. C. **99**. e. **27**.
pp. 44. 22 cm. △
Printed at the Eragny Press.

BROWNING (ROBERT) *the Poet.* [*Smaller Collections.*]
—— Some Poems by Robert Browning. [With a coloured frontispiece by Lucien Pissarro.] pp. 64. *Eragny Press: London*, 1904. 8°. C. **99**. e. **16**.

COLERIDGE (SAMUEL TAYLOR) [*Smaller Collections.*—III. *Verse.*]
—— Christabel, Kubla Khan, Fancy in Nubibus, and Song from Zapolya. (The frontispiece designed and engraved on the wood by L. Pissarro; the border and initial letters designed by L. Pissarro and engraved by E. Pissarro.) pp. 41. *Eragny Press: London*, 1904. 8°.
C. **99**. e. **17**.

MILTON (JOHN) [*Prose Works. — Areopagitica.*] Areopagitica, *etc.* (The border & initial letters ...designed by Lucien Pissarro.) pp. 37. *Eragny Press: London*, 1904. 4°. C.**99**.i.**1**.

BINYON (ROBERT LAURENCE) *Keeper of Prints and Drawings, British Museum.*
—— Dream Come True. Poems. (Frontispiece ... designed ... by L. Binyon ... decorations designed by Lucien Pissarro & engraved by Esther Pissarro.) pp. 28. *Eragny Press: London; John Lane: New York*, 1905. 8°. C. **99**. b. **7**.

MOORE (THOMAS STURGE)
—— The Little School. A posy of rhymes. pp. 45. *Eragny Press: London*, 1905. 8°. C. **99**. b. **8**.

STEELE (ROBERT REYNOLDS)
—— Some Old French and English Ballads, edited by Robert Steele. [Music and words.] (Frontispiece designed and engraved on the wood by L. Pissarro.) pp. 60. *Eragny Press: London*, [1905.] 8°. C. **99**. e. **15**.
The date in the colophon is misprinted MCCCCMV.

JONSON (BEN) [*Poems.*]
—— Songs by Ben Jonson. A selection from the plays, masques, and poems, with the earliest known settings of certain numbers. (The coloured frontispiece ... designed and engraved on the wood by L. Pissarro. The border & initial letters ... designed by L. Pissarro and engraved by E. Pissarro.) [With musical notes.] pp. 59. *Eragny Press: London*, 1906. 8°. C. **99**. e. **18**.

KEATS (JOHN) [*Single Poems.*]
La Belle Dame sans Merci.
pp. **xxviii**. *Eragny Press: Hammersmith*, 1906. *obl.* 16°. C.**99**.a.**21**.

ROSSETTI (CHRISTINA GEORGINA) Verses ... re-printed from G. Polidori's edition of 1847. Edited by J. D. Symon. (The decorations by Lucien Pissarro.) pp. v. 75. *Eragny Press: London*, 1906. 8°.

C.99.e.19.

PERRAULT (CHARLES)

[Contes des fées.]

—— Riquet à la houppe. Deux versions d'un conte de ma Mère Loye. (The first version is by Ch. Perrault and the second, taken from a manuscript in the Magazine Library, Paris, is by an unknown author of the XVIIth century.) [With designs by Lucien Pissarro.] *London: printed & sold by E. & L. Pissarro at the Eragny Press*, 1907.

C. 99. a. 18.

pp. 48. 14 cm. △

One of seventy-five paper copies printed in red and black, out of a total edition of eighty copies on paper and eight on vellum.

PO YÜ SHIH SHU.

—— Album de poèmes tirés du Livre de jade. (Translated by Mme. Judith Gautier.) [The preface signed: Diana White.] *London: Eragny Press*, 1911. **11094. a. 33.**

ff. 27 ; illus. 20 cm. △

Printed, on one side of the leaf only, on Japanese vellum.

PO YÜ SHIH SHU.

—— [Another copy.] Album de poèmes tirés du Livre de jade. 1911. C. 104. a. 9.

△

No. 3 of ten copies printed, on one side of the leaf only, on Roman vellum. Campbell Dodgson's copy.

FIELD (MICHAEL) *pseud.* [i.e. KATHARINE HARRIS BRADLEY and EDITH EMMA COOPER.]

—— Whym Chow, Flame of Love. pp. 58. *Eragny Press: London*, 1914. 8°. C. 99. e. 21.

One of 27 copies privately printed.

ESSEX HOUSE PRESS, London:
Chipping Camden, Glos.

CELLINI (BENVENUTO) *the Artist.*

—— The Treatises of Benvenuto Cellini on Goldsmithing and Sculpture. (Made into English from the Italian of the Marcian codex by C. R. Ashbee.) [With plates.] pp. xiv. 164. *Edward Arnold: London*, 1898. 4°.

C. 99. k. 4.

BARDEISAN.

—— The hymn of Bardaisan rendered into English by F. Crawford Burkitt. [*London:*] *Edward Arnold*, 1899.

753. a. 56.

pp. 30. 16 cm. △

Printed at the Essex House Press.

BUNYAN (JOHN) [*Pilgrim's Progress.—Pt. 1.—English.*]

—— The pilgrim's progress, *etc.* (Pt. I. Collated from the earlier editions by Janet E. Ashbee.) [*London:*] *Edward Arnold*, 1899. C. 99. a. 6.

pp. 426 : plate. 16 cm. △

Printed at the Essex House Press.

LONDON.—III. *Art Workers Guild.*

—— Beauty's Awakening, a Masque of Winter and of Spring. (Written, designed & contrived by the members of the Art Workers Guild.) pp. 38. *Printed for the Art Workers Guild at the Press of the Guild of Handicraft: Bow*, 1899. 4°.

Cup.510.bbc.5

No. 17 of an edition of twenty-four copies.

SHAKESPEARE (WILLIAM) [*Collected Poems.*]

—— The poems of William Shakespeare, according to the text of the original copies, including the lyrics, songs, and snatches found in his dramas. (Arranged, and carefully collated with the originals, by F. S. Ellis.) [*London:*] *Edward Arnold*, 1899. C. 99. f. 5.

pp. 253. 23 cm. △

Printed at the Essex House Press.

BOURDILLON (FRANCIS WILLIAM)

—— Through the Gateway. [Poems.] pp. 48. *Privately printed for the Author at the Press of the Guild of Handicraft: Bow*, 1900. 4°. Cup.510.bbc.6.

CASTIGLIONE (BALDASSARE) *Count.* [*Libro del Cortegiano.*]

—— The courtyer ... Done into Englyshe by Thomas Hoby. (The work has been edited ... by Janet E. Ashbee, and carried out under the supervision of C. R. Ashbee.) [*London:*] *Edward Arnold*, 1900. C. 99. f. 4.

pp. 391. 23 cm. △

Printed at the Essex House Press.

GRAY (THOMAS) *the Poet.* [*Elegy written in a Country Churchyard.*] Gray's Elegy ... Printed ... under the care of C. R. Ashbee, *etc.* pp. 13. ON VELLUM. *Edward Arnold: London*, 1900. 8°. C.99.c.11.

HILLS (OSBORN CLUSE)

—— Saint Mary Stratford Bow ... With an introductory chapter by C. R. Ashbee. [*London:*] *Edward Arnold*, 1900. L.C.C. **122.**

pp. 48, vi : pl. XXVII. 29 cm. (Committee for the survey of the memorials of Greater London. Monograph no. 2.)

△

Printed at the press of the Guild of Handicrafts, Essex House, Bow.

KEATS (JOHN) [*Single Poems.*]

[The eve of St. Agnes.]

—— Keats' eve of St. Agnes. (With a frontispiece by Reginald Savage.) [*London:*] *Edward Arnold*, 1900. C. 99. c. 10.

pp. 23. 20 cm. △

The title is taken from the spine. Printed on vellum at the Essex House Press.

LINCOLN (ABRAHAM) *President of the United States of America.*

—— President Lincoln's Funeral Hymn [by Walt Whitman]. Reprinted ... under the care of C. R. Ashbee, *etc.* ON VELLUM. pp. 18. *Edward Arnold: London*, 1900. 8°.

C. 99. c. 14.

SHELLEY (Percy Bysshe) [*Adonais.*]

—— [Adonais. By P. B. Shelley.]   [*London :*] *Edward Arnold,* 1900.   C. **99**. c. **13**.

pp. 30 ; illus. 20 cm.   △

One of an edition of fifty copies, printed on vellum at the Essex House Press.

ASHBEE (Charles Robert)

—— An Endeavour towards the Teaching of John Ruskin and William Morris. pp. 52.   *Edward Arnold: London,* 1901. 8°.   C. **99**. e. **26**.

ENGLAND.—*National Trust for Places of Historic Interest or Natural Beauty.*

—— A Report by Mr. C. R. Ashbee to the Council of the National Trust . . . on his visit to the United States in the Council's behalf. October, MDCCCC, to February, MDCCCCI. pp. 24. *Essex House Press: [London?]* 1901. 4°.
C. **104**. i. **1**.

No. 31 of fifty fine paper copies signed by the author.

ERASMUS (Desiderius) [*Moriae Encomium.*] The Praise of Folie. Moriae Eucomium . . . Englished by Sir T. Chaloner (and edited from the Black Letter edition of 1549 by Janet E. Ashbee, *etc.*) pp. vi. 87. *Edward Arnold: London,* 1901. 4°.   C. **99**. k. **3**.

MILTON (John) [*Comus.*] Comus, a mask. (Printed under the care of C. R. Ashbee, *etc.*) pp. 47. *Edward Arnold: [London;] Samuel Buckley & Co.: New York,* 1901. 8°.   C. **99**. c. **16**. *Printed on vellum.*

PENN (William) *Founder of Pennsylvania.* Some Fruits of Solitude . . . Printed . . . under the care of C. R. Ashbee, *etc.* pp. xiv. 257.   *Edward Arnold: [London,]* 1901. 8°.   C. **99**. a. **5**.

SHELLEY (Percy Bysshe) [*Letters.*]

—— A Letter from Percy B. Shelley to T. Peacock, July, MDCCCXVI. pp. 15.   *Privately printed at the Essex House Press for the Owner of the Manuscript: [London,]* 1901. 8°. C. **104**. b. **4**.

One of an edition of fifty copies.

SPENSER (Edmund) [*Epithalamium.*] The Epithalamium of Spenser. With a woodcut by Reginald Savage. Printed at the Essex House Press, *etc.* pp. 21 *Edward Arnold: [London,]* 1901. 8°. *Printed on vellum.*   C. **99**. c. **15** .

STRANG (William) The Doings of Death. [A series of woodcuts.]   [*Essex House Press : London,* 1901.] obl. fol.   **Print Room.**

WOOLMAN (John) *Member of the Society of Friends.*

—— A journal of the life and travels of John Woolman in the service of the Gospel. [*London :*] *Edward Arnold,* [1901].
C. **99**. a. **7**.

pp. 387 ; illus. 16 cm.   △

Printed at the Essex House Press.

ASHBEE (Charles Robert)

—— American Sheaves & English Seed Corn : being a series of addresses mainly delivered in the United States, 1900–1901. pp. 134. *Edward Arnold: London,* [1902.] 8°.
C. **99**. d. **22**.

ASHBEE (Charles Robert)

—— The Masque of the Edwards of England : being a Coronation Pageant to celebrate the crowning of the King. (The drawings . . . by Edith Harwood.) pp. 45. *Edward Arnold: [London;] S. Buckley & Co.: New York,* 1902. obl. fol.   C. **99**. l. **21** .

BIBLE.—*Psalms.* [*English.—Prose Versions.*]

—— The Psalter or Psalms of David from the Bible of Archbishop Cranmer. (Edited . . . by Janet E. Ashbee, and reprinted . . . at the Essex House Press . . . under the care of C. R. Ashbee, who has . . . drawn the woodcuts.) [*London :*] *Edward Arnold ; New York: Samuel Buckley & Co.,* 1902.   C. **99**. k. **6**.

pp. 87. 30 cm.   △

BURNS (Robert) *the Poet.* [*Single Poems.*]
[Tam o' Shanter.]

—— *End.* Here ends Robert Burns' Tam o' Shanter, *etc. London: Edward Arnold ; New York: Samuel Buckley & Co.,* 1902.   C. **99**. c. **8**.

pp. 12 ; illus. 19 cm.   △
On vellum.

CHAUCER (Geoffrey) [*Doubtful or Supposititious Works. —The Flower and the Leaf.*]

—— The Flower and the Leaf. (Printed under the care of C. R. Ashbee. The ornamental letters drawn and coloured in by Edith Harwood.) pp. 45. ON VELLUM. *Edward Arnold: London; S. Buckley & Co.: New York,* 1902. 8°. C. **99**. c. **8**.

Printed at the Essex House Press.

GODMAN (Ernest)

—— The Old Palace of Bromley-by-Bow. [*London :*] *Edward Arnold ; New York: Samuel Buckley & Co.,* 1902.
L.C.C. **122**.

pp. 21 : pl. 37 ; illus. 29 cm. (Committee for the survey of the memorials of Greater London. no. 3.)   △

Printed at the Essex House Press.

STEVENSON (Robert Louis)

—— Three Letters from Robert Louis Stevenson. pp. 6. *Essex House Press: [Chipping Campden,]* 1902. 4°.
Cup. **510**. bbc. **2**.

One of an edition of sixty copies.

ASHBEE (Charles Robert) and ASHBEE (Janet Elizabeth)

—— The Essex House song book, being the collection of songs formed for the singers of the Guild of Handicraft by C. R. and Janet E. Ashbee, and edited by her. *London: Essex House Press,* 1903–1905.   Music K. **10**. a. **8**.

10 pt. ; music. 24 cm.   △

COLERIDGE (Samuel Taylor) [*Lyrical Ballads.—Rime of the Ancient Mariner.*]

—— The Rime of the Ancient Mariner. (Printed at the Essex House Press . . . under the care of C. R. Ashbee.) pp. 30.   *Edward Arnold: London; S. Buckley & Co.: New York,* 1903. 8°.   C. **99**. c. **9**. *Printed on vellum.*

GUNN (EDWIN)

—— The Great House, Leyton. [*London :*] *Edward Arnold ; New York : William Buckley & Co.*, 1903. L.C.C. **122.**

pp. 24 : pl. 25. 29 cm. (Committee for the Survey of the memorials of Greater London. Monograph no. 4.) △

Printed at the Essex House Press.

LITURGIES.—*Church of England.* [*Common Prayer.*]

—— The Book of Common Prayer . . . Together with the Psalter, *etc.* (The designs and the type . . . by C. R. Ashbee.) pp. 387. *Eyre & Spottiswoode ; Edward Arnold : London ; Samuel Buckley & Co. : New York*, 1903. fol. C. **99.** l. **4.**

WORDSWORTH (WILLIAM) [*Ode. Intimations of Immortality, etc.*]

—— Intimations of immortality from recollections of early childhood. (With a frontispiece by Walter Crane.) [*London :*] *Edward Arnold ; New York : Samuel Buckley & Co. ; Campden : printed at the Essex House Press*, 1903. C. **99.** c. **12.**

pp. 12. 20 cm.
On vellum.

WREN (CHRISTOPHER) *Son of Sir Christopher Wren.*

—— Life and Works of Sir Christopher Wren. From the Parentalia or Memoirs by his son Christopher. (Edited from the original edition by E. J. Enthoven and carried out under the supervision of C. R. Ashbee . . . Twenty drawings of Wren's Churches . . . by E. H. New.) pp. 259. viii. *Edward Arnold : [London ;] Samuel Buckley & Co. : New York*, 1903. 4°. C. **99.** k. **5.**

BISHOP (GERALD)

—— A May-Day Interlude. (Written by Gerald Bishop for the Campden children.) pp. 19. *Essex House Press : Campden*, [1904.] 8°. Cup. **510.** bbc. **7.**

One of an edition of twenty-four copies.

CICERO (MARCUS TULLIUS) [LAELIUS.—*Latin and English.*]

—— The Booke of Freendeship of Marcus Tullie Cicero. (With the English translation of Sir John Harryngton [or rather John Harington of Kelston], edited by E. D. Ross & printed . . . under the care of C. R. Ashbee.) pp. viii. 51. 51. *Essex House Press : London*, 1904. 8°. C. **99.** d. **19.**

DRYDEN (JOHN) [*Poetical Works.—Single Works.*] Alexander's Feast, *etc.* (Printed . . . under the care of C. R. Ashbee.) pp. 11. *Edward Arnold : London*, 1904. 8°. C.99.c.5.

Printed on vellum.

ESSEX HOUSE PRESS.

—— A Bibliography of the Essex House Press, with notes on the designs, blocks, cuts, bindings, etc., from the year 1898 to 1904. [With illustrations.] pp. 23. *Essex House Press : Campden*, 1904. 8°. **11919.** bb. **11.**

GOLDSMITH (OLIVER) *the Poet.* [*The Deserted Village.*] *End.* Here ends Oliver Goldsmith's Deserted Village, printed . . . under the care of & with a frontispiece by C. R. Ashbee. pp. 22. *Essex House Press : Campden*, 1904. 8°. C.99.c.3.

Printed on vellum.

HOOD (THOMAS) *the Elder.*

—— Miss Kilmansegg and her Precious Leg. A golden legend. (Printed with three drawings by R. Savage under the care of C. R. Ashbee.) pp. 94. *Edward Arnold : London ; Samuel Buckley & Co. : New York*, 1904. 8°. C. **99.** e. **29.**

JESUS CHRIST. [*De Imitatione Christi.—English.*]

—— Of the Imitation of Christ, *etc.* (Edited by Ernest Godman from the earliest English translations, the first three are from that of Thomas Rogers 1580, the fourth from that of the Lady Margaret, Countess of Richmond . . . 1504 . . . Printed . . . under the care of C. R. Ashbee.) pp. 215. *Essex House Press : London*, 1904. 4°. C. **99.** k. **2.**

One of 100 copies.

SHELLEY (PERCY BYSSHE) [*Prometheus Unbound.*] Prometheus Unbound, *etc.* (Printed under the care of C. R. Ashbee.) pp. 96. *Edward Arnold : [London ;] Samuel Buckley & Co. : New York*, 1904. 4°. C.99.k.9.

WESTON SUBEDGE. The Last Records of a Cotswold Community : being the Weston Subedge Field Account Book for the final twenty-six years of the famous Cotswold Games, hitherto unpublished, and now edited with a study on the old time sports of Campden and the village community of Weston, by C. R. Ashbee. pp. lvi. 59. *Essex House Press : Campden*, 1904. 4°. *Only 75 copies printed.* C.99.f.22.

ASHBEE (CHARLES ROBERT)

—— Echoes from the City of the Sun : being poems and songs by C. R. Ashbee. pp. 58. *Essex House Press : London*, 1905. 8°. C. **99.** f. **15.**

BROWNING (ROBERT) *the Poet.* [*Single Poems not originally published separately.*]

—— The Flight of the Duchess. (Printed under the care of C. R. Ashbee.) pp. 42. *Essex House Press : London*, 1905. 8°. C. **99.** c. **7.**

GODMAN (ERNEST)

—— Mediæval architecture in Essex. *Banstead : the Author*, 1905. C. **99.** i. **7.**

pp. 33 : plates ; illus. 26 cm. △

Printed at the Essex House Press.

GODMAN (ERNEST)

—— Norman architecture in Essex. *Banstead : the Author*, 1905. C. **99.** i. **8.**

pp. 44 : plates ; illus. 26 cm. △

Printed at the Essex House Press.

H., F. A.

—— An Octet of Sonnets by F. A. H. [i.e. F. A. Hyett.] With Christmas greetings from the author. *Essex House Press : [Chipping Campden,]* 1905. 8°. Cup. **510.** bbc. **4.**

One of an edition of fifty copies, printed for private circulation. Author's presentation copy to Roland Austin.

MITFORD (ALGERNON BERTRAM FREEMAN) *Baron Redesdale.*

—— The Second Address of Lord Redesdale ... at the Campden School of Arts and Crafts. Delivered at the opening of the winter session on October 7, MDCCCCV. pp. 14. *Essex House Press: Campden,* 1905. Cup.510.bbc.10. *Privately printed.*

TENNYSON (ALFRED) *Baron Tennyson.* [*Maud.*] Maud. (The frontispiece from a design by Laurence Housman.) ON VELLUM. pp. 75. *Essex House Press: Campden,* 1905. 8°. C.99.c.4.

'UMAR KHAIYĀM. [*FitzGerald's Version.*]

—— Rubáiyát of Omar Khayyám of Naishápur. (Rendered into English verse by Edward FitzGerald, and printed for the Omar Khayyam Club ... under the care of C. R. Ashbee.) [With an introduction by Clement K. Shorter.] pp. vii. 26. *Essex House Press: London,* 1905. 4°. C. 99. f. 3.

ASHBEE (CHARLES ROBERT)

—— A Book of Cottages and Little Houses: for landlords, architects, builders and others: with suggestions as to cost, the housing difficulty, & the improvement of taste in these matters. pp. 130. pl. 25. *B. T. Batsford: London,* 1906. 4°. C. 99. e. 32. *Printed at the Essex House Press.*

ASHBEE (CHARLES ROBERT)

—— On the Need for the Establishment of Country Schools of Arts & Crafts. [Signed: C. R. Ashbee. With plates.] pp. 11. *Essex House Press: Campden, Glos.,* 1906. 8°. Cup. 510. bbc. 9.

ASHBEE (CHARLES ROBERT)

—— Socialism and Politics: a study in the readjustment of the values of life. pp. 68. *Brimley Johnson & Ince: London,* 1906. 8°. Cup.510.bbc.3.

CEBES. [*English.*]

—— Κεβητος ... Πιναξ. The Picture of Kebes the Theban, *etc.* (Translated by Hugh E. Seebohm.) pp. 52. *Essex House Press: Chipping Campden,* 1906. 8°. C. 99. a. 9.

HOUSMAN (LAURENCE) Mendicant Rhymes. pp. 56. *London,* 1906. 4°. C.99.e.30.

JOHN [FISHER], *Saint, Cardinal, Bishop of Rochester.*

—— A mornynge remembraunce, *etc.* (Printed under the care of C. R. Ashbee.) *London: Essex House Press,* 1906. C. 99. a. 8.

pp. 85: plate. 16 cm. △

MITFORD (ALGERNON BERTRAM FREEMAN) *Baron Redesdale.* A Tale of Old and New Japan, being a lecture delivered before the Japan Society, *etc.* pp. 40. *Privately printed: Campden,* 1906. 8°. Cup.510.bbc.1.

COOMARASWAMY (ANANDA KENTISH)

—— The Deeper Meaning of the Struggle (between Englishmen and Indians). pp. 26. *Essex House Press: Broad Campden,* 1907. 8°. C. 99. d. 2. *One of an edition of seventy-five copies.*

ASHBEE (CHARLES ROBERT)

—— Conradin: a philosophical ballad. (The pictures by P. A. Mairet.) pp. 26. *Essex House Press: Broad Campden, Gloucestershire,* 1908. 4°. C. 99. i. 3.

ASHBEE (CHARLES ROBERT)

—— Craftsmanship in Competitive Industry, being a record of the workshops of the Guild of Handicraft, and some deductions from their twenty-one years' experience. [With illustrations.] pp. 258. *Essex House Press: Campden, Glos. & London,* [1908.] 8°. X. 510/215. *With a copy of a letter from L. W. Hodson to the author inserted.*

COOMARASWAMY (ANANDA KENTISH)

—— The Aims of Indian Art. pp. 22. *Essex House Press: Broad Campden,* 1908. 4°. C. 99. i. 6. *One of fifty copies printed on hand-made paper.*

COOMARASWAMY (ANANDA KENTISH)

—— Mediæval Sinhalese Art ... Being a monograph of mediæval Sinhalese arts and crafts, mainly as surviving in the eighteenth century, with an account of the structure of society and the status of the craftsmen. pp. xvi. 340. pl. LIII. *Essex House Press: Broad Campden,* 1908. fol. C. 99. l. 3. *No. 14 of twenty-five copies printed on hand-made paper.*

COOMARASWAMY (ANANDA KENTISH)

—— Nētra Maṅgalya; or Ceremony of Painting the Eyes Images, as performed by craftsmen in Ceylon. (Extra from "Mediæval Sinhalese Art.") pp. 7. *Essex House Press: Broad Campden,* 1908. fol. 4504. l. *One of an edition of twenty-five copies.*

ASHBEE (CHARLES ROBERT)

—— The Private Press: a study in idealism. To which is added a bibliography of the Essex House Press. [With illustrations.] pp. 86. [*C. R. Ashbee:*] *Broad Campden,* 1909. 4°. Cup. 510. bbc. 8.

ASOKA, *Maurya, Emperor of Northern India.*

—— The Edicts of Asoka. Edited in English, with an introduction and commentary, by Vincent A. Smith. pp. xx. 77. *Henry Frowde: London,* 1909. 4°. C. 99. i. 2.

EDDA. [*Poetic Edda.—English.*]

—— Völuspa: done into English ... by A. K. Coomaraswamy. pp. 29. *Essex House Press: Broad Campden,* 1909. 8°. C. 99. c. 20.

COOMARASWAMY (ANANDA KENTISH)

—— The Oriental View of Women. pp. 23. *Essex House Press: Broad Campden; Probsthain & Co.: London,* 1910. 16°. 08415. e. 15. (1.) *No. 11 of twenty-five copies printed on hand-made paper.*

COOMARASWAMY (ANANDA KENTISH)

—— Selected Examples of Indian Art. [With an introduction and a description of the plates.] pp. vii. 19. pl. XL. *Essex House Press: Broad Campden; Bernard Quaritch: London,* 1910. fol. C. 99. l. 5. *No. 6 of twenty-five copies printed on hand-made paper.*

HOKUSAI. Two Drawings by Hok'sai from the collection of W. Rothenstein. [With a preface by W. Rothenstein.] *Essex House Press: Broad Campden,* 1910. fol. Tab. **687**. a. **3**.
One of ten copies printed on hand-made paper.

LONDON.—III. *Royal India and Pakistan Society.*
—— Indian Drawings. By Ananda K. Coomaraswamy. pp. vii. 32. pl. XXIX. *Essex House Press: Broad Campden; Probsthain & Co.: London,* 1910. 4°.
K.T.C. **26**. b. **5**.
No. 12 of 25 copies printed on hand-made paper.

ASHBEE (CHARLES ROBERT)
—— Where the Great City stands. A study in the new civics. [With plates.] pp. xii. 164. *Essex House Press, & B. T. Batsford: London,* 1917. 4°. C. **99**. k. **12**.

FANFARE PRESS, London

BARING (Hon. MAURICE)
—— Poems, 1892–1929. pp. 128. *Privately printed at the Fanfare Press: [London,]* 1930. 8°. Cup. **510**. bap. **1**.
No. 38 of an edition of fifty copies.

COLERIDGE (SAMUEL TAYLOR) [*Lyrical Ballads.—Rime of the Ancient Mariner.*]
—— The rime of the ancient mariner. With ten engravings on copper by David Jones. pp. 37. *Bristol: Douglas Cleverdon,* 1929. C. **100**. k. **20**.
pp. 37. 33 cm. △
One of a limited issue signed by the artist and containing a set of the engravings in first state, a set in final state, and proofs of the discarded engravings.

WILDE (OSCAR FINGALL O'FLAHERTIE WILLS)
—— Salome . . . Translated from the French . . . by Lord Alfred Douglas, and illustrated by Aubrey Beardsley. With a new introduction by Holbrook Jackson. pp. 105. *Printed for the members of the Limited Editions Club at the Fanfare Press: London,* 1938. fol. C. **105**. e. **3**.

FANFROLICO PRESS, London

ARISTOPHANES, *the Poet.* [*Lysistrata.—English.*]
Lysistrata . . . Done into English by Jack Lindsay. Illustrations by Norman Lindsay. *London: Fanfrolico Press,* 1926. fol. Cup. **803**. f. **7**.
pp. xii, 51 : plates. 39 cm. △
Printed at the Chiswick Press. For sale to subscribers only.

SLESSOR (KENNETH)
—— Earth-Visitors. Poems. [With plates.] pp. 75. *Fanfrolico Press: London,* 1926. 4°. C. **98**. f. **7**.

HARINGTON (Sir JOHN)
—— The metamorphosis of Aiax . . . Reprinted from the original editions. Edited by Peter Warlock and Jack Lindsay. *London: Fanfrolico Press,* 1927. C. **98**. f. **12**.
pp. xxviii, 143 : plate ; port. 25 cm. △

HERRICK (ROBERT) *the Poet.* [*Smaller Collections.*]
—— Delighted earth. A selection by Peter Meadows from Herrick's ' Hesperides '. With illustrations by Lionel Ellis. *London: Fanfrolico Press,* 1927. **11633**. f. **54**.
pp. 170. 24 cm. △
Printed at the Curwen Press.

HERRICK (ROBERT) *the Poet.* [*Smaller Collections.*]
—— [Another copy.] Delighted earth, *etc.* 1927.
C. **99**. g. **39**.
△
One of twenty-five copies printed on Japanese vellum.

LANDOR (ROBERT EYRES) [*Selections.*]
—— Robert Eyres Landor. Selections from his poetry and prose. With an introduction biographical & critical by Eric Partridge. [With a portrait.] pp. 286. *Fanfrolico Press: London,* 1927. 8°. **012273**. b. **19**.

LANDOR (ROBERT EYRES) [*Selections.*]
—— Selections from Robert Landor. Edited by Eric Partridge. pp. 176. *Fanfrolico Press: London,* 1927. 8°. **012273**. b. **18**.

LINDSAY (JACK)
—— Helen Comes of Age. Three plays (in verse). pp. 221. *Fanfrolico Press: London,* 1927. 4°. **11781**. i. **24**.

LINDSAY (JACK) Marino Faliero. (A tragedy [in verse.) pp. 104. *Fanfrolico Press: London,* 1927. 4°. C. **98**. f. **8**.

PETRONIUS ARBITER (TITUS) [*English.*]
—— The Complete Works of Gaius Petronius done into English by Jack Lindsay. With one hundred illustrations by Norman Lindsay. Comprising The Satyricon and Poems. pp. viii. 151. *Franfrolico Press: London,* [1927]. 4°.
Cup. **803**. f. **5**.
Privately printed for sale to subscribers only.

PROPERTIUS (SEXTUS)
—— Propertius in Love. [Selections.] Done into English verse . . . by Jack Lindsay. With XVIII illustrations by Norman Lindsay. fol. lxxxviii. *Fanfrolico Press: London,* 1927. fol. C. **99**. l. **13**.
One of an edition of 60 copies.

TOM, *Mad.*
—— Loving Mad Tom. Bedlamite verses of the XVI and XVII centuries. With five illustrations by Norman Lindsay. Foreword by Robert Graves. The texts edited, with notes, by Jack Lindsay, *etc. London: Fanfrolico Press,* 1927. C. **123**. ff. **14**.
pp. 110. 29 cm. △

BEDDOES (THOMAS LOVELL) [*Collections.*]
—— The Complete Works of Thomas Lovell Beddoes. Edited, with a memoir, by Sir Edmund Gosse, and decorated by the " Dance of Death " of Hans Holbein. [With a portrait.] pp. xxxv. 590. *Fanfrolico Press: London* 1928. 8°. **12271**. i. **19**.
No. 39 of an edition of 75 copies.

ELIOT (JOHN) *Translator*.

—— The Parlement of Pratlers. A series of Elizabethan dialogues and monologues . . . extracted from Ortho-epeia Gallica, *etc.* (Edited by Jack Lindsay and illustrated by Hal Collins.) pp. 119. *Fanfrolico Prrss: London*, 1928. 8°. C. **99**. e. **40**.
One of an edition of 75 copies.

FANFROLICO PRESS.

—— Fanfrolicana, June 1928. Being a statement of the aims of the Fanfrolico Press both typographical and aesthetic with a complete bibliography and specimen passages and illustrations from the books. pp. 36. *Fanfrolico Press: London*, 1928. 8°. Cup. **502**. c. **11**.

LINDSAY (JACK)

—— Dionysos. Nietzsche contra Nietzsche. An essay in lyrical philosophy, *etc.* [With plates.] pp. xi. 243. *Fanfrolico Press: London*, [1928.] 4°. **8485**. ff. **16**

LINDSAY (JACK) Inspiration. An anthology of utterances by creative minds defining the creative act and its lyrical basis in life. Edited by J. Lindsay. pp. 124. *Fanfrolico Press: London*, 1928. 8°. **012305**. m. **45**.

LINDSAY (NORMAN ALFRED WILLIAM)

—— Hyperborea. Two fantastic travel essays. [With illustrations.] pp. 27. *Fanfrolico Press: London*, 1928. 4°. Cup. **503**. f. **4**.

MACCRAE (HUGH) Satyrs and Sunlight: being the collected poetry of Hugh McCrae. Illustrated and decorated by Norman Lindsay. With an introduction by Thomas Earp. pp. xix. 176. *Fanfrolico Press: London*, 1928. 4°. C. **98**. gg. **15**.

NIETZSCHE (FRIEDRICH WILHELM)

—— [Der Antichrist.] The Antichrist . . . A new version in English by P. R. Stephensen. With illustrations by Norman Lindsay. *Fanfrolico Press: London*, [1928.] fol. C. **103**. k. **6**.

PERIODICAL PUBLICATIONS.—*London*.

—— The London Aphrodite. Edited by Jack Lindsay & P. R. Stephensen. no. 1–6. Aug. 1928—July 1929. *London*, 1928, 29. 25 cm. P.P. **5938**. ban.
△

SAPPHO. [*English*.]

A Homage to Sappho. Made by Norman and Jack Lindsay. [Poems, embodying translations of the fragments by J. Lindsay, illustrated with fifteen etchings by N. Lindsay.] pp. 64. *Fanfrolico Press: London*, 1928. 4°. C. **100**. a. **5**.
One of an edition of 70 copies, privately printed.

SKELTON (JOHN) *Poet Laureate*.

—— The Tunning of Elynour Rumming . . . With decorations from drawings . . . by Pearl Binder. pp. 46. *Fanfrolico Press: London*, 1928. 4°. C. **100**. a. **15**.

ARISTOPHANES, *the Poet*. [*Ecclesiazusae.—English*.]

—— Women in Parliament by Aristophanes. Done into English by Jack Lindsay. With illustrations by Norman Lindsay and a foreword by Edgell Rickword. pp. xiv. 59. *Fanfrolico Press: London*, 1929. fol. C. **100**. l. **9**.
For sale to subscribers only.

BYRON (GEORGE GORDON NOEL) *Baron Byron*. [*Manfred*.]

—— Manfred. A tragedy . . . Decorated by Frederick Carter, with an introduction by the artist. *London: issued for the subscribers of the Fanfrolico Press*, 1929. C. **100**. k. **17**.

Pages not numbered. 28 cm. △
One of an edition of thirty copies.

CATULLUS (CAIUS VALERIUS) [*Works.—English*.]

—— The Complete Poetry of Gaius Catullus, translated by Jack Lindsay, with decorations engraved on wood by Lionel Ellis, and an essay by the translator, *etc.* *Fanfrolico Press: London*, [1929.] 8°. C. **98**. f. **20**.

HERODAS.

—— The Mimiambs of Herondas. Translated [in verse] by Jack Lindsay. Decorated by Alan Odle. With a foreword by Brian Penton. *Fanfrolico Press: London*, [1929.] 4°. C. **100**. k. **19**.

LINDSAY (JACK)

—— William Blake. Creative will and the poetic image . . . Second edition, enlarged. pp. 89. *Fanfrolico Press: London*, 1929. 8°. **11853**. s. **15**.

LINDSAY (NORMAN ALFRED WILLIAM) ——————

Madam Life's Lovers. A human narrative embodying a philosophy of the artist in dialogue form, *etc.* pp. 188. *Fanfrolico Press: London*, [1929.] 8°. **08416**. dd. **5**.

THEOCRITUS. [*English*.]

—— Theocritos. The Complete Poems, translated by Jack Lindsay, with wood cuts by Lionel Ellis and an introduction by Edward Hutton. pp. xxiv. 162. *Fanfrolico Press: London*, [1929.] 4°. C. **98**. h. **29**.
One of an edition of thirty copies.

AUSONIUS (DECIMUS MAGNUS) [*Smaller Collections*.]

—— Patchwork Quilt. [Selected poems.] (Done into English by Jack Lindsay. With decorations by Edward Bawden.) *Fanfrolico Press: London*, [1930.] 8°. **11386**. gg. **13**.

BOTTOMLEY (GORDON)

—— Festival Preludes. (Poems.) *Fanfrolico Press: London*, 1930. 8°. **11642**. eee. **44**.

DE LOCRE (ELZA)

—— Older than Earth. Record of a lyrical experience. [In verse.] *Fanfrolico Press: London*, 1930. 8°. **11642**. eee. **45**.

DONNE (JOHN) *Dean of St. Paul's*.

A Defence of Women for their Inconstancy & their Paintings . . . With five decorations by Norman Lindsay. *Fanfrolico Press: London*, [1930.] 8°. **08416**. ff. **73**.

FLEAS.

—— Fleas in Amber. Verses and one fable in prose on the philosophy of vermin. A miscellany. *Fanfrolico Press: London*, 1930. 8°. **11662**. e. **7**.

HOMER. [*Hymns.—English*.]

—— Homer's hymns to Aphrodite. Translated by Jack Lindsay. [*London:*] *Fanfrolico Press*, [1930]. C. **100**. c. **2**.

Pages not numbered : plates. 27 cm. △

LINDSAY (JACK) Hereward. A play, *etc.* pp. 114. *Fanfrolico Press: London & Aylesbury,* [1930.] 8°.
11781. i. 34.

LINDSAY (JACK) The Passionate Neatherd. A lyric sequence. pp. 63. *Fanfrolico Press: London,* [1930.] 8°. **11644. h. 54.**
One of 50 copies printed on Japanese vellum.

LINDSAY (PHILIP) Morgan in Jamaica. (Being an account . . . of the latter days of Sir Henry Morgan . . . With a poem panegyrical by Mr. Jack Lindsay and some portraits by Mr. Raymond Lindsay.) *Fanfrolico Press: London,* 1930. fol. **10825. f. 45.**

MORRIS (WILLIAM) *Poet.* Guenevere. Two poems . . . The Defence of Guenevere, and King Arthur's Tomb. With eight decorations by Dante Gabriel Rossetti and a foreword by Gordon Bottomley. *Fanfrolico Press: London,* 1930. 8°. **11642. eee. 43.**

STANHOPE (PHILIP) *2nd Earl of Chesterfield.*
—— Philip Stanhope, second Earl of Chesterfield: his correspondence with various ladies, among whom is notably Barbara Villiers, later Lady Castlemaine & Duchess of Cleveland, and letters exchanged with Sir Charles Sedley, John Dryden, Charles Cotton, Mr. Bates, &c., *etc. Fanfrolico Press: London,* [1930.] 4°. **10906. i. 18.**

TOURNEUR (CYRIL) [*Collections.*]
—— The Works of Cyril Tourneur. Edited by Allardyce Nicoll. With decorations by Frederick Carter. pp. ix. 344. *Fanfrolico Press: London,* [1930.] 8°. **11774. k. 18.**

FANTASY PRESS, Eynsham, Oxon, *etc.*

HALL (DONALD)
—— Exile. The Newdigate Prize Poem, 1952. *Fantasy Press: Eynsham,* [1952?] 8°. **Cup. 510. cab. 6.**
Privately printed for the author by Oscar Mellor. With the author's signature.

GUNN (THOM)
—— Fighting Terms. Poems. pp. 44. *Fantasy Press: Swinford,* 1954. 8°. **Cup.510.cab.2.**

MAC BETH (GEORGE)
—— A Form of Words. Poems. pp. 25. *Fantasy Press: Swinford,* 1954. 4°. **Cup.510.cab.3.**

OVIDIUS NASO (PUBLIUS) [*Amores.—English.*]
—— The Elegies of Ovid. From the translation by Christopher Marlowe. With line drawings by Oscar Mellor. (Text by C. F. Tucker Brooke.) pp. 112. *Fantasy Press: Swinford,* 1954. 8°. **Cup.510.cab.1.**

DAVIE (DONALD)
—— Brides of Reason. [Poems.] pp. 39. *Fantasy Press: Eynsham,* 1955. 8°. **Cup.510.cab.7.**

TOMLINSON (ALFRED CHARLES)
—— The necklace, *etc. Oxford: Fantasy Press,* [1955]. **Cup. 510. cab. 8.**
pp. 28. 24 cm. △
Poems.

AMIS (KINGSLEY WILLIAM)
—— The Evans Country. (Poems.) pp. 8. *Fantasy Press: Oxford,* 1962. 8°. **Cup. 510. cab. 4.**

WILLIAMS (ROBERT COLEMAN)
—— Ladycross. Poems. pp. 33. *Fantasy Press: Oxford,* 1962. 8°. **Cup. 510. cab. 5.**

FAVIL PRESS, London

ENGLAND.—*English Bookplate Society.*
—— The Bookplate. Edited by James Guthrie, *etc.* no. 1–3. Sept. 1920—Sept. 1921. *Flansham,* 1920, 21. 26 cm. & 29 cm.
△

—— New series. no. 1; supplementary number. Dec. 1922; June 1923. *Flansham,* 1922, 23. 26 cm.
△

—— New series. no. 1–3. July 1924—July 1925. [*London,*] 1924, 25. 24 cm.
△

—— New series. no. 1. *London.* [1927]. 24 cm.
Ac. 9672. c.
△

From 1920 to 1923 published at the Pear Tree Press and from 1924 to 1925 at the Favil Press.

SAINSBURY (HESTER)
—— Holy Women, and other poems & wood cuts. *Favil Press: London,* 1921. 8°. **11651. cc. 48.**

SAMSON (HILLEL) A.D. 1583.
—— Sir Humphrey Gilbert. A record & a surmise. pp. 41. *Favil Press: Kensington,* 1921. 8°. **Cup. 510. acb. 1.**

SITWELL (*Sir* OSBERT) *Bart.*
—— At the House of Mrs. Kinfoot. Consisting of four satires by Osbert Sitwell. With two drawings by William Roberts. pp. 14. *Favil Press: Kensington,* 1921. 8°.
Cup. 401. c. 23.
No. 56 of an edition of 101 copies, signed by the author.

SITWELL (*Sir* SACHEVERELL) *Bart.*
—— Doctor Donne and Gargantua. First (–Third) canto, *etc. London: Favil Press,* 1921. **11633. f. 56.**
3 pt. 19–26 cm. △
Privately printed. Pt. 2 is one of an edition of thirty-five copies; pt. 3 is one of an edition of sixty-five copies, and bears the imprint "Stratford-upon-Avon: Shakespeare Head Press".

DAVIS (ROSAMUND) Rambling Reveries, *etc.* [Poems.] pp. 31. *Favil Press: London,* 1922. 8°. **011648. g. 109.**

FRENCH (CECIL) *Writer of Verse.* Between Sun and Moon. Poems and wood-cuts. pp. 47. *Favil Press: London,* 1922. 8°. **11646. h. 25.**

ORAC, *pseud.* How & Why. [Poems.] By Orac. pp. 27. *Privately printed for the Author at the Favil Press: Kensington,* 1922. 8°. **011648. g. 120.**

SAINSBURY (GEOFFREY)
—— Polarity. [Philosophical essays.] pp. 48. *For the Author: London,* 1922. 8°. **08463. e. 56.**

SITWELL (*Dame* EDITH) *D.B.E.*

—— Facade, *etc.* [Poems.] pp. 27. *Favil Press:* London, 1922. 8°. Cup. 510. acb. 2.
Privately printed.

HILL (FRANCES ELLERTON)

—— Before the Dawn. Ten poems and three drawings. pp. 20. *Favil Press:* London, 1923. 8°. 011649. i. 119.

MONTAGU (*Right Hon.* EDWIN SAMUEL) [*Appendix.*]

—— Edwin S. Montagu. Born February 6th, 1879. Died November 15th, 1924. [Obituary notices. With a portrait.] *Favil Press:* [London, 1925.] 4°. 10823. k. 45.

PALMER (AMY CHRISTINA) *Lady.*

—— The Invisible Betrothal. [Tales.] pp. 55. *Privately printed for the Author:* [London,] 1925. 8°. 12646. i. 6.

HOLLAND (GRAHAM MICHAEL STEWART)

—— Poems by Michael Holland. [With a portrait.] pp. 21. *Privately printed:* London, 1926. 8°. Cup. 510. acb. 5.

MARCH EVENING.

—— March Evening and other Verses. [By L. A. G. Strong.] *Favil Press:* [London,] 1932. 8°. Cup. 510. acb. 3.
No. 9 of an edition of 100 copies issued as a Christmas greeting for 1932. Author's presentation copy to Seumas O'Sullivan.

STRONG (LEONARD ALFRED GEORGE)

—— The Nice Cup O'Tea. [A tale, issued as a Christmas greeting for 1938.] *Favil Press:* [London,] 1938. 8°. Cup. 510. acb. 4.
With a card bearing the signature Sylvia and Leonard Strong inserted.

BIBLE.—*Judith.* [*English.*]

—— Judith the Widow of Bethulia. The drawings and script of Richard Ziegler. [An abridgment of the Book of Judith, in the text of the Authorised Version.] *Dennis Dobson:* London, 1946. 4°. C. 103. i. 11.
Lithographed.

KEOWN (ANNA GORDON) [*Collections.*]

—— Collected Poems ... Four wood-engravings and decorations by Guy Worsdell. pp. 71. *Caravel Press:* London, 1953. 8°. Cup. 510. age. 4.

EVELYN (CECIL JOHN ALVIN)

—— Pandora. [Poems.] pp. 195. *Favil Press:* London, 1954. 8°. 11659. cc. 16.

LEWIS (CECIL DAY)

—— The newborn. D.M.B. 29th April, 1957. [*London:*] *Favil Press of Kensington,* [1957]. Cup. 510. acb. 16.
Pages not numbered. △

HARWOOD (ANTHONY)

—— Swan Songs, and other poems. pp. 53. *Favil Press:* London, 1961. 8°. Cup. 510. acb. 6.

FLORENCE PRESS, London

LORRIS (GUILLAUME DE) The Romaunt of the Rose [by Guillaume de Lorris and Jehan de Meung], rendered out of the French into English by Geoffrey Chaucer. Illustrated by Keith Henderson and Norman Wilkinson. pp. 108. *Chatto & Windus:* London, 1908. 8°. K.T.C. 107. b. 16.

ALBERTINI (FRANCESCO DEGLI)

—— Memoriale di molte statue et picture sono nella inclyta cipta di Florentia per mano di sculptori et pictori excellenti moderni et antiqui tracto dalla propria copia di messer Francesco Albertini prete fiorentino anno Domini 1510, *etc.* pp. 23. *Chatto & Windus:* [London,] 1909. 8°. K.T.C. 33. a. 12.

FRANCIS [BERNARDONI], *of Assisi, Saint.* [*Appendix.* *I Fioretti di San Francesco.*] The Little Flowers of S. Francis. Translated from the Italian by T. W. Arnold. (With illustrations reproduced from a manuscript in the Laurentian Library, Florence.) pp. xv. 135. pl. xxix. *Published for the Florence Press by Chatto & Windus:* London, 1909. 4°. K.T.C. 37. b. 15.

SWINBURNE (ALGERNON CHARLES) Songs before Sunrise. pp. ix. 209. *For the Florence Press, by Chatto & Windus:* London, 1909. 4°. K.T.C. 27. b. 6.

CARMAN (WILLIAM BLISS)

—— Sappho. One hundred lyrics by Bliss Carman. [With an introduction signed: C. G. D. Roberts.] *London: published for the Florence Press by Chatto & Windus,* 1910. 11686. k. 33.

pp. xviii, 116. 19 cm. △

STEVENSON (ROBERT LOUIS) Virginibus Puerisque and other papers. (With twelve illustrations in colour after designs by Norman Wilkinson.) pp. 120. *Chatto & Windus:* London, 1910. 4°. 12352. y. 13.

BLAKE (WILLIAM) *Artist.*

—— The marriage of Heaven and Hell and A song of liberty . . . With an introduction by Francis Griffin Stokes. *London: published for the Florence Press by Chatto & Windus,* 1911. 11646. g. 64.
pp. 79. 19 cm. △

BOCCACCIO (GIOVANNI) [*Eclogae.*]

—— Boccaccio's Olympia. Edited, with an English rendering, by Israel Gollancz. *Lat. & Eng.* pp. 56. *Chatto & Windus:* London, 1913. 4°. K.T.C. 101. a. 18.

STEVENSON (ROBERT LOUIS) Poems. pp. xvi. 399. *Chatto & Windus; Longmans & Co.:* London, 1913. 8°. K.T.C. 101. a. 1.

DELSTANCHE (ALBERT)

—— The Little Towns of Flanders. Twelve woodcuts by A. Delstanche. With notes by the artist, and a prefatory letter from Émile Verhaeren. (Translated from the French by Geoffrey Whitworth.) pp. 56. *Published for the Florence Press by Chatto & Windus:* London, 1915. 4°. K.T.C. 28. b. 22.

KEATS (JOHN) [*Poetical Works.*]

       The Poems of John Keats, arranged in chronological order with a preface by Sidney Colvin. 2 vol. *Chatto & Windus: London*, 1915. 4°.

       K.T.C.103.b.11.

SHELLEY (PERCY BYSSHE) [*Poetical Works.*]

—— The lyrical poems and translations (The dramatic poems—The narrative poems) of Percy Bysshe Shelley, arranged in chronological order with a preface by C. H. Herford. *London: Chatto & Windus at the Florence Press*, 1918 [1917]–27.   Tab. 501. a. 10.

   4 bk. 23 cm.   △

The "Lyrical poems" only are printed on large paper.

BLAKE (WILLIAM) *Artist.* [*Collected Poems.*]

—— The Poems of William Blake. Edited and arranged with a preface by John Sampson. pp. xxxviii. 343. *Florence Press, for Chatto & Windus: London*, 1921. 8°.

       K.T.C. 8. a. 26.

STEVENSON (ROBERT LOUIS) Virginibus Puerisque, and other papers . . . Illustrated after designs by Norman Wilkinson. pp. vi. 193. *Chatto & Windus: London*, 1921. 8°.   012352. ee. 12.

BYRON (GEORGE GORDON NOEL) *Baron Byron.* [*Smaller Collections.*]

—— Poems of Lord Byron. Selected and arranged in chronological order, with a preface, by H. J. C. Grierson. pp. xxx. 397. F.P. *Chatto & Windus: London*, 1923. 8°.   11642. g. 47.

Printed at the Florence Press.

MILTON (JOHN) [*Poetical Works.*] The Poems of John Milton ... Arranged in chronological order with a preface by H. J. C. Grierson. 2 vol. *Chatto & Windus: London*, 1925* . 8°.   2302.g.7.

HUXLEY (ALDOUS LEONARD) Essays New and Old. pp. viii. 257. *Chatto & Windus: London*, 1926. 8°.   012352. i. 6.

FLYING FAME, London

FLYING FAME. [Booklets, leaflets and sheets, issued by "Flying Fame": being short pieces in prose and verse by Ralph Hodgson, Lovat Fraser, Holbrook Jackson, Oliver Davies, James Stephens and Richard Honeywood. Illustrated with woodcuts by Lovat Fraser.] *London*, 1913. 8° & 4°.

       L.R.271.b.22.

Nearly all the pieces are in duplicate, one copy of each having the illustrations coloured; the coloured copies of the booklets are on large paper.

FOREST PRESS, Breamore

MACFALL (CHAMBERS HALDANE COOKE)

—— The Art of Hesketh Hubbard. [With twenty-six plates.] pp. 87. *Morland Press: London*, 1924. 4°.   8760. cc. 21.

HUBBARD (ERIC HESKETH) The Gateways of Salisbury Cathedral Close. With five colour prints by the author, etc. *Forest Press: Breamore*, 1925. fol.

No. 72 of an edition of 100 copies. L.R. 39. d. 2.

HUBBARD (ERIC HESKETH) Colour Block Print Making from Linoleum Blocks. pp. xv. 211. *Forest Press: Breamore*, 1927. 8°. 07943. bb. 32.

FORTUNE PRESS, London

HARRIS (FRANK) *Editor of the "Fortnightly Review."* New Preface to "The Life and Confessions of Oscar Wilde." By F. Harris and Lord Alfred Douglas. pp. 55. *Fortune Press: London*, 1925. 8°.   010856. b. 31.

HARRIS (FRANK) *Editor of the "Fortnightly Review."*

—— [Another copy.] New preface to "The life and confessions of Oscar Wilde". 1925. 010856. d. 35.

        △

Large paper.

PLATO. [*Symposium.—English.*] Plato's Symposium ... Newly translated by Francis Birrell & Shane Leslie. [Revised by R. G. Bury.] pp. 130. *Fortune Press: London*, [1925.] 8°. Cup.510.as.6.

CLELAND (JOHN) *Miscellaneous Writer.*

—— Memoirs of a coxcomb. *London: Fortune Press*, 1926.   Cup. 510. as. 5.

   pp. 273. 23 cm.   △
Printed at Dijon.

DOUGLAS (*Lord* ALFRED BRUCE) The Collected Satires of Lord Alfred Douglas. pp. vi. 61. *Fortune Press: London; Dijon* printed, 1926. fol.

   Cup.510.as.9.

APULEIUS (LUCIUS) *Madaurensis.* [*Asinus Aureus.—Selections.—English.*]

—— Cupid and Psyches. The excellent narration of their marriage translated into English by William Adlington ... 1566. *Fortune Press: London*, 1927. 8°. Cup. 510. as. 1.

No. 16 of an edition of which only 100 copies were printed.

B., A.

—— Covent Garden drollery. (Collected by A. B.) Edited by the Rev. Montague Summers. *London: Fortune Press*, 1927.   Cup. 510. as. 11.

   pp. vi, 123 : plate ; illus. 20 cm.   △

CICERO (MARCUS TULLIUS) [*De Republica.—Somnium Scipionis.—Latin and English.*]

—— The Dream of Scipio. Translated from the sixth book of the de Republica of Cicero, together with the Latin text, introduction & notes by Edward Henry Blakeney. pp. 48. *Fortune Press: London*, 1927. 4°. Cup.510.as.13.

HARRIS (FRANK) *Editor of the "Fortnightly Review."*

—— New Preface to "The Life and Confessions of Oscar Wilde." By F. Harris and Lord Alfred Douglas. (Second edition.) pp. 63. *Fortune Press: London*, 1927. 8°.   Cup. 363. e. 42.

SECUNDUS (JOANNES)
[*Basia.*]

—— Kisses, being the Basia of Iohannes Secundus rendered into English verse by Thomas Stanley, 1647. *Fortune Press: London*, 1927. fol. Cup. 510. as. 19.

SHADWELL (THOMAS) *Poet Laureate*. The Complete Works of Thomas Shadwell. Edited by Montague Summers. [With a portrait.] 5 vol. *Fortune Press: London*, 1927. 8°. **Cup.510.as.10.**
One of 90 copies printed on hand-made paper.

SINISTRARI DE AMENO (LUDOVICUS MARIA) Demoniality... Translated... with introduction and notes, by the Rev. Montague Summers. pp. xliii. 127. **F. P.** *Fortune Press: London*, [1927.] 8°. **Cup.510.as.12.**

CROSLAND (THOMAS WILLIAM HODGSON)
—— Last Poems. pp. 115. *Fortune Press: London; Bruges* printed, 1928. 8°. **Cup.510.as.14.**

DACRE, afterwards BYRNE (CHARLOTTE)
—— Zofloya; or, the Moor... With an introduction by ... Montague Summers. [With a portrait.] pp. xxvii. 264. **F.P.** *Fortune Press: London*, [1928.] 8°. **Cup.510.as.3.**

LOUŸS (PIERRE) Aphrodite. A novel of ancient morals... With an introduction by Shane Leslie. pp. xix. 262. *Fortune Press: London; Liége* printed, 1928. 8°, **Cup.510.as.16.**

LOUŸS (PIERRE)
—— The Songs of Bilitis, *etc.* pp. x. 163. *Fortune Press: London*, [1928.] 8°. Cup. 510. as. 15.

LOUŸS (PIERRE)
—— The Twilight of the Nymphs... Translated by Phillis Duveen, *etc.* [With plates.] pp. 105. *Fortune Press: London; Liége* printed, 1928. 8°. Cup. 510. as. 4.

MAUGE (GILBERT) *pseud.* [i.e. EDMÉE DE LA ROCHEFOUCAULD.]
—— [Fonction d'X.] The Unknown Quantity... Translated ... by Shane Leslie. pp. xiii. 68. *Fortune Press: London*, [1928.] 8°. **Cup.510.as.8.**

PERRAULT (CHARLES) Histories or Tales of Past Times told by Mother Goose, with Morals... Englished by G. M. Gent. [i.e. Guy Miege?] [Reprinted from the twelfth edition of 1802.] pp. 108. *Fortune Press: London*, 1928. 8°. **Cup.510.as.2.**

SUMMERS (ALPHONSUS JOSEPH-MARY AUGUSTUS MONTAGUE)
—— Essays in Petto. [With a portrait.] pp. ix. 183. **F.P.** *Fortune Press: London*, [1928.] 8°. Cup. 510. as. 7.

DE SHANE (BRIAN) De Sade. Being a series of wounds, inflicted with brush and pen, upon sadistic wolves garbed in masochists' wool. [The text by B. de Shane. The plates by Beresford Egan.] **F.P.** *Fortune Press: London*, [1929.] 4°. C. 98. gg. 20.

LOUŸS (PIERRE)
—— The Adventures of King Pausole... Translated by Charles Hope Lumley. Drawings by Beresford Egan. pp. 312. *Fortune Press: London*, 1929. 8°. Cup. 510. as. 17.
One of 75 copies printed on handmade paper.

LUCIAN, *of Samosata.* [*Dialogues.—Collections.—English.*]
—— Cyprian Masques... Translated [from the French version of Pierre Louÿs] by Ruby Melvill. Drawings by Beresford Egan. pp. xxi. 137. *Fortune Press: London*, [1929.] 8°. Cup. 510. as. 18.

GREEK ANTHOLOGY.
—— Strato's Boyish Muse. (The twelfth book of the Greek Anthology.) Now first translated wholly into English. [The introduction signed: Ion Ionicos. With etchings by Jean de Bosschère.] *London: Fortune Press*, [1932]. Cup. 510. asb. 1.

pp. 79: plates. 23 cm. △

PETRONIUS ARBITER (TITUS) [*English.*]
—— The Satyricon of Petronius. The only complete translation into English, with introduction and notes. pp. lx. 222. *Fortune Press: London*, [1933.] 8°. Cup.800.f.52.

JOHNSON (STOWERS)
—— The Mundane Tree. Fiftyone poems. [With a portrait.] pp. 488. *Fortune Press: London*, 1947. 8°. Cup. 402. g. 17.

FOUNTAIN PRESS, New York

CABELL (JAMES BRANCH)
—— Sonnets from Antan with an editorial note by J. B. Cabell. *Fountain Press: New York*, 1929. 8°. Cup. 510. pb. 3.

HUXLEY (ALDOUS LEONARD)
—— Arabia Infelix, and other poems. pp. 35. *Fountain Press: New York; Chatto & Windus: London*, 1929. 8°. Cup. 510. pl. 2.

MILNE (ALAN ALEXANDER)
—— The Secret, and other stories. pp. 70. *Fountain Press: New York; Methuen & Co.: London*, 1929. 8°. Cup. 510. pk. 2.

WOOLF (VIRGINIA)
—— A Room of one's own. [An essay on women in relation to literature.] pp. 159. *Fountain Press: New York; Hogarth Press: London*, 1929. 8°. Cup. 503. c. 21.

YEATS (WILLIAM BUTLER)
—— The Winding Stair. pp. 25. **F.P.** *Fountain Press: New York*, 1929. 8°. 011686. h. 89.

ELIOT (THOMAS STEARNS)
—— Ash-Wednesday. [A poem.] pp. 28.   *Fountain Press: New York; Faber & Faber: London; printed in Great Britain*, 1930. 8°.   **011644. g. 145.**

HUXLEY (ALDOUS LEONARD)
—— Brief Candles. [Short stories.] pp. 320.   *Fountain Press: New York; Chatto & Windus: London*, 1930. 8°.   **012603. bb. 23.**

STEPHENS (JAMES) *Author of "The Crock of Gold."* Theme and Variations. pp. 31.   F. P.   *Fountain Press : New York ;* printed in England, 1930. 8°.   **11640. cc. 3.**

WOLFE (HUMBERT)
—— Homage to Meleager. [Translations from Greek poems.] *Gr. & Eng.* pp. vii. 129.   *Fountain Press: New York;* Oxford printed, 1930. 8°.   **11340. de. 59.**

HUXLEY (ALDOUS LEONARD) Music at Night, and other essays. pp. 146.   *Fountain Press : New York*, 1931. 8°.   **Cup.510.pd.4.**

FULCRUM PRESS, Strand-on-the-Green, Middx.

BIBLE.—*Daniel.—Selections.* [*English.*]
—— Nebuchadnezzar and the Story of the Fiery Furnace. From the Authorised Version of the Holy Bible, *etc.* *Fulcrum Press: Strand on the Green*, [1929.] 8°.   **03051. ee. 23.**

PLATO. [*Lysis.—English.*]
—— Lysis. A dialogue of Plato. (Translated by K. A. Matthews & illustrated by Lynton Lamb.)   *Fulcrum Press: Strand on the Green*, 1930. 8°.   **C. 99. f. 37.**

GABERBOCCHUS PRESS, London

AESOP. [*Adaptations, Imitations, etc.*]
—— The Eagle & the Fox. The Fox & the Eagle. Two semantically symmetrical versions followed by a revised application. Drawings by Franciszka Themerson. (After the translation by Samuel Croxall.) pp. 33.   *Gaberbocchus Press: London*, [1949.] 4°.   **C. 103. b. 14.**

AESOP. [*English.—Adaptations, Imitations, etc.*]
—— [Another copy.] The Eagle & the Fox, the Fox & the Eagle, *etc.* London, [1949.] 4°.   **Cup. 510. com. 1.**

CROSBY GAIGE, New York

O'FLAHERTY (LIAM)
—— The Fairy Goose, and two other stories. pp. 58.   *Crosby Gaige: New York*, 1927. 8°.   **012603. f. 48.**

ALDINGTON (RICHARD)
—— Fifty Romance Lyric Poems. Now collected and translated by R. Aldington. pp. xxiv. 240.   *Crosby Gaige : New York*, 1928. 8°.   **11427. i. 8.**

CONRAD (JOSEPH) [*Letters.*]
—— **Letters. Joseph Conrad to Richard Curle. Edited with an introduction and notes by R. C. (Richard Curle.) [With a portrait.]** *Crosby Gaige: New York*, 1928. 8°.   **Ashley 2962.**

CONRAD (JOSEPH)
[Tales of Unrest.]
—— The Sisters. (A story published in " Tales of Unrest.") With an introduction by Ford Madox Ford. pp. 69.   *Crosby Gaige: New York*, 1928. 8°.   **Cup.510.pc.14.**

DE LA MARE (WALTER JOHN) [*Single Works.*]
—— At First Sight. A novel. pp. 142.   *Crosby Gaige: New York*, 1928. 8°.   **Cup. 510. pc. 3.**

E., A.
—— Midsummer Eve. [Poems.] By A. E. [i.e. G. W. Russell.] *Crosby Gaige: New York*, 1928. 8°.   **Cup. 510. pc. 5.**

GOR'KY (MAKSIM) *pseud.* [i.e. ALEKSEI MAKSIMOVICH PESHKOV.] [*Single Works.*]
[Воспоминания.]
—— Reminiscences of Leonid Andreyev ... Translated ... by Katherine Mansfield and S. S. Koteliansky. pp. 84. *Crosby Gaige: New York*, 1928. 8°.   **X. 908/4272.**

JOYCE (JAMES AUGUSTINE ALOYSIUS)
Anna Livia Plurabelle... With a preface by Padraic Colum. pp. xviii. 60. *Crosby Gaige : New York*, 1928. 8°. **012601. bb. 49.**

O'FLAHERTY (LIAM)
—— Red Barbara. and other stories . . . Illustrations by Cecil Salkeld. pp. 49.   *Crosby Gaige: New York; Faber & Gwyer: London*, 1928. 8°.   **012611. k. 110.**

SANDBURG (CARL)
—— Good Morning, America. pp. x. 251.   *Crosby Gaige: New York*, 1928. 8°.   **X. 909/3162.**

STRACHEY (GILES LYTTON)

—— Elizabeth and Essex.　　*New York: Crosby Gaige; London: Chatto & Windus,* 1928.　　**10807. df. 2.**

　　pp. 244 : plates : ports.　23 cm.　　△

WOLFE (HUMBERT)

—— The Craft of Verse.　Oxford poetry essay.　pp. 45. *Crosby Gaige: New York,* 1928.　4º.　　Cup. **510. pd. 3.**

WOOLF (VIRGINIA)

—— Orlando.　A biography.　[With plates.]　pp. 333.　*Crosby Gaige: New York,* 1928.　8º.　　Cup. **503. c. 20.**

HARDY (THOMAS) O.M.　[*Miscellaneous Prose.*]

—— Old Mrs. Chundle.　A short story.　　*New York: Crosby Gaige; Boston: printed by D. B. Updike, the Merrymount Press,* 1929.　　Cup. **510. sac. 10.**

　　pp. 26.　22 cm.　　△

MOORE (GEORGE) *Novelist.*

—— Letters from George Moore to Ed. Dujardin, 1866–1922.　[Translated from the French, with an introduction, by John Eglinton.]　pp. 116.　　*Crosby Gaige: New York,* 1929.　8º.　　**10906. g. 15.**

STEPHENS (JAMES) *Author of " The Crock of Gold."*

—— Julia Elizabeth.　A comedy in one act.　pp. 24.　*Crosby Gaige: New York,* 1929.　8º.　　Cup. **510. pd. 2.**

TOMLINSON (HENRY MAJOR)

—— Thomas Hardy.　(Lithograph drawn by Zhenya Gay.)　pp. xxx.　*Crosby Gaige: New York,* 1929.　8º.　　Cup. **502. b. 24.**

GARDEN CITY PRESS, Letchworth, Herts.

MASEFIELD (JOHN EDWARD)

—— Good Friday.　A play in verse.　pp. 77.　*Garden City Press: Letchworth,* 1916.　8º.　　Cup. **500. a. 30.**

MASEFIELD (JOHN EDWARD)

—— The Locked Chest.　The Sweeps of Ninety-Eight.　Two plays in prose.　pp. 100.　*Garden City Press: Letchworth,* 1916.　8º.　　**11773. h. 12.**

MASEFIELD (JOHN EDWARD)

　　　　　　　　Sonnets and Poems.　pp. 51. *Garden City Press: Letchworth,* 1916.　8º.　　**11646. h. 53.**

SYNGE (JOHN MILLINGTON)　[*Appendix.*]

　　　　　　　John M. Synge : a few personal recollections with biographical notes.　[By John Masefield.]　pp. 32.　　*Garden City Press: Letchworth,* 1916.　8º.　　**010826. h. 13.**

GARSWOOD PRESS, Leicester

BOORDE (ANDREW)

—— The Wisdom of Andrew Boorde.　(An abridged version of The Dyetary of Helth.)　Edited with an introduction and notes by H. Edmund Poole.　Illustrated by A. E. Christopherson.　pp. 63.　　*Edgar Backus: Leicester,* 1936.　8º.　　**7383. t. 32.**

GAUTHIER (August), Press of New York

DREISER (THEODORE)

—— Epitaph.　A poem . . . Decorations by Robert Fawcett. *Heron Press: New York,* [1929.]　4º.　　**C. 106. k. 10.**

GAZEBO PRESS, Huncote

FELMINGHAM (MICHAEL)

—— Alphabet.　[Linocuts.]　　*Gazebo Press: Huncote,* 1965.　8º.　　Cup. **510. da. 1.**

　　One of an edition of thirty copies.

GEHENNA PRESS, Worcester; Northampton, Mass.

SKELTON (JOHN) *Poet Laureate.*

—— A Poem called the Tunning of Elynour Rummynge, *etc.* (The text from Dyce's edition of 1843.　The illustrations engraved by L. Baskin.)　pp. 34.　　*Gehenna Press: Worcester,* 1953.　fol.　　Cup. **510. nax. 1.**

OWEN (WILFRED EDWARD SALTER)

—— Thirteen Poems . . . With drawings by Ben Shahn [including a portrait].　*Gehenna Press: Northampton, Mass.,* 1956.　fol.　　**C. 104. k. 6.**

BROWNE (Sir THOMAS)

[Certain Miscellany Tracts.]

—— Of Garlands and Coronary or Garland Plants.　Thomas Browne to John Evelyn, Esq., F.R.S.　[No. 2 of "Certain Miscellany Tracts".]　*Printed for the Smith College Museum of Art at the Gehenna Press: Northampton, Mass.,* 1962.　8º.　　Cup. **510. nax. 2.**

KENNEDY (RUTH WEDGWOOD)

—— Four portrait busts by Francesco Laurana.　Photographs by Clarence Kennedy with an introductory biographical essay by Ruth Wedgwood Kennedy.　*Northampton, Mass.: Gehenna Press,* 1962.　　Cup. **510. nax. 5.**

　　Pages not numbered.　25 cm.　(Gehenna essays in art. vol. I.)　　△

　　The plates were printed on Tovil paper, handmade in England.

BURNS (ROBERT) *the Poet.* [*The Jolly Beggars.*]
—— The Jolly beggars, a cantata. Edited by John C. Weston.
[With a portrait by Gillian Lewis and a musical score.]
Gohenna Press: Northampton, Mass., 1963. 4°.
Cup. **510.** nax. **3.**

GEMINI PRESS, Higham, Colchester, Essex

GRAVES (IDA)
—— Epithalamion. A poem . . . With associate wood-
engraving by Blair Hughes-Stanton.   *Gemini Press:*
Higham, Colchester, 1934. fol.   C. **100.** l. **17.**
No. 49 of 50 copies printed on Japanese vellum.

M., H. H.
—— Pastoral, or, Virtue requited. By H.H.M. With wood-
engravings by B.-H.-S. [i.e. Blair Hughes-Stanton.] [A
poem.] pp. 38. *Gemini Press: Higham,* 1935. 8°.
Cup. **502.** e. **6.**

GEORGIAN PRESS, Westport, Conn.

ALLEN (WILLIAM HERVEY)
—— Sarah Simon, Character Atlantean. [A poem.] pp. 71.
Doubleday, Doran & Co.: Garden City, N.Y., 1929. 8°.
Cup. **510.** nak. **1.**

GOLDSMITH (OLIVER) *the Poet.* [*Retaliation.*]
—— Retaliation, *etc.* pp. 23. *Richard W. Ellis: Westport, Ct.,*
1929. 4°.   Cup.**510.**nak.**5.**

STEVENSON (ROBERT LOUIS)
—— The Charity Bazaar. An allegorical dialogue. pp. 11.
Georgian Press: Westport, 1929. 8°. Cup.**510.**nak.**3.**

MACHEN (ARTHUR LLEWELYN JONES)
—— Tom o'Bedlam and his Song. [With the text.] pp. 47.
Apellicon Press: [*Glen Rock, Pa.,*] 1930. 8°.
Cup. **510.** nak. **4.**
With the autograph signature of the author.

O'HIGGINS (HARVEY JARROLD)
—— Alias Walt Whitman. pp. 49.   *Carteret Book Club:*
Newark, N.J., 1930. 8°.   Cup.**510.**nak.**6.**
The date in the colophon is 1929.

VENUS.
[*Pervigilium Veneris.*]
—— The Vigil of Venus. Englished by Joseph Auslander.
[With the Latin text, an introduction, and an essay
" Concerning the Pervigilium Veneris," from Walter
Pater's " Marius the Epicurean."] pp. 31.   *Cheshire*
House: New York, 1931. 8°. Cup.**510.**nak.**2.**

GILLISS PRESS, New York

ANDREWS (WILLIAM LORING)
—— The Old Booksellers of New York, and other papers.
pp. 84. *Gilliss Press: New York,* 1895. 8°.
011899. i. 16.

ANDREWS (WILLIAM LORING)
—— An Essay on the Portraiture of the American Revolu-
tionary War : being an account of a number of the
engraved portraits connected therewith . . . To which is
added an appendix, containing lists of portraits of Revolu-
tionary characters to be found in various . . . publications
. . . Illustrated, *etc.* pp. viii. 100.   *Dodd, Mead & Co.:*
New York, 1896. 8°.   7875. r. 7.

ANDREWS (WILLIAM LORING)
—— New Amsterdam, New Orange, New York. A chrono-
logically arranged account of engraved views of the city
from the first picture published in MDCLI until the year
MDCCC. [With plates.] pp. xxx. 143.   *Dodd, Mead*
& Co.: New York, 1897. 8°.   10410. dd. 30.

ANDREWS (WILLIAM LORING)
—— Sextodecimos et infra. *Eng.* pp. xiii. 117.   *Charles*
Scribner's Sons: New York, 1899. 8°.   **11917.** e. **20.**

ANDREWS (WILLIAM LORING)
—— Gossip about Book Collecting. [With plates. 2 vol.
Dodd, Mead & Co.: New York, 1900. 8°.   11917. c. 43.

LYNE (JAMES) *Surveyor.*
James Lyne's Survey or, as it is more
commonly known, the Bradford Map. A plan of the
city of New York at the time of the granting of the
Montgomery Charter in 1731. An Appendix to an
account of the same compiled in 1893 by W. L.
Andrews. pp. 38.   *Dodd, Mead & Co.:*
New York, 1900. 8°.   Maps 199.d.65.

ANDREWS (WILLIAM LORING)
—— The Iconography of the Battery and Castle Garden.
[With maps and illustrations.] pp. xvi. 43.   *Charles*
Scribner's Sons: New York, 1901. 8°. Cup.**510.**naa.**1.**

ANDREWS (WILLIAM LORING)
—— Bibliopegy in the United States, and kindred subjects.
[With reproductions.] pp. 128.   *Dodd, Mead & Co.:*
New York, 1902. 8°.   667. c. 7.
The titlepage is engraved.

GILLISS (WALTER) The Story of a Motto and a
Mark. Being a brief sketch of a few printers' " marks "
and containing the facts concerning the mark of the
Gilliss Press. pp. 42.   *Gilliss Press:*
New York, 1902. 8°.   Cup.**510.**naa.**2.**

ANDREWS (WILLIAM LORING)

—— An English XIX Century Sportsman, Bibliopole and Binder of Angling Books. [On the work of Thomas Gosden. With illustrations.] pp. xvii. 59. 8. *Dodd, Mead & Co.: New York*, 1906. 8°. **667**. d. **5**.

NEW YORK.—*Grolier Club*.

—— DRAKE (JOSEPH RODMAN) The Culprit Fay, and other poems. [With a portrait.] pp. xv. 49. *Printed at the Gilliss Press: New York*, 1923. 8°. C. **99**. d. **32**.
One of a series of six books printed by eminent American printers.

GLEN (Duncan), Hemel Hempstead; Glasgow

MACDIARMID (HUGH) *pseud.* [i.e. CHRISTOPHER MURRAY GRIEVE.]

[In Memoriam James Joyce.]

—— Poetry like the Hawthorn. From In Memoriam James Joyce. pp. 5. *Duncan Glen: Hemel Hempstead*, 1962. 8°. Cup. **510**. ca. **1**.

MAC DIARMID (HUGH) *pseud.* [i.e. CHRISTOPHER MURRAY GRIEVE.]

—— The ministry of water. Two poems. *Glasgow: Duncan Glen*, 1964. Cup. **510**. ca. **3**.

Pages not numbered. 26 cm. △

MACDIARMID (HUGH) *pseud.* [i.e. CHRISTOPHER MURRAY GRIEVE.]

—— The Fire of the Spirit. Two poems. pp. 13. *Duncan Glen: Glasgow*, 1965. 8°. Cup. **510**. ca. **2**.

GOGMAGOG PRESS, London

COX (MORRIS)

—— Yule Gammon. [A poem.] pp. 16. *[The Author:]* *London*, 1957. 8°. Cup. **510**. bcc. **5**.
No. 5 of an edition of twenty copies.

COX (MORRIS)

—— The Slumbering Virgin. A serio-comic version of an old tale. [With illustrations.] ff. 27. *Gogmagog Press: London*, 1958. 8°. Cup. **510**. bcc. **1**.
No. 20 of an edition of forty five copies.

COX (MORRIS)

—— 9 Poems from Nature. [Designed and illustrated by the author.] *The Author: London*, 1959. 8°. Cup. **510**. bcc. **2**.
No. 5 of an edition of thirty-five copies.

COX (MORRIS)

—— The Curtain, *etc.* (With nine original phantographs.) *Morris Cox: London*, 1960. 8°. Cup. **510**. bcc. **4**.
No. 3 of an edition of twenty-six copies.

COX (MORRIS)

—— War in a Cock's Egg. (A poem in three parts. Illustrated with hand-impressed intaglio & surface offsets.) pp. 34. *Gogmagog Press: London*, [1960.] 8°. Cup. **510**. bcc. **3**.

COX (MORRIS)

—— Conversation Pieces. Humorous situations revealed in fragments of dialogue. 1st series. [Illustrations, with captions.] *Gogmagog Press: London*, 1962. 8°. Cup. **510**. bcc. **6**.
No. 19 of an edition of fifty copies.

COX (FRANK LIONEL)

—— The Lost Fisherman. A child's story. . *Gogmagog Press: London*, 1963. 8°. Cup. **510**. bcc. **9**.
No. 44 of an edition of forty-five copies.

COX (MORRIS)

—— Crash ! An experiment in blockmaking and printing. *Gogmagog Press: London*, [1964.] 8°. Cup. **510**. bcc. **8**.
One of an edition of eighty copies.

COX (MORRIS)

—— A Web of Nature. A printbook illustrating a principle. [With a prospectus inserted.] *Gogmagog Press: London*, 1964. 8°. Cup. **510**. bcc. **10**.
No. 5 of an edition of fifty copies. Printed on Japanese Hosho paper.

COX (MORRIS)

—— An Impression of winter: a landscape panorama. *Gogmagog Press: London*, [1965.] 8°. Cup. **510**. bcc. **11**.
No. 10 of an edition of 100 copies.

COX (MORRIS)

—— Mummer's fool. (Poem.) *Gogmagog Press: London*, 1965. 8°. Cup. **510**. bcc. **13**.
No. 60 of an edition of sixty copies.

GOLDEN COCKEREL PRESS, Waltham St. Lawrence, Berks; London

BERESFORD (JOHN DAVYS)

—— Signs & Wonders. [Tales.] pp. 151. *Golden Cockerel Press: Waltham Saint Lawrence*, 1921. 8°. C. **99**. c. **23**.

COPPARD (ALFRED EDGAR)

—— Adam & Eve & Pinch Me. Tales. pp. 140. *Golden Cockerel Press: Waltham St. Lawrence*, 1921. 8°. C. **99**. c. **22**.

GERY (HENRY THEODORE WADE)

—— Terpsichore, & other poems. pp. 67. *Golden Cockerel Press: Waltham St. Lawrence*, 1921. 8°. C. **99**. b. **14**.

ARMSTRONG (MARTIN DONISTHORPE)

—— The Puppet Show. (Stories.) pp. 153. *Golden Cockerell Press: Waltham St. Lawrence*, 1922. 8°. C. **99**. c. **27**.

COPPARD (ALFRED EDGAR)

—— Clorinda Walks in Heaven [and other tales]. pp. 130. *Golden Cockerel Press: Waltham St. Lawrence*, 1922. 8°. C. **99**. c. **24**.

COPPARD (ALFRED EDGAR)
—— [Another copy.] Clorinda walks in Heaven, *etc.* 1922.
C. **99**. c. **28**.

△

*Fine paper. A copy "not for sale" out of series to an
edition of which twenty copies were printed for sale.*

COPPARD (ALFRED EDGAR)
—— Hips & Haws. Poems. pp. 44. *Golden Cockerel Press :
Waltham St. Lawrence,* 1922. 8°. C. **99**. c. **26**.
One of twenty copies signed by the author.

ELLIS (HENRY HAVELOCK)
—— Kanga Creek. An Australian idyll. (Special edition.)
pp. 68. *Golden Cockerel Press : Waltham St. Lawrence,*
1922. 8°. C. **99**. c. **25**.
One of 29 copies printed.

GERY (HENRY THEODORE WADE) Terpsichore, &
other poems. (Second edition.) pp. 67.
Golden Cockerel Press : Waltham St. Lawrence, 1922. 12°.
C. **99**. b. **15**.
One of 20 copies printed on hand-made paper.

HUGHES (RICHARD ARTHUR WARREN)
—— Gipsy-Night, and other poems. pp. 69. *Golden Cockerel
Press : Waltham St. Lawrence,* [1922.] 12°.
C. **99**. b. **13**.

QUENNELL (PETER COURTNEY)
—— Masques & Poems. pp. 53. *Golden Cockerel Press :
Waltham St. Lawrence,* 1922. 4°. C. **99**. e. **34**.

SCHNITZLER (ARTHUR)
—— Casanova's Homecoming. (Translation . . . by Eden &
Cedar Paul.) pp. 175. **F. P.** *Golden Cockerel Press :
Waltham St. Lawrence* [printed]; *Brentano's: London,*
1922. 8°. C. **99**. h. **4**.

APULEIUS (LUCIUS) *Madaurensis.* [*Asinus Aureus.—
English.*]
—— The XI Bookes of the Golden Asse . . . Translated . . .
by William Adlington. pp. 250. *Golden Cockerel Press :
Waltham Saint Lawrence,* 1923. 4°. C. **99**. i. **21.**

BROWNE (*Sir* THOMAS) [*Two or more Works.*]
—— A Letter to a Friend upon the Occasion of the Death of
an Intimate Friend, together with Christian Morals.
pp. 67. *Golden Cockerel Press : Waltham St. Lawrence,*
1923. fol. C. **99**. i. **15**.

BROWNE (*Sir* THOMAS) [*Single Works.*]
—— The Garden of Cyrus, *etc.* pp. 58. *Golden Cockerel
Press : Waltham St. Lawrence,* 1923. 4°. C. **99**. i. **14**.

BROWNE (*Sir* THOMAS) *M.D.* [*Single Works.*]
—— Hydriotaphia, *etc. Waltham Saint Lawrence : printed &
sold at the Golden Cockerel Press,* 1923. C. **99**. i. **12**.
pp. 47. 28 cm. △

BROWNE (*Sir* THOMAS) *M.D.* [*Single Works.*]
—— Religio medici. *Waltham Saint Lawrence : printed & sold
at the Golden Cockerel Press,* 1923. C. **99**. i. **13**.
pp. 81. 28 cm. △

LONGUS. Daphnis & Chloe . . . Translated by
G. Thornley. (From the edition of mdclvij.) pp. 108.
Golden Cockerell Press :
Waltham Saint Lawrence, 1923. 4°. C. **99**. i. **24**.

MAUPASSANT (HENRI RENÉ ALTERT GUY DE)
—— Doctor Heraclius Gloss . . . Translated by Jeffery E.
Jeffery. pp. 127. *Brentano's : London,* 1923. 8°.
012547. cc. **14**.

SPENSER (EDMUND) [*Prothalamion.*] The Wedding
Songs of Edmund Spenser : being the Prothalamion &
the Epithalamion . . . With wood-cuts by Ethelbert
White. pp. 46. *Golden Cockerel Press :*
Waltham Saint Lawrence, 1923. 8°. C. **99**. b. **16**.
No. 10 of 25 copies printed on Japanese vellum.

TAYLOR (JEREMY) *Bishop of Down and Connor, and
of Dromore.* [*Selections.*] Jeremy Taylor : a selection
from his works, made by Martin Armstrong. pp. 132.
Golden Cockerel Press :
Waltham Saint Lawrence, 1923. 4°. C. **99**. i. **22**.

BENNETT (ENOCH ARNOLD)
—— The Bright Island. [A play.] pp. xii. 128. *"Bookman's
Journal"; printed at the Golden Cockerel Press : London,*
1924. 8°. C. **99**. f. **35**.
No. 5 of "The Vine Books."

BOURDEILLE (PIERRE DE) *Seigneur de Brantôme.*
—— The lives of gallant ladies . . . Translated . . . by H. M.
& embellished with woodcuts by Robert Gibbings. (vol. 2.
Translated . . . by F. M.) [The preface signed : Francis
Macnamara.] *Waltham Saint Lawrence : Golden Cockerel
Press,* 1924. C. **98**. g. **2**.
2 vol. : plates. 26 cm. △
Privately printed.

CAREY (HENRY) *Dramatic Writer.*
—— Songs & Poems. [Selected by Moira Gibbings from
" Poems on Several Occasions," 1713, 1723 and 1729.]
With decorations by Robert Gibbings. [With musical
notes.] pp. 64. *Golden Cockerel Press :*
Waltham Saint Lawrence, 1924. 4°. C. **99**. i. **26**.

HENRY VIII., *King of England.* Miscellaneous
Writings . . . In which are included Assertion of the
Seven Sacraments ; Love letters to Anne Boleyn ;
Songs ; Letter to the Emperor ; two Proclamations ;
Will. Edited by Francis Macnamara. pp. 218.
Golden Cockerel Press : Waltham St. Lawrence, 1924. 4°.
C. **98**. g. **4**.

LA ROCHEFOUCAULD (FRANCOIS DE) *2nd Duke.*
—— Moral Maxims. pp. 133. *Golden Cockerel Press :
Twyford,* 1924. 8°. C. **99**. h. **7**.

SIMON (INGO)
—— Roving Shafts. [Poems.] pp. 166. *Thornton
Butterworth : London,* [1924.] 8°. **11643**. cc. **15**.

THOREAU (HENRY DAVID) Where I Lived & What I Lived For. (From "Walden.") [With woodcuts.] pp. 45.	*Golden Cockerel Press:* *Waltham St. Lawrence,* 1924. 16°.	C. 99. a. 24.

BIBLE.—*Judges.*—*Selections.* [*English.*] Samson and Delilah...According to the authorised version. (Illustrated by Robert Gibbings.) pp. 17. *Golden Cockerel Press: Waltham Saint Lawrence,* 1925. 4°.	C. 98. g. 12.

BIBLE.—*Song of Solomon.* [*English.*]

—— The Song of Songs, *etc.* (Illustrations . . . by Eric Gill.) pp. 42.	*Golden Cockerel Press:* *Waltham St. Lawrence,* 1925. 4°.	C. 98. g. 13.

BIBLE.—*Luke.*—*Selections.* [*English.*]

—— The Birth of Christ, from the Gospel according to Saint Luke. [With woodcuts by Noel Rooke.] pp. 43. *Golden Cockerel Press: Waltham St. Lawrence,* 1925. 8°.	C. 99. d. 30.

BROWNING (ROBERT) *the Poet.* [*Smaller Collections.*]

—— Pictor Ignotus, Fra Lippo Lippi, Andrea del Sarto. pp. 39.	*Golden Cockerel Press: Waltham St. Lawrence,* 1925. 4°.	C. 98. g. 8.

BURNS (ROBERT) *the Poet.* [*Smaller Collections.*]

—— Songs from Robert Burns. Selected by A. E. Coppard, with wood engravings by Mabel M. Annesley. pp. xvi. 112. *Golden Cockerel Press: Waltham St. Lawrence,* 1925. 8°.	C. 99. d. 28.

CIBBER (COLLEY)

—— An apology for the life of Colley Cibber, *etc.* *Waltham Saint Lawrence: Golden Cockerel Press,* 1925.
	C. 98. g. 11.

2 vol. 27 cm.	△

CLAY (ENID)

—— Sonnets and Verses. (With wood-engravings by Eric Gill.) pp. 35.	*Golden Cockerel Press:* *Waltham St. Lawrence,* 1925. 8°.	C. 99. d. 27.

ELLIS (HENRY HAVELOCK) Sonnets, with Folk Songs from the Spanish. pp. xiv. 81. *Golden Cockerel Press:* *Waltham St. Lawrence,* 1925. 8°.	C. 99. d. 26.

SWIFT (JONATHAN) *Dean of St. Patrick's.* [*Collections.*—*Prose.*]

—— Selected essays . . . Decorated with engravings on wood by Jon Farleigh. Edited by R. Ellis Roberts. *Waltham Saint Lawrence: Golden Cockerel Press,* 1925. C. 98. g.

vol. 1.: pp. 80. 27 cm.	△

No more published.

SWIFT (JONATHAN) *Dean of St. Patrick's.* [*Gulliver's Travels.*] Travels into several Remote Nations of the World . . . By Lemuel Gulliver. (Illustrations by David Jones.) 2 vol. F. P. *Golden Cockerel Press:* *Waltham St. Lawrence,* 1925. 4°.	C. 98. g. 15.

No. 9 of 30 copies printed on hand-made paper.

SWIFT (JONATHAN) *Dean of St. Patrick's.* [*Miscellaneous Single Works.*] Directions to Servants, *etc.* (Wood engravings by John Nash.) pp. 35. *Golden Cockerel Press: Waltham St. Lawrence,* 1925. 4°.	C. 98. g. 7.

TALLEMANT (GÉDÉON) *Sieur des Réaux.*

—— Love-Tales from Tallemant, *etc.* pp. 247.	*Grafton & Co.: London,* 1925. 4°.	10657. dd. 45.

AESOP. [*English.—Collections.*]

—— The Fables of Æsop. Translated by Sir Roger L'Estrange. [With woodcuts by Celia M. Fiennes.] pp. v. 94.	*Golden Cockerel Press :* *Waltham St. Lawrence,* 1926. 8°.	C. 98. h. 9.

BIBLE.—*Jonah.* [*English.*]

—— The Book of Jonah . . . With engravings on wood by David Jones. pp. 15.	*Golden Cockerel Press:* *Waltham Saint Lawrence,* 1926. 4°.	C. 98. g. 18.

BIBLE.—*Matthew.—Selections.* [*Latin.*]

—— Passio Domini Nostri Jesu Christi : being the 26th and 27th chapters of Saint Matthew's Gospel, *etc.* [With woodcuts by Eric Gill.] pp. 15.	*Golden Cockerel Press:* *Waltham Saint Lawrence,* 1926. 4°.	C. 98. g. 16.

CARLELL (LODOWICK)

—— The Fool would be a Favourit . . . Printed from the edition of 1657 ; with an introduction by Allardyce Nicoll. pp. xii. 88. *Golden Cockerel Press: Waltham Saint Lawrence,* 1926. 8°. [*Berkshire Series.* vol. 3.] C. 98. a. 1/3.

CARLELL (LODOWICK)

—— The Tragedy of Osmond the Great Turk . . . Printed from the edition of 1657 ; with an introduction by Allardyce Nicoll. pp. xii. 59.	*Golden Cockerel Press:* *Waltham Saint Lawrence,* 1926. 8°. [*Berkshire Series.* no. 2.]	C. 98. a. 1/2.

CHAMFORT (SÉBASTIEN ROCH NICOLAS)

—— Maxims and Considerations . . . Translated, with an introduction, by E. Powys Mathers. 2 vol.	*Golden Cockerel Press: Waltham Saint Lawrence,* 1926. 8°.	C. 99. g. 37.

COPPARD (ALFRED EDGAR)

—— Pelagea, and other poems. (Illustrated by Robert Gibbings.) pp. 44.	*Golden Cockerel Press: Waltham St. Lawrence,* 1926. 8°.	Cup. 510. af. 2.

COVENTRY (FRANCIS)

	The History of Pompey the Little, *etc.* (With an introduction by Armdell del Re.) pp. xvi. 225.	*Golden Cockerel Press: Waltham Saint Lawrence,* 1926. 8°.	C. 99. h. 11.

FIELDING (HENRY) An Apology for the Life of Mrs. Shamela Andrews...With an introduction by R. Brimley Johnson. pp. x. 80. *Golden Cockerel Press: Waltham St. Lawrence, 1926.* 8°. Cup. 510. af. 1.

GILL (ARTHUR ERIC ROWTON)
—— Id quod visum placet. A practical test of the beautiful. [With plates.] pp. 19. *Golden Cockerel Press: Waltham St. Lawrence, 1926.* 8°. Cup. 510. af. 3.

MARSTON (JOHN) *Dramatist.* The Metamorphosis of Pigmalions Image...With engravings by Rene Ben Sussan. pp. 17. *Golden Cockerel Press: Waltham St. Lawrence, 1926.* 8°. C. 99. c. 31.

MATHERS (EDWARD POWYS) Procreant Hymn. [With engravings by Eric Gill.] pp. 20. *Golden Cockerel Press: Waltham St. Lawrence, 1926.* 8°. C. 99. g. 36.

MATHERS (EDWARD POWYS) Red Wise. (Illustrated by Robert Gibbings.) pp. 98. *Golden Cockerel Press: Waltham St. Lawrence, 1926.* 8°. C. 99. d. 29.

SHARPHAM (EDWARD)
—— Cupid's Whirligig ... Edited from the first quarto of 1607, with an introduction & textual notes, by Allardyce Nicoll. pp. ix. 94. *Golden Cockerel Press: Waltham St. Lawrence, 1926.* 8°. [*Berkshire Series.* no. 1.] C. 99. a. 1/1.

BIBLE.—*Psalms.* [*English.—Prose Versions.*]
—— The Psalter ; or, Psalms of David. Taken from the Book of Common Prayer. pp. 126. *Golden Cockerel Press: Waltham St. Lawrence, 1927.* 8°. C. 99. h. 17.

BRETON (NICHOLAS)
—— The Twelve Moneths. [Reprinted from "Fantasticks."] Edited by Brian Rhys, with wood engravings by Eric Ravilious. pp. 26. *Golden Cockerel Press: Waltham St. Lawrence, 1927.* 8°. C. 99. h. 16.

CAREW (THOMAS) *the Poet.*
—— A Rapture ... With engravings by J. E. Laboureur. pp. 14. *Golden Cockerel Press: Waltham Saint Lawrence, 1927.* 8°. C. 99. c. 32.

CHAUCER (GEOFFREY) [*Troilus and Cressida.*]
—— Troilus and Criseyde ... Edited by Arundell del Re. With wood engravings by Eric Gill. pp. xi. 309. *Golden Cockerel Press: Waltham Saint Lawrence, 1927.* fol. C. 98. gg. 4.

CHESTER PLAYS.
—— The Chester Play of the Deluge. Edited by J. Isaacs. With engravings ... by David Jones. pp. iv. 16. *Golden Cockerel Press: Waltham St. Lawrence, 1927.* 4°. C. 98. gg. 5.

GILL (ARTHUR ERIC ROWTON)
—— Art & Love. [With plates.] pp. 26. *Douglas Cleverdon: Bristol ; Golden Cockerel Press: Waltham Saint-Lawrence, 1927.* 8°. C. 99. c. 35. *No. 23 of 35 copies issued with an extra set of the engravings.*

LUCIAN, *of Samosata.* [*Vera Historia.*]
—— The true historie of Lucian the Samosatenian. Translated ... by Francis Hickes ... Together with the Greeke and decorated with wood engravings by Robert Gibbings. *Waltham Saint Lawrence: Golden Cockerel Press, 1927.* C. 98. gg. 27.

vol. 1 : pp. 43. 33 cm. △
No more published.

SHENSTONE (WILLIAM) Men & Manners... Selected and introduced by Havelock Ellis. pp. xxiii. 97. *Golden Cockerell Press: Waltham Saint Lawrence, 1927.* 8°. Cup. 510. af. 5.

SUCKLING (*Sir* JOHN) A Ballad upon a Wedding ... With engravings by Eric Ravilious. pp. 8. *Golden Cockerel Press: Waltham Saint Lawrence, 1927.* 8°. C. 99. c. 34.

COPPARD (ALFRED EDGAR)
—— Count Stefan. pp. 56. *Golden Cockerel Press: Waltham Saint Lawrence, 1928.* 8°. C. 100. i. 23.

EARLE (JOHN) *successively Bishop of Worcester and of Salisbury.* Micro-cosmographie ... Edited by Gwendolen Murphy. pp. vi. 73. *Golden Cockerel Press: Waltham St. Lawrence, 1928.* 4°. C. 98. h. 19.

F., A. The Ladies' Pocket Book of Etiquette. By A. F. With engravings by Hester Sainsbury. pp. 55. *Golden Cockerel Press: Waltham St. Lawrence, 1928.* 8°. C. 99. b. 19.

GILL (ARTHUR ERIC ROWTON)
Art & Prudence. An essay. pp. 18. *Golden Cockerel Press: Waltham St. Lawrence, 1928.* 8°. C. 99. c. 40.

GOLDEN COCKEREL PRESS. A Catalogue of an Exhibition held at the Whitworth Art Gallery, Manchester, Spring 1928, of engravings on wood & copper from books printed and published by the Golden Cockerel Press at Waltham Saint Lawrence, Berkshire. [With a preface by Campbell Dodgson.] pp. 7. [*Manchester, 1928.*] 4°. Cup. 510. af. 4.

KEATS (John) [*Single Works.*]

Lamia, Isabella, The Eve of St. Agnes, and other poems. With engravings by Robert Gibbings. pp. 100. *Golden Cockerel Press : Waltham St. Lawrence*, 1928. fol. **C. 98. gg. 16.**

LAMB (Charles) [*A Tale of Rosamund Gray.*]

—— A Tale of Rosamund Gray and Old Blind Margaret . . . With introduction by R. Brimley Johnson. [With a portrait.] pp. ix. 71. *Printed by the Golden Cockerel Press for Frank Hollings: London*, 1928. 8°.
C. 99. b. 24.

STERNE (Laurence) [*Sentimental Journey.*] A Sentimental Journey through France and Italy . . . With six engravings . . . by J. E. Laboureur. pp. 151. *Golden Cockerel Press : Waltham Saint Lawrence*, 1928. 8°. **C. 99. d. 31.**

SWIFT (Jonathan) *Dean of St. Patrick's.* [*Collections.—Verse.*] Miscellaneous Poems . . . Edited by R. Ellis Roberts; decorated with engravings on wood by Robert Gibbings. pp. viii. 67. *Golden Cockerel Press : Waltham St. Lawrence*, 1928. 4°. **C. 98. e. 7.**

TELLIER (Juzes)

—— [*Les Deux Paradis.*] Abd-er-Rhaman in Paradise . . . Translated by Brian Rhys. With wood-engravings by Paul Nash. pp. 34. *Golden Cockerel Press: Waltham St. Lawrence*, 1928. 8°. **C. 100. i. 24.**

ANDREEV (Leonid Nikolaevich) [*Separate Works.*]

—— Abyss . . . Translated by John Cournos. With engravings by Ivan Lebedeff. pp. 31. *Golden Cockerel Press : Waltham St. Lawrence*, 1929. 8°. **C. 99. c. 44.**

CHAUCER (Geoffrey) [*Canterbury Tales.*]

—— The Canterbury Tales . . . With wood engravings by Eric Gill. 4 vol. *Golden Cockerel Press : Waltham St. Lawrence*, 1929–31. fol. **C. 98. gg. 26.**

KĀLIDĀSA. [*Ṛitusaṃhāra.—English.*] A Circle of the Seasons. A translation of the Ritu-Samhāra of Kālidāsa made from various European sources by E. Powys Mathers. With engravings by Robert Gibbings. pp. 28. *Golden Cockerel Press : Waltham Saint Lawrence*, 1929. 8°. **C. 99. g. 43.**

MEEK (Charles) *of Bisley, Glos.*

—— The Will to Function. A philosophical study. pp. 134. *The Author: Bisley, Glos.*, 1929. 8°. **08486. eee. 16.**

SMITH (Aaron) *Seaman.* The Atrocities of the Pirates . . . Decorated . . . with engravings by Eric Ravilious. pp. v. 156. *Golden Cockerel Press : Waltham St. Lawrence*, 1929. 8°. **Cup. 510. af. 6.**

STERNE (Laurence) [*Tristram Shandy.*] The Life & Opinions of Tristram Shandy...With...engravings ...by J. E. Laboureur. 2 vol. *Golden Cockerel Press : Waltham Saint Lawrence*, 1929–30. 8°. **C. 99. d. 35.**

THOMAS [More] *Saint, Lord High Chancellor of England.* [*Utopia.—English.*]

A frutefull, pleasant, and wittie worke, of the beste state of a publique weale, & of the new yle, called Utopia . . . Translated . . . by Raphe Robynson . . . Edited by A. W. Reed. pp. xiii. 137. *Golden Cockerel Press : Waltham St. Lawrence*, 1929. 8°. **C. 98. h. 25.**

COPPARD (Alfred Edgar)

—— The Hundredth Story of A. E. Coppard. With engravings by Robert Gibbings. pp. 57. *Golden Cockerel Press: Waltham Saint Lawrence*, 1930. 8°. **C. 99. g. 44.**

FIELDING (Henry) A Journey from this World to the Next...With six etchings...by Denis Tegetmeier. pp. 175. *Golden Cockerel Press : Waltham St. Lawrence*, 1930. 8°. **C. 100. g. 23.**

GANTILLON (Simon) Maya. A play . . . Paraphrased into English by Virginia & Frank Vernon. With xiii wood engravings by Blair Hughes-Stanton. pp. viii. 93. *Golden Cockerel Press : Waltham Saint Lawrence*, 1930. 8°. **C. 100. c. 8.**

GIBBINGS (Robert John)

—— The 7th Man. A true cannibal tale . . . Told in fifteen wood-engravings and . . . one hundred and eighty nine words. pp. 14. *Golden Cockerel Press: Waltham St. Lawrence*, 1930. **Cup. 510. af. 7.**

GOLDEN COCKEREL PRESS.

—— The Golden Cockerel Press, Spring 1930 (1931). [Prospectuses.] 2 pt. [*Waltham Saint Lawrence,*] 1930, 31. fol. **Cup. 510. af. 25.**

JOHNSON (Abraham) *pseud.* [i.e. Sir John Hill, M.D.]

Lucina sine concubitu...With 3 engravings on copper by Hester Sainsbury. pp. 40. *Golden Cockerel Press : Waltham Saint Lawrence*, 1930. 8°. **C. 99. b. 27.**

PLATO. [*Phædo.—English.*] The Phaedo of Plato. Translated...by William Jowett. pp. 78. *Golden Cockerel Press : Waltham Saint Lawrence*, 1930. fol. **C. 100. c. 6.**

BIBLE.—*Gospels.* [*English.*]

—— The Four Gospels of the Lord Jesus Christ according to the Authorized Version . . . With decorations by Eric Gill. pp. 268. *Golden Cockerel Press : Waltham St. Lawrence*, 1931. fol. **C. 102. l. 5.**

FLAUBERT (GUSTAVE) Salambo. Translated by E. Powys Mathers. Decorated with engravings on wood by Robert Gibbings, *etc.* pp. 317.
Golden Cockerell Press :
Waltham Saint Lawrence, 1931. 4°.   C. 100. c. 14.

GILL (ARTHUR ERIC ROWTON) Clothing without Cloth : an essay on the nude...With engravings on wood by the author. pp. 16. *Golden Cockerel Press :*
Waltham St. Lawrence, 1931. 8°. Cup.510.af.8.¯

GOLDEN COCKEREL PRESS.
—— [A collection of prospectuses, book lists, and specimen pages from works published by the Golden Cockerel Press.] [1931–58].   Cup. 510. af. 26.

53 pt.   △

POWYS (THEODORE FRANCIS) When Thou wast Naked. A story...With engravings by John Nash.   pp. 65.
Golden Cockerel Press :
Waltham Saint Lawrence, 1931. 8°.   C. 99. h. 32.

BATES (HERBERT ERNEST)
—— A German Idyll . . . With wood engravings by Lynton Lamb. pp. 39.   *Golden Cockerel Press :*
Waltham St. Lawrence, 1932. 8°.   C. 99. h. 34.

CONSEQUENCES. Consequences. A complete story in the manner of the old parlour game in nine chapters each by a different author. pp. 66. *Golden Cockerel Press :*
Waltham Saint Lawrence, 1932. 8°.   C. 100. g. 32.

COPPARD (ALFRED EDGAR)
—— Crotty Shinkwin. A tale . . . The Beauty Spot. A tale . . . Engravings by Robert Gibbings. pp. 67.
Golden Cockerel Press : Waltham St. Lawrence, 1932. 8°.
C. 100. g. 31.

COPPARD (ALFRED EDGAR)
—— Rummy : that noble game expounded in prose, poetry, diagram and engraving, by A. E Coppard and Robert Gibbings. With an account of certain diversions into the mountain fastnesses of Cork and Kerry. [Text by A. E. Coppard, illustrations by R. Gibbings.] pp. 49.
Golden Cockerel Press : Waltham Saint Lawrence, 1932. 8°.
C. 100. g. 33.

DAVIES (RHYS) *Novelist.*
—— Daisy Matthews, and three other tales . . . With wood engravings by Agnes Miller Parker. pp. 63.   *Golden Cockerel Press : Waltham St. Lawrence,* 1932. 8°.
C. 99. h. 37.

DRIBERG (JACK HERBERT)
—— Initiation. Translations from poems of the Didinga & Lango tribes by J. H. Driberg. Decorations by Robert Gibbings. pp. 29.   *Golden Cockerel Press :*
[*Waltham St. Lawrence,*] 1932. 8°.   C. 100. g. 29.

FIELDING (HENRY)
—— The Life of Mr. Jonathan Wild the Great . . . With seven etchings on copper by Denis Tegetmeier. pp. viii. 278.   *Golden Cockerel Press :*
Waltham St. Lawrence, 1932. 8°.   C. 99. h. 36.

OVIDIUS NASO (PUBLIUS) [*Amores.—English.*]
—— The Amores of P. Ovidius Naso. Newly translated by E. Powys Mathers. With five engravings on copper by J. E. Laboureur. pp. 81.   *Golden Cockerel Press :*
Waltham St. Lawrence, 1932. 8°.   C. 99. h. 35.

SHAKESPEARE (WILLIAM) [*Twelfth Night.*]
—— Twelfth Night ; or, What you Will . . . With engravings by Eric Ravilious. pp. 75.   *Golden Cockerel Press :*
Waltham St. Lawrence, 1932. fol.   C. 102. l. 7.

WALPOLE (HUGH SEYMOUR)
—— The Apple Trees. Four reminiscences . . . With wood-engravings by Lynton Lamb. pp. 73.   *Golden Cockerel Press : Waltham St. Lawrence,* 1932. 8°.
C. 99. h. 38.

BATES (HERBERT ERNEST)
—— The House with the Apricot, and two other tales. pp. 59. *Golden Cockerel Press : London,* 1933. 8°.
C. 100. g. 40.

CUMBERLAND HOTEL. Cumberland Hotel. [A descriptive brochure. By Philip Page and others. With illustrations.] pp. 30.   *Golden Cockerel Press : London,* [1933.] 8°.   C. 102. e. 9.

DICKENS (CHARLES) [*The Cricket on the Hearth.*]

—— The Cricket on the Hearth . . . Seven posthumous illustrations by Hugh Thomson. [With an introduction by Walter de la Mare.] pp. x. 70.   *Golden Cockerel Press :*
[*London ?*] 1933. fol.   C. 105. c. 7.
Printed for the members of the Limited Editions Club.

PLUNKETT (EDWARD JOHN MORETON DRAX) 18*th Baron Dunsany.*
—— Lord Adrian. A play in three acts . . . . Engravings by Robert Gibbings. pp. 73.   *Golden Cockerel Press :*
Waltham St. Lawrence, 1933. 8°.   C. 99. h. 40.

APULEIUS (LUCIUS) *Madaurensis.* [*Asinus Aureus.— Selections.—English.*]
—— Cupid & Psyches : the most pleasant and delectable tale of their marriage. Engravings by Lettice Sandford. (Translated by William Adlington ; reprinted from the Quarto of 1639.) pp. 47.   *Golden Cockerel Press :*
London, 1934. 8°.   C. 99. h. 32.

BIBLE.—*Ecclesiastes.* [*English.*]
—— Ecclesiastes; or, the Preacher. (The engravings by Blair Hughes-Stanton.) pp. 21. *Golden Cockerel Press:* [*Waltham St. Lawrence,*] 1934. fol.
C. 102. i. 11.

BLIGH (WILLIAM)
—— The Voyage of the Bounty's Launch, as related in William Bligh's Despatch to the Admiralty, and the Journal of John Fryer. With an introduction by Owen Rutter and wood-engravings by Robert Gibbings. pp. 86. *Golden Cockerel Press: London,* 1934. fol.
C. 102. h. 12.

CLAY (ENID) The Constant Mistress . . . With engravings by Eric Gill. [Poems.] pp. 40. *Golden Cockerel Press: London,* 1934. 8°.
Cup. 510. af. 9.

COSMETICS. Cosmetics for my Lady & Good Fare for my Lord. Collected recipes. pp. 75. *Golden Cockerel Press: London,* 1934. 8°. C. 100. g. 45.

GILL (ARTHUR ERIC ROWTON)
—— The Lord's Song. A sermon. pp. 15. *Golden Cockerel Press: London,* 1934. 8°. C. 100. g. 41.

MARSHALL (ARTHUR CALDER)
—— A Crime against Cania. (The wood-engravings by Blair Hughes-Stanton.) pp. 65. *Golden Cockerel Press: London,* 1934. 8°.
C. 99. h. 41.

MOTTRAM (RALPH HALE)
—— Strawberry Time, and The Banquet. (Wood-engravings by Gertrude Hermes.) pp. 87. *Golden Cockerel Press: London,* 1934. 8°.
C. 100. g. 43.

POWYS (LLEWELYN)
—— Glory of Life . . . With wood engravings by Robert Gibbings. pp. 34. *Golden Cockerel Press: London,* 1934. fol.
C. 102. l. 10.

SERMONS.
—— Sermons by Artists, *etc.* pp. 79. *Golden Cockerel Press: London,* 1934. 8°.
C. 100. g. 42.

TOUSSAINT (FRANZ)
—— The Garden of Caresses . . . Now rendered into English by Christopher Sandford. pp. 91. *Golden Cockerel Press:* [*London,*] 1934. 4°. C. 100. e. 15.

BATES (HERBERT ERNEST)
—— Flowers and Faces . . . Engravings by John Nash. pp. 52. *Golden Cockerel Press:* [*Waltham St. Lawrence,*] 1935. 8°.
C. 102. e. 8.

GIBBINGS (ROBERT JOHN)
—— Narratives of the Wreck of the Whale-Ship Essex, of Nantucket, which was destroyed by a Whale in the Pacific Ocean in the year 1819. Told by Owen Chase . . . Thomas Chappell . . . and George Pollard . . . Together with an introduction & twelve engravings on wood by R. Gibbings. pp. 87. *Golden Cockerel Press: London,* 1935. fol. C. 102. f. 9.

GLASSPOOLE (RICHARD)
—— Mr. Glasspoole and the Chinese Pirates. Being the narrative of Mr. R. Glasspoole of the ship Marquis of Ely . . . Together with extracts from the China records and the log of the Marquis of Ely: and some remarks on Chinese pirates . . . by Owen Rutter; and four engravings on wood by Robert Gibbings. pp. 57. *Golden Cockerel Press: London,* 1935. 4°.
C. 100. e. 16.

GOLDEN COCKEREL PRESS.
—— [A collection of titlepages designed for the Golden Cockerel Press, together with trial pages with engravings by Robert Gibbings.] [*Waltham Saint Lawrence,* c. 1935.] 8°.
Cup. 510. af. 18.

GRAMMONT (DE) *Sieur.*
—— Heartsease and Honesty, being the Pastimes of the Sieur de Grammont, steward to the Duc de Richelieu in Touraine. Taken from his notebooks written in French . . . & here made English by Helen Simpson. pp. 77. *Golden Cockerel Press: London,* [1935.] 8°.
C. 102. a. 5.

LASCARIS (EVADNE) *pseud.*
—— The Golden Bed of Kydno. Translated from the modern Greek of Evadne Lascaris by P. M., & illustrated with twelve line-engravings by Lettice Sandford. pp. 41. *Printed for subscribers at the Golden Cockerel Press:* [*Waltham St. Lawrence,*] 1935. fol. C. 100. a. 6.

LINDSAY (JACK)
—— Storm at Sea . . . [A novel.] Wood-engravings by John Farleigh. pp. 75. *Golden Cockerel Press: London,* 1935. 8°. C. 100. g. 47.

MORRISON (JAMES) *Boatswain's Mate of the Bounty.*
—— The Journal of James Morrison, Boatswain's Mate of the Bounty, describing the mutiny & subsequent misfortunes of the mutineers together with an account of the island of Tahiti. With an introduction by Owen Rutter, *etc.* pp. 242. *Golden Cockerel Press: London,* 1935. fol.
C. 100. k. 26.

STRONG (LEONARD ALFRED GEORGE)
—— The Hansom Cab and the Pigeons. Being random reflections upon the silver jubilee of King George V. pp. 42. *Golden Cockerel Press: London,* 1935. 8°.
C. 99. h. 43.

BIBLE.—*Song of Solomon.* [*English.*]
—— The Song of Songs. The Authorised Version together with a new translation, an introduction and notes by W. O. E. Oesterley . . . With engravings on copper by Lettice Sandford. [*London:*] *Golden Cockerel Press,* 1936. C. **102. l. 18.**

pp. 59. 38 cm. △

BLIGH (WILLIAM)
—— The Log of the Bounty. Being Lieutenant William Bligh's log of the proceedings of His Majesty's armed vessel Bounty in a voyage to the South Seas . . . Now published for the first time from the manuscript in the Admiralty records, with an introduction and notes by Owen Rutter, comments on Bligh's navigation by Rear-Admiral J. A. Edgell . . . and four engravings on wood by Lynton Lamb. 2 vol. *Golden Cockerel Press: London,* [1936], 37. fol. C. **102. h. 15.**

GOLDEN COCKEREL PRESS.
—— Chanticleer. A bibliography of the Golden Cockerel Press, April 1921–1936 August. Introduction by Humbert Wolfe. Foreword & notes by the partners. Illustrations from the books. pp. 47. *Golden Cockerel Press: London,* 1936. 8º. C. **100. b. 7.**

LAWRENCE, afterwards **SHAW** (THOMAS EDWARD)
—— Crusader Castles. (I. The thesis.—II. The letters.) [With plates.] 2 vol. *Golden Cockerel Press: London,* 1936. 4º. C. **98. i. 14.**

MATHERS (EDWARD POWYS)
—— Love Night. A Laotian gallantry . . . Engravings by Buckland Wright. pp. 140. *Golden Cockerel Press: London,* 1936. 8º. C. **100. c. 17.**
With a set of six extra plates.

MILLER (PATRICK) *pseud.* [i.e. GEORGE GORDON MAC-FARLANE.]
—— The Green Ship. (With eight wood-engravings by Eric Gill.) pp. 181. *Golden Cockerel Press:* [*London,*] 1936. 4º. C. **100. b. 6.**

QUENNELL (NANCY)
—— The Epicure's Anthology. Collected by Nancy Quennell. With an essay on the Epicure and the Epicurean by A. J. A. Symons and decorations by Osbert Lancaster. pp. 187. **F.P.** *Golden Cockerel Press: London,* 1936. 8º. Cup.**510.af.10.**

BIBLE.—*Old Testament.—Selections.* [*English.*]
—— Roses of Sharon. Poems chosen from the flower of ancient Hebrew literature, with an introduction, by W. O. E. Oesterley . . . 12 wood-engravings by Mary Groom. pp. 58. *Golden Cockerel Press:* [*London,*] 1937. 8º. C. **102. e. 14.**

BLIGH (WILLIAM)
—— Bligh's Voyage in the Resource from Coupang to Batavia, together with the log of his subsequent passage to England in the Dutch packet Vlydt and his remarks on Morrison's Journal . . . From the manuscripts in the Mitchell Library of New South Wales, with an introduction and notes by Owen Rutter, & engravings on wood by Peter Barker-Mill. [With facsimiles.] pp. 159. *Golden Cockerel Press: London,* 1937. fol. C. **98. c. 10.**

DAVID (JACOB VILLIERS PEVERIL)
—— A Winter Firework . . . With decorations by Osbert Lancaster. pp. 20. *Golden Cockerel Press:* [*London,*] 1937. 8º. Cup. **510. af. 24.**

GEDDES (ELIZABETH)
—— Animal Antics. [Verses. With illustrations by the author.] *Golden Cockerel Press: London,* 1937. 16º. Cup.**510.af.11.**

GREEK ANTHOLOGY.
—— The Golden Cockerel Greek Anthology. A selection of the poems, edited, with translations into English verse and an introduction, by F. L. Lucas . . . Line-engravings . . . by Lettice Sandford. pp. 81. [*Golden Cockerel Press: London,* 1937.] fol. C. **103. h. 2.**
No. 18 of an edition of 216 copies, of which no. 1–80 contain six more illustrations than the rest.

JONSON (BEN)
—— A Croppe of Kisses. Selected lyrics . . . chosen, with an appreciation, by John Wallis. pp. 48. *Golden Cockerel Press: London,* 1937. fol. C. **100. a. 7.**

LACOMBE (JEAN DE)
—— [Compendiare du Levant.] A Compendium of the East, being an account of voyages to the Grand Indies . . . Now published for the first time, from the Bordeaux manuscript of 1681, in an English translation by Stephanie & Denis Clark. Edited, with an introduction and notes, by Ashley Gibson. Contemporary engravings . . . from Schultzen's Ost-indische Reyse . . . 1676. pp. 208. *Golden Cockerel Press: London,* 1937. 4º. C. **103. i. 1.**

MILLER (PATRICK) *pseud.* [i.e. GEORGE GORDON MAC-FARLANE.]
—— Ana the Runner. A treatise for princes & generals attributed to Prince Mahmoud Abdul . . . Engravings by Clifford Webb. pp. 108. *Golden Cockerel Press: London,* 1937. 8º. C. **99. d. 50.**

MILTON (JOHN) [*Paradise Lost.*]
—— Paradise Lost . . . The text of the first edition, prepared for press by J. Isaacs. [With engravings by Mary Groom.] pp. 378. *Golden Cockerel Press:* [*London,*] 1937. fol. C. **102. l. 20.**

POWYS (LLEWELYN) [*Selections.*]
—— The Book of Days of Llewelyn Powys. Thoughts from his philosophy selected by John Wallis . . . With an introduction by Llewelyn Powys and twelve etchings by Elizabeth Corsellis. pp. 85. *Golden Cockerel Press: London*, 1937. fol. C. 100. l. 18.
No. 14 of 55 copies signed by the artist. With a second set of the etchings inserted.

POWYS (THEODORE FRANCIS)
—— Goat Green; or, the Better Gift . . . Engravings by Gwenda Morgan. pp. 61. *Golden Cockerel Press: London*, 1937. 8°. C. 102. a. 9.

PUSHKIN (ALEKSANDR SERGYEEVICH)
—— The Tale of the Golden Cockerel. (Translated by Hannah Waller, with a note on Pushkin and the Tale by Raïssa Lomonossova.) pp. 22. *Golden Cockerel Press: London*, [1937.] 16°. C. 100. h. 26.
No. 20 of 100 copies printed on hand-made paper.

RUTTER (JOAN)
—— Here's Flowers. An anthology of flower poems. Compiled by Joan Rutter, *etc.* pp. 197. *Golden Cockerel Press: London*, 1937. 8°. C. 102. a. 11.

RUTTER (OWEN)
—— The First Fleet. The record of the foundation of Australia from its conception to the settlement at Sydney Cove. Compiled from the original documents in the Public Record Office, with extracts from the log-books of H.M.S. Sirius and an introduction and notes, by Owen Rutter . . . Five engravings by Peter Barker-Mill. pp. 149. *Golden Cockerel Press: London*, 1937. fol. C. 100. a. 8.

WHITFIELD (CHRISTOPHER)
—— Mr. Chambers and Persephone. A tale . . . With wood-engravings by Dorothea Braby. pp. 62. *Golden Cockerel Press: London*, 1937. 8°. C. 102. a. 8.

BINYON (ROBERT LAURENCE) *Keeper of Prints and Drawings, British Museum.*
—— Brief Candles . . . [A play.] With six engravings by Helen Binyon. pp. 49. *Golden Cockerel Press: London*, [1938.] 16°. C. 103. a. 1.
No. 24 of an edition of 100 copies.

BYNG (LANCELOT ALFRED CRANMER)
—— Tomorrow's Star. An essay on the shattering and remoulding of a world. pp. 179. *Golden Cockerel Press: [London,]* 1938. 8°. Cup.510.af.12.

COPPARD (ALFRED EDGAR)
—— Tapster's Tapestry . . . [A tale.] Engravings by Gwenda Morgan. pp. 58. F.P. *Golden Cockerel Press: London*, 1938. 8°. C. 103. e. 3.
No. 64 of an edition of seventy-five copies.

GARCÍA CALDERÓN (VENTURA)
—— The White Llama. Being La Venganza del Condor . . . translated . . . by Richard Phibbs. Engravings by Clifford Webb. pp. 123. *Golden Cockerel Press: [London,]* 1938. 8°. C. 99. d. 51.
No. 49 of an edition of seventy-five copies.

GAUTIER (THÉOPHILE) *the Elder.*
—— Mademoiselle de Maupin . . . Translated by R. & E. Powys Mathers. Engravings by John Buckland Wright. pp. 284. *Golden Cockerel Press: [London,]* 1938. 4°. C. 103. b. 2.
No. 17 of 50 copies " specially bound and illustrated with twelve plates."

JOHN [DE BRÉBEUF], *Saint and Martyr.*
—— The Travels & Sufferings of Father Jean de Brébeuf among the Hurons of Canada, as described by himself. Edited & translated from the French and Latin by Theodore Besterman. pp. 196. *Golden Cockerel Press: London*, 1938. fol. C. 103. i. 5.

JONES (GEORGE W.) *Printer.*
—— Catalogue of the Library of George W. Jones at the Sign of the Dolphin . . . Gough Square . . . London, E.C.4. [With plates, including a portrait.] pp. ix. 131. *Printed for the Members of the Limited Editions Club by George W. Jones: London*, 1938. fol. C. 105. g. 10.
Printed for private circulation. Author's presentation copy.

KARN (C.)
—— Armagnac, Beaune, Bordeaux, *etc.* (Ex cellariis C. Karn, consulting wine merchant.) [A wine catalogue.] *Golden Cockerel Press: [London,]* 1938. 4°. Cup.510.af.22.

QUENNELL (NANCY)
—— A Lover's Progress. Seventeenth century lyrics: selected by N. Quennell. pp. 84. *Golden Cockerell Press: [London,]* 1938. fol. C. 103. i. 2.
Privately printed.

SWIRE (HERBERT)
—— The Voyage of the Challenger. A personal narrative of the historic circumnavigation of the globe in the years 1872–1876. By . . . H. Swire . . . Illustrated with reproductions from paintings and drawings in his journals, *etc.* 2 vol. *Golden Cockerel Press: London*, 1938. fol. C. 103. i. 3.

'UMAR KHAIYAM. [*English and Latin.*]
—— The Golden Cockerel Rubáiyát of Omar Khayyám. Translated by Edward Fitzgerald. The first edition reprinted: together with Fitzgerald's Monk-Latin version, now printed for the first time. Translations of the Latin & of the Persian originals, and a critical essay, by Sir E. Denison Ross. Introduction by Charles Ganz. Line-engravings by John Buckland-Wright. pp. 99. *Golden Cockerel Press: London*, 1938. fol. C. 103. i. 4.
One of thirty copies accompanied by five additional engravings, and a collotype facsimile of Fitzgerald's Monk-Latin MS., on eight sheets.

FRYER (Mary Ann)
—— John Fryer of the Bounty. Notes on his career. Written by his daughter Mary Ann. With an introduction and commentary by Owen Rutter, and wood-engravings by Averil Mackenzie-Grieve. pp. 53. *Golden Cockerel Press:* [London,] 1939. fol. C. **103**. i. **6**.

LAWRENCE, afterwards **SHAW** (Thomas Edward)
—— Secret Despatches from Arabia by T. E. Lawrence . . . Foreword by A. W. Lawrence. [With a portrait.] pp. 173. *Golden Cockerel Press:* [London, 1939.] 4º.
C. **103**. b. **5**.
One of thirty copies accompanied by a collotype reproduction of part of the manuscript of " The Seven Pillars of Wisdom."

PLYMOUTH, *Massachusetts.* [*Appendix.*]
—— The Pilgrim Fathers. A journal of their coming in the Mayflower to New England and their life and adventures there : edited, with preface and notes, by Theodore Besterman : eight engravings by Geoffrey Wales. Reprinted, from the rare 1622 edition [of " A Relation or Journall of the beginning and proceedings of the English Plantation setled at Plimoth "], *etc.* pp. 87. *Golden Cockerel Press:* London, 1939. 8º. C. **103**. b. **3**.

VENUS.
—— Pervigilium Veneris. Engravings by John Buckland-Wright. (The Vigil of Venus. Translation by F. L. Lucas.) *Lat. & Eng.* pp. 27. *Golden Cockerel Press:* London, 1939. 4º. C. **102**. g. **7**.
No. 33 of an edition of 100 copies.

WELLS (Herbert George)
—— The Country of the Blind, 1939 . . . [A revised version.] With engravings by Clifford Webb. pp. 67. *Golden Cockerel Press:* London, 1939. 4º.
C. **103**. b. **6**.

WHITFIELD (Christopher)
—— Lady from Yesterday . . . With wood-engravings by Lettice Sandford. pp. 70. *Golden Cockerel Press:* London, 1939. 8º. C. **102**. a. **15**.
No. 30 of an edition of fifty copies.

BELL (Gertrude Margaret Lowthian)
—— The Arab War. Confidential information for General Headquarters from Gertrude Bell. Being despatches reprinted from the secret " Arab Bulletin ", *etc.* *London: Golden Cockerel Press,* 1940. C. **99**. i. **28**.
pp. 50. 26 cm. △
No. 13 of thirty copies. Bound in full Niger and containing " A facsimile reproduction of Gertrude Bell's handwriting. The manuscript of an essay on Romance in the Iraq ".

LAWRENCE, afterwards **SHAW** (Thomas Edward)
—— Men in Print. Essays in literary criticism . . . Introduction by A. W. Lawrence. pp. 58. *Golden Cockerel Press:* [London,] 1940. 4º. C. **99**. g. **51**.
No. 18 of thirty copies bound in full Niger and accompanied by a facsimile reproduction of T. E. Lawrence's manuscript of one of the essays.

WELSH TRIADS.
—— The Wisdom of the Cymry. Translated from the Welsh Triads by Winifred Faraday. [Selected, and arranged according to topic.] pp. 47. *Golden Cockerel Press:* [*Waltham St. Lawrence,* 1940.] 16º. C. **99**. a. **30**.
No. 26 of an edition of sixty copies.

FÊNG (Mêng-lung)
—— Glue and Lacquer. Four cautionary tales [selected from the collection " Hsing Shi Hêng Yen," edited by Fêng Mêng-lung]. Translated . . . by Harold Acton & Lee Yi-hsieh . . . With illustrations from drawings by Eric Gill interpreted on copper by Denis Tegetmeier. pp. 139. *Golden Cockerel Press:* London, 1941. 8º.
C. **99**. g. **53**.
One of a limited edition printed on hand-made paper and containing collotype reproductions of the drawings by Eric Gill.

HUDSON (William Henry) *C.M.Z.S.* [*Letters.*]
—— W. H. Hudson's Letters to R. B. Cunninghame Graham. With a few to Cunninghame Graham's mother, Mrs Bontine. Edited, with an introduction, by Richard Curle. Drawings of Hudson and Cunninghame Graham by Sir William Rothenstein. pp. 128. *Golden Cockerel Press:* London, 1941. 8º. Cup. **510**. al. **13**

LAWRENCE, afterwards **SHAW** (Thomas Edward) [*Letters.*]
—— Shaw-Ede. T. E. Lawrence's letters to H. S. Ede, 1927–1935. Foreword and running commentary by H. S. Ede. (Accompanied by facsimile reproductions of five of the letters.) pp. 62. *Golden Cockerel Press:* London 1942. 4º. C. **100**. g. **50**.

SWINBURNE (Algernon Charles)
—— Lucretia Borgia. The Chronicle of Tebaldeo Tebaldei . . . Commentary and notes by Randolph Hughes. Engravings by Reynolds Stone. [With a facsimile of part of Swinburne's manuscript.] pp. 191. *Golden Cockerel Press:* London, 1942. fol. C. **99**. k. **28**.

TENBURY.—*St. Michael's College.*
—— The Tenbury Letters. Selected & edited by Edmund H. Fellowes . . . & Edward Pine. [With facsimile reproductions.] pp. 223. *Golden Cockerel Press:* London, 1942. 8º. C. **121**. b. **22**.

DE CHAIR (Somerset Struben)
—— The Golden Carpet, *etc.* [With a portrait.] pp. 128. *Golden Cockerel Press:* London, 1943. 4º. C. **99**. g. **48**.

DE CHAIR (Somerset Struben)
—— The Silver Crescent, *etc.* [An account of the author's experiences during the Syrian campaign in 1941. With plates, including portraits.] pp. 126. *Golden Cockerel Press:* London, 1943. 8º. C. **99**. g. **47**.

GOLDEN COCKEREL PRESS.

—— Pertelote. A sequel to Chanticleer. Being a bibliography of the Golden Cockerel Press, October 1936–1943 April. Foreword & notes by the partners [i.e. Christopher Sandford and Owen Rutter]. Illustrations from the books. pp. 51. *London*, 1943. 8º.

C. 99. g. 46.

PHILBY (Harry St. John Bridger)

—— A Pilgrim in Arabia. [With plates, including portraits.] pp. 191. *Golden Cockerel Press: London*, 1943. 4º.

C. 99. g. 49.

No. 19 of thirty copies containing a short photographic supplement.

SCOTT (Walter Sidney)

—— The Athenians. Being correspondence between Thomas Jefferson Hogg and his friends Thomas Love Peacock, Leigh Hunt, Percy Bysshe Shelley, and others. Edited by W. S. Scott. [With a portrait.] pp. 86. *Golden Cockerel Press: London*, 1943. 4º. C. 99. f. 40.

No. 34 of fifty copies specially bound and containing collotype facsimiles.

BIBLE.—*Psalms.—Selections. [English.—Single Psalms.]*

—— The Ninety-First Psalm. With wood-engravings by Dorothea Braby. *Golden Cockerel Press: London*, 1944. 8º. C. 99. d. 55.

SCOTT (Walter Sidney)

—— Harriet & Mary. Being the relations between Percy Bysshe Shelley, Harriet Shelley, Mary Shelley, and Thomas Jefferson Hogg, as shown in letters between them now published for the first time. Edited by W. S. Scott. [With a portrait of Shelley.] pp. 84. *Golden Cockerel Press: London*, 1944. 4º. C. 99. f. 41.

No. 24 of fifty copies specially bound and containing collotype facsimiles.

SCOTT (Walter Sidney)

—— Shelley at Oxford. The early correspondence of P. B. Shelley with his friend T. J. Hogg together with letters of Mary Shelley and T. L. Peacock and a hitherto unpublished prose fragment by Shelley. Edited by W. S. Scott. [With plates, including portraits.] pp. 79. *Golden Cockerel Press: London*, 1944. 4º. C. 99. f. 38

No. 43 of fifty copies specially bound and with additional plates.

SPARRMAN (Anders)

—— A Voyage round the World with Captain James Cook in H.M.S. Resolution . . . Introduction & notes by Owen Rutter. Wood-engravings by Peter Barker-Mill. [A translation, by Averil Mackenzie-Grieve and Huldine V. Beamish, of " Resa omkring jordklotet i sällskap med kapit. J. Cook och hrr. Forster," forming pt. 2 of " Resa till Goda Hopps-Udden." With a map.] pp. 218. *Golden Cockerel Press: London*, 1944. fol. C. 99. k. 27.

No. 4 of an edition of fifty copies, specially bound.

SWINBURNE (Algernon Charles)

—— Hymn to Proserpine . . . [From " Poems and Ballads," first series.] Engravings by John Buckland-Wright. pp. 9. *Golden Cockerel Press: London*, 1944. 8º. C. 99. d. 53.

No. 8 of fifty copies with an additional engraving and specially bound.

FRANKS

—— The First Crusade. The deeds of the Franks and other Jerusalemites. " Gesta francorum et aliorum hierosolimitanorum." Translated . . . by Somerset de Chair. Engravings by Clifford Webb. pp. 92. *Golden Cockerel Press: London*, 1945. fol. C. 103. i. 8.

GARCÍA CALDERÓN (Ventura)

—— The Lottery Ticket . . . Done into English by Richard Phibbs with engravings by Dorothea Braby. pp. 11. *Golden Cockerel Press: [London*, 1945.] 8º. C. 99. d. 54.

No. 28 of 100 copies bound in ¼ white morocco.

NAPOLEON I., *Emperor of the French. [Works.]*

—— Napoleon's Memoirs. [With portraits.] 2 vol.

vol. 1. Corsica to Marengo. Edited by Somerset de Chair. pp. 422.
vol. 2. Waterloo Campaign. Edited and translated by Somerset de Chair. pp. 78.

Golden Cockerel Press: [London,] 1945. fol. C. 103. i. 7.

No. 28 of fifty copies bound in full morocco.

NAPOLEON I., *Emperor of the French. [Works.]*

—— Supper at Beaucaire . . . Translated . . . by Somerset de Chair. [With a portrait.] pp. 38. *Golden Cockerel Press: London*, 1945. 16º. Cup. 510. af. 14.

WHITFIELD (Christopher)

—— Together and alone. Two short novels . . . With engravings by John O'Connor. *London: Golden Cockerel Press*, 1945. C. 99. f. 39.

pp. 109. 26 cm. △

No. 43 of an edition of one hundred copies bound in quarter-white morocco.

FLINDERS (Matthew)

—— Matthew Flinders' Narrative of his Voyage in the Schooner Francis : 1798. Preceded and followed by notes on Flinders, Bass, the wreck of the Sidney Cove, &c., by Geoffrey Rawson. With engravings by John Buckland Wright. [With a map.] pp. 100. *Golden Cockerel Press: London*, 1946. fol. C. 102. h. 16.

GRAY (Thomas) *the Poet. [Elegy written in a Country Churchyard.]*

—— Gray's Elegy written in a Country Church-yard. With . . . eight engravings by Gwenda Morgan. pp. 19. *Golden Cockerel Press: London*, 1946. 8º. C. 99. b. 38. *No. 54 of an edition of eighty copies specially bound.*

JONES (Gwyn)

—— The Green Island. A novel . . . Engravings by John Petts. pp. 84. *Golden Cockerel Press: London*, 1946. 8º. C. 103. b. 7.

RUTTER (Owen)

—— We Happy Few. An anthology by O. Rutter . . . [Edited by Dorothy Rutter.] With eleven engravings by John O'Connor. pp. 150. *Golden Cockerel Press: London*, 1946. 8º. C. 99. c. 48.

DE HERIZ (PATRICK) La Belle O'Morphi. A brief biography . . . With illustrations by François Boucher [including portraits]. pp. 35. *Golden Cockerel Press:* [*London*, 1947.] 8°. **C. 99. c. 49.**

KEATS (JOHN) [*Single Poems.*]
—— Endymion . . . With engravings by John Buckland-Wright. pp. 150. *Golden Cockerel Press: London,* 1947. fol. **C. 103. i. 9.**
No. 30 of 100 copies specially bound by Sangorski and Sutcliffe.

MILLER (PATRICK) *pseud.* [i.e. GEORGE GORDON MAC-FARLANE.]
—— Woman in Detail. A scientific survey . . . With drawings by Mark Severin. pp. 63. *Golden Cockerel Press: London,* 1947. 8°. **Cup.820.aa.1.**

BANNET (IVOR)
—— The Amazons. A novel . . . Engravings by Clifford Webb. pp. 252. *Golden Cockerel Press: London,* 1948. fol. **C.103.g.11.**

HOMER. [*Hymns.—Greek and English.*]
—— The Homeric Hymn to Aphrodite. A new translation by F. L. Lucas . . . With ten engravings by Mark Severin. pp. 35. *Golden Cockerel Press: London,* 1948. fol. **C. 103. i. 12.**
No. 53 of 100 copies specially bound.

JOHNSON (SAMUEL) *Author of "A Compleat Introduction to the Art of Writing Letters."*
—— The New London Letter Writer . . . Foreword and decorations by Averil Mackenzie-Grieve. pp. 63. *Golden Cockerel Press: London,* 1948. 8°. **C. 103. c. 6.**
No. 76 of an edition of 100 copies specially bound.

LUCAS (FRANK LAURENCE)
—— Gilgamesh, King of Erech . . . With twelve engravings by Dorothea Braby. pp. 63. *Golden Cockerel Press: London,* 1948. 8°. **C. 104. e. 6.**
No. 19 of an edition of 60 specially bound copies.

MABINOGION.
—— The Golden Cockerel Mabinogion. A new translation from the White Book of Rhydderch and the Red Book of Hergest by Gwyn Jones and Thomas Jones. With illustrations by Dorothea Braby. pp. 266. *Golden Cockerel Press: London,* 1948. fol. **C. 108. i. 6.**

SWINBURNE (ALGERNON CHARLES)
—— Laus Veneris . . . Engravings by John Buckland-Wright. pp. 27. *Golden Cockerel Press: London,* 1948. 8°. **C. 103. b. 11.**
No. 70 of an edition of 100 copies with an additional engraving and specially bound.

CABELL (JAMES BRANCH)
—— Jurgen . . . With wood engravings by John Buckland Wright. pp. 349. *Golden Cockerel Press: London,* 1949. 8°. **C. 99. i. 31.**
No. 80 of an edition of 100 specially bound copies.

MUSAEUS, *the Grammarian.* [*English.*]
—— Hero and Leander. Translated . . . by F. L. Lucas. (The engravings are by John Buckland Wright.) [*London:*] Christopher Sandford, 1949. **C. 103. b. 15.**
pp. 47 : plate. 24 cm. △
No. 58 of one hundred specially bound copies with one extra engraving. Signed by the translator and the engraver.

KOMENSKÝ (JAN AMOS)
—— The Labyrinth of the World and the Paradise of the Heart . . . Translated by Count Lutzow. Illustrations by Dorothea Braby. pp. 271. *Golden Cockerel Press: London,* 1950. 8°. **C. 103. c. 8.**

SWINBURNE (ALGERNON CHARLES)
—— Pasiphaë. A poem. [Edited with an introduction by Randolph Hughes. With engravings by John Buckland-Wright.] pp. 40. *Golden Cockerel Press: London,* 1950 [1951]. 8°. **C. 103. f. 4.**

BEAUMONT (FRANCIS)
—— Salmacus and Hermaphroditus. A poem attributed to F. Beaumont. Edited by Gwyn Jones. With ten engravings in colour by John Buckland-Wright. pp. 44. *Golden Cockerel Press: London.* 1951. fol. **C. 104. i. 12.**

CAESAR (CAIUS JULIUS) [*Works.—English.*]
—— Julius Caesar's Commentaries. A modern rendering by Somerset de Chair. Engravings by Clifford Webb. pp. 311. *Golden Cockerel Press: London,* 1951. 8°. **Cup.510.af.15.**

GOLDEN COCKEREL PRESS.
—— Cockalorum. A sequel to Chanticleer and Pertelote. Being a bibliography of the Golden Cockerel Press, June 1943—December 1948. Foreword and notes by Christopher Sandford. Illustrations from the books. pp. 112. *Golden Cockerel Press:* [*London,* 1951.] 8°. **C. 103. b. 23.**

GAWAINE, *Knight of the Round Table.*
—— Sir Gawain and the Green Knight. A prose translation, with an introductory essay by Gwyn Jones. With six engravings in colour by Dorothea Braby. **F.P.** pp. 95. *Golden Cockerel Press: London,* 1952. fol. **C. 100. a. 16**

HARTNOLL (PHYLLIS MAY)
—— The Grecian Enchanted . . . with eight aquatints by John Buckland-Wright. pp. 79. *Golden Cockerel Press:* [*London,*] 1952. fol. **C. 104. i. 11.**

ARAITH.
—— [Araith ddychan i'r gwragedd.] Against Women. A satire translated from the old Welsh by Gwyn Williams. Engravings by John Petts. pp. 25. *Golden Cockerel Press: London,* 1953. 8°. **C. 103. f. 6.**

EDGEWORTH (MARIA) [*Letters.*]
—— Letters of Maria Edgeworth and Anna Letitia Barbauld selected from the Lushington papers and edited by Walter Sidney Scott. Illustrations by Lettice Sandford. pp. 86. *Golden Cockerel Press: London,* 1953. 8°. **C. 103. e. 23.**

NELSON (HORATIO) *Viscount Nelson.* [*Letters.*]
—— Nelson's Letters from the Leeward Islands, and other original documents in the Public Record Office and the British Museum : edited by Geoffrey Rawson, with notes by Professor Michael Lewis and engravings by Geoffrey Wales. pp. 73. *Golden Cockerel Press: London*, 1953. fol.
10921. m. 23.

NELSON (HORATIO) *Viscount Nelson.* [*Letters.*]
—— [Another copy.] Nelson's Letters from the Leeward Islands, *etc.* 1953. **C. 103. g. 28.**
△

BARCLAY (JOHN) *Poet, Author of the " Argenis."*
—— Euphormio's Satyricon. " Euphormionis satyricon " . . . Translated . . . for the first time, from the 1605 edition by Paul Turner . . . Ten wood engravings by Derrick Harris. pp. 158. *Golden Cockerel Press: London*, 1954. 8º. **C. 103. g. 30.**

BROWNE (WILLIAM) *of the Inner Temple.*
—— Circe and Ulysses. The Inner Temple masque presented by the gentlemen there January 13, 1614. Written by William Browne of Tavistock and now edited, with an essay on W. Browne and the English masque, by Gwyn Jones. Seven wood-engravings by Mark Severin. pp. 61. *Golden Cockerel Press: [London,]* 1954. 8º.
C. 100. g. 49.

DE CHAIR (SOMERSET STRUBEN)
—— The Story of a Lifetime . . . Engravings by Clifford Webb. pp. 93. *Golden Cockerel Press: [London,]* 1954. fol. **C. 103. i. 14.**
No. 3 of an edition of one hundred copies.

STEWART (CECIL)
—— Topiary . . . An historical diversion. With colour engravings by Peter Barker-Mill. pp. 33. *Golden Cockerel Press: London,* [1954.] 8º. **C. 99. g. 54.**

WALTERS (EUROF)
—— The Serpent's Presence . . . With eight wood-engravings by Clifford Webb. pp. 105. *Golden Cockerel Press: London,* 1954. 8º. **Cup. 510. af. 16.**

FLINT (Sir WILLIAM RUSSELL)
—— Minxes admonished ; or, Beauty reproved. An album of deplorable caprices faithfully narrated & modestly embellished by W. R. Flint. pp. 123. *Golden Cockerel Press: London,* 1955. fol. **C. 102. h. 17.**
With eight special plates.

HERRICK (ROBERT) *the Poet.* [*Smaller Collections.*]
—— One Hundred and Eleven Poems by Robert Herrick. Selected, arranged & illustrated by Sir William Russell Flint. pp. 127. *Golden Cockerel Press: [London,]* 1955. 8º. **C. 98. c. 12.**

LLYWARCH, *Hen.*
—— The Saga of Llywarch the Old. A reconstruction by Glyn Jones with the verse interludes translated by T. J. Morgan . . . With colour engravings by D. Braby. pp. 38. *Golden Cockerel Press: London,* 1955. 8º.
C. 103. f. 10.

SHELLEY (PERCY BYSSHE) [*Zastrozzi.*]
—— Zastrozzi. A romance . . . With . . . engravings by Cecil Keeling. pp. 131. *Golden Cockerel Press: London,* 1955. 8º. **C. 103. f. 11.**

APOLLONIUS, *Tyrius.*
—— Apollonius of Tyre. Histoiria Apollonii Regis Tyri. Translated from the Latin by Paul Turner. Line-engravings by Mark Severin. pp. 68. *The Golden Cockerel Press: London,* 1956. 4º. **C. 104. e. 12.**

GRIMM (JACOB LUDWIG CARL) and **GRIMM** (WILHELM CARL) [*Kinder- und Hausmärchen.—Selections.*]
—— Grimms' Other Tales. A new selection by Wilhelm Hansen : Translated & edited by Ruth Michaelis-Jena and Arthur Ratcliff : illustrated with ten wood-engravings by Gwenda Morgan. pp. 160. *Golden Cockerel Press: London,* 1956. 8º. **Cup. 510. af. 23.**

MALLARMÉ (STÉPHANE)
—— L'Après-midi d'un faune . . . The translation by Aldous Huxley. Drawings by John Buckland Wright. [Foreword by Mary Buckland Wright.] pp. 10. *Golden Cockerel Press: London,* 1956. fol. **Cup. 510. af. 19.**

DRYDEN (JOHN) [*Poetical Works.—Smaller Collections.*]
—— Songs and Poems of John Dryden. Chosen and introduced by Gwyn Jones. Drawings by Lavinia Blythe. pp. 64. *Golden Cockerel Press: London,* 1957. fol.
C. 104. l. 1.

XENOPHON, *the Ephesian.*
—— The Ephesian story . . . Translated . . . by Paul Turner. With illustrations by Eric Fraser. *London: Golden Cockerel Press,* 1957. **Cup. 510. af. 27.**
pp. 61 : plates. 25 cm.
△

'UMAR KHAIYĀM. [*English.—Fitzgerald's Version.*]
—— The Rubáiyát of Omar Khayyam. Edward Fitzgerald's translation reprinted from the first edition with his preface and notes. Drawings by J. Yunge Bateman. pp. 35. *Golden Cockerel Press: [London,]* 1958. fol.
C. 104. i. 13.

SHAKESPEARE (WILLIAM) [*Collected Poems.*]
—— The Poems & Sonnets of William Shakespeare. Edited by Gwyn Jones. pp. 245. **F.P.** *Golden Cockerel Press: London,* 1960. fol. **C. 100. a. 17.**

CYNWAL (WILLIAM)
—— [Araith ddychan i'r gwragedd.] In Defence of Woman. A Welsh poem translated by Gwyn Williams. Engravings by John Petts. pp. 28. *Golden Cockerel Press: London,* [1961.] 8º. **C. 104. d. 6.**

PARADIS DE MONCRIF (François Augustin)
[Les Chats.]

—— Moncrif's Cats. Les Chats de François Augustin Paradis de Moncrif translated by Reginald Bretnor. [With plates.] pp. 187. *Golden Cockerel Press: London,* 1961. 8°. Cup. **510**. af. **20**.

SUDHĪNDRA-NĀTHA GHOSHA.

—— Folk Tales and Fairy Stories from India . . . With illustrations by Shrimati E. Carlile. pp. 147. *Golden Cockerel Press: London,* 1961. fol. Cup. **510**. af. **21**.

GOLDEN CROSS PRESS, New York

BIBLE.—*Esther.* [*English.*]

—— The Book of Esther. From the King James version of the Holy Bible. Designed & hand illuminated by Valenti Angelo. pp. 36. *Golden Cross Press: New York,* 1935. 8°. C. **104**. b. **5**.

GOLDEN EAGLE PRESS, Mount Vernon, N.Y.

CUMMINGS (Edward Estlin)

—— Puella mea. (Poem. With reproductions of drawings and paintings by Klee [and others].) *S. A. Jacobs, Golden Eagle Press:* [*Mount Vernon, N.Y.,* 1923.] 8°. Cup. **510**. sat. **1**.

GOLDEN HEAD PRESS, Cambridge, *etc.*

LISTER (Raymond George)

—— A Title-List of Books on Miniature Painting, *etc.* pp. 18. *The Author: Cambridge,* 1952. 8°. Cup. **510**. al. **26**.
One of an edition of sixty copies.

LISTER (Raymond)

—— Thomas Gosse. A biographical sketch of an itinerant miniature painter of the early nineteenth century. [With a portrait.] pp. 23. *Raymond Lister, at the Sign of the Golden Head: Linton, Cambs.,* 1953. Cup. **510**. al. **3**.
No. 3 of an edition of sixty copies signed by the author.

BAX (Clifford)

—— Who's Who in Heaven. A sketch. *Golden Head Press: Meldreth,* 1954. 8°. Cup.**510**.al.**5**.

LISTER (Raymond)

—— The Muscovite Peacock. A study of the art of Léon Bakst . . . With a memoir by Simon Lissim. [With plates.] pp. 52. *Golden Head Press: Meldreth,* 1954. 8°. Cup.**510**.al.**4**.

LISTER (Raymond)

—— Decorated Porcelains of Simon Lissim. pp. 32. pl. XIII. *Golden Head Press: Cambridge,* 1955. 8°. Cup.**510**.al.**7**

S., S.

—— An Adjustment. By S. S. [i.e. Siegfried L. Sassoon.] With a foreword by Philip Gosse. *Golden Head Press: Royston,* 1955. 8°. Cup.**510**.al.**10**.

STAGEMAN (Peter)

—— A Bibliography of the First Editions of Philip Henry Gosse . . . With introductory essays by Sacheverell Sitwell and Geoffrey Lapage. [With plates.] pp. xi. 87. *Golden Head Press: Cambridge,* 1955. 8°. Cup.**510**.al.**6**.

LISTER (Raymond)

—— The Loyal Blacksmith. Being the story of William Houlbrook of Marlborough, newly written by R. Lister with copious quotations from Houlbrook's own narrative. pp. 32. *Golden Head Press: Cambridge,* 1957. 8°. Cup.**510**.al.**8**.
One of an edition of ninety copies printed on hand-made paper.

CHANTER (Phyllis)

—— Saltfleet, and other poems. pp. 25. *Golden Head Press: Cambridge,* 1958. 8°. Cup.**510**.al.**25**.
One of an edition of one hundred copies.

VIRGILIUS MARO (Publius) [*Bucolica.—English.*]

—— Virgil's Second Eclogue. [Illustrated by Raymond and Pamela Lister.] ff. 9. *Golden Head Press: Cambridge,* [1958.] 8°. Cup.**510**.al.**1.**—
No. X *of 10 presentation copies signed by Raymond Lister.*

DURHAM (John Francis Langton)

—— Telegraphs in Victorian London. pp. 30. *Golden Head Press: Cambridge,* 1959. 8°. Cup.**510**.al.**9**.

MOORE (Thomas) *the Poet.* [*Selections.*]

—— The Song of Fionnuala, and nine other songs. (Printed from photo-line engraved blocks taken from original designs by Raymond Lister.) *Golden Head Press: Cambridge,* 1960. 8°. Cup. **510**. al. **2**.
No. 8 of ten copies printed for presentation, these and a further twenty-six copies being illuminated, coloured and signed by Raymond Lister.

LISTER (Raymond George)

—— Ehon. A nocturne in wood and words. [Woodcuts with accompanying text.] *Golden Head Press: Cambridge,* 1962. 8°. Cup. **510**. al. **13**.
Printed on blue Natsume paper. One of an edition of twenty-six copies.

LISTER (Raymond George)

—— The First Book of Theodosius, called The Gate. [With illustrations by the author.] *Golden Head Press: Cambridge,* 1962. Cup. **510**. al. **11**.
No. 5 of an edition of five copies, on hand-made Japanese paper, signed by the author. Printed on one side of the paper only.

LISTER (Raymond George)

—— Scroll of Proverbs. Calligraphy by Albert Cousins. Proverbs & monotype by R. Lister. *Golden Head Press: Cambridge*, [1962.] *s.sh.* fol. Cup. **510**. al. **12**.
One of an edition of ninety copies.

WARNER (Francis) *Writer of Verse.*

—— Perennia ... [A poem.] Decorated with wood-engravings by Raymond Lister. pp. 27. *Golden Head Press: Cambridge*, 1962. 8⁰. Cup. **510**. al. **14**.

DYER (John) *Poet.*

—— Grongar Hill. With woodcuts by Pamela Hughes. *Golden Head Press: Cambridge*, 1963. 8⁰. Cup. **510**. al. **16**.

LISTER (Raymond George)

—— The Miniature defined. pp. 20. pl. vi. *Golden Head Press: Cambridge*, 1963. 8⁰. Cup. **510**. al. **15**.

LISTER (Raymond George)

—— The Song of Theodosius. On Vellum. [*Golden Head Press*:] *Cambridge*, 1963. 8⁰. Cup. **510**. al. **17**.
One of an edition of fifteen copies signed by the author.

LISTER (Raymond George) [*Appendix.*]

—— Raymond Lister. Five essays, by Charles Richard Cammell [and others], *etc.* [With portraits.] pp. 22. pl. xviii. *Golden Head Press: Cambridge*, 1963. 8⁰. Cup. **510**. al. **19**.

CAMMELL (Charles Richard)

—— Ars poetica. An ode. *Golden Head Press: Cambridge*, 1964. 8⁰. Cup.**510**.a1.**24**.

HENN (Thomas Rice)

—— Shooting a Bat, and other poems. pp. 42. F.P. *Golden Head Press: Cambridge*, 1964. 8⁰. Cup. **510**. al. **20**.
One of a fine paper issue of which twenty-six copies were printed for sale.

LISTER (Raymond George)

—— Gabha. (Written and designed by R. Lister.) *Golden Head Press: Cambridge*, 1964. 8⁰. Cup. **510**. al. **18**.

LISTER (Raymond George)

—— Ghazal. (Written and designed by R. Lister.) *Golden Head Press: Cambridge*, 1964. 8⁰. Cup. **510**. al. **21**.

BLUNDEN (Edmund Charles)

—— Eleven poems. pp. 21. *Golden Head Press: Cambridge*, 1965. 8⁰. Cup. **510**. al. **23**.
Signed by the author.

LISTER (Raymond George)

—— Tao. (Written and designed by Raymond Lister.) *Golden Head Press: Cambridge*, 1965. 8⁰. Cup. **510**. al. **22**.
The colophon states: "Six impressions, each with an original drawing; thirty-four impressions on Natsume paper, each signed by the artist and numbered".

GOLDEN HIND PRESS, Madison, N.J.

BOWIE (Walter Russell)

—— When Jesus was Born. The story of Christmas for little children ... Illustration ... by Charles B. Falls. pp. 20. *Harper & Bros.: New York & London*, 1928. 16⁰. Cup. **510**. pm. **1**.

RUSHMORE (Elsie Mitchell)

—— Songs and other verses. pp. 29. *Printed by A. W. Rushmore at the Golden Hind Press: Madison, N.J.*, 1928. 8⁰. Cup. **510**. pm. **5**.
One of an edition of which 100 copies were printed for sale.

BLUNDEN (Edmund Charles)

—— Near and far. New poems. pp. viii. 64. *Harper & Bros.: New York & London*, 1930. 8⁰. Cup. **510**. pm. **4**.

LAMB (Charles)
[*Essays of Elia.*]

—— Grace before Meat, from the Essays of Elia. pp. 18. *Privately printed by Arthur W. Rushmore at the Golden Hind Press: Madison, N.J.*, 1931. 8⁰. Cup. **503**. e. **11**.
No. 46 of an edition of seventy-five copies.

MILLAY (Edna St. Vincent)

—— "There are no Islands, any more." Lines written in passion and in deep concern for England, France and my own country, by E. St. Vincent Millay. pp. 10. *Harper & Bros.: New York & London*, 1940. 8⁰. Cup. **510**. pm. **2**.

THOMAS [More], *Saint, Lord High Chancellor of England.* [*Miscellaneous Works.*]

—— A letter from Sir Thomas More to Conrad Goclenius, London, c. November 1522. Translated by Robert Samuel Rogers. With a note by Elizabeth Frances Rogers. *Madison, N.J.: Golden Hind Press*, 1949. Cup. **510**. pm. **6**.

Pages not numbered ; port. 23 cm. △

On Goclenius's dedication to More of his translation of Lucian's Hermotimus. With a facsimile of the original letter in the Archives générales du Royaume, Brussels.

HUNTINGTON (Archer Milton)

—— Tapestry. [Poems.] pp. viii. 75. *New York*, 1951. 8⁰. Cup. **510**. pm. **3**.
One of an edition of 100 copies printed by hand on all rag paper at the Golden Hind Press.

GOLDEN HOURS PRESS, London

MARLOWE (Christopher) *the Dramatist.* [*Doctor Faustus.*]

—— The Tragicall History of Doctor Faustus ... With engravings by Blair Hughes-Stanton. pp. 55. *Golden Hours Press: London*, 1932. 4⁰. C. **98**. e. **19**.

MARLOWE (Christopher) *the Dramatist.* [*Hero and Leander.*]

—— The Amorous Poem entitled Hero & Leander. Begun by Christopher Marlowe and finished by George Chapman. Printed by Felix Kingston for Paul Linley, 1598. Together with two lyrics by Chr. Marlowe ... With engravings by Lettice Sandford. pp. 85. *Golden Hours Press: London*, 1933. 4⁰. C. **102**. f. **5**.

MARLOWE (CHRISTOPHER) *the Dramatist.* [*The Jew of Malta.*]

—— The Famous Tragedy of the Rich Jew of Malta . . . With engravings by Eric Ravilious. pp. 86. *Golden Hours Press: London,* 1933. 4°. C. 102. f. 4.

REMEDY.

—— A Remedy for Sedition. Which rare and witty book is now reprinted for the first time. With a foreword by E. M. Cox. pp. 60. *Golden Hours Press: London,* 1933. 8°. C.103.b.9.

No. 7 of an edition of 100 copies.

GOLDEN STAR PRESS, New York

HUGHES (JAMES LANGSTON)

—— The Negro mother, and other dramatic recitations . . . With decorations by Prentiss Taylor. pp. 20. *Golden Stair Press: New York,* [1931.] 8°. Cup. 510. ncl. 1.

GOLIARD PRESS

JONAS (STEPHEN)

—— The Music master, *etc.* [A poem by Stephen Jonas. With an original print by Barry Hall.] *Andrew Crozier, Ferry Press: London,* 1965. 8°. Cup. 510. dak. 1.

No. 24 of a limited edition of thirty-three copies, signed by the author and the illustrator.

SMITH (EDWARD LUCIE)

—— A game of French and English. *London: Turret Books,* 1965. Cup. 510. dak. 43.

    Pages not numbered. 20 cm. △

A poem. No. 24 of an edition of one hundred copies, printed at the Goliard Press and signed by the author.

SMITH (EDWARD LUCIE)

—— Three experiments. *London: Turret Books,* 1965. 29 cm. Cup. 510. dak. 44.

    △

Verse. A single sheet. No. 24 of an edition of eighty copies, printed at the Goliard Press, and signed by the author.

GRABHORN PRESS, San Francisco

HARTE (FRANCIS BRET)

—— Dickens in Camp . . . With a foreword by Frederick S. Myrtle. pp. 15. *John Howell: San Francisco,* 1922. 8°. Cup. 510. pb. 1.

BISSETT (CLARK PRESCOTT)

—— Abraham Lincoln. A universal man. pp. xiii. 230. *John Howell: San Francisco,* 1923. 8°. Cup.510.pb.2.

TAGGARD (GENEVIÈVE)

—— Hawaiian Hilltop. [Poems.] pp. 15. *Wyckoff & Gelber: San Francisco,* 1923. 8°. Cup. 510. pb. 39. *Flight.* no. 1.

ANDERSON (SHERWOOD)

—— The Modern Writer. pp. 44. *Gelber, Lilienthal: San Francisco,* 1925. 8°. Cup. 510. pb. 38.

BENSON (STELLA)

—— The Awakening. A fantasy. pp. 15. *Printed by Edwin and Robert Grabhorn for the Lantern Press: San Francisco,* 1925. 8°. Cup. 510. pb. 31.

BIBLE.—*Job.* [*English.*]

—— The Book of Job according to the Authorized Version of 1611, *etc.* pp. xxix. *E. & R. Grabhorn:* [*San Francisco,*] 1926. fol. L.R. 37. d. 13.

VESPUCCI (AMERIGO)

—— [Lettera di Amerigo Vespucci delle isole nuouamente trouate.] The letter of Amerigo Vespucci describing his four voyages to the New World, 1497–1504. (Initials, drawings and hand-colored map, adapted from contemporary sources, by Valenti Angelo.) [The introduction signed: Oscar Lewis.] *San Francisco: Book Club of California ; printed by Edwin & Robert Grabhorn,* 1926. Cup. 510. pb. 18.

    pp. 28. 31 cm. △

WILDE (OSCAR FINGAL O'FLAHERTIE WILLS)

—— Salome, *etc.* (Frontispiece and marginal decorations from word blocks designed and cut by Valenti Angelo.) [Translated by Lord Alfred Douglas.] *Edwin & Robert Grabhorn: San Francisco,* 1927. 8°. Cup. 510. pb. 6.

ROBINSON (EDWIN ARLINGTON)

—— Fortunatus. *Reno: Slide Mountain Press ; San Francisco:* [*printed at*] *the Grabhorn Press,* 1928. Cup. 510. pb. 7.

    Pages not numbered. 24 cm. △

A poem. Printed on one side of the leaf only.

ANDERSON (SHERWOOD)

—— Nearer the Grass Roots . . . An Account of a Journey: Elizabethton. pp. 34. *Westgate Press: San Francisco,* 1929. 8°. Cup. 510. pb. 36.

CABELL (JAMES BRANCH)

—— Sonnets from Antan with an editorial note by J. B. Cabell. *Fountain Press: New York,* 1929. 8°. Cup. 510. pb. 3.

DEARDEN (ROBERT ROWLAND) and **WATSON** (DOUGLAS SLOANE) An Original Leaf from the Bible of the Revolution, and an essay concerning it by Robert R. Dearden, Jr. and Douglas S. Watson. [On the edition of the Bible printed by R. Aitken, Philadelphia, 1782. With a facsimile of a letter of George Washington with reference to its publication.] pp. 34. *John Howell: San Francisco,* 1930. 8° Cup.510.pb.8.

SAN FRANCISCO.—*Roxburghe Club of San Francisco.*
Eden Anto. By Antonio Fogazzaro.
Translated by Theodore Wesley Koch. [With a preface concerning the edition of Ariosto's "Orlando Furioso" published by Francesco Rosso at Ferrara in 1532, and facsimiles and illustrations.] pp. 29.
San Francisco, 1930. 8°.   C. 98. e. 13.

WOOLF (VIRGINIA)
—— Street Haunting. pp. 35. *Westgate Press: San Francisco*, 1930. 8°.   Cup.510.pb.30.

CRANE (STEPHEN) *Novelist.*
—— The Red Badge of Courage, *etc.* (Decorations by Valenti Angelo.) pp. 142. *Random House: New York*, 1931. fol.   Cup. 510. pb. 47.

STODDARD (CHARLES WARREN)
—— Charles Warren Stoddard's Diary of a Visit to Molokai in 1884, with a letter from Father Damien to his brother in 1873. Introduction by Oscar Lewis. [With a portrait of Father Damien.] pp. xi. 52.   *Book Club of California: San Francisco*, 1933. 8° Cup.510.pb.9.

BAER (WARREN)
—— The Duke of Sacramento. A comedy in four acts . . . reprinted from the rare edition of 1856, to which is added a sketch of the early San Francisco stage by Jane Bissell Grabhorn, and illustrations by Arvilla Parker. pp. 77. *Grabhorn Press: San Francisco*, 1934. 8°.
     Cup.510.pb.10.
Ser. 3. vol. 1 of " Rare Americana."

BOTTOME (PHYLLIS)
—— Stella Benson.   *Printed for Albert M. Bender: San Francisco*, 1934. 8°.   Cup. 510. gb. 46.

JEFFERS (JOHN ROBINSON)
—— Return. An unpublished poem.   *Grabhorn Press for Gelber, Lilienthal: San Francisco*, 1934. fol.
     Cup. 510. pb. 34.

ROBERTSON (JOHN WOOSTER)
—— Bibliography of the Writings of Edgar A. Poe. (Commentary on the bibliography of Edgar A. Poe.) [With facsimiles.] 2 vol.   *Russian Hill Private Press: San Francisco*, 1934. 8°.   2784.ms.2.

JEFFERS (JOHN ROBINSON)
—— Solstice, and other poems. pp. 151.   *Random House: New York; printed by the Grabhorn Press: San Francisco*, 1935. 8°.   Cup. 510. pb. 35.
With the author's autograph.

MERCER (ASA SHINN)
—— The Banditti of the Plains ; or, the Cattlemen's invasion of Wyoming in 1892 . . . Foreword by James Mitchell Clarke and illustrations by Arvilla Parker. pp. xiv. 136. *George Fields: San Francisco*, 1935. 8°. Cup.510.pb.12.

PARSONS (GEORGE FREDERIC)
—— The Life and Adventures of James W. Marshall, the discoverer of gold in California . . . Introduction and notes by G. Ezra Dane. [With a portrait.] pp. xvi. 144. *George Fields: San Francisco*, 1935. 8°. Cup.510.pb.11.

DELANO (ALONZO)
—— A Sojourn with Royalty, and other sketches by " Old Block "—Alonzo Delano. Collected and edited by G. Ezra Dane. Foreword by Edmund G. Kenyon. Illustrated by Charles Lindstrom. pp. 96.   *George Fields: San Francisco*, 1936. 8°.   Cup.510.pb.13.

LAWRENCE (DAVID HERBERT)
—— D. H. Lawrence's Unpublished Foreword to " Women in Love," 1919.   *Gelber, Lilienthal: San Francisco*, 1936. 4°.   Cup. 510. pb. 20.
One of an edition of 100 copies printed at the Grabhorn Press.

SUTRO (ALFRED)
—— The Batheaston Parnassus Fairs [i.e. the literary contests organised by Lady Anne Miller at Batheaston]. A manuscript identified. [On the poem "Bath Sets" by Miss Waters of Bath-Easton. With the text.] pp. 15. *Grabhorn Press: San Francisco*, 1936. 4°.
     Cup. 510. pb. 32.
Privately printed.

GESNER (CONRAD) *Professor in the University of Zurich.*
—— Conrad Gesner. On the Admiration of Mountains, the prefatory letter addressed to Jacob Avienus . . . in Gesner's pamphlet " On Milk and Substances prepared from Milk " . . . A Description of the Riven Mountain, commonly called Mount Pilatus, addressed to J. Chrysostome Huber, originally printed with another work of Gesner's at Zürich in 1555. Translated by H. B. D. Soulé. Together with: On Conrad Gesner and The Mountaineering of Theuerdank, by J. Monroe Thorington. Bibliographical notes by W. Dock and J. M. Thorington. [Edited by W. Dock. With illustrations.] pp. 54.   *Grabhorn Press: San Francisco*, 1937. fol.   C.99.g.50.

KANE (THOMAS LEIPER)
—— A Friend of the Mormons. (The private papers and diary of Thomas Leiper Kane.) With an introduction and edited by Oscar Osburn Winther. [With plates, including a portrait.] pp. ix. 78.   *Gelber-Lilienthal: San Francisco*, 1937. 8°.   Cup.510.pb.15.

SAN FRANCISCO.—*Bohemian Club.*
—— A Brief Catalog of the Published Works of Bohemian Club Authors. pp. 50. *San Francisco*, 1937. 8°.
     2784. mt. 18.

SCHUENEMANN-POTT (FRIEDRICH)

—— The Story of my Life. A translation from the original German of the autobiography of Friedrich Schuenemann-Pott, as made by his daughter, Ida Denicke. (Original published in 1873 in "Blaetter fur freies religiöses Leben".) pp. 132. *Grabhorn Press: San Francisco*, 1937. 8°.   Cup. 510. pb. 33.
Privately printed. No. 28 of an edition of 100 copies.

WAGNER (HENRY RAUP)

—— The Plains and the Rockies. A bibliography of original narratives of travel and adventure, 1800–1865. Revised and extended by Charles L. Camp. pp. 299. *Grabhorn Press: San Francisco*, 1937. 8°.   2774. m. 8.

FRANCE. [*Appendix.—History and Politics.—Miscellaneous.*]

—— Joan the Maid of Orleans. Being that portion of the Chronicles of St. Denis which deals with her life and times, from the Chroniques de France printed in Paris in 1493. Now translated by Pauline B. Sowers with reproductions of woodcuts from the original edition and a bibliographical note on the work of Antoine Vérard [by Roy Vernon Sowers]. pp. xxv.   *R. V. Sowers: San Francisco*, 1938. fol.   C. 103. k. 1.

ROGERS (FRED B.)

—— Soldiers of the Overland. Being some account of the services of General Patrick Edward O'Connor & his volunteers in the West. [With plates, including portraits, and with maps.] pp. 290. *Grabhorn Press: San Francisco*, 1938. 8°.   Cup. 510. pb. 14

SAN FRANCISCO.—*Book Club of California.*

—— An original issue of "The Spectator". Together with the story of the famous English periodical and of its founders, Joseph Addison & Richard Steele, by Eric Partridge.   [*San Francisco:*] *printed by the Grabhorn Press*, 1939.   L.R. 261. b. 18.

pp. 49; ports. 34 cm.   △
The issue of "The Spectator" inserted in this copy is no. 82.

SAN FRANCISCO.—*Golden Gate International Exposition.*

—— Fine Bookbindings exhibited at the Golden Gate International Exposition, San Francisco: MCMXXXIX. [A catalogue. By Morgan A. Gunst.] pp. 32. *Privately printed: San Francisco*, 1939. fol. Cup. 510. pb. 16.

SAN FRANCISCO.—*Society of California Pioneers.*

—— New Helvetia Diary. A record of events kept by John A. Sutter and his clerks at New Helvetia, California, from September 9, 1845, to May 25, 1848. [With plates.] pp. xxvii. 138. *San Francisco*, 1939. fol.   Ac. 8381. b.

WILDE (OSCAR FINGALL O'FLAHERTIE WILLS)

—— The Fisherman and his Soul. (Reprinted from "A House of Pomegranates.") pp. 65.   *Printed for Ransohoffs by the Grabhorn Press: San Francisco*, 1939. 8°.
C. 102. f. 12.

ELWOOD (LOUIE BUTLER)

—— Queen Calafia's Land. An historical sketch of California. [With plates.] pp. 108. *Grabhorn Press: San Francisco*, 1940. 8°.   Cup. 510. pb. 21.

HELLER (ELINOR RAAS) and **MAGEE** (DAVID)

—— Bibliography of the Grabhorn Press. 1915–1940. (1940–1956. By Dorothy and David Magee. With a checklist, 1916–1940.) [With specimen pages.] 2 vol. [*Grabhorn Press:*] *San Francisco*, 1940, 57. fol.   C. 99. l. 18.

LAWRENCE (DAVID HERBERT)

—— Fire and Other Poems . . . With a foreword by Robinson Jeffers and a note on the poems by Frieda Lawrence. pp. xi. 36. *Printed at the Grabhorn Press for the Book Club of California: San Francisco*, 1940. 8°.
Cup. 510. pb. 19.

MELVILLE (HERMAN)
[The piazza tales.]

—— The Encantadas or, Enchanted isles . . . With an introduction, critical epilogue & bibliographical notes by Victor Wolfgang von Hagen. *Burlingame: William P. Wreden; San Francisco: printed at the Grabhorn Press*, 1940.
C. 99. g. 52.

pp. xxiii, 118: plates; illus. 28 cm.   △
From "The piazza tales".

SANDBURG (CARL)

—— Bronze Wood. [On a mask carved by Leon Gelber. With a reproduction.]   *Gelber, Lilienthal: San Francisco*, 1941. 4°.   Cup. 510. pb. 23.

WHEAT (CARL IRVING)

—— The Maps of the California Gold Region, 1848–1857. A biblio-cartography of an important decade. [With facsimiles.] pp. xlii. 152. *Grabhorn Press: San Francisco*, 1942. fol.   Maps. Ref. L. 4.

FARQUHAR (FRANCIS PELOUBET)

—— A Brief Chronology of Discovery in the Pacific Ocean from Balboa to Capt. Cook's First Voyage, 1513 to 1770. pp. 14. *Grabhorn Press: San Francisco*, 1943. 8°.
Cup. 510. pb. 22.

GAUGUIN (PAUL) [*Letters.*]

—— Letters to Ambroise Vollard & André Fontainas. Edited by John Rewald. With reproductions of ten woodcuts. pp. 67. *Grabhorn Press: San Francisco*, 1943. fol.
L.R. 294. d. 10.

METZGAR (JUDSON D.)

—— Adventures in Japanese Prints . . . A Story of Oriental print collecting in the early years of the present century with some technical criticisms on prints and observations on forming a collection. [With plates.] pp. 116. *Grabhorn Press for Dawson's Book Shop: Los Angeles*, [1944.] fol.   L.R. 295. c. 2.

SHAKESPEARE (WILLIAM) *[Selections and Extracts.]*
—— VIII Lyrics by William Shakespere. *[Grabhorn Press]: San Francisco,* 1946. 8°. Cup.510.pb.25.

LEVY (HARRIET LANCE)
—— " I love to talk about myself " & other verses concerning God & man & me. *San Francisco: Grabhorn Press,* 1947. Cup. 510. pb. 51.
pp. 96. 23 cm. △

BIBLE.—*Susannah. [English.]*
—— The History of Susanna. (Engravings by Mallette Dean.) *Grabhorn Press : San Francisco,* [1948.] 8°. Cup. 510. pb. 40.

BOK (CURTIS)
—— Commonwealth v. Gordon et al. The opinion of Judge Bok, March eighteenth, 1949. [Judgment in the case arising out of the confiscation by the Philadelphia police of books alleged to be obscene.] pp. 57. *Blanche & Alfred Knopf; printed by the Grabhorn Press:* [San Francisco,] 1949. 4°. Cup.510.pb.41.

DICKENS (CHARLES) *[A Christmas Carol,]*
—— A Christmas Carol, *etc.* (Initials by Malletto Dean.) pp. 74. *Ransohoffs: San Francisco,* 1950. fol. C. 104. k. 4.

MACHEN (ARTHUR LLEWELYN JONES)
—— Bridles & Spurs ... With a preface by Nathan van Patten. [With a portrait.] pp. xv. 70. *Rowfant Club : Cleveland,* 1951. 8°. Cup. 510. pb. 24.

STEVENSON (ROBERT LOUIS)
—— The Silverado Squatters. pp. 181. *Grabhorn Press : San Francisco,* 1952. 8°. Cup.510.pb.4.

REICHERT (IRVING FREDERICK)
—— Judaism & the American Jew. Selected sermons & addresses. pp. xii. 245. *Grabhorn Press : San Francisco.* 1953. 4°. Cup.510.pb.42.

SAN FRANCISCO.—*Book Club of California.*
—— [An annual series of publications, or " keepsakes ", sent to members.] 1954, 1955, 1958–1963, 1966, 1967.
  1954. Early Transportation in Southern California. 13 pt.
    Cup. 500. p. 13. (1.)
  1955. The Vine in Early California. 12 pt.
    Cup. 500. p. 13. (2.)
  1958. Gold Rush Steamers. 12 pt.
    Cup. 500. p. 13. (3.)
  1959. California Sheet Music Covers. 12 pt.
    Cup. 500. p. 13. (4.)
  1960. Early California Mail-bag. 12 pt.
    Cup. 500. p. 13. (5.)
  1961. Early California Firehouses and Equipment. 12 pt.
    Cup. 500. p. 13. (6.)

SAN FRANCISCO.—*Book Club of California.*
—— [An annual series of publications, or " keepsakes ", sent to members.]—*cont.*
  1962. Portfolio of Book Club Printers, 1912–1962. 14 pt.
    Cup. 500. p. 13. (7.)
  1963. The California Government Seals. 12 pt.
    Cup. 500. p. 13. (8.)
  1966. Early California Trade Cards. 9 pt.
    Cup. 500. p. 13. (9.)
  1967. Homes of California authors. 12 pt.
    Cup. 500. p. 13. (10.)
San Francisco, 1954–67. 8° & *obl.* 8°. Cup. 50 13.

SAN FRANCISCO.—*Roxburghe Club of San Francisco.*
—— Chronology of Twenty-Five Years. (1928–1953. Geo. E. Dawson, editor.) pl. XXVI. *San Francisco,* 1954. fol. Cup.500.g.12.

STANFORD, *California.—Leland Stanford Junior University.—Libraries.*
—— Catalogue of an exhibition of the typographic work of Jane Grabhorn in the Albert M. Bender Room of the Stanford University Libraries, March 4 to April 7, 1956. *[Stanford,* 1956]. Cup. 510. pb. 43.
pp. 27. 26 cm. △

STANFORD, *California.—Leland Stanford Junior University.—Library.*
—— Les Architectes du livre. Contemporary creative French bookbinding from the collection of Mr. and Mrs. Morgan A. Gunst and Mr. and Mrs. Edward H. Heller in an exhibition by the Stanford University Libraries . . . September 23—October 20, 1956. (Catalogue compiled by J. Terry Bender.) *Grabhorn Press : San Francisco,* 1956. fol. Cup.510.pb.44.

DANTE ALIGHIERI. *[Divina Commedia.—Complete Texts.—English.]*
—— The Comedy of Dante Alighieri, translated into English unrhymed hendecasyllabic verse by Mary Prentice Lillie. 3 vol. pp. 535. *Grabhorn Press : San Francisco,* 1958. fol. Cup.510.pb.26.

RACINE (JEAN) *[Phèdre.]*
—— Phaedra. Translated . . . by Agnes Tobin. pp. 80. *Printed at the Grabhorn Press for John Howell: San Francisco,* 1958. 8°. Cup. 510. pb. 17.

RAPP (ALBERT) *Professor of Classical Languages at the University of Tennessee.*
—— The Ancient Greeks & Joe Miller . . . A prolegomenon by Nat Schmulowitz. pp. 32. *Privately printed for Members of the Roxburghe Club of San Francisco:* [San Francisco,] 1958. fol. Cup.510.pb.28.
Anecdota Scowah. no. 3.

SCHULZ (H. C.)
—— French Illuminated Manuscripts . . . With an original leaf from a miniature Book of Hours. pp. 30. *Printed for David Magee by the Grabhorn Press: San Francisco,* 1958. 8°. Cup.510.pb.27.

TOBIN (AGNES)

—— Agnes Tobin. Letters [mostly to Alice Meynell], translations, poems. With some account of her life. [With a biographical sketch, signed : J. S., and an essay by Sir Francis Meynell. With plates, including portraits.] pp. xxi. 99. *Printed at the Grabhorn Press for John Howell: San Francisco*, 1958. 4°. **10601. y. 53.**

TOBIN (AGNES) [*Collections.*]

—— [Another copy.] Agnes Tobin, *etc.*   *San Francisco,* 1958. 4°.   **Cup. 510. pb. 5.**

GRABHORN PRESS.

—— Nineteenth Century Type, displayed in 18 fonts, cast by United States Founders, now in the cases of the Grabhorn Press, *etc.* [With an introduction by Robert Grabhorn.] *San Francisco,* 1959. *obl.* 8°.   **Cup.510.pb.29.**

BRACCIOLINI (POGGIO) [*Single Works.—Facetiae.*]

—— The Facetiae of Poggio, the Florentine. By Albert Rapp. [With translations of selected stories.] Praefatio & bibliography by Nat Schmulowitz. [With portraits.] pp. 37. *Privately printed for Members of the Roxburghe Club of San Francisco :* [*San Francisco,*] 1962. fol.   **L.R. 409. pp. 5.**

Anecdota Scowah. no. 5.

BRANSTEN (JOSEPH)

—— MDCCCLXXVII—Ave, Robinson Jeffers . . . Vale, MCMLXII. (Presented by Joseph Bransten [and others].) pp. 30. *Grabhorn Press : San Francisco,* [1962.] 4°.   **Cup. 510. pb. 45.**

STEVENSON (ROBERT LOUIS) [*Letters.*]

—— R.L.S. to J. M. Barrie. [A letter.] A Vailima portrait. With an introduction by Bradford A. Booth. (Sketches of Stevenson and his household at Vailima by Isobel Strong.) pp. xiv. 15.   *Book Club of California : San Francisco,* 1962. fol.   **Cup. 510. pb. 37.**

VAN WIE (CARRIE)

—— The Wonderful city of Carrie Van Wie. Paintings of San Francisco at the turn of the century. With text by Oscar Lewis. [Reproductions. With a portrait.] *Book Club of California : San Francisco,* 1963. fol.   **C. 119. k. 9.**

KITAGAWA (UTAMARO)

—— Twelve wood-block prints of Kitagawa Utamaro, illustrating the process of silk culture, with an introductory essay by Jack Hillier. Reproduced in facsimile from the originals in the collection of Edwin & Irma Grabhorn. *Book Club of California : San Francisco,* 1965. fol.   **Cup. 510. pb. 49.**

GRAFTON PRESS, New York

CHAUCER (GEOFFREY) [*Canterbury Tales.—Single Tales.— Nun's Priest's Tales.*]

—— The Nonnes Preestes Tale of the Cok and Hen . . . With introduction by William Cushing Bamburgh. **B.L.** pp. iii. 64. *Grafton Press : New York,* 1902. 4°.   **11626. ee. 36.**

GRAVESEND PRESS, Lexington, Ky.

POWYS (LLEWELYN)

—— Thomas Bewick, 1753–1828. An essay (from Thirteen Worthies) by L. Powys, To which is now added : a letter from England from Alyse Powys. Illustrated. pp. vii. 16. *Gravesend Press : Lexington, Ky.,* 1951. 16°.   **11870. a. 13.**

KOCH (RUDOLF) *Writer on Typography.*

—— Wer ist Victor Hammer? (Translation by Ulrich Middeldorf together with the text of the original manuscript.) *Eng. & Ger.* pp. 11.   *Gravesend Press : Lexington, Ky.,* 1952. 4°.   **Cup. 510. nap. 4.**

BOCCACCIO (GIOVANNI) [*Decamerone.—English.—Single Tales.*]

—— The Three Admirable Accidents of Andrea de Piero, from the first Englyshed edition of the Decameron . . . with woodcuts by Fritz Kredel. pp. 48.   *Gravesend Press : Lexington, Ky.,* 1954. 8°.   **Cup.510.nap.1.**

AUCASSIN. [*English.*]

—— The Song-Story of Aucassin & Nicolette. [Translated by Andrew Lang. The woodcuts by Fritz Kredel.] pp. 78. *Gravesend Press : Lexington,* 1957. 8°.   **Cup.510.nap.3.**

KREDEL (FRITZ)

—— Dolls and Puppets of the Eighteenth Century, as delineated in twenty four drawings by F. Kredel. With a preface by Joseph C. Graves.   *Gravesend Press : Lexington, Ky. ; Frankfurt am Main* printed, 1958. 8°.   **Cup. 502. a. 1.**

KREDEL (FRITZ)

—— [Another copy.] Dolls and Puppets of the Eighteenth Century, *etc.*   *Lexington, Ky. ; Frankfurt am Main* printed, 1958. 8°.   **Cup. 510. nap. 2.** *With the artist's autograph.*

GRAYHOUND PRESS, Fisher's Pond, *etc.*

GAY (JOHN) *the Poet.*

—— Seven Songs from " The Beggars Opera." *Grayhound Press: Fisher's Pond*, 1925. 8⁰. **11774. bb. 54.**

H., N.

—— The Closet of Beauty; or, An old Way to procure new Loveliness. By N. H., 1694. [Extracts from " The Ladies' Dictionary ".] pp. 31. *The Grayhound: Fisher's Pond*, 1925. 8⁰. **Cup. 510. bac. 2.**

W., H. H.

—— The Wonderful Adventures of Tobias and Jemima in Nonesuch Land. By H. H. W. pp. 47. *Grayhound Press: Fisher's Pond*, 1925. 8⁰. **Cup. 510. bac. 1.** *No. 16 of an edition of forty copies.*

GIBBON (MONK) The Tremulous String. [Prose poems.] *A. W. Mathews: Fair Oak*, 1926. 8⁰. **012352. ff. 52.**

R., T. Exploits and Wonders. [Extracts from " The Amazement of Future Ages," by T. R.] pp. 13. *Grayhound Press: Fair Oak*, 1926. **Cup. 510. bac. 3.**

GIBBON (MONK) The Branch of Hawthorn Tree. [Poems.]...Colour designs by Picart Le Doux. pp. 83. *Grayhound Press: London; Paris* [printed], 1927. 8⁰. **C. 100. k. 14.**

GIBBON (MONK) A Ballad. *Grayhound Press: Winchester; Paris* printed, 1930. fol. **C. 98. gg. 23.**

GREENWOOD PRESS, San Francisco

BIBLE.—*Psalms.—Selections.* [*English.—Single Psalms.*]

—— Psalm the Twenty-third. (With a woodcut from Gorricio's Contemplaciones, 1495.) *Bern Porter: Berkeley*, [1945?] 4⁰. **C. 106. h. 4.** *Prayer Book version.*

RUKEYSER (MURIEL)

—— The Children's Orchard. [A poem.] *Book Club of California:* [*San Francisco,*] 1947. 8⁰. **Cup. 510. net. 1.** *California Poetry Folders.* pt. 9.

GREGYNOG PRESS, Newtown, Montgomeryshire

HERBERT (GEORGE) *the Poet.* [*Smaller Collections.*]

—— Poems. (Selected by Sir H. Walford Davies.) [With a woodcut.] *Gregynog: Gregynog Press*, 1923. **C. 99. e. 35.**

pp. xv, 26. 21 cm. △

GREGYNOG.

—— [Programmes of concerts and music festivals held at Gregynog.] [*Newtown, Montgom.:*] *Gregynog Press*, 1924–33. **C. 102. f. 3.**

7 pt. △

VAUGHAN (HENRY) *the Silurist.* [*Selections.*]

—— Poems. [Selected and with an introduction by Ernest Rhys. With woodcuts by Robert Ashwin Maynard and Horace Walter Bray.] pp. xxxv. 85. *Gregynog Press: Gregynog*, 1924. 8⁰. **C. 99. e. 37.**

HUGHES (JOHN CEIRIOG) Caneuon Ceiriog. Detholiad. [Edited by John Lloyd Jones. With a portrait and illustrations.] pp. xxx. 87. *R. A. Maynard: Gwasg Gregynog*, 1925. 4⁰. **C. 98. h. 8.**

JONES (THOMAS GWYNN) Detholiad o Ganiadau. pp. xiii. 169. *Gwasg Gregynog: y Drenewydd*, 1926. 8⁰. **C. 99. e. 38.**

THOMAS (PHILIP EDWARD) [*Selections.*]

—— Chosen essays. (Selected by Ernest Rhys ... The wood engravings are by Robert Ashwin Maynard & Horace Walter Bray.) [*Newtown, Montgom.:*] *Gregynog Press*, 1926. **C. 98. f. 5.**

pp. 102: port. 26 cm. △

BIBLE.—*Ecclesiastes.* [*Welsh.*]

—— Llyfr y Pregeth-wr. [The text of the Bible version of 1588. With woodcuts by David Jones.] pp. 20. *Gwasg Gregynog: Gregynog*, 1927. 4⁰. **C. 98. f. 14.**

RHYS (ERNEST) The Life of St. David. [Compiled by E. Rhys from the life by Rhygyfarch and other sources. With woodcuts by Robert Ashwin Maynard and Horace Walter Bray.] pp. 41. *Gregynog Press: Gregynog*, 1927. 4⁰. **C. 100. k. 16.**

THOMAS (PHILIP EDWARD) [*Selections.*]

—— Selected Poems ... With an introduction by Edward Garnett. pp. xix. 95. *Gregynog Press: Newtown*, 1927. 8⁰. **C. 99. g. 41.**

DAVIES (RICHARD) *Quaker.* An Account of the Convincement, Exercises, Services and Travels of... Richard Davies, *etc.* pp. xx. 162. *Gregynog Press: Newtown, Montgomeryshire*, 1928. 8⁰. **C. 99. d. 34.**

DAVIES (WILLIAM HENRY) [*Collections.*]

—— Selected Poems of W. H. Davies. Arranged by Edward Garnett. With a foreword by the author. [With a portrait engraved by R. A. Maynard from the original by Augustus John.] pp. vii. 91. *Gregynog Press:* [*Gregynog,*] 1928. 8⁰. **C. 99. h. 26.**

HERBERT (Edward) *Baron Herbert of Cherbury.*
The Autobiography of Edward, Lord Herbert of
Cherbury. With an introduction by C. H. Herford
(Wood-engravings by Horace Walter Bray).
pp. xv. 93.   *Gregynog Press :*
Newtown, Montgomeryshire, 1928. fol. C. 100. l. 10.

PEACOCK (Thomas Love)
—— The Misfortunes of Elphin. (Wood-engraving by Horace
Walter Bray.) pp. 119.   *Gregynog Press : Newtown,*
Montgomeryshire, 1928. 8°.   C. 100. g. 54.

'UMAR KHAIYĀM. [*Welsh.*]
—— Penillion Omar Khayyâm, wedi eu cyfieithu o'r Berseg
i'r Gymraeg gan John Morris-Jones. [With woodcuts by
R. A. Maynard.]   [*Newtown, Montgom. :*] *Gwasg y*
Gregynnog, 1928.   C. 100. c. 12.
   pp. xvi, 30.   25 cm.   △

BIBLE.—*Psalms.* [*Welsh.—Prose Versions.*]

—— Psalmau Dafydd, yn ol William Morgan, 1588. [Edited
by Ifor Williams.] pp. 189.   *Gwasg Gregynnog :*
Newtown, 1929. 4°.   C. 100. k. 24.

JONES (Thomas) *C.H.*
—— Elphin Lloyd Jones. [A memoir by Thomas and Eirene
Theodore Jones. With a facsimile of an essay by E. L.
Jones and a portrait.] pp. 16.   *Gregynog Press :*
[*Newtown,*] 1929. 4°.   010825. g. 52.
   Privately printed.

JONES (Thomas) *C.H.*
—— [Another copy.]. Elphin Lloyd Jones.   [*Newtown,*]
1929. 4°.   C.99.d.52.

LAMB (Charles) [*Essays of Elia.*]
—— Elia and the Last Essays of Elia . . . With wood-
engravings adapted from contemporary prints. 2 vol.
Gregynog Press : Newtown, 1929, 30. 8°. C. 100. g. 30.

ABU ZAID, *al-Hilālī.* The Celebrated Romance of
the Stealing of the Mare. [An episode from the
romance of Abu Zaid.] Translated...by Lady Anne
Blunt and done into verse by Wilfrid Scawen Blunt.
pp. ix. 73. *Gregynog Press : Newtown,* 1930. 4°.
                                          C. 102. l. 4.

ROSSETTI (Christina Georgina) [*Selections.*] ——
                          Poems. Chosen
by Walter de la Mare. [With an introduction by
W. de la Mare.] pp. xliii. 107.   *Gregynog Press :*
Newtown, 1930. 8°.   C. 99. h. 28.

AESOP. [*English.—Collections.*]
—— The Fables of Esope. Translated out of Frensshe in to
Englysshe by: William Caxton. With engravings on
wood by Agnes Miller Parker. pp. 146. *Gregynog Press :*
Newtown, 1931. 4°.   C. 102. h. 11.

EURIPIDES. [*Works.—English.*]
—— The Plays of Euripides. [Eight plays.] . . . Trans-
lated into English rhyming verse by Gilbert Murray . . .
With wood-engravings from the Greek vase paintings by
Robert Ashwin Maynard and Horace Walter Bray. 2 vol.
Gregynog Press : Newtown, 1931. fol.   C. 102. l. 8.

MILTON (John) [*Comus.*]
—— Comus . . . With a frontispiece and the six characters
in costume designed and engraved on wood by Blair
Hughes-Stanton. pp. 25.   *Gregynog Press : Newtown,*
1931. 8°.   C. 98. e. 29.

BIBLE.—*Revelation.* [*English.*]
—— The Revelation of Saint John the Divine. (The
format was arranged, the wood-engravings and title
page designed and engraved by Blair Hughes-Stanton.)
Gregynog Press : Newtown, 1932. fol.   C. 102. l. 19.

BUTLER (Samuel) *Philosophical Writer.*
—— Erewhon . . . The wood-engravings by Blair Hughes-
Stanton. *Newtown : Gregynog Press,* 1932. C. 99. h. 44.
   pp. 266.   23 cm.   △

GRUFFYDD (William John)
—— Caniadau. (Torrwyd y darluniau gan Blair Hughes-
Stanton.) pp. vii. 101.   *Gwasg Gregynog : Trenewydd,*
1932. 8°.   C. 69. g. 9.

VANSITTART (Robert Gilbert) *Baron Vansittart.*

—— The Singing Caravan, *etc.* (With decorations and
frontispiece by William MacCance.) pp. vii. 142.
Gregynog Press : Newtown, 1932. 8°.   C. 100. a. 3.

BIBLE.—*Lamentations.* [*English.*]
—— The Lamentations of Jeremiah. (Wood-engravings,
title page and initial letters designed and engraved by Blair
Hughes-Stanton.) [*Newtown,*] *Montgom.: Gregynog Press,*
1933.   C. 100. l. 19.
   Pages not numbered.   39 cm.   △

DAVIES (William Henry)
—— The Lovers' Song-Book. pp. v. 30.   *Gregynog Press :*
[*Gregynog,*] 1933. 8°.   C. 69. ee. 13.

EDWARDS (Sir Owen Morgan)
—— Clych atgof, *etc.* [With woodcuts by William MacCance.]
Ger y Drenewydd : Gwasg Gregynog, 1933. C. 102. a. 10.
   pp. 95.   22 cm.   △

JONES (Thomas) *C.H.*
—— A Theme with Variations. [Speeches and articles on
Welsh subjects.] pp. 221.   *Gregynog Press : Newtown,*
1933. 8°.   12301. p. 1.
   Printed for private circulation.

MILTON (JOHN) [*Minor Poems.*]

—— Four Poems by John Milton. L'Allegro, Il Penseroso, Arcades, Lycidas. With wood-engravings by Blair Hughes-Stanton. pp. 33. *Gregynog Press: Newtown,* 1933. 8°.   C. 102. e. 13'

SAMPSON (JOHN) *Librarian in the University of Liverpool.*

—— XXI Welsh Gypsy Folk-Tales. Collected by: John Sampson. (Edited by Miss Dora E. Yates.) With engravings on wood by: Agnes Miller Parker. pp. xi. 108. *Gregynog Press: Newtown,* 1933. 8°.   C. 102. f. 11.

HABERLY (LOYD)

—— Anne Boleyn, and other poems. pp. 77.   *Gregynog Press: Newtown,* 1934. 4°.   C. 100. e. 21.

MADARIAGA Y ROJO (SALVADOR DE)

—— [Guía del lector del " Quijote."] Don Quixote . . . Translated . . . by the author and Constance H. M. de Madariaga. pp. xv. 136.   *Gregynog Press:* [*Newtown, Montgomery,*] 1934. 8°.   C. 103. b. 1.

APULEIUS (LUCIUS) *Madaurensis.* [*Asinus Aureus.— Selections.—English.*]

—— Eros and Psyche. A poem . . . By Robert Bridges: with wood-cuts from designs by Edward Burne-Jones. *Newtown, Montgom.: Gregynog Press,* 1935. C. 102. g. 8. pp. 141 : illus. 29 cm.   △

FORTESCUE (*Hon. Sir* JOHN WILLIAM)

—— The Story of a Red-Deer . . . With decorations by Dorothy Burroughes. pp. 125.   *Gregynog Press: Newtown,* 1935. 4°.   C.108.g.2.

VEGA CARPIO (LOPE FELIX DE) [*Plays.—Separate Plays.*]

—— The Star of Seville. A drama . . . attributed to Lope de Vega.. Translated out of Spanish by Henry Thomas. pp. xii. 108. *Gregynog Press: Newtown,* 1935. 8°.   C. 102. e. 16.

WADDELL (HELEN JANE)

—— New York City, *etc.* [A poem.]   *Gregynog Press:* [*Newtown,*] 1935. fol.   20020. k. 28.

GREVILLE (FULKE) *Baron Brooke.*

—— Cælica . . . Edited by Una Ellis-Fermor. · pp. xiii. 149. *Gregynog Press: Newtown, Montgomeryshire,* 1936. 8°.   C.108.g.5.

XENOPHON, *the Historian.* [*Cyropaedia.—English.*]

—— Cyrupædia . . . Translated . . . by Philemon Holland . . . Fully reprinted from the 1632 edition. pp. xvii. 321. *Gregynog Press: Newtown,* 1936. fol.   C.108.h.3.

JOINVILLE (JEAN DE)

—— The History of Saint Louis . . . Translated from the French text edited by Natalis de Wailly, by Joan Evans. pp. 157. *Gregynog Press: Newtown,* 1937. fol.   C. 103. h. 4.

GUEVARA (ANTONIO DE) successively *Bishop of Guadix and of Montoñedo.*

—— [Vitae Rusticae Encomium.] The Praise and Happinesse of the Countrie-Life . . . Put into English by H. Vaughan . . . Reprinted from the edition of 1651, with an introduction by Henry Thomas, and wood engravings by Reynolds Stone. pp. xv. 37. *Gregynog Press: Newtown,* 1938. 8°.   C. 108. b. 3.

HARTZENBUSCH (JUAN EUGENIO)

—— The Lovers of Teruel. A drama in four acts in prose and verse . . . Translated from the Spanish by Henry Thomas. pp. x. 112. *Gregynog Press: Newtown,* 1938. 8°.   C. 100. e. 23.

HARTZENBUSCH (JUAN EUGENIO)

—— [Another copy.] The lovers of Teruel, *etc.* 1938.   C. 100. b. 9.

       △

SHAW (GEORGE BERNARD) [*Selections.*]

—— Shaw Gives Himself Away. An autobiographical miscellany. [With a portrait.] pp. xi. 188.   *Gregynog Press: Newtown, Montgomeryshire,* 1939. 8°.   C. 109. g. 7.

ABERCROMBIE (LASCELLES)

—— Lyrics and unfinished poems. [With " A note on the poetry of Lascelles Abercrombie " signed: Wilfrid Gibson.] *Newtown: Gregynog Press,* 1940. C. 108. f. 1. pp. xii, 82. 29 cm.   △

WYNNE (ELLIS)

—— Gweledigaetheu y Bardd Cwsc . . . Visions of the Sleeping Bard. Translated by T. Gwynn Jones. 'Welsh & Eng. pp. xi. 213. *Gregynog Press: Newtown,* 1940. 4°.   C. 100. k. 27.

GUTHRIE (Stuart), Horsham, Sussex

CHESSHIRE (MAY)

—— An Anthology. Extracts from letters written by Miss May Chesshire, a West Country Poet, to Llewelyn Powys, selected and arranged by Diana Harding. [With a preface by John Cowper Powys.] pp. 23.   *Stuart Guthrie: Horsham,* 1937. 4°.   10923. k. 6.

HABERLY (Loyd), Corfe Mullen, Dorset

HABERLY (LOYD)

—— The Crowning Year, and other poems. pp. 59.   *Loyd Haberley: Corfe Mullen,* 1937. 8°.   C. 100. h. 27.

HALCYON PRESS, Maastricht

KEATS (JOHN) [*Selections.*] Odes. · pp. 21.
A. A. M. Stols: Bussum, 1927. 4°. C. 98. f. 21.

KEATS (JOHN) [*Selections.*]
—— [Another copy.] Odes by John Keats. *Bussum*,
1927. 8°. Cup. 510. g 6.

DOUGLAS (*Lord* ALFRED BRUCE)
—— Two Loves and other Poems. pp. 22. [*A. A. M. Stols:*
Maastricht,] 1928. 8°. Cup. 510. g. 19.
One of an edition of fifty copies.

ROSSETTI (DANTE GABRIEL)
—— Hand and Soul. pp. 36. *Halcyon Press: Maastricht*,
1928. 8°. Cup. 510. g. 9.

EVERYMAN.
—— Everyman. A Dutch morality play of the xvth century
translated into English. (The text follows the better of the
two editions printed at London in Paul's Churchyard by
John Skot, about Mdxxxvii, edited some years ago by
Mr. C. F. Tucker Brooke.) pp. xlv. *Halcyon Press:*
Maastricht, 1929. 8°. Cup. 510. g. 18.

HOMER. [*Hymns.—Greek and English.*]
—— Six Hymns of Homer. The English translation [of
selected portions] by Percy Bysshe Shelley, facing the
original Greek. pp. 19. *Halcyon Press: Maastricht*,
1929. 8°. Cup. 510. g. 10.

MILTON (JOHN) [*Sonnets.*]
—— The sonnets of Mr. John Milton, both English and Italian.
Maastricht: Halcyon Press, 1929. Cup. 510. g. 28.
pp. 28. 27 cm. △

KEATS (JOHN) [*Selections.*]
—— The Collected Sonnets of John Keats. Illustrated by
John Buckland Wright. *A. A. M. Stols: Maastricht*,
1930. 8°. Cup. 510. g. 26.

KEATS (JOHN) [*Selections.*]
—— [Another copy.] The collected sonnets of John Keats,
etc. 1930. C. 98. f. 23.
  △
One of fifteen copies on hand-made vellum, containing three
extra sets of the illustrations and of five rejected woodcuts, and
signed by the artist.
  △

MELVILLE (JOHN) *Writer of Verse.*
—— Batavia. A poem. *Maastricht: Halcyon Press*, 1930.
  Cup. 510. g. 27.
pp. 34. 26 cm. △
No. 67 of an edition of one hundred copies.

MELVILLE (JOHN) *Writer of Verse.*
—— [Another copy.] Batavia, *etc.* 1930. C. 98. i. 8.
  △
A copy " out of series " to an edition of ten copies on vellum.

MOORE (THOMAS STURGE)
—— Nine Poems. pp. 36. *Halcyon Press: Maastricht*,
1930. Cup. 510. g. 12.

POE (EDGAR ALLAN) [*Tales.*]
—— The Fall of the House of Usher. With 10 aquatints by
Alexandre Alexeïeff. pp. 68. *A. A. M. Stols:*
Maastricht, 1930. 4°. C. 100. c. 10.
One of 10 copies printed on antique Japanese vellum, and
containing three supplementary sets of proofs of the en-
gravings.

KEATS (JOHN) [*Letters.*]
—— Letters of John Keats to Fanny Brawne. With three
poems and three additional letters. Introductory note by
J. F. Otten. [With a portrait.] pp. 117. *Halcyon*
Press: Maastricht, 1931. 8°. C. 99. h. 30.
No. XXXI of 30 copies, numbered II–XXXI, printed on hand-
made paper and containing two additional proofs of the wood-
cut portrait.

DUMAS (ALEXANDRE) *the Elder.*
—— The Three Musketeers . . . The translation by William
Robson with an introduction by Ben Ray Redman and
illustrations by Pierre Falké. [With plates.] 2 vol.
Halcyon Press for Members of the Limited Editions Club:
Maastricht, 1932. 8°. C. 105. f. 11.
With the autograph signature of the illustrator.

POE (EDGAR ALLAN) [*Tales.*]
—— The Masque of the Red Death, and other tales. Wood
engravings by J. Buckland Wright. pp. 170. *Halcyon*
Press: Maastricht & London, 1932. 4°. C. 98. i. 12.
One of 30 copies containing two additional sets of the
illustrations and of three rejected engravings, which have
been removed and placed in the Department of Prints &
Drawings.

BYRON (GEORGE GORDON NOEL) *Baron Byron.* [*Smaller*
Collections.]
—— Lyrical Poems. Selected and arranged in chronological
order (by E. du Perron). Wood engraving by J. Buckland
Wright. pp. 67. *Halcyon Press: [London ;]*
Maastricht printed, 1933. 8°. C. 100 e. 10.

HAMMER (Victor), Florence

MILTON (JOHN) [*Samson Agonistes.*]
—— Samson Agonistes. A dramatic poem. *Stamperia*
del Santuccio: Florence, 1931. fol. C. 98. c. 9.

HAMPDEN PRESS, Derby; London

BIGGS (JOHN REGINALD)
—— Sinfin Songs and other poems. by J. R. Biggs. With ten
wood-engravings by the same hand. pp. vi. 32. *Privately*
printed at the Hampden Press: Derby, 1932. 12°.
  Cup. 510. am. 1.
No. 7 of an edition of thirty copies.

BIGGS (JOHN REGINALD)
—— Three Sonnets . . . Being three youthful effusions printed
for amusement in May 1932. *Hampden Press: Derby*,
1932. 8°. Cup. 510. am. 5.
No. 3 of an edition of fifteen copies. With a MS letter
from the author inserted.

BINYON (ROBERT LAURENCE) *Keeper of Prints and Drawings, British Museum.*

—— Three Poems. *Hampden Press: Derby,* 1934. 8⁰.
Cup. **510**. am. **2**.

No. 28 of an edition of 90 copies.

GIBSON (WILFRID WILSON)

—— A Leaping Flame—a Sail! [Poems.] *Hampden Press: Derby,* 1935. 8⁰. Cup. **510**. am. **3**.

No. 59 of an edition of sixty copies.

ARISTOPHANES, *the Poet.* [*Aves.—English.*]

—— The Hoopoe's Call . . . Translated by T. F. Higham. *Hampden Press: London,* 1945. 8⁰. Cup. **510**. am. **4**.

No. 15 of an edition of forty copies.

HAMPERMILL PRESS, Oxley, Herts.

HAMPERMILL PRESS.

—— Book papers. no. 6–9. *Oxhey, Herts.,* 1962, 63.
Cup. **510**. dax. **2**.

4 pt. 13 cm. △

Selections of fine mill papers produced in booklet form at the Hampermill Press.

WHITEMAN (YVONNE)

—— Poems. *Oxhey [Herts.]: Hampermill Press,* 1964.
Cup. **510**. dax. **1**.

Pages not numbered ; illus. 20 cm. △

No. 60 of an edition of sixty-five copies.

HAND AND FLOWER PRESS, Cobham, Kent, *etc.*

JAMES (HENRY) *Novelist.*

—— The Turn of the Screw. Illustrated by Mariette Lydis. pp. 138. *Hand & Flower Press: [Cobham,]* 1940. fol.
C. **99**. k. **30**.

FASSAM (THOMAS)

—— The Shrapnel in the Tree. Poems, 1940 1941. pp. 22. *Hand & Flower Press: Cobham,* 1945. 8⁰. **11657**. d. **14**.

FASSAM (THOMAS)

—— An Herbarium for the Fair. Being a book of common herbs with etchings by Betty Shaw-Lawrence. Together with curious notes on their histories and uses for the furtherance of loveliness and love by T. Fassam. pp. 90. *Hand & Flower Press: London,* 1949. 4⁰. **7034**. c. **39**.

FASSAM (THOMAS)

—— My Tongue is my own. Selected poems. pp. xiii. 92. *Hand & Flower Press: Aldington,* 1950. 8⁰.
011641. ee. **141**.

SHAKESPEARE (WILLIAM) [*Sonnets.*]

—— An Explanatory Introduction to Thorpe's Edition of Shakespeare's Sonnets, 1609. With text transcription. ([By] C. Longworth de Chambrun.) pp. 135. *Hand & Flower Press: Aldington; Paris printed,* 1950. fol.
11765. k. **15**.

No. 35 of an edition of eighty copies.

LYLE (ROB)

—— Heroic Elegies. pp. **xxx**. *Hand & Flower Press: Aldington,* 1957. 8⁰. **11662**. d. **1**.

BORROW (ANTONY)

—— Don Juan. A comedy, with shadows, in three acts. pp. 60. *Hand & Flower Press: Lympne,* 1963. 8⁰.
Cup. **500**. b. **39**.

HARBOR PRESS, New York

HOW (LOUIS) *Narcissus, and two other poems, etc.*
Harbor Press: New York, 1928. 8⁰. C. **99**. e. **45**.

LANDAUER (BELLA CLARA)

—— Some Early American Lottery Items. [With facsimiles.] pp. 19. *Harbor Press: New York,* 1928. 8⁰.
Cup. **510**. pl. **1**.

Privately printed.

PAYNE (ROGER)

—— Extracts from the Diary of Roger Payne. [A fictitious work.] pp. 28. *Harbor Press: New York,* 1928. 8⁰.
C. **99**. b. **28**.

HAZARD (CAROLINE)

—— The Homing to " This Precious Stone set in a Silver Sea ". [Poems.] pp. 50. *Harbor Press: New York,* 1929. 8⁰. Cup. **510**. pl. **3**.

HOOVER (HERBERT CLARK) *President of the United States of America.*

—— A Remedy for Disappearing Game Fishes . . . [With " Address of President Hoover at Madison Courthouse, Virginia."] Foreword by French Strother. Woodcuts by Harry Cimino. pp. viii. **41**. *Huntington Press: New York,* 1930. 8⁰. Cup. **510**. pl. **8**.

LA MOTTE FOUQUÉ (FRIEDRICH HEINRICH CARL DE) *Baron.*

—— Undine . . . Translated . . . by Edmund Gosse. Woodcuts by Allen Lewis. *New York: Limited Editions Club; printed by the Harbor Press,* 1930. C. **105**. c. **1**.

pp. vii, 141. 32 cm. △

LANDAUER (BELLA CLARA)

Bookplates from the Aeronautica Collection of B. C. Landauer. *Privately printed at the Harbor Press: New York,* 1930. 8⁰. Cup.**510**.pl.**4**.

LANDAUER (BELLA CLARA)

" Chalking the Hat," *etc.* [Early American railway passes.] From the collections of B. C. Landauer. [With plates.] pp. 28. *Privately printed at the Harbor Press: New York,* 1930. 8⁰. **11907**. d. **52**.

LANDAUER (BELLA CLARA)

Some Early Vermont Invitations from the Collection of B. C. Landauer. [Facsimiles.] *Harbor Press: New York,* 1930. 8⁰. *Privately printed.* Cup.**510**.pl.**5**.

MOORE (GEORGE) *Novelist.*

—— A Flood. pp. 33. *G. C. [Groff Conklin] at The Harbor Press: New York,* 1930. 8⁰. Cup.**510**.pl.**6**.

FAULKNER (William) *Novelist*.
—— Idyll in the Desert. pp. 17.   *Random House: New York*,
1931. 8º.   Cup. 403. h. 23.
With the author's autograph.

LANDAUER (Bella Clara)
—— Some Alcoholic Americana. From the Collection of
B. C. Landauer. [With plates.]
Privately printed at the Harbor Press: New York, 1932. fol.
Cup.510.pl.7.
No. 29 of an edition of sixty copies.

ADAMS (Léonie)
—— This Measure . . . Illustrations by George Plank. [A
poem.] *Alfred A. Knopf: New York*, [1933.] 8º.
Cup. 510. pl. 9.
Borzoi Chap Books. no. 7.

LANDAUER (Bella Clara)
—— Some Ephemeral Portraits of Lincoln and Franklin
from the Collections of B. C. Landauer. [Plates, with
an introduction by B. C. Landauer.] pp. 8.   *Privately
printed: New York*, 1935. 8º.   10883. i. 25.
No. 18 of an edition of sixty copies.

WILDE (Oscar Fingall O'Flahertie Wills)
—— The Ballad of Reading Gaol . . . With an introduction by
Burton Rascoe and lithographs by Zhenya Gay. pp. xii. 42.
*Printed for the members of the Limited Editions Club at the
Harbor Press: New York*, 1937. 8º.   C. 104. i. 3.

HARRISON OF PARIS, Paris

HARTE (Francis Bret)
—— The Wild West. Stories . . . Pictures by Pierre Falké.
pp. 187. *Harrison: Paris*, 1930. 8º.   C. 100. c. 19.

MANN (Thomas) *Novelist*.
—— [Lebensabriss.] A sketch of my life. (The translation
. . . has been made by H. T. Lowe-Porter.) *Paris: Harrison*, 1930.   010703. e. 55.
pp. 69. 21 cm.   △
*Printed in Darmstadt. One of fifteen copies not printed for
sale.*

SHAKESPEARE (William) [*Venus and Adonis.*]
—— Shakespeare's Venis and Adonis. pp. 70.   *Harrison:
Paris*, 1930. 8º.   C. 98. i. 9.

WESCOTT (Glenway)
—— The Babe's Bed. pp. 46. *Harrison: Paris*, 1930. 4º.
012604. c. 6.

AESOP. [*English.—Collections.*]
—— Fables of Æsop according to Sir Roger L'Estrange.
With fifty drawings by Alexander Calder. pp. 124.
Harrison: Paris, 1931. 4º.   Cup.500.bb.26.

BYRON (George Gordon Noel) *Baron Byron.* [*Childe
Harold's Pilgrimage.—Cantos* I–IV.]
—— Childe Harold's pilgrimage . . . With illustrations by Sir
Francis Cyril Rose.   *Paris: Harrison; New York:
Minton, Balch & Co.*, 1931.   11641. h. 18.
pp. 236. 27 cm.   △
One of twenty-five copies not printed for sale.

DOSTOEVSKY (Theodor Mikhailovich) [Кроткая.]
—— A Gentle Spirit . . . Translated . . . by Constance Garnett,
etc. pp. 85. *Harrison: Paris; Darmstadt printed*, 1931. 8º.
012591. aaa. 57.

MÉRIMÉE (Prosper)
—— Carmen and Letters from Spain. Newly translated.
With ten monochrome water-colours by Maurice Barraud.
pp. 175. *Harrison: Paris*, 1931. 8º.   12239. cc. 7.

MOTIER (Marie Madeleine) *Countess de La Fayette.*
—— The Death of Madame [i.e. Henrietta Anna, Consort of
Philip, Duke of Orleans.] [An extract from the " Histoire
de Madame Henriette d'Angleterre." Translated by
Monroe Wheeler.] pp. 25.   *Harrison: Paris;
Darmstadt printed*, 1931. 16º.   Cup.501.a.2.

PORTER (Katherine Anne)
—— Hacienda. [A novel.] pp. 81.   *Harrison of Paris:
New York*, 1934. 8º.   012604. d. 42.

HART (James D.), Berkeley, Calif.

NASH (Ogden)
—— Scrooge rides again. (Illustrated by Victor R. Anderson.)
Hart Press: Berkeley, Cal., 1960. 8º.   Cup. 510. ney. 1.

HARTMUS HANDPRESS, San Francisco

MORENO (Ralph)
—— A Man's Estate. [A play.] pp. 63.   *Hartmus
Handpress: San Francisco*, 1962. 4º. Cup. 510. neb. 1.

HAWK'S WELL PRESS, New York

GUNN (Thom)
—— Fighting Terms. [Poems. Revised edition.] pp. 46.
Hawk's Well Press: New York; Barcelona printed, 1958.
11455. d. 39.

HAWORTH PRESS, Halifax

LA ROCHEFOUCAULD (FRANÇOIS DE) *Duke.*

—— Maxims of La Rochefoucauld. A . . . translation by G. Kenneth Pratt. pp. xvi. 87. *Haworth Press:* [*Halifax*], 1933. 8°. **8409. cc. 16.**

SHEFFIELD (JOHN) *Duke of Buckingham and Normanby.*

—— Miscellanea from the Works of John Sheffield, Earl of Mulgrave, Marquis of Normanby and Duke of Buckingham. pp. 120. *Haworth Press:* [*Halifax,*] 1933. 8°. **012272. bb. 5.**

SUCKLING (Sir JOHN)

—— Poems. [*Halifax:*] *Haworth Press*, 1933. **11632. ccc. 6.** pp. 120. 19 cm. △

SUCKLING (Sir JOHN)

—— [Another issue.] Poems. *Halifax · Haworth Press*, 1933. 23 cm. **11633. cc. 27.** △

WILMOT (JOHN) *Earl of Rochester.* [*Collections.*]

—— The Poetical Works of John Wilmot, Earl of Rochester. Edited by Quilter Johns. [With a portrait.] pp. xxxii. 238. *Haworth Press:* [*Halifax,*] 1933. 8°. **11609. s. 2.**

PAGET (JOHN) *Barrister at Law.*

—— The New "Examen" . . . [Essays criticizing certain portions of Macaulay's "History of England."] With a critical introduction by . . . Winston S. Churchill. pp. xv. 235. *Haworth Press:* [*Halifax,*] 1934. 8°. **09525. f. 2.**

HAWTHORN HOUSE, Windham, Conn.

SÉVIGNÉ (MARIE DE) *Marchioness.*

—— Horace Walpole's Letter from Madame de Sévigné. By W. S. Lewis. [With text and facsimiles.] pp. iii. 21. *Privately printed: Farmington, Conn.*, 1933. 8°. [*Miscellaneous Antiquities.* no. 8.] **W.P. D. 527/8.** *One of an edition of a hundred copies.*

STANHOPE (PHILIP) *2nd Earl of Chesterfield.*

—— Some Short Observations for the Lady Mary Stanhope concerning the Writing of Ordinary Letters . . . Edited by W. S. Lewis. [With a portrait.] pp. 16. *Privately printed: Farmington, Conn.*, 1934. 8°. [*Miscellaneous Antiquities.* no. 9.] **W.P. D. 527/9.** *One of an edition of a hundred copies.*

BELOT, afterwards **DUREY DF MEINIÈRES** (OCTAVIE)

—— Le Triomphe de l'amitié, ou l'Histoire de Jacqueline et de Jeanneton. By W. S. Lewis. [With an abridged English translation of the text of Mme. de Meinières.] pp. 19. *Privately printed: Farmington, Conn.*, 1935. 8°. [*Miscellaneous Antiquities.* no. 10.] **W.P. D. 527/10.** *One of an edition of a hundred copies.*

LEWIS (WILMARTH SHELDON)

—— Bentley's Designs for Walpole's Fugitive Pieces. [With illustrations.] pp. 22. *Privately printed: Farmington, Conn.*, 1936. 8°. [*Miscellaneous Antiquities.* no. 12.] **W.P. D. 527/12.** *One of an edition of a hundred copies.*

WALPOLE (HORACE) *Earl of Orford.*

—— Memoranda Walpoliana. With an introduction by W. S. Lewis. [With plates.] pp. ix. 21. *Privately printed: Farmington, Conn.*, 1937. 8°. [*Miscellaneous Antiquities.* no. 13.] **W.P. D. 527/13.** *One of an edition of a hundred copies.*

NEW YORK.—*Grolier Club.*

—— The Duchess of Portland's Museum. By Horace Walpole. With an introduction by W. S. Lewis. *New York; Windham, Ct.: printed by Edmund Burke Thompson at Hawthorn House*, 1936. **W.P. D. 527/11.** pp. viii, 15; illus. 26 cm. (Miscellaneous antiquities. no. 11.) △

WALPOLE (HORACE) *Earl of Orford.*

—— The Impenetrable Secret, probably invented by Horace Walpole. An explanation of the secret. With a note on the original by W. S. Lewis. [With ten printed cards.] pp. 15. *Privately printed: Farmington, Conn.*, 1939. 12°. [*Miscellaneous Antiquities.* no. 15.] **W.P. D. 527/15.** *One of an edition of a hundred copies.*

OXFORD.—*University of Oxford.*—*Clarendon Press.*

—— A Newly-Discovered Broadside Specimen of Fell Type printed at Oxford about 1685. Reproduced in collotype facsimile with a bibliographical note by Philip Hofer. (An Advertisement of several Bibles and Common-Prayer Books lately printed at the Theatre in Oxford, a specimen of the letter on which every book is printed followeth underneath.) *Department of Printing and Graphic Arts, Harvard College Library: Cambridge, Mass.; Columbiad Club: Meriden.* 1940. fol. **11909. w. 27.**

WALPOLE (HORACE) *Earl of Orford.*

—— Notes . . . on several Characters of Shakespeare. Edited by W. S. Lewis. pp. viii. 21. *Privately printed: Farmington, Conn.*, 1940. 8°. [*Miscellaneous Antiquities.* no. 16.] **W.P. D. 527/16.** *One of a hundred copies.*

FRANCK (PETER)

—— A Lost Link in the Technique of Bookbinding, and how I found it. pp. 18. *Gaylordsville*, 1941. 8°. **7946. b. 20.**

MORSE (WILLIAM INGLIS)

—— Bliss Carman. Bibliography. Letters. Fugitive verses and other data. [With portraits.] pp. 86. *Hawthorn House: Windham, Conn.*, 1941. 8°. **11908. d. 10.**

HAWTHORN PRESS, Melbourne

MILLS (OLIVE MILDRED LILLIAN)

—— Why should their Honour fade? (The history of John and Charles Mills.) [With plates, including portraits.] pp. 39. *Hawthorn Press: Melbourne*, 1960. 8°. **10818. w. 14.** *Privately printed.*

HAWTHORNDEN PRESS, London

DRUMMOND (WILLIAM) of *Hawthornden.* A Cypress Grove ... Introduction and notes by Samuel Clegg. [With a portrait.] pp. 78.
At the Hawthornden Press, published by C. J. Sawyer : London, 1919. 8°.   4256. dd. 16.

GIFFORD (HUMFREY)
—— A Posie of Gilloflowers, each differing from other in colour and odour, yet all sweet. (Edited, with an introduction, by F. J. Harvey Darton.) pp. xxx. 168.
Hawthornden Press : London, 1933. 8°.   11630. ff. 9.

HAYMARKET PRESS, London

BIBLE.—*Judith.* [*English.*]
—— Judith. Reprinted from the Revised Version ... With an introduction by Dr. Montague R. James ... and colour-plates after drawings by W. Russell Flint. pp. xvii. 49. F.P. *Haymarket Press : London,* 1928. 4°.
C. 98. e. 8.
No. 11 of an edition of twelve copies.

CONGREVE (WILLIAM)
—— The way of the world ... An unexpurgated edition, including an original signed etching by A. R. Middleton Todd ... and a foreword by Malcolm C. Salaman. *London : Haymarket Press,* 1928.   L.R. 33. a. 13.
pp. xxi, 79 : plate. 27 cm.   △
One of an edition of one hundred copies.

BIBLE.—*Apocrypha.* [*English.*]
—— The Book of Tobit and the History of Susanna. Reprinted from the Revised Version of the Apocrypha, with an introduction by ... Montague R. James ... and four colour-plates after drawings by W. Russell Flint. pp. xvi. 45.   *Haymarket Press : London,* 1929. 4°.
C. 98. i. 7.
With a duplicate set of the plates.

BIBLE.—*Psalms.* [*English.—Prose Versions.*]
—— The Book of Psalms. From the version of Miles Coverdale as published in the " Great Bible " of 1539. With an introduction by Francis Wormald ... and facsimile reproductions of eight illuminated folios from the fourteenth century manuscript known as Queen Mary's Psalter. pp. xvi. 156.   *Haymarket Press : London,* 1930. fol.   C. 100. l. 13.
No. 24 of an edition of fifty copies. With a duplicate set of the plates.

HERMES PRESS, London

EGAN (BERESFORD) The Sink of Solitude : being a series of satirical drawings occasioned by some recent events [viz. the attacks by James Douglas in the " Sunday Express " on the novel " The Well of Loneliness " by Marguerite Radclyffe Hall and its subsequent withdrawal from publication] performed by B. Egan, Gent, to which is added a preface by P. R. Stephensen, Gent, and a verse lampoon composed by several hands, *etc.*   *Hermes Press : London,* 1928. 4°.   L.R.33.a.19.

HESPERIDES PRESS, London

BEROALDE DE VERVILLE (FRANCOIS)
—— The Way to Succeed ... Newly done into English by Oliver Stonor, *etc.* 2 vol.   *Hesperides Press : [London] ; printed in France,* 1930. 4°.
T.C.6.b.23.

MAPLET (JOHN) A Greene Forest ; or, a naturall historie ... Reprinted from the edition of 1567, *etc.* pp. viii. 183. *Hesperides Press : London,* 1930. 4°
Cup.510.cef.1.

MARLOWE (CHRISTOPHER) the *Dramatist.* [*Tamburlaine the Great.*]
The Life and Death of Tamburlaine the Great ... Illustrated by R. S. Sherriffs. *Hesperides Press : London,* 1930. 4°.   11771. l. 9.

HIGH HOUSE PRESS, Shaftesbury, Dorset; Bristol

IBBETT (WILLIAM JOSEPH) Twenty-four Sonnets. *J. E. Masters : Shaftesbury,* 1924. 16°. Cup.510.ab.1.

RAAD (N. C.) Rocky Valley, and other poems. pp. 20. *J. E. Masters : Shaftesbury,* 1924. 8°.
Cup.510.ab.2.

VENUS.
—— The Eve of Venus. A version of the Pervigilium Veneris. By W. J. Ibbett. pp. 13.   *J. E. Masters : Shaftesbury,* 1924. 8°.   Cup. 510. ab. 3.

FARJEON (ELEANOR) Young Folk and Old. [Poems.] pp. 20. *High House Press : Shaftesbury,* 1925. 8°.
Cup.510.ab.6.

GREEK ANTHOLOGY. A Greek Garland of Amorous Trifles, re-wove into English [from the Greek Anthology] by William J. Ibbett. pp. 17.
High House Press : Shaftesbury, 1925. 8°.
Cup.510.ab.4.

HUTTON (DAVID GRAHAM)
—— Twilight Corners. [Verses.] pp. 13.   *J. E. Masters : Shaftesbury,* 1925. 8°.   Cup.510.ab.27.

SHEPHERD. The Shepheards Holy Day. A pastoral. (Reprinted from " Witt's Recreations," first published MDCXL.) pp. 8.   *High House Press : Shaftesbury,* 1925. 8°.   Cup.510.ab.7.

SUCKLING (Sir JOHN)
—— A Ballade upon a Wedding. A discourse between two country-men. pp. 12. *High House Press: Shaftesbury,* 1925. 4°.
Cup.510.ab.8.

TOWNSEND (LEWIS W.) Poems. pp. 20. *High House Press: Shaftesbury,* 1925. 8°.
Cup.510.ab.5.

GOSSIPS. The Gossips...From a manuscript of the fifteenth century. [A ballad.] pp. 10. *High House Press: Shaftesbury,* 1926. 8°.
Cup.510.ab.9.
No. 13 of an edition of 100 copies.

PETRARCA (FRANCESCO) [*Canzoniere. — English.*] Some Sonnets & Songs...made in Laura's lifetime and now done into English by William J. Ibbett. pp. 31. *High House Press: Shaftesbury,* 1926. 8°.
Cup.510.ab.10.

SHENSTONE (WILLIAM) [*Selections.*]
Twenty Songs...With decorations by Philip Ainsworth. pp. 36. *High House Press: Shaftesbury,* 1926. 8°.
Cup.510.ab.12.

WALLER (EDMUND) *the Poet.* [*Selections.*]
Songs and Verses selected from the works of Edmund Waller, *etc.* pp. 22. *High House Press: Shaftesbury,* 1926. 8°.
Cup.510.ab.11.
One of 25 copies printed on hand-made paper.

ANACREON. [*English.*]
—— The First Three Odes of Anacreon. Done into English by Ambrose Philips. pp. 8. *High House Press: Shaftesbury,* 1927. 8°.
Cup.510.ab.15.
One of an edition of 100 copies.

SONGS. Rymes of the Minstrels. Selected [by J. E. Masters] from a manuscript of the fifteenth century [now in the Bodleian Library, previously edited by Thomas Wright, under the title "Songs and Carols, *etc.*"] pp. 30. *High House Press: Shaftesbury,* 1927. 8°.
C. 99. h. 21.
One of 30 copies printed on hand-made paper.

VENUS. The Vigil of Venus. A rendering of the Pervigilium Veneris into English verse. By Thomas Parnell. pp. 14. *High House Press: Shaftesbury,* 1927. 16°.
Cup.510.ab.13.
One of 30 copies printed on hand-made paper.

WHITE (ERIC WALTER) The Room, and other poems, 1921–1926. pp. 23. *High House Press: Shaftesbury,* 1927. 8°.
Cup.510.ab.14.
One of 30 copies printed on hand-made paper.

HARMONY. The Harmony of Birds. A poem printed by John Wight in the middle of the sixteenth century, *etc.* pp. 31. **F. P.** *J. E. Masters: Shaftesbury,* 1928. 8°.
Cup.510.ab.17.

MARTIN (E. M.) *Essayist.*
—— The Reckoning, and other poems. pp. 26. *High House Press: Shaftesbury,* 1928. 8°.
Cup. **510**. ab. 36.
Printed on mould-made paper.

SHENSTONE (WILLIAM)
—— A Pastoral Ballad in four parts. pp. 15. *High House Press : Shaftesbury,* 1928. 8°.
Cup.510.ab.18.

WINE.
—— Good Wine. A song from a fifteenth-century manuscript in the Bodleian Library. pp. 5. *Privately printed by James E. Masters & Beatrice M. Masters for their friends: Shaftesbury,* 1928. 8°.
Cup.510.ab.37.
No. 13 of an edition of ninety copies.

DONNE (JOHN) *Dean of St. Paul's.* An Anatomie of the World, *etc.* pp. 32. *High House Press : Shaftesbury,* 1929. 4°.
Cup.510.ab.20.

PETRARCA (FRANCESCO) [*Canzoniere.—Sonetti.— English.*] Twenty-six Sonnets of the Divine Poet M. Francesco Petrarca made on Laura dead, and now done into English by William J. Ibbett. pp. 30. *High House Press: Shaftesbury,* 1929. 8°.
Cup.510.ab.19.

THEOCRITUS. [*English.*] Hylas. The XIIIth idyll of Theokritos. Rendered into English verse by S. Matthewman. pp. 8. *High House Press : Shaftesbury,* 1929. 8°.
Cup.510.ab.28.

IMRU' AL-ḰAIS IBN ḤUJR.
—— The poem of Amriolkais, one of the seven Arabian poems or moallaka which were suspended on the temple at Mecca. Rendered into English by Sir William Jones . . . With four wood-engravings by Eileen Mayo. *Shaftesbury: James E. Masters at the High House Press,* 1930.
14570. c. 7.
pp. 27. 23 cm. △
A copy out of series to an edition of fifty copies containing an extra set of the engravings, and signed by the artist and the printer.

LYLY (JOHN) *the Euphuist.* [*Selections.*]
—— Twelve Songs from the Plays of John Lyly. pp. 16. *High House Press: Shaftesbury,* 1930. 4°. Cup.510.ab.

MATTHEWMAN (SYDNEY)
—— The High House Press. A short history and an appreciation. *High House Press: Shaftesbury,* 1930. 8°.
Cup.510.ab.26.

MILTON (JOHN) [*Arcades.*]
—— Arcades. pp. 80. *High House Press: Shaftesbury.*
1930. 8°. Cup.510.ab.30.
One of an edition of 100 copies.

IBBETT (WILLIAM JOSEPH)
—— A Medley. Some verses. pp. 14. *High House Press:*
Shaftesbury, 1931. 8°. Cup.510.ab.21.

IBBETT (WILLIAM JOSEPH)
—— One Hundred Facets of Winter and Spring, *etc.* [Poems.]
pp. 38. *High House Press: Shaftesbury,* 1931. 8°.
Cup.510.ab.22.

BIGGS (JOHN REGINALD)
                Shaftesbury: the Shaston of Thomas
Hardy. Twelve wood-engravings by J. R. Biggs and
James E. Masters. [With explanatory letterpress.] *High*
House Press: Shaftesbury, 1932. 8°. Cup.510.ab.31.
One of an edition of sixty copies on hand-made paper.

FARJEON (ELEANOR)
—— Pannychis. pp. 14. *High House Press: Shaftesbury,*
1933. 8°. Cup.510.ab.23.

HIGH HOUSE PRESS.
—— [A collection of specimens, advertisements and proof
pages of items printed by the High House Press.] *Shaftes-*
bury, 1933–39. Cup. 510. ab. 39.
5 pt.
Some items were printed at Bristol.

MERCHANT.
—— How a Merchant did his wife betray. A 15th-century
ballad, *etc.* pp. 22. *High House Press: Shaftesbury,*
1933. 8°. Cup.510.ab.32.
One of an edition of 100 copies.

HORATIUS FLACCUS (QUINTUS) [*Selections.—Latin*
and English.]
—— Three Hundred & Sixty-Five Short Quotations from
Horace. With modern titles and varied metrical versions
in English by H. Darnley Naylor. pp. vii. 91. *High*
House Press: Shaftesbury, 1935. 8°. Cup.510.ab.33.
One of fifteen copies printed on hand-made paper.

HEYWOOD (THOMAS) *Dramatist.*
—— A Marriage Triumphe solemnized in an Epithalamium,
in memorie of the happie nuptials betwixt the high and
mightie Prince Count Palatine and the most excellent
Princesse the Lady Elizabeth. pp. 31. *High House Press:*
Bristol, 1936. fol. Cup.510.ab.25.
No. 35 of an edition of 65 copies.

MARLOWE (CHRISTOPHER) *the Dramatist.* [*Hero and*
Leander.]
—— Hero & Leander. The divine poem of Musaeus . . .
Translated . . . by George Chapman [or rather, adapted
from Musaeus by George Chapman and completed by
Marlowe]. pp. 28. *High House Press: Shaftesbury,*
1936. 4°. Cup. 510. ab. 38.

RATCLIFFE, afterwards **MAC GRIGOR PHILLIPS**
(DOROTHY UNA)
—— Romany Joter. [Poems.] pp. 15. *High House Press:*
Bristol, 1937. 8°. Cup.510.ab.34.

BRIGHT (N. L.)
—— Six Poems, *etc. High House Press: Bristol,* 1938. 8°.
Cup.510.ab.24.

GRISELDA.
—— The Pleasant and Sweet History of Patient Grissell,
etc. (Translated out of Italian.) pp. 24. *Reprinted by*
James E. Masters at the High House Press: Bristol, 1939.
fol. Cup. 510. ab. 35.
No. 32 of sixty-five copies printed on Arnold hand-made
paper.

RATCLIFFE, afterwards **MACGRIGOR PHILLIPS**
(DOROTHY UNA)
—— From All the Airts. Poems. [With a portrait.] pp. 49.
Eyre & Spottiswoode: London, 1940. 8°. **11656.** e. 30.

HILTON (John), Hadlow

YALDING.
—— Yalding. A village history. [By John Anthony Hilton.
With plates.] pp. 11. *John Hilton: Hadlow,* [1965.] 8°.
Cup. 510. cug. 1.

HOGARTH PRESS, Richmond, Surrey; London

WOOLF (VIRGINIA)
—— Two Stories. Written and printed by Virginia Woolf
and L. S. Woolf. (Three Jews, by L. S. Woolf. The Mark
on the Wall, by Virginia Woolf.) pp. 31. *Hogarth Press:*
Richmond, 1917. 8°. Cup. 401. f. 24.

ELIOT (THOMAS STEARNS)
—— Poems. *L. & V. Woolf at the Hogarth Press: Richmond,*
1919. 8°. Cup. 510. afa. 1.
The first issue of the first edition published in a limited
edition.

MIRRLEES (HOPE) Paris. A poem. pp. 23.
Hogarth Press: Richmond, 1919. 16°. Cup.510.afa.4.

MURRY (JOHN MIDDLETON)
—— The Critic in Judgment; or, Belshazzar of Baronscourt.
[Verses.] pp. 26. *Hogarth Press: Richmond,* [1919.] 8°.
Cup. 510. afa. 23.

WOOLF (VIRGINIA)
—— Kew Gardens. [A short story. With woodcuts by
Vanessa Bell.] *Hogarth Press: Richmond,* 1919. 8°.
Cup.510.afa.2.

WOOLF (VIRGINIA) The Mark on the Wall . . .
Second edition. pp. 10. *Hogarth Press:*
Richmond, 1919. 8°. Cup.510.afa.5.

FORSTER (EDWARD MORGAN)
—— The story of the siren. *Richmond: Leonard &*
Virginia Woolf at the Hogarth Press, 1920.
Cup. **510**. afa. **6**.

    pp. 14. 24 cm. △

MANSFIELD (KATHERINE) *pseud.* [i.e. KATHLEEN BEAU-
CHAMP, afterwards MURRY.]
—— Prelude. *Richmond: Hogarth Press,* [1920].
Cup. **510**. afa. **24**.

    pp. 68. 19 cm. △

BELL (ARTHUR CLIVE HEWARD)
—— Poems. pp. 29. *L. & V. Woolf: Richmond,* 1921. 8°.
Cup.510.afa.7.

WOOLF (LEONARD SIDNEY)
—— Stories of the east. *Richmond: Leonard & Virginia*
Woolf at the Hogarth Press, 1921. Cup. **510**. afa. **25**.
    pp. 55. 20 cm. △

SANDERS (RUTH MANNING) Karn. [A poem.]
pp. 45. *L. & V. Woolf: Richmond,* 1922. 8°.
Cup.510.afa.8.

SHOVE (FREDEGOND) Daybreak. [Poems.] pp. 43.
L. & V. Woolf: Richmond, 1922. 8°. Cup.510.afa.9.

BELL (ARTHUR CLIVE HEWARD)
—— The Legend of Monte della Sibilla; or, le Paradis de la
reine Sibille. [A poem.] pp. 25. *L. & V. Woolf:*
Richmond, 1923. fol. Cup.510.afa.13.

ELIOT (THOMAS STEARNS)
—— The waste land. *Richmond, Surrey: Leonard &*
Virginia Woolf at the Hogarth Press, 1923.
Cup. **510**. afa. **22**.

    pp. 35. 23 cm. △
    A poem.

FORSTER (EDWARD MORGAN) Pharos and Pharillon.
[Sketches from the history of Alexandria.] pp. 80.
L. & V. Woolf: Richmond, 1923. 8°. Cup.510.afa.10.

GRAVES (ROBERT VON RANKE)
—— The Feather Bed, *etc.* [A poem.] pp. 28. *L. & W.*
Woolf: Richmond, 1923. 8°. Cup. **510**. afa. **12**.

LIMEBEER (ENA)
—— To a proud phantom. *Richmond: Leonard & Virginia*
Woolf at the Hogarth Press, 1923. Cup. **510**. afa. **26**.
    pp. 32. 20 cm. △
    Poems.

READ (HERBERT E.) Mutations of the Phœnix.
[Poems.] pp. 51. *L. & V. Woolf:*
Richmond, 1923. 4°. Cup.510.afa.11.

RANSOM (JOHN CROWE) Grace after Meat [Selections
from "Poems about God"] . . . With an introduction
by Robert Graves. pp. 57. *L. & V. Woolf:*
London, 1924. 8°. Cup.510.afa.14.

CUNARD (NANCY)
—— Parallax. *London: Leonard & Virginia Woolf at the*
Hogarth Press, 1925. Cup. **510**. afa. **15**.
    pp. 24. 23 cm. △
    A poem.

RYLANDS (GEORGE HUMPHREY WOLFESTAN)
—— Russet and Taffeta. [In verse.] pp. 8. *L. & V. Woolf:*
London, 1925. 4°. Cup. **510**. afa. **17**.

TREVELYAN (ROBERT CALVERLEY) Poems and
Fables. pp. 23. *L. & V. Woolf: London,* 1925. 8°.
Cup.510.afa.16.

MUIR (EDWIN) Chorus of the Newly Dead. pp. 16.
L. & V. Woolf: London, 1926. 8°. Cup.510.afa.20.

SANDERS (RUTH MANNING) Martha Wish-You-Ill
[and other poems]. pp. 16. *L. & V. Woolf:*
London, 1926. 8°. Cup.510.afa.18.

SNAITH (STANLEY) April Morning. [Poems.]
pp. 24. *L. & V. Woolf: London,* 1926. 8°.
Cup.510.afa.19.

RIDING (LAURA) [i.e. LAURA RIDING GOTTSCHALK.]
Voltaire. A biographical fantasy. [In free verse.]
pp. 30. *L. & V. Woolf: London,* 1927. 8°.
Cup.510.afa.21.

HOLLY HILL PRESS, Fredericksburg, Va.

SUMNER (LAURA VOELKEL)
—— Sonnets. pp. 127. *Privately printed at the Holly Hill*
Press: Fredericksburg, Va., 1961. 8°. Cup. **510**. sak. **1**.

HOURS PRESS, Paris

ALDINGTON (RICHARD)
—— Hark the Herald. [A poem.] *Hours Press:*
[*Paris,* 1928.] 8°. Cup.510.f.2.

DOUGLASS (GEORGE NORMAN)
—— Report on the Pumice Stone Industry of the Lipari Islands. pp. 6. *Reprinted in France on hand-press by Nancy Cunard at the author's request:* [*Réanville,*] 1928. 8º.
Cup. **510**. f. **23**.
One of an edition of eighty copies. A presentation copy from the author.

GUEVARA (ALVARO)
—— St. George at Silene. [A poem.] *Hours Press:* [*Chapelle-Réauville,*] 1928. fol. Cup. **500**. g. **6**.

GUEVARA (ALVARO)
—— [Another copy.] St. George at Silene. [1928].
Cup. **510**. f. **3**.
△

MOORE (GEORGE) *Novelist.*
—— Peronnik the Fool ... Revised edition. pp. 63. *Hours Press: Chapelle-Réauville,* 1928. 8º. Cup.510.f.1.

ALDINGTON (RICHARD)
—— The Eaten Heart. [A poem.] pp. 17. *Hours Press: Chapelle-Réanville,* 1929. 4º. Cup.510.f.5.

CARROLL (LEWIS) *pseud.* [i.e. CHARLES LUTWIDGE DODGSON.]
  —— La Chasse au Snark ... Traduit ... par Aragon. pp. 29. *Chapelle-Réanville,* 1929. fol. Cup.510.f.4.

DOUGLASS (GEORGE NORMAN) One Day. [With portraits.] pp. 55. *Hours Press: Chapelle-Réanville,* 1929. 8º. Cup.510.f.7.

ACTON (HAROLD MARIO MITCHELL)
—— This Chaos. [Poems.] pp. 31. *Hours Press: Paris,* 1930. fol. Cup.510.f.15.
Privately printed.

ALDINGTON (RICHARD)
—— Last Straws. [A tale.] pp. 61. *Hours Press: Paris,* 1930. 8º. Cup.510.f.17.

BECKETT (SAMUEL) Whoroscope. pp. 4. *Hours Press: Paris,* 1930. 8º. Cup.510.f.12.

CAMPBELL (IGNATIUS ROY DUNNACHIE)
—— Poems. pp. 18. *Hours Press: Paris,* 1930. fol. Cup.510.f.13.
Privately printed.

CROWDER (HENRY)
—— Henry-music by Henry Crowder. Poems by ... Nancy Cunard [and others], *etc. Paris: Hours Press,* 1930.
Music. H. **2012**.
pp. 20; port. 33 cm. △
The leaves containing the poems are unnumbered. No. 53 of an edition of one hundred copies, signed by Henry Crowder.

CUNARD (NANCY)
—— The Hours Press Booklet. Being a list of books published by Nancy Cunard at the Hours Press during 1929 & 1930, with a detailed description of each, *etc. Hours Press: Paris,* [1930.] 16º. Cup.510.f.21.

GRAVES (ROBERT VON RANKE)
—— Ten Poems More. pp. 17. *Hours Press: Paris,* 1930. fol. Cup.510.f.9.
Privately printed.

HOWARD (BRIAN)
—— God save the King. *Paris: Hours Press,* [1930]. Cup. **510**. f. **20**.
pp. 40. 30 cm. △
The cover bears the title "First poems".

HOWARD (BRIAN)
—— [Another copy.] God save the King. [1930].
Cup. **510**. f. **22**.
△

LOWENFELS (WALTER)
—— Apollinaire. An elegy. (Covers by Yvres Tanguy.) pp. 16. *Hours Press: Paris,* 1930. fol. Cup.510.f.8.

POUND (EZRA LOOMIS)
—— A Draft of xxx Cantos. pp. 141. *Hours Press: Paris,* 1930. 8º. Cup. **510**. f. **14**.

RIDING (LAURA) [i.e. LAURA RIDING GOTTSCHALK.]
—— Four Unposted Letters to Catherine. pp. 50. *Hours Press: Paris,* [1930.] 4º. Cup.510.f.11.

RIDING (LAURA)
—— [Another copy.] Four Unposted Letters to Catherine. *Paris,* [1930.] 4º. 8411. d. **37**.

RIDING (LAURA) [i.e. LAURA RIDING GOTTSCHALK.] Twenty Poems Less. pp. 33. *Hours Press: Paris,* 1930. fol. Cup.510.f.10.

RODKER (JOHN) [*Collections.*]
Collected Poems, 1912–1925.
Hours Press: Paris; printed in England, 1930. 8º. Cup.510.f.16.

BROWN (ROBERT CARLTON) *the Younger.*
—— Words. [Poems.] pp. 23. *Hours Press: Paris,* 1931. fol. Cup.510.f.18
Privately printed.

MOORE (GEORGE) *Novelist.*
—— The Talking Pine. *Hours Press: Paris,* 1931. 8º. Cup.510.f.19.

SYMONS (ARTHUR) Mes souvenirs. *Eng.* pp. 41.
Hours Press : Chapelle-Réanville, [1931.] 8°.
Cup.510.f.6.

HUNTER (Dard), Chillicothe, Ohio

HUNTER (DARD)
—— Papermaking through Eighteen Centuries. [With illustrations.] pp. xvii. 358. *W. E. Rudge: New York,* 1930. 8°. **7941. s. 4.**

HUNTER (DARD)
—— Old Papermaking in China and Japan. [With plates, and with specimens of old Oriental papers.] pp. 71. *Mountain House Press: Chillicothe,* 1932. fol.
Tab. 1280. a. 4.

HUNTER (DARD)
—— A Papermaking Pilgrimage to Japan, Korea and China. [With plates, and 50 specimens of paper.] pp. 148. *Pynson Printers: New York,* 1936. 4°. **7943. w. 20.**

HUNTER (DARD)
—— Chinese Ceremonial Paper. A monograph relating to the fabrication of paper and tin foil and the use of paper in Chinese rites and religious ceremonies. [With specimens.] pp. 79. *Mountain House Press: Chillicothe, Ohio,* 1937. fol. **C. 102. f. 10.**

HUNTER (DARD)
—— Papermaking by Hand in India. [With specimens of paper and with plates.] pp. 129. *Pynson Printers: New York,* 1939. 4°. **L.R. 280. b. 12.**

HUNTER (DARD)
—— Before Life Began. 1883–1923. [An autobiography.] pp. 115. *Rowfant Club: Cleveland,* 1941. 8°.
10889. c. 8.

INVICTA PRESS, Newbury, Berks.

LELAND (JOHN) *the Antiquary.*
[The Itinerary.]
—— John Leland at Reading. (Taken from the "Itinerary".] *Invicta Press: Newbury,* 1965. 8°. **Cup. 510. azb. 1.** *No. 20 of an edition of twenty-four copies.*

JAMES PRESS, London

BETJEMAN (JOHN)
—— Mount Zion ; or, In touch with the infinite. [Verses. With illustrations.] pp. 57. *James Press: London,* [1931.] 8°. **Cup.510.bef.1.** *Printed on blue paper. Author's presentation copy.*

EDWARD. [i.e. EDWARD JAMES.]
—— Twenty Sonnets to Mary. By Edward. *James Press: [London,* 1933.] fol. **C. 102. h. 9.**

JAMES (EDWARD FRANK WILLIS)
—— The Next Volume . . . [Verses.] With decorations by Rex Whistler. pp. vii. 83. *James Press: London,* 1933. fol. **C. 102. h. 8.** *No. 12 of an edition of 25 copies on hand-made paper. With a decorated inscription to the British Museum by Rex Whistler.*

JONGLEUR PRESS, Bradford

ARNELL (CHARLES JOHN)
—— On Divers Strings. Selected poems. pp. 23. *Poetry Publishing Co.: Exeter,* 1927. 8°. **11643. d. 44.** *One of an edition of 100 copies.*

VICKRIDGE (ALBERTA) The Adoration of the Star. A Christmas poem. *Printed for private circulation: Bradford,* 1927. 8°. **011644. eee. 8.** *One of an edition of 100 copies.*

JOHNES (EDITH M.) The Cup. [A poem.] pp. 4. *Alberta Vickridge: Frizinghall,* 1929. 8°.
011644. h. 5.

RATCLIFFE afterwards MACGRIGOR PHILLIPS (DOROTHY UNA)
—— Four Letters from Lesley of Winpenie. [in verse.] pp. 11. *Alberta Vickridge: Bradford,* 1929. 8°.
11644. h. 55. *No. 60 of an edition of 60 copies, privately printed.*

SPEIGHT (ROSE EMMA)
Fiddler Jan, and other poems, *etc.* pp. 15. [*A. Vickridge :*] *Bradford,* 1929. 8°. *Privately printed.* **011644. h. 35.**

VICKRIDGE (ALBERTA) The Glass Slipper. [*A. Vickridge:*] *Bradford,* 1929. 8°. **011644. h. 49.** *Privately printed.*

WINTLE (IRENE) Harvest. [Verses.] pp. 36. *Alberta Vickridge : Frizinghall,* 1929. 8°.
011644. h. 6.

HENDERSON (FLORENCE LESLIE) The Unbroken Line, & other poems. pp. 40. *Beamsley House: Bradford,* 1930. 8°. **011644. i. 54.**

JOHNES (EDITH M.) A Book of Ballads. pp. 38. *Jongleur Press: Bradford,* 1930. 8°. **11644. k. 28.**

LANG (ERDA) Mirrors. [Verses.] pp. 50. *Beamsley House: Bradford,* 1930. 8°. **011644. h. 138.**

VICKRIDGE (ALBERTA) Printer's Ink. [Poems.]
pp. 17. [*Alberta Vickridge :*] *Bradford*, 1930. 8°.
        11640. ee. 6.

WAKEFIELD (JESSIE HARE) Fourteen Poems.
pp. 17. [*Alberta Vickridge :*] *Bradford*, [1930.] 8°.
        11640. ee. 5.

KESSLER (JEAN) Maiden Voyage. [Poems.]
pp. 28. *Beamsley House : Bradford*, 1931. 8°.
        11640. ee. 23.

RASPIN (ELSIE HARRIET) Poems. pp. 23.
Beamsley House : Bradford, 1931. 8°. **11644. k. 44.**

VICKRIDGE (ALBERTA)
—— Goatfoot, and other poems, *etc.* pp. 45.
Beamsley House : Bradford, 1931. 8°. **11644. k. 63.**

COVELL (CLARICE M.) The Drinking Cup . . . [A poem.]
Illustrated by Ashford Hatherly. pp. 22. *Beamsley
House : Bradford*, 1932. 8°. **11640. ee. 37.**

GIBSON (WILFRID WILSON)
—— Highland Dawn. pp. 17. *Beamsley House : Bradford,*
1932. 8°.
        11644. k. 60.

HOUSMAN (A. W.)
—— Poems. pp. 40. *Alberta Vickridge : Bradford,*
1932. 8°.
        11640. h. 43.

BENINGTON (WILSON)
—— The Phial. [A poem.] pp. 9. *Alberta Vickridge :
Bradford*, 1933. 8°.
        011641. ee. 43.

GALLETLEY (LEONARD)
—— An English Village. [Poems.] pp. 36. *Beamsley House :
Bradford*, 1933. 8°.
        011641. ee. 45.

ORMSBY (IËRNE)
—— Egypt's Gold. [Poems.] pp. 36. *Beamsley House :
Bradford*, 1933. 8°.
        '011641. ee. 47.

SPEIGHT (ROSE EMMA)
—— Broad Acres. [Poems.] pp. 9. *Beamley House :
Bradford*, [1933.] 8°.
        011641. ee. 44.

VICKRIDGE (ALBERTA)
—— Eden Gate, *etc.* [Verse.] pp. 35. *Jongleur Press :
Bradford*, [1933.] 8°.
        11640. i. 31.

LUBBOCK (PHYLLIS M.)
—— Poems. pp. 27. *Beamsley House : Bradford*, 1934. 8°.
        11654. aaa. 9.

TREVOR (ROSE)
—— The Barrier, and other poems. pp. 28. *The Author :
Guisborough*, 1934. 8°. **11654. b. 27.**

VICKRIDGE (ALBERTA)
—— The Unending Dream. A book for maidens . . .
[Verses.] With decorations by Marygold Cecilia Crowe.
pp. 39. *Beamsley House : Bradford*, 1934. 8°.
        11654. aaa. 8.

CHILDE (WILFRED ROWLAND)
—— Fountains & Forests, *etc.* [Poems.] pp. 36.
Beamsley House : Bradford, 1935. 8°. **11655. bb. 23.**

JOHANSEN (MARGUERITE)
—— The Zemorrites. [A poem.] pp. 23. *Jongleur Press :
Bradford*, 1935. 8°.
        011653. o. 36.

KESSLER (JEAN)
—— Star-Wagon. [Poems.] pp. 23. *Jongleur Press :
Bradford*, 1936. 8°.
        11654. c. 72.

VICKRIDGE (ALBERTA)
—— Over the Moon. Poems. *Beamsley House : Bradford,*
[1939.] 8°.
        11657. bb. 19.

WILKINSON (EMILY)
—— From My Window, and other poems. *Bradford,*
1939. 8°.
        11657. bb. 23.

BRATTON (FREDERICK)
—— Dust of War. [Poems.] *Printed for the Author :
Bradford*, [1947.] 16°. **11657. e. 75.**

SACKVILLE (*Lady* MARGARET)
—— Miniatures. [Poems.] pp. 18. *Beamsley Press :
Bradford*, 1947. 12°. **11657. e. 74.**

DOBELL (EVA)
—— A Gloucestershire Year. [Poems.] pp. 37. *For the
Author at the Jongleur Press : Bradford*, 1949. 8°.
        11662. eee. 12.

SACKVILLE (*Lady* MARGARET)
—— Country verse. *Bradford : [A. Vickridge,]* [1950].
        11659. b. 8.

  Pages not numbered. 20 cm.   △

KARUBA PRESS, San Francisco

JUNG (M. Ruth)
—— Haiku from Telegraph Hill . . . [Poems.] With linocuts by Mary Ellen Cranston. *Karuba Press: San Francisco,* 1963. 8°.   Cup. **510**. new. **1**.

KEEPSAKE PRESS, London

LOWBURY (Edward Joseph Lister)
—— Metamorphoses. (Poems.) pp. 15. *Keepsake Press: London,* 1958. 8°.   Cup. **510**. agb. **9**.
One of the "Keepsake Limited Editions".

LEWIS (Roy) *Journalist.*
—— The Death of God. A curious narrative dream dreamed by Roy Lewis in the year Mcmxliij, *etc.* B. L. *Printed [by the author] on his private press: Hammersmith,* 1959. 8°.   Cup. **510**. agb. **10**.

SYMES (Gordon)
—— Whither shall I wander? A sheaf of six poems. pp. 11. *Keepsake Limited Editions: Hammersmith,* 1959. 8°.   Cup. **510**. agb. **1**.

AḤMAD 'ALI, *Novelist.*
—— Purple Gold Mountain. Poems from China. pp. 16. *Keepsake Press: London,* 1960. 8°.   Cup. **510**. agb. **5**.

SAINT OLAVE (E.)
—— An Octet of Verse. pp. 12. *Keepsake Press: London,* 1960. 8°.   Cup. **510**. agb. **6**.

SHORE (Charles St. J.)
—— Reminiscences of a tax inspector. *etc.* pp. 15. *Keepsake Press: London,* 1960. 16°.   Cup. **510**. agb. **11**.
One of the " Keepsake limited editions ".

KEEPSAKE PRESS.
—— The Keepsake Press. Report and adieux. [By Roy Lewis.] pp. 7. *Roy Lewis & Daughters: London,* [1961.] 8°.   Cup. **510**. agb. **12**.

WATSON (Francis)
—— Poems in India. pp. 11. *Keepsake Press: London,* [1962.] 8°.   Cup. **510**. agb. **2**.

RUSSELL (Irwin Peter)
—— The Spirit & the Body. An orphic poem. *Keepsake Press: London,* 1963. 8°.   Cup. **510**. agb. **3**.

HEADLAND (Ian)
—— Non tantum nomine Barbaræ. [A poem.] *Eng. Keepsake Press: London,* 1964. 8°.   Cup. **510**. agb. **13**.

PENNATI (Camillo)
—— Landscapes . . . English translation by Peter Russell, *etc.* [Poems.] *Ital. & Eng. Keepsake Press: London,* [1964.] 8°.   Cup. **510**. agb. **4**.

LOWBURY (Edward Joseph Lister)
—— New Poems. *Keepsake Press: London,* 1965. 8°.   Cup. **510**. agb. **7**.

LOWBURY (Edward Joseph Lister)
—— [Another copy.] New poems. *London,* 1965. 8°.   Cup. **510**. agb. **15**.

MOMENTS.
—— Moments of truth. Nineteen short poems by living poets. *London: Keepsake Press,* 1965. Cup. **510**. agb. **18**. pp. 23. 18 cm.
One of an edition of which 100 copies are for sale.

MOMENTS.
—— [Another copy.] Moments of truth. Nineteen short poems by living poets. 1965.   Cup. **510**. agb. **28**.
                                        △

PEAKE (Mervyn Laurence)
—— Poems and Drawings, *etc.* *Keepsake Press: London,* 1965. 8°.   Cup. **510**. agb. **8**.

KELMSCOTT PRESS, Hammersmith, London

KELMSCOTT PRESS.
—— [A collection of proofs and trial pages of works printed by William Morris at the Kelmscott Press. Compiled by Sir Sydney Cockerell and including various important items mentioned by him in his printed account of the Press. With other printed and MS. material, and with photographs of William Morris and of the Kelmscott Press staff.] ms. notes [by Sir Sydney Cockerell]. [c. 1870–1930.] 8° & 4°.   C. **102**. h. **18**.

MORRIS (William) *the Poet.* [A collection of proof-sheets, woodcut illustrations and borders, fly-sheets, circulars, and book-labels, printed by William Morris at the Kelmscott Press, with his autograph notes, and with ms. lists of contents by Robert Proctor, etc.] 25 vol.   *William Morris: Hammersmith,* [1891–98.] fol., 4° & 8°.   C. **43** c. **26**, f. **24**. g. **11**, & h. **22**.

KELMSCOTT PRESS.
—— [Specimen pages, advertisements, etc., of printed matter issued by the Kelmscott Press.]   *London,* [1891 ?–98 ?]. 8°, *etc.*   C. **99**. k. **29**.

MORRIS (William) *Poet.* Poems by the way. pp. 197. *Reeves & Turner: London,* 1891. 8°.   C. **43**. e. **2**.
Printed by the author at his private press

MORRIS (WILLIAM) *Poet.* The Story of the Glittering Plain. Which has been also called the Land of Living Men or the Acre of the Undying. pp. 188. *Reeves & Turner: London*, 1891. 4°.   C.43.e.1.
    Printed by the author at his private press.

MORRIS (WILLIAM) *Poet.*
—— [Another copy.] The Story of the Glittering Plain, *etc.* *London*, 1891. 4°.   C. 102. a. 19.
    With a pull of the first trial page printed at the Kelmscott Press, Jan. 31, 1891, and another variant of the same page; pulls of the last two leaves sig. bb 1, 2, the last leaf containing a different initial and setting of type in the text and colophon; and with the original drawings for two initials. A presentation copy from Morris to Sir Sydney Cockerell.

BLUNT (WILFRID SCAWEN)
—— The Love-Lyrics & Songs of Proteus by W. S. Blunt. With the Love-Sonnets of Proteus by the same author, now reprinted in their full text with many sonnets omitted from the earlier editions. pp. vii. 251.   *Reeves & Turner: London; printed by William Morris at the Kelmscott Press*, 1892. 4°.   C. 43. e. 3.

BLUNT (WILFRID SCAWEN)
—— [Another copy.] The love-lyrics & songs of Proteus, *etc.* 1892.   C. 72. b. 7.
                               △

    Bound by Birdsall in a style after Mr. Douglas Cockerell's.

JACOBUS, *de Voragine, Archbishop of Genoa.* The Golden Legend of master William Caxton done anew. [Edited by F. S. Ellis. With "memoranda, bibliographical and explanatory, concerning the Legenda Aurea of Jacobus de Voragine and some of the translations of it."] pp. 1286.   *Printed by me William Morris at the Kelmscott Press: London*, 1892. 4°.   C.43.f.1.

LE FÈVRE (RAOUL)
—— The recuyell of the historyes of Troye. (Translated ... by Willyam Caxton.) *Hammersmith: printed by William Morris at the Kelmscott Press; [London:] sold by Bernard Quaritch*, 1892.   C. 43. f. 2.
    2 vol.: pp. xv, 717; illus.   30 cm.   △

MACKAIL (JOHN WILLIAM)
—— Biblia Innocentium; being the story of God's chosen people, before the coming of our Lord Jesus Christ upon earth, written anew for children. pp. viii. 249. *W. Morris: Hammersmith*, 1892. 8°.   C. 43. e. 7.

MORRIS (WILLIAM) *Poet.*
—— Child Christopher and Goldilind the Fair. [A tale.] 2 vol.   *W. Morris: at the Kelmscott Press, Hammersmith*, 1892. 8°.   C. 43. dd. 6.

MORRIS (WILLIAM) *the Poet.*
—— [A collection of catalogues, prospectuses, leaflets, worksheets, paper accounts and proof-sheets from the Kelmscott Press of William Morris.]   *London*, [1892–97.] 8°, 4° & fol.   C.43.g.19.

MORRIS (WILLIAM) *Poet.*
—— The Defence of Guenevere and other poems. pp. 169. *Reeves and Turner: London*, 1892. 4°.   C. 43. e. 5.
    Printed by the Author at his private press.

MORRIS (WILLIAM) *Poet.* A Dream of John Ball; and, A King's Lesson, pp. 123. *Reeves & Turner: London*, 1892. 8°.   C.43.e.6.
    Printed by the author at his private press.

MORRIS (WILLIAM) *Poet.* News from Nowhere, *etc.* pp. 305. *Reeves & Turner: London*, 1892. 8°.   C.43.e.9.
    Printed by the Author at the Kelmscott Press.

ORDER.
—— The Order of Chivalry. [A translation of Ramon Lull's "Libre del Orde de Cauayleria".] (Translated from the French by William Caxton, edited by F. S. Ellis.) (L'Ordene de Chevalerie [by Hugues de Tabarie], with translation [into verse] by William Morris.) 2 pt. *William Morris, Kelmscott Press: London*, 1892, 93. 8°.   C. 43. e. 10.

REYNARD THE FOX. [*English.—Caxton's Translation.*] The History of Reynard the Foxe, [translated] by William Caxton. B. L. pp. v. 163. *B. Quaritch: London*, 1892. fol.   C.43.f.3.
    A Reprint of the edition of 1481. *Printed by William Morris at the Kelmscott Press, Hammersmith.*

RUSKIN (JOHN) The Nature of Gothic: a chapter of the Stones of Venice. [With a preface by W. Morris.] pp. iv. 127. *G. Allen: London*, [1892.] 8°.   C.43.e.4.
    Printed by William Morris at the Kelmscott Press.

CAVENDISH (GEORGE)
—— The Life of Thomas Wolsey, Cardinal, *etc.* [Transcribed from the original manuscript by F. S. Ellis.] pp. iv. 287. *William Morris: Kelmscott Press, Hammersmith*, 1893. 8°.   C. 43. e. 11.

FLORUS, *King of Ausay.*
—— The Tale of King Florus and the fair Jehane. pp. 96. *W. Morris: Hammersmith*, 1893. 8°.   C. 43. dd. 9.

FLORUS, *King of Ausay.*
—— [Another copy.] The Tale of King Florus, *etc.* *Hammersmith*, 1893. 4°.   Ashley 1234.

GODFREY [DE BOUILLON], *King of Jerusalem.*
—— The History of Godefrey of Boloyne and of the Conquest of Iherusalem. [Translated by William Caxton from a French version of the "Historia rerum in partibus transmarinis gestarum" of Gulielmus, Archbishop of Tyre.] (Corrected for the press by H. Halliday Sparling.) B. L. pp. xxii. 450.   *William Morris, at the Kelmscott Press: Hammersmith*, 1893. 4°.   C. 43. f. 4*.

—— [Another copy.] ON VELLUM.   *Hammersmith*, 1893. 4°.   C. 43. f. 4.

MEINHOLD (WILHELM) Sidonia the Sorceress ... Translated by Francesca Speranza Lady Wilde. pp. xiv. 455.   *W. Morris: Kelmscott Press*, [*London*], 1893. 8°.   C.43.f.5.

MEINHOLD (Wilhelm)

—— [Another copy.] Sidonia the Sorceress, *etc.* on vellum.
W. Morris: Kelmscott Press, London, 1893. 4°.
C. **43**. f. **6**.

MORRIS (William) *Poet.*

—— Gothic Architecture: a lecture for the Arts and Crafts
Exhibition Society. pp. 68. *Kelmscott Press:*
London, 1893. 8°. C. **43**. dd. **2**.

MORRIS (William) *Poet. Gothic Architecture.*
[Proof-sheets, with the author's corrections.] ff. 67.
[Kelmscott Press: London, 1893.] 8°. C. **39**. g. **38**.

ROSSETTI (Dante Gabriel)

—— Ballads and Narrative Poems. pp. 227. *Ellis & Elvey:*
London, 1893. 8°. C. **43**. e. **14**.
Printed by William Morris at the Kelmscott Press.

SHAKESPEARE (William) [*Collected Poems.*]

—— The Poems of William Shakespeare printed after the
original copies of Venus and Adonis, 1593, the Rape of
Lucrece, 1594, Sonnets, 1609, the Lover's Complaint.
(Edited by F. S. Ellis.) pp. 216. *Reeves & Turner:*
London, 1893. 8°. C. **43**. e. **8**.
Printed by William Morris at the Kelmscott Press.

TENNYSON (Alfred) *Baron Tennyson.* [*Maud.*]

Maud, a
Monodrama. pp. 69. *MacMillan & Co.:*
(*London,*) 1893. 4°. C. **43**. e. **13**.
Printed by William Morris at the Kelmscott press.

THOMAS [More] *Saint, Lord High Chancellor of England.*

Utopia. [Robinson s translation. Revised by F. S.
Ellis.] (Foreword by W. Morris.) pp. xiv. 282.
Reeves & Turner: [London], 1893. 8°. C. **43**. e. **12**.
Printed by W. Morris at the Kelmscott Press.

AMIS, *Hero of Romance.* [*Prose Versions.*]

—— Of the Friendship of Amis and Amile. (Done out of
the ancient French into English, by William Morris.)
pp. 67. *W. Morris, Kelmscott Press: Hammersmith,*
1894. 16°. C. **43**. dd. **4**.

BIBLE. — *Psalms.* — *Selections.* [*Polyglott.* — *Penitential*
Psalms.]

—— Psalmi Penitentiales. (Rhymed version of the Peni-
tential Psalms, found in a Manuscript of Horæ Beatæ
Mariæ Virginis, written at Gloucester about the year 1440,
and now transcribed and edited by F. S. Ellis.) Lat. &
Eng. pp. 63. *William Morris, at the Kelmscott Press:*
Hammersmith, 1894. 8°. C. **43**. e. **20**.

CONSTANTIUS I, *Emperor of Rome.*

—— The Tale of the Emperor Coustans; and of Over Sea.
(Done out of the ancient French into English by William
Morris.) pp. 130. *William Morris, at the Kelmscott*
Press: Hammersmith, 1894. 8°. C. **43**. dd. **5**.

KEATS (John) [*Poetical Works.*]

—— The Poems of John Keats. (Overseen after the text of
foregoing editions by F. S. Ellis.] pp. 384. *Kelmscott*
Press: Hammersmith, 1894. 8°. C. **43**. e. **16**.

MORRIS (William) *Poet.* The Story of the Glittering Plain, *etc.* (With 23 pictures by Walter Crane.)
pp. 177. *W. Morris, Kelmscott Press:*
Hammersmith, 1894. 8°. C.**43**.f.**8**.

MORRIS (William) *Poet.*

—— [Another copy.] The Story of the Glittering Plain, *etc.*
Hammersmith, 1894. 4°. C. **69**. h. **9**.

MORRIS (William) *Poet.*

—— The Wood beyond the World. [A tale.] pp. 261.
W. Morris, at the Kelmscott Press: Hammersmith, 1894. 8°.
C. **43**. e. **17**.

ROSSETTI (Dante Gabriel) Sonnets and Lyrical
Poems. pp. x. 197. *Ellis & Elvey: London*, 1894. 8°.
C.**43**.e.**15**.
Printed by William Morris at the Kelmscott Press.

SAVONAROLA (Girolamo) [*Letters.—Single Letters.*]

—— Epistola de Contemptu Mundi, *etc.* pp. 15. [*Printed*
for private circulation] *Per G. Morris alla stamperia Kelm-*
scott: [*Hammersmith,*] 1894. 8°. C. **43**. e. **21**.

SAVVA, *Monk* [*Prince* Sulkhan Orbeliani].

—— The Book of Wisdom and Lies. (Translated, with notes
by O. Wardrop.) pp. xvi. 256. *B. Quaritch: London,*
1894. 8°. C. **43**. e. **18**.
Printed by William Morris at the Kelmscott Press.

SWINBURNE (Algernon Charles)

—— Atalanta in Calydon, *etc.* pp. 81. *W. Morris, at the*
Kelmscott Press: Hammersmith, 1894. 4°. C. **43**. f. **7**.

BEOWULF.— [*English.*]

—— The Tale of Beowulf. (Done out of the Old English
tongue by William Morris & A. J. Wyatt.) pp. 119.
Kelmscott Press: Hammersmith, 1895. 4°. C. **43**. f. **9**.

HERRICK (Robert) *the Poet.* [*Smaller Collections.*]

Poems chosen out of the works
of Robert Herrick. (Edited by F. S. Ellis from the
text of the edition put forth by the author in 1648.)
pp. xiv. 296. *Printed by W. Morris at the*
Kelmscott Press: London, 1895. 8°. C.**43**.e.**23**.

KELMSCOTT PRESS.

—— [A collection of trial pages and proofs of illustrations
of works published or projected by the Kelmscott Press,
compiled by Sir Sydney Cockerell, including one of two
known copies of the trial page, Macbeth, of a projected
volume of Shakespeare's works.] 21 pt.
[1895–98.] fol. & 8°. C. **102**. l. **22**.

MORRIS (WILLIAM) *Poet.*

—— Child Christopher and Goldilind the fair.   *Hammer-smith: printed & sold by William Morris at the Kelmscott Press*, 1895.   C. **43**. dd. **6**.

   2 vol.   15 cm.   △

MORRIS (WILLIAM) *Poet.*   **The Life and Death of** Jason.   pp. 353.   *William Morris, Kelmscott Press: Hammersmith*, 1895.   4°.   C. **43**. f. **10**

PERCEVAL, *le Gallois, Knight of the Round Table.* Syr Perecyvelle of Gales.   (Overseen by F. S. Ellis, after the edition printed by J. O. Halliwell from the MS. in the Library of Lincoln Cathedral.)   pp. 98.
          William Morris: Kelmscott Press, Hammersmith, 1895.   8°.   C. **43**. e. **22**.

ROSSETTI (DANTE GABRIEL)   Hand and Soul. Reprinted from "The Germ."   pp. 56.
Kelmscott Press: Hammersmith, 1895.   12°.

                     C. **43**. dd. **7**.

ROSSETTI (DANTE GABRIEL)

—— Hand and Soul.   pp. 56.   *Way & Williams: Chicago; Kelmscott Press* printed, 1895.   8°.   C. **43**. dd. **1**.

SHELLEY (PERCY BYSSHE)   [*Poetical Works.*]

—— The poetical works of Percy Bysshe Shelley.   *Hammer-smith: printed & sold by William Morris at the Kelmscott Press*, 1895 [1894, 95].   C. **43**. e. **19**.

   3 vol.   21 cm.   △

CHAUCER (GEOFFREY)   [*Works and Complete Poetical Works.*]

—— The Works of Geoffrey Chaucer now newly imprinted. (Edited by F. S. Ellis; ornamented with pictures designed by Sir Edward Burne-Jones, and engraved on wood by W. H. Hooper.)   pp. ii. 554.   *Kelmscott Press: Hammersmith*, 1896.   fol.   C. **43**. h. **19**.

CHAUCER (GEOFFREY)   [*Works and Complete Poetical Works.*]

—— [Another copy.]   The works of Geoffrey Chaucer, *etc.* 1896.   Ashley **5170**.

                     △

CHAUCER (GEOFFREY)   [*Works and Complete Poetical Works.*]

—— [Another copy.]   The works of Geoffrey Chaucer, *etc.* 1896.   C. **42**. l. **12**.

                     △

On vellum.   In a white blind-tooled pigskin binding designed by William Morris and bound at the Doves Bindery.

CHAUCER (GEOFFREY)   [*Works and Complete Poetical Works.*]

—— [Another copy.]   The works of Geoffrey Chaucer, *etc.* 1896.   C. **43**. h. **17**.

                     △

On vellum.   Imperfect; wanting 108 out of 278 sheets.

COLERIDGE (SAMUEL TAYLOR) *Smaller Collections.*—III. *Verse.*

—— Poems chosen out of the works of S. T. Coleridge. (Edited by F. S. Ellis.)   pp. 100.   *Sold by William Morris at the Kelmscott Press: Hammersmith*, 1896.   8°.   C. **43**. e. **24**.

DEGREVANT, *Sir.*

—— The Romance of Sir Degrevant.   (Edited by F. S. Ellis after the edition printed by J. O. Halliwell from the Cambridge MS., with some additions & variations from that in the Library of Lincoln Cathedral.)   pp. 81.   *Kelmscott Press: London*, 1896.   8°.   C. **43**. c. **13**.

FLOWER.   The Floure and the Leafe, & the Boke of Cupide, god of love, or the Cuckow and the Night-ingale.   [The latter by Sir T. Clanvowe.]   (Edited by F. S. Ellis.)   pp. 47.   *Kelmscott Press: Hammersmith*, 1896.   8°.   C. **43**. c. **11**.

FLOWER.

—— [Another copy.]   The Floure and the Leafe, & the Boke of Cupid, God of Love, *etc.*   *Hammersmith*, 1896.   4°.   C. **68**. g. **10**.

FROISSART (JEAN)

—— *Begin.* Here begynneth the prologe of Sir Johan Froissart, *etc.*   *End.* Incomplete sheets of the Froissart.   32 copies printed at the Kelmscott Press on Dec. 24, 1896, before the distribution of the type.   Not for sale.   [Reprinted from the edition of 1525.]   *Kelmscott Press:* [*Hammersmith*,] 1896.   fol.   C. **43**. h. **21**.

MARY, *the Blessed Virgin.*   Laudes beatae Mariae Virginis.   (Taken from a Psalter written ... early in the 13th century.)   pp. 33.   *William Morris: Kelmscott Press, Hammersmith*, 1896.   4°.
                     C. **43**. f. **12**.

MORRIS (WILLIAM) *Poet.*

—— The earthly paradise.   [*Hammersmith:*] *printed by William Morris at the Kelmscott Press*, 1896, 97.   C. **43**. e. **25**.

   8 vol.; illus.   24 cm.   △

Vol. 4–8 bear the colophon " Printed by the trustees of William Morris at the Kelmscott Press ".

MORRIS (WILLIAM) *Poet.*   **The Well at the World's End.**   (With four pictures designed by Sir E. Burne-Jones)   pp. 496.
        Printed by W. Morris at the Kelmscott Press: Hammersmith, 1896.   8°.   C. **43**. f. **11**.

SPENSER (EDMUND)   [*Shepheardes Calender.*]   The Shepheardes Calender, *etc.*   pp. 98.
        Trustees of William Morris, Kelmscott Press: London, 1896.   8°.   C. **43**. c. **12**.

COCKERELL (Sir SYDNEY CARLYLE)

—— Some German Woodcuts of the Fifteenth Century. [Thirty-five reproductions from printed books in the library of William Morris, preceded by extracts from an article by him on the early illustrated books of Ulm and Augsburg, and followed by a list of the principal books with woodcuts in his library.   Compiled and edited by S. C. Cockerell.]   ff. 23.   pp. 24–36.   *Printed at the Kelmscott Press: Hammersmith*, 1897.   4°.   C. **43**. f. **14**.

FROISSART (Jean)

—— *Begin.* These two trial pages of the projected edition of Lord Berners' translation of Froissart were printed . . . to preserve the designs made for the work by William Morris, *etc. Kelmscott Press: [Hammersmith,]* 1897. fol.
C. **43.** h. **18.**

ISUMBRAS, *Sir.* The Romance of Sir Isumbras. (Edited by F. S. Ellis after the edition printed by J. O. Halliwell, *etc.*) pp. 41. *Trustees of William Morris: Kelmscott Press, London,* 1897. 8°. C.43.c.14.

MORRIS (William) *Poet.* Love is Enough, *etc.* (With two pictures designed by Sir E. Burne-Jones.) pp. 90. *Kelmscott Press: Hammersmith,* 1897. 4°.
C.43.f.15.

MORRIS (William) *Poet.* [Sigurd the Volsung.] *Begin.* In this book is told, *etc. End.* Incomplete sheet of Sigurd the Volsung. 32 copies printed at the Kelmscott Press on Jan. 11, 1897, before the distribution of the type. Not for sale. *Kelmscott Press: [Hammersmith,]* 1897. fol. C. **43.** h. **20.**

MORRIS (William) *Poet.* The Sundering Flood. (Romance . . . overseen by May Morris.) pp. 507. *Trustees of William Morris, Kelmscott Press: Hammersmith,* 1897. 8°. C.43.c.15.

MORRIS (William) *Poet.* The Water of the Wondrous Isles. L. P. pp. 340. *Trustees of William Morris: Kelmscott Press, Hammersmith,* 1897. 4°.
C.43.f.13.

KELMSCOTT PRESS.

—— [A set of proofs, compiled by Sir Sydney Cockerell, of type, initials, borders and ornaments designed by William Morris for the Kelmscott Press.] [1898.] *obl.* fol.
C. **109.** bb. **1.**

MORRIS (William) *Poet.* A Note by William Morris on his aims in founding the Kelmscott Press. Together with a short description of the Press by S. C. Cockerell, and an annotated list of the books printed thereat. pp. 70. *Sold by the Trustees of the late William Morris at the Kelmscott Press: Hammersmith,* 1898. 8°.
C.43.c.16.
The last book printed at the Kelmscott Press.

MORRIS (William) *Poet.* [Another copy.] A Note by William Morris, *etc. Kelmscott Press: Hammersmith,* 1898. 8°.
C. **43.** c. **17.**

MORRIS (William) *Poet.* The Story of Sigurd the Volsung and the Fall of the Niblungs. (With two pictures designed by E. Burne-Jones.) pp. 207. *Trustees of the late William Morris: Kelmscott Press, Hammersmith,* 1898. 8°. C.43.g.9.

KENNELS PRESS, Milngavie, Scotland

CLIFTON (Violet Mary)

—— Marymas, and other poems . . . with a colour block decoration after Roublev by John Laurie. pp. 29. *Kennels Press: Milngavie,* 1956. 8°. Cup. **510.** bek. **2.**
Privately printed. No. 28 of an edition of forty-five copies.

BURNS (Robert) *the Poet.* [*Single Poems.*]

—— Tam O'Shanter. pp. 20. *Kennels Press: Milngavie,* 1959. 12°. Cup. **510.** bek. **1.**
No. 6 of an edition of fifty copies.

SHAKESPEARE (William) [*Phœnix and the Turtle.*]

—— The phœnix and the turtle. *Milngavie: Kennels Press,* 1964. Cup. **510.** bek. **3.**
Pages not numbered. 19 cm. △

KIRGATE PRESS, Canton, Pa.

HAVENS (Munson Aldrich) Horace Walpole and the Strawberry Hill Press, 1757–1789. [With facsimiles.] pp. 86. *Kirkgate Press: Canton, Pennsylvania,* 1901. 8°. 011900. g. **19.**

HAWTHORNE (Nathaniel) Main-Street . . . With a preface by Julian Hawthorne. pp. 61. *Kirkgate Press: Canton, Pennsylvania,* 1901. 8°.
012331. k. **13.**

MACKINLEY (William) *President of the United States of America.*

—— The Last Speech of William McKinley, *etc.* [With a portrait.] pp. 15. *Lewis Buddy: Canton, Pa.,* [1901.] 8°. 12302. de. **3.**

CARLYLE (Thomas) [*Essays.—Collections.*]

—— Collectanea . . . 1821–1855. Edited by Samuel Arthur Jones. [Contributions to periodicals.] pp. 142. *Kirgate Press: Canton, Pa.,* 1903. 8°. 12273. g. **11.**

EMERSON (Ralph Waldo) Tantalus . . . With a memorial note by F. B. Sanborn. pp. 41. *Kirgate Press: Canton, Pennsylvania,* 1903. 8°.
012356. i. **58.**

KIT-CAT PRESS, Bushey, Herts;
King's Langley, Herts.

PALMER (Frederick) *Writer of Verse*

—— Poems. *Kit-Cat Press: Bushey,* 1958. 8°.
11662. b. **4.**

HARDACRE (Kenneth)

—— [A collection of leaflets printed by K. Hardacre at the Kit-Cat Press.] *Bushey,* 1959–61. 14 pt.
Cup. **510.** caw. **6.**
△

PINE (George Edward)

—— Last Things, and other poems. *Kit-Cat Press: Bushey*, 1962. 8°. Cup. **510**. caw. **2**.

LYON (Peter)

—— Tulips, Stilts & Balloons. [On wine-glasses.] *Kit-Cat Press: [King's Langley,]* 1963. 16°. Cup. **510**. caw. **1**.

KLANAK PRESS, Vancouver

SCOTT (Francis Reginald)

—— Signature. [Poems.] pp. 56. *Klanak Press: Vancouver*, 1964. 8°. X. **900/2617**.

KLYCE (Scudder), Winchester, Mass.

KLYCE (Scudder) Universe, *etc.* [A philosophical treatise.] pp. x. 251. *S. Klyce: Winchester, Mass.*, 1921. fol. **8462**. i. **26**.

KYNOCH PRESS, Birmingham

MORISON (Stanley) and **JACKSON** (Holbrook)

—— A Brief Survey of Printing History and Practice. pp. 87. *The Fleuron: London*, 1923. 8°. **011904**. aa. **19**.

SMITH (Sheila Kaye)

—— Saints in Sussex. [Poems.] pp. 29. *Elkin Mathews: Birmingham*, 1923. 8°. **011648**. h. **54**.

LABORATORY PRESS, Pittsburgh

FLANNER (Hildegarde) That Endeth Never, *etc.* [A tale.] pp. xi. 28. *Laboratory Press: Pittsburgh*, 1926. 8°. **012634**. ccc. **49**.
One of an edition of 49 copies.

PITTSBURGH.—*Carnegie Institute.*—*Carnegie Institute of Technology.*—*Laboratory Press.*

—— A Documentary Account of the Beginnings of the Laboratory Press, Carnegie Institute of Technology. By Porter Garnett. [With type-specimens.] pp. x. 131. *For private distribution: Pittsburgh*, 1927. 8°. **11907**. c. **24**.

GARNETT (Porter)

—— What is it? An aesthetical investigation. To which is added some " don'ts " for beginners, and others. pp. 20. *Laboratory Press: Pittsburgh*, 1931. 8°. **7812**. df. **29**.

GARNETT (Porter)

—— The Fine Book. A symposium . . . Edited with an introduction by P. Garnett. pp. xxxiii. 189. *Laboratory Press: Pittsburgh*, 1934. 8°. C. **100**. e. **18**.

PITTSBURGH.—*Carnegie Institute.*—*Carnegie Institute of Technology.*—*Laboratory Press.*

—— A Laboratory Press Anthology, unfinished. A collection of texts . . . originally used as projects in typography for students . . . at Carnegie Institute of Technology. Compiled by Porter Garnett. pp. 46. ms notes. *Pittsburgh*, 1935. 8°. **11912**. c. **35**.
One of an edition of fifty-two copies.

LAKESIDE PRESS, Chicago

MELVILLE (Herman) Moby Dick . . . Illustrated by Rockwell Kent. 3 vol. *Lakeside Press: Chicago*, 1930. 4°. L.R. **50**. b. **1**.

BRONTË (Emily Jane)

—— Wuthering Heights . . . Illustrated with twelve wood engravings by Clare Leighton. pp. xvii. 325. *Duckworth: London; Chicago printed*, 1931. 4°. **012604**. d. **20**.

FRANCE (Anatole) *pseud.* [i.e. Jacques Anatole Thibault.]

—— [La Rôtisserie de la Reine Pédauque.] At the Sign of the Queen Pédauque. Translated by Mrs. Wilfrid Jackson. With an introduction by Ernest Boyd and illustrations by Sylvain Sauvage. pp. xii. 174. *Printed for the Members of the Limited Editions Club by the Lakeside Press: Chicago*, 1933. 4°. C. **105**. h. **4**.

LANTERN PRESS, San Francisco

TAGGARD (Genévieve)

—— Hawaiian Hilltop. [Poems.] pp. 15. *Wyckoff & Gelber: San Francisco*, 1923. 8°. Cup. **510**. pb. **39**.
Flight. no. 1.

ANDERSON (Sherwood)

—— The Modern Writer. pp. 44. *Gelber, Lilienthal: San Francisco*, 1925. 8°. Cup. **510**. pb. **38**.

BENSON (Stella)

—— The Awakening. A fantasy. pp. 15. *Printed by Edwin and Robert Grabhorn for the Lantern Press: San Francisco.* 1925. 8°. Cup. **510**. pb. **31**.

BATES (Herbert Ernest)

—— The Spring Song, and In View of the Fact that. Two stories. [With a portrait.] pp. 15. *"Lantern Press": San Francisco*, 1927. 4°. Cup. **403**. h. **8**.
Privately printed. No. 23 of an edition of fifty copies, signed by the author.

LATIN PRESS, Langford, Somerset, *etc*; Saint Ives, Cornwall

PERIODICAL PUBLICATIONS.—*Langford, Somerset.*

—— Loquela Mirabilis. vol. 1. no. 1—vol. 2. no. 1. Nov. 1936—May 1937. *Langford*, 1936, 37. 16 cm. P.P. **5939**. bgy.

△

WADDELL (Helen Jane)

[Peter Abelard.]

—— Sylvestris discourses. [A proof copy of an extract from "Peter Abelard," forming part of vol. 1. no. 1 of the periodical "Loquela Mirabilis".] *Guido Morris: Langford*, 1936. 8°. Cup. **510**. acd. **7**.

BLACKETT (*Sir* Basil Phillott) *K.C.B.*

—— Translations from the Greek of Saint Gregory Nazianzen, and the Latin of Aurelius Prudentius Clemens, Hildebert of Le Mans, and St. Peter Damiani, Cardinal Bishop of Ostia. [With the original texts.] pp. 31. *Guido Morris: [London,]* 1937. 8°. Cup. 510 . acd . 8.

HESELTINE (Nigel)

—— Violent Rain. A poem. *Latin Press: London*, 1938. 8°. Cup.510.acd.2.

Printed on pink hand-made paper. The heading on the wrapper reads "Published for the Companionate of the Independent Poets by the Latin Press. no. 1."

LEVINE (Albert Norman)

—— The tight-rope walker. [Verses.] *London: Totem Press; Saint Ives, Cornwall: printed by Guido Morris at the Latin Press*, 1950. Cup. **510**. acd. **10**.

pp. 30; illus. 26 cm. △

Verses.

APHRODITE.

—— Aphrodite's Garland. Five ancient love poems. Translated by John Heath-Stubbs. *Latin Press: Saint Ives*, 1951. 8°. [*Crescendo Poetry Series.* no. 2.]

Cup.510.acd.3/2.

CADDICK (Arthur)

—— The Speech of Phantoms. pp. 14. *Latin Press: Saint Ives*, 1951. 8°. [*Crescendo Poetry Series.* no. 1.]

Cup.510.acd.3/1.

LONDON.—III. *Spanish and Portuguese Jews' Congregation.*

—— Treasures of a London Temple. A descriptive catalogue of the ritual plate, mantles and furniture of the Spanish and Portuguese Jews' Synagogue in Bevis Marks. Published by authority of the Wardens and Elders of the Congregation on the occasion of the 250th anniversary of its opening. Compiled by A. G. Grimwade [and others], *etc.* pp. xii. 68. v. pl. xx. *Taylor's Foreign Press: London*, 1951 [1952]. 4°. Cup.510.acd.9.

With a corrigenda slip.

MORRIS (Guido)

—— Songs at High Noon. *Latin Press: Saint Ives*, 1951. 8°. [*Crescendo Poetry Series.* no. 3.] Cup.510.acd.3/3.

BERGONZI (Bernard)

—— Godolphin, & other poems. *Latin Press: Saint Ives*, 1952. 8°. [*Crescendo Poetry Series.* no. 6.] Cup. **510**. acd. **3/6**.

DE BEER (*Sir* Gavin Rylands) [*Appendix.*]

—— G. R. de Beer . . . Publications, 1922–1952 (1952–1960), *etc.* 2 pt. pp. 24. *Private Press of Guido Morris: Saint Ives, [Cornwall,]* 1952, [62]. 4°. Cup. **510**. acd. **5**. *Pt. 2 was printed at Edinburgh by Thomas Nelson & Sons.*

KENYON (Katherine Mary Rose)

—— Thirteen Poems. pp. 15. *Latin Press: Saint Ives*, 1952. 8°. Cup.510.acd.4.

NEWTON (Brean Leslie Douglas)

—— Metamorphoses of Violence. *Latin Press: Saint Ives*, 1952. 8°. [*Crescendo Poetry Series.* no. 7.] Cup.510.acd.3/7.

ROLFE (Frederick William Serafino Austin Lewis Mary) *calling himself* Baron Corvo.

—— Letters to Grant Richards. pp. 46. *Peacocks Press: [Hurst, Berks.,]* 1952. 8°. Cup.510.acd.6.

TRAKL (Georg)

—— Decline. Twelve poems by G. Trakl, 1887–1914. Translated by Michael Hamburger. *Latin Press: Saint Ives*, 1952. 8°. [*Crescendo Poetry Series.* no. 8.] Cup. **510**. acd. **3/8**.

WELCH (Noel)

—— Ten Poems. *Latin Press: St. Ives*, 1952. 8°. [*Crescendo Poetry Series.* no. 5.] Cup.510.acd.3/5. *With an errata and an addenda slip.*

WRIGHT (David John Murray) *Poet.*

—— Moral Stories. *Latin Press: Saint Ives*, 1952. 8°. [*Crescendo Poetry Series.* no. 4.] Cup. **510**. acd. **3/4**.

HOMA (Bernard)

—— A Fortress in Anglo-Jewry. The story of the Machzike Hadath. [With photostats of documents and an appendix in Hebrew.] pp. xvi. 160. xlviii. c-q. pl. xii. *Shapiro, Vallentine & Co.: London*, 1953. 8°. **04034**. p. **61**.

SAPPHO. [*Greek and English.*]

—— The poems of Sappho. Containing nearly all the fragments printed from the restored Greek texts. Translated by P. Maurice Hill. *London, New York: Staples Press*, 1953. Cup. **500**. k. **11**.

pp. xxii, 73. 23 cm. △

Printed by Guido Morris at the Latin Press, Saint Ives, Cornwall, in collaboration with Worden Printers, Marazion.

LAVEROCK PRESS, Welwyn, Herts, *etc.*

BAIN (Iain)

—— John Sharpe, Publisher & Bookseller, Piccadilly. A preliminary survey of his activities in the London book trade, 1800–1840. [With plates.] pp. 21. *Laverock Press: Welwyn*, 1960. 8°. Cup. **510**. bef. **1**. *One of an edition of 40 copies.*

BAIN (James) *Bookseller.*

—— James Bain Ltd. . . Retrospectus and Prospectus, 1961. pp. 8. *London,* [1961.] 12°. **2713**. ct. **8**.

WHITFIELD (Christopher)

—— The Kinship of Thomas Combe II, William Reynolds and William Shakespeare. [With genealogical tables.] pp. 16. *Laverock Press: Newnham*, 1961. 8º. Cup. **510.** bef. **2.**
One of an edition of one hundred copies.

BAIN (Iain)

—— John Bell's " Album de Novo Castro ". A description of a commonplace book together with a brief life of its first owner . . . 1783-1864. [With a portrait.] pp. 23. *Laverock Press: Newnham*, 1963. 8º. Cup. **510.** bef. **3.**
One of an edition of eighty copies.

LECRAM PRESS, Paris

WOLFE (Thomas Clayton)

—— To Rupert Brooke. [A poem.] *Privately printed:* [*Paris*,] 1948. 8º. Cup. **510.** fap. **1.**
No. 9 of an edition of 100 copies.

LEICESTER COLLEGE OF ART, Leicester

MASON (John) *Instructor in Bookbinding at the Leicester College of Arts and Crafts.*

—— Twelve by eight. Some adventures in papermaking. A talk to the Double Crown Club, 11 December, 1957. [With illustrations.] pp. 8. *College of Art: Leicester*, 1958. 8º. Cup.510 cak 2.

DAVIES (J. Michael)

—— The Private Press at Gregynog . . . Illustrations by Rigby Graham. pp. 19. *Leicester College of Art:* [*Leicester*,] 1959. 8º. Cup. **510.** cak. **1.**

GWILLIM (Peter) and **WHITMORE** (Christopher)

—— Slate Engraving. [With illustrations.] *Leicester College of Art, School of Printing: Leicester*, 1964. fol. Cup. **510.** cak. **4.**

LILAC TREE PRESS, Wallasey, Cheshire

LEA (George) *Writer of Verse.*

—— Canticles at evensong. [Poems.] *Lilac Tree Press:* [*Wallasey*, 1960.] 8º. Cup. **510.** dal. **1.**
One of an edition of twelve copies.

LINDLEY (Kenneth A.) Swindon

LINDLEY (Kenneth Arthur)

—— A Sequence of Downs. [Engravings with explanatory text.] *Kenneth A. Lindley: Swindon*, 1962. fol. Cup. **510.** bak. **1.**
No. 19 of an edition of twenty-four copies.

LION AND UNICORN PRESS, London

FUGGER (Wolfgang)

—— Wolffgang Fugger's Handwriting Manual entitled A Practical and Well-grounded Formulary for Divers Fair Hands . . . Translated by Frederick Plaat, *etc.* [Edited by Harry Carter.] *Lion & Unicorn Press: London*, 1955. obl. 8º. C. **103.** a. **4.**

WILKES (John) *M.P.*

[John Wilkes.]

—— The Life of John Wilkes. Patriot. An unfinished autobiography. With illustrations by Donald Higgins. [Edited with preface and introduction by R. des Habits.] pp. 72. *Lion & Unicorn Press: London*, 1955. fol. Cup. **510.** beg. **6.**

CASSON (Sir Hugh Maxwell)

—— Red Lacquer Days. An illustrated journal describing a recent journey to Peking. *Lion & Unicorn Press: London*, 1956. 4º. Cup 510.beg 10.

CASSON (Sir Hugh Maxwell)

—— [Another copy.] Red lacquer days, *etc.* 1956. Cup. **510.** beg. **11.**
△

CLARK (Kenneth Mackenzie) *Baron Clark.*

—— Five Speeches. An address at the Royal College of Art convention. *Lion & Unicorn Press:* [*London*,] 1956. 8º. Cup. **510.** beg. **5.**

EPSTEIN (Sir Jacob)

—— Epstein 1956. A camera study of the sculptor at work by Geoffrey Ireland. Introduction by Laurie Lee. *London: Lion & Unicorn Press*, [1957]. Cup. **501.** g. **18.**
Pages not numbered: plates; ports. 38 cm. △

FIERA (Baptista) *Mantuanus.*

—— [Hymni divini.] De Iusticia pingenda. On the painting of justice. A dialogue between Mantegna and Momus . . . The Latin text of 1515 reprinted with a translation, an introduction, and notes by James Wardrop. [From " Hymni divini." With a portrait.] *Eng. & Lat.* pp. 50. *Lion & Unicorn Press: London*, 1957. 8º. Cup. 510.beg 1.

WELCH (Maurice Denton)

—— I left my Grandfather's House. An account of his first walking tour . . . Illustrations by Leslie Jones. [With " Letters from D. Welch to Helen Roeder on the publication of his first book ' Maiden Voyage ' during 1942-3."] [With a portrait.] pp. 82. *Lion & Unicorn Press: London*, 1958. 4º. Cup. **503.** f. **17.**

YCIAR (Juan de)

—— [Orthographia practica.] Arte subtilissima. With a translation by Evelyn Shuckburgh, etc. (A facsimile of the 1550 edition.) *Lion & Unicorn Press: London,* 1958. 8°. Cup.510.beg.2.

MOMMENS (Norman)

—— Zoz. A story of glory. Written and illustrated by N. Mommens. *Lion & Unicorn Press: London,* 1959. fol. Cup.510 beg.3.

OXFORD.—*University of Oxford.—Bodleian Library.*

—— A Newe Booke of Copies 1574. ' A facsimile of a unique Elizabethan writing book in the Bodleian Library, Oxford. (Bodleian Don. c. 379). Edited with an introduction and notes by Berthold Wolfe. pp. 99. pl. 32. *Lion & Unicorn Press: London,* 1959. 4°. Cup.510,beg.4.

CHAUCER (Geoffrey) [*Canterbury Tales.—Single Tales.—Merchant's Tale.*]

—— The Merchant's Tale. Translated into modern English by Neville Coghill. With illustrations by Derek Cousins. *London: Lion and Unicorn Press,* 1960. Cup. **510**. beg. **9**.

pp. 64 : coll. 64. 28 cm. △

With the version printed in the 1868–79 edition of the Ellesmere manuscript.

GAINSBOROUGH (Thomas) [*Letters.*]

—— The Letters of Thomas Gainsborough. Edited by Mary Woodall. [With reproductions, including a self-portrait.] pp. 175. pl. 26. *Lion & Unicorn Press: London.* 1961. 4°. Cup. **510**. beg. **7**.

GIRLING (Frank Aldous)

—— English Merchants' Marks. A field survey of marks made by Merchants and Tradesmen in England between 1400 and 1700. [With illustrations.] pp. 119. *Lion & Unicorn Press: London,* 1962. 4°. **2740**. s. **4**.

PAOLOZZI (Eduardo)

—— Eduardo Paolozzi. The metallization of a dream. [Reproductions.] With a commentary by Lawrence Alloway. (Compiled, with the assistance of the sculptor, by John Munday.) pp. 63. *Lion & Unicorn Press: London,* 1963. 4°. Cup. **510**. beg. **8**.

SPENCER (Sir Stanley)

—— Scrapbook Drawings of Stanley Spencer. Selected and introduced by Colin Hayes. pp. 16. pl. 60. *Lion & Unicorn Press: London,* 1964. fol. L.R. **409**. d. **20**.

LOUJON PRESS, New Orleans

BUKOWSKI (Charles)

—— It catches my heart in my hands . . . New & selected poems, 1955–1963, etc. pp. 97. *Loujon Press: New Orleans,* [1963.] 8°. Cup. **510**. pae. **2**.
Gypsy Lou series. no. 1. Printed partly on coloured paper.

BUKOWSKI (Charles)

—— Crucifix in a deathhand . . . New poems, 1963–1965 . . . With etchings by Noel Rockmore. pp. 101. *Lyle Stuart: New York,* 1965. fol. Cup. **510**. pae. **1**.

LUDGVAN PRESS, London

NEWTON (Brean Leslie Douglas)

—— The Annunciation to the Virgin Mary. [A poem.] *Anthony Froshaug: London,* 1947. 8°. **11658**. c. **55**.

THEMERSON (Stefan)

—— The Lay Scripture ; or, a draft for a preface to a text-book of physics. *Anthony Froshaug: London,* 1947. 8°. **11658**. bb. **61**.

GRAHAM (William Sydney)

Writer of Verse.

—— The Voyages of Alfred Wallis. [A poem.] *Anthony Froshaug: London,* 1948. 8°. **11657**. b.

POTWOROWSKI (Peter)

—— 5 Letters. pp. 14. *Anthony Froshaug: London,* 1948. 8°. **10923**. aaa. **19**.

MALL PRESS, Hammersmith, London

NEW YORK.—*Grolier Club.*

—— Of the just shaping of letters. From the Applied geometry of Albrecht Dürer, book III. (Translated by R. T. Nichol from the Latin text.) *New York; Hammersmith: printed by Emery Walker & Wilfred Merton at the Mall Press,* 1917. C. **98**. gg. **11**.

pp. 40; illus. 32 cm. △

MANDRAKE PRESS, London

BIBLE.—*Tobit.* [*English.*]

—— The Book of Tobit. Decorated by Ann Gillmore Carter. *Mandrake Press: London,* 1929. 8°. Cup. **503**. e. **25**.

CROWLEY (Edward Alexander) calling himself Aleister Crowley.

—— The Spirit of Solitude. An autohagiography. Subsequently re-antichristened The Confessions of Aleister Crowley. [With plates, including portraits.] 2 vol. *Mandrake Press: London,* 1929. 8°. **10855**. g. **37**.

DAVIES (Rhys) *Novelist.*

—— A Bed of Feathers . . . Frontispiece wood-engraving by Lionel Ellis. pp. 93. *Mandrake Press: London,* [1929.] 16°. Cup.510.h.17.

LAWRENCE (DAVID HERBERT)
—— The Paintings of D. H. Lawrence. [Plates, with an introduction.] *Mandrake Press: London*, [1929.] 4º.
Cup. **820**. dd. **1**.

MIDDLETON (RICHARD BARHAM) [*Letters.*]
—— Richard Middleton's Letters to Henry Savage. Edited with an introduction and comments by the recipient. [With a portrait.] pp. 200. *Mandrake Press: London.* 1929. 8º. **010905**. i. **21**.

STEPHENSEN (PERCY REGINALD)
—— The Bushwhackers. Sketches of life in the Australian Outback. pp. 122. *Mandrake Press: London*, [1929.] 16º. Cup. **501**. h. **16**.

FLAUBERT (GUSTAVE)
—— Salammbo . . . The translation of J. W. Matthews with . . . illustrations by Haydn Mackey. pp. xi. 299. *Mandrake Press: London*, 1930. 4º. **12550**. k. **29**.

MANOR HOUSE PRESS, Sonning-on-Thames, Oxon.

THOMAS (*Sir* HENRY) *Principal Keeper of Printed Books, British Museum.*

—— Monster & Miracle. [On the legendary miracle of Santo Domingo de la Calzada. With plates.] pp. 12. *Printed for the Author; Manor House Press: Sonning-on-Thames*, 1935. 8º. **20020**. a. **35**.

MARCHBANKS PRESS, New York

STEVENSON (ROBERT LOUIS)
[New Arabian nights.]
—— Two mediaeval tales. (Introduction by Clayton Hamilton. Illustrations by C. B. Falls.) [*New York:*] *Limited Editions Club*, 1930. Cup. **510**. pah. **1**.
pp. xvii, 67. 24 cm. △
From "New Arabian nights".
CONTENTS: *A lodging for the night.—The Sire de Malétroit's door.*

MARDALE PRESS, Manchester

WHITTAKER (KENNETH)
—— A History of Withington. [With illustrations.] pp. 41. *The Author: [Manchester,]* 1957. 8º Cup.510.bav.1.

WHITTAKER (KENNETH)
—— The Limerick Book of Kenneth Whittaker. *Mardale Press: Manchester*, 1958. 16º. Cup. **510**. bav. **2**.
Privately printed.

MARION PRESS, New York

ARNOLD (WILLIAM HARRIS)
—— A Record of Books & Letters collected by W. H. Arnold [and sold at auction by Messrs. Bangs & Co., May 7 and 8, 1901.] With an essay on The Collector's Point of View by Leon H. Vincent. [With facsimiles and prices.] pp. xvi. 106. **F.P.** *Marion Press: New York*, 1901. 4º.
Ashley **2318**.
No. 4 of twenty-nine copies on Japan paper.

MEREDITH (GEORGE)
—— George Meredith's "Chillianwallah." [A poem. With a prefatory note by William E. Comfort.] *Marion Press: Jamaica, N.Y.*, 1909. 4º. Ashley **3641**.
Printed on one side of the leaf only.

MARLBOROUGH COLLEGE PRESS, Marlborough, Wilts.

GRAVES (ROBERT VON RANKE)
—— The More Deserving Cases. Eighteen old poems for reconsideration. [With a portrait.] *Marlborough College Press: [Marlborough,]* 1962. 8º.
Cup. **510**. bag. **1**.

IBBERSON (DORA)
—— Two Wiltshire Villages. An approach to the history of Oare with Rainscombe, and Huish. [Edited by Phyllis Steeds. With a map.] pp. 94. *Marlborough College Press: [Marlborough,]* 1963. 8º. Cup. **510**. bag. **2**.

MARVELL PRESS, Hessle, E. Riding, Yorks.

LARKIN (PHILIP)
—— The Less Deceived. Poems. pp. 43. *Marvell Press: Hessle*, 1955. 8º. **11659**. cc. **51**.

HOLLOWAY (CHRISTOPHER JOHN)
—— The Minute, and longer poems. pp. 72. *Marvell Press: Hessle*, 1956. 8º. **11660**. eee. **35**.

THWAITE (ANTHONY)
—— Home Truths. [Poems.] pp. 61. *Marvell Press: Hull*, 1957. 8º. **11661**. eee. **41**.

POUND (EZRA LOOMIS)
—— Gaudier-Brzeska, *etc.* pp. 147. pl. xxx. *Marvell Press: Hessle*, 1960. 8º. **7873**. bb. **54**.

MATRIX PRESS, London

BALL (DAVID)
—— Two Poems. (Drawing by Gene Mahon.)   *Matrix Press: London*, 1964. 8º.   Cup. **510**. cog. **3**.

DORN (EDWARD MERTON)
—— From Gloucester out . . . Drawing by Barry Hall. *Matrix Press: London*, [1964.] 8º.   Cup. **510**. cog. **2**.

HOLLO (PAUL ANSELM ALEXIS)
—— History . . . Drawings by Ken Landsdowne & Gregory Corso. *Matrix Press:* [*London*, 1964.] 8º.
Cup. **510**. cog. **1**.

MAVERICK PRESS, New York

EMMONS (EARL H.)
—— Strange Devices. A group of designs done for the Typophile Year Book.   *Maverick Press: New York*, 1938. 16º.   **011899**. e. **21**.

MEDBOURNE PRESS, Leicester

PICKERING (CHARLES) *Writer of Verse.*
—— Three Poems.   *Medbourne Press: Leicester*, [1965.] 8º.
Cup. **510**. cud. **1**.

MELISSA PRESS, Draguignan, Var, France; Dorchester

POTOCKI (GEOFFREY WLADISLAS VAILE) *Count de Montalk.*
—— [Christmas cards, containing poems by Count Potocki.] 3 pt.   *London; Draguignan*, 1945, [59.] 8º & 16º.
Cup.510.fad.11.

POTOCKI (GEOFFREY WLADISLAS VAILE) *Count de Montalk.*
—— [Miscellaneous pamphlets.] 7 pt.   *London, Draguignan,* [1945-50.] 8º.   Cup 510,fad.10.

POTOCKI (GEOFFREY WLADISLAS VAILE) *Count de Montalk.*
—— Mel meum. [Poems. With a portrait.] pp. 45. *Printed by hand and foot at the Mélissa Press: Draguignan*, 1959. 8º.   Cup. **510**. fad. **1**.

POTOCKI (GEOFFREY WLADISLAS VAILE) *Count de Montalk.* [Mel meum.]
—— Music is Immortal. (Part of Mel Meum.)   *Mélissa Press: Draguignan*, 1959. 8º.   Cup.510.fad.17. *One of an edition of a hundred copies.*

POTOCKI (GEOFFREY WLADISLAS VAILE) *Count de Montalk.*
—— The Fifth Columnist. A short story by Jim Goodleboodle, ex-convict [i.e. Count Potocki]. pp. 35.   *Mélissa Press: Draguignan*, 1960. 8º.   Cup. **510**. fad. **9**.

POTOCKI (GEOFFREY WLADISLAS VAILE) *Count de Montalk.*
—— [Another copy.] The fifth columnist, *etc.* 1960.
Cup. **510**. fad. **2**.
△

POTOCKI (GEOFFREY WLADISLAS VAILE) *Count de Montalk.*
—— YTT YZZ . . . A surrealist poem.   *Mélissa Press: Draguignan*, 1960. 8º.   Cup. **510**. fad. **7**.

ALDINGTON (RICHARD)
—— A Letter from Richard Aldington [to G. W. V. Potocki], and a summary bibliography of Count Potocki's published works. *Mélissa Press: Draguignan*, [1961.] 8º.
Cup. **510**. fad. **15**.

ALDINGTON (RICHARD)
—— [Another copy.] A Letter from Richard Aldington, *etc. Draguigan*, [1961.] 8º.   Cup. **510**. fad. **16**.

ALDINGTON (RICHARD)
—— [Another copy.] A letter from Richard Aldington, *etc.* [1961].   Cup. **510**. fad. **8**.
△

ALDINGTON (RICHARD)
—— A Tourist's Rome. pp. 24.   *Mélissa Press: Draguignan*, [1961.] 8º.   Cup. **510**. fad. **6**.

ALDINGTON (RICHARD)
—— A Letter from Richard Aldington, and a summary bibliography of Count Potocki's published works.   *Mélissa Press: Draguignan*, [1963.] 8º.   Cup. **510**. fad. **3**.

POTOCKI (GEOFFREY WLADISLAS VAILE) *Count de Montalk.*
—— Lulu's Lullaby, czyli-jak wiersz powstaje. Another surrealist poem.   *Mélissa Press: Dorchester*, 1964. 8º.
Cup. **510**. fad. **14**.

POTOCKI (GEOFFREY WLADISLAS VAILE) *Count de Montalk.*
—— One more Folly. Observations on the Hinton St. Mary mosaic. pp. 13.   *Mélissa Press: Dorchester, Dorset*, [1964.] 8º.   Cup. **510**. fad. **4**.

POTOCKI (GEOFFREY WLADISLAS VAILE) *Count de Montalk.*
—— The Whirling River. (Poems.) pp. 40.   *Mélissa Press: Dorchester*, 1964. 8º.   Cup. **510**. fad. **5**.

DE MALION (PETER)

—— Thomas Hardy from behind, and other memories. Introduction by Peter de Malion [or rather, written by P. de Malion]. pp. 14. *Mélissa Press: Dorchester*, 1965. 8º.
Cup. **510.** fad. **13.**

MAURRAS (CHARLES MARIE PHOTIUS)

—— Dear Garment. Six poems by Charles Maurras & one by Charles d'Orléans. Translated by Count Potocki of Montalk. pp. 19. *Mélissa Press: Dorchester*, 1965. 8º,
Cup. **510.** fad. **12.**

MERLE PRESS, Thames Ditton

CORKE (HELEN)

—— D. H. Lawrence's 'Princess.' A memory of Jessie Chambers. [With a portrait.] pp. 47. *Merle Press: Thames Ditton*, 1951. 8º.
10861. e. **53.**

MERCER (THOMAS STANLEY)

—— James Elroy Flecker: from school to Samarkand . . . With a bibliography. [With a portrait.] pp. 56. *Merle Press: Thames Ditton*, 1952. 8º.
10863. aa. **37.**

MERCER (THOMAS STANLEY)

—— St. Scandalbags. By Mrs. Amanda M. Ros. Together with Meet Irene, by D. B. Wyndham Lewis, & At the Sign of the Harrow, by F. Anstey. Edited with notes by T. S. Mercer. [With a portrait.] pp. 47. *Merle Press: Thames Ditton*, 1954. 8º.
11861. cc. **38.**

ROS (AMANDA M'KITTRICK)

—— Donald Dudley, the Bastard Critic. [A novel.] pp. 64. *Merle Press: Thames Ditton*, 1954. 8º. Cup.**401.f.7.**

MERRION PRESS, London

MOZLEY (CHARLES)

—— Wolperiana. An illustrated guide to Berthold L. Wolpe, *etc.* [With portraits.] *Merrion Press: London*, 1960. 8º.
Cup. **510.** a. **1.**

ELIOT (THOMAS STEARNS)

—— Geoffrey Faber, 1889–1961. pp. 19. *Faber & Faber: London*, 1961. 8º.
Cup. **510.** a. **2.**
No. 96 of an edition of 100 copies printed for private distribution. Printed on one side of the paper only.

MERRYMOUNT PRESS, Boston, Mass.

LITURGIES.—*Episcopal Church of America.* [*Common Prayer.—Communion Office.*]

—— The altar book: containing the order for the celebration of the Holy Eucharist according to the use of the American Church: MDCCXCII. (By Daniel Berkeley Updike and Harold Brown . . . The plain-song is arranged by Sir John Stainer.) *London: A. P. Watt & Son; New York: printed at the De Vinne Press*, 1896. K.T.C. **41.** b. **4.**
Pages not numbered; illus. 39 cm. △
"The type for this volume was set at the Merrymount Press, Boston."

ALBANY, *N.Y., Diocese of.* A Description of the Pastoral Staff given to the Diocese of Albany New York, Anno Domini. M.DCCCXCVII : with representations of the chief parts of the staff. [*Merrymount Press: Boston*, 1900.] fol.
Crach. **1.** Tab. **6.** b. **4.**

SANBORN (FRANKLIN BENJAMIN) The Personality of Thoreau. pp. 71. *Charles E. Goodspeed: Boston* [*Mass.*], 1901. 8º.
Cup.**510.** sac.**1.**

THOREAU (HENRY DAVID) The Service...Edited by F. B. Sanborn. pp. x. 30. *C. E. Goodspeed: Boston* [*Mass.*], 1902. 8º.
Cup.**510.** sac.**2.**

NORTON (CHARLES ELIOT) The Poet Gray as a Naturalist. With selections from his notes on the Systema Naturæ of Linnæus and facsimiles of some of his drawings. pp. lxvi. *Charles E. Goodspeed: Boston, Mass.*, 1903. 8º.
Cup **510.** sac.**3.**

ERASMUS (DESIDERIUS) [*Adagia.—Chil. IV. Cent. I.*] Erasmus against War. With an introduction by J. W. Mackail. pp. xxxiii. 64. *Merrymount Press: Boston* [*Mass.*], 1907. 8º. Cup.**510.** sac **4.**
Part of "The Humanists' Library.

UPDIKE (WILKINS) A History of the Episcopal Church in Narragansett, Rhode Island. Including a history of other Episcopal Churches in the State . . . With a transcript of the Narragansett Parish Register, from 1718 to 1774; an appendix containing a reprint of a work entitled "America Dissected" by the Revᵈ James MacSparran, and copies of other old papers . . . Second edition, newly edited, enlarged and corrected by the Reverend Daniel Goodwin. 3 vol. *D. B. Updike: Boston* [*Mass.*], 1907. 8º.
4745. dd. **24.**

BULWER, afterwards **BULWER-LYTTON** (EDWARD GEORGE EARLE LYTTON) *Baron Lytton.* [*Letters.*]

—— Letters of Bulwer-Lytton to Macready. With an introduction by Brander Matthews, 1836–1866. pp. xx. 180. *Carteret Brook Club: Newark, N.J.*, 1911. 8º.
Cup.**510.** sac.**5.**
No. 34 of an edition of 100 copies privately printed by D. B. Updike at the Merrymount Press.

SIDNEY (Sir PHILIP) [*Letters.*]

—— The Correspondence of Philip Sidney and Hubert Languet. [Collected and translated from the Latin by S. A. Pears.] Edited by William A. Bradley. pp. xxxi. 229. *Merrymount Press: Boston*, 1912. 8º. Cup. **510.** sac. **6.**
No. 5 of "The Humanists Library".

DUERER (Albrecht) [*Literary Works.*]

—— Records of Journeys to Venice and the Low Countries . . . Edited by Roger Fry. pp. xxv. 117. *Merrymount Press: Boston*, 1913. 8°. Cup. **510**. sac. **7**.
    Vol. 6 of " The Humanists' Library ".

LITURGIES.—*Episcopal Church of America.—Common Prayer.—Communion Office.* Ordinary and Canon of the Mass, together with the Order for the Administration of the Lord's Supper or Holy Communion and the Holy Chant. (Prepared by Maurice W. Britton.) *H. W. Gray Co.: New York*, 1913. fol. **3408**. i. **25**.

CLEVELAND, *Ohio.—Rowfant Club.*

—— A lover's moods. By Bertram Dobell. [The foreword signed : Charles C. Bubb.] *Cleveland*, 1914.
            Cup. **510**. sac. **13**.
    pp. ix, 61. 18 cm. △
    Printed by D. B. Updike at the Merrymount Press, Boston.

BOSTON, *Massachusetts.—Museum of Fine Arts.—Department of Prints.*

—— A Catalogue of the Collection of Prints from the Liber Studiorum of Joseph Mallord William Turner formed by the late Francis Bullard . . . and bequeathed by him to the Museum of Fine Arts in Boston. [Edited by W. A. Bradley. With illustrations.] pp. 203. *Privately printed: Boston*, 1916. fol. L.R. **38**. b. **1**.

MERRITT (Percival)

—— The parochial library of the eighteenth century in Christ Church, Boston. By a proprietor of Christ Church. (The preface signed : Percival Merritt.) *Boston: privately printed at the Merrymount Press*, 1917. **011904**. aaa. **40**.
    pp. 81. 22 cm. △

PROVIDENCE, *Rhode Island.—Brown University.—John Carter Brown Library.*

—— Catalogue of the John Carter Brown Library, *etc.* (Bibliotheca Americana.) 3 vol. *Providence*, 1919–31. 8°. **N.L.5.b.**
    Vol. 1 and 2 are each in two parts.

NEW YORK.—*Grolier Club.*

—— Notes and journal of travel in Europe, 1804–1805, by Washington Irving. With an introduction by William P. Trent and . . . illustrations in aquatint . . . by Rudolph Ruzicka. *New York; Boston: printed by D. B. Updike at the Merrymount Press*, 1921. Ac. **4714/2**.
    3 vol.: plates. 18 cm. △

AMORY (Martha Babcock) [*Letters.*]

—— The Wedding Journey of Charles and Martha Babcock Amory. Letters of Mrs. Amory to her mother, Mrs. Gardiner Greene, 1833–1834. 2 vol. *Privately printed: Boston*, 1922. 4°. **10906**. c. **5**.

BOSTON, *Massachusetts.—Club of Odd Volumes.*

—— The Felicities of Sixty. By Isaac H. Lionberger. pp. 35. *Boston*, 1922. 8°. Cup. **510**. sac. **9**.

LAMB (Charles) [*Smaller Collections.*]

—— Letter regarding Roast Pig to William Hazlitt and a Letter on Friendship to Robert Lloyd, together with A Dissertation on Roast Pig. [With facsimiles of the letters.] *W. K. Bixby: Boston*, 1922. 8°. Cup. **510**. sac. **8**.
    Privately printed at the Merrymount Press.

GRAHAM (Robert Bontine Cunninghame)

—— Inveni portam. Joseph Conrad. *Cleveland: Rowfant Club*, 1924. Cup. **510**. sac. **12**.
    pp. 14. 21 cm. △
    English. A tribute to Conrad, reprinted from "The Saturday Review".

NEW YORK.—*Grolier Club.*

—— A dissertation upon English typographical founders and founderies. By Edward Rowe Mores . . . With appendix by John Nichols . . . Edited by D. B. Updike. *Boston: printed by D. B. Updike at the Merrymount Press*, 1924. Ac. **4714/25**.
    pp. xl, 103; port. 25 cm. △

UPDIKE (Daniel Berkeley)

—— In the Day's Work. [Three papers on printing] . . . Limited edition. pp. 69. *Harvard University Press: Cambridge*, 1924. 8°. **2703**. ba. **67**.

BOSTON, *Massachusetts. — Public Latin School.* The Public Latin School of Boston in the World War, 1914–1918. A roll of honor. *D. B. Updike: Boston*, 1925. fol. L.R. **262**. c. **6**.
    One of an edition of 26 copies.

UNITED STATES OF AMERICA. — *National Society of the Colonial Dames of America.* The Record of those who gave to an Endowment Fund collected by the...Society...for the maintenance of Sulgrave Manor, the home of the ancestors of George Washington, in Sulgrave, Northamptonshire, England. pp. . 108. *Boston*, 1925. fol. **1785**. b. **14**.
    No. 44 of an edition of 48 copies.

W., G. P.

—— A Chronological List of the Books printed at the Kelmscott Press. With illustrative material from a collection made by William Morris and Henry C. Marillier, now in the library of Marsden J. Perry, *etc.* [Preface signed: G. P. W., i.e. George Parker Winship.] pp. 42. *Merrymount Press: Boston*, 1928. 8°. **011899**. aaa. **25**.

HARDY (Thomas) O.M. [*Miscellaneous Prose.*]

—— Old Mrs. Chundle. A short story. *New York: Crosby Gaige; Boston: printed by D. B. Updike, the Merrymount Press*, 1929. Cup. **510**. sac. **10**.
    pp. 26. 22 cm. △

LA FONTAINE (Jean de) [*Fables.—English.*]

—— The Fables of Jean de La Fontaine. Newly translated into English verse by Joseph Auslander and Jacques le Clercq. With title-page and decorations engraved on copper by Rudolph Ruzicka. 2 vol. *Limited Editions Club: New York*, 1930. 8°. C. **105**. a. **2**.

OPUS.

—— Opus v. [Poems.] [By ♪] pp. v. 82.
    Privately printed: Boston, 1931. 8°. C. **103**. b. **13**.
    No. 10 of twenty-five copies printed by D. B. Updike.

SMITH (Sidney Lawton) Sidney Lawton Smith : Designer, Etcher, Engraver. [A memoir by Amy G. Smith and an appreciation by Gardner Teall.] With extracts from his diary and a check-list of his book-plates. [With plates, including portraits.] pp. xi. 135. *C. E. Goodspeed & Co.: Boston*, 1931. 8°.
           Print Room.

UPDIKE (DANIEL BERKELEY)

—— Notes on the Merrymount Press & its Work. By D. B. Updike. With a bibliographical list of books printed at the Press, 1893-1933. By Julian Pearce Smith. With views of the press at various periods, etc. pp. vi. 279. *Harvard University Press: Cambridge, Mass.*, 1934. 8°.
11911. b. 21.

SAN FRANCISCO.—*Book Club of California.*

—— An Original Issue of "The Spectator." Together with the story of the famous English periodical and of its founders, Joseph Addison & Richard Steele, by Eric Partridge. pp. 49. [*San Francisco,*] 1939. fol.
L.R. 261. b. 18.

The issue of "The Spectator" inserted in this copy is no. 82.

NEW YORK.—*American Institute of Graphic Arts.*

—— Daniel Berkeley Updike and the Merrymount Press. [By various authors.] pp. 47. *New York,* 1940. 8°.
Cup. 510. sac. 11.

UPDIKE (DANIEL BERKELEY)

—— Some Aspects of Printing Old and New. [With a portrait.] pp. 72. *W. E. Rudge: New Haven,* 1941. 8°.
11907. bb. 34.

MERRYTHOUGHT PRESS, London

MORGAN (EDWARD GUY TRICE)

—— Off the Record. [Tales.] 6 no.

No. 1 The Story of William McShakespeare, etc. [With a portrait.] pp. 19. 1960. Cup. 510. bam. 1/1.
No. 2 Judgement Day . . . Wood engraving by Cecil Gill. pp. 22. 1960. Cup. 510. bam. 1/2.
No. 3. The Bird . . . Linocut by John Tribe. pp. 19. 1961. Cup. 510. bam. 1/3.
No. 5. Mr. Christmas Strikes Back. Frontispiece by Jane Brown. pp. 17. 1962. Cup. 510. bam. 1/5.
No. 6. The Commissar . . . Frontispiece by Bernard Lodge. pp. 22. 1962. Cup. 510. bam. 1/6.

Merrythought Press: London, 1960–62. 8°.
Cup. 510. bam. 1.

The collective title is taken from a portfolio in which the six booklets are enclosed.

CRON (BRIAN SAWYER)

—— The Recent owners of the Golden Psalter. *Merrythought Press: London,* 1963. 8°. Cup. 510. bam. 3.
Printed for private circulation. One of an edition of fifty copies.

GARLICK (RAYMOND ERNEST) [*Selections.*]

—— Landscapes and Figures. Selected poems, 1949–63. pp. 44. *Merrythought Press: Ealing,* 1964. 8°.
Cup. 510. bam. 2.

MEYNELL (Francis), London

MEYNELL (EVERARD)

—— From a Hospital Journal, 1921–1922. pp. 61. *Printed for G. M., J. M., A. M., W. M. & V. M.: London,* 1928. 8°.
Cup. 510. be 1.1.

THOMPSON, afterwards **MEYNELL** (ALICE CHRISTIANA)

—— A.M. A Keepsake for the A.I.G.A. from Francis Meynell. [A collection of verse and prose by Alice Meynell, with three poems written in her praise. With an introduction by Sir Francis Meynell.] pp. vii. 29. *Francis Meynell: London,* 1930. 12°. **Cup. 510. be 1.2.**
Presentation copy from Wilfred Meynell to Ethel Herdman.

MIGRANT PRESS, Worcester

FINLAY (IAN HAMILTON)

—— The Dancers inherit the Party. Selected poems . . . With two woodcuts by Zeljko Kujundzic. pp. 35. *Migrant: Worcester,* 1960. 8°. Cup. 510. bca. 1.

HILL (HUGH CREIGHTON)

—— Latterday Chrysalides. [Poems.] *Migrant Press: Worcester, Ventura,* 1961. 8°. Cup. 510. bca. 2.

MILL HOUSE PRESS, Stanford Dingley, Berks.

HARDY (Hon. ROBERT GATHORNE)

—— Village symphony. *Stanford Dingley: Mill House Press,* 1926. Cup. 510. ap. 24.

Pages not numbered. 21 cm. △

A poem. No.7 of an edition of fifteen copies. Author's presentation copy.

HARDY (Hon. ROBERT GATHORNE)

—— John Donne sits for his portrait. (By R. G-H. [i.e. R. Gathorne-Hardy.]) *Stanford Dingley: Mill House Press,* 1927. Cup. 510. ap. 23.

Pages not numbered; illus. 23 cm. △

A poem. No. 3 of an edition of twenty-five copies. Author's presentation copy to Roger Senhouse.

HARDY (Hon. ROBERT GATHORNE)

—— The old companion. A poem by R. G-H. [i.e. R. Gathorne-Hardy.] *Stanford Dingley: Mill House Press,* 1927. Cup. 510. ap. 25.

Pages not numbered; illus. 24 cm. △

No. 22 of an edition of twenty-five copies. Author's presentation copy.

HUME (DAVID) *the Historian.* [*Biography.*]

—— My Own Life. pp. 27. *Mill House Press: Stanford Dingley,* 1927. 12°. Cup. 510. ap. 2.
One of an edition of eighty copies.

DARIAN.

—— Darian. [In verse.] *Stanford Dingley: Mill House Press,* 1928. Cup. 510. ap. 26.

Pages not numbered. 16 cm. △

In verse. One of an edition of twenty-five copies. A slip reading "Now ready. Darian, by the author of The Old Companion", and bearing the date 1929, is affixed to the titlepage.

GLANVILL (JOSEPH)

—— The Story of a Languishment. [From "Saducismus Triumphatus".] *Mill House Press: Stanford Dingley,* 1928. 8°. Cup. 510. ap. 18.

GLANVILL (JOSEPH)

—— The Story of Mr. John Bourne. [From " Saducismus Triumphatus ".] *Mill House Press: Stanford Dingley,* 1928. 8°. Cup. **510**. ap. **17**.

JAMES (MONTAGU RHODES)

—— Wailing Well. pp. 20. *Mill House Press: Stanford Dingley,* 1928. 4°. Cup. **510**. ap. **4**.

BOSWELL (JAMES) the Elder. [*Life of Johnson. Selections and Extracts.*]

—— Conjugal fidelity. A suppressed dialogue between Boswell & Johnson. *Mill House Press: Stanford Dingley,* 1929. Cup. **510**. ap. **27**.

 Pages not numbered. 23 cm.   △

 '*Reprinted . . . from the . . . uncancelled state of page 302 of volume II of the first edition of Boswell's "Life of Johnson" '*
One of an edition of thirty copies.

SITWELL (*Sir* OSBERT) *Bart.*

     MISS Mew. [Poems.]
Mill House Press: Stanford Dingley, 1929. 8°.
     Cup.510.ap.7.

BRIDGES (ROBERT SEYMOUR)

—— On receiving Trivia from the Author. [A poem addressed to Logan Pearsall Smith.] *Mill House Press: Stanford Dingley,* 1930. 8°. Cup.510.ap.3.
One of thirty-six copies printed for private circulation only.

PALMER (HERBERT EDWARD)

—— Jonah comes to Nineveh. A ballad. pp. 17. *Mill House Press: Stanford Dingley,* 1930. 8°. Cup. **510**. ap. **5**.

HARDY (Hon. ROBERT GATHORNE)

—— The White Horse. [Poems.] pp. 23. *Mill House Press: [Stanford Dingley,]* 1931. 8°. Cup. **510**. ap. **6**.
One of an edition of fifty copies, privately printed.

LENG (KYRLE)

—— Juvenilia. *Stanford Dingley: Mill House Press,* 1931.
     Cup. **510**. ap. **21**.

 pp. 26. 19 cm.   △
 Two tales. No. 16 of an edition of thirty-five copies. Author's presentation copy.

BOOTH (DIGBY HAWORTH) Kleinias. Poems. pp. 30. *At the Sign of the Boar's Head: Manaton,* 1932. 8°.
     Cup.510.aga.2.

TREVELYAN (*Lady* HILDA)

—— The Lady Hilda Trevelyan Rescue Fund Balance Sheet, *etc.* [By Logan Pearsall Smith.] [*Mill House Press: Stanford Dingley,* 1932.] 4°. Cup. **510**. ap. **1**. (1.)

SMITH (ROBERT PEARSALL)

—— How Little Logan was brought to Jesus. Edited with a preface by Logan Pearsall Smith. (Second edition.) [With a portrait.] pp. 9. *Mill House Press: Stanford Dingley,* 1934. 8°. Cup. **510**. ap. **15**.
One of an edition of sixty-five copies. Presentation copy to Max Beerbohm from Logan Pearsall Smith.

BRIDGES (ROBERT SEYMOUR) [*Two or more Works.*]

—— Four Collects. *Mill House Press: Stanford Dingley,* 1947. 8°.   Cup.510.ap.8.
No. 12 of an edition of forty-two copies.

H., R. G.

—— Seven Poems written in War-Time by R. G.-H. [i.e. Robert Gathorne-Hardy.] pp. 7. *Mill House Press: Stanford Dingley,* 1947. 4°. Cup. **510**. ap. **9**.
 One of an edition of forty-five copies printed for private circulation.

GRAY (THOMAS) *the Poet.* [*Miscellanea.*]

—— Occasional Memorandums. Being extracts from a journal for the year 1767 now first printed from the original manuscript, *etc.* [With an introduction by Roger Senhouse.] *Mill House Press: Stanford Dingley,* 1950. 8°. Cup. **510**. ap. **10**.
 One of an edition of a hundred copies.

SASSOON (SIEGFRIED LORAINE)

—— Common Chords. [Poems.] pp. 18. *Mill House Press: Stanford Dingley,* 1950. 8°. Cup.510.ap.11.

FORSTER (EDWARD MORGAN)

—— Desmond MacCarthy.   *Mill House Press: Stanford Dingley,* 1952. 8°. Cup.510.ap.12.
 One of an edition of seventy-two copies.

FORSTER (EDWARD MORGAN)

—— [Another copy.] Desmond MacCarthy. 1952.
     Cup. **510**. ap. **20**.
        △

BRIDGES (ROBERT SEYMOUR) [*Letters.*]

—— XXI Letters: correspondence between Robert Bridges and R. C. Trevelyan on New Verse and The Testament of Beauty. [With a foreword by Robert Gathorne-Hardy.] pp. 27. *Mill House Press: Stanford Dingley,* 1955. 8°.
     Cup.510.ap.13.
 One of an edition of sixty-eight copies.

FITZGERALD (EDWARD) *Translator of Omar Khayyam.* [*Single Works.*]

—— White Sauce. Now first printed from the original manuscript, *etc.* *Mill House Press: [Stanford Dingley,* 1956.] 4°. Cup. **510** ap. **1**. (2.)
 Printed on one side of the leaf only.

HARDY (Hon. ROBERT GATHORNE)

—— A Month of Years by R. G. H. [Poems. With a prefatory note signed: Kyrle Leng, Robert Gathorne-Hardy.] pp. 59. *Mill House Press: Stanford Dingley,* 1956. 4°.
     Cup. **501**. e. **25**.

HARDY (Hon. ROBERT GATHORNE)

—— [Another copy.] A Month of Years. By RGH (R. Gathorne-Hardy). *Stanford Dingley,* 1956. 4°.
     Cup. **501**. e. **2**.

HARDY (Hon. ROBERT GATHORNE)

—— [Another copy.] A month of years, *etc.* 1956.
     Cup. **510**. ap. **14**.
        △

HILL (Anne Catherine Dorothy)
—— Trelawny's Strange Relations. An account of the domestic life of Edward John Trelawny's mother & sisters in Paris and London, 1818–1829. [With plates.] pp. 36. *Mill House Press: Stanford Dingley,* 1956. 8°.
Cup. **510**. ap. **19**.

SMITH (Logan Pearsall)
—— Cousin Crowe. (The decoration on the title designed and cut by Reynolds Stone.) [On Henry James and his cousin Theophilus Crowe.] pp. 4. *Mill House Press: [Stanford Dingley,* 1960.] 8°. Cup. **510**. ap. **16**.
One of an edition of twenty-two copies with the titlepage ornament printed in blue. Presentation copy from Robert Gathorne-Hardy to his brother Edward.

ROSSETTI (Christina Georgina)
—— Familiar correspondence newly translated from the Italian of Christina G. Rossetti. [Translated by Robert Gathorne-Hardy.] *Stanford Dingley: Mill House Press,* 1962. Cup. **510**. ap. **22**.
pp. 17. 22 cm. △
One of an edition of sixty-seven copies.

MINORCA PRESS, Dublin

DONAGHY (John Lyle) Primordia Caeca. Poems. pp. 33. *Eason & Son: Dublin,* 1927. 8°. *Privately printed.* **11643**. d. **40**.

DONAGHY (John Lyle)
—— Ad Perennis Vitae Fontem. Poems. pp. 32. *Minorca Press: Dublin,* 1928. 8°. Cup. **501**. bb. **27**. *Privately printed.*

MONK'S HEAD PRESS, Philadelphia

HOUSMAN (Laurence) and **SIMONS** (L.)
The Tale of a Nun. (Done out of the Old Dutch by L. Housman and L. Simons.) pp. 43. *Privately Printed by E. S. P. of the Monk's Head: Philadelphia,* 1901. 12°. **12403**. a. **49**.

MONKTON COMBE SCHOOL PRESS, Monkton Combe, Wilts.

MONKTON COMBE.—*Monkton Combe School.*
—— The Valley. An anthology of verse by members of Monkton Combe School, 1875–1960. [With illustrations.] pp. 44. *Monkton Combe School Press: Monkton Combe,* 1962. 8°. Cup. **510**. bad. **1**.

MONTAGUE PRESS, Montague, Mass.

WINSHIP (George Parker)
—— Luther S. Livingston: a biographical sketch (with bibliography. Reprinted from Bibliographical Society of America.—Papers, vol. VIII. no. 3–4). [1914.] 8°. **010883**. h. **37**.

MORLAND PRESS, London

SPARE (Austin Osman)
—— A Book of Satyrs. [Thirteen plates. With an introduction by James Guthrie.] *John Lane: London, New York,* [1909.] fol. **1755**. b. **21**.

BIBLE.—*Job.* [*English.*]
—— The Book of Job. With an introduction by G. K. Chesterton & illustrated in colour by C. Mary Tongue. pp. xxvi. 101. *C. Palmer & Hayward: London,* 1916. 8°. **3052**. dd. **18**.

PHILLPOTTS (Eden)
—— The Girl and the Faun . . . Illustrated by Frank Brangwyn. pp. 78. *C. Palmer & Hayward: London,* 1916. 4°. **12410**. r. **2**.

SQUIRE (Sir John Collings)
—— Twelve Poems. Decorations by A. Spare, cut on wood by W. Quick. pp. 28. *Morland Press: London,* 1916. 8°. **011649**. i. **23**.

YEATS (William Butler)
—— Eight Poems . . . Transcribed by Edward Pay. "*Form*": London, 1916. fol. **11647**. g. **62**.

FARJEON (Eleanor) All the Way to Alfriston. [Poems.]...With drawings by Robin Guthrie. pp. 16. *Morland Press: London,* 1918. 8°. **011648**. ee. **68**.

BRANGWYN (Sir Frank William)
—— Bruges. [Drawings by Frank Brangwyn, cut on wood by Yoshijiro Urushibara. With six poems written for this work by R. L. Binyon.] *Morland Press: London,* [1919.] fol. Dept. of Prints & Drawings. *No. 35 of an edition of fifty copies.*

BRANGWYN (Sir Frank William)
—— Bookplates. [With a foreword by Eden Phillpotts and a technical note by E. H. Hubbard.] pp. 19. pl. 69. *Morland Press: London,* 1920. 4°. **7960**. cc. **7**.

SPARE (Austin Osman) The Focus of Life: the mutterings of Aäos: written and illustrated by A. O. Spare. With an introduction by Francis Marsden. pp. 44. *Morland Press: London,* 1920. 4°. L.R. **33**. c. **6**.

RODO (LUDOVIC) *pseud.* [i.e. LUDOVIC RODOLPHE PISSARRO.]
—— Ex-libris and Marks, *etc.*   *Morland Press: London,*
1921. 8°.   **7860**. dd. **6**.

WALLER (PICKFORD)
—— Bookplates by Pickford Waller. (Introduction by W. G.
Blaikie Murdoch.) *Morland Press: London,* 1921. 4°.
                                                       9907. f. **23**.

WALLER (PICKFORD)
—— Pickford Waller's Bookplates. (Second book . . . Introduction by W. G. B. Murdoch.) *Morland Press: London,*
1922. fol.   **9907**. gg. **5**.
One of twenty-five copies printed.

CONRAD (JOSEPH)
—— Laughing Anne. A play. pp. 66.   *"The Bookman's
Journal" Office: London,* 1923. 8°.   **011779**. l. **33**.
No. 4 of "The Vine Books."

CONRAD (JOSEPH)
—— [Another copy.] Laughing Anne, *etc.*   1923.
                                                       Ashley **2952**.
                                                              △

DE LA MARE (WALTER JOHN)
—— Lispet, Lispett and Vaine. [A short story.] (Decorated
by W. P. Robins.) pp. 47.   *"Bookman's Journal":*
London, 1923. 8°.   **012630**. m. **28**.
Vine Books. no. 3.

MAC EVOY (AMBROSE)
—— The Work of Ambrose Mc Evoy . . . Compiled by
"Wigs". pp. 31. pl. 12. *Colour Magazine: London,*
1923. 4°.   L.R. **33**. c. **15**.

MACFALL (CHAMBERS HALDANE COOKE)
—— The Book of Lovat Claud Fraser. [With portraits,
illustrations and coloured plates.] pp. 183. *J. M. Dent &
Sons: London,* 1923. 4°.   L.R. **33**. c. **11**.

MACFALL (CHAMBERS HALDANE COOKE)
—— The art of Hesketh Hubbard.   *London: Morland
Press,* 1924.   **7860**. cc. **21**.
pp. 87; illus. 26 cm.   △

MOSHER (Thomas B.), Portland, Me.

BRIDGES (ROBERT SEYMOUR) [*Single Works.*]
—— The Growth of Love. [With an introductory essay by
Lionel Johnson.]   *Thomas B. Mosher: Portland, Me.*
1894. 8°.   Cup. **402**. c. **36**.

DOWSON (ERNEST CHRISTOPHER)
—— The Poems of Ernest Dowson. [With a memoir of
Dowson by Arthur Symons, reprinted from the "Fort-
nightly Review".] pp. xxxvii. 161. *Thomas B. Mosher:
Portland, Me.,* 1902. 8°.   Cup. **500**. a. **19**.
No. 2 of an edition of fifty copies.

MACLEOD (FIONA)
—— By Sundown Shores: studies in spiritual history. pp. 94.
Thomas B. Mosher: Portland, Maine, 1902. 16°.
                                                       K.T.C. **41**. a. **3**.

Printed on Japanese vellum.

MAC LEOD (FIONA) *pseud.* [i.e. WILLIAM SHARP.]
The Wayfarer. pp. xi. 47.   *Thomas B. Mosher:
Portland, Maine,* 1905. 16°.   K.T.C. **41**. a. **5**.

CELTIC VERSE.
—— A Little Garland of Celtic Verse. pp. viii. 41.   *Thomas
B. Mosher: Portland, Me.,* 1907. 12°.   Cup. **500**. a. **11**.

JEFFERIES (JOHN RICHARD)
—— Nature and Eternity: with other uncollected papers.
pp. 91. *Thomas B. Mosher: Portland, Maine,* 1907. 16°.
                                                       Cup. **501**. aa. **25**.

MAC LEOD (FIONA) *pseud.* [i.e. WILLIAM SHARP.]
The Tale of the Four White Swans. (Second edition.)
pp. 96.   *Thomas B. Mosher:
Portland, Maine,* 1907. 8°.   K.T.C. **41**. a. **4**.
Printed on Japan vellum.

MAC LEOD (FIONA) *pseud.* [i.e. WILLIAM SHARP.]
Ulad of the Dreams. pp. 70.   *Thomas B. Mosher:
Portland, Maine,* 1907. 8°.   K.T.C. **41**. a. **6**.
Printed on Japan vellum.

SYMONS (ARTHUR)
—— Lyrics. (Second edition.) pp. viii. 36.   *Thomas B.
Mosher: Portland, Me.,* 1907. 12°.   Cup. **500**. a. **25**.

DOBSON (HENRY AUSTIN)
—— Proverbs in Porcelain and other Poems. pp. vi. 63.
Thomas B. Mosher: Portland, Me., 1909. 8°.
                                                       Cup. **501**. aa. **15**.
No. 85 of an edition of 100 copies.

SYMONS (ARTHUR)
—— Silhouettes. pp. xiv. 94. *Thomas B. Mosher: Portland,
Me.,* 1909. 8°.   Cup. **500**. a. **26**.
Part of the "Old World Series".

YEATS (WILLIAM BUTLER)
—— The Land of Heart's Desire. pp. 31.   *Thomas B.
Mosher: Potland, Me.,* 1909. 4°.   Cup. **503**. aa. **1**.

THOMPSON (FRANCIS) *Poet.*
—— The hound of Heaven. (Third edition.) [With a foreword signed: T. B. M., i.e. T. B. Mosher.]   *Portland,
Me.: Thomas B. Mosher,* 1911.   Cup. **503**. a. **1**.
pp. viii, 11. 15 cm.   △

MOUNT ST. BERNARD ABBEY, Coalville, Leics.

WILDE (Oscar Fingall O'Flahertie Wills)
[The Happy Prince, and other tales.]
—— The Nightingale and the Rose. A fairy tale. [From The Happy Prince, and other tales.] *Percival & Graham: [Leicester,]* 1961. 8°. **Cup. 510. coz. 1.**
Privately printed by the Cistercian Monks of Mount Saint Bernard Abbey. Designed and produced by George Percival and Rigby Graham. Edition limited to a few copies for circulation among their friends.

G., P. M.
—— An Autumn Anthology. Illustrations by Rigby Graham. [The compiler's note signed: P. M. G., i.e. Patricia M. Graham.] *Privately printed by the Cistercians of Mount Saint Bernard Abbey: Coalville,* 1964 [1965]. 8°. **Cup. 510. coz. 2.**

MYRIAD PRESS, Twinstead Green; Sudbury, Suffolk

BEECHING (Jack)
—— Truth is a Naked Lady. [Poems.] pp. 32. *Myriad Press: Twinstead Green,* 1957. 8°. **11661. de. 54.**

LINDSAY (Jack)
—— Three Elegies. *Myriad Press: Sudbury, Suff.,* 1957. 8°. **11661. de. 36.**

NAG'S HEAD PRESS, Christchurch, N.Z.

DADDS (E.)
—— The Centennial history of Barnego Flat. General editor: E. Dadds. *Nag's Head Press: Christchurch,* 1964– . 8°. **X. 0708/77.**

NAPLES PRESS, London

HORNER (William) *Writer of Verse.*
—— Sequence of Seven. *Naples Press: London,* 1964. 12°. **Cup. 510. cot. 1.**
One of an edition of 100 copies.

NASH (John Henry), San Francisco

THOMPSON (Susan F.)
—— The Twins and the Whys. A fairy tale worth while. pp. 26. *Paul Elder & Co.: San Francisco & New York,* 1906. 8°. **Cup. 510. nag. 2.**

NEW YORK.—*Grolier Club.*
—— Quattrocentisteria . . . By Maurice Hewlett. *New York: printed by John Henry Nash, San Francisco,* 1921. **C. 98. gg. 10.**
pp. v, 19. 31 cm. △
One of a series of six books printed by eminent American printers.

BALFOUR, afterwards **STEVENSON** (Margaret Isabella)
—— Stevenson's baby book: being the record of the sayings and doings of Robert Louis Balfour Stevenson, *etc.* [With " A note to the reader " signed: Katharine D. Osbourne.] *San Francisco: printed for John Howell by John Henry Nash,* 1922. **Cup. 510. nag. 3.**
pp. 58: plate; port. 24 cm. △
Lithographed from the MS., with a transcription.

WILDE (Oscar Fingal O'Flahertie Wills) [*Letters.*]
—— Some letters from Oscar Wilde to Alfred Douglas, 1892–1897, heretofore unpublished. With illustrative notes by Arthur C. Dennison, Jr., & Harrison Post and an essay by A. S. W. Rosenbach. [With " A bibliographical preface by William Andrews Clark, Jr."] *San Francisco: printed for William Andrews Clark, Jr., by John Henry Nash,* 1924. **MS. Facs. 750.**
pp. xli: plates; facsims., port. 32 cm. △
Privately printed. Including a facsimile of one letter from Lord Alfred Douglas to Oscar Wilde.

BARRETT, afterwards **BROWNING** (Elizabeth Barrett) [*Single Works.*]
—— Sonnets from the Portuguese . . . With some observations and a bibliographical note by William Andrews Clark, *etc.* pp. xxxi. 45. *J. H. Nash: San Francisco,* 1927. fol. **C. 98. gg. 21.**

DRYDEN (John) [*Dramatic Works.*]
—— All for Love, *etc.* [With " Bibliographical note and prefatory remarks " by William Andrews Clark, with plates, including a portrait, and with a facsimile of the first edition, 1678.] 2 pt. *W. A. Clark, Jr.: San Francisco,* 1929. fol. & 4°. **C. 102. l. 2.**

PHILLIPS (Catherine Coffin) Cornelius Cole, Californian pioneer and United States senator, *etc.* [With plates, including portraits.] pp. vii. 379. *J. H. Nash: San Francisco,* 1929. fol. **C. 98. e. 10.**

SANDERSON (Thomas James Cobden)
—— Cobden-Sanderson and the Doves Press. The History of the Press and the story of its types, told by Alfred W. Pollard. The Character of the Man, set forth by . . . Edward Johnston. With The Ideal Book or Book Beautiful, by T. J. Cobden-Sanderson, and a list of the Doves Press printings. pp. xviii. 35. *J. H. Nash: San Francisco,* 1929. fol. **C. 100. k. 23.**

KENNEDY (Hugh Ankerell Studdert)
—— The Visitor. Of his coming and of his sojourning and concerning the manner of his going away. pp. 50. *John Henry Nash: San Francisco,* 1930. 4°. **Cup. 510. nag. 4.**
A copy signed by the author.

STEVENSON (ROBERT LOUIS)
—— Father Damien. An open letter to the Reverend Dr. Hyde of Honolulu, *etc.* [With an introduction by William Andrews Clark, a facsimile of the original edition, Sydney, 1890, and portraits.] 2 pt. *J. H. Nash: San Francisco,* 1930. fol.   C. **102.** l. **3.**

ANDERSON (MELVILLE BEST)
—— The Fate of Virgil as conceived by Dante. A dialogue of the dead and the living between Walter Savage Landor and Willard Fiske. pp. v. 19.   *John Henry Nash: San Francisco,* 1931. fol.   Cup. **510.** nag. **1.**

FRANKLIN (BENJAMIN) *LL.D.*
—— The Autobiography of Benjamin Franklin. With an introduction and marginal glosses by Edward F. O'Day. [With " Notes to the Autobiography by John Byelow." With a portrait.] pp. vii. 243.   *Printed for the Limited Editions Club by John Henry Nash: San Francisco,* 1931. fol.   C. **105.** c. **14.**

GRAY (THOMAS) *the Poet.* [*Ode on the Pleasure arising from Vicissitude.*]
—— Ode on the Pleasure arising from Vicissitude. Left unfinished by Mr. Gray, and since completed [by William Mason]. With an introduction by Leonard Whibley. [Edited by William Andrews Clark. With a facsimile of the original edition.] 2 vol. *J. H. Nash: San Francisco,* 1933. 4°.   C. **102.** h. **10.**

EMERSON (RALPH WALDO)
—— The Essays of Ralph Waldo Emerson. With critical introduction by Edward F. O'Day. The First series, MDCCCXLI and the Second series, MDCCCXLIV, in one volume. pp. x. 262.   *John Henry Nash for the Limited Editions Club: San Francisco,* 1934. fol.   C. **105.** c. **13.**

RAY (MILTON SMITH)
—— The Farallones, the Painted World, and other poems of California. With fifty-three illustrations and with a supplementary history and description of the Farallones, including notes on their plant, bird, and animal life. 2 vol. *J. H. Nash: San Francisco,* 1934. fol.   C. **102.** h. **14.**

MILTON (JOHN) [*Smaller Collections of Works.*]
—— Paradise Lost and Paradise Regain'd . . . with an introduction by William Rose Benét and illustrations by Carlotta Petrina. pp. xiii. 441.   *Printed for the Members of The Limited Editions Club by John Henry Nash: San Francisco,* 1936. fol.   Cup. **510.** nag. **5.**

NONESUCH PRESS, London

ANACREON. [*English.*]
—— Anacreon done into English out of the original Greek, by Abraham Cowley and S. B. [or rather by Francis Willis, Thomas Wood, Abraham Cowley and John Oldham] . . . With copperplate engravings by Stephen Gooden. pp. 52. *Nonesuch Press: London,* 1923. 12°.   C. **99.** f. **33.**

APULEIUS (LUCIUS) *Madaurensis.* [*Asinus Aureus.— Selections.—English.*] Cupid and Psyche . . . Translated . . . by W. Adlington . . . 1566.   *Nonesuch Press: London,* 1923. 8°.   C. **99.** d. **25.**

BIBLE.—*Ruth.* [*English.*]
—— The Book of Ruth, *etc.*   *Nonesuch Press: London,* 1923. 8°.   C. **99.** h. **6.**

CONGREVE (WILLIAM)

COMPLETE WORKS.
—— The Complete Works of William Congreve. Edited by Montague Summers. 4 vol.   *Nonesuch Press: London,* 1923. 4°.   C. **99.** i. **18.**
     No. 60 of seventy-five copies printed on English hand-made paper.

DONNE (JOHN) *Dean of St. Paul's.* [*Collections.*]
—— Love Poems of John Donne. With some account of his life taken from the writings in 1639 of Izaak Walton. [With portrait.] pp. xxiii. 91.   *Nonesuch Press: London,* 1923. 8°.   C. **99.** l. **19.**

DONNE (JOHN) *Dean of St. Paul's.* Paradoxes and Problemes . . . with two Characters and an Essay of Valour . . . Reprinted from the editions of 1633 and 1652 with one additional Probleme. [Edited by Geoffrey Keynes] pp. viii, 80.   *Nonesuch Press: London,* 1923. 8°.   C. **99.** h. **5.**

DONNE (JOHN) *Dean of St. Paul's.*
—— X Sermons . . . Chosen from the whole body of Donne's Sermons by Geoffrey Keynes. pp. 162.   *Nonesuch Press: London,* 1923. fol.   C. **99.** k. **17.**

HUDSON (WILLIAM HENRY) *C.M.Z.S.* 153 Letters from W. H. Hudson. Edited and with introduction and explanatory notes by Edward Garnett. [With portrait.] pp. 191. *Nonesuch Press: London,* 1923. 8°.   C. **99.** i. **23.**

MARVELL (ANDREW) Miscellaneous Poems. [With portrait.] pp. 148. *Nonesuch Press: London,* 1923. 4°.   C. **99.** i. **20.**

SECUNDUS (JOANNES)
—— Kisses . . . Rendered into English verse by Thomas Stanley, 1647. *Nonesuch Press: London,* 1923. 8°.
C. **99**. i. **25**.

BIBLE.—*Genesis.—Selections.* [*English.*]
—— Genesis. Twelve woodcuts by Paul Nash, with the first chapter of Genesis in the Authorised Version. *Nonesuch Press: London,* 1924. 8°. C. **98**. h. **2**.

MENDEL, afterwards **MEYNELL** (VERA) and **MEYNELL** (*Sir* FRANCIS)
—— The Week-End Book. [An anthology of poems, songs, games, *etc.*] (V. Mendel, F. Meynell, general editors. John Goss, music editor.) pp. xii. 319. *Nonesuch Press: London,* 1924. 8°. C. **99**. c. **29**.

MOORE (GEORGE) *Novelist.* Pure Poetry. An anthology. Edited by G. Moore. pp. ix. 128. *Nonesuch Press: London,* 1924. 8°. C. **98**. f. **1**.

PLATO. [*Symposium.—English.*] Plato's Symposium or Supper. Newly translated by Francis Birrell & Shane Leslie. [Revised by R. G. Bury.] pp. 106. *Nonesuch Press:* [*London,* 1924.] 8°. C. **99**. b. **17**.

VAUGHAN (HENRY) *the Silurist.* [*Collections.*]
—— Henry Vaughan, Silurist. Poems . . . An Essay . . . Two Letters, *etc.* pp. 164. *Nonesuch Press: London,* 1924. 8°. C. **98**. h. **1**.

WYCHERLEY (WILLIAM) [*Collections.*]
—— The Complete Works of William Wycherley. Edited by Montague Summers. 4 vol. *Nonesuch Press: Soho,* 1924. 4°. C. **98**. g. **3**.

BIBLE. [*English.*]
—— The Holy Bible, *etc.* 5 pt. *Nonesuch Press: London ; Dial Press: New York,* 1925–27, 24. fol.
C. **99**. k. **19**.
Version of 1611. With Apocrypha, which bears the date 1924. The titlepages are engraved.

BLAKE (WILLIAM) *Artist.* [*Works.*]
—— The writings of William Blake. Edited . . . by Geoffrey Keynes. *London: Nonesuch Press,* 1925. C. **98**. h. **5**.
3 vol.: pl. LVIII: plate; port. 28 cm. △

BURTON (ROBERT) *Author of " The Anatomy of Melancholy".*
—— The anatomy of melancholy . . . Illustrated by E. McKnight Kauffer. *London: Nonesuch Press,* 1925.
C. **99**. k. **21**.
pp. xv, 588. 31 cm. △
An extra copy to an edition of forty copies on vellum.

HOTSON (JOHN LESLIE) The Death of Christopher Marlowe. (Second impression.) [With plates and facsimiles.] pp. 76. *Nonesuch Press: London ; Harvard University Press: Cambridge [Mass.],* 1925. 8°.
C. **99**. h. **8**.

KING (HENRY) *Bishop of Chichester.* The Poems of Bishop Henry King. Edited by John Sparrow. pp. xxvii. 197. *Nonesuch Press: London,* 1925. 8°.
C. **98**. g. **10**.

MENDEL, afterwards **MEYNELL** (VERA) and **MEYNELL** (*Sir* FRANCIS)
—— The Week-End Book. (Second edition.) pp. xii. 360. *Nonesuch Press: London,* 1925. 8°. C. **99**. c. **30**.

COWLEY (ABRAHAM) [*Smaller Collections.*]
—— The Mistress, with other select poems . . . Edited by John Sparrow. [With a portrait after C. F. Zincke.] pp. xx. 213. *Nonesuch Press: London,* 1926. 8°.
C. **98**. g. **19**.

MELVILLE (HERMAN) Benito Cereno . . . With pictures by E. McKnight Kauffer. pp. 122. *Nonesuch Press: London,* 1926. 4°. C. **98**. gg. **3**.

MILTON (JOHN) [*Poetical Works.*]
—— Poems in English. With illustrations by William Blake. 2 pt. *Nonesuch Press: London,* 1926. 8°. C. **98**. f. **4**.

MOORE (GEORGE) *Novelist.* Ulick and Soracha. pp. 286. *Nonesuch Press: London,* 1925. 8°.
C. **99**. h. **9**.

OTWAY (THOMAS) [*Works.*]
—— The Complete Works of Thomas Otway. Edited by Montague Summers. 3 vol. **F. P.** *Nonesuch Press: London,* 1926. 8°. C. **98**. g. **21**.

WILMOT (JOHN) *Earl of Rochester.* [*Collections.*]
—— Collected Works . . . Edited by John Hayward. pp. l. 407. **F. P.** *Nonesuch Press: London,* 1926. 4°.
C. **98**. h. **7**.
One of 75 copies printed on hand-made paper.

BLAKE (WILLIAM) *Artist.* [*Works.*]
—— Poetry and prose of William Blake. Edited by Geoffrey Keynes. *London: Nonesuch Press,* 1927. C. **99**. c. **33**.
pp. xi, 1152. 20 cm. △

BLAKE (WILLIAM) *Artist.* [*Illustrations, Drawings, etc. by Blake.*]
—— Pencil Drawings . . . Edited by Geoffrey Keynes. pp. xvi. pl. 82. *Nonesuch Press:* [*London,*] 1927. 4°.
C. **98**. h. **14**.

HERBERT (GEORGE) *the Poet.* The Temple . . . [Edited by Francis Meynell.] Printed from the manuscript in the Bodleian Library, *etc.* pp. x. 213. *Nonesuch Press: London,* 1927. 8°.　C. **98.** *f.* **10.**

LAVER (JAMES) Love's Progress; or, the Education of Araminta. [A poem.] pp. 30.　*Nonesuch Press: London,* 1927. 8°.　C. **98.** h. **28.**

LAVER (JAMES) A Stitch in Time; or, Pride prevents a fall. [A poem.] pp. 27. *Nonesuch Press: London,* 1927. 4°.　C. **98.** h. **16.**

SARDA (DANIEL)
—— Conte de Maître Espapidour.　*Vincent Brooks, Day & Son, sous la direction de la Nonesuch Press, pour Mrs. Fern L. Bedaux: Londres,* 1927. 8°.　C. **99.** c. **51.**

THOMSON (JAMES) *the Poet.* [*The Seasons.*] The Seasons . . . With five pictures by Jacquier and an introduction by John Beresford. pp. xx. 198. *Nonesuch Press: London,* 1927.　C. **98.** e. **4.**

VANBRUGH (*Sir* JOHN) [*Collections.*]
—— The Complete Works of Sir John Vanbrugh. The plays edited by Bonamy Dobrée. The letters edited by Geoffrey Webb. 4 vol. **F. P.**　*Nonesuch Press: London,* 1927. 4°.　C. **98.** e. **5.**

VOLTAIRE (FRANÇOIS MARIE AROUET DE) [*La Princesse de Babylone.*]
—— The Princess of Babylon . . . With decorations by Thomas Lowinsky. pp. 156.　*Nonesuch Press: London,* 1927. 8°.　C. **99.** c. **36.**

WILSON (MONA) The Life of William Blake. [With plates, including portraits.] pp. xv. 397. *Nonesuch Press: London,* 1927. 4°.　C. **98.** h. **12.**

AESOP. [*English.—Selections.*]
—— Twenty Four Fables of Aesop and other eminent mythologists, as rendered into English by Sir Roger L'Estrange . . . With illustrations after the etchings of Marcus Gheeraerts. pp. 52.　*Ernest Benn: London,* 1928. 4°.　Cup. **510.** caf. **8.**
No. 50 of 50 copies printed on hand-made paper.

BEEDOME (THOMAS)
—— Select Poems Divine and Humane. pp. 51. iv. *Nonesuch Press: London,* 1928. 8°.　C. **99.** c. **42.**

BUNYAN (JOHN) [*Two or more Works.*]
—— The Pilgrim's Progress and The Life & Death of Mr. Badman. (Wood-cuts by Karl Michel.) [Edited, with an introduction, by George B. Harrison.] pp. 22. viii. 450. *Nonesuch Press:* [*London,*] 1928. 8°.　C. **100.** e. **1.**

DANTE ALIGHIERI. [*Divina Commedia.—Italian and English.*] La Divina Commedia...The Italian text edited by Mario Casella . . . With the English version of H. F. Cary and 42 illustrations after the drawings by Sandro Botticelli. pp. 324. *Nonesuch Press:* [*London,*] 1928. fol.　C. **98.** gg. **6.**

HARVEY (WILLIAM) *M.D.* [*Two or more Works.*]
　　　　　　　　　The Anatomical Exercises of Dr. William Harvey. De Motu Cordis, 1628: De Circulatione Sanguinis, 1649: the first English text of 1653...Edited by Geoffrey Keynes, *etc.* pp. xvi. 202.　　*Nonesuch Press: London; printed in Holland,* [1928.] 8°.　C. **99.** c. **37.**

MENDEL, afterwards **MEYNELL** (VERA) and **MEYNELL** (*Sir* FRANCIS)
—— The Week-End Book. (New edition. Illustrated by Albert Rutherston.) pp. xii. 516.　*Nonesuch Press: London,* 1928. 8°.　C. **99.** b. **26.**

PINDAR. [*English.*] Pythian Odes. Translated by H. T. Wade-Gery & C. M. Bowra. pp. xlv. 165. *Nonesuch Press: London,* 1928. 8°.　C. **99.** b. **22.**

DONNE (JOHN) *Dean of St. Paul's.* [*Collections.*]
—— Complete Poetry and Selected Prose. Edited by John Hayward. pp. xxiii. 793.　*Nonesuch Press: London,* 1929. 8°.　C. **100.** e. **3.**

LE BOVIER DE FONTENELLE (BERNARD) A Plurality of Worlds. John Glanvill's translation. With a prologue by David Garnett. pp. ix. 138. *Nonesuch Press: London,* 1929. 8°.　C. **99.** c. **45.**

PLUTARCH. [*Vitæ Parallelæ.—English.—North's Translation.*]
—— The lives of the noble Grecians & Romanes . . . Translated . . . by Thomas North: the illustrations by T. L. Poulton: with the fifteen supplementary lives of 1603. *London: Nonesuch Press,* 1929, 30.　C. **100.** k. **25.**
5 vol.: plates. 31 cm.　　　　　　△

SHAKESPEARE (WILLIAM) [*Works.*]
—— The works of Shakespeare. The text of the First Folio with Quarto variants and a selection of modern readings: edited by Herbert Farjeon. [*London:*] *Nonesuch Press; New York: Random House,* 1929–32.　C. **100.** b. **1.**
6 vol. 24 cm.　　　　　　△

WALTON (IZAAK) *the Angler.* [*Works.*]

The Compleat Angler. The Lives of Donne, Wotton, Hooker, Herbert & Sanderson. With Love and Truth & Miscellaneous Writings. Edited by Geoffrey Keynes. Illustrations by Thomas Poulton and Charles Sigrist. [With plates, including portraits.] pp. x. 631. *Nonesuch Press: London,* 1929. 8º. C. 99. e. 43.

CERVANTES SAAVEDRA (MIGUEL DE) [*Single Works.* —DON QUIXOTE.—*English.—Motteux's Translation.*]

—— Don Quixote de la Mancha . . . Motteux' translation revised anew—1743—& corrected . . . by J. Ozell, who likewise added the explanatory notes . . . Reprinted with twenty-one illustrations by E. McKnight Kauffer. 2 vol. *Nonesuch Press: London,* 1930. 8º. C. 99. h. 29.

DONNE (JOHN) *Dean of St. Paul's.* The Courtier's Library, or Catalogus librorum aulicorum incomparabilium et non vendibilium...Edited by Evelyn Mary Simpson. With a translation [by Percy Simpson]. pp. 93. *Nonesuch Press: London,* 1930. 8º. **Cup.510.bec.5.**

FARQUHAR (GEORGE) [*Works.*]

The Complete Works of George Farquhar...Edited by Charles Stonehill. 2 vol. F. P. *Nonesuch Press: London,* 1930. 4º. C. 100. c. 9.

LAWRENCE (DAVID HERBERT) Love Among the Haystacks, & other pieces...With a reminiscence by David Garnett. pp. xiii. 96. *Nonesuch Press: London,* 1930. 8º. C. 99. d. 36.

DRYDEN (JOHN) [*Dramatic Works.*]

—— Dryden. The dramatic works . . . Edited by Montague Summers. *London: Nonesuch Press,* 1931, 32. C. 100. c. 16.

6 vol. 26 cm. △

No. 2 of an edition of fifty copies printed on fine paper.

HOMER. [*Iliad. Greek and English.*]

—— The Iliad. [The Greek text, with Pope's translation.] pp. 926. *Nonesuch Press: [London:] Haarlem* printed, 1931. 8º. C. 100. e. 13.

HOMER. [*Odyssey.—Greek and English.* Odyssey. [The Greek text with Pope's translation. pp. 759. *Nonesuch Press: London ;] Haarlem* printed, 1931. fol. C. 98. e. 16.

MONTAIGNE (MICHEL DE) Montaigne's Essays. John Florio's translation...Edited by J. I. M. Stewart. 2 vol. *Nonesuch Press: London,* 1931. 8º. C. 100. e. 5.

SIDNEY (*Sir* PHILIP) Astrophel & Stella...Edited by Mona Wilson. pp. xxxviii. 193. *Nonesuch Press: [London,]* 1931. 8º. C. 99. h. 31.

BUTLER (SAMUEL) *Philosophical Writer.*

—— Butleriana. [Compiled, mainly from previously unpublished portions of Butler's "Note-Books," by A. T. Bartholomew.] pp. xvi. 172. *Nonesuch Press: London,* 1932. 8º. C. 99. d. 40.

DONNE (JOHN) *Dean of St. Paul's.*

—— Complete Poetry and Selected Prose. Edited by John Hayward. (Third impression.) pp. xxiii. 794. *Nonesuch Press: London ; Random House: New York,* 1932. 8º. C. 99. b. 29.

DONNE (JOHN) *Dean of St. Paul's.*

—— Donne's Sermon of Valediction at his Going into Germany, preached at Lincoln's Inn, April 18, 1619. Printed from the original version in the Lothian and Ashmole manuscripts and from XXVI Sermons. Edited by Evelyn Mary Simpson. pp. 79. *Nonesuch Press: London,* 1932. 8º. C. 102. h. 6.

MAC KENNA (MICHAEL) *of Trinity College, Cambridge.*

—— Michael. 31st January, 1910–6th October, 1931. [Extracts from the letters and diaries of M. McKenna, compiled by Pamela McKenna. With plates, including portraits.] pp. ix. 488. *Nonesuch Press: [London,]* 1932. 8º. 10864. de. 55. *Privately printed. A letter from Pamela McKenna to L. A. G. Strong is inserted.*

RICKETTS (CHARLES S.)

—— Oscar Wilde. Recollections by Jean Paul Raymond & Charles Ricketts. [Written by Charles Ricketts.] pp. 59. *Nonesuch Press: London,* 1932. 8º. C. 98. c. 18.

COLERIDGE (SAMUEL TAYLOR) [*Smaller Collections.*—I. *Prose and Verse.*]

—— Coleridge. Select Poetry & Prose. Edited by Stephen Potter. pp. xxx. 821. *Nonesuch Press: London,* 1933. 8º. C. 98. a. 4.

LAVER (JAMES)

—— Ladies' Mistakes : Cupid's Changeling, A Stitch in Time, Love's Progress . . . [Poems.] With nine illustrations by Thomas Lowinsky. pp. 106. *Nonesuch Press: Bloomsbury,* 1933. 8º. C. 100. e. 9.

MOORE (GEORGE) *Novelist.*

—— A Communication to my Friends. pp. 86. *Nonesuch Press: [London,]* 1933. 8º. C. 99. d. 47.

TENNYSON (ALFRED) *Baron Tennyson.* [*In Memoriam.*]

—— In Memoriam, *etc.* [With an introduction by John H. A. Sparrow.] pp. xxii. 145. *Nonesuch Press: London,* 1933. fol. C. 100. a. 2.

YOUNG (ANDREW JOHN)
—— Winter Harvest. [Poems.] pp. 51. *Nonesuch Press:*
London, 1933. 8°. C. 99. d. 48.

COLERIDGE (SARA) *the Elder*. Minnow among Tritons.
Mrs. S. T. Coleridge's letters to Thomas Poole, 1799–
1834. Edited by Stephen Potter. [With portraits and a
facsimile.] pp. xxxvi. 185. *Nonesuch Press: London*,
1934. 8°. C. 100. g. 44.

ELLIS (HENRY HAVELOCK)
—— Chapman . . . With illustrative passages. pp. 146.
Nonesuch Press: London, 1934. 8°. C. 102. e. 6.

HAMILTON (*Sir* GEORGE ROSTREVOR)
—— The Greek Portrait. An anthology of English verse
translations from the Greek poets—Homer to Meleager—
with the corresponding Greek text . . . Illustrated by
Mariette Lydis. Edited by G. R. Hamilton. pp. 235.
Nonesuch Press: London, 1934. 8°. C. 102. f. 7.

HOOPINGTON (AMBROSE)
—— A Letter to a Young Lady on her Approaching Marriage.
pp. 41. *Nonesuch Press: London*, 1934. 8°.
C. 99. g. 45.

BLAKE (WILLIAM) *Artist*
—— The Note-Book of William Blake called the Rossetti
Manuscript. Edited by Geoffrey Keynes. [With a facsi-
mile of the note book.] pp. xii. 162. *Nonesuch Press:*
London; printed in France, 1935. 4°. C. 100. c. 20.

COLERIDGE (SAMUEL TAYLOR) [*Smaller Collections.*—I. -
Prose and Verse.]
—— Selected Poems of Coleridge. [Chosen by Stephen
Potter. With three engravings by Stefan Mrozewski.]
pp. 130. *Nonesuch Press:* [*London,*] 1935. 8°.
C. 100. a. 4.

COLLIER (JOHN) *Novelist*.
—— The Devil and All, *etc.* [Six short stories.] pp. 123.
Nonesuch Press: [*London*, 1935.] 8°. C. 100. g. 48.

HERODOTUS. [*English.*]
—— The History of Herodotus of Halicarnassus. The translation of G. Rawlinson, revised & annotated by A. W.
Lawrence. With nine wood engravings by V. Le Campion
and a series of new maps by T. Poulton. To which is
added a life of Herodotus and the Behistun inscription.
pp. xxvi. 778. *Nonesuch Press: London*, 1935. fol.
C. 102. h. 13.

POPE (ALEXANDER) *the Poet*. [*Two or more Works.—*
English.]
—— Pope's Own Miscellany. Being a reprint of " Poems on
Several Occasions," 1717, containing new poems by
Alexander Pope and others. Edited by Norman Ault.
pp. xcvii. 165. *Nonesuch Press: London*, 1935. 8°.
C. 102. e. 7.

NONESUCH PRESS.
—— The Nonesuch Century. An appraisal, a personal note
and a bibliography of the first hundred books issued by the
Press, 1923–1934. [By A. J. A. Symons, Francis Meynell
and Desmond Flower. With plates.] pp. 80.
Nonesuch Press: London, 1936. fol. C. 102. g. 5.

BLAKE (WILLIAM) *Artist*. [*Illustrations, Drawings, etc. by*
Blake.]
—— The Illustrations of William Blake for Thornton's Virgil,
with the first eclogue and the imitation by Ambrose
Philips. The introduction by Geoffrey Keynes. pp. 38.
Nonesuch Press: London, 1937. 8°. C. 102. a. 13.

DICKENS (CHARLES) [*Works.*]
—— The Nonesuch Dickens. Published under the editorial
direction of Arthur Waugh, Hugh Walpole, Walter Dexter
and Thomas Hatton. [The text from the Charles Dickens
Edition, 1867–[75]: the plates chiefly printed from the
original plates and blocks.] 23 vol.

Nonesuch Press: Bloomsbury, 1937, 38. 8°.

MILTON (JOHN) [*Comus.*]
—— The Mask of Comus. The poem . . . Edited by E. H.
Visiak. The airs of the five songs [by Henry Lawes] . . .
edited by Hubert J. Foss . . . Ornamented by M. R. H.
Farrar. pp. xxiv. 44. *Nonesuch Press: London*,
1937. fol. C. 102. l. 21.

ROUSSEAU (JEAN JACQUES) [*Les Confessions.*]
—— The Confessions of J. J. Rousseau in an anonymous
English version first published in two parts in 1783 & 1790,
now revised and completed by A. S. B. Glover. With an
introduction by Havelock Ellis, *etc.* 2 vol. *Nonesuch*
Press: London, 1938. 8°. C. 102. a. 14.

WHITE (GILBERT) *of Selborne*.
—— The Writings of Gilbert White of Selborne. Selected
and edited with an introduction by H. G. Massingham.
(With wood-engravings by Eric Ravilious.) 2 vol.
Nonesuch Press: London, 1938. 8°. C. 102. e. 15.

VOLTAIRE (FRANÇOIS MARIE AROUET DE) [*Candide.*]
—— Candide; or, Optimism. Translated . . . by Richard
Aldington. With an introduction by Paul Morand and
twenty illustrations in colour by Sylvain Sauvage.
pp. xix. 147. *Nonesuch Press: London; Mâcon* printed.
1939. 8°. C. 99. i. 29.

SHAKESPEARE (WILLIAM) [*Works.*]

—— The Complete Works of William Shakespeare. The text and order of the first folio with quarto variants & a choice of modern readings noted marginally : to which are added Pericles and the first quartos of six of the plays with three plays of doubtful authorship : also the poems according to the original quartos and octavos. The Nonesuch text established MCMXXIX by Herbert Farjeon. With a new introduction by Ivor Brown. 4 vol. *Nonesuch Press : London*, 1953. 8º.   C. **100**. e. **24**.

BELLOC (JOSEPH HILAIRE PIERRE) [*Collections.*]

—— The Verse of Hilaire Belloc. Edited by W. N. Roughead. pp. xxv. 296.   *Nonesuch Press : [London ;] printed in Holland*, 1954. 8º.   Cup. **500**. b. **13**.

HOPKINS (GERARD MANLEY) [*Selections.*]

—— Selected Poems. (Chosen by Francis Meynell.) pp. v. 104. *Nonesuch Press : London*, 1954. 8º.
Cup. **510**. aa. **1**.

CAVENDISH (WILLIAM) *Duke of Newcastle.*

—— The Phanseys of William Cavendish, Marquis of Newcastle, addressed to Margaret Lucas, and her letters in reply. Edited by Douglas Grant. pp. xxxiii. 127. *Nonesuch Press : London*, 1956. 8º.   C. **129**. c. **11**.

MEYNELL (*Sir* FRANCIS)

—— Poems & Pieces, 1911 to 1961. pp. 59.   *Nonesuch Press : London*, 1961. 8º.   C. **100**. g. **53**.

BIBLE. [*English.*]

—— The Holy Bible. The Authorized or King James Version of 1611 now reprinted with the Apocrypha . . . With reproductions of 105 of the sixteenth-century woodcuts of Bernard Salomon. 3 vol.   *Nonesuch Press : London ; Random House : New York*, 1963. 8º. Cup. **510**. bec. **4**.

CARROLL (LEWIS) *pseud.* [i.e. CHARLES LUTWIDGE DODGSON.] [*Collections.*]

—— Alice's Adventures in Wonderland & Through the Looking Glass. Both with the illustrations of John Tenniel & The Hunting of the Snark. All by Lewis Carroll. pp. 292.   *Nonesuch Press : London*, 1963. 8º.
Cup. **501**. bb. **13**.
Part of the series " Nonesuch Cygnet ".

LANG (ANDREW) [*Collections.*]

—— Fifty Favourite Fairy Tales. Chosen from the Colour Fairy Books . . . by Kathleen Lines. With illustrations by Margery Gill. pp. 363.   *Nonesuch Press : London*, 1963. 8º.   Cup. **501**. bb. **9**.
Part of the series " Nonesuch Cygnet ".

MACDONALD (GEORGE) *LL.D.*

—— At the Back of the North Wind . . . with illustrations by Charles Mozley. pp. 276.   *Nonesuch Press : London*, 1963. 8º.   Cup. **501**. bb. **11**.
Part of the series " Nonesuch Cygnet ".

STEVENSON (ROBERT LOUIS)

—— Treasure Island . . . Illustrated by Robert Micklewright. pp. 266. *Nonesuch Press : London*, 1963. 8º.
Cup. **501**. bb. **3**.
Part of the series " Nonesuch Cygnet ".

MEYNELL (*Sir* FRANCIS)

—— By Heart. An anthology of memorable poems chosen from all periods by Francis Meynell. pp. 338.   *Nonesuch Press : [London,]* 1965. 8º.   X. **909**/5530.
A "Nonesuch Cygnet".

NESBIT, afterwards **BLAND** (EDITH) [*Smaller Collections.*]

—— The Bastables. The Story of the Treasure Seekers. The Wouldbegoods . . . Illustrated by Susan Einzig. pp. 368. *Nonesuch Press : London*, 1965. 8º.   X. **990**/248.
Part of the series "Nonsuch Cygnet".

NONPAREIL PRESS, Urmston, Lancs; Manchester

HORNE (HERBERT PERCY)

—— Amata loquitur. [In verse.]   *Nonpareil Press : Urmston*, 1961. 8º.   Cup. **510**. cof. **2**

D'ISRAELI (ISAAC)

[Curiosities of Literature.]

—— Early Printing. [Extracted from vol. 1 of "Curiosities of Literature."] pp. 8.   *Nonpareil Press : Manchester*, 1963. 16º.   Cup. **510**. cof. **1**.
Privately printed.

OFFICINA BODONI, Montagnola di Lugano; Verona

SHELLEY (PERCY BYSSHE) [*Epipsychidion.*]

—— Epipsychidion. pp. 38. *Officina Bodoni : Montagnola*, 1923. fol.   Cup. **510**. ee. **1**.

SHAKESPEARE (WILLIAM) [*The Tempest.*]

—— The Tempest. pp. 151.   *Officina Bodoni : Montagnola di Lugano*, 1924. fol.   Cup. **510**. ee. **2**.

HENRICIS (LODOVICI DE) The Calligraphic Models of Ludovico degli Arrighi surnamed Vicentino. A complete facsimile and introduction by Stanley Morison. pp. xvi. 63.   *Frederic Warde : Paris ; Montagnola di Lugano* printed, 1926. 8º.
Cup. **510**. ee. **3**.

PLATO. [*Crito.—English.*]

—— Crito . . . Translated by Henry Cary. pp. xxxvi.   *The Pleiad : Paris*, 1926. 4º.   Cup. **510**. ee. **4**.

WALPOLE (Horace) *Earl of Orford.*

—— Hieroglyphic Tales. pp. 85. *Elkin Mathews: London; Montagnola* printed, 1926. 8°. Cup. **510.** ee. **5.**

A. A Newly Discovered Treatise on Classic Letter Design [beginning : Questo A si caua del tondo & del quadro], printed at Parma by Damianus Moyllus, circa 1480. Reproduced in facsimile with an introduction by Stanley Morison. pp. 81. *Pegasus Press : Paris; Montagnola* printed, 1927. 8°. Cup.**510**.ee.**8.**

STANHOPE (Philip Dormer) *Earl of Chesterfield.* [*Collections.*]

The Poetical Works of Philip Dormer Stanhope, Earl of Chesterfield. pp. 46. *E. Mathews & Marrot : London ; Montagnola* printed, 1927. 8°. Cup.**510**.ee.**7.**

MONOTYPE CORPORATION.

Pastonchi. A specimen of a new letter for use on the " Monotype." pp. 65. *Lanston Monotype Corporation : London ; Verona* printed, [1929.] 8°. Cup.**510**.ee.**10.**

MORISON (Stanley)

—— Eustachio Celebrino da Udene, calligrapher, engraver and writer for the Venetian printing press . . . With . . . a . . . facsimile of The way of learning to write the lettera Merchantescha, *etc.* *Paris: Pegasus Press; Verona: printed at the Officina Bodoni,* 1929. Cup. **510.** ee. **12.**

pp. 23. 26 cm. △

OFFICINA BODONI.

—— The Officina Bodoni. The operation of a hand-press during the first six years of its work. [With a preface by Hans Mastersteig, woodcuts by Frans Mascreel, and facsimiles.] pp. 79. *Paris, New York; printed in Italy,* 1929. fol. Cup. **510.** ee. **13.**

THOMAS (Sir Henry) *Principal Keeper of Printed Books, British Museum,* and **MORISON** (Stanley)

—— Andres Brun, calligrapher of Saragossa. Some account of his life and work . . . With a facsimile in collotype of the surviving text and plates of his two writing books, 1583 & 1612. *Paris: Pegasus Press; Verona: printed at the Officina Bodoni,* 1929. Cup. **510.** ee. **11.**

pp. 29. 31 cm. △

The date in the colophon is 1928.

MERCATOR (Gerardus)

—— The Treatise of Gerard Mercator, Literarum Latinarum, quas Italicas, cursoriasque vocant, scribendarum ratio . . . Edited in facsimile with an introduction by Jan Denucé . . . and a note by Stanley Morison. *De Sikkel : Antwerp; Pegasus Press: Paris; Verona* printed, 1930. 8°. Cup. **510.** ee. **14.**

DANTE ALIGHIERI. [*Divina Commedia. — Complete Texts.—English.*]

—— The Divine Comedy of Dante Alighieri, translated into English verse by Melville Best Anderson, with notes and elucidations by the translator and with an introduction by Arthur Livingston. pp. xxi. 491. *Limited Editions Club : New York; Verona* printed, 1932. fol. C. **105.** c. **18.**

LANDOR (Walter Savage)

—— Imaginary Conversations. Selected & introduced by R. H. Boothroyd. pp. xi. 303. *Printed for Members of the Limited Editions Club:* [*New York;*] *Verona* printed, 1936. 8°. C. **105.** d. **12.**

VALÉRY (Paul Ambroise Toussaint Jules)

—— Le Cimetière marin. (The Graveyard by the Sea.) [The original Text with a verse translation by C. Day Lewis.] pp. 19. *Martin Secker & Warburg: Londres; Verona* printed, 1946. 8°. Cup. **510.** ee. **16.**

MANSFIELD (Katherine) *pseud.* [i.e. Kathleen Beauchamp, afterwards Murry.]

—— The Garden Party, and other stories. With coloured lithographs by Marie Laurencin. pp. 315. *Verona Press: London ; printed in Italy,* [1947.] 4° Cup.**510**.ee.**23.**

The date of printing is given in the colophon as 1939.

MONTANO (Lorenzo) *pseud.* [i.e. Danilo Lebrecht.]

—— [San Zeno vescovo, patrono di Verona.] Bishop San Zeno, Patron of Verona. [With woodcuts by G. Boehmer.] pp. 14. *Officina Bodoni : Verona,* 1949. 8°. Cup.**510**.ee.**18.**

One of an edition of sixty copies.

THOMAS (Dylan)

—— Twenty-six Poems. pp. 76. *J. M. Dent & Sons : London ; printed in Italy,* 1949. fol. Cup.**510**.ee.**20.**

BOCCACCIO (Giovanni) [*Ninfale Fiesolano.— English.*]

—— The Nymphs of Fiesole . . . With the woodcuts made by Bartolommeo di Giovanni for a lost Quattrocento edition . . . now . . . reassembled and recut (by Fritz Kredel). [Translated by John Goubourne from the French version of A. Guerein du Crest.] pp. xi. 127. *Editiones Officinae Bodoni : Verona,* 1952. 4°. Cup.**510**.ee.**21.**

POUND (Ezra Loomis) [*Collections.*]

—— Diptych Rome-London. Homage to Sextus Propertius & Hugh Selwyn Mauberley, Contacts and Life. pp. 76. *Faber & Faber: London, Verona* printed, 1957 [1958]. 4°. Cup.**510**.ee.**25.**

Part of a limited edition signed by the author.

ELIOT (Thomas Stearns) [*Collections.*]

—— Four Quartets. pp. 53. *Faber & Faber: London ; Verona* printed, 1960. fol. Cup. **510.** ee. **27.** *Printed by Giovanni Mandersteig at the Officina Bodoni. With the author's signature.*

ELIOT (Thomas Stearns)

—— The Waste Land. pp. 51. *Faber & Faber: London,* 1961. fol. Cup. **510.** ee. **28.** *Printed by Giovanni Mardersteig at the Officina Bodoni in Verona. With the author's signature.*

MACDIARMID (Hugh) *pseud.* [i.e. Christopher Murray Grieve.]

—— The Kind of Poetry I want. [In verse.] pp. 57. *K. D. Duval: Edinburgh,* 1961. fol. Cup. **510.** ee. **29.** *Signed by the author. Printed at the Officina Bodoni, Verona.*

BIBLE.—*Gospels.* [*English.*]

—— The Holy Gospel according to Matthew, Mark, Luke and John. [With woodcuts recut by Bruno Bramanti after the original illustrations by Bartolommeo di Giovanni of 1495.] pp. 369. *Officina Bodoni: Verona*, 1962. fol.

Cup. 510. ee. 30.

OLD BOURNE PRESS, London

MILTON (JOHN) [*Ode on the Morning of Christ's Nativity.*]

—— Hymn on the morning of Christ's nativity. [*London:*] *Old Bourne Press*, [1903]. Cup. 510. bfa. 1.

Pages not numbered. 15 x 18 cm. △

ORIOLE PRESS, Berkeley Heights, N.J.

ELLIS (EDITH MARY OLDHAM)

Personal Impressions of Edward Carpenter. [With portrait.] pp. 15. *Free Spirit Press: Berkeley Heights*, [1922.] 8°.

Cup.510.pe.1.

ELLIS (EDITH MARY OLDHAM)

—— Stories and essays. With . . . notes by Havelock Ellis.

Stories . . . With a preface by Charles Marriott, reminiscences by Mrs. Clifford Bax, *etc.* pp. xviii, 88.
Essays . . . With a preface by George Ives, reminiscences by F. W. Stella Browne, *etc.* pp. xviii, 86.

Berkeley Heights: privately printed by the Free Spirit Press, [1924]. Cup. **510**. pe. **2**.

2 vol.: plates; illus., ports. 21 cm. △

The title is taken from the covers.

ELLIS (HENRY HAVELOCK) Havelock Ellis. In appreciation . . . [Articles by various authors.] Compiled . . . by Joseph Ishill. [With portraits and facsimiles.] pp. xlvi. 299. *Oriole Press: Berkeley Heights, N.J.*, 1929. 8°. Cup.510.pe.3.

RECLUS (ÉLIE)

—— [Physionomies végétales.] Plant Physiognomics . . . Translated from a collection of unpublished MSS. by Rose Freeman-Ishill. With introductory appreciations by Élie Faure & Havelock Ellis. Including woodengravings by Louis Moreau. [With "Biblio-biographical data on the life and works of Élie Reclus" by Paul Reclus. With a portrait.] pp. xxi. 132. *Published & printed privately by the Oriole Press: Berkeley Heights, N.J.*, 1931. 8°.

Cup.510.pe.4.

JACKSON (HOLBROOK)

—— William Morris & the Arts & Crafts. (An address.) pp. 17. *Oriole Press: Berkeley Heights*, 1934. 8°.

Cup. 510. pe. 18.

MESNIL (JACQUES)

—— Frans Masereel . . . Translated from the French by Rose Freeman-Ishill. [With reproductions of woodcuts.] pp. 20. *Published & printed privately by Oriole Press: Berkeley Heights*, 1934. 8°. Cup. 510. pe. 15.

SLEIGH (BERNARD)

—— Witchcraft. [With an introduction by Bertram June.] pp. x. 89. *Published & printed privately by the Oriole Press: Berkeley Heights, N.J.*, 1934. 8°. Cup.510.pe.5.

WEINBERGER (HARRY)

—— The Liberty of the Press. Two addresses, *etc.* pp. 38. *Oriole Press: Berkeley Heights, N.J.*, 1934. 8°.

Cup.510.pe.6.

ORIOLE PRESS.

—— The Oriole Press: a bibliography. Comprising: book reviews, essays, unpublished letters by distinguished authors, bibliographical data and the complete check list . . . Illustrated, compiled and printed by Joseph Ishill. [With plates, including portraits.] pp. xxvi. 477. *Oriole Press: Berkeley Heights, N.J.*, 1953. 8°. Cup.510.pe.8. *No. 15 of an edition of fifty copies.*

BASKETTE (EWING C.)

—— Springtime! . . . *Berkeley Heights, N.J.: privately printed by the Oriole Press*, 1958. Cup. 510. pe. 36.

Pages not numbered. 20 cm. △

A poem. With a poem entitled " Moon and moonlight " inserted. No. 76 of an edition of one hundred copies.

ISHILL (JOSEPH)

—— Benjamin R. Tucker. A bibliography. With an appreciation by G. Bernard Shaw. Compiled & edited by Joseph Ishill. [With portraits.] pp. 27. *Oriole Press: Berkeley Heights*, 1959. 8°. Cup. 510. pe. 16. *One of an edition of sixty copies.*

ISHILL (ROSE FREEMAN)

—— Havelock Ellis . . . and a letter by Havelock Ellis, *etc. Berkeley Heights, N.J.: Oriole Press*, [1959].

Cup. 510. pe. 35.

Pages not numbered; port. 20 cm. △

No. 60 of an edition of one hundred copies.

BROWN (MARIAN C.)

—— Joseph Ishill & the Oriole Press. Poem by Samuel Duff McCoy. *Berkeley Heights, N.J.*, [1960].

Cup. 510. pe. 34.

Pages not numbered; port. 21 cm.

ORLEANS (ILO LOUIS)

—— Johnny Appleseed. A poem *Berkeley Heights. N.J.: Oriole Press*, [1960]. Cup. 510. pe. 37.

Pages not numbered. 21 cm. △

SHAW (GEORGE BERNARD) [*Miscellaneous Works.*]

—— Anarchism versus State socialism. *Berkeley Heights: Oriole Press*, 1960. Cup. 510. pe. 28.

Pages not numbered. 17 cm. △

Printed for private circulation.

BASSETT (WILLIAM BURNET KINNEY) [*Collections.*]

—— Darien's World. (A compendium of poems by Peter Darien—W. B. K. Bassett.) [With a portrait.] 10 vol. *Oriole Press: Berkeley Heights, N.J.*, 1961, 62. 8°.

Cup. 510. pe. 9.

With a prospectus and photocopies of press-cuttings inserted.

HAY (John Milton)

—— In praise of Omar. An address before the Omar Khayyam Club (1897). *Berkeley Heights: Oriole Press,* 1961. Cup. **510**. pe. **27**.

Pages not numbered. 15 cm. △
Printed for private circulation.

JACKSON (Holbrook)

—— Ulysses à la Joyce. *Berkeley Heights: Oriole Press,* 1961. Cup. **510**. pe. **25**.

Pages not numbered. 20 cm. △

WHITMAN (Walt)

—— The People and John Quincy Adams ... With a note by William White. [Reprinted from the "Daily Crescent" of New Orleans. With a facsimile of a proof of the original article with the author's corrections.] pp. 21. *Privately printed by the Oriole Press: Berkeley Heights, N.J.,* 1961. 8°. Cup. **510**. pe. **7**.
No. 8 of an edition of 100 copies. Printed on one side of the leaf only.

ZANGWILL (Israel)

—— Israel. A poem. *Berkeley Heights: New Jersey,* 1961. Cup. **510**. pe. **26**.

Pages not numbered. 20 cm. △

GROVER (Edwin Osgood)

—— Christmas living, *etc.* [*Berkeley Heights:*] *Oriole Press,* 1962. Cup. **510**. pe. **30**.

Pages not numbered; illus. 21 cm. △
Printed on one side of the leaf only.

ISHILL (Joseph)

—— For the Thoreau Centennial, 1862–1962. A variorum from the Oriole Press. 6 pt. *Oriole Press: Berkeley Heights, N.J.,* 1962. 8°. Cup. **510**. pe. **10**.
Printed for private distribution.

ELLIS (Henry Havelock)

—— Kropotkin. A tribute. *Oriole Press: Berkeley Heights,* 1963. 8°. Cup. **510**. pe. **14**.
One of an edition of sixty copies.

FISHBEIN (I. Leo)

—— The gentle art of equanimity. The making of character. Enthusiasm an essential to greatness. *Berkeley Heights: Oriole Press,* 1963. Cup. **510**. pe. **29**.

Pages not numbered. 21 cm. △
Three essays.
No. 34 of an edition of seventy-five copies, printed for private circulation.

ISHILL (Joseph)

—— Ishill's Variorum. A compendium of thoughts and reflections culled from Goudy's Ars typographica and other literary sources. [With illustrations, including a portrait.] pp. xii. 201. *Oriole Press: Berkeley Heights, N.J.,* 1963. 8°. Cup. **510**. pe. **24**.
No. 5 of an edition of 100 copies printed for private distribution.

STRACHEY (Lionel)

——Anarchism in literature. pp. 18. *Oriole Press: Berkeley Heights,* 1963. 8°. Cup. **510**. pe. **12**.
One of an edition of thirty-eight copies.

WILDE (Oscar Fingall O'Flahertie Wills) [*Appendix.*]

—— The Story of Oscar Wilde's life and experience in Reading gaol. By his warder. With a tribute by Rose Freeman-Ishill. [Reprinted from "Bruno's Weekly". With a portrait.] pp. 21. *Oriole Press: Berkeley Heights, N.J.,* 1963. 8°. Cup. **510**. pe. **22**.
One of an edition of fifty copies.

ELLIS (Henry Havelock)

[Impressions and comments.]

—— A Revelation. [An extract from "Impressions and comments, Third-and final-series, 1920–1923".] ... With a letter by the author to Joseph Ishill. [With a portrait.] *Oriole Press: Berkeley Heights,* 1964. 8°. Cup. **510**. pe. **19**.

ISHILL (Rose Freeman)

—— Seer in Darkness. A group of three poems. *Oriole Press: Berkeley Heights, N.J.,* 1964. 8°. Cup. **510**. pe. **21**.

JACKSON (Holbrook)

—— The Eighteen-nineties. Prelude to the nineteen-hundreds. The recapture of something of a remarkable era. *Oriole Press: Berkeley Heights,* 1964. 8°. Cup. **510**. pe. **13**.
One of an edition of sixty copies.

NORDHOFF (Evelyn Hunter)

—— The Doves bindery ... With an unpublished letter by Anne Cobden Sanderson to Joseph Ishill. [With illustrations.] pp. 21. *Oriole Press: Berkeley Heights,* 1964. 8°. Cup. **510**. pe. **20**.
One of an edition of fifty copies.

SILVERMAN (Hirsch Lazaar)

—— Requiem in memory of John Fitzgerald Kennedy, 1917–1963. [*Berkeley Heights, N.J.:*] *Oriole Press,* 1964. Cup. **510**. pe. **31**.

Pages not numbered; illus. 22 cm. △
Printed on one side of the leaf only. One of an edition of thirty copies, printed for private distribution.

THOREAU (Henry David)

—— Love. An essay ... Woodcuts by Bernard Sleigh. [With a portrait.] *Oriole Press: Berkeley Heights,* 1964. 8°. Cup. **510**. pe. **11**.
One of an edition of fifty copies.

WOOD (Charles Erskine Scott)

[Debs and the poets.]

—— Debs has visitors in jail ... with a poem by Witter Bynner. (Extracted from Debs and the poets.) pp. 22. *Oriole Press: Berkeley Heights,* 1964. 8°. Cup. **510**. pe. **17**.
One of an edition of seventy-five copies.

ISHILL (Rose Freeman)

—— Wellspring & later poems. *Oriole Press: Berkeley Heights, N.J.,* 1965. 8°. Cup. **510**. pe. **23**.
No. 47 of an edition of 100 copies.

ORPHEUS PRESS, Leicester

CLARE (John) *Poet.*

—— Lines written in Northampton County Asylum. (Second edition. Illustrations by Rigby Graham.) *Orpheus Press: [Leicester,]* 1959. 8°. Cup.510.asa.1.
One of an edition of 100 copies.

MASON (JOHN) *Instructor in Bookbinding at the Leicester College of Arts and Crafts.*
—— Papermaking. [With notes by Douglas Martin and illustrations by Rigby Graham.] pp. 11.   *Leicester,* 1959. fol.   Cup. **510**. asa. **4.**
One of an edition of seventeen copies on handmade paper. With proof sheets inserted.

TYCHBORNE (CHIDIOCK)
—— My Prime of Youth is but a Frost of Cares. (Illustrations by Rigby Graham.)   *Printed by Douglas Martin at the Orpheus Press:* [*Leicester,*] 1959. 8⁰. Cup. **510**. asa. **5.**
With proof-sheets, containing a variant transcript of the poem and an anonymous "Answer to Mr. Tichborne", inserted.

TYCHBORNE (CHIDIOCK)
—— My Prime of Youth is but a Frost of Cares. (Illustrations by Rigby Graham.) *Privately printed by Douglas Martin at the Orpheus Press:* [*Leicester,*] 1959. 8⁰.
                              Cup. **510**. asa. **6.**
One of an edition of twenty-five copies.

TYCHBORNE (CHIDIOCK)
—— [A reissue.] My Prime of Youth is but a Frost of Cares. [*Leicester,*] 1959. 8⁰.   Cup. **510**. asa. **7.**
One of an edition of twenty-five copies. The illustrations are in a later state.

BEST (JOHN)
—— Poems and Drawings in Mud Time. [Text by J. Best, illustrations by Rigby Graham.] *Orpheus Press: Leicester,* 1960. 8⁰.   Cup. **510**. asa. **3.**

CHURCHYARD (THOMAS)
—— Lovesong to an Inconstant Lady. Graphically embellished by Rigby Graham. *Orpheus Press: Leicester,* 1961. 8⁰.   Cup. **510**. asa. **2.**

SONG.
—— A song in favour of bundling; illustrations by Rigby Graham. *Leicester: designed and produced at the Orpheus Press for the Twelve by Eight,* 1961.   Cup. **510**. asa. **8.**
    Pages not numbered. 32 cm.   □
Two anonymous poems.

OSBOURNE (S. L.), Davos, Switzerland

STEVENSON (ROBERT LOUIS) Not I, and other poems. pp. 8. *S. L. Osbourne: Davos,* 1881. 16⁰.
                              C. **58**. a. **37.**

STEVENSON (ROBERT LOUIS) Moral Emblems. A second collection of cuts and verses.
S. L. Osbourne & Company: Davos-Platz, [1882.] 16⁰.
                              C. **58**. a. **36.**

OUTPOSTS PUBLICATIONS, Dulwich Village

BRUNT (MURIEL)
—— Personal Perspective. [Poems.] pp. 12.   *Outposts Publications: Dulwich Village,* 1962. 8⁰.
                              Cup. **510**. bat. **1.**

BRYANT (NANCY)
—— Mr. Zells of Tunbridge Wells, and other poems. pp. 12. *Outposts Publications: Dulwich Village,* 1962. 8⁰.
                              Cup. **510**. bat. **4.**

CLARKE (GERALD)
—— Fragments. [Poems.] pp. 12.   *Outposts Publications: Dulwich Village,* 1962. 8⁰. Cup. **510**. bat. **10.**

COLE (MAURICE)
—— Probes and Journeys. [Poems.] pp. 12.   *Outposts Publications: Dulwich Village,* 1962. 8⁰.
                              Cup. **510**. bat. **8.**

EDWARDS (BARBARA CATHERINE)
—— Poems from Hospital. pp. 12.   *Outposts Publications: Dulwich Village,* 1962. 8⁰. Cup. **510**. bat. **5.**

GARVIN (KATHARINE)
—— The Bright Rock Crystal. [Poems.] pp. 12.   *Outposts Publications: Dulwich Village,* 1962. 8⁰.
                              Cup. **510**. bat. **7.**

JOHNS (ROBERT) *Poet.*
—— First Light. pp. 12.   *Outposts Publications: Dulwich Village,* 1962. 8⁰. Cup. **510**. bat. **6.**

TUGWELL (SIMON)
—— Eternity's too Long. pp. 12.   *Outposts Publications: Dulwich Village,* 1962. 8⁰. Cup. **510**. bat. **3.**

WILLIAMS (HERBERT LLOYD)
—— Too Wet for the Devil, and other poems. pp. 12. *Outposts Publications: Dulwich Village,* 1962. 8⁰.
                              Cup. **510**. bat. **9.**

HENDERSON (REGINALD COLLINGWOOD)
—— Reconciliation. [Poems.] pp. 12. *Outposts Publications: Dulwich Village,* 1963. 8⁰. Cup. **510**. bat. **2.**

OVERBROOK PRESS, Stamford, Conn.

SAVILE (GEORGE) *Marquis of Halifax.*
—— The Lady's New-Year's-Gift, or: Advice to a Daughter, etc. pp. 107. *Overbrook Press: Stamford, Conn.,* 1934. 8⁰.
                              08108. g. **61.**

MANN (THOMAS) *Novelist.* [*Letters.*]
[Briefwechsel.]
—— An Exchange of Letters … With a foreword by J. B. Priestley. (Printed on the occasion of a dinner given by the Yale Library Associates in honour of Thomas Mann.) ff. 15. *Overbrook Press: Stamford, Conn.,* 1938. 8⁰.
                              Cup. **510**. nab. **3.**
Printed on one side of the leaf only.

ADAMS (FREDERICK BALDWIN)
—— Radical Literature in America. An address . . . To which is appended a catalogue of an exhibition held at the Grolier Club in New York City. [With plates.] pp. 61. *Overbrook Press: Stamford, Conn.,* 1939. 4°.
                                      12301. s. 43.

CHURCHILL (*Right Hon. Sir* WINSTON LEONARD SPENCER) *K.G.* [*Speeches and Addresses.*]
—— An Address by the Right Hon. Winston S. Churchill (before the members of the Senate & of the House of Representatives of the United States) . . . December 26th, 1941. pp. 15. *Overbrook Press: Stamford, Conn.,* 1942. 8°.
                                      Cup.510.nab.1.

PRÉVOST D'EXILES (ANTOINE FRANÇOIS)
—— Histoire du Chevalier des Grieux et de Manon Lescaut . . . suivant l'édition de 1753. Illustrations dessinées et imprimées par T. M. Cleland. [With a portrait.] pp. 204. *Stamford, Conn.,* 1958. 4°.   Cup.510.nab.2.

OVID PRESS, London

GAUDIER-BRZESKA (HENRI) H. Gaudier-Brzeska, *etc.* (20 drawings from the notebooks of H. Gaudier-Brzeska.) *Ovid Press: London,* [1919.] fol.
                                      Print Room.

ELIOT (THOMAS STEARNS)
                Ara Vus Prec. [Poems.] pp. 54.
Ovid Press: [*London,* 1920.] 4°.   11646. v. 6.

P., E.
—— Hugh Selwyn Mauberley. By E. P. [i.e. Ezra Pound.] *London: Ovid Press.* 1920.   C. 123. ff. 11.
pp. 28. 26 cm.   △

RODKER (JOHN) Hymns. pp. 39.   *Ovid Press:*
London, 1920. 8°.   11645. h. 32.

WADSWORTH (EDWARD) The Black Country, *etc.* (Drawings.) pl. xx. *Ovid Press: London,* 1920. 4°.
                                      K.T.C. 41. b. 28.

OYEZ PRESS, Berkeley, Cal.

DUNCAN (ROBERT EDWARD)
—— Medea at Kolchis. The maiden head. [A play.] pp. 44. *Oyez: Berkeley,* 1965. 8°.   Cup. 510. nez. 1.

PANDANUS PRESS, Miami, Fla.

COMBS (TRAM)
—— Ceremonies in mind: artists, boys, cats, lovers, judges, priests. *St. Thomas, V.I.,* [1959].   Cup. 510. ss. 4.
30 p. 25 cm.   □
Poems.

PANDORA PRESS, Leicester

CLARE (JOHN) *Poet.* [*Collections.*]
[The Prose of John Clare.]
—— The Natural World. [From " The Prose of John Clare ".] Drawings by Rigby Graham. *Pandora Press: Leicester,* 1961. 8°.   Cup. 510. ase. 4.
One of an edition of forty copies.

DE VERE (EDWARD) *Earl of Oxford.*
—— The Sheepheard's Commendation of his Nimph. Illustrations by Rigby Graham. *Pandora Press: Leicester,* 1961. 8°.   Cup. 510. ase. 15.

SCOTT (THEA)
—— Fingal's Cave . . . Illustrated by Rigby Graham. *Toni Savage: Leicester,* 1961. 4°.   Cup. 510. ase. 6.

SHELLEY (PERCY BYSSHE) [*Lines written among the Euganean Hills.*]
—— Lines written among the Euganean Hills . . . Drawings by Rigby Graham. *Pandora Press: Leicester,* 1961. 8°.
                                      Cup. 510. ase. 1.
One of an edition of sixty copies.

SWINBURNE (ALGERNON CHARLES)
[Poems and Ballads.]
—— The Garden of Proserpine. [From " Poems and Ballads ", first series.] Drawings by Rigby Graham. *Pandora Press: Leicester,* 1961. 8°.   Cup. 510. ase. 5.

BYRON (GEORGE GORDON NOEL) *Baron Byron.* [*Poems,* 1816.]
—— When We Two parted . . . [Extracted from Poems, 1816.] Drawings by Rigby Graham. *Toni Savage: Leicester,* 1962. 8°.   Cup. 510. ase. 3.
One of an edition of 100 copies.

CAMPION (THOMAS)
—— The Man of Life Upright . . . Illustrated by Rigby Graham. *Pandora Press: Leicester,* 1962. 8°.
                                      Cup. 510. ase. 13.

LEICESTER.—*Living Theatre.*
—— The Living Theatre. Drawings by Rigby Graham. (Written by, and produced for, the Living Theatre.) *Pandora Private Press: Leicester,* 1962. 8°.
                                      Cup. 510. ase. 12.
Printed on blue paper.

MARVELL (ANDREW) *Poet.*

—— Thoughts in a Garden . . . Illustrated by Rigby Graham. *Pandora Private Press: Leicester,* 1962. 8°.
Cup. **510**. ase. **7.**

SWINBURNE (ALGERNON CHARLES)

—— A Match. Drawings by Rigby Graham. [A poem.] *Pandora Press: Leicester,* 1962. 8°. Cup. **510**. ase. **2**

WILDE (OSCAR FINGALL O'FLAHERTIE WILLS)

—— Serenade . . . Illustrated by Rigby Graham. *Pandora Press: Leicester,* 1962. 8°. Cup. **510**. ase. **8.**
One of an edition of 100 copies.

HOLT (PENELOPE)

—— A Sicilian Memory. Drawings by Rigby Graham. *Toni Savage at the Pandora Press: Leicester,* 1963. 8°.
Cup. **510**. ase. **9.**
One of an edition of seventy copies.

LADY.

—— Where his Lady keepes his Hart. [By] Arthur Warren? Andrew Willet? Ambrose Willoughby? Arthur Wingfield? [A poem originally published in " A Poetical Rapsodie ", compiled by Francis Davison.] *Pandora Private Press: Leicester,* 1963. 8°. Cup. **510**. ase. **10.**
One of an edition of about seventy copies.

SAVAGE (TONI)

—— Rigby Graham . . . With a mural painting note by Hugh Collinson. [With reproductions.] *Gadsby Gallery; Pandora Private Press: Leicester,* [1963.] 8°.
Cup. **510**. ase. **11.**

BEST (JOHN)

—— Nine Gnats. [Illustrated by Rigby Graham.] *Pandora Press: Leicester,* 1964. 8°. Cup. **510**. ase. **14.**
One of an edition of fifty copies.

EPITAPH.

—— An Epitaph. An inscription from a headstone in a churchyard in the county of Norfolk. Illustrated by Rigby Graham. *Pandora Press:* [*Leicester,*] 1965. 8°.
Cup. **510**. ase. **16.**
One of an edition of fifty copies.

PARAGON PRESS, Chicago

LEVINE (ISAAC)

—— 100 Quatrains. *Paragon Press: Chicago,* 1946. 8°.
Cup. **510**. nal. **1.**
No. 20 of an edition of sixty-two copies. Author's presentation copy to Edmund Blunden, with autograph letter inserted.

PARDOE (F. E.), Birmingham

PEIGNOT (ÉTIENNE GABRIEL)
[Manuel du bibliophile.]

—— Establishing a library. A translation of an extract from Le manuel du bibliophile, *etc. Birmingham: printed by F. E. Pardoe,* [1961]. Cup. **510**. cax. **4.**
pp. 4. 19 cm. △
One of fifty copies, privately printed.

WHISTLER (LAURENCE)

—— Fingal's Cave. [A poem.] [*F. E. Pardoe: Birmingham,*] 1963. 8°. Cup. **510**. cax. **1.**

BLACHFORD (R. D.)

—— Poems. *F. E. Pardoe: Birmingham,* 1965. 12°.
Cup. **510**. cax. **2.**
Produced for the Private Libraries Association Society of Private Printers.

PARIS PRESS, London

DAMOGLOU (EFFIE)

—— The Three Stages of Love, or L'Education d'amour. An essay. pp. 8. *Paris Press: London,* 1960. 8°.
Cup. **510**. aaa. **1.**
No. 1 of an edition of twenty-five copies. Bound in velvet.

DAMOGLOU (EFFIE)

—— Fragments. Ten poems. *Paris Press: London,* 1962. 8°. Cup. **510**. aaa. **3.**

DAMOGLOU (EFFIE)

—— Art and Ideas & their Relation to Life. An essay. pp. 24. 3. *Paris Press: London,* 1963. 8°.
Cup. **510**. aaa. **2.**

PEACOCKS PRESS, Hurst, Berks.

ROLFE (FREDERICK WILLIAM SERAFINO LEWIS MARY) calling himself *Baron Corvo.*

—— Amico di Sandro. A fragment of a novel. pp. 44. *Privately printed:* [*London,*] 1951. 8°. Cup. **500**. b. **2.**

ROLFE (FREDERICK WILLIAM SERAFINO AUSTIN LEWIS MARY) calling himself *Baron Corvo.*

—— Letters to Grant Richards. pp. 46. *Peacocks Press:* [*Hurst, Berks.,*] 1952. 8°. Cup.**510**.acd.**6.**

ALDINGTON (RICHARD)

—— Ezra Pound & T. S. Eliot. A lecture. pp. 20. *Peacocks Press: Hurst, Berks.,* 1954. 8°. Cup.**510**.bd.**3.**
No. 5 of ten copies signed by the author.

ALDINGTON (RICHARD)

—— A. E. Housman & W. B. Yeats. Two lectures. pp. 35. *Peacocks Press: Hurst,* 1955. 8°. 11875. c. **41.**

ALDINGTON (RICHARD)

—— [Another copy.] A. E. Housman & W. B. Yeats. 1955.
Cup. **510**. bd. **1.**
△
No. 10 of ten copies on fine paper, numbered and signed by the author.

ALDINGTON (RICHARD)

—— The Berkshire Kennet. [A poem.] *Printed for distribution to selected customers and friends by G. F. Sims, the Peacocks Press: Hurst,* [c. 1955.] 8°. Cup. **510**. bd. **2.**
One of 10 copies on hand-made paper printed for A. A. and G. S.

PEAR TREE PRESS, Shorne, near Gravesend, *etc*; Flansham, Bognor

GUTHRIE (JAMES JOSHUA)

An Album of Drawings.
pp. 24.   *The White Cottage,*
Shorne, nr. Gravesend, 1900. fol.   **7858. r. 44.**

WALLER (EDMUND) *the Poet.* [Selections.] —————
Songs and Verses
selected from the works of Edmund Waller. (Decorated
by P. Waller and printed ... under the supervision of
J. Guthrie.) pp. 33.   *Pear Tree Press :*
South Harting, 1902. 8º.   **Cup.510.aka.1.**

WILLIAMS (   ) *Mrs.* An Alphabet for little
men and little women, *etc.*   *Pear-Tree-Press :*
South Harting, [1902.] 16º.   **12802. aa. 10.**

"MINIMUM." The Conquest of Camborne, April
9th 1903, by Sir Wilfrid Lawson, Bart., M.P. Verses
before the conquest by "Minimum." Drawings after
the conquest by C. Richardson. *For private circulation :*
Petersfield, [1903.] 8º.   **011651. ccc. 111.**

VIRGILIUS MARO (PUBLIUS) [*Bucolica.—Eclogue* II.—
English.]
——— Alexis, a pastoral of Virgil. Translated by John
Dryden. *South Harting : printed for the Harting Guild,*
1904.   **Cup. 510. aka. 28.**
ff. 4; *illus.* 28 cm.   △
Printed, on one side of the paper only, by James Guthrie
at the Pear Tree Press.

BOTTOMLEY (GORDON)
——— Midsummer Eve ... With drawings by James Guthrie.
(A play in one act.) pp. 34.   *Pear Tree Press :*
Petersfield, 1905. 8º.   **Cup.510.aka.2.**

GUTHRIE (JAMES JOSHUA)
——— An Account of the Aims and Intentions of his Press,
with a List of Books, by James Guthrie. [With illustrations.] pp. 32. *Pear Tree Press : Harting,* 1905. 8º.
Cup. 502. d. 8.

HODGKIN afterwards HOLDSWORTH (LUCY VIOLET)
——— Holy Poverty: the message of St. Francis for to-day.
[A summary of Paul Sabatier's " S. François et le mouve-
ment religieux au treizième siècle".] pp. 15.   *Pear Tree*
Press : Petersfield, 1905. 8º.   **4152. cc. 58.**

MACLOGHLIN (EDWARD PERCY PLANTAGENET)
——— Deliberate Writings ... With preface, a brief memoir,
and appendix, by his wife, Eliza Macloghlin. [With
portraits.] pp. xvii. 99. *Privately printed,* 1906. 4º.
12358. g. 4.

TYNAN, afterwards HINKSON (KATHARINE) A
Little Book for John O'Mahony's Friends. pp. 25.
Pear Tree Press : Petersfield, 1906. 8º. **10827. cc. 25.**

TYNAN, afterwards HINKSON (KATHARINE) A
Little Book for Mary Gill's Friends. pp. 17.
Peartree Press : Petersfield, 1906. 8º.   **4908. a. 17.**
Only 75 copies printed.

BLAKENEY (EDWARD HENRY)
——— The Angle of the Hours, and other poems. pp. 64.
Elkin Mathews : London, 1907. 8º.   **11648. ff. 24.**

B., J. D.
——— Echoes of Poetry, by J. D. B. With drawings by James
Guthrie. pp. 59. *Pear Tree Press : [Bognor,]* 1908. 8º.
Cup.510.aka.3.
One of an edition of sixty copies.

BOTTOMLEY (GORDON)
——— The Riding to Lithend. (Play in one act.) ... With
drawings by James Guthrie. pp. 38.   *Pear Tree Press :*
Flansham, 1909. 4º.   **Cup.510.aka.4.**

OSMASTON (FRANCIS P. B.)   The Paradise of
Tintoretto. An essay. pp. xi. 87. pl. XXIX.
Pear Tree Press : Flansham, Bognor, 1910. 4º.
Cup.510.aka.27.

PERIODICAL PUBLICATIONS.—*Flansham.*
——— Root and Branch : a seasonal of the arts. Edited by
James Guthrie. [vol. 1. no. 1]—vol. 3. no. 1. Spring
1912[—Sep. 1919.] *Flansham,* 1912-19. 8º & 4º.
Cup. 510. aka. 16.

BLAKE (WILLIAM) *Artist.*
——— Auguries of Innocence. (Proverbs. Written out by
Lillian Frost.) pp. 11.   *Printed at the Pear Tree Press by*
James Guthrie & S. J. Housley : Flansham, 1914. 8º.
Cup. 510. aka. 5.
Printed from etched plates on one side of the leaf only.

ENGLAND.—*English Bookplate Society.*
——— The Bookplate. Edited by James Guthrie, *etc.* no. 1–3.
Sept. 1920—Sept. 1921. *Flansham,* 1920, 21. 26 cm. &
29 cm.
△
——— New series. no. 1 ; supplementary number. Dec.
1922 ; June 1923. *Flansham,* 1922, 23. 26 cm.
△
——— New series. no. 1–3. July 1924—July 1925.
[*London,*] 1924, 25. 24 cm.
△
——— New series. no. 1. *London.* [1927]. 24 cm.
Ac. 9672. c.
△
From 1920 to 1923 published at the Pear Tree Press
and from 1924 to 1925 at the Favil Press.

GUTHRIE (STUART)
——— A Little Anthology of hitherto uncollected poems by
modern writers. Edited ... by S. Guthrie.   *Stuart*
Guthrie : Flansham, [1922.] 4º.   **Cup. 510. aka. 11.**

GUTHRIE (JAMES JOSHUA)
A Book of Intaglio Book-
plates... A selection of 20 designs printed in colour, *etc.*
Pear Tree Press : [Harting, 1923.] 4º   **C.102.f.8.**
One of fifty copies only printed.

GUTHRIE (JOHN) *of Flansham, Sussex.*

—— First designs for the theatre. *Bognor: hand printed at the Pear Tree Press by John Guthrie,* 1923. 32 cm.
Cup. **510**. aka. **29**.

△

Plates, numbered I–XIX, *with an introduction by Eleanor Farjeon. No. 49 of an edition of fifty-five copies, signed by the artist.*

IBBETT (WILLIAM JOSEPH)

—— Ibbett's Jessie. [Poems.] pp. 9. *Pear Tree Press: Flansham,* 1923. 4°. Cup.**510**.aka.**24**.
No. 2 of an edition of 100 copies.

IBBETT (WILLIAM JOSEPH)

——- Ibbett's Jessie. [Poems.] pp. 9. *Pear Tree Press: Flansham,* 1923. 8°. Cup.**510**.aka.**20**.
Proof sheets.

IBBETT (WILLIAM JOSEPH) Ten Lyrics. pp. 12. *James Guthrie: Bognor,* 1924. 8°. Cup.**510**.aka.**26**

GUTHRIE (JAMES JOSHUA)

—— Ten Designs for the Two Gentlemen of Verona, *etc. Pear Tree Press: Flansham,* 1925. fol. C. **102**. l. **12**.
Only 50 copies printed.

GUTHRIE (JAMES JOSHUA)

—— Twelve Madrigals. [With an introduction signed: James Guthrie.] Designed, cut, and printed by, David Graves. *Swanbourne Press: Yapton,* 1925. 8°.
11603. h. **26**.

No. 33 of 50 copies printed.

GUTHRIE (JAMES JOSHUA)

Last Bookplates : being a collection of designs. *Pear Tree Press: Flansham,* 1929. 8°. C.**99**.b.**34**.

LITURGIES.—*Church of England.*—*Common Prayer.*—*Morning and Evening Prayer.*—*Canticles.*

—— Te Deum Laudamus and Nunc Dimittis, from the Book of Common Prayer. *Pear Tree Press: Bognor Regis,* 1929. 16°. C. **99**. a. **29**.

TOMALIN (MILES) Fool's Luck. Ten Poems, *etc.* pp. ix. *Pear Tree Press: Flansham,* 1929. 8°.
C.**102**.a.**2**.

BIBLE.—*Matthew.*—*Selections.* [*English.*]

—— The Sermon on the Mount, from the Gospel of St. Matthew. pp. 19. *Pear Tree Press: Bognor Regis,* 1930. 16°. Cup.**510**.aka.**6**.

BOTTOMLEY (GORDON)

—— The Viking's Barrow at Littleholme. [A poem.] ff. 3. *Hand-printed at his Press by James Guthrie:* [*Flansham,*] 1930. fol. Cup. **510**. aka. **25**.
Engraved throughout on one side of the paper only. No. 1 of an edition of twenty copies.

GREEN (ARTHUR ROMNEY)

—— A Strange Visit. (The actual behaviour of a corncrake.) [A poem.] pp. 2. *Pear Tree Press: Flansham,* [1930.] 8°. Cup.**510**.aka.**21**.
Printed on one side of the leaf only. Printer's rough trial copy, presented by James Guthrie to Seumas O'Sullivan.

GUTHRIE (JAMES JOSHUA)

—— Frescoes from Buried Temples. A portfolio of drawings . . . With poems by Gordon Bottomley. *Pear Tree Press: Flansham,* [1930.] fol. C. **102**. l. **13**.

MILTON (JOHN) [*Ode on the Morning of Christ's Nativity.*] On the Morning of Christ's Nativity. *Pear Tree Press: Bognor Regis,* 1930. 16°.
No. 1 of an edition of 100 copies. C.**99**.a.**28**.

DAVIDSON (ALEXANDER MACKENZIE)

—— The weaver's loom. *Bognor Regis: Pear Tree Press,* 1931. **11643**. n. **67**.

pp. 23. 24 cm. (New Scottish series. no. 1.) △
Poems. The date in the colophon is 1932.

MURPHY (G. H.)

—— Change. [Poems.] pp. 26. *Pear Tree Press: Bognor Regis,* 1931. 8°. C. **102**. a. **3**.
Printed for the author. One of an edition of 100 copies.

O'SULLIVAN (SEUMAS)

—— Twenty-Five Lyrics, *etc.* pp. iv. 27. *Pear Tree Press: Bognor Regis,* 1933. 8°. C.**102**.a.**4**.

BIBLE.—*Ruth.* [*English.*]

—— The Book of Ruth. (Designed and hand printed by Vincent Stuart.) pp. 23. *Flansham,* 1934. fol. **3049**. g. **12**.

One of an edition of fifty copies.

PERIODICAL PUBLICATIONS.—*Flansham.*

—— The Book Craftsman. A technical journal for printers & collectors of fine editions. Edited by James Guthrie. vol. 1. no. 1–4. Oct. 1934–Summer 1935. *Flansham: Pear Tree Press,* 1934, 35. 28 cm. P.P. **1622**. bmb.

△

STRODE (WILLIAM) *D.D.*

—— Four Poems . . . In Commendation of Musick. On Westwell Downes. A Watch sent home to Mrs. Eliz. King wrapt in theis verses. A Sonnet. ff. 6. *Pear Tree Press: Flansham,* 1934. fol. Cup.**510**.aka.**22**.
No. 14 of an edition of 100 copies.

ECKERT (ROBERT PAUL)

—— These things the poets said. [The editor's foreword signed: Robert P. Eckert.] *Bognor Regis: Pear Tree Press,* 1935. Cup. **510**. aka. **7**.

pp. iii, 21; illus. 23 cm. △
Tributes in verse to Philip Edward Thomas.

ECKERT (ROBERT PAUL)

—— [Another copy.] These Things the Poets said. *Bognor Regis,* 1935. 8°. Cup. **510**. aka. **23**.
John Gawsworth's copy, with a revised MS. *version of his poem "To E.T." on the half-title. With prospectuses of this work of of other publications of the Pear Tree Press inserted.*

COLLINS (WILLIAM) *Poet.* [*Single Poems not originally published separately.*]

—— Ode to Evening. [With decorations by James J. Guthrie.] pp. 3. *Pear Tree Press: Flansham,* 1937. fol. C. **103**. h. **1**.

GUTHRIE (JAMES JOSHUA)

—— To the Memory of Edward Thomas. [With plates.] pp. 32. *Pear Tree Press: Flansham*, 1937. fol.
C. 100. a. 9.

MANNER.

—— The Manner to Dance Base Dances. (Translated out of French by Robert Coplande.) pp. 14. *Pear Tree Press: Flansham*, 1937. 4°.
Cup.510.aka.8.
One of an edition of 100 copies.

HOUSMAN (LAURENCE .)

—— Hop-o'-me-Heart. A grown-up fairy tale, *etc.* [In verse.] pp. 15. *Pear Tree Press: Flansham*, [1938.] 8°.
Cup.510.aka.10.

SHAKESPEARE (WILLIAM) [*Phœnix and the Turtle.*]

—— The Phœnix and the Turtle . . . Edited with an introduction by Gerald Bullett. pp. 14. *Pear Tree Press: Flansham*, 1938. 8° *Green Pastures Series.* no. 1.
Cup.510.aka.9.

THOMAS (PHILIP EDWARD)

—— The Friend of the Blackbird. (Reprinted from the author's corrected copy. Newly written out by Helen Hinkley. Decorations & plate printing by James Guthrie.) ff. 14. *Pear Tree Press: Flansham*, 1938. fol.
C. 103. g. 2.
Engraved. No. 22 of an edition of 100 copies.

BLAKE (WILLIAM) *Artist.*

—— Songs of Innocence. (Decorated and hand-printed in colours from intaglio plates by James Guthrie.) *Pear Tree Press: Bognor*, 1939. fol.
Cup.510.aka.19.
Specimen plates.

FARJEON (ELEANOR)

—— A Sussex Alphabet . . . With illustrations in colour by Sheila M. Thompson. *Pear Tree Press: Bognor Regis*, 1939. fol.
Cup.510.aka.18.

GUTHRIE (JAMES JOSHUA)

—— From a Sussex Village. [Essays and poems.] pp. 16. *Pear Tree Press: Bognor Regis*, 1951. 8°. 12360. ff. 45.

PELICAN PRESS, London

TREVELYAN (ROBERT CALVERLEY)

—— The Pterodamozels. An operatic fable. pp. 64. *Printed for the Author at the Pelican Press: London*, [1916.] 8°. 11785. ee. 22.

BELL (ARTHUR CLIVE HEWARD)

—— Ad Familiares. [Verses.] pp. 27. *Printed by Fr. Mey.* [*Francis Meynell*] *at the Pelican Press:* [*London*,] 1917. 8°.
Cup. 510. agh. 1.

GARNETT (EDWARD WILLIAM)

—— Papa's War, & other satires. pp. 119. *At the Office of the Herald;* [*printed by Francis Meynell*] *at the Pelican Press: London*, [1918.] 4°. Cup.510.agh.2.
Inscribed "Bertram Russell with the author's compliments."

PECHEY (E. P.) The Twin Brethren: a mystery play. pp. 14. *Printed for the Author: London*, [1918.] 8°. 11778. k. 51.

ALDINGTON (RICHARD) Images. [Taken from "Images, 1910–1915," with additional poems.] pp. 59. *The Egoist: London*, [1919.] 8°. 011649. f. 122.

LEWIS (PERCY WYNDHAM)

The Caliph's Design, *etc.* pp. 70. *The Egoist: London*, 1919. 8°. 07816. h. 63.

MASSINGHAM (HAROLD JOHN) People and Things: an attempt to connect art and humanity. pp. 223. *Headley Bros.: London*, 1919. 8°. 012350. df. 60.

COCTEAU (JEAN)

—— [Le Coq et l'Arlequin.] Cock and Harlequin. Notes concerning music . . . Translated . . . by Rollo H. Myers. With a portrait of the author and two monograms by Pablo Picasso. pp. 57. *Egoist Press: London*, 1921. 8°.
7894. b. 49.

CRAFT.

—— The Craft of Printing. Notes on the history of type-forms, etc. [By Stanley Morison. With facsimiles.] pp. 14. *Pelican Press: London*, 1921. 8°.
011900. b. 71.

D., H. Hymen. [With other poems.] By H. D. [i.e. Hilda Doolittle, afterwards Aldington.] pp. 46. *Egoist Press: London*, 1921. 8°. 011649. i. 101.

MOORE (MARIANNE) Poems. pp. 23. *Egoist Press: London*, 1921. 8°. 011649. i. 99.

PELICAN PRESS. The Types, Borders, Ornaments, Initial Letters, Flowers, & Decorations of the Pelican Press, *etc. London*, 1921. fol. 1887. c. 27.

ANACREON. [*English.*]

—— Anacreon done into English out of the original Greek, by Abraham Cowley and S. B. [or rather by Francis Willis, Thomas Wood, Abraham Cowley and John Oldham] . . . With copperplate engravings by Stephen Gooden. pp. 52. *Nonesuch Press: London*, 1923. 12°.
C. 99. f. 33.

HORATIUS FLACCUS (QUINTUS) [*Carmina.—English.*]

—— The Odes of Quintus Horatius Flaccus. Book I. Translated by Patrick Branwell Brontë, with an introduction by John Drinkwater. pp. xxii. 47.   *Privately printed: London*, 1923. 8°.   Ashley 2470.
   No. 14 of an edition of fifty copies.

PELICAN PRESS. Typography. The written word and the printed word, *etc.* [With specimens of types in use at the Pelican Press. Compiled by Francis Meynell.] pp. xlv. ff. 20.   *Pelican Press: London*, 1923. 8°.   **011899. d. 9.**

VENUS. Pervigilium Veneris…The Eve of Venus. In Latin and in English. Edited and translated with a commentary by R. W. Postgate.   *Grant Richards: London*, 1924. 8°.   C. **98.** g. **5.**

MAC ARTHUR, afterwards **ANDERSON** (FLORENCE MARY)

—— Tribute. [Poems. With illustrations.] pp. 37. *Pelican Press: London*, [1925 ?] fol.   **11656.** r. **14.**
   The title and the name of the author are taken from the cover.

HIGHAM (*Sir* CHARLES FREDERICK)

—— Tittle tattle, being old saws resharpened with one or two new ones. [*Iver Heath*, 1927 ?]   Cup. **510.** agh. **3.**
   pp. 23. 20 cm.   △
   Privately printed at the Pelican Press.

PELICAN PRESS. Typography . . . Second impression, to which has [*sic*] been added examples of new faces. (Compiled by Francis Meynell.) pp. 96. *Pelican Press: London*, [1927.] 8°.   **011899. c. 33.**

BIBLE.—*Daniel.—Selections.* [*English.*]

—— Nebuchadnezzar and the Story of the Fiery Furnace. From the Authorised Version of the Holy Bible, *etc. Fulcrum Press: Strand on the Green*, [1929.] 8°.
   03051. ee. 23.

ALLEN (EDWARD HERON)

—— The Gods of the Fourth World, being Prolegomena towards a discourse upon the Buddhist Religion and its acquired Pantheon, *etc.* [With plates.] pp. xii. 54. *London*, 1931. 16°. [*Privately Printed Opuscula issued to Members of the Sette of Odd Volumes.* No. 92.]
   Ac. **9128.**

PENGUIN PRESS, London

BRATHWAIT (RICHARD)

—— Barnabae Itinerarium: Barnabees journall. To which is added the Song of Bessie Bell. [The introduction signed: D. B. Thomas.] *London: Penguin Press*, 1932.
   C. **99.** d. **42.**
   pp. xv, 175. 23 cm.   △
   Latin and English. No. 41 of an edition of forty-five copies.

JOBSON (RICHARD)

—— The Golden Trade ; or, a Discovery of the River Gambra, and the Golden Trade of the Aethiopians, *etc.* [With an introduction by David Biron Thomas.] pp. xix. 217. *Penguin Press: London*, 1932. 8°.   C. **99.** d. **43.**
   No. 41 of an edition of 45 copies.

LIBER.

—— The Book of Vagabonds and Beggars, with a vocabulary of their language and a preface by Martin Luther. (Von der falsche betler büeberey.) First translated into English by J. C. Hotten and now edited anew by D. B. Thomas. [The German text of the 1529 edition, with the English translation. With illustrations and a bibliography.] pp. xvi. 188.   *Penguin Press: London*, 1932. 8°.   C. **99.** d. **44.**
   No. 41 of an edition of 45 copies.

PERPETUA PRESS, Bristol

TYLER (FROOM)

—— A Note on Irving. The great actor's association with the West Country. pp. 6.   *Coleridge Bookshop: Bristol*, 1931. 8°.   **010822.** de. **22.**
   Privately printed.

HOPES (REX F.)

—— The Garden. [Poems. With illustrations.]   *R. F. Hopes: Bristol*, 1934. 8°.   **11654.** b. **49.**

WHITE (ERIC WALTER)

—— Wander Birds. [A tale.] With ten silhouettes, *etc.* pp. 29. *Perpetua Press: Bristol*, 1934. 8°.
   012614. aa. **33.**

NICHOLSON (HUBERT)

—— Date. Poems . . . Drawings by Molly Moss. *Coleridge Bookshop: Bristol*, 1935. 8°.   **11655.** aaa. **11.**

NICHOLSON (HUBERT)

—— Date. Poems . . . Drawings by Molly Moss. *Coleridge Bookshop: Bristol*, 1935. 8°.   **11655.** aaa. **20.**
   One of an edition of twenty-five copies.

WHITE (ERIC WALTER)

—— The Little Chimney Sweep . . . After the silhouette film by Lotte Reiniger. pp. 29. pl. 8.   *White & White: Bristol*, 1936. 8°.   **11794.** i. **36.**

PETER KAVANAGH HAND PRESS, New York

KAVANAGH (PATRICK)

—— Recent poems. *New York: Peter Kavanagh Hand-Press*, 1958.   Cup. **510.** sad. **7.**
   pp. 28. 23 cm.   △
   No. 9 of an edition of twenty-five copies.

KAVANAGH (PETER)

—— Irish Mythology. A dictionary. (With an essay by Patrick Kavanagh.) 3 vol. pp. 152.   *Peter Kavanagh Hand-Press: New York*, [1958, 59.] 8°. Cup. 510. sad.
   No. 47 of an edition of 100 copies.

KAVANAGH (PETER)

—— Hermeneutics of Kednaminsha.   *New York: Peter Kavanagh Hand-Press*, [1960].   Cup. **510**. sad. **8**.

pp. 12.   23 cm.   △

Reminiscences.   No. 11 of an edition of one hundred copies.

BYRNS (LOIS)

—— Recusant Books in America, 1640–1700.   pp. 69.   *Peter Kavanagh Hand-Press: New York*, [1961.]   4°.
2726. ac. **3**.

No. 47 of an edition of 100 copies.

KAVANAGH (PETER)

—— Saint Jerome.   A dissertation in two acts.   pp. 82.   *Peter Kavanagh Hand-Press: New York*, [1961.]   8°.
Cup. **510**. sad. **2**.
No. 59 of an edition of one hundred copies.   With a prospectus of the Peter Kavanagh Hand Press inserted.

KAVANAGH (PETER)

—— Saint Patrick linking with Saint Jerome in a catena.   *New York: Peter Kavanagh Hand-Press*, [1961].
Cup. **510**. sad. **1**.

pp. 78.   23 cm.   △

No. 7 of an edition of one hundred copies.

KAVANAGH (PETER)

—— John Scotus Eriugena.   Number three in a catena.   [A play.]   pp. 73.   *Peter Kavanagh Hand Press: New York*, [1962.]   8°.   Cup. **510**. sad. **4**.
No. 20 of an edition of 100 copies.

KAVANAGH (PETER)

—— Oliver Plunkett.   Number five—ending a catena.   *New York: Peter Kavanagh Hand Press*, [1963].
Cup. **510**. sad. **6**.

pp. 55.   23 cm.   △

No. 14 of an edition of one hundred copies.

KAVANAGH (PETER)

—— Saint Malachy.   Number four in a catena.   pp. 68.   *Peter Kavanagh Hand-Press: New York*, 1963.   8°.
Cup. **510**. sad. **5**.

No. 28 of an edition of 100 copies.

BYRNS (LOIS)

—— Recusant books in America, 1700–1829.   pp. 71   *Peter Kavanagh Hand-Press: New York*, [1964.]   8°.
2726. ac. **6**.

No. 47 of an edition of 100 copies.

PETER PAUPER PRESS,
New Rochelle, N.J.; Mount Vernon, N.Y.

HOUSMAN (ALFRED EDWARD)

—— A Shropshire Lad.   pp. v. 74.   *Peter Pauper Press: New Rochelle*, [1934.]   8°.
11660. bb. **37**.

CRANE (STEPHEN) *Novelist.*

—— A Battle in Greece . . . Decorated by Valenti Angelo.   pp. 30.   *Peter Pauper Press: Mount Vernon, N.Y.*, 1936.   8°.   Cup. **510**. p. **13**.

HAAS (IRVIN)

—— Bruce Rogers: a bibliography.   Hitherto unrecorded work, 1889–1925 ; complete work, 1925–1936, *etc.*   pp. vii. 72.   *Peter Pauper Press: Mount Vernon, N.Y.*, 1936.   8°.
11914. e. **10**.

KNOWLTON (CHARLES)

—— Fruits of Philosophy, or the private companion of adult people . . . Edited with an introductory notice by Norman E. Himes . . . With medical emendations by Robert Latou Dickinson.   pp. xv. 107.   *Peter Pauper Press: Mount Vernon*, 1937.   8°.   Cup. **363**. d. **2**.

HAWTHORNE (NATHANIEL)

—— The Golden Touch . . . Decorated & illuminated by Valenti Angelo, *etc.*   pp. 39.   *Peter Pauper Press: Mount Vernon, N.Y.*, [1939.]   4°.   Cup. **510**. p. **4**.

DEFOE (DANIEL)   [*Robinson Crusoe.—Part 1.—The Life and Strange Surprising Adventures of Robinson Crusoe.*]

—— The Life & Strange Surprising Adventures of Robinson Crusoe . . . Illustrated by Richard Floethe.   pp. 284.   *Peter Pauper Press: Mount Vernon, N.Y.*, [1945.]   8°.
Cup. **510**. p. **9**.

CHINESE FAIRY TALES.

—— Chinese Fairy Tales.   Newly gathered from many sources.   With illustrations by Sonia Roetter.   pp. 76.   *Peter Pauper Press: Mount Vernon, N.Y.*, [1946.] obl. 8°.
C. **104**. a. **2**.

PLATO.   [*Symposium.—English.*]

—— The Symposium . . . Translated by Percy B. Shelley.   pp. 77.   *Peter Pauper Press: Mount Vernon, N.Y.*, [1946.]   8°.
Cup. **510**. p. **5**.

BARRETT, afterwards **BROWNING** (ELIZABETH BARRETT)

—— Sonnets from the Portuguese . . . Centennial variorum edition.   Edited with an introduction by Fannie Ratchford, and notes by Deoch Fulton.   pp. 123.   *Philip C. Duschnes: New York*, 1950.   8°.   C. **106**. c. **3**.
Designed and printed by Peter Beilenson.

DICKENS (CHARLES)   [*Pickwick   Papers. — Adaptations, Abridgments and Extracts.*]

—— Christmas with Mr. Pickwick . . . Being chapters from The Pickwick Papers, illustrated by Fritz Kredel.   pp. 77.   *Peter Pauper Press: Mount Vernon, N.Y.*, [c. 1950.]   8°.
Cup. **510**. p. **2**.

FRANKLIN (BENJAMIN) *LL.D.*

—— The Autobiography of Benjamin Franklin.   Illustrated by Raymond Lufkin.   pp. 219.   *Peter Pauper Press: Mount Vernon, N.Y.*, [c. 1950.]   8°.   Cup. **510**. p. **10**.

FRANKLIN (Benjamin) *LL.D.*
—— Poor Richard's Almanack. Being the choicest morsels of wit and wisdom, written during the years of the Almanack's publication, *etc*. [Edited by P. L. Ford. With illustrations.] pp. 79.   *Peter Pauper Press : Mount Vernon*, [*N.Y.*,] [c. 1950.] 8⁰.   Cup.510.p.11.

HANNA (Boyd)
—— The Story of the Nativity in Wood Engravings, *etc*. *Peter Pauper Press : Mount Vernon, N.Y.*, [c. 1950.] 8⁰.   Cup.510.p.1.

SMITH (Alexander) *Poet.*
—— Dreamthorp. Eight essays . . . With wood-engravings by Boyd Hanna. pp. 138.   *Peter Pauper Press : Mount Vernon, N.Y.*, [c. 1950.] 8⁰.   Cup.510.p.6.

STILES (Henry Reed)
—— Bundling : its origins, progress and decline in America . . . With cuts by Herb Roth, *etc*. pp. 88.   *Peter Pauper Press : Mount Vernon, N.Y.*, [c. 1950.] 8⁰.   C. 104. d. 1.

THOMAS (Dylan)
—— In Country Sleep, and other poems. [With a portrait.] pp. 34. *James Laughlin : New York*, [1952.] 8⁰.   Cup.510.p.8.
      One of the " New Directions Books.'

BRADLEY (Will)
—— Will Bradley, his Chap Book. An account, in the words of the dean of American typographers, of his graphic arts adventures : as boy printer in Ishpeming ; art student in Chicago, *etc*. pp. vii. 104. *The Typophiles : New York*, 1955. 8⁰.   Cup.510.p.12.
      Typophile Chap Books. no. 30.

GREEK ANTHOLOGY.
—— Love Poems from the Greek Anthology. Translated by Jacques Le Clercq. [With plates.] *Peter Pauper Press : Mount Vernon, N.Y.*, [1955.] 8⁰.   Cup.510.p.7.

WHITMAN (Walt)
—— Leaves of Grass . . . Illustrated by John Steuart Curry. pp. 374. *Peter Pauper Press : Mount Vernon*, [1955.] 8⁰.   Cup.510.p.3.

SEASONS.
—— The four seasons. Japanese haiku written by Basho, Buson, Issa, Shiki and many others. (Decorations by Marion Morton.)   *Mount Vernon : Peter Pauper Press*, [1958].   15235. bb. 26.
      Pages not numbered. 19 cm.   △

PHILOSOPHER PRESS, Wausau, Wisc.

JOHNSON (Samuel) *LL.D.* [*Rasselas.*]
      The History of Rasselas, Prince of Abissinia. pp. 191. *Van Vechten & Ellis : Wausau, Wisconsin*, 1902. 8⁰.   12613. i. 24.

MADAN (Falconer) The Daniel Press. pp. 25. *Philosopher Press : Wausau, Wisconsin*, 1904. 8⁰.
      Only 50 copies printed.   011901.h.18

PHOENIX PRESS, London

CARPENTER (Maurice)
—— ix poems. [*London :*] *Phoenix Press*, 1935.   Cup. 510. bev. 1.
      pp. 30. 30 cm.   △

MANNING (Hugo)
—— Beyond the Terminus of Stars. A sequence. [In verse.] pp. 26. *Phœnix Press : London*, 1949. 8⁰.   11658. c. 70.

PIAZZA PRESS, London

CATULLUS (Caius Valerius) [*Works.*].—*Latin and English.*]
      —— Catulli Carmina. The Poems of Catullus. With complete verse translations and notes by F. C. W. Hiley . . . Illustrations by Véra Willoughby. pp. xvi. 215. *Piazza Press : London*, 1929. 8⁰.   11355. d. 31.

PARTS. The Middle Parts of Fortune. Somme & Ancre, 1916. [By Frederic Manning.] 2 vol. pp. 453. F. P. *Piazza Press : London*, 1929. 8⁰.   T.C.4.a.16.

PICCOLO PRESS, Stroud, Glos.

CRAIG (John) *of the Piccolo Press.*
—— These women all. A medieval ballad newly decorated. *Piccolo Press : Stroud*, 1965. 8⁰.   Cup. 510. dam. 1.
      No. 40 of fifty copies reserved for friends of the author and members of the Society of Private Printers.

ZUKOFSKY (Louis)
—— Finally a valentine. A poem.   *Stroud : Piccolo Press*, 1965.   Cup. 510. dam. 3.
      Pages not numbered. 23 cm. (Opening. no. 1.) △

PIGEONHOLE PRESS, Savannah, Ga.

GIGNILLIAT (Thomas Heyward)
—— Merlinson ; a play in verse. By Genillat [pseudonym of T. H. Gignilliat]. *Savannah : Pigeonhole Press*, [1963].   Cup. 510. nie. 1.

PITCHFORK PRESS, Hanbury

OWEN (CHARLES) *D.D.*
—— [An Essay towards a Natural History of Serpents.] A Booklet of Dragons. (Text taken from An Essay towards a Natural History of Serpents by Owen.) *C. J. K. Cunningham & J. Stafford-Baker at the Pitchfork Press: Hanbury,* 1965. 8°. Cup. **510**. cux. **1**.

PLEIAD (The), London

PLATO. [*Crito.—English.*]
—— Crito . . . Translated by Henry Cary. pp. xxxvi. *The Pleiad: Paris,* 1926. 4°. Cup. 510. co. 4.

LYND (ROBERT) The Silver Book of English Sonnets. A selection of less-known sonnets, with an introduction. pp. 53. *The Pleiad: London; Haarlem* printed, 1927. 8°. C. **98**. h. **20**.

MUSSET (LOUIS CHARLES ALFRED DE) Fantasio. A comedy in two acts...Translated by Maurice Baring. [With illustrations by Fernand Giauque.] pp. 57. *The Pleiad : [London ;] Haarlem* printed, 1927. 8°. C. **100**. k. **21**.

URQUHART (*Sir* THOMAS) The Life and Death of the Admirable Crichtoun . . . From the original text of The Discovery of a most Exquisite Jewel, 1652, and with an introduction by Hamish Miles. pp. xxi. 103. *The Pleiad: Paris,* 1927. 8°. 010855. df. **16**.

PLIMPTON PRESS, Norwood, Mass.

HOWELLS (WILLIAM DEAN)
[Impressions and experiences.]
—— The country printer. An essay. *Norwood, Mass.: Plimpton Press,* [1916]. Cup. **500**. m. **33**.
pp. 48 : plate ; port. 21 cm. △
From " Impressions and experiences". Privately printed.

CABELL (JAMES BRANCH)
—— The White Robe. A saint's summary . . . With illustrations by Robert E. Locher. *John Lane: London ; R. M. McBride & Co.: New York ; Norwood, Mass.* printed, [1928.] 8°. C. **98**. h. **23**.

ORCUTT (WILLIAM DANA) The Book in Italy during the Fifteenth and Sixteenth Centuries, shown in facsimile reproductions from the most famous printed volumes . . . With an introduction by . . . Guido Biagi . . . Explanatory text and comment by W. D. Orcutt. pp. 220. *G. G. Harrap & Co.: London; Norwood, Mass.* printed, 1928. 4°. L.R. **41**. b. **6**.

MACLEISH (ARCHIBALD)
—— Before March [A poem.] . . . Drawings by Leja Gorska. *Alfred A. Knopf: New York,* [1932.] 12°. Cup. **510**. pd. **9**.
Borzoi Chap Books. no. **3**.

FROST (ROBERT LEE)
—— The Lone Striker. *Alfred A. Knopf: New York,* [1933.] 8°. Cup. **501**. b. **48**.
Borzoi Chap Books. no. **8**.

KNOPF (ALFRED A.) [*Appendix.*]
—— Alfred A. Knopf. Quarter century. [By various authors. With a portrait.] pp. 52. *Plimpton Press: [New York,]* 1940. 8°. 2712. l. **32**.

POET & PRINTER, London

BLUNDELL (GORDON JAMES)
—— The Swan & other poems. (Collected verse.) pp. 16. *Poet & Printer: London,* 1965. 8°. Cup. **510**. cut. **3**.

FRY (COLIN RICHARD)
—— Words from the Land of the Living. Some of the verse of Colin R. Fry. pp. 19. *Poet & Printer: London,* 1965. 8°. Cup. **510**. cut. **1**.

POINTING FINGER PRESS, Swindon

LINDLEY (KENNETH ARTHUR)
—— A sequence of downs. *Swindon: Kenneth A. Lindley,* 1962. 33 cm. Cup. **510**. bak. **1**.
△
Engravings with explanatory text. No. 19 of an edition of twenty-four copies.

LINDLEY (JOYCE) and **LINDLEY** (KENNETH ARTHUR)
—— Urns and angels. An anthology of epitaphs and engravings. (Compiled from material collected by Joyce & Kenneth Lindley.) [*Pointing Finger Press :*] *Swindon,* 1965. obl. 8°. C. **99**. h. **47**.
One of an edition of twenty-two copies.

POULK PRESS, Tytherington; Sutton Veny

KIDDIER (WILLIAM)
—— The Profanity of Paint. pp. 44. *Poulk Press: Tytherington,* 1933. 8°. Cup. **510**. amb. **1**.

TAYLOR (GEOFFREY BASIL)
—— Seven simple poems. By G. T. [i.e. G. B. Taylor.] *Sutton Veny: Poulk Press,* 1937. Cup. **510**. amb. **2**.
Pages not numbered; illus. 15 cm. △

POUND PRESS, Tunbridge Wells

VILLON (FRANÇOIS)

—— Seeven Poems o Maister Francis Villon made owre intil scots bi Tom Scott. pp. 12. *Peter Russell: Tunbridge Wells*, 1953. 4°. Cup.510.ceb.1.

RUSSELL (IRWIN PETER)

—— Three Elegies of Quintilius. pp. 26. *Pound Press: Tunbridge Wells*, 1954. 8°. Cup. 510. ceb. 2.

PRARIE PRESS, Iowa City

HALL (JAMES NORMAN)

—— The Friends. [In verse.] pp. 34. *Prairie Press: Muscatine*, 1939. 8°. Cup.510.sab.1.

BRINNIN (JOHN MALCOLM)

—— The Lincoln Lyrics. [Poems on Abraham Lincoln.] *New Directions: Norfolk, Conn.*, 1942. 8°. Cup. 510. sab. 3.
Part of a series entitled " Poet of the Month."

HEINE (HEINRICH) [*Buch der Lieder.—Die Nordsee.*]

—— The North Sea. Translated by Vernon Watkins. *New York: New Directions; Iowa City: printed at the Prairie Press*, [1951]. Cup. 510. sab. 5.

pp. 95. 25 cm. △
German and English.

VAN DOREN (MARK)

—— In that Far Land. [Poems.] pp. 28. *Prairie Press: Iowa City*, 1951. 8°. Cup. 510. sab. 7.

DERLETH (AUGUST WILLIAM)

—— Country Poems . . . With wood-engravings by J. J. Lankes. pp. 44. *Prairie Press: Iowa City*, [1956.] 8°. Cup. 510. sab. 4.

WEST (HERBERT FAULKNER)

—— ·For a Hudson Biographer. (New material.) pp. 37. *Westholm Publications: Hanover, N.II.*, 1958. 8°. Cup.510.sab.2.

DERLETH (AUGUST WILLIAM)

—— This Wound . . . [Poems.] Wood engravings by Frank Utpatel. pp. 43. *Prairie Press: Iowa City*, [1962.] 8°. Cup. 510. sab. 6.

BLUMENTHAL (WALTER HART)

—— Who knew Shakespeare ? What was his reputation in his lifetime ? pp. 97. *Prairie Press: Iowa City*, [1965.] 8°. Cup. 510. sab. 8.

PRIORY PRESS, Tynemouth

KING (MADGE) of *Tynemouth*, and **KING** (ROBERT) of *Tynemouth*.

—— Street Games of North Shields Children. pp. 40. *Priory Press: Tynemouth*, 1926. 8°. Cup. 510. afd. 1.
One of twenty copies printed on hand-made paper.

GRANT (GWEN)

—— Alps of Gold. Poems. pp. 15. *Printed by Robert King at the Priory Press: Tynemouth*, 1927. 8°. Cup.510.afd.3.
No. 3 of an edition of twenty copies on unbleached Arnold hand-made paper.

JOHNSON (LEWIS) *Writer of Verse.*

—— Recreations in Verse. pp. 34. *Priory Press: Tynemouth*, 1928. 8°. Cup. 510. afd. 8.
Author's presentation copy.

NEWCASTLE-UPON-TYNE.—*Trinity House.*

—— The North Shields Lighthouses, *etc.* [Extracts from the books of Trinity House, Newcastle. Edited by Madeleine H. Dodds.] pp. 34. *Priory Press: Tynemouth*, 1928. 8°. Cup. 510. afd. 6.
No. 8 of an edition of 100 copies.

BARNES (BARNABE)

—— Ten Poems from " Parthenophil and Parthenophe." With an introduction by Madeleine Hope Dodds. pp. vi. 10. *Priory Press: Tynemouth*, 1929. 8°. 11643. cc. 59.
No. 19 of an edition of 20 copies printed on hand-made paper.

KING (ROBERT) of *Tynemouth*. The Last Judgment. A theological farce. pp. 47. *Priory Press: Tynemouth*, 1929. 8°. Cup.510.afd.7.

KING (MADGE) of *Tynemouth*, and **KING** (ROBERT) of *Tynemouth*.

—— Street Games of North Shields Children. Second series. [With musical notes.] pp. 45. *Priory Press: Tynemouth*, 1930. 8°. Cup. 510. afd. 2.
No. 20 of 20 copies on hand-made paper.

HYETT (FLORENCE B.) Spring's Garden. Flower verses for children. pp. 15. *Priory Press: Tynemouth*, 1927. 8°. Cup.510.afd.5.

JOHNSON (REGINALD BRIMLEY)

—— Poems. pp. 16. *Priory Press: Tynemouth*, 1927. 4°. Cup.510.afd.4.
No. 4 of an edition of 100 copies.

PROKOSCH (Frederick), New Haven, Conn.

AUDEN (WYSTAN HUGH)

—— Two Poems. [Reprinted from "New Verse".] *Printed for the Author: [New Haven, Conn.,]* 1934. 8°. Cup. 510. saf. 1.
One of four trial copies for an edition of twenty-two copies privately printed by Frederic Prokosch.

PUNCH PRESS, Corsham

BLOMFIELD (RICHARD C.)
—— ABC. Picture book of colour wood-cuts. (Printed by hand from wood-cuts by R. Blomfield.) pp. 13.   *Punch Press:* [*Bath,*] 1961. 4°.   Cup. **510**. cox. **2**.

COCK ROBIN. [*The Nursery Rhyme.*]
—— The Death and Burial of Cock Robin. An old nursery rhyme with new illustrations by Richard Blomfield. pp. 16. [*R. C. Blomfield:*] Corsham, 1961. 8°.
                              Cup. **510**. cox. **1**.

PUSHKIN PRESS, London

PUSHKIN (ALEKSANDR SERGYEEVICH)
—— Evgeny Onegin. Translated by Oliver Elton and illustrated by M. V. Dobujinsky, *etc.* pp. xxxiii. 255. *Pushkin Press: London,* 1937. fol.   C. **103**. g. **1**.

BOURDEILLE (PIERRE DE) *Seigneur de Brantôme.*
—— The Lives of Gallant Ladies . . . Translated . . . by H. M. [and F. M.] pp. 508.   *Pushkin Press:* [*Twickenham,*] 1943. 4°.   **08415** de. **83**.

FLAUBERT (GUSTAVE)
—— Salambo . . . Translated by E. Powys Mathers. pp. 337. *Pushkin Press: London,* 1947. 8°.
                              012550. n. **16**.

VILLON (FRANÇOIS) [*Collections — English.*]
—— The Testaments of François Villon. Translated by John Heron Lepper. pp. 154.   *Pushkin Press: London,* 1947. 8°.   **11484**. c. **33**.

PYNSON PRINTERS, New York

MACHEN (ARTHUR LLEWELYN JONES)
—— Ornaments in Jade. pp. 46.   *Alfred A. Knopf: New York,* 1924. 8°.   Cup. **510**. pd. **8**.

NEW YORK.—*Grolier Club.*
—— PLUNKETT (Edward John Moreton Drax) 18*th Baron Dunsany.* The compromise of the King of the Golden Isles. *New York,* 1924. 4°.   C. **98**. gg. **12**.
pp. 25; illus. 29 cm.   △
Printed by T. N. Cleland.

HITCHENER (ELIZABETH) [*Letters.*]
                    Letters of Elizabeth Hitchener to Percy Bysshe Shelley. [With an introduction by W. E. Peck.] pp. 39.
          Privately printed for C. H. Pforzheimer: New York, 1926. 8°.   C. **98**. f. **17**.

MAC LEISH (ARCHIBALD)
—— Nobodaddy. A play.   *Cambridge* [*Mass.*]: *Dunster House; New York: printed by the Pynson Printers,* 1926.
                              11793. b. **2**.
pp. 67. 21 cm.   △

MORLEY (CHRISTOPHER DARLINGTON)
—— The Worst Christmas Story. [Reprinted from " The Bookman."] pp. 22.   *Privately uttered at Random House for thirteen Gentlemen of the Trade: Novi Eboraci,* 1928. 8°.   Cup. **510**. pd. **1**.

WOLFE (HUMBERT)
—— The Craft of Verse. Oxford poetry essay. pp. 45. *Crosby Gaige: New York,* 1928. 4°.   Cup. **510**. pd. **3**.

LAWRENCE (DAVID HERBERT)
—— My Skirmish with Jolly Roger . . . Written as an introduction to and a motivation of the Paris edition of " Lady Chatterley's Lover." pp. 11.   *Random House: New York,* 1929. 8°.   Cup. **510**. pd. **6**.

MORLEY (CHRISTOPHER DARLINGTON)
—— The Palette Knife . . . Illustrated by René Gockinga. *Chocorua Press: New York,* 1929. 8°. Cup. **510**. pd. **10**.

STEPHENS (JAMES) *Author of " The Crock of Gold."*
—— Julia Elizabeth. A comedy in one act. pp. 24.   *Crosby Gaige: New York,* 1929. 8°.   Cup. **510**. pd. **2**.

STEVENSON (ROBERT LOUIS)
—— Strange case of Dr. Jekyll and Mr. Hyde . . . With illustrations by W. A. Dwiggins.   *New York: Random House; printed by the Pynson Printers,* 1929.
                              Cup. **510**. pd. **7**.
pp. 161. 21 cm.   △
" *Facsimile sheet of author's manuscript is inserted.*"

TOMLINSON (HENRY MAJOR)
—— Thomas Hardy. (Lithograph drawn by Zhenya Gay.) pp. xxx. *Crosby Gaige: New York,* 1929. 8°.
                              Cup. **502**. b. **24**.

HUXLEY (ALDOUS LEONARD) **Music at Night, and** other essays. pp. 146.   *Fountain Press: New York,* 1931. 8°.   Cup. **510**. pd. **4**.

BIRD (ROBERT MONTGOMERY) *M.D.*
—— The City Looking Glass. A Philadelphia comedy . . . Edited, with an introduction, by Arthur Hobson Quinn. pp. xxi. 137. *The Colophon: New York,* 1933. 8°.
                              11351. g. **34**.

HUNTER (DARD)
—— A Papermaking Pilgrimage to Japan, Korea and China. [With plates, and 50 specimens of paper.] pp. 148. *Pynson Printers: New York,* 1936. 4°.   **7943**. w. **20**.

PFORZHEIMER (WALTER LIONEL)

—— Stocktoniana. An essay. By Walter L. Pforzheimer . . . The Lady, or the Tiger? By Frank R. Stockton. [With a portrait.] pp. 42. *Privately printed: New York,* 1936. 8°.   Cup. **510**. pd. **5**.
  Inserted in this copy is a leaflet entitled "Stocktoniana Number Two", describing Stockton's work as a wood-engraver.

HUNTER (DARD)

—— Papermaking by Hand in India. [With specimens of paper and with plates.] pp. 129.   *Pynson Printers: New York,* 1939. 4°.   L.R. **280**. b. **12**.

NEW YORK.—*American Institute of Graphic Arts.*

—— Daniel Berkeley Updike and the Merrymount Press. [By various authors.] pp. 47. *New York,* 1940. 8°.
                    Cup. **510**. sac. **11**.

QUARTO PRESS, St. Andrews

DAVIDSON (ALAN) *Poet.*

—— So many Kinds of Yes. By Alan Davidson & Andrew Lothian. (Poems.) pp. 27.   *The Authors: St. Andrews,* 1963. 8°.   Cup. **510**. cob. **1**.

ROBERTSON (ALASTAIR HOWARD DAVIS)

—— The haunted house of love.   *St. Andrews: Quarto Press,* 1965.   Cup. **510**. cob. **2**.
  20 p. 19 cm.   □

QUEEN ANNE PRESS, London

WAUGH (EVELYN)

—— The Holy Places . . . With wood engravings by Reynolds Stone. pp. 37.   *Queen Anne Press: London,* 1952. 8°.   C. **103**. f. **5**.
  No. 36 of fifty copies specially bound and signed by the author and artist.

FERMOR (PATRICK MICHAEL LEIGH)

—— A Time to keep Silence. [Meditations on monastic life.] pp. xvii. 92. *Queen Anne Press: London,* 1953. 8°.
                    Cup. **510**. aff. **1**.
  No. 11 of an edition of fifty copies specially bound and signed by the author.

QUERCUS PRESS, San Mateo, Calif.

JEFFERS (JOHN ROBINSON)

—— Natural music. [A poem.]   *[Book Club of California: San Francisco,]* 1947. 8°.   Cup. **510**. nep. **1**.
  Book Club of California Poetry Folios. no. 12.

QUOTA PRESS, Belfast

HOUGHTON (CLAUDE) *pseud.* [i.e. CLAUDE HOUGHTON OLDFIELD.]

—— The Beast . . . Illustrations by Alfred E. Kerr. pp. 44. *Quota Press: Belfast,* 1936. 4°.   12625. s. **9**.

RACCOON PRESS, Arcadia, Calif.

WAYLAND (VIRGINIA) and **WAYLAND** (HAROLD)

—— Of Carving, Cards & Cookery; or, the Mode of carving at the table, as represented in a pack of playing cards originally designed & sold by Joseph & James Moxon, London, 1676-7. Together with divers recipes . . . collected from 17th century masters at the art of cookery by Virginia & Harold Wayland, etc. [With reproductions.] pp. 122. *Printed for V. & H. Wayland by Carol Allen Cockel at the Raccoon Press: Arcadia, Cal.,* 1962. 4°.
                    Cup. **510**. nav. **1**.

DOUGAN (OLIVE CONSTANT)

—— Shadows, and other poems. [Edited by Robert O. Dougan.]   *Carol A. Cockel: Arcadia, Calif.,* 1963. 8°.
                    Cup. **510**. nav. **2**.
  Printed for private distribution.

RAMPANT LIONS PRESS, Cambridge

NICHOLS (ROBERT MALISE BOWYER)

—— A Spanish Triptych. Being three poems of compassion. pp. 18. *Rampant Lions Press: Cambridge,* 1936. 8°.
                    Cup.**510**.ac.**1**.

BIBLE.—*Song of Solomon.* [*English.*]

—— The Song of Solomon according to the Authorised Version. Illustrated with lino-cuts by Harry Hicken, *etc.* pp. 19. *Rampant Lions Press: Cambridge,* 1937. fol.
                    C. **98**. gg. **25**.

MARTIN (JAMES) *Convict.*

—— Memorandoms by James Martin. Edited by Charles Blount. [With illustrations and a map.] pp. xv. 45. *Rampant Lions Press: Cambridge,* 1937. 16°.
                    Cup.**510**.ac.**2**

CARTER (JOHN WAYNFLETE)

—— Clerihews. An unofficial supplement to "Biography for beginners" [by E. C. Bentley]. [The editor's note signed: John Carter.]   *Cambridge: printed by Will Carter at the Rampant Lions Press,* 1938.   Cup. **510**. ac. **3**.
  Pages not numbered. 12×19 cm.   △
  Printed on tinted paper.

BROWNE (*Sir* THOMAS)
[Hydriotaphia.]

—— The last chapter of Urne buriall. (Edited by John Carter. Cover and title page designs by John Piper.) *Cambridge: Rampant Lions Press,* 1946.
                    Cup. **510**. ac. **36**.
  Pages not numbered. 21 cm.   △

YOUTH.

—— Youth. Translated from the Old French by Arnold Moon. [A poem. With the original text.] *Cyril Edwards:* [London,] 1947. 8°. Cup. **510**. ac. **17**.
Printed on one side of the leaf only.

RAMPANT LIONS PRESS.

—— [A collection of programmes, handbills, invitation cards, book plates and other ephemera printed at the Rampant Lions Press.] 59 pt. *Cambridge,* [1950–56.] 8°, *etc.*
Cup.510.ac.13.

JOHNSON, afterwards **CORY** (WILLIAM)

—— Lucretilis. [With an introduction by John Sparrow and a bibliographical note signed : J. W. C., i.e. J. W. Carter.] *Rampant Lions Press: Cambridge,* 1951. 8°. C. **102**. i. **2**.

SASSOON (SIEGFRIED LORAINE)

—— Emblems of Experience. [Poems.] pp. 13. *Rampant Lions Press: Cambridge,* 1951. 8°. Cup.510.ac.4.
No. 10 of a limited edition of seventy-five copies.

MUNBY (ALAN NOEL LATIMER)

—— Floreat Bibliomania. (Reprinted from the New Statesman & Nation.) pp. 10. *Printed for private distribution: Cambridge,* 1953. 8°. Cup.510.ac.5.

PARKER (BARRETT)

—— Collects and Prayers in Wartime. pp. 16. *Newman Neame:* [London,] 1953. 8°. Cup.510.ac.6.
One of an edition of one hundred copies.

RAMPANT LIONS PRESS.

—— [A collection of prospectuses, leaflets, invitation cards, etc. printed by Will Carter at the Rampant Lions Press.] *Cambridge,* [1953–59.] 8°, *etc.* Cup.510.ac.13

FARROW (JOHN)

—— Seven Poems in Pattern, *etc. Rampart Lions Press: Cambridge,* 1955. 4°. Cup.510.ac.8.

PARKER (BARRETT)

—— William Belmont Parker. A memoir. pp. 25. *Rampant Lions Press: Cambridge,* 1955. 8°.
Cup.510.ac.7.
One of an edition of seventy-five copies.

GOFF (CECILIE) *Lady.*

—— Three generations of a loyal house. [*Cambridge:*] *Rampant Lions Press,* 1957. X. **809/10861**.

pp. 176: plates; ports. 22 cm.

On Peregrine Bertie, 12th Baron Willoughby d'Eresby, Robert Bertie, 1st Earl of Lindsey, and Montagu Bertie, 2nd Earl of Lindsey. Privately printed.

HECKSCHER (AUGUST)

—— Memorial Day Address. Prepared for delivery at Fort Hill Cemetry, Auburn. 30th May 1956. pp. 12. *Privately printed for Philip Hofer at the Rampant Lions Press: Cambridge,* 1957. 8°. Cup.510.ac.9.

KEYNES (*Sir* GEOFFREY LANGDON) [*Appendix.*]

—— Three Tributes to Sir Geoffrey Keynes on his Seventieth Birthday, 25th March 1957. *Rampant Lions Press:* [Cambridge,] 1957. 8°. **10864**. ttt. **8**.

KEYNES (*Sir* GEOFFREY LANGDON) [*Appendix.*]

—— [Another copy.] Three Tributes to Sir Geoffrey Keynes on his Seventieth Birthday, *etc.* [Cambridge, 1957.] 8°. **11919**. b. **12**.

BEDFORD (STEPHEN)

—— The Food of Love. [Poems.] *Sebastian Carter: Cambridge,* 1958. 8°. Cup.510.ac.14.

CARTER (WILL) *Calligrapher.*

—— The First 10. Some ground covered at the Rampant Lions Press by Will Carter, 1949–58. [With reproductions.] pp. 12. *Rampant Lions Press: Cambridge,* [1958.] 8°. **2707**. ct. **3**.

CARTER (WILL) *Calligrapher.*

—— [Another copy.] The First 10, *etc. Cambridge,* [1959.] 8°. Cup. **510**. ac. **11**.

CAMBRIDGE.—*University of Cambridge.*—*King's College.*

—— Luncheon in Honour of Sir Winston Churchill, the Trustees, Master and Fellows of Churchill College, 17th Oct. MCMLIX. [A menu.] *Will Carter: Cambridge,* 1959.] 8°. Cup. **510**. ac. **18**.

JOHNSON, afterwards **CORY** (WILLIAM) [*Appendix.*]

—— William Johnson Cory, 1823–1892. (Article first published in The Times Literary Supplement, as a review of Faith Compton Mackenzie's biography.) [By J. W. Carter.] pp. 8. *Rampant Lions Press: Cambridge,* 1959. 8°. Cup. **510**. ac. **10**.

SHIRE (HELENA MENNIE)

—— Poems from Panmure House. Edited, with an introduction, by H. M. Shire. pp. 23. *Sebastian Carter: Cambridge,* 1960. 8°. Cup.510.ac.19.

SKELTON (ROBIN)

—— Two Ballads of the Muse. pp. 10. *Rampant Lions Press: Cambridge,* 1960. fol. Cup. **510**. ac. **12**.
No. 75 of an edition of one hundred copies.

SMART (CHRISTOPHER)

—— A Song to David. Edited by J. B. Broadbent. pp. xxi. 40. *Rampant Lions Press: Cambridge; distributed by the Bodley Head: London,* 1960. fol. Cup. **510**. ac. **15**.

AYTON (*Sir* ROBERT)

—— Poems and Songs of Sir Robert Ayton. (Edited with a commentary by Helena Mennie Shire.) pp. 30. *Ninth of May: Cambridge,* 1961. 8°. Cup. **510**. ac. **16**.

BARING (RUBY FLORENCE MARY) *Countess of Cromer.*

—— The Hospital of St. John in Jerusalem. pp. 47. *Printed by Will Carter at the Rampant Lions Press: Cambridge,* 1961. 8º. Cup. 510. ac. 23.

BRAIN (WALTER RUSSELL) *Baron Brain.*

—— Poems and Verses. pp. 48. *Privately printed: Cambridge,* 1961. 8º. Cup. 510. ac. 25. *One of an edition of 100 copies.*

DANIEL (GLYN EDMUND)

—— The Pen of my Aunt. *[Glyn Daniel:] Cambridge,* 1961. 8º. Cup. 510. ac. 22.

JONES (*Sir* WILLIAM) *the Orientalist.*

—— Poems. Selected by Jonathan Benthall. [With a portrait.] *Sebastian Carter: Cambridge,* 1961. 8º. Cup. 510. ac. 20.

S., C. R.

—— A Letter to John Fairfax-Ross, 16th April 1944. [The postcript signed: C. R. S., i.e. C. R. Stone.] pp. 14. *Printed for Christopher Stone by Will Carter at the Rampant Lions Press: Cambridge,* 1961. 8º. Cup. 510. ac. 24. *One of an edition of fifty copies.*

MORISON (STANLEY)

—— Tact in typographical design, etc. *[Cambridge: printed by Will Carter at the Rampant Lions Press,* 1962]. Cup. 510. ac. 32.

pp. 6. 22 cm. △

With a "Printer's introductory note", and with a card containing an autograph note from Will Carter to Charles Batey inserted.

MORISON (STANLEY)

—— Tact in typographical design . . . A type specimen. *Cambridge: printed by Will Carter at the Rampant Lions Press,* 1962. Cup. 510. ac. 33.

pp. 6. 23 cm. △

One of an edition of one hundred advance copies printed for the 165th meeting of the Double Crown Club at Magdalene College, Cambridge.

SHIRE (HELENA MENNIE)

—— The Thrissil, the Rois and the Flour-de-lys. A sample-book of state poems and love-songs showing affinities between Scotland, England and France in the sixteenth and seventeenth centuries. Several texts were never before printed. The poems are edited with a commentary by H. M. Shire. pp. 31. *Rampant Lions Press: Cambridge,* 1962. 8º. Cup. 510. ac. 21. *The Ninth of May.* vol. 3.

LELIÈVRE (FRANK JAMES)

—— Cory's Lucretilis. *Cambridge: Rampant Lions Press,* 1964. Cup. 510. ac. 31.

pp. 13. 26 cm. △

COLT (ARMIDA MARIA THERESA)

—— Weeds and wild flowers. Some irreverent words . . . With wood-engravings by George Mackley. *London: Two-Horse Press; Cambridge: printed by Will Carter at the Rampant Lions Press,* [1965]. Cup. 510. ac. 37.

2 vol.: pp. 54. 31 cm.

Vol. 2 consists of separate prints of the wood-engravings from vol. 1.

DANIEL (GLYN EDMUND)

—— Oxford chicken pie. *The Author: Cambridge,* 1965. 8º. Cup. 510. ac. 26.

GREEK ANTHOLOGY.

—— Translations from the Greek Anthology. ([By] David M. Mitchell.) *Cambridge: Rampant Lions Press,* 1965. Cup. 510. ac. 35.

pp. 36. 22 cm. △

JONES (DAVID MICHAEL)

—— The Fatigue: c. A.U.C. DCCLXXXIV. pp. xii. 20. *Rampant Lions Press: Cambridge,* 1965. 8º. Cup. 510. ac. 28. *Privately printed.*

RANSOM (Will R.) (Private Press of) Chicago

SIMONS (HI)

—— Orioles & Blackbirds. [Poems.] pp. 71. *Will Ransom: Chicago,* 1922. 8º. Cup. 510. na. 1.

ACHAD, *Frater, pseud.* [i.e. CHARLES ROBERT STANSFIELD JONES.]

—— XXXI Hymns to the Star Goddess Who is Not. pp. 38. *Will Ransom: Chicago,* 1923. 8º. Cup. 510. na. 2.

FUJITA (JUN)

—— Tanka. Poems in exile. pp. 61. *Covici-McGee Co.: Chicago,* 1923. 4º. Cup. 510. na. 3. *Printed by Will R. Ransom at his private press.*

RAVEN PRESS, Harrow Weald, Middx.

BIBLE.—*Tobit.* [*English.*]

—— The Book of Tobit from the Apocrypha according to the Authorised Version. With wood-engravings by Horace Walter Bray. pp. 34. *Raven Press: Harrow Weald,* 1931. 8º. C. 100. g. 28.

MILTON (JOHN) [*Samson Agonistes.*] Samson Agonistes...With wood-engravings by Robert Ashwin Maynard. pp. xi. 63. *Raven Press: Harrow Weald,* 1931. 4º. C. 98. e. 14.

SHAKESPEARE (WILLIAM) [*Venus and Adonis.*] Venus and Adonis. With wood-engravings by Horace Walter Bray. pp. 43. *Raven Press: Harrow Weald,* 1931. 4º. C. 98. e. 15.

TUSSER (THOMAS) Five Hundred Points of Good Husbandry, *etc.* [With notes by Daniel Hilman.] pp. xii. 336. *J. Tregaskis & Son: London,* 1931. 8º. C. 100. c. 15.

SOUTHEY (ROBERT) [*A Vision of Judgment.*]

—— A Vision of Judgement. By Robert Southey. And The Vision of Judgement. By Lord Byron. Here printed in one volume with an introduction by R. Ellis Roberts and wood-engravings by the printers. *R. A. Maynard & H. W. Bray: Harrow Weald,* 1932. 8º. C. 98. f. 24.

CECIL (*Lord* EDWARD CHRISTIAN DAVID GASCOYNE)
—— Sir Walter Scott. [With a portrait.] pp. 59.
Constable & Co.: London, 1933. 8°. [*Raven Miscellany.*]
C. 100. g. 38/2.

WADDELL (HELEN JANE)
—— The Abbé Prévost. A play. pp. 57. *Constable & Co.: London*, 1933. 8°. [*Raven Miscellany.*] C. 100. g. 38/1.

MITCHISON (NAOMI MARGARET) *Baroness Mitchison.*
—— The Alban goes out . . . With wood-engravings by Gertrude Hermes. [Verse.] pp. 11. *Raven Press: [Harrow]*, 1939. 4°. 11656. f. 78.

ALLFREY (PHYLLIS SHAND)
—— In Circles. Poems. pp. 19. *Raven Press: [Harrow Weald,]* 1940. 8°. 011653. h. 61.

RECLUSE PRESS, Athol, Mass.

LONG (FRANK BELKNAP)
—— A Man from Genoa, and other poems. pp. 31. *W. P. Cook: Athol, Mass.*, 1926. 8°. 011686. f. 76.

LOVEMAN (SAMUEL) The Hermaphrodite. A poem, *etc.* pp. 33. *W. P. Cook: Athol, Mass.*, 1926. 8°. 011686. aa. 26.

RED APPLE PRESS, Evesham, Worcs.

BOOK.
[The Book of Days.]
—— Heigh for Cotswold. A brief account of the Cotswold games. (Extracted from The Book of Days [edited by Robert Chambers].) *Red Apple Press: Evesham*, 1965. 8°. Cup. 510. aaf. 2.

RED LION PRESS, London

SACKVILLE (*Lady* MARGARET)
—— Twelve Little Poems. pp. 18. *E. Lahr: London*, 1931. 16°. 11640. f. 10.

BINYON (ROBERT LAURENCE) *Keeper of Prints and Drawings, British Museum.*
—— Koya San. Four poems from Japan. pp. 15. *Red Lion Press: London*, 1932. 8°. Cup.510.bk.3

LAY (CECIL HOWARD)
—— April's Foal. [Poems.] pp. 20. *Red Lion Press: London*, 1932. 8°. Cup. 510. bk. 2.
No. 14 of an edition of 59 copies.

SACKVILLE (*Lady* MARGARET)
—— Ariadne by the Sea . . . Decorated by Albert Wainright. [Poems.] pp. 22. *Red Lion Press: London*, 1932. 8°. Cup.510.bk.1.

LAY (CECIL HOWARD)
—— Samples. [Poems.] pp. 14. *Red Lion Press: London*, 1934. 8°. 11654. d. 29.
The date in the colophon is 1935.

MÉGROZ (RODOLPHE LOUIS)
—— From the Scrip of Eros . . . Poems. pp. 16. *Fenland Press: London*, 1934. 8°. 11654. b. 33.

REDLYNCH PRESS, Ealing, Middx.

WOOD (PHYLLIS TAUNTON)
—— Pilgrim's Elixir. [Poems.] pp. 29. *Redlynch Press: [Ealing,]* 1938. 8°. Cup.510.bbe.1.
The book-plate of Walter De La Mare is inserted.

REDPATH PRESS, Montreal

HERSON (BENJAMIN)
—— Journey of a soul. [Poems.] pp. 158. *Redpath Press of the McGill University Press: Montreal*, 1965. 8°. X. 902/476.

Author's presentation copy.

REED PALE PRESS, London

BIBLE.—*Ruth.* [*English.*]
—— The Book of Ruth. pp. xvi. *Reed Pale Press: London*, 1934. 4°. C. 100. e. 17.

SHELLEY (PERCY BYSSHE) [*Adonais.*]
—— Adonais, *etc.* pp. 31. *Reed Pale Press: London*, 1935. 4°. C. 99. e. 48.

REIGATE PRESS, Reigate

TEMPLE (JOHN SCOTT)
—— Sonnets. pp. 38. *Priory Press: Reigate*, 1903. 8°. 11648. cc. 59.

BUNSTON, afterwards **DE BARY** (ANNA)
—— Leaves from a Woman's Manuscript. [Poems.] pp. 58. *Priory Press: Reigate*, 1904. 8°. 11652. dd. 42.

WILSON (GEORGE FRANCIS) The Amarant: a winter's dream. pp. 58. *Priory Press: Reigate*, 1904. 8°. 011651. e. 91.

WILSON (GEORGE FRANCIS)

—— Cricket Poems. pp. 65. *Simpkin, Marshall & Co.: London*, 1905. 8°. **011651**. g. **67**.

RICCARDI PRESS, London

AURELIUS ANTONINUS (MARCUS) called *the Philosopher, Emperor of Rome.—[Meditations.—English.]*

—— The Thoughts of the Emperor Marcus Aurelius Antoninus. Translated by George Long. Illustrated by W. Russell Flint. pp. 108. *P. L. Warner: London*, 1909. 4°. [*Riccardi Press Books.*] **C. 98. k. 2.**

BIBLE.—*Song of Solomon.* [*English.*]

—— The Song of Songs, which is Solomon's. Now printed in the Authorised Version and illustrated after drawings by W. Russell Flint. pp. 16. *P. L. Warner: London*, 1909. 4°. [*Riccardi Press Books.*] **C. 98. k. 1.**

BOCCACCIO (GIOVANNI) [*Decamerone.—English.—Single Tales.*]

—— The Story of Griselda. Being the tenth story of the tenth day . . . Translated by J. M. Rigg. pp. 20. *P. L. Warner: London*, 1909. 8°. **C. 98. i. 2.**

ARTHUR, *King of Britain.—[Sir Thomas Malory's Morte darthur.]*

—— Le Morte Darthur: the book of King Arthur and of his noble Knights of the Round Table. By Sir Thomas Malory. (Illustrations by W. Russell Flint.) 4 vol. *P. L. Warner: London*, 1910, 11. 4°. [*Riccardi Press Books.*] **C. 98. k. 3.**

HORATIUS FLACCUS (QUINTUS) [*Works.—Latin.*]

—— Quinti Horati Flacci opera omnia cura E. C. Wickham. *Londini: apud P. H. Lee Warner*, 1910. **C. 98. i. 3/1.**

pp. 290. 25 cm. (Scriptorum classicorum Bibliotheca Riccardiana.) △

CATULLUS (CAIUS VALERIUS) [*Works.] –Latin.*]

—— Catulli, Tibulli, Properti carmina quae extant omnia, cura Robinson Ellis, Joannis P. Postgate, Joannis S. Phillimore. pp. 318. *Apud P. H. Lee Warner, Mediceæ Societatis Librarium: Londini*, 1911. 4°. [*Scriptorum Classicorum Bibliotheca Riccardiana.* no. 2.] **C. 98. i. 3/2.**

EVERYMAN.

—— Everyman. A morality play. Illustrated after drawings by John H. Amschewitz. (Edited by Frank Sidgwick.) *London: Philip Lee Warner, publisher to the Medici Society*, 1911. **C. 98. k. 4.**

pp. xiii, 36: plates. 28 cm. (Riccardi Press books.) △

R., O.

—— The King who knew not fear, a tale of other days. By O. R. *London: Philip Lee Warner, publisher to the Medici Society*, 1912. **012210.** c. **1/1.**

pp. 30. 27 cm. (Riccardi Press booklets. no. 1.) △ *No. 3 of twenty-five copies printed on large paper.*

STEELE (ROBERT REYNOLDS) The Revival of Printing. A bibliographical catalogue of works issued by the chief modern English presses. With an introduction by R. Steele. [With facsimiles.] pp. xxxiii. 89. *Macmillan & Co.: P. Lee Warner: London*, 1912. 8°. **2036.a.** *One of "The Riccardi Press Books."*

STEELE (ROBERT REYNOLDS)

—— [Another copy.] The Revival of Printing, *etc. London*, 1912. 8°. **C. 98. i. 1.**

APULEIUS (LUCIUS) *Madaurensis.—[Asinus Aureus.— Selections.—Latin.]*

—— Apulei Psyche et Cupido, cura Ludovici C. Purser. pp. 41. *Apud P. H. Lee Warner: Londini*, 1913. 8°. [*Scriptorum classicorum Bibliotheca Riccardiana.* no. 4.] **C. 98. i. 3/4.**

BAIN (FRANCIS WILLIAM)

—— The Indian Stories of F. W. Bain. 13 vol. *London*, 1913–20. 4°. [*Riccardi Press Books.*] **C. 98. k. 8.**

CHAUCER (GEOFFREY) [*Canterbury Tales.*]

—— The Canterbury Tales . . . Illustrated after drawings by W. Russell Flint. (The text of Professor W. W. Skeat.) *London: Philip Lee Warner for the Medici Society*, 1913. **C. 98. k. 6.**

3 vol.: plates. 27 cm. (Riccardi Press books.) △ *With a prospectus inserted in vol.* 1.

PATER (WALTER HORATIO)

—— Marius the Epicurean, *etc. London: Philip Lee Warner, publisher to the Medici Society*, 1913. **C. 98. k. 7.**

2 vol. 24 cm. (Riccardi Press books.) △

SHAKESPEARE (WILLIAM) [*Sonnets.*]

—— The sonnets of Mr. William Shakespeare, *etc. London: published for the Medici Society by Philip Lee Warner*, 1913. **012210.** c. **1/2.**

pp. 78. 24 cm. (Riccardi Press booklets.) △

'UMAR KHAIYĀM. [*English.—Fitzgerald's Version.*]

—— Rubáiyát of Omar Khayyám . . . Rendered into English verse by Edward Fitzgerald. *London: Philip Lee Warner, publisher to the Medici Society*, 1913. **012210.** c. **1/3.**

pp. xxiv, 22. 24 cm. (Riccardi Press booklets.) △

BARRETT, afterwards **BROWNING** (ELIZABETH BARRETT) [*Single Works.*] [*Poems.*]

—— Sonnets from the Portuguese. *London: published for the Medici Society by Philip Lee Warner*, 1914. **012201.** c. **1/5.**

pp. 27. 23 cm. (Riccardi Press booklets.) △

BIBLE.—*Genesis.* [*English.*]

—— The Book of Genesis now printed in the Authorised Version and illustrated after drawings by F. Cayley Robinson. pp. xv. 88. *Medici Society: London*, 1914. 4°. [*Riccardi Press Books.*] **C. 98. k. 12.**

CAESAR (Caius Julius) [*De Bello Gallico.—Latin.*]

—— Gai Iuli Caesaris commentarii rerum in Gallia gestarum VII. Accedit Auli Hirti commentarius. Ex recensione T. Rice Holmes. pp. xi. 249. *P. H. L. Warner: Londini*, 1914. 8°. [*Scriptorum classicorum bibliotheca Riccardiana.* no. 15.] **C. 98. i. 3/5.**

CARROLL (Lewis) *pseud.* [i.e. Charles Lutwidge Dodgson.]

—— Alice's adventures in Wonderland ... With the original illustrations by John Tenniel. *London: Philip Lee Warner for the Medici Society*, 1914. **C. 98. k. 9.**

pp. xi, 131. 23 cm. (Riccardi Press books.) △

HOUSMAN (Alfred Edward)

—— A Shropshire lad. *London: Philip Lee Warner, publisher to the Medici Society*, 1914. **012210. c. 1/4.**

pp. viii, 48. 23 cm. (Riccardi Press booklets.) △

IRVING (Washington)

[The sketch book.]

—— Knickerbocker Papers, being Rip van Winkle & The legend of Sleepy Hollow. *London: Philip Lee Warner, publisher to the Medici Society*, 1914. **012210. c. 1/6.**

pp. vii, 53. 23 cm. (Riccardi Press booklets.) △

KINGSLEY (Charles) [*Miscellaneous Works.*]

—— The Heroes . . . Illustrated after the water-colour drawings by W. Russell Flint. pp. xviii. 166. *P. L. Warner: London*, 1914. 8°. **04503. k. 6.**

TENNYSON (Alfred) *Baron Tennyson.* [*In Memoriam.*]

—— In memoriam. *London: Philip Lee Warner, publisher to the Medici Society*, 1914. **012201. c. 1/7.**

pp. vii, 92. 23 cm. (Riccardi Press booklets.) △

BROOKE (Rupert Chawner) [*Collections.*]

—— The Collected Poems of Rupert Brooke. The titlepage and portrait cut on wood by G. Raverat. (Edited by E. M. [i.e. Sir Edward H. Marsh.) pp. x. 156. *P. L. Warner: London*, 1919. 8°. **11646. p. 14.**
One of the Riccardi Press Books.

FAIRLESS (Michael) [i.e. Margaret Fairless Barber.] The Roadmender. pp. ix. 107. *London & Boston*, 1920. 8°. [*Riccardi Press Books.*] **C. 98. k. 11.**

ETON COLLEGE.

—— List of Etonians who fought in the Great War, 1914–1919. (Compiler: E. L. Vaughan.) *London: privately printed in the Riccardi Press fount*, 1921. **8366. l. 4.**

pp. xi, 281. 28 cm. △
With supplements inserted.

HARDY (Thomas) *O.M.* Selected Poems ... With portrait & title page design...by William Nicholson. pp. x. 144. *London*, 1921. 8°. [*Riccardi Press Books.*] **C. 98. k. 10.**

THEOCRITUS. [*English.*]

—— Theocritus, Bion and Moschus. (Rendered into English prose by Andrew Lang. Illustrated [in colour] . . . by W. Russell Flint.) 2 vol. *London*, 1922. 4°. [*Riccardi Press Books.*] **C. 98. k. 13.**

SWINBURNE (Algernon Charles)

—— Atalanta in Calydon, *etc.* pp. xix. 79. *London*, 1923. 8°. [*Riccardi Press Booklets.*] **012210. c. 1/8.**

WHARTON (Edith Newbold)

—— Twelve Poems. pp. 51. *Medici Society: London*, 1926. 8°. [*Riccardi Press Books.*] **C. 98. k. 14.**

ROBIN PRESS, Hull

DENNIS (Edward James) Of a Son, and other verses. pp. 48. *Robin Press: Hull*, 1950. 8°. **Cup. 510. at. 1.**

RONSARD (Pierre de) [*Selections.*]

—— Salute to Ronsard. Salut, ô Ronsard! Selected poems of Pierre de Ronsard, with English verse translations by E. J. Dennis. With six drawings by J. M. Dennis. pp. 28. *Robin Press: Hull*, [1960.] 8°. **Cup. 510. at. 2.**
With the autograph signature of the translator.

DENNIS (Edward James)

—— Voici mon coeur. A diversity of French poems, with English verse translations by E. J. Dennis and with six new drawings by J. M. Dennis. pp. 28. *E. J. Dennis at the Robin Press: Hull*, [1961.] 8°. **Cup. 510. at. 3.**

ROCHESTER PRESS, London

ROFFE (Robert Cabbell)

—— " My diary of sixty-three days: with memorandums of occasional trips into Kent." By Robert Cabbell Roffe ... With notes and illustrations by Alfred, Felix and Edwin Roffe. *London: imprinted by Edwin Roffe*, 1858. **10826. d. 20.**

ff. 40; illus. 23 cm. △
One of an edition of fifty copies, privately printed, on one side of the leaf only, at the Rochester Press.

ROFFE (Alfred Thomas)

—— Leeds; our grandfather's native village. With divers remains, gathered in memory of Robert Cabell Roffe, engraver. By Alfred, Felix and Edwin Roffe. *London: imprinted by Edwin Roffe*, 1859 [1862]. **10826. cc. 7.**

pp. 64: plates; illus., ports. 22 cm. △
The colophon bears the date 1862. One of an edition of thirty copies, privately printed at the Rochester Press.

ROFFE (Edwin)

—— British monumental inscriptions, gathered occasionally from divers churchyards by Edwin Roffe *London: imprinted by Edwin Roffe*, 1859, 61. **1266. d. 67.**

2 pt. 22 cm. △
One of an edition of sixteen copies, privately printed at the Rochester Press.

MAIDSTONE MISCELLANY.

—— The Maidstone miscellany, or Leeds and Fairleigh archæologia. [The compilers identified as Edwin, Arthur and Robert Roffe, the editor as Edwin Roffe.] *London: imprinted by Edwin Roffe*, 1860. **10826. d. 15.**

pp. 69; illus. 22 cm. △
One of an edition of twelve copies, privately printed at the Rochester Press.

ROFFE (ROBERT CABBELL)

—— The grand master. Being some extracts from the short-hand correspondence of Robert Cabbell Roffe . . . with . . . Thomas Molineux . . . Edited by Alfred Roffe. *London: set up and imprinted by Edwin Roffe, 1860.* **10920**. f. **25**.

pp. 76. 22 cm. △

On the short-hand system invented by John Byrom. One of an edition of twenty copies, privately printed at the Rochester Press.

ROFFE (EDWIN)

—— A ryghte goodlie lyttle booke of frisket fancies set forth for bibliomaniacs *London: imprinted by Edwin Roffe, 1861 [1864].* **10826**. d. **17**.

7 pt.: illus. 22 cm. △

One of an edition of twelve copies, privately printed at the Rochester Press.

CROOKEDSTAFF (CAMDEN)

—— Time's Tunefull Tabor, being divers diary notes! Selected from the original MS. of Master Camden Crookedstaff, by his trusty friend, Edwin Roffe. [In fact written by Roffe himself.] 6 pt. *Edwin Roffe: London*, 1862. 4°. **10826**. d. **19**.

One of an edition of twelve copies. Privately printed.

ROFFE (EDWIN)

—— Walks in the way of Old Weever! *London: imprinted by Edwin Roffe, 1862.* **10826**. d. **18**. **(1.)**

7 bk.; illus. 22 cm. △

One of an edition of sixteen copies, privately printed at the Rochester Press.

ROFFE (EDWIN)

—— The tomb seeker. *London: imprinted by Edwin Roffe, 1863 [1864].* **10826**. d. **16**.

2 pt.; illus. 22 cm. △

Pt. 2 bears the title " Funeral records ". One of an edition of sixteen copies, privately printed at the Rochester Press.

ROFFE (EDWIN)

—— A basket of bright berries from the yew trees of Paradise. Gathered by Edwin Roffe. *[London:] printed by Edwin Roffe, [1864].* **10826**. d. **18**. **(3.)**

pp. 6; illus. 22 cm. △

ROFFE (EDWIN)

—— Sundry slips of yew, set to the memory of divers citizens of London . . . Inscriptions from church-yard tombs, copied by Edwin Roffe, *etc.* *[London: printed by Edwin Roffe, 1864].* **10826**. d. **18**. **(2.)**

pp. 11; illus. 22 cm. △

ROFFE (EDWIN)

—— A perambulating survey, or Topographical and historical account of the Parish of Saint Pancras, *etc.* *London: imprinted by Edwin Roffe, at his private press, 1865.* **10826**. d. **14**.

3 bk.; illus. 22 cm. △

Half-title " Pancredge." One of an edition of sixteen copies.

ROFFE (ALFRED THOMAS)

—— A musical triad from Shakespeare: the Clown in Twelfth Night; Autolycus; the Lord of Amiens. Also Shakespeare upon art and nature. To which is added Old English singers, and Mr. Bowman—actor, singer, and ringer. [Edited by Edwin Roffe.] *London: printed by Edwin Roffe, 1872 [1874].* **11766**. g. **1**.

pp. 92. 22 cm. △

The titlepage headed: Ye Rochester Press. The colophon bears the date 1874. One of an edition of twenty copies, privately printed.

ROFFE (ALFRED THOMAS)

—— The real religion of Shakespeare. Also an essay on Prospero and his philosophy. To which is added a lecture concerning Jacob Behmen, *etc.* [The editor's name revealed in the book as Edwin Roffe.] *London: privately printed, 1872* **11766**. g. **2**.

pp. 82. 22 cm. △

The titlepage headed: Ye Rochester Press. One of an edition of twenty copies, privately printed.

WILLE (JOHANN GEORGE)

—— The autobiography of the early years of . . . John George Wille . . . Translated from the French, by Alfred Roffe. *London: privately printed, 1872.* **10708**. f. **43**.

pp. 27: plate; port. 23 cm. △

The titlepage headed: Ye Rochester Press.

RODALE PRESS, London

STEVENSON (ROBERT LOUIS)

—— The Treasure of Franchard. Illustrated by Laszlo Matulay. pp. xiv. 73. *Rodale Press: London*, 1954. 8°. Cup.510.afc.3.

WILDE (OSCAR FINGALL O'FLAHERTIE WILLS)

—— Lord Arthur Savile's Crime . . . With wood-engravings by Dorothea Braby. pp. 99. *Rodale Press: London*, 1954. 8°. Cup.510.afc.1.

LA FONTAINE (JEAN DE) [*Minor Works.*]

—— Adonis. Translated . . . by David M. Glixon with nine colour lithographs by Ru Van Rossem. pp. 83. *Rodale Press: London*, 1957. 8°. Cup.510.afc.2.

ROMNEY STREET PRESS, London

THOMPSON, afterwards **MEYNELL** (ALICE CHRISTIANA) Ten Poems . . .1913–1915. pp. 15. *Romney Street Press: London*, 1915. 8°. C. 99. h. 13.
One of an edition of 50 copies.

CAREY (MARY)

—— Meditations from the Note Book of Mary Carey, 1649–1657. [Edited by Sir Francis Meynell.] pp. xii. 53. ON VELLUM. *Printed & sold by Francis Meynell: Westminster*, 1918. 12°. C. 104. a. 4.
One of an edition of 100 copies.

RONALD ISHILL PRESS, Staten Island

MARKHAM (EDWIN)

—— The Man with the Hoe ... With an unpublished letter [in facsimile] by the author to Howard W. May. *Ronald Ishill Press: Staten Island*, 1961. 8°. Cup. **510.** sae. **1.**
No. 41 of an edition of 100 copies.

ROSEMARY PRESS, Leicester

OUTRAM (ALBERT ERNEST)

—— The Limitations of Science. pp. 15. *Printed by the Author at the Rosemary Press: Leicester*, 1959 [1960]. fol. Cup. 510. ay. **1.**

One of fourteen presentation copies.

ROYCROFTERS (The), East Aurora, N.Y.

HUBBARD (ELBERT) A Message to Garcia. Being a preachment. pp. 9. *The Roycrofters: East Aurora, New York*, [1899.] 8°. Cup.510.pa.**14.**

BROWNING (ROBERT) *the Poet.* [*Single Poems not originally published separately.*]

—— [The last ride together.] So here then is The last ride. *East Aurora, N.Y.: The Roycrofters*, 1900.
Cup. **510.** pa. **21.**

Pages not numbered. 20 cm. △

HUBBARD (ELBERT)

—— Little Journeys to the Homes of English Authors ... Robert Burns. [With a portrait.] *The Roycrofters: East Aurora*, 1900. 8°. Cup.510.pa.**12.**

STEVENSON (ROBERT LOUIS)
[Familiar Studies of Men and Books.]

—— The Essay on Walt Whitman. [From 'Familiar Studies of Men and Books.'] By R. L. Stevenson. With a little journey to the home of Whitman by Elbert Hubbard. pp. 91. *Roycroft Shop: East Aurora, N.Y.* 1900. 8°. Cup. **510.** pa. **1.**
With two press-cuttings inserted.

TENNYSON (ALFRED) *Baron Tennyson.* [*Maud.*]

—— This then is Maud, being a monodrama, as writ & arranged by Alfred Tennyson. (Illumined by Elsie Whitney.) pp. 80. *Roycroft Press: East Aurora, N.Y.*, 1900. 8°. Cup. **510.** pa. **19.**
No. 21 of an edition of 100 copies

HUBBARD (ELBERT)

—— Little Journeys to the Homes of English Authors. Robert Browning. [With a portrait.] *Roycrofters: East Aurora*, 1901. 8°. Cup.510.pa.**16.**

HUBBARD (ELBERT)

—— Little Journeys to the Homes of Great Musicians. Handel. *The Roycrofters: East Aurora*, 1901. 8°. Cup.510.pa.**2**

HUBBARD (ELBERT)

—— A Message to Garcia and thirteen other Things. As written by Fra Elbertus. [With a portrait.] pp. iii. 166. *Roycrofters: East Anvora*, 1901. 8°. Cup.510.pa.**18.**

HUBBARD (ELBERT)

—— Little Journeys to the Homes of Eminent Artists: Cellini. [With a portrait.] *The Roycrofters: East Aurora, N.Y.*, 1902. 8°. Cup.510.pa.**3**

ROYCROFT SHOP.

—— The Roycroft Books. A catalog and some comment concerning the shop at East Aurora, New York, and its workers. [With plates, including portraits.] pp. 32. *East Aurora*, [1902.] 8°. 2712. l. **15.**
The cover bears the title " The Book of the Roycrofters."

SHAKESPEARE (WILLIAM) [*Hamlet.*]

—— Shakespeare's Tragedy of Hamlet, Prince of Denmark. pp. 172. **F.P.** *Roycroft Shop: East Aurora, N.Y.*, 1902. 4°. Cup. **510.** pa. **7.**

STEVENSON (ROBERT LOUIS)

—— Virginibus Puerisque. An essay in four parts. pp. 77. *The Roycrofters: East Aurora*, 1903. 8°. Cup.510.pa.**8**

INGERSOLL (ROBERT GREEN)

—— Crimes against Criminals. [With portraits.] pp. 59. *The Roycrofters: East Aurora*, 1906. 8°. C.**99.b.35.**

OUIDA, *pseud.* [i.e. MARIE LOUISE DE LA RAMÉE.]

—— A Dog of Flanders. Being a story of friendship closer than brotherhood. pp. 90. *The Roycrofters: East Aurora*, 1906. 8°. Cup.510.pa.**9.**
Printed on Japan vellum.

HUBBARD (ELBERT)

—— So here cometh White Hyacinths—being a book of the Heart, etc. *Roycrofters: East Aurora, N.Y.*, 1907. 8°. Cup. **510.** pa. **5.**

HUBBARD (ELBERT) *the Elder.*

—— This then is a William Morris Book. Being a little journey by Elbert Hubbard, & some letters, heretofore unpublished, written to his friend & fellow worker, Robert Thomson, etc. [With plates, including portraits.] pp. 67. *The Roycrofters: East Aurora*, 1907. 8°. Cup. 502. c. 9.

HUGO (VICTOR MARIE) *Viscount.* [*Les Misérables.*]

—— So this then is the Battle of Waterloo, etc. (Translated by Lascelles Wraxall.) [With a portrait.] pp. 105. *The Roycroft Shop: East Aurora, N.Y.*, 1907. 8°. C.**99.b.36.**

HUBBARD (ELBERT)

—— Little Journeys to the Homes of Great Teachers. Moses (Confucius.—Pythagoras.—Plato.—King Alfred.—Friedrich Froebel). [With portraits.] pp. 150. *The Roycrofters: East Aurora*, 1908. 8°. Cup.510.pa.**15**

HUBBARD (ELBERT)

—— The Doctors. A satire in four seizures. [With plates.] pp. 123. *The Roycrofters: East Aurora, N.Y.*, 1909. 8°. C.**99.b.37.**

HUBBARD (ELBERT)
—— The Roycroft Shop. A history. pp. 31. *The Roycrofters:*
East Aurora, 1909. 8°. Cup. **510.** pa. **20.**

HUBBARD (ELBERT)
—— So here then cometh Pig-Pen Pete, or, Some chums of
mine. Being stories truthfully related by Elbert Hubbard
about some of our dumb brothers, *etc.* [With plates.]
pp. 221. *The Roycrofters: East Aurora, N.Y.,* [1914.] 8°.
Cup.510.pa.11.

HUBBARD (ELBERT) Who lifted the Lid off of
Hell? pp. 15. [*The Author:*
East Aurora, N.Y., 1914.] 16°. Cup.510.pa.13

HUBBARD (ELBERT)
—— A Little Journey to a Builder of Men: being an apprecia-
tion of Grenville Kleiser. pp. 23. *The Roycrofters:*
East Aurora, N. Y., 1915. 8°. Cup. **510.** pa. **4.**

EAST AURORA, *New York.—Roycrofters.*
—— Roycroft. vol. 4. no. 3. May 1919. *East Aurora,*
N.Y., 1919. 8°. Cup. **510.** pa. **6.**

HUBBARD (ELBERT)
—— The Liberators; being adventures in the city of fine
minds. [With a portrait.] pp. 266. *The Roycrofters:*
East Aurora, 1919. 4°. Cup.510.pa.10

HUBBARD (ELBERT)
—— The Olympians. A tribute to "tall sun-crowned men."
(Compiled from The Fra Magazine.) pp. 150. [*The*
Roycrofters: East Aurora, 1921.] 8°. Cup.510.pa.17.

RUDGE (William Edwin), New York

KNIGHT (SARAH)
—— The Journal of Madam Knight. With an introductory
note by George Parker Winship. [With a map.]
pp. xiv. 72. *Printed by Bruce Rogers for Small, Maynard*
& Co.: Boston, 1920. 8°. Cup.510.pc.15.

COLE (TIMOTHY)
—— Considerations on Engraving. pp. 15. *W. E. Rudge:*
New York, 1921. 8°. C. 100. k. 11.

SLATER (JOHN ROTHWELL)
—— Printing and the Renaissance: a paper, *etc.* pp. 35.
W. E. Rudge: New York, 1921. 8°. C. 100. k. 10.

BEATTY (JOHN WESLEY)
—— The Relation of Art to Nature. pp. 71. *William*
Edwin Rudge: New York, 1922. 8°. 07806. fff. 22.

IRVING (WASHINGTON)
—— The Christmas Dinner. From "The Sketch Book".
pp. 29. *W. E. Rudge: New York,* 1923. 8°.
Cup. **510.** pc. **2.**

LAMB (CHARLES) [*Essays of Elia.*] [*Selections.*]
New Year's Eve. [From "The
Essays of Elia."] pp. 15. *W. E. Rudge:*
New York, 1923. 8°. Cup.510.pc.11.

BARRIE (*Sir* JAMES MATTHEW) *Bart.* [*Single Works.*]
—— George Meredith, 1909. pp. 13. *William Edwin Rudge:*
New York, 1924. 8°. Cup.510.pc.12

NEW YORK.—*Grolier Club.*
PLUNKETT (Edward John Moreton Drax) *18th Baron*
Dunsany. The Compromise of the King of the Golden
Isles. pp. 25. *New York,* 1924. 4°. C.98.gg.12.

QUINN (JOHN)
—— Complete Catalogue of the Library of John Quinn, sold
by auction [12 Nov. 1923–20 Mar. 1924], *etc.* [With
portraits and facsimiles.] 2 vol. pp. 1205. *Anderson*
Galleries: New York, 1924. 8°. 011904. aa. 44.

SIMSON (THEODORE SPICER) Men of Letters of the
British Isles. Portrait medallions from the life by
T. Spicer-Simson. [Twenty-nine plates.] With
critical essays by Stuart P. Sherman and a preface
by G. F. Hill. pp. 133. *W. E. Rudge:*
New York, 1924. 8°. 7757. k. 20.

ADAMS (ELBRIDGE L.)
—— Joseph Conrad: the Man. By E. L. Adams. A Burial in
Kent. By John Sheridan Zelie. Together with some biblio-
graphical notes. [With a portrait.] pp. 71. *William*
Edwin Rudge: New York, 1925. 8° Cup.510.pc.17.

KUYUMJIAN (DIKRĀN) *afterwards* ARLEN (MICHAEL)
—— [The Green Hat.] The Acting Version of the Green
Hat, *etc.* pp. 108. *George H. Doran Co.: New York,*
1925. 8°. Cup. **510.** pc. **1.**
Printed on green paper.

MOORE (THOMAS STURGE)
—— Roderigo of Bivar. pp. 51. *William Edwin Rudge:*
New York, 1925. 8°. Cup.510.pc.13.

SYMONS (ARTHUR) Studies on Modern Painters.
pp. 88. *W. E. Rudge: New York,* 1925. 8°.
7853. t. 17.

BATES (DAVID HOMER)
—— Lincoln Stories. Told by him in the Military Office in the War Department during the Civil War. Recorded by . . . D. H. Bates. [With a portrait.] pp. 64. *William Edwin Rudge: New York*, 1926. 8º. 9618. aa. 5.

CABELL (JAMES BRANCH)
—— The Music from behind the Moon. An epitome . . . With eight wood engravings by Leon Underwood, *etc.* pp. 54. *John Day Co.: New York*, 1926. 8º. Cup. 510. pc. 19.

CHURCHWARD (JAMES)
—— The Lost Continent of Mu, the motherland of man, *etc.* pp. 315. *W. E. Rudge: New York*, 1926. 8º. 07704. ccc. 29.

DRINKWATER (JOHN) *Poet.* Persephone. [A poem.] *W. E. Rudge : New York*, 1926. 8º. C. 98. e. 6.

MOORE (GEORGE) *Novelist.*
—— Peronnik the Fool. pp. 68. *William Edwin Rudge : New York*, 1926. 8º. Cup.510.pc.9.

NEW YORK.—*American Institute of Graphic Arts.*
—— Fifty Prints of the Year. Selected for exhibition by the American Institute of Graphic Arts, 1925–1926 (1926–1927). 2 pt. [*New York*, 1926, 27.] 8º. 7864. p. 46.

PARK (LAWRENCE) Gilbert Stuart: an illustrated descriptive list of his works. . . With an account of his life by John Hill Morgan and an appreciation by Royal Cortissoz. [With portraits.] 4 vol. pp. 982. pl. 606. *W. E. Rudge : New York*, 1926. 4º. L.R. 262. b. 8.

BINYON (ROBERT LAURENCE) *Keeper of Prints and Drawings British Museum.*
—— The Wonder Night. *William Edwin Rudge : New York*, 1927. 8º. [*Ariel Poets.*] Cup. 510. pc. 10/7. *One of an edition of twenty-seven copies.*

CHESTERTON (GILBERT KEITH)
—— Gloria in Profundis. *William Edwin Rudge : New York*, 1927. 8º. [*Ariel Poets.*] Cup. 510. pc. 10/1. *One of an edition of twenty-seven copies.*

CHICAGO.—*Caxton Club.*
—— Ancient Books and Modern Discoveries. By Frederic G. Kenyon. pp. 83. pl. 30. *Chicago; printed by Bruce Rogers at the Press of W. E. Rudge : Mount Vernon*, 1927. 4º. C. 98. gg. 8.

DE LA MARE (WALTER JOHN) [*Single Works.*]
—— Alone. *William Edwin Rudge : New York*, 1927. 8º. [*Ariel Poets.*] Cup. 510. pc. 10/8. *One of an edition of twenty-seven copies.*

ELIOT (THOMAS STEARNS)
—— Journey of the Magi. *William Edwin Rudge : New York*, 1927. 8º. [*Ariel Poets.*] Cup. 510. pc. 10/3. *One of an edition of twenty-seven copies.*

FORD (FORD MADOX) *pseud.* [i.e. JOSEPH LEOPOLD FORD HERMANN MADDOX HUEFFER.]
—— New Poems. pp. 38. *William Edwin Rudge : New York*, 1927. 8º. Cup. 510. pc. 16.

GIBSON (WILFRID WILSON)
—— The Early Whistler. *William Edwin Rudge : New York*, 1927. 8º. [*Ariel Poets.*] Cup. 510. pc. 10/4. *One of an edition of twenty-seven copies.*

HARDY (THOMAS) *O.M.*
—— Yuletide in a Younger World. *William Edwin Rudge : New York*, 1927. 8º. [*Ariel Poets.*] Cup. 510. pc. 10/5. *One of an edition of twenty-seven copies.*

NEW YORK.—*Armor and Arms Club.*
—— A Miscellany of Arms and Armor. (Papers.) Presented by fellow members of the Armor and Arms Club to Bashford Dean in honor of his sixtieth birthday. [With plates, including a portrait.] pp. ix. 109. *New York*, 1927. 4º. 7804. t. 11.

NEW YORK.—*Grolier Club.*
—— Champ Fleury. By Geofroy Tory. Translated . . . and annotated by George B. Ives. *New York: printed by William Edwin Rudge*, 1927. C. 98. gg. 13.
pp. xxiii, 208; illus. 32 cm. △

NEWBOLT (*Sir* HENRY JOHN)
—— The Linnet's Nest. *William Edwin Rudge : New York*, 1927. 8º. [*Ariel Poets.*] Cup. 510. pc. 10/6. *One of an edition of twenty-seven copies.*

SASSOON (SIEGFRIED LORAINE)
—— Nativity. *William Edwin Rudge : New York*, 1927. 8º. [*Ariel Poets.*] Cup. 510. pc. 10/2. *One of an edition of twenty-seven copies.*

CONRAD (JOSEPH)
[Tales of Unrest.]
—— The Sisters. (A story published in " Tales of Unrest.") With an introduction by Ford Madox Ford. pp. 69. *Crosby Gaige: New York*, 1928. 8º. Cup. 510. pc. 14.

DE LA MARE (WALTER JOHN) [*Single Works.*]
—— At First Sight. A novel. pp. 142. *Crosby Gaige: New York*, 1928. 8º. Cup. 510. pc. 3.

E., A.
—— Midsummer Eve. [Poems.] By A. E. [i.e. G. W. Russell.] *Crosby Gaige: New York*, 1928. 8º. Cup. 510. pc. 5.

MORLEY (CHRISTOPHER DARLINGTON)
—— Really, My Dear . . . A play in one act . . . with drawings by Johan Bull. pp. 28. *William Edwin Rudge: New York*, 1928. 8°. Cup. 510. pc. 14.

PARRISH (MORRIS LONGSTRETH)
—— A List (Supplementary List) of the Writings of Lewis Carroll—Charles L. Dodgson—in the Library at Dormy House, Pine Valley, New Jersey, collected by M. L. Parrish. [With a portrait and illustrations.] 2 pt. FEW MS. NOTES [by M. B. Forman]. *Privately printed:* [*Pine Valley ?*] 1928, 33. 8°. Cup.510.pc.8.
No. 62 of an edition of sixty-six copies.

STEVENSON (ROBERT LOUIS)
—— Monmouth. A tragedy . . . With an introduction and some notes by Charles Vale. pp. xi. 75. *W. E. Rudge: New York*, 1928. 8°. Cup. 510. pc. 6.

MORLEY (CHRISTOPHER DARLINGTON)
—— The Palette Knife . . . Illustrated by René Gockinga. *Chocorua Press: New York*, 1929. 8°. Cup. 510. pd. 10.

ALDINGTON (RICHARD)
—— Love and the Luxembourg. [A poem.] pp. 53. *Covici, Friede: New York*, 1930. 8°. Cup.510.pc.18.
Signed by the author and by the designer

CORNER.
—— From a Corner of the Housetop. [In verse.] pp. 66. *William Edwin Rudge: New York*, 1930. 8°. C. 102. a. 1.
One of a privately printed edition of twenty-five copies.

RUSKIN (JOHN) The King of the Golden River . . . With an introduction by Eugene A. Noble. Illustrations by Ferdinand Huszti Horvath. pp. 65. *Studio: London; W. E. Rudge: New York*, 1930. 8°. Cup.510.pc.7.

PENNELL (JOSEPH) Joseph Pennell. [Plates.] Introduction by Malcolm C. Salaman. pp. 12. pl. 12. *The Studio : London ; W. E. Rudge : New York*, 1931. obl. fol. [*Modern Masters of Etching.* no. 28.] L.R.281.a.1/28.

LAWRENCE afterwards **SHAW** (THOMAS EDWARD) [*Letters.*]
—— Letters from T. E. Shaw to Bruce Rogers. [Concerning T. E. Shaw's translation of Homer's Odyssey.] *Privately printed:* [*New York*, 1933.] 8°. 010920. bbb. 13.

MANN (THOMAS) *Novelist.*
[Rede und Antwort.]
—— Sleep, sweet sleep. Privately printed by Phyllis Baldwin Browne. [*Mount Vernon, N.Y.:*] *William E. Rudge's Sons*, 1934. Cup. 510. pc. 20.
pp. 10. 22 cm. △
A translation of "Süsser Schlaf", originally published in "Rede und Antwort". One of an edition of sixty copies.

RUGBY PRESS, Rugby

MARSH MARIGOLDS.
—— Marsh Marigolds. By the author of Primulas and pansies, *etc* [i.e. Norman R. Gale.] [Poems.] *George E. Over: Rugby*, 1888. 8°. Cup.510.ata.9.
One of an edition of sixty copies. Author's presentation copy.

ANEMONES.
—— Anemones. A collection of simple songs from Unleavened Bread, Primulas and Pansies, Marsh Marigolds, with fresh flowers from the author's garden. [By Norman R. Gale.] *George E. Over: Rugby*, 1889. 8°. Cup.510.ata.10.
One of an edition of sixty copies.

SAYLE (CHARLES)
—— Erotidia. [Poems.] pp. xii. 99. *G. E. Over: Rugby*, 1889. 8°. 011653. e. 70.

CRICKET SONGS.
—— Cricket Songs, and other Trifling Verses penned by one of the authors of "Thistledown" [i.e. Norman R. Gale]. pp. 55. *George E. Over: Rugby*, 1890. 8°. Cup.510.ata.2.
One of an edition of eighty copies.

RUSTICUS, *pseud.* [NORMAN ROWLAND GALE.]
—— Thistledown. A set of six essays. By Rusticus and a friend of his. pp. 133. *George E. Over: Rugby*, 1890. 8°. Cup. 510. ata. 1.
One of an edition of forty copies.

GALE (NORMAN ROWLAND)
—— The Candid Cuckoo. [Verses.] pp. 54. *Norman Gale: Old Bilton*, 1891. 8°. 11659. bb. 86.
One of an edition of one hundred copies.

GORILLAS.
—— Gorillas. [A poem. By Norman R. Gale.] *George E. Over: Rugby*, [1891.] 12°. Cup.510.ata.3.
One of an edition of sixty copies.

RADFORD (DOLLIE) A Light Load. [Poems.] pp. xi. 64. *E. Mathews: London*, 1891. 12°. 11653. l. 47

REDCHEEK, *Prince.*
—— Prince Redcheek. [A tale. By Norman R. Gale.] pp. 16. *G. E. Over: [Rugby*, 1891.] 12°. Cup.510.ata.4.
One of an edition of fifty copies.

VIOLETS. Here be blue and white Violets from the garden wherein grew Meadowsweet. [Poems.] L. P. *G. E. Over: Rugby*, [1891.] 8°. 11653. o. 47.
Only 25 copies printed on large paper.

GALE (NORMAN ROWLAND)
—— A Country Muse. [Poems.] pp. 109. *D. Nutt: London*, 1892. 12°. 11652. d. 37.

GALE (NORMAN R.) A June Romance. pp. 107. *G. E. Over: Rugby*, [1892.] 12°. 012634. f. 98.

GALE (NORMAN ROWLAND)

—— [Another copy.] A June Romance. *Rugby*, 1892. 8°.
Cup.510.ata.5.
In the original box as issued, with a letter from the author inserted.

LOVE.

—— Love's memorial. [By Theodore Wratislaw.] *Rugby: Geo. E. Over, printer, the Rugby Press*, 1892.
11651. g. 47.

pp. 60. 20 cm. △

Poems. No. 22 of an edition of thirty-five copies.

VERSES.

—— Some verses. By the author of Love's memorial [i.e. Theodore Wratislaw]. *Rugby: printed at the Rugby Press by George E. Over*, 1892. 11653. e. 48.

pp. 21. 21 cm. △

DE GRUCHY (AUGUSTA CHAMBERS DE)

—— Under the hawthorn, and other verse. *London: Elkin Mathews & John Lane*, 1893. K.T.C. 8. a. 11.

pp. 83 [82]. 22 cm. △

No. 28 of an edition of thirty copies printed on Japanese vellum.

FELLOWSHIP.

—— A Fellowship in Song. [By] Alfred Hayes, Richard Le Gallienne, Norman Gale. [Poems.] 3 pt. *George E. Over: Rugby; Elkin Mathews & John Lane: London*, 1893. 12°. Cup.510.ata.6.
In the original box, as issued.

HAZLITT (WILLIAM) *the Elder.*

—— Liber Amoris . . . With an introduction by R. Le Gallienne. pp. xciii. 182. *E. Mathews & J. Lane: London*, 1893. 8°. 12355. r. 21.

WRATISLAW (THEODORE WILLIAM GRAF)

—— Caprices. Poems. *London: Gay & Bird*, 1893.
Cup. 403. tt. 10.

pp. 48. 19 cm. △

No. 1 of an edition of one hundred copies. A presentation copy to Charles Kains-Jackson from the author. MS. notes. With an MS. letter pasted in before the back cover.

WRATISLAW (THEODORE WILLIAM GRAF)

—— [Another copy.] Caprices, *etc.* 1893. 011652. ee. 2.
△

No. 7 of an edition of twenty copies printed on vellum.

WRATISLAW (THEODORE WILLIAM GRAF)

—— Caprices. Poems. pp. 48. *Gay & Bird: London*, 1893. 8°. 11658. aa. 75.
No. 29 of an edition of 100 copies. A different issue from the preceding, containing " Paradox " and " At Midnight " on pp. 31 and 32 in place of " To a Sicilian Boy " and " L'Eternel Féminin."

GALE (NORMAN ROWLAND) A June Romance. **L. P.** pp. 107. *G. E. Over: Rugby*, 1894. 12°.
Cup.510.ata.8.

GALE (NORMAN ROWLAND) and **LEATHER** (ROBINSON KAY)

—— On Two Strings. [In verse.] pp. 71. *Privately printed by G. E. Over: Rugby*, 1894. 8°. Cup. 510. ata. 7.

WRATISLAW (THEODORE WILLIAM GRAF)

The Pity of Love. A tragedy [in one act and in verse]. pp. 43. *Swan Sonnenschein & Co.: London*, 1895. 8°.
11781. cc. 58.

CLARE (JOHN) *Poet.* [*Selections.*]

—— Poems . . . Selected and introduced by Norman Gale . . . With a bibliography by C. Ernest Smith. pp. xliv. 156. *G. E. Over: Rugby*, 1901. 8°.
011649. ff. 74.

RUSSELL (T. C.), San Francisco

MAC GOWAN (EDWARD) *of San Francisco.*

—— Narrative of E. McGowan, including a full account of the author's adventures and perils while persecuted by the San Francisco Vigilance Committee of 1856; together with a with a report of his trial . . . Reprinted . . . from the original edition . . . 1857, *etc.* pp. 6. 240. *T. C. Russell: San Francisco*, 1917. 8°. 10884. bb. 3.

MAURELLE (FRANCISCO ANTONIO)

—— Voyage of the Sonora in the Second Bucareli Expedition . . . The Journal . . . Translated by the Hon. Daines Barrington . . . Reprinted line for line . . . from Barrington's Miscellanies, 1781. With concise notes . . . by Thomas C. Russell, *etc.* pp. xii. 120. *T. C. Russell: San Francisco*, 1920. 4°. 10497. g. 21.

SAINT ALBERT'S PRESS, Aylesford, Kent

THOMAS [MORE], *Saint, Lord High Chancellor of England.*

—— Of Pilgrimage. Being chapter the third of The Dialogue concerning Tyndale. [With portraits.] *Carmelite Fathers at St. Albert's Press: Aylesford*, 1955. 8°.
The colophon bears the date 1956. Cup.510.bes.1.

FARJEON (ELEANOR)

—— Elizabeth Myers. With a sonnet by Sara Jackson. [With a portrait.] pp. 22. *St. Albert's Press: Aylesford*, 1957. 8°. Cup. 510. bes. 2.
No. 20 of an edition of one hundred copies.

LITURGIES.—*Latin Rite.*—*Ceremonials.*—III. *Carmelite Nuns.*

—— Ceremoniale . . . Sororum Carmelitarum . . . pro senescentibus et infirmis. (Ceremonial . . . of the Carmelite Sisters . . . for the Aged and Infirm.) *Llandeilo: St. Albert's Press*, 1960. Cup. 510. bes. 4.

pp. 47. 23 cm. △

Latin & English.

DELTEIL (JOSEPH) [*Appendix.*]

—— Joseph Delteil. Essays in tribute. By Eugène Louis Julien, Jacques Madaule, Henry Miller, Henry de Montherlant, Fr. Brocard Sewell and F. J. Temple. (Reprinted from The Aylesford Review, Volume IV, Number 7.) [Edited by Brocard Sewell.] *Eng. & Fr.* pp. 39. *St. Albert's Press: [Aylesford,]* 1962. 8°. Cup. 510. bes. 3.

RUSSELL (IRWIN PETER)
—— Visions and ruins, *etc.* *Aylesford: Saint Albert's Press,* 1964. Cup. **501**. k. **36**.

pp. 27. 25 cm. △

Poems. No. 19 of an edition of fifty copies, signed by the author. With a list of Peter Russell's publications and a prospectus for " The golden chain " inserted.

SAINT ANTHONY PRESS, Leicester

BAYLDON (OLIVER)
—— Morning. A poem. *St. Anthony Press: Leicester,* [1959.] 8°. Cup. **510**. bbg. **2**.

SEATON (RAY)
—— Russia . . . With illustrations by Rigby Graham. pp. 7. *St. Anthony Press: Leicester,* 1959. 8°.
Cup. **510**. bbg. **1**.

BERGSTROM (HILDEFRED INVENTIO)
—— My Island Star. *St. Anthony Press: Leicester,* 1960. 8°.
Cup. **510**. bbg. **1**.

One of an edition of fifty copies.

HEALEY (CHARLES PATRICK)
—— Solma-ri . . . Illustration by Julius Stafford-Baker. [Verses.] *St. Anthony Press: Leicester,* [1960.] 8°.
Cup. **510**. bbg. **3**.

GARCÍA LORCA (FEDERICO)
—— Llanto por Ignacio Sánchez Mejías. Translated . . . by A. L. Lloyd. (Rigby Graham . . . did the illustrations.) *Leicester: St. Anthony Press,* 1961. Cup. **510**. bbg. **6**.

Pages not numbered. 27 cm. △

English. On wrapper: " Federico Garcia Lorca's Lament of the death of a bullfighter ". One of an edition of one hundred copies, not for sale.

BEDFORD (PATRICK EDWARD LLOYD)
—— Sebastien Melmoth, and other poems. *Leicester: St Anthony Private Press,* [1963 ?] Cup. **510**. bbg. **5**.

Pages not numbered ; illus. 21 cm. △

ST. DOMINIC'S PRESS, London; Ditchling, Sussex

COOMARASWAMY, afterwards. **MAIRET** (ETHEL MARY PARTRIDGE)
—— A Book on Vegetable Dyes. pp. 153. *Douglas Pepler: London,* 1916. 8°. Cup. **510**. bed. **21**.

GILL (ARTHUR ERIC ROWTON)
—— Serving at Mass: being instructions and directions for laymen as to the manner of serving at Low Mass. (Compiled chiefly from " Ceremonial according to the Roman Rite," by Joseph Baldeschi.) pp. 35. *Douglas Pepler: Ditchling,* 1916. 16°. Cup. **510**. bed. **32**.

JOHNSTON (PRISCILLA) *Author of " The Mill Book."* The Mill Book. [With woodcuts.] pp. 21. *Douglas Pepler: Hammersmith & Ditchling,* 1915. 16°. Cup. **510**. bed. **16**.

P., H. D. C. Concerning Dragons: a rhyme by H. D. C. P[epler]. Emblems by A. E. R. G[ill]. *Douglas Pepler: Ditchling,* 1916. 16°. Cup. **510**. bed. **20**.

PERIODICAL PUBLICATIONS.—*Ditchling.*
—— The Game. An occasional magazine. no. 1. Oct. 1916. *Ditchling,* 1916. 19 cm. P.P. **3558**. p.
△

STEVENSON (MATTHEW)
—— An Elegy upon Old Freeman, us'd hardly by the Committee, for lying in the Cathedral, and in church porches, praying the Common-Prayer by heart, *etc.* *Everard Meynell: London,* 1916. 8°. Cup. **510**. bed. **81**.

A., F.
—— Christ. (A Christian parody of Swinburne's Hertha.) [The foreword signed : F. A. i.e. Faith Ashford.] pp. 7. *Printed by Douglas Pepler: Ditchling,* [1918.] 8°.
Cup. **510**. bed. **75**.

ASHFORD (FAITH)
—— Poor Man's Pence. [Poems.] pp. 84. *Douglas Pepler: Ditchling,* 1917. 16°. Cup. **510**. bed. **2**.

P., H. D. C.
—— God and the Dragon. Rhymes by H. D. C. P[epler]. Engravings by A. E. R. G[ill]. pp. 44. *Douglas Pepler: Ditchling,* 1917. 16°. Cup. **510**. bed. **22**.

STATIONS OF THE CROSS. The Way of the Cross: being devotions on the progress of our Lord Jesus Christ from the Judgment Hall to Calvary as traditionally venerated by the Catholic Church. [With illustrations.] *Douglas Pepler: Ditchling,* 1917. 8°.
Cup. **510**. bed. **31**.

GILL (ARTHUR ERIC ROWTON) [*Appendix.*]
—— Catalogue of Drawings and Engravings by Eric Gill. Alpine Club Gallery, 5th to 14th May, A.D. 1918. [With a foreword signed D.P., i.e. Douglas Pepler.] pp. 11. *Douglas Pepler: Ditchling,* [1918.] 8°. Cup. **510**. bed. **5**.

GREEN (ARTHUR ROMNEY)
—— Woodwork in principle and practice. *Ditchling: Douglas Pepler,* 1918. Cup. **510**. bed. **11**.

vol. 1.: pp. xvi, 110; illus. 20 cm. △
No more published.

M., P. A.
—— January 14th . . . Press Supper: 2nd. anniversary of the foundation of the Ditchling Press. The song of the evening. (Written and sung by P. A. M. [i.e. Philippe A. Mairet.]) [1918.] 8°. Cup. **510**. bed. **4**.

MAIRET (PHILIPPE AUGUSTE) and **COOMARASWAMY**, afterwards **MAIRET** (ETHEL MARY PARTRIDGE)
—— Crafts and Obedience. pp. 8. *Ditchling,* 1918. 4°. An Essay on *Douglas Pepler:* Cup. **510**. bed. **19**.

SCOTT (Margaret) *Mrs.*
—— Happiness and other essays. pp. 41.   *Printed for the Author by Douglas Pepler: Ditchling,* 1918. 12º.
Cup. **510.** bed. **59.**

THOMPSON (Francis) *Poet.*
—— The Mistress of Vision . . . Together with a commentary by the Rev. John O'Connor . . . and with a preface by Father Vincent McNabb. pp. 23.   *Douglas Pepler: Ditchling,* 1918. 4º.   Cup. **510.** bed. **45.**

ASHFORD (Faith)
—— A Soul Cake . . . Verses. pp. 53.   *Douglas Pepler: Ditchling,* 1919. 8º.   Cup.510.bed.33.

P., H. D. C. Nisi Dominus . . . Rimes : H. D. C. P[epler]. Engravings : E. P. J. G. pp. 56.
S. Dominic's Press: Ditchling, 1919. 8º.
Cup.510.bed.23.

WELFARE HANDBOOK.
—— Welfare handbook. no. 2–10.   *Ditchling: S. Dominic's Press,* 1919–23. 14–16 cm.   Cup. **510.** bed. **6.**
△

COOMARASWAMY (Ananda Kentish)
—— Three Poems . . . With a woodcut by Eric Gill. pp. 6. *S. Dominic's Press: Ditchling,* 1920. 4º. Cup.510.bed.46.

MARY, *the Blessed Virgin.*
—— Songs to our Lady of Silence. [By Mary Elise Woellwarth.] *Ditchling: S. Dominic's Press,* 1920.
Cup. **510.** bed. **34.**
pp. 71; illus. 21 cm.   △

STATIONS OF THE CROSS.
—— The Way of the Cross: being devotions on the progress of Our Lord Jesus Christ from the Judgment Hall to Calvary, *etc.* [With woodcuts.] pp. 33.   *St. Dominics Press: Ditchling,* 1920. 16º.   **03456.** df. **57.**

GEORGE, *Saint and Martyr.*
—— King George and the Turkish Knight. Old Sussex play collected by Osobel Horn. pp. 16.   *S. Dominic's Press: Ditchling,* 1921. 8º.   Cup. **510.** bed. **35.**

GILL (Arthur Eric Rowton)
—— Songs without Clothes: being a dissertation on the Song of Solomon, and such-like songs, *etc.* pp. 46. *S. Dominic's Press: Ditchling,* 1921. 8º.   Cup. **510.** bed. **8.**

MARY, *the Blessed Virgin.*
—— Songs to Our Lady of Silence. [By M. E. Woellwarth.] pp. 55. *S. Dominic's Press: Ditchling,* 1921. 8º.
Cup. **510.** bed. **67.**

CORNFORD (Frances Crofts) Autumn Midnight. [Poems.] pp. 23. *Poetry Bookshop: London,* 1923. 8º.
Cup.510.bed.9.

DAISY.
—— Daisy and Marguerite. [Two tales. By Cyril and Mr Cyril Andrews.] pp. 22. [*S. Dominic's Press*]: *Ditchlin* 1923. 8º.   Cup.510.bed.1
No. 50 of an edition of sixty copies.

GILL (Arthur Eric Rowton)
—— Sculpture. An essay . . . With a preface about God. pp. 41. *Saint Dominic's Press: Ditchling,* [1923.] 16º.
Cup. **510.** bed. **10.**

GILL (Arthur Eric Rowton) and **PEPLER** (Hilary Douglas Clark)
—— In Petra. [Poems.] Being a sequel to ' Nisi Dominus', *etc.* pp. vii. 26.   *St. Dominic's Press: Ditchling,* 1923. 16º.   Cup. **510.** bed. **13.**

HERNAMAN (Irene) Child Mediums: being an exposure...with an introduction by G. K. Chesterton. pp. 38. *S. Dominic's Press: Ditchling,* 1923. 8º.
Cup.510.bed.12.

LITURGIES.—*Latin Rite.*—*Hours.*—III. *Dominicans.* Horae Beatae Virginis Mariae juxta ritum Sacri ordinis praedicatorum. [With woodcuts.] pp. 73. *Typographia S. Dominici: Ditchling,* 1923. 4º.
Cup.510.bed.41.

ASHFORD (Faith)
—— Things Unseen. A book of verse. pp. 28.
S. Dominic's Press: Ditchling, 1924. 8º. Cup.510.bed.

CHRISTMAS PLAY.
—— A Christmas Play. [By H. D. C. Pepler.] pp. 15. [*Saint Dominic's Press :*] *Ditchling,* [1924.] 16º.
Cup. **510.** bed. **77.**

MARY, *the Blessed Virgin.* A Child's Rosary Book: being the fifteen mysteries of the Most Holy Rosary of the Blessed Virgin Mary, *etc.* pp. 37.
S. Dominic's Press: Ditchling, 1924. 8º. Cup.510.bed.51.

P., H.
—— Libellus Lapidum . . . The first part of a collection of verses and wood-engravings made by H. P. and D. J. [i.e. the verses by H. D. C. Pepler, the engravings by David Jones], *etc.* pp. 24.   *S. Dominic's Press: Ditchling & London,* 1924. 8º.   Cup. **510.** bed. **55.**

CAROL BOOK.
—— The Common Carol Book. A collection of Christmas and Easter hymns. [With the airs.] pp. 75.   *S. Dominic's Press: Ditchling,* 1926. 8º.   Cup. **510.** bed. **66.**

DITCHLING.
—— Guide book of Ditchling. Illustrated with wood-cuts.
pp. 16. *Ditchling*, 1926. 8°. Cup. 510. bed. 82.

DRESSMAKER.
—— The Dressmaker and Milkmaid. [Two poems by H. D. C. Pepler. With an engraving by A. E. R. Gill.]
S. Dominic's Press: Ditchling, [1926?] 16°.
Cup. 510. bed. 74.

EPHEMERIDES.
—— St. Thomas Aquinas Calendar. *Ditchling: St. Dominic's Press*, 1926. 1866. c. 16.
illus. 28 × 38 cm. △

LAW.
—— The Law the Lawyers know about. [Poems originally published in " God and the Dragon " by H. D. C. Pepler. With wood engravings, mostly by A. E. R. Gill.]
S. Dominic's Press: Ditchling, [1926?] 16°.
Cup. 510. bed. 71.

PERTINENT. Pertinent & Impertinent. An assortment of verse. [By the author of " Nisi Dominus." With woodcuts.] pp. 69. *St. Dominic's Press: Ditchling*, 1926. 8°. Cup.510.bed.56.

BAKER (Augustine)
—— A Spirituall Life in a Secular State : being an addition to The Abridgment of a Spirituall Life . . . Taken from a manuscript at St. Gregory's Abbey, Downside, *etc.*
pp. 6. *St. Dominic's Press: Ditchling*, 1927. 16°.
Cup.510.bed.54.

BATEMAN (Gerald Cooper) A Countryman's Calendar. Sayings for the months. Compiled by G. C. Bateman. pp. 31. *St. Dominic's Press: Ditchling*, 1927. 8°. Cup.510.bed.3.

JESUS CHRIST. The Jesus Psalter. [Here attributed to Richard Whitford.] *St. Dominic's Press: Hassocks*, 1927. 16°. Cup.510.bed.62,

LITURGIES.—*Latin Rite.—Missals.—*I. *Abridgments and Extracts.* [*English.*] An English Mass Book, *etc.* pp. 40. *St. Dominic's Press: Ditchling*, 1927. 16°. Cup.510.bed.63.

MARY, *the Blessed Virgin.* A Simple Rosary Book. *St. Dominic's Press:* [*Ditchling,*] 1927. 16°. Cup. 510.bed.64.

SAINT DOMINIC'S PRESS,
—— Books, Pamphlets, Altar Cards, Rhyme Sheets, Carol Books. Book Plates, &c. [A catalogue, compiled by H. D. C. Pepler.] pp. 14. *St. Dominic's Press: Ditchling Common*, 1927. 8°. Cup. 510. bed. 78.

SHEWRING (Walter Hayward)
—— The Water Meads. Verses. pp. 15. *S. Dominic's Press: Ditchling*, 1927. 4°. Cup.510.bed.14.
No. 81 of an edition of one hundred copies.

ASPIDISTRAS.
—— Aspidistras and Parlers. [Two poems.] By the author of Concerning Dragons [i.e. H. D. C. Pepler]. *S. Dominic's Press: Ditchling*, 1928. 16°. Cup. 510. bed. 72.

CHRISTMAS GIFTS.
—— Christmas Gifts. [Verses.] By the author of Concerning Dragons [i.e. H. D. C. Pepler]. *S. Dominic's Press: Ditchling*, 1928. 16°. Cup. 510. bed. 73.

LEACH (Bernard)
—— A Potter's Outlook. pp. 25–39. *New Handworkers' Gallery:* [*London,*] 1928. 8°. *Handworkers' Pamphlets.* no. 3. Cup. 510. bed. 76.

LONDON.—III. *Architectural Association.—School of Architecture.*
—— Number Thirty-Five. March 1928—Feb. 1930. *London*, 1928–30. 4°. P.P. 1667. db.

P., H. D. C.
—— Concerning Dragons. A rhyme by H. D. C. P[epler], *etc.* *S. Dominic's Press: Ditchling*, 1928. 16°. Cup. 510. bed. 25.

PILATUS (Pontius)
—— Pilate. A Passion Play. pp. 47. *St. Dominic's Press: Ditchling*, 1928. 16°. Cup. 510. bed. 52.

SWINSTEAD (Margaret Honor)
—— The Affectionate Parent's Gift. A collection of prose and verse made . . . from old books for children. pp. 94. *S. Dominic's Press: Ditchling*, 1928. 8°. Cup. 510. bed. 70.

THOMAS [More] *Saint, Lord High Chancellor of England.* [*Miscellaneous Works.*]
—— The XII Propertees or Condicyons of a Lover, by Johan Picus Erle of Myrandula . . . expressed in balade [or rather, originally written] by Sir Thomas More. ff. 14. *Saint Dominic's Press: Ditchling Common*, 1928. fol. Cup. 510. bed. 49.
Printed on one side of the leaf only.

WAUGH, afterwards HOBHOUSE (Rosa)
—— The diary of a story-maker. *Stanford le Hope: published at the Sign of the Willow;* [*Ditchling:*] *printed by hand at St. Dominic's Press*, 1928. 12805. g. 76.
2 pt. 19 cm. △
Pt. 2 bears the title " Two little tales for round about Christmas time ".

WAUGH, afterwards HOBHOUSE (Rosa)
—— The Man with the Leather Patch, and five other tales: being parts I, II & III of The Diary of a Story Maker. pp. 41. *Stanford le Hope*, 1928. 8°. 12812. k. 28.

HAEMMERLEIN (Thomas) *a Kempis.* [*Selections.*]

—— Meditations on Our Lady. [Selections from Johannes Mercator's " Quae de Beata Maria Virgine passim scripsit Thomas a Kempis ".] Translated by W. H. F. S., *etc.* pp. 41. *St. Dominic's Press: Ditchling*, 1929. fol.
4807. ff. 21.

No. 9 of 100 copies printed on hand-made paper.

P., H. D. C. Plays for Puppets. By H. D. C. P[epler]. *St. Dominic's Press: Ditchling*, 1929. 16°.
CuP.510.bed.27.

PEPLER (Hilary Douglas Clark)

—— Saint Dominic. Scenes from the life of the saint in the form of a play. pp. ix. 62. *St. Dominic's Press: Ditchling*, 1929. 16°. **Cup. 510. bed 26.**

SAINT DOMINIC'S PRESS.

—— Catalogue of Books, St. Dominic's Press, *etc.* [Compiled by Hilary D. C. Pepler.] *Ditchling*,1929. 16°.
Cup.510.bed.18.

STATIONS OF THE CROSS. Via Crucis. [In English. With woodcuts.] pp. 32.
Privately printed at St. Dominic's Press : Ditchling, 1929. 8°. **Cup.510.bed.65.**
With a metal crucifix attached.

THOMAS (More) *Saint, Lord High Chancellor of England.* [*Miscellaneous Works.*]

—— A Godly Meditation and two Prayers written in the Tower of London, *etc.* *St. Dominic's Press: Ditchling*, 1929. 16°. **Cup. 510. bed. 53.**

CHESTERTON (Gilbert Keith)

—— The Turkey and the Turk . . . [A dramatic poem.] Arranged and pictured by Thomas Derrick. **F.P.** [*St. Dominic's Press: Ditchling*,] 1930. 4°.
Cup.510.bed.40.
One of an edition of which 100 copies were published for sale.

EPHEMERIDES.

—— A Rosary Calendar. Engravings by David Jones. 1931. *St. Dominic's Press: Ditchling*, [1930.] 8°.
Cup. 510. bed. 58.

Printed on one side of the leaf only.

JOYCE (James Augustine Aloysius)

—— Ibsen's New Drama [" When We Dead Awaken "]. From " The Fortnightly Review", *etc.* pp. 36. *Ulysses Bookshop: London*, 1930. 8°. **Cup. 510. bed. 61.**
No. 10 of an edition of 40 copies printed for private circulation.

JOYCE (James Augustine Aloysius)

—— James Clarence Mangan. From St. Stephen's, Dublin, *etc. London: Ulysses Bookshop*, 1930.
Cup. 510. bed. 60.

pp. 15. 15 cm. △
No. 6 of an edition of forty copies printed by H. D. C. Pepler for private circulation.

MAC NABB (Vincent Joseph)

—— God's Book and other Poems. [With illustrations, and a portrait.] pp. 39. *St. Dominic's Press: Ditchling*, 1930. 8°. **Cup. 510. bed. 24.**

PEPLER (Hilary Douglas Clark)

—— Le Bœuf et l'âne, et deux autres pièces pour marionnettes. (Le Bœuf et l'âne. Traduction de " Plays for Puppets ", de H. D. Pepler, par Henri Gibon.—La Naissance . . . Par Alexis Deitz.—Orlando Furioso. Tragédie burlesque . . . par Adrien van der Horst . . . Traduction par Paul Jeanne.) pp. 72. *S. Dominic's Press: Ditchling*, 1930. 4°. **Cup. 510. bed. 43.**

SARGENT (Daniel) *Roman Catholic Writer.*

—— My Account of the Flood. By Noah's brother-in-law. With authentic illustrations as lately discovered and newly transcribed [or rather written] by D. Sargent. *St. Dominic's Press: Ditchling*, 1930. 4°.
Cup. 510. bed. 44.

SHEWRING (Walter Hayward) Hermia, and some other poems. pp. 32. *St. Dominic's Press : Ditchling*, 1930. 8°. **Cup.510.bed.15.**

SMITH (Judith Florence)

—— The Mary Calendar . . . Engravings by M. Dudley Short. pp. 49. *St. Dominic's Press: Ditchling*, 1930. 8°.
Cup. 510. bed. 30.

COLLIER (John) *Novelist.*

—— Gemini. Poems. pp. 33. *Ulysses Press: London*, 1931. 8°. **Cup.510.bed.48.**

DOUGLAS (Alice Margaret)

—— Margaret Douglas. A selection from her writings. Together with appreciations of her life and work by Charlotte Balfour . . . Nesta Sawyer, *etc.* [With a portrait and illustrations by Sylvia Packard.] pp. 283. *Privately printed : Ditchling Common*, 1931. 8°.
012273. d. 14.

GOODMAN (Richard)

—— Poems. *St. Dominic's Press: Ditchling*, 1931. 4°.
11642. ccc. 52.

No. 56 of an edition of 100 copies.

GREEN (F. H.) *Writer on Clocks.* Old English Clocks. Being a collector's observations on some seventeenth century clocks...Together with over fifty plates taken from photographs of the finest specimens. pp. 89. *St. Dominic's Press : Ditchling*, 1931. 4°.
Printed for the author. **Cup.510.bed.47.**

MEYERSTEIN (Edward Harry William) Beauty and the Beast. A poem. pp. 12. *St. Dominic's Press : Ditchling*, 1931. 8°.
No. 7 of an edition of 100 *copies.* **Cup.510.bed.37.**

P., H. D. C.

—— The Four Minstrels of Bremen and " The Two Robbers," being more plays for puppets by H. D. C. P. [i.e. H. D. C. Pepler.] (Second impression.) pp. 47. *St. Dominic's Press: Ditchling*, [1932.] 8°. **Cup.510.bed.57.**

PEPLER (Hilary Douglas Clark)

—— Mimes Sacred & Profane. pp. 139. *Saint Dominic's Press: Hassocks*, 1932. 8°. Cup.510.bed.42.

SARGENT (Daniel) *Roman Catholic Writer.*

—— The Song of the Three Children. [A poem.] pp. 14. *South Natick; Ditchling* printed, 1932. 8°. Cup.510.bed.39.

THOMAS [More] *Saint. Lord High Chancellor of England.* [*Miscellaneous Works.*]

—— The XII Propertees or Condicyons of a Lover. By Johan Picus, Erle of Myrandula . . . Expressed in balade by Sir T. More, *etc.* ff. 14. *St. Dominic's Press: Ditchling Common*, 1933. 8°. Cup.510.bed.69. *Printed on one side of the leaf only.*

MAC NABB (Vincent Joseph)

—— Geoffrey Chaucer. A study in genius and ethics. *Pepler & Sewell: Ditchling & London*, 1934. 8°. [*Stones from the Brook.* no. 1.] Cup. 510. bed. 7/1.

PEPLER (Hilary Douglas Clerk)

—— The hand press. An essay written and printed by hand for the Society of Typographic Arts, Chicago, by H. D. C. Pepler, printer, founder of St Dominic's Press. *Ditchling Common*, 1934. 11911. b. 25.

pp. 79; illus. 24 cm. △

PEPYS (Samuel) [*Diary.—Abridgements and Extracts.*]

—— Christmas Day with Mr. Pepys. Extracts, from the Braybrooke—1851—edition of the diary, *etc.* *St. Dominic's Press : Ditchling*, [1934.] 16°. Cup.510.bed.28.

BONIFACE (Eleanor)

—— Welsh ways & days. *Ditchling: Pepler & Sewell*, 1935 [1934]. Cup. 510. bed. 38.

pp. 10; illus. 19 cm. △

JOHN [Fisher], *Saint, Cardinal, Bishop of Rochester.*

—— Sermon against Luther . . . Reprinted from the first edition. pp. 14. *Pepler & Sewell: Ditchling ; E. Walters: London*, 1935. 8°. Cup.510.bed.50.

KELLY (Bernard William)

—— The Mind and Poetry of Gerard Manley Hopkins, S.J. *Pepler & Sewell: Ditchling & London*, 1935. 8°. [*Stones from the Brook.* no. 2.] Cup.510.bed.7/2.

ROPE (Henry Edward George)

—— Pugin. pp. 42. *Pepler & Sewell: Ditchling.* 1935. 8°. Cup.510.bed.29.

MARITAIN (Raïssa)

—— The Prince of This World. Done into English by Gerald B. Phelan, *etc.* pp. 16. *St. Dominic's Press: Ditchling*, 1936. 8°. Cup.510.bed.36.

DITCHLING PRESS.

—— Christmas, 1939. A list of Christmas cards published by the Ditchling Press, *etc.* *Ditchling*, 1939. 8°. Cup. 510. bed. 79.

CAMMELL (Charles Richard)

—— XXI Poems. pp. 28. *Poseidon Press: Edinburgh*, 1943. 8°. 11656. d. 63.

MARY DOMINIC, *Sister, O.P.*

—— A Rosary Chain. pp. 40. *Blackfriars Publications: Oxford*, [1947.] 8°. Cup. 510. bed. 68.

WAUGH, afterwards **HOBHOUSE** (Rosa)

—— Out of the Years. Poems. [With a portrait.] pp. 77. *Ditchling Press: Ditchling*, [1953.] 8°. 11659. c. 19.

SAINT MARY'S ABBEY, Haslemere

CHRISTMAS CRIB.

—— How to make my own Christmas Crib. By a Benedictine of Haslemere. pp. 1–9, ff. 10–19. *A. R. Mowbray & Co.: London*, [1965.] 8°. Cup. 510. cuz. 1.

SAINT NICOLAS PRESS, Cambridge

VERSTEGAN (Richard) *the Elder.*

—— The Original Story of the Pied Piper of Hamelin . . . being an extract from " A Restitution of Decayed Intelligence in Antiquities concerning the British Nation." *Saint Nicolas Press: Cambridge*, 1949. 8°. Cup.510.aac.1.

CORBET (Richard) successively *Bishop of Oxford* and *of Norwich.*

—— Three Poems by Richard Corbet. *St. Nicolas Press: Cambridge*, 1951. 8°. Cup.510.aac.2.

WELLESLEY (Arthur) *Duke of Wellington.*

—— The Conversations of the First Duke of Wellington with George William Chad. Edited by the 7th Duke of Wellington. [With a portrait.] pp. 23. *Saint Nicolas Press: Cambridge*, 1956. 8°. Cup. 510. aac. 4.

CORNFORD (Frances Crofts)

—— On a Calm Shore. Poems . . . Designs by Christopher Cornford. pp. 95. *Printed by hand at the Saint Nicolas Press: Cambridge*, [1960.] 8°. Cup. 510. aac. 3. *One of a limited edition of 150 copies.*

SAINT WILLIAM HAND PRESS, Norwich

MONCK (WALTER NUGENT)

—— The interlude of holly and ivy, made by Nugent Monck from fifteenth century sources. *Norwich: Saint William Hand-Press*, 1913. Cup. **510**. agk. **1**.

pp. 11. 23 cm. △

MONCK (WALTER NUGENT) and **KINDER** (MARTIN)

—— Aucassin and Nicolette, a play from the 12th century French song-story. *Norwich: Saint William Press*, 1913. Cup. **503**. n. **37**.

pp. 40. 22 cm. △

SALAMANDER PRESS, Edinburgh

GLEN (MICHAEL HAMISH)

—— Once upon a Thyme . . . With illustrations by Isobel and Rosemary Johnstone. pp. 32. *Salamander Press: Edinburgh*, 1962. 8º. Cup. **510**. cok. **2**.

YOUNG (VERONICA HAZEL)

—— Tomorrow and other poems . . . with illustrations by Isobel Johnstone. pp. 32. *Salamander Press: Edinburgh*, 1964. 8º. Cup. **510**. cok. **1**.

FINLAY (IAN HAMILTON)

—— Cythera. *Wild Hawthorn Press:* [*Edinburgh*,] 1965. 4º. Cup. **510**. cop. **2**.

SAMSON PRESS, Warlingham; Woodstock

GRIERSON (HERBERT JOHN CLIFFORD)

—— The Flute. With other translations and a poem by H. J. C. Grierson. pp. 36. *Samson Press: Warlingham*, 1931. 8º. **11644**. l. **24**.

MUIR (WILLA) 5 Songs from the Auvergrat, done into modern Scots by Willa Muir. *Samson Press: Warlingham*, 1931. 8º. **11640**. ee. **29**.

No. 12 of an edition of 100 copies.

RAMSAY (ANNA AUGUSTA WHITTALL) The Wee Apollo. Twelve pre-Burnsian Scottish songs. Collected and introduced by A. A. W. Ramsay. *J. M. Shelmerdine: Warlingham*, 1931. 8º. ·*No. 28 of an issue of 100 copies.* **11601**. l. **11**.

MUIR (EDWIN)

—— Six Poems, etc. pp. 22. *Samson Press: Warlingham*, 1932. 8º. **11640**. i. **8**.

NIGHT.

—— Nicht at Eenie. The bairns' Parnassus. With wood-engravings by Iain Macnab. pp. 37. *Samson Press: Warlingham*, 1932. 8º. **11645**. i. **28**. *With musical notes.*

WEST (*Hon.* VICTORIA MARY SACKVILLE) afterwards **NICOLSON** (*Hon.* VICTORIA MARY)

—— Sissinghurst. pp. 5. *Samson Press: Warlingham*, 1933. 4º. **11643**. n. **58**.

BURNS (ROBERT) *the Poet.* [*Single Poems.*]

—— Tam o' Shanter . . . with wood-engravings by Iain Macnab. pp. 13. *Samson Press: Warlingham*, 1934. 8º. **11654**. b. **52**.

GEORGE (DANIEL) *pseud.* [i.e. DANIEL GEORGE BUNTER.]

—— Roughage. *Samson Press: Warlingham*, 1935. 8º. **11654**. b. **79**.

BOUTENS (PETRUS CORNELIS)

—— The Christ Child. A poem: translated from the Dutch . . . by H. J. C. Grierson with wood-engravings by Tom Chadwick. *Samson Press: Woodstock*, 1938. 8º. **11565**. cc. **43**.

SAMURAI PRESS, Cranleigh

GIBSON, afterwards **CHEYNE** (ELIZABETH)

Author of "The Evangel of Joy." From the Shadow : a book of poems. pp. 63. *Samurai Press: Cranleigh*, 1907. 8º. **11648**. i. **26**.

MONRO (HAROLD EDWARD)

—— Judas. [A poem.] pp. 31. *Samurai Press: Cranleigh*, 1907. 4º. Cup. **510**. bfd. **2**.

SABIN (ARTHUR KNOWLES)

The Wayfarers. pp. 34. *Samurai Press: Cranleigh*, 1907. 8º. Cup. **510**. bfd. **4**.

STOCKER (RICHARD DIMSDALE) Seership and Prophecy. pp. 31. *Samurai Press: Cranleigh, Surrey*, 1907. 8º. **12352**. r. **15**.

DRINKWATER (JOHN) *Poet.*

—— Lyrical and other poems. *Cranleigh: Samurai Press*, 1908. Cup. **510**. bfd. **5**.

pp. 56. 20 cm. △

ELIOT (NEVILL) Ideala and First Love, and some minor poems. pp. 51. *Samurai Press: Cranleigh*, 1908. 8º. **11649**. gg. **35**.

FICKE (ARTHUR DAVISON) The Earth Passion, Boundary, & other poems. pp. vii. 59. *Samurai Press: Cranleigh*, 1908. 4º. **11648**. g. **15**.

GIBSON, afterwards **CHEYNE** (ELIZABETH)

Author of " The Evangel of Joy."
The Day's Journey. [Poems.] pp. 76.
Samurai Press: Cranleigh, 1908. 8°. . **11648. i. 38.**

GIBSON, afterwards **CHEYNE** (ELIZABETH)

Author of " The Evangel of Joy."
A Pilgrim's Staff. [Poems.] pp. 61. *Samurai Press :*
Cranleigh, 1908. 8°. **11649. gg. 15.**

GUTHRIE (JAMES JOSHUA)
—— An Album of Drawings . . . With an introduction by
Daniel Phaër. pp. 23. *Samurai Press: Cranleigh,*
[1908.] 4°. **7857. v. 20.**

HILL (NORMAN) Lyrics by a Briton in Gallia.
pp. 63. *Samurai Press: Cranleigh*, 1908. 8°.
11647. ccc. 26.

MONTGOMERY (ALBERTA VICTORIA) The Rose
and the Fire. (Poems and chants.) pp. 35.
Samurai Press: Cranleigh, 1908. 4°. **Cup.510.bfd.7.**

RAWNSLEY (HARDWICKE DRUMMOND)
—— Milton tercentenary sermon preached in Peterborough
Cathedral. *Cranleigh: A. K. Sabin*, [1908].
Cup. 510. bfd. 1.
pp. 13. 23 cm. △
One of fifty hand-printed copies.

SABIN (ARTHUR KNOWLES)

Dante and Beatrice. pp. 40.
Samurai Press: Cranleigh, 1908. 8°. **Cup.510.bfd.6.**

THURLOCKE (A. R.) *pseud.* [i.e. ARTHUR LOCKE.]

The Rustic Choir, and other
poems. pp. 54. *Samurai Press: Cranleigh*, 1908. 8°.
Cup.510.bfd.3.

SANDFORD, (Christopher), London

MUSAEUS, *the Grammarian.* [English.]
—— Hero and Leander. Translated . . . by F. L. Lucas.
(Engravings by John Buckland Wright.) pp. 47.
Christopher Sandford: London,] 1949. 8°.
C. 103. b. 15.
No. 58 of 100 specially bound copies with one extra
engraving.

SCHOLARTIS PRESS, London

BLAKE (WILLIAM) *Artist.* [*Single Works.*]
—— Poetical sketches . . . With an essay on Blake's metric
by Jack Lindsay. [The introduction signed: Eric Partridge.] *London: Scholartis Press*, 1927. **11633. g. 51.**
pp. xxiv, 85. 27 cm. △
A copy "out of series" to an edition of seventy-five copies
printed on hand-made paper.

PARTRIDGE (ERIC HONEYWOOD) The Three War-
tons [Thomas the Elder, Joseph, and Thomas the
Younger]. A choice of their verse, edited with a note
by Eric Partridge. pp. 192. *Scholartis Press :*
London, 1927. 8°. **C. 99. g. 38.**

MARTIN (DOROTHY) *Translator.* Sextette. Translations from the French symbolists . . . With a preface
by L. C. Martin. pp. xiv. 99. *Scholartis Press :*
London, 1928. 8°. **C. 99. h. 22.**

FIELDING (HENRY) The Adventures of Joseph
Andrews...Edited, with introduction and notes, by
J. Paul de Castro. pp. 409. *Scholartis Press :*
London, 1929. 8°. **C. 98. h. 24.**
One of 80 copies printed on handmade paper.

PARTRIDGE (ERIC HONEYWOOD) The First Three
Years. An account and a bibliography of the
Scholartis Press. pp. ix. 54. *Scholartis Press :*
London, 1930. 8°. **011900. b. 22.**

ALEXANDER, *Aphrodisæus.* Ἀλεξάνδρου Ἀφροδι-
σιέως πρὸς τοὺς αὐτοκράτορας περὶ εἱμαρμένης. Alexander
of Aphrodisias on Destiny, addressed to the Emperors.
Translated...by Augustine FitzGerald. *Gr. & Eng.*
pp. 163. *Scholartis Press : London*, 1931. 8°.
08458. b. 11.

BENINGTON (WILSON) Love in London, and the Tidal
Town. [Poems.] pp. v. 100. *Scholartis Press: London*,
1931. 8°. **11644. k. 57.**

BLAKESTON (OSWELL) and **BRUGUIÈRE**
(FRANCIS) Few are Chosen. Studies in the theatrical
lighting of life's theatre. [With plates.] pp. 116.
Eric Partridge : London, 1931. 8°. **12625. pp. 6.**

FITZGERALD (AUGUSTINE) Peace and War in
Antiquity. A selection of passages from ancient Greek
and Latin authors, presented in English, with the
originals appended, by A. Fitzgerald. [Edited by
Alexander Souter.] pp. 123. *Scholartis Press :*
London, 1931. 8°. **08425. f. 37.**

GROSE (FRANCIS) *F.A.S.* A Classical Dictionary of
the Vulgar Tongue...Edited with a biographical and
critical sketch and an extensive commentary by Eric
Partridge. pp. ix. 396. *Scholartis Press :*
London, 1931. 8°. **12980. dd. 25.**
Issued for private subscribers.

BINDER (FRANK) Dialectic ; or, the Tactics of thinking.
pp. 299. *Eric Partridge : London*, 1932. 8°.
08458. bb. 49.

MILTON (JOHN) [*Paradise Regained.*]
—— Paradise Regained . . . Newly edited with an intro-
duction and commentary by E. H. Blakeney. pp. ix. 187.
Eric Partridge : London, 1932. 8°. **11633. h. 20.**

B., W. M.

—— Love-Letters of a Sentimentalist. By W. M. B. [i.e. W. M. Bocquet. In verse.] pp. 22.   *Scholartis Press:* *London,* 1933. 8°.   **011641. cc. 118.**

GROOM (G. LAURENCE)

—— Grecian Nocturne. Poems. pp. 64.   *Scholartis* *Press: London,* 1933. 8°.   **011641. c. 10.**

THEOCRITUS. [*Greek and English.*]

—— The Festival of Adonis. Being the xvth Idyll . . . Edited with a revised Greek text, translation and . . . notes by E. H. Blakeney . . . to which is added a rendering in English verse of the Lament for Adonis attributed to Bion. pp. 37.   *Eric Partridge: London,* 1933. 8°.   **11340. ee. 13.**

GOETHE (JOHANN WOLFGSNG VON) [*Faust.—Thl. 1.—* *English.*]

—— The First Part of Goethe's Faust. Translated . . . by John Shawcross, *etc.* pp. vi. 189.   *Eric Partridge:* *London,* 1934. 8°.   **20018. d. 9.**

SCHOOL OF FINE ARTS PRESS, Reading

MONTALE (EUGENIO) [*Selections.*]

—— Poems from Eugenio Montale. Translated by Edwin Morgan. pp. 57.   *School of Art, University of Reading:* [*Reading,*] 1959. 8°.   **11392. aaa. 22.**

SPENCER (BERNARD)

—— The Twist in the Plotting. Twenty five poems. pp. 31. *School of Art, University of Reading:* [*Reading,*] 1960. 8°.   **Cup. 510. afb. 1.**

FLETCHER (IAN)

—— Motets. Twenty one poems. pp. 47. *School of Fine Art, University of Reading: Reading,* 1962. 8°.
                          Cup. 510. afb. 2.

SCREW PACKET PRESS, Newport, Mon.

NEWPORT, *Monmouthshire.—Newport, Monmouthshire, College of Art.*

—— Typographic Variations on 14 epitaphs. (Excusemy.— Designed and produced by graphic design students of Newport, Monmouthshire, College of Art.) 2 pt.   *Screw Packet Press:* [*Newport,*] 1965. obl. 8°. Cup. 510. dap. 1. *One of an edition of eighty copies.*

SEIZIN PRESS, Majorca

RIDING (LAURA) [i.e. LAURA RIDING GOTTSCHALK.] Love as Love, Death as Death. [Poems.] pp. 64. *Seizin Press: London,* 1928. 8°. **Cup.510.bab.1.**

GRAVES (ROBERT VON RANKE)   Poems, 1929. pp. 33. *Seizin Press: London,* 1929. 8°.
                       Cup.510.bab.3.

STEIN (GERTRUDE) An Acquaintance with Description. pp. 50. *Seizin Press: London,* 1929. 8°.
                       Cup.510.bab.2.

LYE (LEN)   No Trouble. pp. 27. *Seizin Press: Deya, Majorca,* 1930. 4°.
                       Cup.510.bab.5.

RIDING (LAURA) [i.e. LAURA RIDING GOTTSCHALK.] Though Gently. [Reflections in prose and verse.] pp. 29. *Seizin Press: Deya, Majorca,* 1930. 4°.
                       Cup.510.bab.7.

GRAVES (ROBERT VON RANKE)

—— To Whom Else? (A seizin.) [Poems.] pp. 19. *Seizin Press: Deyá,* 1931. 4°.   **Cup.510.bab.4.**

RIDING (LAURA) [i.e. LAURA RIDING GOTTSCHALK.]

—— Laura and Francisca. [In free verse.] pp. 22.   *Seizin* *Press: Deyá, Majorca,* 1931. 4°.   **Cup.510.bab.6.**

RIDING (LAURA) [i.e. LAURA RIDING GOTTSCHALK.]

—— The First Leaf. [A poem.]   *Seizin Press:* *Deyá, Majorca,* 1933. 4°.   **Cup.510.bab.8.**

RIDING (LAURA) [i.e. LAURA RIDING GOTTSCHALK.]

—— The Second Leaf. [A poem.]   *Seizin Press:* *Deyá, Majorca,* 1935. 4°.   **Cup.510.bab.9.**

SEVEN ACRES PRESS, Long Crendon

VERSES.

—— Verses on Mans Mortalitie with an other of the hope of his resurrection. Reprinted with woodcuts by L. H. (Reprinted from Michael Spark's Crums of Comfort. *Seven* *Acres Press: Long Crendon,* 1925. 8°. **Cup.500.bb.4.** *The cover bears the title " Like as the Damaske Rose."*

AUDELAY (JOHN) Alia Cantalena de Sancta Maria. [With woodcuts by Loyd Haberly.] *Seven Acres Press: Long Crendon,* 1926. 8°.
                       C. 99. h. 15.

H., L. Cymberina. An unnatural history in woodcuts and verse. By L. H. [i.e. Loyd Haberly.] pp. 45. *Seven Acres Press: Long Crendon,* 1926. 4°.
                       C. 98. e. 1.

FAREWELLS. Farewells. [A verse anthology.] ff. 47. *Seven Acres Press : Long Crendon*, 1927. 8°. C. **99. e. 39.**
Printed on one side of the leaf only.

H., L. The Sacrifice of Spring. A masque of queens. By L. H. [i.e. Loyd Haberly.] pp. 19. *Seven Acres Press : Long Crendon*, 1927. 4°. C. **98. e. 2.**

H., L. When Cupid Wins, None Lose; or, a True Report of Fairy Sport...By L. H. [i.e. Loyd Haberly.] pp. 7. *Seven Acres Press : Long Crendon*, 1927. 4°. C. **98. e. 3.**

HABERLY (LOYD) John Apostate, an Idyl of the Quays. pp. 10. *Seven Acres Press : Long Crendon*, 1927. 8°. **11645. dd. 56.**

HABERLY (LOYD) Daneway. A fairy play ... Written and illustrated by L. Haberly. pp. 45. *Seven Acres Press : Long Crendon*, 1929. 8°. *No. 32 of an edition of 60 copies.* C. **98. k. 19.**

HABERLY (LOYD) Poems. pp. 210. *Seven Acres Press : Long Crendon*, 1930. 8°. C. **99. c. 46.**

NICLAS (HENDRIK) calling himself *Father of the Family of Love*. A New Balade or Songe of the Lambes Feast. (By Henrick Niclaes. Reprinted from a ballad sheet of the year MDLXXIIII.) pp. 9. *Seven Acres Press : Long Crendon*, [1930.] 8°. **11630. bbb. 36.**

HABERLY (LOYD) The Copper Coloured Cupid ; or, the Cutting of the Cake. The second book of Oregon's Orpheus: twelve poems made to match as many months. (Illustrated with woodcuts...by Loyd Haberly.) pp. 31. *Loyd Haberly : Long Crendon*, 1931. 8°. **11644. l. 21.**

HABERLY (LOYD)
—— The boy and the bird. An Oregon idyll, written and decorated by Loyd Haberly. *Long Crendon: Seven Acres Press*, 1932. C. **99. h. 39.**
    pp. 18. 24 cm. (Oregon's Orpheus. bk. 12.) △

HABERLY (LOYD)
—— The Keeper of the Doves. A tale of Notley Abbey. Written and decorated with designs from tiles of its ancient pavement by L. Haberley. pp. 24. *Seven Acres Press : Long Crendon*, 1932. 4°. Cup. **501. e. 24.** *No. 56 of an edition of 100 copies.*

BELLOC (HILAIRE)
—— [The praise of wine.] In praise of wine. [*Long Crendon:*] *privately printed at the Seven Acres Press*, 1933. C. **98. k. 17.**
    pp. 11; illus. 24 cm. △
Author's presentation copy to Maurice Baring.

HABERLY (LOYD)
—— The Antiquary. A poem written in Waterperry Church and decorated with designs from the glass of its ancient windows. [With woodcuts.] pp. 19. *Seven Acres Press : Long Crendon*, 1933. 4°. Cup. **501. e. 16.**
One of an edition of 100 copies.

SHAPCOTT PRESS, Brisbane

GAULTIER, Bon., *pseud.* [i.e. *Sir* THEODORE MARTIN.]
[The book of ballads.]
—— The convict and the lady. An Australian fantasy. [By Sir Theodore Martin and William E. Aytoun. The foreword signed: B. D., i.e. Brian S. Donaghey.] *Brisbane: Shapcott Press*, 1965. Cup. **510. va. 4.**
    Pages not numbered. 19 cm. △
    An extract from " The book of ballads " edited by Bon Gaultier. No. 40 of an edition of one hundred copies.

SHAW, COLLINS & HARVEY, Ipswich

BUTLER (MICHAEL) *Writer of Verse.*
—— Nails and other poems, *etc. David Shaw, Paul Collins & Stephen Harvey: Ipswich*, 1964. obl. 8°. Cup. **510. daf. 1.**

SHELTER PRESS, Moreton Wirral

CHARNOCK (JOHN) *of Moreton, Wirral.*
—— A Little Book of Castles and Cathedrals. pp. 34. *Shelter Press : Moreton*, 1961. 8°. **7825. b. 18.**

SHENVAL PRESS, London

GRIVOLIN (JEANNE AURÉLIE)
—— Breviary of Love. Being the private journal written at Lyon and Cherbourg during the years 1802-3 of Jeanne Aurélie Grivolin. [A translation of " Les Oraisons amoureuses de Jeanne-Aurélie Grivolin, Lyonnaise," by Roger Pillet.] pp. xix. 79. *Constable & Co.: London*, 1938. 8°. **010655. aa. 29.**

JONES (DAVID) *Illustrator.*
—— The Anathemata. Fragments of an attempted writing. [With plates.] pp. 243. *Faber & Faber: London*, 1952. 8°. **012635. c. 30.**

CONNOLLY (CYRIL VERNON)
—— Bond strikes camp. *London: Shenval Press*, 1963. Cup. **510. das. 3.**
    pp. 16 : plate. 25 cm. △
    On the character James Bond in the novels of Ian Fleming. No. 6 of an edition of fifty copies, signed by the author.

SHINGLE STREET PRESS, Ipswich

BIBLE.—*Judges.*—*Selections.* [*English.*]
—— How the Hosts of Sisera were Discomforted [*sic*], and How Sisera was Slain by the Treachery of Jael. (Adapted from Judges, 4.) pp. 8. *V. C. Calver: Ipswich,* 1932. 16º. **03051. de. 60.**

SHIPYARD PRESS, Whitstable

WOODMAN (GEORGE DAVID)
—— The Heretic. [With a woodcut.] pp. 10. *Shipyard Press: Whitstable,* 1963. 8º. **Cup. 510. bal. 1.**

SHOESTRING PRESS, Whitstable

CARROLL (LEWIS) *pseud.* [i.e. CHARLES LUTWIDGE DODGSON.]
[Through the Looking-Glass.]
—— The Walrus and the Carpenter. A poem from ' Through the Looking Glass ' . . . Illustrated with colour gradated lino-cuts by Ben Sands. *Shoestring Press: London,* 1958. obl. 8º. **Cup.510.bcb.2.**
No. 2 of an edition of sixty copies.

EVANS (CHARLES)
—— My Path. (Illustrated by Ben Sands.) [A tale.] pp. 11. *Shoestring Press: London,* 1958. 8º. **Cup.510.bcb.1.**

CAREY (HENRY) *Dramatic Writer.*
—— The Dragon of Wantley. A rendition in Regency dress of a burlesque opera in three acts by Henry Carey . . . The whole embellished with 20 cuts by Ben Sands, *etc.* pp. 26. *Shoestring Press: Whitstable,* 1960. 8º. **Cup. 510. bcb. 3.**

SIGN OF THE GEORGE, Charles River, Mass.

STEVENSON (ROBERT LOUIS)
—— Confessions of a Unionist. An unpublished ' Talk on Things Current '. Written in . . . 1888 and equally pertinent to events at the opening of the Belfast Parliament. [With a prefatory note signed: F. V. L.] pp. 19. *Privately printed: Cambridge, Mass.,* 1921. 8º. **C. 57. i. 20.**

KIPLING (RUDYARD) [*Single Tales and Poems.*]
—— "After." A false start. [A facsimile of the original draft of the first three stanzas of the poem afterwards published as " Recessional." With an introductory note by F. V. Livingston.] [*G. P. Winship: Cambridge, Mass.,*] 1924. 16º. **11655. c. 96.**

SIGNET PRESS, Greenock

CHATTO (WILLIAM ANDREW)
—— Thomas Bewick, Wood Engraver, Newcastle upon Tyne, 1753–1828. (Text taken from " A Treatise on Wood Engraving, Historical and Practical.") [With illustrations, including a portrait.] pp. 20. *Signet Press: Greenock,* 1956. 8º. **Cup.510.bcd.1.**

WORDSWORTH (WILLIAM) *Poet Laureate.* [*Selections.*]
—— Wordsworth in Scotland. A selection from the poems of W. Wordsworth inspired by his visit to Scotland in 1803. *Signet Press: Greenock,* 1957. 8º. **Cup.510.bcd.2.**

RAE (THOMAS)
—— Androw Myllar. A short study of Scotland's first printer. pp. viii. 14. *Signet Press: Greenock,* 1958. 8º. **Cup.510.bcd.3**

SEYMOUR (WILLIAM KEAN)
—— The First Childermas. A play in five scenes. pp. 36. *Signet Press: Greenock,* 1959. 8º. **Cup.510.bcd.5.**

MARY, *Queen of Scotland.* [*Appendix.*]
—— The Death of Mary Queen of Scots. From " The Life of Mary Stewart, Queen of Scotland & France [by Pierre Le Pesant, sieur de Bois-Guillebert] . . . done into English by James Freebairn," *etc.* *Signet Press: Greenock,* [1960.] 8º. **Cup. 510. bcd. 4.**
No. 74 of an edition of " about one hundred copies".

BEWICK (THOMAS) [*Works written and works containing illustrations by T. Bewick.*]
[A Memoir of Thomas Bewick.]
—— Some Notes on Wood Engraving . . . Selected from his ' Memoir ' and edited by Thomas Rae. [With illustrations including a portrait.] pp. 19. vi. *Signet Press: Greenock,* 1961. 8º. **Cup.510.bcd.8.**

DICKENS (CHARLES) [*Sketches by Boz.*—*Selections.*]
—— Public Dinners. (Reprinted from "Sketches by Boz".) pp. 16. *Signet Press: Greenock,* 1962. 8º. **Cup. 510. bcd. 6.**

WATSON (JAMES) *Printer at Edinburgh.*
—— Preface to the History of Printing, 1713. Edited by James Munro. pp. xiii. 35. *Signet Press: Greenock,* 1963. 8º. **Cup. 510. bcd. 7.**

SILVER UNICORN PRESS, Middleton, Sussex

ROSSETTI (CHRISTINA GEORGINA)
—— Goblin Market. (Drawings by Sheila Thompson.) pp. 25. *Silver Unicorn Press: Middleton, Sussex,* 1931. 8º. **Cup.510.adb.1.**
No. 56 of an edition of 100 copies.

SLIDE MOUNTAIN PRESS, Gaylordsville, Conn.

ROBINSON (Edwin Arlington)
—— Fortunatus. *Reno: Slide Mountain Press; San Francisco: [printed at] the Grabhorn Press, 1928.*
Cup. **510**. pb. **7**.

Pages not numbered. 24 cm. △

A poem. Printed on one side of the leaf only.

STEPHENS (James) *Author of " The Crock of Gold."*
—— Optimist. [A poem.] *Slide Mountain Press · Gaylordsville, 1929. 8⁰.*
Cup.510.nad.4.

DE LA MARE (Walter John) [*Single Works.*]
[Peacock Pie.]
—— Silver. [From " Peacock Pie ".] *Slide Mountain Press: Gaylordsville, Conn., 1930. 16⁰.* Cup. **510**. nad. **2**.
One of an edition of nine copies, privately printed.

HARE (Amory)
—— Tristram and Iseult. A play by Amory Hare with scenes by Wharton Esherick. *Gaylordsville: Slide Mountain Press, 1930.* Cup. **510**. nad. **5**.
pp. 104. 30 cm. △

HUXLEY (Aldous)
—— Apennine. [A poem.] *Slide Mountain Press: Gaylordsville, 1930. 4⁰.* Cup. **510**. nad. **1**.
No. 28 of an edition of ninety-one copies. With an errata slip inserted.

MAC FEE (William Morley Punshon)
—— Born to be hanged. [A tale.] pp. 13. *Slide Mountain Press: Gaylordsville, 1930. 8⁰.* Cup.510.nad.3.
One of an edition of ninety-one copies.

SNAIL'S PACE PRESS, Amherst

HOUSMAN (Alfred Edward)
—— Fragment of a Greek Tragedy . . . Now for the second time reprinted from the Cornhill Magazine, *etc.* pp. 7. *Snail's Pace Press: Amherst, 1925. 8⁰.* Cup. **503**. i. **12**.
No. 13 of an edition of ninety-two copies.

SOPHISTOCLES PRESS, London

BAUDELAIRE (Charles Pierre)
—— Fleurs du mal, in pattern and prose. By Beresford Egan and C. Bower Alcock. [A selection.] pp. 142. *Sophistocles Press & T. Werner Laurie: London, 1929. 4⁰.* **11482**. m. **23**.

STEPHENSON (Percy Reginald)
—— Policeman of the Lord. A political satire [on Sir William Joynson-Hicks]. The drawings by Beresford Egan. The preface and lampoon by P. R. Stephensen. **F.P.** *Sophistocles Press: London, [1929.] 4⁰.* **12330**. m. **48**.

SOUTHWORTH-ANTHOENSEN PRESS, Portland, Me.

SANTAYANA (George)
—— Lucifer, or the Heavenly Truce. A theological tragedy. pp. xxi. 128. *Dunster House: Cambridge, Mass., 1924. fol.* Cup.510.neg 1

PROSE QUARTOS.
—— Prose Quartos. 6 pt. *Random House: New York, 1930. 8⁰.* Cup.510.neg.2.

BOGGS (Tom)
—— American Decade. 68 poems for the first time in an anthology . . . Edited by Tom Boggs. pp. 93. *Cummington Press: Cummington, [1943.] 8⁰.* X. **900/1871**.

BENTON (Josiah Henry)
—— John Baskerville, Type-founder and Printer, 1706–1775, *etc.* [With plates, including a portrait.] pp. xxviii. 101. *Printed for The Typophiles: New York, 1944. 8⁰.* **10860**. aa. **18**.

DWIGGINS (William Addison)
—— MSS. by WAD. Being a collection of the writings of Dwiggins on various subjects, *etc.* [Edited by Watson Gordon.] ˙pp. xiv. 152. *Typophiles: New York, 1947. 8⁰.* **11914**. f. **37**.
Typophile Chapbooks. no. 17.

SOWERS (Edwin Uhler), Forstoria, Ohio

PLUNKETT (Edward John Moreton Drax) *Baron Dunsany.*
[The Last Book of Wonder.]
—— Why the Milkman shudders when he perceives the Dawn. (From " The Last Book of Wonder.") pp. 6. *Privately printed, by Edwin Uhler Sowers: Forstoria, Ohio, 1925. 8⁰.* Cup. **510**. sa. **1**.
One of 100 copies printed. With the autograph signature of the printer.

SPIRAL PRESS, New York

WEBER (Max) *Artist.*
—— Primitives. Poems and woodcuts. *Spiral Press: New York, 1926. 8⁰.* Cup. **510**. pk. **1**.

UNTERMEYER (Richard Starr)
—— By Richard Starr Untermeyer. [Poems and sketches. With a portrait.] pp. xi. 152. *Privately printed: [Norwood, Mass., 1927.] 8⁰.* **011686**. aa. **22**.

MILNE (ALAN ALEXANDER)
—— The Secret, and other stories. pp. 70.　　*Fountain Press: New York; Methuen & Co.: London*, 1929.　8°.
　　　　　　　　　　　　　　　Cup. **510**. pk. **2**.

WIGGLESWORTH (MICHAEL)
—— The Day of Doom . . . with other poems . . . Edited with an introduction by Kenneth B. Murdock.　With drawings adapted from early New England gravestones by Wanda Gág.　pp. xi. 94.　*Spiral Press: New York*, 1929.　8°.
　　　　　　　　　　　　　　　Cup. **510**. pk. **6**.

COPPARD (ALFRED EDGAR)
—— Cheefoo.　*Privately printed for Alfred Parsons Sachs for presentation to his friends: Croton Falls, N.Y.*, 1932.　8°.
　　　　　　　　　　　　　　　Cup. **510**. pk. **7**.

GALSWORTHY (JOHN)　[*Single Works.*]
—— Author and Critic.　　*House of Books: New York*, 1933.　8°.　　　　　　　Cup. **510**. pk. **8**.
Crown Octavos.　no. 3.

COPPARD (ALFRED EDGAR)
—— Emergency Exit.　pp. 71.　*Random House: New York*, [1934.]　8°.　　　　　Cup. **510**. pk. **12**.

COPPARD (ALFRED EDGAR)
—— Good Samaritans.　*New York: Spiral Press*, 1934.
　　　　　　　　　　　　　　　Cup. **510**. pk. **17**.

　Pages not numbered; illus.　21 cm.
　"*Privately printed at Christmas 1934 for Albert Parsons Sachs.*"

JOYCE (JAMES AUGUSTINE ALOYSIUS)
—— Collected Poems of James Joyce.　[With a portrait.]　pp. lxv.　*Black Sun Press: New York*, 1936.　8°.
　　　　　　　　　　　　　　　Cup. **510**. pk. **3**.

DAVISON (EDWARD LEWIS)
—— Nine Poems.　　*Privately printed for the author: New York*, 1937.　8°.　　Cup.**510**.pk.**5**.
Author's presentation copy to Sir Hugh Walpole.

NEW YORK.—*Metropolitan Museum of Art.*
—— Addresses on the Occasion of the Opening of the Branch Building, The Cloisters, in Fort Tryon Park, the gift of John D. Rockefeller, Jr.　May tenth.　1938.　pp. 27.　*New York*, 1938.　8°.　　　Cup. **510**. pk. **4**.

BUNYAN (JOHN)　[*Pilgrim's Progress, Pt. 1.—English.*]
—— The Pilgrim's Progress . . . Illustrated with 29 water-color paintings by William Blake now printed for the first time.　Edited by G. B. Harrison.　With a new intro-duction by Geoffrey Keynes.　pp. xxxii. 213.　*Printed at the Spiral Press for the members of the Limited Editions Club: New York*, 1941.　fol.　　　C. **105**. f. **7**.

TODD (FREDERICK P.)
—— Soldiers of the American Army, 1775-1941.　Drawings by Fritz Kredel.　Text by Frederick P. Todd, *etc.　H. Bittner & Co.: New York*, 1941.　fol.
　　　　　　　　　　　　　　　L.R. **294**. b. **13**.

WATERBURY (FLORANCE)
—— Early Chinese Symbols and Literature: Vestiges and Speculations.　With particular reference to the ritual bronzes of the Shang dynasty, *etc.*　pp. 153.　pl. 76.　*E. Weyhe: New York*, 1942.　4°.　　L.R. **295**. b. **7**.

FROST (ROBERT LEE)　[*Collections.*]
—— [A collection of single poems by Robert Frost printed as greeting cards from various persons.]　22 pt.　*Spiral Press: New York*, 1944–62.　8°.　Cup. **510**. pk. **13**.

RUIZ PICASSO (PABLO)
—— Guernica.　[Reproductions.]　(Text by Juan Larrea.　Translated by Alexander H. Krappe and edited by Walter Pach.)　pp. 76.　*Curt Valentin: New York*, 1947.　4°.
　　　　　　　　　　　　　　　L.R. **299**. aa. **25**.

GRAHAM (FRANK PORTER)
—— The Faith and Hope of an American.　*Spiral Press: New York*, 1952.　8°.　　Cup. **510**. pk. **11**.

WILLIAMS (WILLIAM CARLOS)
—— The Desert Music and other poems.　pp. 90.　*Random House: New York*, [1954.]　8°.　Cup.**510**.pk.**9**.
No. 100 of an edition of 100 copies, signed by the author.

LITURGIES.—*Latin Rite.—Hours.*—I.　[*Appendix.*]
—— The Belles Heures of Jean, Duke of Berry, Prince of France.　With an introduction by James J. Rorimer.　(Description of the plates by Margaret B. Freeman.)　[With facsimile reproductions.]　*Metropolitan Museum of Art: New York*, 1958.　8°.　Cup.**510**.pk.**10**.

BLUMENTHAL (JOSEPH)
—— Robert Frost and the Spiral Press.　*Spiral Press: New York*, 1963.　8°.　　Cup. **510**. pk. **14**.

STEUBEN GLASS, INC.
—— Poetry in crystal by Steuben Glass.　(Interpretations in crystal of thirty-one new poems by contemporary American poets.)　*New York: Steuben Glass*, [1963].
　　　　　　　　　　　　　　　Cup. **510**. pk. **16**.

　pp. 86 ; illus.　27 cm.　　　　　　　　　△
　With biographical notes on the poets and artists.

AESOP.　[*English.—Selections.*]
—— Aesop ; five centuries of illustrated fables.　Selected by John J. McKendry.　[New York :] Metropolitan Museum of Art, [1964].　　　　**Cup. 510. pk. 15.**
　95 p.; illus.　24 cm.　　　　　　　　　□

STANBROOK ABBEY PRESS, Stanbrook, Worcester

BENEDICT, *Saint, Abbot of Monte Cassino* [*Regula.*]
—— Sancti benedicti Regula monasteriorum. (Recognovit Cuthbertus Butler.) pp. 91. *Prelis B. V. M. de Consolatione: Stanbrook,* 1930. 4°. Cup. **510**. aab. **5**.

STANBROOK, *Benedictines of.*
—— Christmas Lyrics, *etc.* pp. 30. *Stanbrook Abbey Press: Worcester,* 1957. 8°. Cup.510.aab.2.

LEO I., *Saint,* surnamed *the Great, Pope.*
[Sermo XXI.]
—— On the Birthday of our Lord Jesus Christ. (Translated from the Office of Matins for the Feast of Christmas by the Benedictines of Stanbrook.) [An extract.] pp. 5. *Stanbrook Abbey Press: Worcester,* 1958. 8°. Cup.510.aab.3.

STANBROOK ABBEY PRESS.
—— [A collection of prospectuses, price lists, cards, and other specimens of printing by the Stanbrook Abbey Press.] [*Worcester, ca.* 1958–67]. Cup. **510**. aab. **21**.
22 pt. △
With six manuscript letters, dated from 1958 to 1962, from Dame Hildelith Cumming to Beatrice Warde.

LITURGIES.—*Latin Rite.*—*Combined Offices.*—v. *Paroissiens, etc.*—*Milan.*
—— Magi venerunt. Expositio Sancti Ambrosii Mediolanensis. There came Wise Men, *etc.* (Illustrated & translated by the Benedictines of Stanbrook from the Mass & Office of the sixth day within the octave of the Epiphany.) *Lat. & Eng. Stanbrook Abbey Press: Worcester,* [1959.] 4°. Cup.510.aab.6.
No. 49 of sixty copies printed on Millbourne handmade paper.

SASSOON (SIEGFRIED LORAINE) [*Selections.*]
—— The Path to Peace. Selected poems. pp. 31. *Stanbrook Abbey Press: Worcester,* 1960. 4°. Cup. **510**. aab. **4**.

AUGUSTINE, *Saint, Bishop of Hippo.* [*Selections.*—*English.*]
—— Unless the Grain die, *etc.* (S. Augustine of Hippo: The Grain of Wheat; commentary on John VI, 5–13; commentary on John XII, 24–26. S. Ignatius of Antioch: Letter to the Romans. Translated from the Latin & Greek texts by the Benedictines of Stanbrook.) pp. 18. *Stanbrook Abbey Press: Worcester,* 1961. fol. Cup. **510**. aab. **7**.

CRASHAW (RICHARD) [*Single Poems not originally published separately.*]
—— Caritas nimia. pp. 4. *Stanbrook Abbey Press: Worcester,* [1963.] 8°. Cup. **510**. aab. **10**.

GUIGO, *de Castro Novo, General of the Carthusians.*
[De laude solitarie vite.]
—— The Solitary Life. A letter of Guigo introduced and translated from the Latin by Thomas Merton. pp. 11. *Stanbrook Abbey Press: Worcester,* 1963. 16°. Cup. **510**. aab. **8**.

LITURGIES.—*Latin Rite.*—*Rituals.*—III. *Benedictines.*—*England.*
—— Rituale Abbatum sub regula Sancti Patris Benedicti in congregatione Anglicana. pp. 22. *Typis Abbatiæ de Stanbrook: Wigorniæ,* 1963. fol. Cup. **510**. aab. **16**.

LITURGIES. — *Latin Rite.* — *Missals.* — III. *Augustinian Canons.*—*Lesnes.*
—— Missale de Lesnes. MS L404 in the library of the Victoria and Albert Museum. Edited with introduction and indices by Dom Philip Jebb. pp. xxiv. 214. *Stanbrook Abbey Press: Worcester,* 1964. 8°. [*Henry Bradshaw Society. Publications.* vol. 95.] Ac. **9929/63**.

SHAKESPEARE (WILLIAM) [*Selections and Extracts.*]
—— A Memento of the Quarter-Centenary Year of William Shakespeare, 1564–1964, April 23. *Stanbrook Abbey Press: Worcester,* 1964. 8°. Cup. **510**. aab. **9**.

DREYFUS (JOHN G.)
—— Books from Stanbrook Abbey Press and The Vine Press. Introduced by J. G. Dreyfus. pp. 12. *Times Bookshop: London,* [1965.] 8°. Cup. **510**. aab. **12**.

MARITAIN (RAÏSSA) [*Selections.*]
—— Patriarch tree. (Thirty poems.) Translated into English by a Benedictine of Stanbrook. With a preface by Robert Speaight. *Worcester: Stanbrook Abbey Press,* 1965. Cup. **510**. aab. **11**.
pp. xvii, 81 : plate ; port. 27 cm. △
English and French.

STANTON PRESS, Wembley Hill, Mddx; Chelsfield, Kent

VIDA (MARCUS HIERONYMUS) *Bishop of Alba.* The Game of Chess, done into English [verso]...& printed by Richard Stanton Lambert...& decorated with woodcuts by Nell Lambert. *Lat. & Eng.* pp. 61. *Stanton Press: Wembley Hill,* 1921. 4°. 11408.h.23.

VIDA (MARCUS HIERONYMUS) *Bishop of Alba.*
—— [Another copy.] The Game of Chess, *etc. Wembley Hill,* 1921. 4°. C. 98. h. 4.

DAVIES (Sir JOHN) *Attorney-General for Ireland.*
—— Orchestra, *etc.* (Reprint of the original edition of 1596.) [With introduction by Richard Stanton Lambert and woodcuts by Elinor Lambert.] pp. vii. 61. *Stanton Press: Wembley Hill,* 1922. 4°. C. 99. i. 11.

ROSWITHA. Abraham. A play...Translated... into English prose by Richard S. Lambert, and illustrated by Agnes Lambert. pp. 37. *Stanton Press: Wembley Hill*, 1922. 8°.   C. **99**. f. **30**.

    No. 59 of 100 copies printed.

BIBLE.—*Susannah.* [*English.*]

—— The history of Susanna, *etc.*   [*Wembley Hill:*] Stanton Press, 1923.   C. **99**. a. **26**.

    pp. 19; illus. 15 cm.   △

    No. 3 of eight copies printed on Japanese vellum.

STATUS (PUBLIUS PAPINIUS) [*Silvæ.—English.*]

—— Ode to Sleep. [Silvae v, 4.] Translated . . . into English verse by R. S. Lambert. pp. xiv.   *Stanton Press: Wembley Hill*, 1923. obl. 16°.   C. **99**. a. **25**.

BINYON (ROBERT LAURENCE) *Keeper of Prints and Drawings, British Museum.*

—— The Sirens. An ode. pp. 38.   *Stanton Press: Chelsfield*, 1924. fol.   C. **99**. k. **22**.

STRABO (WALFRIDUS)

—— Hortulus; or, the little garden, *etc.* (Done into English verse . . . by R. S. Lambert.) pp. 38.   *Stanton Press: Wembley Hill*, 1924. 4°.   C. **98**. g. **6**.

STELLAR PRESS, Barnet, Herts.

HOPKINS (GERARD MANLEY) [*Selections.*]

—— Selected Poems. (Chosen by Francis Meynell.) pp. v. 104. *Nonesuch Press: London*, 1954. 8°.   Cup. **510**. aa. **1**.

GOFF (CECILIE) *Lady.*

—— Three generations of a loyal house.   [*Cambridge:*] *Rampant Lions Press*, 1957.   X. **809**/**10861**.

    pp. 176: plates; ports. 22 cm.

    On Peregrine Bertie, 12th Baron Willoughby d'Eresby, Robert Bertie, 1st Earl of Lindsey, and Montagu Bertie, 2nd Earl of Lindsey. Privately printed.

JOYCE (JAMES AUGUSTINE ALOYSIUS)

[*Ulysses.*]

—— Concerning Ulysses and The Bodley Head. (To celebrate the twenty-fifth anniversary of first publication, by The Bodley Head of James Joyce's Ulysses, Charles Mozley has drawn some auto-lithographs.) [With quotations from the text.]   *Printed at the Stellar Press for private distribution: Barnet*, 1961. 8°.   Cup. **510**. aa. **10**.

    The title is taken from the wrapper.

BIBLE.—*Luke.—Selections.* [*English.*]

—— The Gospel according to St. Luke, chapter II, verses 1–20. (Lithographs and initial letters by Charles Mozley.) *London: published by Cyril & Barbara Sweett for their friends; Barnet: printed at the Stellar Press*, 1962.   Cup. **510**. aa. **2**.

    Pages not numbered. 27 cm.   △

    The cover bears the title " The Nativity ".

GREENE (GRAHAM)

—— The Revenge. An autobiographical fragment. pp. 11. *Privately printed: [Barnet,]* 1963. 8°.   Cup. **510**. aa. **7**.

    Presentation copy from the author to John Hayward.

PLOMER (WILLIAM CHARLES FRANKLYN)

—— Conversation with my Younger Self. pp. 27.   [*Simon Nowell-Smith:*] *Ewelme*, 1963. 8°.   Cup. **510**. aa. **3**.

    One of an edition of twenty-five copies.

SPENSER (EDMUND) [*Fowre Hymnes.*]

—— An Hymne of Heavenly Beautie [from "Fowre Hymnes"] made by Edmund Spenser, 1552–1599. (Lithographs by Charles Mozley.)   *Barbara & Cyril Sweett: Barnet*, 1963. 8°.   Cup. **510**. aa. **4**.

RYDER (JOHN STANLEY)

—— Lines of the Alphabet in the Sixteenth Century. [With illustrations.] pp. 79.   *Stellar Press: [Barnet;] Bodley Head: London*, 1965. 8°.   Cup. **510**. aa. **5**.

    The author's name appears only on the spine of the binding.

STINEHOUR PRESS, Lunenberg, Vt.

BEERBOHM (SIR MAX)

—— The Happy Hypocrite, *etc.* pp. 81.   *Bruce Rogers: New Fairfield*, 1955. 8°.   **Cup.510.pac.1.**

EBERHART (RICHARD)

—— Thirteen Dartmouth Poems. Selected by Richard Eberhart.   *Charles Butcher Fund: Hanover, N.H.*, 1958. 8°.   Cup. **510**. pac. **5**.

    With the author's signature on the titlepage.

EBERHART (RICHARD)

—— Forty Dartmouth poems. Selected, and with an introduction, by Richard Eberhart. pp. 51.   *Dartmouth Publications: Hanover*, 1962. 8°.   Cup. **510**. pac. **3**.

EBERHART (RICHARD)

—— Thirty five Dartmouth poems. Selected, and with an introduction, by Richard Eberhart. pp. 44.   *Dartmouth Publications: Hanover, N.H.*, 1963. 8°.

             Cup. **510**. pac. **4**.

MOORE (MARIANNE)

—— Occasionem cognosce. A poem.   *Stinehour Press: Lunenburg, Vt.*, 1963. fol.   Cup. **510**. pac. **2**.

CAMBRIDGE, *Massachusetts.—Harvard University.—University Library.—Houghton Library.*

—— An Annotated list of the publications of the Reverend Thomas Frognall Dibdin . . . Based mainly on those in the Harvard College Library, with notes of others. [By William A. Jackson. With a portrait and facsimiles.] pp. 63. *Cambridge*, 1965. fol.   Cup. **510**. pac. **6**.

STOCKHAM (Anne) & (Peter) Elstree, Herts.

STOCKHAM (ANNE) and STOCKHAM (PETER)

—— [A collection of chapbooks and broadsides reprinted by Anne and Peter Stockham for the amusement of their friends.] *Elstree*, 1965– . 12°, *etc.*   **Cup. 510. dab. 1.**

STOURTON PRESS, London; Capetown

DRYDEN (JOHN) [*Dramatic Works.*]

—— All For Love, *etc.* pp. xxii. 97.   *Stourton Press: London*, 1931. 4°.   **Cup. 510. apa. 2.**

HALL (FAIRFAX)

—— A birthday greeting. *Westminster: Stourton Press*, 1931.   **Cup. 510. apa. 3.**

pp. v; port. 23 cm.   △
Poems. Printed in Gothic type. No. 23 of an edition of fifty-six copies.

DAVID (*Sir* PERCIVAL VICTOR) *Bart.* A Catalogue of Chinese Pottery and Porcelain in the Collection of Sir Percival David, Bt., F.S.A. By R. L. Hobson. pp. xl. 189. pl. CLXXX.   *Stourton Press: London*, 1934. fol.   **Cup. 1247. a. 2.**
No. 6 of thirty copies printed on Imperial Japanese paper.

MARLOWE (CHRISTOPHER) *the Dramatist.* [*Hero and Leander.*]

—— Hero and Leander. pp. 36.   *Stourton Press: London*, 1934. 8°.   **C. 99. h. 42.**

MARLOWE (CHRISTOPHER) *the Dramatist.* [*Hero and Leander.*]

—— [Another copy.] Hero and Leander.   *Westminster*, 1934. 8°.   **Cup. 510. apa. 1.**

USPENSKY (PETR DEM'YANOVICH)

—— Strange life of Ivan Osokin.   *London: Stourton Press*, 1947.   **Cup. 510. apa. 4.**

pp. 179. 26 cm.   △
A novel.

THEORY.

—— The Theory of Eternal Life. By the author of The Theory of Celestial Influence [i.e. Rodney Collin Smith]. [With plates.] pp. 120.   *Stourton Press: Cape Town*, 1950. 8°.   **8473. cc. 49.**

USPENSKY (PETR DEM'YANOVICH)

—— Tertium Organum, *etc.* pp. 192.   *Stourton Press: Cape Town*, 1950. fol.   **8630. l. 12.**

COLLIN (RODNEY) *pseud.* [i.e. RODNEY COLLIN SMITH.]

—— Hellas. A spectacle with music and dances in four acts. pp. 138. *Stourton Press: Cape Town*, 1951. 8°.   **11783. g. 46.**

USPENSKY (PETR DEM'YANOVICH)

—— A record of some of the meetings held by P. D. Ouspensky between 1930 and 1947.   *Cape Town: Stourton Press*, 1951.   **X. 529/14251.**

pp. v. 694. 22 cm.   △
No. 18 of an edition of twenty copies, printed for private circulation.

BLAND (ROSAMUND)

—— Extracts from Nine Letters written by R. Bland at the beginning of P. D. Ouspensky's London work in 1921. pp. 73. *Stourton Press: Cape Town*, 1952. 8°.   **10922.g.39**
Printed for private circulation.

USPENSKY (PETR DEM'YANOVICH)

—— A further record, chiefly of extracts from meetings held by P. D. Ouspensky between 1928 and 1945. *Cape Town: Stourton Press*, 1952.   **X. 529/14250.**

pp. iii, 317. 22 cm.   △
No. 12 of an edition of twenty copies, printed for private circulation.

USPENSKY (PETR DEM'YANOVICH)
[Tertium organum.]

—— An Abridgement of P. D. Ouspensky's Tertium organum made by Fairfax Hall. pp. xiv. 276.   *Stourton Press: Cape Town*, 1961. 8°.   **X. 529/1657.**
One of an edition of one hundred copies printed for private circulation.

GILMAN (HAROLD)

—— Paintings and Drawings by Harold Gilman and Charles Ginner in the Collection of Edward Le Bas. [Selected by Edward Le Bas and B. Fairfax Hall. Text by B. Fairfax Hall, including " The Camden Town Group " by Charles Ginner.] pp. 49. pl. 36.   *B. Fairfax Hall: London*, 1965. fol.   **C. 160. ee. 1.**
Privately printed.

STOVEPIPE PRESS, New York

WILLIAMS (WILLIAM CARLOS)

—— William Zorach: two drawings. William Carlos Williams: two poems. *Stovepipe Press*, 1937. 8°.   **Cup. 510. nef. 1.**

SUMAC PRESS, La Crosse

WULLING (FREDERICK JOHN)

—— Pharmacy Forward . . . Being selections, mostly not published before, from the diary, autobiography, speeches, & reports, significant of a lifetime effort in the profession of pharmacy. Edited & published by Emerson G. Wulling. [With illustrations, including portraits.] pp. 123. *Sumac Press: La Crosse*, 1948. 8°.   **7682. b. 37.**

SWALLOW (Alan) Denver

SWALLOW (ALAN)

—— Anthology 1(–111). Edited by A. Swallow. 3 vol. [*Alan Swallow: Denver*, 1959.] 8°.   **Cup. 510. naf. 1–3.**
The works contained in these volumes have various imprints and dates.

CUNNINGHAM (James Vincent)
—— To what strangers, what welcome. A sequence of short poems. *Alan Swallow: Denver*, [1964.] 8⁰.
Cup. 510. naf. 10.

SWAN PRESS, Leeds

CHILDE (Wilfred Rowland)
—— The Hills of Morning. Poems. pp. 31. *W. Brierley: Leeds*, [1921.] 16⁰.
011648. de. 117.

MATTHEWMAN (Sydney)
—— The Gardens of Meditation. [Verses.] pp. 18. *Swan Press: Leeds*, 1921. 12⁰.
Cup. 510. bce. 3.

ARNOLD (Matthew)
—— The Forsaken Merman . . . Illustrated by Violet Dinsdale. *Swan Press: Leeds*, 1922. 16⁰.
11644. dd. 49.

MATTHEWMAN (Sydney)
—— The Lute of Darkness. [Verses.] pp. 13. *Swan Press: Leeds*, 1922. 16⁰.
Cup. 510. bce. 4.

MILNES (Thomas Wray)
—— Salt for the Goose. A comedy. *Leeds*, 1922. 12⁰.
11784. a. 29.

SEVEN. Seven. A book of verses [by various authors]. Decorated by Albert Wainwright. *Swan Press: Leeds*, 1922. 8⁰.
011645. de. 94.

BOYLE (Douglas Jackson)
—— Marcus Aurelius: a tragedy, *etc. Swan Press: Leeds*, 1923. 12⁰.
011779. de. 24.

CHILDE (Wilfred Rowland)
—— The Garland of Armor. Sixteen poems, *etc.* pp. 20. *Swan Press: Leeds*, 1923. 8⁰.
011645. df. 150.

COLLARD (Lorna Keeling)
—— Two Sonnets, *etc. Swan Press: Leeds*, 1923. 16⁰.
011644. de. 36.

SMITH (Albert Hugh) The Merry Shire. Poems in the Yorkshire dialect, *etc.* pp. 18. *Swan Press: Leeds*, 1923. 8⁰.
011645. df. 149.

COLLARD (Lorna Keeling)
—— The Uncharted Coast. Poems . . . Illustrated by Joyce E. J. Collard, *etc.* pp. 39. *Swan Press: Leeds*, 1924. 8⁰.
011645. g. 12.

MATTHEWMAN (Sydney,) The Crystal Casket. A fantasy, *etc. Swan Press: Leeds*, 1924. 16⁰.
Cup. 510. bce. 5.

MATTHEWMAN (Sydney) Six Epigrams, *etc. Swan Press: Leeds*, 1924. 16⁰.
Cup. 510. bce. 9.

MILNES (Thomas Wray)
—— The Thorn's Reflowering, *etc.* [Poems.] pp. 55. *Swan Press: Leeds*, 1924. 8⁰.
011645. de. 96.

NORTH-COUNTRY CHAP-BOOKS.
—— North-Country chap-books. (Swan Press chap-books.) *Leeds: Swan Press*, 1924. Cup. 510. bce. 10.
7 pt.; illus. 15 cm.
△

RATCLIFFE, afterwards MAC GRIGOR PHILLIPS (Dorothy Una)
—— Nathaniel Baddeley, bookman. A play for the fireside in one act . . . Illustrated by Fred Lawson. *Leeds: Swan Press*, 1924.
11779. h. 47.
pp. 50. 23 cm.
△

RATCLIFFE, afterwards MAC GRIGOR PHILLIPS (Dorothy Una)
—— [Another copy.] Nathaniel Baddeley, bookman, *etc.* 1924.
11783. ff. 29.
△

SWINBURNE (Algernon Charles) Cleopatra . . . Decorated by Albert Wainwright. *Swan Press: Leeds*, 1924. 8⁰.
11646. b. 64.

VICKRIDGE (Alberta) The Forsaken Princess (Poems) . . . Decorated by Albert Wainwright, *etc.* pp. 45. *Swan Press: Leeds*, 1924. 8⁰.
Cup. 510. bce. 12.

BOTTERILL (Denis)
—— This Garland for Mabel: five poems. pp. v. *Thetan Press: Ben-Rhydding*, 1925. 8⁰.
11643. cc. 58.
Privately printed. No. 77 of an edition of 100 copies.

COKE (Percival Hale)
—— What you will. A volume of verse. pp. 24. *Swan Press: Leeds*, 1925. 8⁰.
11645. dd. 23.

COLLETT (T. W.) Consuela y Raffell, and other poems. pp. 80. *Swan Press: Leeds*, 1925. 8⁰. 011649. i. 140.

HARLAND (Oswald Henry)
—— Inhabitants. Poems, *etc.* pp. 19. *Swan Press: Leeds*, 1925. 8⁰.
11645. dd. 22.

HUMMERSTON (M. M.) The Battle of Briggate, etc. pp. 20. *Swan Press: Leeds*, 1925. 8°. [*Cameos of Leeds Life.* no. 1.] W.P. 8535/1.

MILNES (THOMAS WRAY) The Widow of Ephesus. The delectable tale from the Satyricon of Titus Petronius Arbiter done into a play, etc. pp. 29. *At the Sign of the Swan: Leeds*, 1925. 8°. 011781. e. 40.

SYMONS (ARTHUR) Notes on Joseph Conrad. With some unpublished letters [and a portrait]. pp. 38. *Myers & Co.: London*, 1925. 4°. Cup.510.bce.1.

SYMONS (ARTHUR)
—— [A reissue.] Notes on Joseph Conrad, etc. *London*, 1926. 8°. Cup. 510. bce. 2. *Author's presentation copy to Selwyn Image.*

WAKEFIELD (JESSIE HARE) The Happy Isle. Poems. pp. 47. *Swan Press: Leeds*, 1925. 8°. 11649. de. 53.

GROOM (G. LAURENCE) The Ship of Destiny, etc. [Poems.] pp. 64. *Swan Press: Leeds*, 1926. 8°. 011644. e. 109.

MATTHEWMAN (SYDNEY)
—— Sketches in Sunshine, etc. pp. 23. *Swan Press: Leeds*, 1926. 16°. Cup. 510. bce. 6.

PEACOCK (MARION) Quiet Ladies. A book of poems. pp. vii. 32. *Swan Press: Leeds*, 1926. 8°. 11643. d. 35.

SACKVILLE (*Lady* MARGARET) Epitaphs. pp. 29. *Swan Press: Leeds*, 1926. 8°. 011645. h. 8.

STRONG (AYLMER) Mon Autel. Poème. pp. 11. *Swan Press: Leeds*, 1926. 4°. 11481. i. 42.

WAINWRIGHT (ALBERT) Café Noir. [Poems] . . . Decorations by the author. pp. 24. *Printed by S.M. at the Sign of the Swan: Leeds*, 1926. 8°. 011648. h. 85.

CHILDE (WILFRED ROWLAND)
—— The Country of Sweet Bells . . . Decorated by Albert Wainwright. [Poems.] pp. 47. *Swan Press: Leeds; Gay & Hancock: London*, 1927. 8°. X. 907/1405.

GROOM (G. LAURENCE) The Singing Sword. A poem, etc. pp. 61. *Swan Press: Leeds; Gay & Hancock: London*, 1927. 8°. 011644. ee. 66.

HYDE (FRANCIS AUSTIN) Wireless and sike-like. A comedy in one act. pp. 24. *Swan Press: Leeds; Gay & Hancock: London*, 1927. 16°. 011779. de. 53.

KERR (WILLIAM) *Writer of Verse.* The Apple Tree. Poems. pp. 48. *Swan Press: Leeds; Gay & Hancock: London*, 1927. 12°. 011644. de. 141.

MATTHEWMAN (SYDNEY) Poems, 1927...Decorated by Albert Wainwright. pp. 103. *Swan Press: Leeds*, 1927. 8°. Cup.510.bce.7.

WOOD (CLAUDIA L.) *Dramatist.*
—— The plays of Claudia L. Wood. *Swan Press: Leeds; Gay & Hancock: London*, 1927, 31. W.P. 8883. 3 pt. 16 cm. △

BOTTERILL (DENIS) Dedications. Poems by D. Botterill. pp. 63. *Swan Press: Leeds; Gay & Hancock: London*, 1928. 8°. Cup.510.bce.11.

MATTHEWMAN (SYDNEY)
—— Epithalamion : an ode written upon the occasion of the marriage of his dear friends Geoffrey Woledge and Hilda Vickridge, May the seventeenth MCMXXIX, by S. Matthewman. *Sydney Matthewman & Chas H. Dixon: Leeds*, [1929.] 8°. Cup.510.bce.8. *One of an edition of thirty copies.*

SWAN PRESS, London

BACON (FRANCIS) *Viscount St. Albans.*—[ESSAYS]
—— Of Truth, Beautye, and Goodnesse. pp. ix. *Swan Press: London*, 1926. 4°. C. 98. h. 11. *One of an edition of 50 copies. The half-title reads " Three Essays by Francis Bacon."*

MILTON (JOHN) [Sonnets.]
—— The English Sonnets of Mi. John Milton. Wood engravings by Rachel Russell. *Swan Press: London*, 1926. 4°. C. 98. g. 20. *One of an edition of 100 copies.*

ANDERSEN (HANS CHRISTIAN) *the Novelist.* [*Other Works.*] Nove quadri presi da cio che vide la luna... Traduzione di Penelope Eyre, etc. *Swan Press: Chelsea*, 1927. 4°. Cup.510.ala.3. *One of an edition of 100 copies.*

FRANCIS [BERNARDONI], *of Assisi, Saint.* The Hymn of the Sun, etc. *Ital. & Eng.* *Swan Press: [London,]* 1927. 8°. Cup.ala.1. *No. 35 of an edition of 100 copies.*

GOSSE (HELEN) *and* (PHILIP) Gathered Together, etc. [A collection of words signifying a gathering together of a number of individuals of the same kind.] pp. 14. *Swan Press: Chelsea*, 1927. 8°. Cup.510.ala.5.

MARY, *Queen of Scotland.* [*Letters.*]

—— The Last Letter of Mary Queen of Scotland, *etc.* [With an English translation.] *Fr. & Eng.* *Swan Press: Chelsea*, 1927. 4°. Cup. **510**. ala. **2**.

BACON (FRANCIS) *Viscount St. Albans.* [*Essays. Single Essays.*]

—— Of Gardens. pp. ix. *Swan Press: London*, 1928 [1927]. 4°. Cup. **510**. ala. **4**.
   One of an edition of 100 copies.

BIBLE.—*Old Testament.—Selections.* [*English.*]

—— The Canticles of the Old Testament. Arranged and edited by Edward Henry Blakeney. *Swan Press: Chelsea*, 1928. 8°. Cup.**510**.ala.**6**.
   One of an edition of 100 copies.

E., M. P., and **WALTERS** (LETTICE D'OYLEY)

—— In Praise of Phillis. An anthology of sixteenth & seventeenth century verse. Arranged by M. P. E. and L. D'O. W(alters). *Swan Press: London*, 1928. 8°. Cup. **510**. ala. **11**.
   One of an edition of 100 copies.

STEVENSON (ROBERT LOUIS)

—— Ten Fables. With twenty one illustrations by Rachel Russell. *Swan Press: London*, 1928. 8°. C. **98**. i. **5**.
   One of 10 copies with the illustrations coloured by hand.

EVELYN (JOHN) *F.R.S.*

—— Fumifugium: or, the Inconvenience of the Aer, and Smoake of London dissipated, *etc.* [A reprint of the edition of 1772.] pp. 49. *Swan Press: London*, [1929.] 4°. Cup. **510**. ala. **13**.
   One of an edition of 100 copies printed on hand-made paper.

GOLDSMITH (OLIVER) *the Poet.* [*Poems.*]

—— The Traveller and The Deserted Village. *Swan Press: Chelsea*, 1929. 4°. Cup.**510**.ala.**10**.
   No. 2 of an edition of 100 copies on hand-made paper.

LYDGATE (JOHN)

—— The Chorle and the Birde. Done into English from the French by Master John Lydgate. 𝕭.𝕷. *Swan Press: London*, 1929. 4°. C. **98**. gg. **17**.
   One of an edition of 100 copies.

CHILDE (WILFRED ROWLAND)

—— Blue Distance. [Sketches.] pp. 94. *Swan Press: London*, 1930. 16°. 012352. bbb. **42**.

COLLARD (LORNA KEELING)

—— The voyage. A sonnet sequence. *London: Swan Press*, 1930. Cup. **510**. ala. **7**.
   pp. 21. 21 cm. △

DUCK (STEPHEN) The Thresher's Labour. *Swan Press: London*, 1930. 8°. [*Swan Poets.* no. 1.]
   One of an edition of 100 copies. Cup.**510**.ala.**9/1**.

DYER (JOHN) *Poet.* Grongar Hill. *Swan Press: London*, 1930. 8°. [*Swan Poets.* no. 4.]
   One of an edition of 100 copies. Cup.**510**.ala.**9/4**.

LAY (CECIL HOWARD) In and Out. Thirty-six poems ...With brush drawings by the author. pp. 45. *Swan Press: London*, 1930. 8°. Cup.**510**.ala.**8**.

POPE (ALEXANDER) *the Poet.* [*Pastorals.*] Pastorals. *Swan Press: London*, 1930. 8°. [*Swan Poets.* no. 5.]
   One of an edition of 100 copies.
   Cup.**510**.ala.**9/5**.

SHENSTONE (WILLIAM) Songs. *Swan Press: London*, 1930. 8°. [*Swan Poets.* no. 2.]
   One of an edition of 100 copies. Cup.**510**.ala.**9/2**.

GOSSE (IRENE) A Florilege. Chosen from the old Herbals by I. Gosse, and illustrated with twenty wood engravings by Gertrude Hermes. *Swan Press: London*, 1931. 4°. 1822. b. **22**.

JOHNSON (SAMUEL) *LL.D.* [*Letters.*]

—— Forty Four Letters from Samuel Johnson. Annotated by L. D'O. Walters. *Swan Press: Chelsea*, 1931. fol.
   One of an edition of 100 copies. Cup.**510**.ala.**12**.

EDGEWORTH (MARIA) [*Selections and Extracts.*]

—— Angelina: or, l'Amie Inconnue . . . [Extracted from "Moral Tales for Young People".] Wood engravings by Helen Binyon. pp. 85. *Swan Press: London*, 1933. 4°. C. **102**. e. **3**.
   One of an edition of 100 copies.

TALKARRA PRESS, Cremorne, Australia

STEPHENSON (PERCY REGINALD)

—— Philip Dinmock. A memoir of a poet. *Sydney: Talkarra Press*, 1958. Cup. **501**. i. **49**.
   pp. 39. 23 cm. △

FITZGERALD (ROBERT DAVID)

—— The Wind at your Door. A poem. *Talkarra Press: Cremorne*, 1959. 8°. 12229. a. **38**.

TAURUS PRESS, Kenton, Middx.

PIECH (PAUL PETER)

—— War and Misery. A portfolio of 12 original woodcuts. pl. 12. *Paul Peter Piech at the Taurus Press: Kenton*, [1960.] 16°. Cup. **510**. bea. **1**.

EPHEMERIDES.

—— Poor Richard's Almanack. Being the choicest morsels of wit and wisdom written during the years of the almanack's publication, by . . . Benjamin Franklin. *Paul Peter Piech at the Taurus Press: London*, [1961.] 8°. Cup. **510**. bea. **3**.

PIECH (Paul Peter)

—— Poem to Rene. Written and illustrated by Paul Peter Piech. *Taurus Press: Kenton,* [1963.] 8⁰. [*Taurus Poems.* no. 1.]   Cup. 510. bea. 2/1.

TEMPLE SHEEN PRESS, East Sheen, Surrey

COLERIDGE (Samuel Taylor) [*Christabel; Kubla Khan; The Pains of Sleep.—Kubla Khan.*]

—— Kubla Khan. pp. 4.   *Lamley & Co.: London,* 1910. 16⁰.   Cup.510.aya.2.

MONRO (Harold Edward)

Before Dawn. Poems and impressions. pp. 144. *Constable & Co.: London,* 1911. 8⁰.   011650. i. 59.

SABIN (Arthur Knowles) ——————————

Medea and Circe, and other poems . . . With an introduction by Richard G. Moulton. ff. vii. 55. *Temple-Sheen Press,* 1911. 16⁰. *Printed on one side of the leaf only.*   011651. h. 84.

SABIN (Arthur Knowles)———————————

Christmas, 1914: a poem. pp. 17. *The Author: East Sheen,* 1914. 8⁰.   011649. eee. 63.

SABIN (Arthur Knowles) ——————————

Five Poems. ff. 5. *Temple Sheen Press: London,* [1914.] 8⁰.   011604. ee. 2. (3.)

SABIN (Arthur Knowles)———————————

New Poems. pp. 50. *Temple Sheen Press: East Sheen,* 1914. 16⁰.   011650. de. 113.

SABIN (Arthur Knowles)

War Harvest, 1914. [Sonnets.] pp. 13. *Temple Sheen Press: East Sheen,* [1914.] 8⁰.   11649. cc. 61.

SABIN (Arthur Knowles)

The Death of Icarus . . . New separate edition. pp. 16.   *The Author: East Sheen,* 1915. 8⁰.   11648. g. 58.

SABIN (Arthur Knowles)

New Poems . . . Second edition. pp. 50. *Temple Sheen Press: East Sheen,* 1915. 16⁰.   011652. i. 113.

DANCE OF DEATH. [*Pictorial Representations.—*II. *Representations originally published in book form or as sets of engravings.—Holbein.—Totentanz.*]

Enlarged facsimiles of the original wood engravings by Hans Lützelberger in the first complete edition: Lyons 1547. [With the French text, accompanied by an English verse translation. Edited, with a preface, by Frederick H. Evans.] *Privately printed: London,* 1916. 8⁰.   7859. c. 5.

MONRO (Harold Edward)

Trees. [Poems.] pp. 14. *Poetry Bookshop: London,* 1916. 8⁰.   Cup.510.aya.4.

BIBLE.—*Job.* [*English.*]

—— The Book of Job. [With a prefatory note signed: W. R., i.e. Walter Runciman.] pp. 94. *Printed at the Temple Sheen Press by Arthur K. Sabin: East Sheen,* 1918. 4⁰.   Cup. 510. aya. 1. *One of an edition of 100 copies.*

RUNCIMAN (Thomas)

—— Songs, Sonnets & Miscellaneous Poems. [With an introductory note by Walter Runciman and with a portrait.] pp. 43. *Printed for Walter Runciman at the Temple Sheen Press:* [*London,*] 1922. 4⁰.   Cup.510.aya.3. *Privately printed.*

THREE CANDLES PRESS, Dublin

LESLIE (Sir John Randolph Shane) *Bart.*

—— Saint Patrick's Purgatory . . . With an appendix: Saint Patrick's breastplate in modern Irish and a new English translation by Colm O. Lochlainn. [With plates, including maps.] pp. 27. [*Colm O Lochlainn, at the Sign of the Three Candles: Dublin,* 1961.] 8⁰. Cup.510.cam.2.

O LOCHLAINN (Colm)

—— Cnuac ρáoραιc. Ireland's holy mountain. pp. 47. *Three Candles: Dublin,* 1961. 8⁰.   X. 108/1097.

FALLER (Kevin)

—— Island Lyrics. pp. 46.   *Colm O Lochlainn: Dublin,* [1963.] 8⁰.   Cup. 510. cam. 1.

THREE KINGS PRESS, Mindelheim, Bavaria

SHAKESPEARE (William) [*Works attributed to Shakespeare. —A Lover's Complaint.—German.*]

—— A Lover's Complaint . . . Woodcuts by O. W. Leuenberger. pp. 18.   *Three Kings Press: Mindelheim,* 1964. 8⁰.   Cup. 510. ge. 3. *No. 17 of an edition of fifty copies.*

GRAY (Thomas) *the Poet.* [*Elegy written in a Country Churchyard.*]

—— Elegy written in a Country Churchyard. (Linocuts by Milan Kerac.) *Melchior William Mittl: Mindelheim,* [1965.] 8°. Cup. **510**. ge. **4**.
No. 4 of an edition of ninety-nine copies.

THREE MOUNTAINS PRESS, Paris

ADAMS (B. M. G.) England. [Sketches.] pp. 31. *Shakespeare & Co. : Paris,* 1923. 8°. Cup.**510**.fac.**5**.

FORD (Ford Madox) *pseud.* [i.e. Joseph Leopold Ford Hermann Madox Hueffer.]
—— Women & Men. pp. 61. *Three Mountains Press: Paris,* 1923. 8°. Cup. **510**. fac. **2**.

POUND (Ezra Loomis)
—— Indiscretions ; or, une Revue de deux mondes. pp. 62. *Three Mountains Press: Paris,* 1923. 8°. Cup.**510**.fac.**1**.

WILLIAMS (William Carlos)
—— The Great American Novel. pp. 79. *Three Mountains Press : Paris,* 1923. 8°. Cup. **510**. fac. **4**.
A slip, bearing the imprint " Contact Editions : Paris ", is pasted on to the titlepage.

WINDELER (B. Cyril)
—— Elimus : a story . . . With twelve designs by D. Shakespear. pp. 45. *Three Mountains Press: Paris,* 1923. 8°. Cup.**510**.fac.**3**.
A slip with the imprint " Contact Editions : Paris," has been pasted on the titlepage.

POUND (Ezra Loomis)
—— Antheil and the Treatise on Harmony. [Articles, mostly reprinted from periodicals.] pp. 105. *Three Mountains Press : Paris,* 1924. 8°. Cup. **402**. b. **32**.

THREE STAR PRESS, Crumlin

DAVENPORT (Leonard)
—— Medicine & Surgery at Sea . . . A tribute to the medical services of the Mercantile Marine Service. [With plates.] pp. 36. *Printed by the author at the Three Star Press: Crumlin,* 1960. 8°. X. **329/405**.

TINTERN PRESS, Chepstow

CHUBB (Ralph Nicholas)
—— Songs Pastoral and Paradisal. ff. 28. *Tintern Press : Brockweir,* 1935. fol. Tab. **535**. b. **14**.
Engraved throughout. One of an edition of 100 copies.

COPPARD (Alfred Edgar)
—— Cherry Ripe. Poems. (Wood engravings by Sylvia Marshall.) pp. 47. *Tintern Press: Chepstow,* 1935. 8°. Cup.**510**.ag**1**.**1**.

DAVIES (Rhys) *Writer of Fiction.*
—— The Skull. pp. 14. *Tintern Press: Chepstow,* 1936. 4°. C. **102**. e. **11**.

TORCH PRESS, Cedar Rapids, Iowa

STARRETT (Vincent)
—— Ambrose Bierce. pp. 50. *Walter M. Hill: Chicago,* 1920. 8°. **11456**. d. **7**.

BAY (Jens Christian Ballieu)
—— The Leigh Hunt Collection of Luther Albertus Brewer. pp. 38. *Privately printed: Cedar Rapids, Iowa,* 1933. 8°. **11913**. aa. **60**.

TOUCAN PRESS, Beaminster

BLUNDEN (Edmund Charles)
—— A Wessex Worthy, Thomas Russell. pp. 11. *Toucan Press: Beaminster,* 1960. 8°. Cup. **510**. ace. **2**.
One of an edition of which 100 copies were printed for sale. :

CURLE (Richard Henry Parnell)
—— The Richard Curle Collection of the Works of Cicely Veronica Wedgwood. [A list of items.] pp. 19. *J. Stevens Cox at the Toucan Press: Beaminster,* 1961. 16°. Cup. **510**. ace. **1**.
One of an edition of sixty-five copies.

BLUNDEN (Edmund Charles)
—— A Corscombe inhabitant. *Beaminster : Toucan Press,* 1963. Cup. **510**. ace. **6**.
Pages not numbered. 21 cm. △
Part of an edition of fifty-three copies, privately printed.

SLEE (Daphne)
—— Poems. pp. 59. *Toucan Press: Beaminster,* 1963. 8°. Cup. **510**. ace. **3**.

STANBOROUGH (Pamela)
—— Eleven Poems. pp. 8. *J. Stevens Cox, Toucan Press : Beaminster,* 1964. 8°. Cup. **510**. ace. **4**.

TOYON PRESS, San Francisco

WINTERS (Yvor)
—— To the Holy Spirit. A poem. *Book Club of California:* [*San Francisco,*] 1947. 8°. Cup. **510**. nem. **1**.
California Poetry Folios. pt. 8.

TRAGANA PRESS, Edinburgh

O'SULLIVAN (VINCENT)

—— In Quiet. [Reprinted from " The Dublin Magazine."] *Tragana Press: Edinburgh*, 1956. 8°. Cup.510.afg.2.
No. 25 of an edition of twenty-five copies.

ROLFE (FREDERICK WILLIAM SERAFINO AUSTIN LEWIS MARY) calling himself *Baron Corvo. [Letters.]*

—— A letter to Father Beauclerk. *Edinburgh: Tragara Press*, 1960. Cup. 510. afg. 5.

  Pages not numbered. 21 cm. △
  Dated 10 Feb. 1906. Printed on one side of the leaf only. Proof sheets of an edition of twenty copies printed for private distribution.

BEARDSLEY (AUBREY VINCENT) *[Letters.]*

—— A letter to Smithers from Aubrey Beardsley. With a note by Patricio Gannon. *Edinburgh: Tragara Press*, 1963. Cup. 510. afg. 4.

  Pages not numbered. 26 cm. △
  No. 17 of an edition of fifty-five copies.

TRIANON PRESS, Clairvaux, Jura

BLAKE (WILLIAM) *Artist. [Single Works.]*

—— Jerusalem. A facsimile of the illuminated book (printed in, or soon after, 1820). pp. viii. pl. 100. *Published by the Trianon Press for William Blake Trust: London; Paris printed*, [1951.] fol. L.R. 301. de. 1.
  Reproduced by collotype in orange, and with hand-coloured plates. Printed on one side of the leaf only, and divided into six parts and an introduction.

CAMBRIDGE.— *University of Cambridge.—Fitzwilliam Museum.*

—— The Fitzwilliam Museum. An illustrated survey. With an introduction and commentary by the Director, Carl Winter. pp. ix. 431. *Trianon Press: Clairvaux; printed in France and England*, 1958. 4°. L.R. 261. b. 29.

BLAKE (WILLIAM) *Artist. [Single Works.]*

—— Visions of the Daughters of Albion. [Facsimile reproduction of the 1793 edition. With a bibliographical note by Sir Geoffrey Keynes.] *Published by The Trianon Press for the William Blake Trust: Clairvaux*, 1959. fol. C. 102. k. 2.

LEBEL (ROBERT)

—— [Sur Marcel Duchamp.] Marcel Duchamp. With chapters by Marcel Duchamp, André Breton & H. P. Roché. Translation by George Heard Hamilton. [With illustrations, including reproductions, and a catalogue raisonné.] pp. 191. *Trianon Press: London; Paris printed*, 1959. fol. L.R. 403. p. 3.

BLAKE (WILLIAM) *Artist. [Single Works.]*

—— The Marriage of Heaven and Hell. [A facsimile of the copy in the Rosenwald collection. With " Description and bibliographical statement " by Sir Geoffrey L. Keynes.] *Trianon Press: Clairvaux; for the William Blake Trust: London*, 1960. fol. C. 104. l. 2.

PALMER (SAMUEL) *Artist.*

—— Samuel Palmer's Sketch-book, 1824. [A reproduction.] An introduction and commentary by Martin Butlin, with a preface by Geoffrey Keynes. 2 pt. *Trianon Press for the William Blake Trust: Clairvaux*, [1962.] obl. 8°. Cup. 500. bb. 14.
  The part containing the introduction and commentary was printed in England.
  No. U of an issue of twenty-six copies numbered A to Z.

TROUTBECK PRESS, Amenia, N.Y.

HUGHES (JAMES LANGSTON)

—— Dear lovely death. [Poems. With a portrait.] *Troutbeck Press: Amenia, N.Y.*, 1931. 8°. Cup. 510. nev. 1.
  One of an edition of 100 copies privately printed, signed by the author.

TROVILLON PRESS, Herrin, Ill.

MUNTHE (AXEL MARTIN FREDRIK)
[Små skizzer.]

—— Vagaries from Munthe. [The foreword signed: Hal W. Trovillion.] *Herrin, Ill.: Violet & Hal W. Trovillion*, 1925. Cup. 510. n. 28.

  pp. 43. 18 cm. △
  " Three selections from Vagaries ".

TROVILLION PRIVATE PRESS.

—— [Catalogues and prospectuses of books, Christmas cards, etc., printed at the Trovillion Private Press.] *Herrin, Ill.*, 1936– . 12° & 8°. Cup. 510. n. 1.

TROVILLION (VIOLET DE MARS) and **TROVILLION** (HAL WEEDEN)

—— The Private Press as a Diversion. pp. viii. 81. *Trovillion Private Press: Herrin, Ill.*, 1937. 8°. Cup.510.n.2.

TROVILLION (VIOLET DE MARS) and **TROVILLION** (HAL WEEDEN)

—— A Keepsake from Thatchcot. [*Trovillion Private Press: Herrin, Ill.*, 1940.] 12°. Cup. 510. n. 3.
  No. 4 of an unnamed series.

TROVILLION (VIOLET DE MARS) and **TROVILLION** (HAL WEEDEN)

—— As a Hobby a Private Press. *Trovillion Private Press: Herrin, Ill.*, [1941.] 12°. Cup.510.n.4.

PLATT (Sir HUGH)

—— Delightes for Ladies . . . Reprinted from the edition of 1627 [i.e. the edition of 1630, printed in 1627]. Illustrations from 1609 edition. Collated and edited by Violet and Hal W. Trovillion. pp. xxii. 120. *Trovillion Private Press: Herrin, Ill.*, 1942. 12°. Cup.510.n.5.

SCHAUINGER (JOSEPH HERMAN)

—— A Bibliography of Trovillion Private Press, operated by Violet & Hal W. Trovillion at the Sign of the Silver Horse. pp. viii. 49. *Trovillion Private Press: Herrin*, 1943. 8°. Cup.510.n.6.
  Privately printed.

BURKE (Harry Rosecrans)
—— Visitation at Thatchcot. A symposium of little journeys
to the home of Trovillion Private Press. By H. R.
Burke and F. A. Behymer. pp. 22. *Trovillion Private
Press: Herrin, Ill.*, 1944. 12º. Cup.510.n.7.

HENRY VIII., *King of England.* [*Letters.*]
—— Love Letters of Henry VIII . . . Gathered by Violet &
Hal W. Trovillion, *etc.* pp. xvi. 26. *Trovillion Private
Press: Herrin*, 1945. 8º. Cup.510.n.8.

WILDE (Oscar Fingal O'Flahertie Wills)
—— The Happy Prince and the Selfish Giant . . . With a foreword by Hal W. Trovillion. (Illustrated by William J.
Goodacre.) pp. x. 35. *Trovillion Private Press: Herrin*,
1945. 8º. Cup.510.n.11.

WILKINSON (Robert) D.D., *Pastor of St. Olave's, South-
wark.*
—— The Merchant Royall. Being a sermon preached in
1607 in praise of the wife wherein she is likened to a
merchant ship. Whereunto is added an introduction by
Stanley Pargellis. pp. 34. *Trovillion Private Press:
Herrin, Ill.*, 1945. 8º. Cup.510.n.10.

HILL (Thomas) *Londoner.*
—— First Garden Book. Being a faithful reprint of A Most
Briefe and Pleasaunt Treatyse teachynge howe to dress,
sowe, and set a garden by Thomas Hyll, Londyner 1563.
Collated and edited by Violet and Hal W. Trovillion.
pp. xv. 98. *Trovillion Private Press: Herrin, Ill.*,
1946. 12º. Cup.510.n.9.

TROVILLION (Violet De Mars) and **TROVILLION**
(Hal Weeden)
—— Recipes & remedies of early England. Garnered from
many and diverse sources and here set forth by Violet &
Hal W. Trovillion. *Herrin, Ill.: Trovillion Private Press*,
1946. Cup. 510. n. 27.
   pp. ix, 76. 20 cm. △

TROVILLION (Violet de Mars) and **TROVILLION**
(Hal Weeden)
—— Christmas at Thatchcot. pp. 26. *Trovillion Private
Press: Herrin*, 1947. 8º. Cup.510.n.12.

FIELD (Roswell Martin)
—— The Passing of Mother's Portrait . . . With biographical
introduction by J. Christian Bay. pp. xvii. 53. *Trovillion
Private Press: Herrin*, 1948. 8º. Cup.510.n.14.

LAWSON (William) *Horticulturist.*
—— The Countrie Houswifes Garden . . . 1617. [Edited by
H. W. Trovillion.] pp. xvii. 53. *Trovillion Private
Press: Herrin*, 1948. 8º. Cup.510.n.13.

RENÉ (Blanche)
—— A Pony Cart of Verse. [With a portrait.] pp. 46.
Trovillion Private Press: Herrin, 1949. 8º. Cup.510.n.15

THOMAJAN (Puzant Kevork)
—— America's Oldest Private Press [i.e. the Trovillion
Private Press, Herrin, owned by Hal W. Trovillion and
Violet de Mars Trovillion]. [With plates, including por-
traits.] *Trovillion Private Press: Herrin*, 1952. 8º. Cup.510.n.16.

TROVILLION (Hal Weeden)
—— Designing a Bookplate. [With plates.] *Trovillion
Private Press: Herrin*, 1953. 8º. Cup.510.n.17.

MORAN (James)
—— An English Appraisal of America's Oldest Private Press
(the Trovillion Press of Herrin, Illinois). [Reprinted from
" Printing World."] *Trovillion Private Press: Herrin*,
1954. 8º. Cup.510.n.26.

TROVILLION (Hal Weeden)
—— Some Mottoes to live by. *Trovillion Private Press:
Herrin*, 1954. 8º. Cup.510.n.18.

TROVILLION (Hal Weeden)
—— An Adventure in Christmas Cards. *Trovillion Private
Press: Herrin, Ill.*, 1955. 8º. Cup.510.n.19.

TROVILLION (Violet de Mars) and **TROVILLION**
(Hal Weeden)
—— The Sundial in our Garden. (Third edition.) pp. 57.
Trovillion Private Press: Herrin, 1955. 8º. Cup.510.n.22.

TROVILLION (Violet de Mars) and **TROVILLION**
(Hal Weeden)
—— The Tussie Mussies. A collection of flower and garden
sentiments in prose and verse, compiled by V. & H. W.
Trovillion. (Third edition.) pp. xiii. 104. *Trovillion
Private Press: Herrin*, 1955. 8º. Cup.510.n.20.

TROVILLION (Hal Weeden)
—— Faces and Places remembered. [With plates, including
portraits.] pp. 82. *Trovillion Private Press: Herrin*,
1956. 8º. Cup.510.n.21.

TROVILLION (Hal Weeden)
[Faces and Places remembered.]
—— Two from the Book. [Two essays from " Faces and
Places remembered."] *Trovillion Private Press:
Hovrin*, 1956. 8º. Cup.510.n.23.

TROVILLION (HAL WEEDEN)

—— Three from the Book. pp. 15. *Trovillion Private Press: Herrin*, 1957. 8°.   Cup.510.n.24.

TROVILLION PRIVATE PRESS.

—— I salute the Silver Horse. By Paul Jordan-Smith. Being the story of Trovillion Private Press, America's oldest private press. Whereunto is added an account of its founding by Hal W. Trovillion. pp. 15.   *Trovillion Private Press: Herrin, Ill.*, 1958. 8°. Cup.510.n.25.

MORAN (JAMES)

—— The Private Press at Home and Abroad. By J. Moran . . . and Henry F. Henrichs. [On the Trovillion Private Press.] *Trovillion Private Press: Herrin, Ill.*, 1959. 8°.   **2706. lt. 3.**

TWO HORSE PRESS, London

COLT (ARMIDA MARIA THERESA)

—— Spring poetry. (Illustrations by Roland Stone.) [Compiled by A. M. T. Colt.] *London: Two Horse Press*, 1960.   Cup. **510.** amd. **1.**

Pages not numbered. 27 cm.   △

Printed on one side of the leaf only. No. 44 of an edition of fifty copies.

COLT (ARMIDA MARIA THERESA)

—— Weeds and wild flowers. Some irreverent words . . . With wood-engravings by George Mackley.   *London: Two-Horse Press; Cambridge: printed by Will Carter at the Rampant Lions Press*, [1965].   Cup. **510.** ac. **37.**

2 vol.: pp. 54. 31 cm.   △

Vol. 2 consists of separate prints of the wood-engravings from vol. 1.

VALE PRESS, London

PERIODICAL PUBLICATIONS.—*London.*

—— The Dial. Edited by Chas. H. Shannon & C. Ricketts. no. 1–5. 1889–1897.   [*London*,] 1889–97. 32 cm. & 36 cm.   C. **99.** l. **2.**
    △

LONGUS.

—— Daphnis and Chloe . . . Done into English by Geo. Thornley, Gent. (The woodcuts drawn on the wood by Charles Ricketts from the designs by Charles Shannon and Charles Ricketts.) *London & Edinburgh: printed by the Ballantyne Press; London; sold by Elkin Matthews & John Lane*, 1893.   C. **99.** k. **13.**

pp. 106. 29 cm.   △

MARLOWE (CHRISTOPHER) *the Dramatist.* [*Hero and Leander.*]

—— Hero and Leander. By Christopher Marlowe and George Chapman. (With decorations . . . by C. Ricketts and C. Shannon.) pp. 112.   *E. Mathews & J. Lane: London*, 1894. 8°.   C. **99.** e. **20.**

ARNOLD (MATTHEW)

—— Empedocles on Etna, *etc.* (The engraved decorations by Charles Ricketts.) pp. 61.   *Hacon & Ricketts: London*, 1896. 4°.   C. **99.** e. **5.**

CAMPION (THOMAS) [*Selections.*]

—— Fifty Songs. (Chosen by John Gray. The border and decorations . . . designed and engraved by Charles Ricketts.) pp. 61. *Hacon & Ricketts: London*, 1896. 8°.   C.**99.**f.**2.**

DRAYTON (MICHAEL) [*Collections.*]

Here ends this edition of Nymphidia and the Muses Elizium . . . Edited from the earliest editions by John Gray and decorated . . . by C. Ricketts, *etc.* pp. 137.   *Hacon & Ricketts: London*, 1896. 8°.   C.**99.**f.**1.**

GRAY (JOHN) *Canon.*   Spiritual Poems, chiefly done out of several languages. pp. 113. *Hacon and Ricketts: London*, 1896. 8°.   C.**99.**e.**7.**

LANDOR (WALTER SAVAGE) Epicurus Leontion and Ternissa. (The build of the book and its decoration . . . by C. Ricketts.) pp. xcix.   *Hacon & Ricketts: London*, [1896.] 8°.   C.**99.**e.**4.**

MILTON (JOHN) [*Minor Poems.*]

—— Milton. Early poems. (Seen through the press by Charles Sturt. The decorations are designed and cut on the wood by Charles Ricketts.) [*London:*] *printed by the Ballantyne Press; sold by Hacon & Ricketts*, [1896].   C. **99.** i. **4.**

pp. ciii. 27 cm.   △

SHAKESPEARE (WILLIAM) [*Works attributed to Shakespeare.*—*The Passionate Pilgrim.*]

—— [*End.*] Here ends this edition of the Passionate Pilgrim and the Songs in Shakespeare's plays, edited by T. S. Moore and decorated . . . by C. Ricketts, *etc.* pp. 79. *Hacon & Ricketts: London*, 1896. 8°.   C. **99.** c. **18.**

SUCKLING (Sir JOHN)

—— The Poems of Sir John Suckling. (Edited by John Gray and decorated by C. Ricketts.) pp. cxvii.   *Hacon & Ricketts: London*, 1896. 8°.   **11603.** h. **49.**

SUCKLING (Sir JOHN)

—— [Another copy.] The poems of Sir John Suckling. 1896.   C. **99.** f. **25.**
    △

APULEIUS (LUCIUS) *Madaurensis.*—[*Asinus Aureus.*—*Selections.*—*Latin.*]

—— The Excellent Narration of the Marriage of Cupide and Psyches . . . Translated . . . by W. Adlington. (The woodcuts . . . engraved on the wood by Charles S. Ricketts.) pp. 56. *Hacon & Ricketts: London*, 1897. 8°.   C. **99.** f. **19.**

BARRETT, afterwards **BROWNING** (ELIZABETH BARRETT)

—— Sonnets from the Portuguese. *London: printed by the Ballantyne Press; sold by Hacon & Ricketts,* 1897.

C. **99**. a. **14.**

pp. 46. 15 cm. △

BLAKE (WILLIAM) *Artist.* [*Smaller Collections.*]

—— The Book of Thel, Songs of Innocence and Songs of Experience. (With decorations by Charles Ricketts.) pp. lxxxi. *Hacon & Ricketts: London,* 1897. 4°.

C. **99**. e. **8.**

CONSTABLE (HENRY) *Poet.* [*Works.*]

—— The Poems and Sonnets of Henry Constable. (Edited from early editions and manuscripts by John Gray, with wood cut border & decorations executed by Charles Ricketts.) pp. cl. *Printed at the Ballantyne Press; sold by Hacon & Ricketts: London,* 1897. 8°.

C. **99**. f. **16.**

FIELD (MICHAEL) *pseud.* [i.e. KATHARINE HARRIS BRADLEY and EDITH EMMA COOPER.]

Fair Rosamund. [A drama.] (The decorations by C. Ricketts.) pp. 75. *Hacon & Ricketts: London,* 1897. 8°. C.99.f.27.

VALE PRESS.

—— [Prospectuses and leaflets relating to books published by Hacon and Ricketts at the Vale Press.] 19 pt. [*London,* 1897–1904.] 4° & 8°. Cup.510.cay.2.

VAUGHAN (HENRY) *the Silurist.* [*Selections.*]

Vaughan's Sacred Poems: being a selection. (C. S. Ricketts the designer and engraver of the decorations.) pp. cxcix. *Hacon & Ricketts: London,* 1897. 8°. C.99.e.3.

CHATTERTON (THOMAS) *the Poet.*

—— The Rowley Poems of Thomas Chatterton. (Edited by Robert Steele, and decorated with woodcut border and initials engraved by Charles Ricketts.) 2 vol. *Hacon & Ricketts: London,* 1898. 8°. C. **99**. f. **24.**

FIELD (MICHAEL) *pseud.* [i.e. KATHARINE HARRIS BRADLEY and EDITH EMMA COOPER.]

The World at Auction, a play...Decorations ...by C. Ricketts, *etc.* pp. cxvi. *Hacon & Ricketts: London,* 1898. 4°. C.99.f.28.

KEATS (JOHN) [*Poetical Works.*]

—— The Poems of John Keats. (Edited by C. J. Holmes, and decorated by C. Ricketts.) 2 vol. *Hacon & Ricketts: London,* 1898. 8°. C. **99**. f. **12.**

RICKETTS (CHARLES DE SOUSY) and **PISSARRO** (LUCIEN)

De la Typographie et de l'harmonie de la page imprimée. William Morris et son influence sur les arts et métiers. pp. 31.

Paris; London [printed], 1898. 4°. C.99,e.6.

ROSSETTI (DANTE GABRIEL) The Blessed Damozel. pp. 27. *Hacon & Ricketts: London,* 1898. *obl.* 16°.

C.99.a.20.

SHELLEY (PERCY BYSSHE) [*Selections.*] Lyrical Poems. pp. 54. *Hacon & Ricketts: London,* 1898. 4°.

C.99.a.16.

SIDNEY (Sir PHILIP) [*Smaller Collections.*]

The Sonnets of Sir Philip Sidney. (The text carefully prepared from the earliest editions by John Gray; the ornaments designed and cut on the wood by C. S. Ricketts.) pp. 67. *Hacon & Ricketts: London,* 1898. 8°. C.99.f.21.

BLAKE (WILLIAM) *Artist.*

—— Poetical sketches. (With decorations designed and cut on the wood by Charles Ricketts.) *London: printed at the Ballantyne Press; sold by Hacon & Ricketts,* 1899.

C. **99**. e. **2.**

pp. xciii. 20 cm. △

BROWNING (ROBERT) *the Poet.*

—— Dramatic Romances and Lyrics. [No. 3 and 7 from "Bells and Pomegranates".] (Decorated with woodcut border and initials by Charles Ricketts.) pp. 121. *Hacon & Ricketts: London,* 1899. 8°. C. **99**. f. **11.**

COLERIDGE (SAMUEL TAYLOR) [*Lyrical Ballads.—Rime of the Ancient Mariner.*]

—— The rime of the Ancient Mariner. (Decorated by Charles Ricketts.) *London: printed at the Ballantyne Press; sold by Hacon & Ricketts,* 1899. C. **99**. c. **19.**

pp. xliv. 20 cm. △

GUÉRIN (GEORGES MAURICE DE) The Centaur. The Bacchante. Translated from the French . . . by T. S. Moore. pp. 35. *Hacon & Ricketts: London,* 1899. 4°. C.99.f.20.

RICKETTS (CHARLES DE SOUSY)

A Defence of the Revival of Printing. [Decorated by the author.] pp. 37. *Hacon & Ricketts: [London,]* 1899. 8°. C.99.c.17.

ROSSETTI (DANTE GABRIEL) Hand and Soul ... (Decorated by C. S. Ricketts.) pp. 44. *Hacon & Ricketts: London,* 1899. 8°. C.99.a.15.

SHAKESPEARE (WILLIAM) [*Sonnets.*] Shakespeare's Sonnets. Reprinted from the edition of 1609. [Edited by T. S. Moore. With border designed and engraved by C. S. Ricketts.] pp. 160.   *Hacon & Ricketts: London,* 1899. 4°.   C.99.d.20.

CELLINI (BENVENUTO) *the Artist.*

—— The life of Benvenuto Cellini. Translated by John Addington Symonds. (Seen through the press by C. J. Holmes and decorated by C. S. Ricketts.)   *London: printed at the Ballantyne Press; sold by Hacon & Ricketts; New York: John Lane,* 1900.   C. 99. k. 8.

2 vol.   30 cm.   △

SHAKESPEARE (WILLIAM) [*Works.*] The Vale Shakespeare. 39 vol.   *Hacon & Ricketts: London,* 1900–03. 8°.   011765. h.

TENNYSON (ALFRED) *Baron Tennyson.* [*In Memoriam.*] In Memoriam. (Seen through the press by C. J. Holmes, and decorated by C. S. Ricketts.) pp. cxxv.   *Hacon & Ricketts: London,* 1900. 8°.   C.99.f.10.

TENNYSON (ALFRED) *Baron Tennyson.* [*Selections and Extracts.*] Poems of Alfred Lord Tennyson. (Seen through the press by C. J. Holmes, and decorated with border designed by C. S. Ricketts.) pp. cxvi.   *Hacon & Ricketts: London,* 1900. 8°.   C.99.f.9.

APULEIUS (LUCIUS) *Madaurensis.* [*Asinus Aureus.—Selections.—Latin.*]

—— De Cupidinis et Psyches amoribus fabula anilis. (Textum recensuit C. I. Holmes. Tabulas invenit et sua manu sculpsit C. Ricketts.)   *Londini: Hacon & Ricketts; Ebor. Nov.: Iohannes Lane,* 1901.   C. 99. k. 11.

pp. xxx.   30 cm.   △

FIELD (MICHAEL) *pseud.* [i.e. KATHARINE HARRIS BRADLEY and EDITH EMMA COOPER.]

—— The Race of Leaves. (A play. [In verse.]) pp. lxxxv.   *Hacon & Ricketts: London,* 1901. 8°.   C. 99. f. 29.

SHELLEY (PERCY BYSSHE) [*Poetical Works.*]

—— The poems of Percy Bysshe Shelley. (Decorated by Charles Ricketts.)   *London: printed at the Ballantyne Press; sold by Hacon & Ricketts, the Vale Press; New York: John Lane,* 1901, 02.   C. 99. f. 14.

3 vol.   24 cm.   △

'UMAR KHAIYĀM. [*English.—Fitzgerald's Version.*]

—— Rubaiyat of Omar Khayyam. (Decoration designed by C. Ricketts.) pp. xxx.   *Hacon & Ricketts: London,* 1901. 8°.   C. 99. d. 21.

BIBLE.—*Hagiographa.* [*English.*]

—— Ecclesiastes; or, The preacher, and The Song of Solomon. *London: printed by the Ballantyne Press for Hacon & Ricketts,* [1902].   C. 99. k. 10.

pp. xxvii.   30 cm.   △

BROWNE (*Sir* THOMAS) [*Two or more Works.*]

—— Religio medici, Urn burial, Christian morals, and other Essays. (Edited by C. J. Holmes; decorated by C. S. Ricketts.)   *London: printed at the Ballantyne Press; sold by Hacon & Ricketts, the Vale Press; New York: John Lane,* 1902.   Cup. 510. cay. 1.

pp. cxcviii.   30 cm.   △

SHANNON (CHARLES HAZLEWOOD)   A Catalogue of Mr. Shannon's Lithographs, with prefatory note by C. Ricketts, *etc.* pp. 32.   *E. J. Van Wisselingh: London,* [1902.] 8°.   C.99.f.17.

WORDSWORTH (WILLIAM) *Poet Laureate.* [*Collections.—II. Poetry.—Smaller Collections.*]

—— Poems from Wordsworth. (Chosen and edited by T. Sturge Moore & illustrated by woodcuts designed & engraved by T. S. Moore.)   *London: Hacon & Ricketts; New York: John Lane; [Edinburgh:] printed at the Ballantyne Press,* [1902].   C. 99. f. 13.

pp. clxxxiii.   24 cm.

BIBLE.—*Gospels.—Selections.* [*English.*]

—— The Parables from the Gospels. With ten original woodcuts designed and engraved on the wood by Charles Ricketts. pp. lxxv. *Hacon & Ricketts: London,* 1903. 8°.   C. 99. e. 23.

FIELD (MICHAEL) *pseud.* [i.e. KATHARINE HARRIS BRADLEY and EDITH EMMA COOPER.]

          Julia Domna, (A play...The decorations are designed and cut on the wood by Charles Ricketts, *etc.*) pp. liii.   *Hacon & Ricketts: London,* 1903. 8°.   C.99.f.26.

JAMES I., *King of Scotland.* Heirefter followis the Quair maid be King Iames of Scotland the First callit the Kingis Quair and maid quhen his Majestie wes in Ingland. (Edited by Robert Steele. Designed by Charles Ricketts.) pp. liv.   *Hacon & Ricketts: London; John Lane: New York,* [1903.] 8°.   C.99.f.18.

MOORE (THOMAS STURGE) Danaë. A poem. (With three illustrations designed and engraved on wood by Charles Ricketts.) pp. xlv.   *Hacon & Ricketts: London; John Lane: New York,* 1903. 8°.   C.99.f.23.

SCHWEIDLER (ABRAHAM)

—— Mary Schweidler, the amber witch. The most interesting trial for witchcraft ever known. Printed from an imperfect manuscript by her father, Abraham Schweidler ... Edited [or rather, written] by William Meinhold ... Translated ... by Lady Duff Gordon.   *London: printed at the Ballantyne Press; sold by Hacon & Ricketts, the Vale Press; London, New York: John Lane,* 1903.   C. 99. k. 1.

pp. clvi.   30 cm.   △

VERONA PRESS, Verona

JOHNSTON (Frederick) *Poet.*
—— Pale Maidens. [Poems.] pp. 70.　　*Verona Press:*
Verona, 1937. 8°.　　　　　　　　**11661. v. 4.**

MANSFIELD (Katherine) *pseud.* [i.e. Katherine Beauchamp, afterwards Murry.]
—— The Garden Party, and other stories. With coloured
lithographs by Marie Laurencin. pp. 315. *Verona Press:*
London; printed in Italy, [1947.] 4° Cup.510.ee.23.

The date of printing is given in the colophon as 1939.

VICKERS (Jonathan), London

POE (Edgar Allan) *Poet.* [*Miscellaneous Works.*]
—— Silence. [With illustrations.] pp. 17.　　*Jonathan*
Vickers: London, 1963. 8°.　　　　**Cup. 510. cal. 1.**
No. 51 of an edition of seventy-five copies.

VILIAGE PRESS, Marlborough on Hudson, N.Y.

MONAHAN (Michael) Heinrich Heine. pp. 47.
Mitchell Kennerley: New York & London, 1911. 8°.
010704. ff. 5.

NEW YORK.—*Grolier Club.*
—— Birrell (*Right Hon.* Augustine)　　Three essays.
I. Book-buying. II. Book-binding. III. The office of
literature. *New York; Marlborough-on-Hudson: printed*
by Frederic & Bertha Goudy at the Village Press, 1924.
C. 98. gg. 9.
pp. xxvi. 30 cm.　　　　　　　　△
One of a series of six books printed by eminent American
printers.

DRINKWATER (John) *Poet.*
—— The World's Lincoln. pp. 34.　*Bowling Green Press:*
New York, 1928. 8°.　　　　　**C. 103. e. 25.**

MACKAYE (Milton)
—— Glorifier of the Alphabet: Frederic W. Goudy. [With
a portrait.]　　*Strathmore Paper Co.: West Springfield,*
Mass., [1933.] 8°.　　　　　**11913. bb. 35.**

VILLAGE PRESS, Thornhill, Ont.

WARDE (Beatrice Lamberton) [*Letters.*]
—— Go to it. An exchange of letters in nineteen fifty eight
on the subject of typography between Beatrice Warde of
the Monotype Corporation of London, England and
Arnold Rockman, then secretary of the Society of Typographic Designers of Canada. [*Thornhill:*] *Guild of Hand*
Printers; privately printed by Gus & Vincent Ructer at the
Village Press, Thornhill, Ontario, 1962.　Cup. 503. 1. 27.
pp. 18. 21×25 cm. (Wrongfount number two, the
collection of Canadian typographica.)　　△
6 letters, 28 Aug., 1957—29 July, 1958.

VINCENT PRESS, Birmingham

JOHNSON (Samuel) *LL.D.* [*Rasselas.*]
—— Rasselas, Prince of Abissinia, *etc.*　　*Vincent Press:*
Birmingham, 1898. 8°.　　　　**C. 100. e. 25.**

VINE PRESS, Hemingford Grey, Huntington

BIBLE.—*Selections.* [*Polyglot.*]
—— Vitis vera. The mystic symbol of the Church of Christ
as used in passages from the Vulgate edition of the Holy
Bible and from the translation of 1611. (Compiled and
printed by Peter Foster and John Peters.)　*Vine Press:*
Hemingford Grey, Huntingdon, 1957. fol.　**C. 103. h. 9.**

SISSON (Marjorie)
—— The Cave . . . With engravings on wood by Frank Martin.
pp. 19. *Vine Press: Hemingford Grey*, 1957. 8°.
Cup.510.bcg.1.

FITZ GIBBON (Constantine)
—— Watcher in Florence. [A novel.] pp. 63.　*Vine Press:*
Hemingford Grey, 1959. 8°.　　**Cup.510.bcg.2.**

READ (*Sir* Herbert Edward)
—— The Parliament of Women. A drama in three acts.
(With designs by Reg Boulton.) pp. 113.　*Vine Press:*
Hemingford Grey, 1960. 8°.　　**Cup. 510. bcg. 3.**
One of an edition of 100 copies.

READ (*Sir* Herbert Edward)
—— Design and Tradition. The Design Oration 1961 of the
Society of Industrial Artists, *etc.* [With a portrait.]
pp. 17. *Vine Press: Hemingford Grey*, 1962. 8°.
Cup. 510. bcg. 4.

ANSELL (Evelyn)
—— Twenty-five Poems. Wood engravings by Diana Bloom-
field. pp. 33. *Vine Press: Hemingford Grey*, 1963. 8°.
Cup. 510. bcg. 5.
One of an edition of 100 copies.

VINE PRESS, Steyning, Sussex

LILLYGAY. Lillygay: an anthology of anonymous
poems. pp. xi. 78. *Vine Press: Steyning*, 1920. 8°.
Cup.510.cub.1.

SONGS. Songs of the Groves: records of the ancient
world. [Poems.] pp. xix. 139.　　*Vine Press:*
Steyning, 1921. 8°.　　　**Cup.510.cub.4.**
No. 37 of forty copies printed on hand-made paper.

SONGS. [Another copy.] Songs of the Groves, *etc.*
[By Victor B. Neuburg.] 1921. 8°. **Cup.510.cub.5.**
No. 35 of 40 copies printed on hand-made paper.

WINGS.

—— Swift wings: songs in Sussex. (Selected from " Star-
craft ".) [By Victor B. Neuburg.]   *Steyning: Vine
Press*, 1921.   Cup. **510**. cub. **2**.

    pp. xiii, 59; illus. 24 cm.   △

    No. 37 of forty copies printed on hand-made paper.

COOKE (RUPERT CROFT)

—— Songs of a Sussex Tramp. pp. xiii. 25.   *Vine Press:*
Steyning, 1922. 8°.   **Cup.510.cub.7.**
    No. 17 of twenty copies printed on hand-made paper.

LARKSPUR.

—— Larkspur: a lyric garland. (Illustrations designed and
cut by Dennis West.) *Steyning: Vine Press*, 1922.
                              Cup. **510**. cub. **13**.

    pp. xi, 101. 23 cm.   △

    No. 11 of forty copies printed on hand-made paper.

HANBURY (ERNEST OSGOOD)   Night's Triumphs :
songs of nature. pp. xi. 106.   *Vine Press :*
Steyning, 1924. 8°.   **Cup.510.cub.6.**

MARTINEAU (GERARD DURRANT) ————
                 The Way of the South
Wind. [Poems.] pp. ix. 25.   *Vine Press :*
Steyning, 1925. 8°.   **Cup.510.cub.10.**
    No. 26 of thirty copies printed on hand-made paper.

URUSOVA (SOFIYA) *Princess*, afterwards **BELLEGARDE**
(SOPHIE DE)

—— Before the storm. Four tales of old Russia . . . With
woodcuts by Eve Rice. *Steyning: Vine Press; London:*
P. J. & A. E. Dobell, 1925.   Cup. **510**. cub. **3**.

    pp. xi, 44. 23 cm.   △

MARTINEAU (GERARD DURRANT)

—— Teams of Tomorrow, *etc.* pp. xi. 56. **F.P.**   *Vine*
Press: Steyning; P. J. & A. E. Dobell: London, 1926. 8°.
                              Cup. **510**. cub. **11**.

    No. 30 of 30 copies printed on hand-made paper.

PRAGNELL (VERA G.) The Story of the Sanctuary.
pp. ix. 78.   *Vine Press : Steyning ;*
P. J. & A. E. Dobell : London, 1928. 8°.
                     Cup.510.cub.12.

TARN (SHIRLEY) *pseud.* [i.e. VICTOR BENJAMIN NEUBURG.]

—— [Poems.] pp. ix. 14.   *Vine Press: Steyning; P. J. &*
A. E. Dobell: London, 1928. 8°. *Hermes Books.* no. 1.
                            Cup. **510**. cub. **14**.

    No. 6 of 16 copies printed on large hand-made paper.

WHITE (ROLD) Day of Life. [Poems.] pp. ix. 32.
    Vine Press : Steyning ; P. J. & A. E. Dobell :
London, 1929. 8°.   **Cup.510.cub.9.**

ARCHER (ETHEL)

—— Phantasy, and other poems.   *Steyning: Vine Press;*
London: P. J. & A. E. Dobell, 1930.
                     Cup. **510**. cub. **15**.

    pp. xii, 32; port. 25 cm. (Hermes books. no. 2.)
                                 △

    No. 14 of sixteen copies printed on large handmade paper.

WHITE (ROLD) Twain One. [Poems.] pp. xi. 37.
    Vine Press: Steyning; P. J. & A. E. Dobell:
London, 1930. 8°.   **Cup.510.cub.8.**

WALLACE (Godfrey), South Tidworth

WALLACE (GODFREY EVERINGHAM)

—— Brief Notes about the Church and Village of Shipton
Bellinger in the Diocese of Winchester.   *Godfrey*
Wallace: South Tidworth, [1965.] 8°. Cup. **510**. cuk. **1**.
    Privately printed.

WALPOLE PRESS, Norwich

MONCK (WALTER NUGENT)

—— The interlude of holly and ivy, made by Nugent Monck
from fifteenth century sources. *Norwich: Saint William*
Hand-Press, 1913.   Cup. **510**. agk. **1**.

    pp. 11. 23 cm.   △

WALPOLE PRESS.

—— [A collection of posters, theatre programmes, etc. printed
by Martin Kinder at the Walpole Press, including an autograph letter.] 16 pt.   *Walpole Press : Norwich,*
[1927–30.] 8°, 4°, & fol.   Cup. **503**. h. **1**.

BROWNE (*Sir* THOMAS) M.D. [*Single Works.*]

—— On dreams.   *Norwich: Martin Kinder at the Walpole*
Press, 1929.   **08486**. ee. **37**.

    pp. 12. 23 cm.   △

NASH (THOMAS) *Satirist.* Thomas Nashe. [Songs
from " Summers Last Will and Testament."] pp. 20.
Martin Kinder : Norwich, 1929. 8°. [*Songs from*
the Dramatists.]   W.P. **8771/1**.

DEKKER (THOMAS) [*Selections and Extracts.*]

—— Thomas Dekker. [Selected songs.] pp. 39.
Martin Kinder: Norwich, 1931. 8°.   [*Songs from the*
Dramatists.]   W.P. S771/2.

SUCKLING (*Sir* JOHN)

—— A Ballad upon a Wedding . . . with decorations by
H. W. Tuck. *Martin Kinder: Norwich*, 1932. 8°.
                     Cup.510.cec.1.

TUCK (HORACE WALT)

—— Norwich. A book of drawings.   *Martin Kinder:*
Norwich, 1932. 8°.   **Cup.510.cec.2.**

BIBLE.—*Tobit.* [*English.*]

—— The Book of Tobit. [With plates.] pp. 31.   *Walpole*
Press: Norwich, 1945. 8°.   **3054**. bb. **7**.

WALTERS PRESS, London

COATES (Ronald Assheton)

—— Several Occasions. Poems . . . Wood-engravings by Edward Walters. pp. 22. *E. Walters & G. Miller: London, 1932.* 8°. 11640. i. 26.

W., E.

—— Silva Civica. Being doggerel verses composed on the occasion of a visit to the Metropolitan common land at Hampstead & Highgate, *etc.* [Signed : E. W., i.e. Edward Walters.] pp. 15. *The Author : London,* [1935.] 8°. 11655. b. 2.

WARD RITCHIE PRESS, South Pasadena; Los Angeles

RONSARD (Pierre de)

—— **Sonnets for Helen.** (Translated by William Van Wyck.) **pp. 142.** *Ward Ritchie : South Pasadena, 1932.* 8°. Cup. 501. aa. 4.
No. 58 of an edition of 100 copies.

BRINTON (Anna Cox)

—— A Pre-Raphaelite Aeneid of Virgil in the Collection of Mrs. Edward Laurence Doheny of Los Angeles [i.e. the manuscript version of the Aeneid executed by William Morris]. Being an essay in honor of the William Morris Centenary, 1934. pp. 39. *Ward Ritchie : Los Angeles, 1934.* 4°. 11912. b. 75.
Printed for private circulation.

FRACASTORO (Girolamo)

—— The Sinister Shepherd. A translation of Girolamo Fracastoro's "Syphilidis sive de Morbo Gallico Libri Tres" by William Van Wyck. [With illustrations.] pp. xxii. 85. *Primavera Press : Los Angeles, 1934.* 8°. 20020. h. 13.

LATIMORE (Sarah Briggs) and **HASKELL** (Grace Clark)

—— Arthur Rackham. A bibliography. [With plates, including a portrait.] pp. xii. 111. *Suttonhouse : Los Angeles, 1936.* 8°. 11914. c. 33.

HOPPER (James Marie)

—— Pepe . . . With a foreword by the author, *etc.* pp. 16. *Book Club of California : [San Francisco,]* 1937. 8°. [*Contemporary California short stories.* no. 5.] Cup. 500. m. 2/5.

CLEMENS' (Samuel Langhorne)

—— The Washoe Giant in San Francisco. Being heretofore uncollected sketches by Mark Twain, published in the "Golden Era" in the sixties . . . With many drawings by Lloyd Hoff. Collected and edited, with an introduction, by Franklin Walker. pp. 143. *George Fields : San Francisco, 1938.* 8°. 12332. d. 1.

HUXLEY (Aldous Leonard)

—— The Most Agreeable Vice. [On reading.] pp. 7. *Jake Zeitlin : Los Angeles, 1938.* 12°. Cup. 510. naz. 2.

VAN WYCK (William)

—— Robinson Jeffers. pp. 17. *Ward Ritchie Press : Los Angeles, 1938.* 8°. 11877. bb. 25.

WAGNER (Henry Raup)

—— The Grabhorn Press. A catalogue of imprints in the collection of H. R. Wagner. [By H. R. Wagner.] pp. 47. *Ward Ritchie Press : Los Angeles, 1938.* 8°. 11914. g. 15.

POWELL (Lawrence Clark)

—— H. Clark Powell, 1900–1938. Memoirs of his life and a bibliography of his writings. Edited by L. C. Powell. [With a portrait.] pp. 18. *Privately printed : Los Angeles, 1939.* 8°. 10858. c. 20.

HUXLEY (Aldous Leonard)

—— Words and their Meanings. pp. 27. *Ward Ritchie Press : Los Angeles,* [1940.] 8°. 12995. bb. 22.

STEIN (Gertrude)

—— What Are Masterpieces. [Three lectures, " Composition as Explanation ", " An American and France " and " What Are Master-Pieces and Why are there so few of them ", with a poem, and other writings. With a foreword by Robert B. Haas and a portrait.] pp. 95. *Conference Press : Los Angeles,* [1940.] 8°. 11863. d. 12.

CHEVALIER (Stuart)

—— The World Charter and the Road to Peace. pp. xi. 179. *Ward Ritchie Press : Los Angeles,* [1946.] 8°. 8007. e. 51.

DAVRIL, afterwards **DAVRIL-HOLDING** (Cynthia)

—— Poems, 1936–1945. pp. ix. 112. *Ward Ritchie Press : Los Angeles, 1946.* 8°. 11689. d. 21.

BIDWELL (John) *of California.*

—— In California before the Gold Rush, *etc.* [With a portrait.] pp. vii. 111. *Ward Ritchie Press : Los Angeles, 1948.* 8°. 10890. fff. 32.

GUILLÉN (Nicolás)

—— Cuba libre. Poems . . . Translated from the Spanish by Langston Hughes and Ben Frederic Carruthers. Illustrated by Gar Gilbert. pp. xi. 96. *Anderson & Ritchie : Los Angeles, 1948.* 4°. Cup. 510. naz. 3.

WILLIAMS (Ames William) and **STARRETT** (Vincent)

—— Stephen Crane. A bibliography. [With plates, including portraits.] pp. xi. 161. *John Valentine : Glendale, Cal., 1948.* 8°. 11917. b. 24.

JEFFERS (JOHN ROBINSON)

—— Poetry, Gongorism and a Thousand Years. (Reprinted from the Times Magazine of January 18, 1948.) pp. 12. *Ward Ritchie Press: [Los Angeles,]* 1949. 8⁰.
Cup. 510. naz. 1.

COWAN (ROBERT ERNEST)

—— Booksellers of Early San Francisco . . . With a biography of the author by Robert G. Cowan. [With plates including portraits.] pp. 111. *Ward Ritchie Press: Los Angeles,* 1953. 8⁰.
2712. laa. 3.

FARQUHAR (FRANCIS PELOUBET)

—— The Books of the Colorado River & the Grand Canyon. A selective bibliography. pp. xi. 75. *Glen Dawson: Los Angeles,* 1953. 8⁰.
2774. m. 2.
Early California Travels. ser. 12.

POWELL (LAWRENCE CLARK)

—— Vroman's of Pasadena. pp. 14. *Privately printed: Pasadena,* 1953. 8⁰.
11919. ccc. 29.

JEFFERS (UNA)

—— Visits to Ireland. Travel-diaries . . . Foreword b⁰ Robinson Jeffers. pp. 56. *Ward Ritchie Press: L⁰ Angeles,* 1954. 4⁰.
X. 709/771.

POWELL (LAWRENCE CLARK)

—— Books, West, Southwest. Essays on writers, their books, and their land. pp. x. 157. *Ward Ritchie Press: Los Angeles,* [1957.] 8⁰.
11879. a. 42.

HANNA (PHIL TOWNSEND)

—— Libros Californianos, or Five feet of California books . . . Revised and enlarged by Lawrence Clark Powell. pp. 87. *Zeitlin & Ver Brugge: Los Angeles,* 1958. 8⁰.
11927. de. 46.

WATER LANE PRESS, Cambridge

DUNCAN (ANDREW) *Printer.*

—— The Glasgow University Printing Office in MDCCCXXVI. [A reprint of the inventory of printing materials and a digest of the inventory of type from a sale catalogue by Andrew Duncan originally published in 1826 under the title "Specimens of Types, and inventory of printing materials, belonging to the University Printing Office of Glasgow," etc.] pp. 15. *Water Lane Press: Cambridge,* 1953. 8⁰.
11914.d.84.
One of an edition of forty copies.

WATSON (Ronald), Dublin

HACKETT (J. P.)

—— Rising from the Mire. Illustrated by Michael Kane. (Poems.) pp. 22. *Ronald Watson: Dublin,* [1963.] 8⁰.
Cup. 510. col. 1.

WATTLE GROVE PRESS, Newnham, Tasmania

EIGER (ALBIN) *pseud.* [i.e. ROLF HENKL, afterwards HENNEQUEL.]

—— Eastward. (A travelogue in verse.) ff. 119. *Wattle Grove Press: Newnham,* [1959.] 4⁰. Cup. 510. v. 2.
Printed on one side of the leaf only. No. 33 of an edition of fifty copies.

EIGER (ALBIN) *pseud.* [i.e. ROLF HENKL, afterwards HENNEQUEL.]

—— Paris. ff. xxxiii. *Wattle Grove Press: [Newnham, Tasmania,* 1960.] 8⁰. Cup. 510. v. 1.
Printed on one side of the leaf only on grey eucalyptus paper.

EIGER (ALBIN) *pseud.* [i.e. ROLF HENKL, afterwards HENNEQUEL.]

—— Red or Purple. A dream of the ancient world. pp. lxix. *Wattle Grove Press: [Newnham, Tasmania,* 1961.] 4⁰.
Cup. 510. v. 4.

EIGER (ALBIN) *pseud.* [i.e. ROLF HENKL, afterwards HENNEQUEL.]

—— The young god: Antinous. A study in portraiture. (Second printing.) *Newnham, Tasmania: Wattle Grove Press,* 1961. X. 415/613.
ff. lxxxix, 13 : plates. 28 cm. △
Reproduced from typewriting. Part of an edition of fifty copies. "Plates. This is a special copy, only partly illustrated"—MS. note, signed: A. E.

HENKL, afterwards **HENNEQUEL** (ROLF)

—— Encounter with Hofmannsthal. [With photographic reproductions of paintings.] pp. xi. *Wattle Grove Press: [Newnham, Tasmania,* 1961.] 8⁰. Cup. 510. v. 3.
No. 17 of an edition of fifty copies, printed in Temple script made in England.

EIGER (ALBIN) *pseud.* [i.e. ROLF HENKL, afterwards HENNEQUEL.]

—— Three Aegyptian stories. [*Newnham, Tasmania: Wattle Grove Press,* 1962]. Cup. 510. v. 16.
pp. 17. 26 cm. △
No. 39 of an edition of one hundred copies.

EIGER (ALBIN) *pseud.* [i.e. ROLF HENKL, afterwards HENNEQUEL.]

—— In Capricornia. Pointless exotic ballads. *Wattle Grove Press: Newham, Tasmania,* [1963.] 4⁰. Cup. 510. v. 6.
Printed on one side of the leaf only.

FLOWER (PAT)

—— Pistils for Two. [Poems.] pp. 38. *Wattle Grove Press: Newnham, Tasmania,* [1963.] 8⁰. Cup. 510. v. 5.

HALL (RODNEY)

—— Forty beads on a hangman's rope. Fragments of memory. [Poems.] *Wattle Grove Press: Newnham,* 1963. 8⁰. Cup. 510. v. 10.

EIGER (ALBIN) *pseud.* [i.e. ROLF HENKL, afterwards HENNEQUEL.]

—— Eastward. (Revised edition.) *Wattle Grove Press: Newnham,* [1964.] 8⁰. Cup. 510. v. 9.
Printed on one side of the leaf only. No. 46 of an edition of 100 copies.

EIGER (ALBIN) *pseud.* [i.e. ROLF HENKL, afterwards HEN-NEQUEL.]

—— Stella matutina. *Newnham, Tas.: Wattle Grove Press,* 1964. Cup. **510**. v. **11**.

    Pages not numbered. 26 cm. △

    " A cycle of twenty-one poems " No. 64 [sic] *of an edition of sixty copies.*

I.L. ENG. Australia. P.

EIGER (ALBIN) *pseud.* [i.e. ROLF HENKL, afterwards HEN-NEQUEL.]

—— [Another copy.] Stella matutina. 1964. Cup. **510**. v. **13**.

△

    No. 27 of an edition of sixty copies. A variant. The word " Southen " has been corrected to " Southern " in the sixth poem.

MITCHAM (HOWARD)

—— Four tales from Byzantium. (Illustrations by the author.) pp. 49. *Wattle Grove Press: Newnham, Tas.,* [1964.] 8⁰. Cup. **510**. v. **12**.

MONTES DE OCA (MARCO ANTONIO) [Delante de la luz cantan los pájaros.]

—— On the Ruins of Babylon with Teiresias . . . Recast into English by Rolf Hennequel. [A poem from "Delante de la luz cantan los pájaros".] pp. xix. *Wattle Grove Press: Newnham, Tasmania,* [1964.] 8⁰. Cup. **510**. v. **7**.

    No. 97 of an edition of 100 copies.

OVIDIUS NASO (PUBLIUS) [*Metamorphoses.—English.—Selections.*]

—— Narcissus and Echo. After Ovid. By Rolf Hennequel. (Drawings by Robert Haberfield.) [A verse translation of part of Book 3 of the Metamorphoses.] *Wattle Grove Press: Newnham, Tasmania,* [1964.] 8⁰. Cup. **510**. v. **8**.

    No. 8 of an edition of thirty-five copies.

WEATHER OAK PRESS, Birmingham

DUGDALE (ROSE SYDENHAM)

—— Fragrant Herbs culled from many gardens . . . Illustrated. pp. 44. *Weather Oak Press: Birmingham,* 1935. 8⁰. 7028. w. **15**.

DUGDALE (ROSE SYDENHAM)

—— A Wreath of Flower Legends . . . Illustrated by I. Anne Ellis. pp. 54. *Weather Oak Press: Birmingham,* 1950. 4⁰. 07030. d. **8**.

WEEKEND PRESS, New York

JENNINGS (HUMPHREY)

—— Poems, *etc.* pp. 10. *Weekend Press: New York,* 1951. 8⁰. Cup.510.sal.**1**.

    No. 81 of an edition of one hundred copies.

RAINE (KATHLEEN)

—— Selected Poems. pp. 20. MS. CORRECTION [by the author]. *Weekend Press: New York,* 1952. Cup.510.sal.**2**.

    Author's presentation copy.

WHITE OWL PRESS, London

COLLIER (JOHN) *Novelist.*

—— No Traveller returns. pp. 62. *White Owl Press: London,* 1931. 8⁰. Cup.510.bez.**2**.

    One of twenty-five copies printed on iridescent Japanese vellum.

MANHOOD (HAROLD ALFRED)

—— Bread and Vinegar. (The Beginning of Wisdom.) [Two tales.] pp. 39. *White Owl Press: London,* 1931. 8⁰. Cup.510.bez.**1**.

    With the addition of two leaves containing the concluding paragraphs of " Bread and Vinegar " in the author's autograph.

BATES (HERBERT ERNEST)

—— Sally Go Round the Moon. [A tale.] pp. 42. *White Owl Press: London,* 1932. 8⁰. Cup.510.bez.**3**.

    One of 21 copies printed on hand-made paper.

BATES (HERBERT ERNEST)

—— The Story Without an End, and The Country Doctor. pp. 51. *White Owl Press: London,* 1932. 8⁰. C. **99**. d. **46**.

    No. 1 of 25 copies printed on hand-made paper, with a leaf of the author's manuscript inserted.

YOUNG (FRANCIS BRETT)

—— Blood Oranges. pp. 40. *White Owl Press: London,* 1932. 8⁰. C. **99**. d. **45**.

MANHOOD (HAROLD ALFRED)

—— Three Nails. pp. 55. *White Owl Press: London,* 1933. 8⁰. Cup.510.bez.**4**.

WHITE RABBIT PRESS, San Francisco

JONAS (STEPHEN)

—— Love, the poem, the sea & other pieces examined. [A poem.] *White Rabbit Press: [San Francisco,]* 1957. 8⁰. Cup. **510**. ned. **4**.

DUNCAN (ROBERT EDWARD)

—— As testimony: the poem & the scene. (A letter referring to a poem by Harold Dull and one by Joan Kyger.) [With the text of the poems.] pp. 20. *White Rabbit Press: San Francisco,* [1964.] 8⁰. Cup. **510**. ned. **6**.

SPICER (JACK)

—— The Holy grail. [A poem.] *White Rabbit Press: San Francisco,* 1964. 8⁰. Cup. **510**. ned. **5**.

LABRUNIE DE NERVAL (GÉRARD)

—— Les Chimères. [Translated by Robin Blaser.] *Open Space: San Francisco,* 1965. 8⁰. Cup. **510**. ned. **1**.

OLSON (CHARLES)

—— O'Ryan, *etc.* *White Rabbit Press: San Francisco,* 1965. 8⁰. Cup. **510**. ned. **3**.

STANLEY (GEORGE) of Berkeley, California.
—— Flowers. [Poems.] *White Rabbit Press: San Francisco,*
1965. 8°. **Cup. 510. ned. 2.**

WHITE RHINOCEROS PRESS, Blacksburgh, Va.

JOHNSTON (GEORGE BURKE)
—— Reflections. *Blacksburg, Va.: White Rhinoceros Press,*
1965. **Cup. 510. nih. 2.**

pp. viii, 32. 18 cm. △
Poems.

WILD HAWTHORN PRESS, Edinburgh

FINLAY (IAN HAMILTON)
—— Glasgow Beasts, an a Burd . . . Papercuts by John Picking
and Pete McGinn, *etc. Wild Flounder Press: [Edinburgh,*
1961.] 8°. **Cup. 510. cop. 1.**

NIEDECKER (LORINE)
—— My friend, tree. (Poems.) Linocuts by Walter Miller.
[With an introduction by Edward Dorn.] *Wild
Hawthorn Press: Edinburgh,* 1961. obl. 8°.
Cup. 510. cop. 4.

NIEDECKER (LORINE)
—— [Another copy.] My Friend Tree, *etc. Edinburgh,*
1961. obl. 8°. **Cup. 510. cop. 3.**

TURNBULL (GAEL)
—— A very particular hill . . . Linocuts: Alexander
McNeish. *Edinburgh: Wild Hawthorn Press,* 1963.
Cup. 510. cop. 5.

Pages not numbered. 15×20 cm. △
Poems.

FINLAY (IAN HAMILTON)
—— Cythera. *Wild Hawthorn Press: [Edinburgh,]*
1965. 4°. **Cup. 510. cop. 2.**

WILDER BENTLEY, Pittsburgh; Berkeley, Cal.

BENTLEY (WILDER) The First Seven Cantos of Helle-
sphere: a vision of the new world. pp. 38.
Printed by the author: Pittsburgh, 1933. 8°.
20003. i. 6.

One of an edition of forty-two copies.

LAMPSON (ROBIN)
—— Terza-rima Sonnets. pp. 53. *Archetype Press:
Berkeley, Cal.,* 1935. 4°. **20029. aaa. 19.**
Printed on one side of the leaf only.

CARR (JOHN) *Blacksmith.* A Vulcan among the Argonauts.
Being . . . excerpts from those most original . .
memoirs of John Carr, blacksmith [viz. " Pioneer Days
in California "]. Edited, with a preface & postscript, by
Robin Lampson . . . Illustrated by " hans." pp. viii. 73.
George Fields: San Francisco, 1936. 8°. **10409. y. 26.**

HARTE (FRANCIS BRET)
—— The Right Eye of the Commander. A New Year's
legend of Spanish California . . . Garnished by Hans, *etc.*
[A story from " Spanish and American Legends."]
W. & E. Bentley: Berkeley, 1937. 8°. **C. 100. b. 8.**

SAROYAN (WILLIAM)
—— A Native American . . . Illustrated by " hans." [Tales.]
pp. 80. *George Fields: San Francisco,* 1938. 8°.
12703. i. 46.

WILSON (Adrian), San Francisco

KEES (WELDON)
—— Poems, 1947–1954. pp. 82. *Adrian Wilson: San
Francisco,* 1954. 8°. **Cup. 510. nam. 1.**
One of a limited edition of twenty five copies.

ALGER (HORATIO)
—— The Young Miner; or, Tom Nelson in California . . .
Introduction and bibliographical note by John Seelye.
[With illustrations.] pp. xxi. 187. *Book Club of
California: [San Francisco,]* 1965. 8°.
Cup. 510. nam. 2.
Publications of the Book Club of California. no. 120.

WILSON (Richard), Chester

WILSON (RICHARD CHARLES)
[High Appreciation.]
—— Kneel on Peas. From High Appreciation. Recollec-
tions of a Captain. [With illustrations.] pp. 40. *The
Author: Chester,* [1961.] 8°. **Cup. 510. can. 3.**

WILSON (RICHARD CHARLES)
—— Imprints. An anthology of new verse by Cheshire poets.
Edited by Richard Wilson. *Richard Wilson: Chester,*
1963. 8°. **Cup. 510. can. 1.**

WHITELOCK (VAL)
—— Conifer, and other poems. *Richard Wilson: Chester,*
1964. 8°. **Cup. 510. can. 2.**

WINCHESTER COLLEGE PRINTING SOCIETY, Winchester

WINCHESTER COLLEGE.
—— A Book of Prayers in Use at the Evening Service of the
Scholars of Winchester College. pp. 30. *College Printing
Society: Winchester,* 1958. 8°. **Cup. 510. c. 1.**

WINDSOR PRESS, San Francisco

APULEIUS (LUCIUS) *Madaurensis.* [*Asinus Aureus.— Selections.—English.*]

—— The most pleasant and delectable tale of the Marriage of Cupid and Psyche, *etc.* [Translated by W. Adlington.] pp. 42. *Windsor Press: San Francisco*, 1926. 4°.

Cup. **510**. pt. **1**.

PHILLIPS (STEPHEN) *the Younger.*

—— Marpessa . . . Together with a foreword by James S. Johnson. pp. vii. 21. *Windsor Press: San Francisco*, 1926. 12°.   Cup. **510**. pt. **7**.
One of the " Benoit Classics."

KIPLING (RUDYARD) [*Single Tales and Poems.*]

—— The Legs of Sister Ursula. pp. 18. *Printed as the first published edition by the Brothers Johnson at the Windsor Press: San Francisco*, 1927. 4°.   Cup. **510**. pt. **2**.

PETRARCA (FRANCESCO) [*Canzoniere.—Trionfi.— English.*]

—— The Triumphs of Petrarch . . . as translated by Boyd, *etc.* pp. vii. 109. *Windsor Press: San Francisco*, 1927. 8°.

Cup. **510**. pt. **3**.

BYNNER (WITTER)

—— The Persistence of Poetry. pp. 29.   *Book Club of California: San Francisco*, 1929. 8°.   Cup.**510**.pt.**4**.

KIPLING (RUDYARD) [*Single Works.*]

—— The Lamentable Comedy of Willow Wood. pp. 27. *Windsor Press: San Francisco*, 1929. 8°.

Cup. **510**. pt. **6**.

No. 1 of an edition of 100 copies.

WILLIAMSON (HENRY) *Novelist.*

—— The Ackymals. pp. 23. *Windsor Press: [San Francisco,]* 1929. 8°.   Cup. **510**. pt. **5**.

FRYER (B. N.)

—— The Obelisk, Macquarie Place. pp. 13. *Windsor Press: [San Francisco,]* 1937. 8°.   Cup. **510**. pt. **8**.

No. 41 of an edition of sixty copies.

WOODLANDS PRESS, Shorne, Gravesend

HALLWARD (REGINALD FRANCIS)

—— Vox humana. *Gravesend: Woodlands Press*, 1900.

11651. m.

no. 1-2; plates; illus. 30 cm.   △
Verses. Lithographed on one side of the leaf only. Imperfect; wanting no. 3-6.

HALLWARD (ADELAIDE)
[With illustrations.] pp. 59. *Shorne, Gravesend*, [1914.] 8°.

The Baby's Quest. *Woodlands Press:* **012621**. ee. **34**.

WOOLY WHALE PRESS, New York

LE GALLIENNE (RICHARD)

—— War. [A poem. With a preface signed: M.B.C., i.e. Melbert B. Cary.] *Press of the Woolly Whale: New York*, 1929. 8°.   Cup. **510**. san. **1**.
One of an edition of fifty copies, printed for private distribution.

EDSCHMID (CASIMIR) *pseud.* [i.e. EDUARD SCHMID.] Lord Byron. The story of a passion...Translated by Eveline Bennett. pp. 413.   *Humphrey Toulmin: London*, 1930. 8°.   **12556**. ppp. **10**.

CARY (MELBERT BRINKERHOFF)

—— A Bibliography of the Village Press . . . (1903–1938.) Including an account of the genesis of the Press by Frederic W. Goudy and a portion of the 1903 diary of Will Ransom, co-founder. [With plates.] pp. 205. *Press of the Woolly Whale: New York*, 1938. 8°.

11900. bbb. **83**.

CARY (MELBERT BRINKERHOFF)

—— The Missing Gutenberg Wood Blocks. [A comic " life " of Gutenberg. Imitations of fifteenth century woodcuts, with accompanying letterpress; with an introduction by M. B. Cary.] *Press of the Woolly Whale: New York*, 1940. 8°.   **12332**. bb. **15**.

YELLOWSANDS PRESS, Bembridge, I.O.W.

MASEFIELD (JOHN EDWARD)

—— John Ruskin. pp. 10. *Printed by H. Whitehouse and E. Daws at the Yellowsands Press, being the private press of Bembridge School: [Bembridge,]* 1920. 4°.

Cup. **501**. k. **29**.

MASEFIELD (JOHN EDWARD)

—— Foundation Day Address [at Bembridge School]. *Yellowsands Press: Bembridge*, 1921. 8°.   **8408**. e. **33**. *Printed for private circulation.*

DE LA MARE (WALTER JOHN) [*Single Works.*]

—— Some Thoughts on Reading. (An address at Bembridge School.) pp. 5.   *Yellowsands Press: [Bembridge,]* 1923. 8°.   Cup. **500**. aa. **11**.

BALDWIN (STANLEY) *Earl Baldwin of Bewdley.*

—— The Bible. [An address.] pp. 9.   *Yellowsands Press: [Bembridge,]* 1928. 8°.   **03126**. e. **21**.

Index